4th edition

CULTURAL ANTHROPOLOGY

WILLIAM A. HAVILAND

CULTURAL ANTHROPOLOGY

WILLIAM A. HAVILAND

University of Vermont

CULTURAL ANTHROPOLOGY

4th edition

Holt, Rinehart and Winston

New York / Chicago / San Francisco / Philadelphia
Montreal / Toronto / London / Sydney
Tokyo / Mexico City / Rio de Janeiro / Madrid

Publisher	*John Michel*
Senior Acquisitions Editor	*David P. Boynton*
Senior Project Manager	*Ruth Stark*
Design Supervisor	*Robert Kopelman*
Text Designer	*Marilyn Marcus*
Production Manager	*Annette Mayeski*

Library of Congress Cataloging in Publication Data
Haviland, William A.
  Cultural anthropology.

  Bibliography: p. 486
  Includes index.
  1. Ethnology. I. Title.
GN316.H38 1983   306   83–4404

ISBN 0-03-062921-7

CBS COLLEGE PUBLISHING
Holt, Rinehart and Winston
The Dryden Press
Saunders College Publishing

COVER PHOTOS:
(front) Napoleon A. Chagnon
(back) Thomas Ives

CREDITS*
We wish to thank the following authors, publishers, and photographers for permission to reprint their work:

p. 2, Arizona State Museum photo, University of Arizona. 9, from "Gentlemen Enthusiasts and Lady Adventurers," by Joan Mark in *Odyssey* (Public Broadcasting Associates, 1980), p. 17. 10 (left), Charles Gatewood, Magnum Photos. (right), from Solomon Asch, "Opinions and Social Pressure," *Scientific American*, November 1955. Reprinted by permission of *Scientific American* and the photographer, William Vandivert. 11, J. Kingston Coleman. 14 (top), *Burlington, Vt., Free Press* photo by Stu Perry; (bottom), courtesy of Wilson W. Hughes, Assistant Director, Garbage Project. 16, from *Yanomamö: The Fierce People* by Napoleon A. Chagnon. Copyright © 1977 by Holt, Rinehart and Winston, Inc. By permission of the publisher. 17, *Voyage to Greenland* by Frederica de Laguna (New York: W. W. Norton, 1977). Copyright Frederica de Laguna; 19, courtesy of Timothy Asch; 22, William A. Haviland photo. 28, Danguole Variakojis. 30 (top), United Press International; (middle), Charles S. Rice; (bottom), Vincent R. Tortora. 33, Photo by Jane Goodall-van Lawick, © National Geographic

Credits continued on p. 495.

Preface

PURPOSE OF THE BOOK

This text is designed for introductory anthropology courses at the college level. It deals primarily with cultural anthropology, presenting the key concepts and terminology of that branch of the discipline, but also brings in related material on physical anthropology and linguistics.

The aim of the text is to give the student a thorough introduction to the principles and processes of cultural anthropology. Because there are many ways to teach anthropology effectively and because anthropologists in general are a pragmatic group, willing to draw on any theoretical approach that offers insights into human behavior, the text draws from the research and ideas of a number of schools of anthropological thought. Therefore, the student will be exposed to a mix of such approaches as evolutionism, historical particularism, diffusionism, functionalism, French structuralism, structural functionalism, and others. Though thorough and scholarly in its coverage, the book is simply written and attractively designed to appeal to students. Thus, they should find that it pleases as it teaches.

UNIFYING THEME OF THE BOOK

Although each chapter has been developed as a self-contained unit of study and may be used in any sequence the instructer wishes, a common theme runs through all the chapters. This, along with part introductions which support that theme, serves to make students aware of how the material in one chapter relates to that in other chapters.

In earlier editions of this book, for want of a better designation, I referred to this common theme as one of environmental adaptation, although I have never been very happy with that phrase. Its principal defect is that it implies a fairly straightforward behavioral response to environmental stimuli. But, of course, people don't just react to an environment as given; rather, they react to it as they perceive it, and different groups of people may perceive the same environment in radically different ways. They also react to things other than the environment: their own biological natures, for one, and their beliefs, attitudes, and the consequences of their own behavior, for others. All of these things present them with problems, and people maintain cultures to deal with problems, or matters that concern them. To be sure, their cultures must produce behavior that is generally adaptive, or at least not maladaptive, but this is not the same as saying that cultural practices necessarily arise because they are adaptive in a particular environment.

v

OUTSTANDING FEATURES OF THE BOOK

1. Readability

The purpose of a textbook is to transmit and register ideas and information, to induce the readers to see old things in new ways and to think about what they see. A book may be the most elegantly written, most handsomely designed, most lavishly illustrated text available on the subject, but if it is not interesting, clear, and comprehensible to the student, it is valueless as a teaching tool.

The readability of the text is also enhanced by the writing style. The book is designed to present even the most difficult concepts in prose that is alive, energetic, and easy to retain. Where technical terms are necessary, they appear in bold-faced type, are carefully defined in the text, and defined again in the glossary in simple, clear language.

Because much learning is based on analogy, numerous and colorful examples have been utilized to illustrate, emphasize, and clarify anthropological concepts. Wherever appropriate, there is a cross-cultural perspective, comparing cultural practices in several different societies, often including the student's own. But while the student should be made aware of the fact that anthropology has important things to say about the student's own society and culture, the emphasis in introductory cultural anthropology should be on non-Western societies and cultures for illustrative purposes. It is a fact of modern life that North Americans share the same planet with great numbers of people who are not only not North Americans but are non-Western as well. Moreover, North Americans constitute a minority, for they account for far less than half of the world's population. Yet traditional school curricula emphasize our own surroundings and backgrounds, saying little about the rest of the world. In its March 8, 1976 issue (p. 32), the *Chronicle of Higher Education* documented an increasing tendency toward cultural insularity and ethnocentrism in North American higher education. More recently, a special presidential commission expressed alarm over the inadequate attention given to the study of foreign languages and cultures by educational institutions in the United States. More than ever college students need knowledge about the rest of the world and its peoples. Such a background gives them the global perspectives they need to better understand their own culture and society and their place in today's world. Anthropology, of all disciplines, with its long-standing commitment to combating ethnocentrism, has a unique obligation to provide this perspective.

2. Original Studies

A special feature of this text is the Original Study that is included with each chapter. These studies consist of selections from case studies and other original works of men and women who have done, or are doing, important anthropological work.

Each study, integrally related to the material in the text, sheds additional light on some important anthropological concept or subject area found in the chapter.

The idea behind this feature is to coordinate the two halves of the human brain, which have rather different functions. While the left (dominant) hemisphere is "logical," and processes verbal inputs in a linear manner, the right hemisphere is "creative" and less impressed with linear logic. Pyschologist James V. McConnell has described it as "an analogue computer of sorts—a kind of intellectual monitor that not only handles abstractions, but also organizes and stores material in terms of Gestalts [that] include the emotional relevance of the experience." Logical thinking, as well as creative problem solving, occurs when the two sides of the brain cooperate. Thus the implication for textbook writers is obvious: To be truly effective, they must reach both sides of the brain. The Original Studies help to do this by conveying some "feel" for humans and their behavior, and how anthropologists actually go about studying them. For example included in Chapter 2 is an Original Study extracted from *Yanomamö: The Fierce People* by Napoleon A. Chagnon, who conveys a real feel for what it is like to be an anthropologist by discussing in vivid detail a unique experience he encountered in the field. There are four new Original Studies in the fourth edition.

3. Illustrations

Another means of appealing to the nondominant hemisphere of the brain is through the use of numerous illustrations and other graphic materials. A number of the illustrations in this text are unusual in that they are not the "standard" anthropological textbook photographs; each has been chosen because it complements the text in some distinctive way. For example, the photos on pages 220–221 depict the market scenes that display various cultures' approaches to trade, our own included. The line drawings, maps, charts, and tables were selected especially for their usefulness in illustrating, emphasizing, or clarifying certain anthropological concepts and should prove valuable teaching aids.

The three full-color portfolios, designed to catch the student's eye and mind, encompass the world of the Eskimo hunter-gatherer, the culture of the Quiché Maya of Chichicastenango, Guatemala, and the North American cowboy.

Each portfolio has a theme, and the accompanying text explains the illustrations and makes some important anthropological point.

4. Previews and Summaries

An old and effective pedagogical technique is repetition: "Tell 'em what you're going to tell 'em, do it, and then tell 'em what you've told 'em." In order to do just this, each chapter begins with a set of "preview" questions, setting up a framework for studying the contents of the chapter. Following each chapter is a summary containing the kernels of the most important ideas presented in the chapter. The summaries provide handy reviews for the student, without being so long and detailed as to seduce the student into thinking that he or she can get by without reading the chapter itself.

5. Suggested Readings and Bibliography

Also following each chapter is a list of suggested readings that will supply the inquisitive student with further information about specific anthropological points which may be of interest. Each reading is fully annotated and provides information as to the content, value, and readability of the book. The books suggested are oriented either toward the general or toward the interested student who wishes to explore further the more technical aspects of some subject. In addition, the bibliography at the end of the book is a complete reference tool in itself; it contains a listing of some 500 books, monographs, and articles from scholarly journals and popular magazines.

6. Glossary

Instead of being in the back of the book, where students rarely look, this book has a running glossary. This catches the student's eye as he or she reads, and so reinforces the meaning of each newly introduced term. Because each term that appears in the glossary is indicated in the index by bold-faced type, the student can readily look up the terms even in the absence of the traditional "back of the book" glossary. The glossary is thus a complete anthropological dictionary in miniature, with each term defined in clear, understandable language.

ADVANTAGES OF THE FOURTH EDITION

The planning of the fourth edition of *Cultural Anthropology* was based on extensive review and criticism by instructors who used the third edition. The changes have improved every feature of the book: readability, continuity, illustrations, Original Studies, summaries, suggested readings, glossary, and bibliography.

While this new edition includes no new chapters, nor have any old chapters been eliminated, their sequence has been altered. Thus what used to be Chapter 10, Economic Systems, now follows directly after Chapter 6, Patterns of Subsistence.

In the third edition, considerable material on modern, complex societies—frequently our own—was added throughout the book. This has been retained and, in some instances, added to, in the present edition. The third edition also saw a chapter on the history of anthropology replaced by boxes on major figures and their contributions to anthropological thought, placed as appropriate throughout the text. These too have been retained and expanded upon by the addition of boxes on Ruth Benedict and Lewis Henry

Morgan. As before, all chapters have been updated as necessary, and new material has been added on such topics as human bio-cultural evolution (Chapter 3), criticism of ape language studies (Chapter 4), Windigo psychosis (Chapter 5), human sexuality and the incest taboo (Chapter 8), the rejection of modernity, global apartheid and structural violence (Chapter 15), studying ones' own culture, anthropological ethics, and the practical value of anthropology (Chapter 16).

Several new illustrations have been added, and captions have been altered or rewritten to ensure that the illustrations supplement the text and clarify concepts that are not easily rendered into words.

In addition to the substantial rewriting and updating of the content of the text, four of the sixteen Original Studies associated with each chapter are new. The topics of these four studies include "A Voyage to Greenland" by Frederica de Laguna (Chapter 1); "The Changing Composition of Camps among the !Kung" by Richard Lee (Chapter 6); "Eskimo Realities: The Act of Artistic Creation" by Edmund Carpenter (Chapter 13); and "Resistance to Modernization among the Kwaio" by Roger Keesing. In addition to the Original Studies, original material developed for a telecourse coordinated with this book has been incorporated into Chapters 1, 8, 11, 15, and 16.

Finally, the Instructor's Manual has been designed to make it an effective tool for both instructors and students. Some of the features are chapter summaries with a statement of objectives, topics for class discussion, ideas for special student assignments, suggested films, and an extensive set of test questions.

ACKNOWLEDGMENTS

Many people assisted in the preparation of this book, some of them directly, some of them indirectly. In the latter category are all of the anthropologists under whom I was privileged to study at the University of Pennsylvania: Robbins Burling, William R. Coe, Carleton S. Coon, Robert Ehrich, Loren Eiseley, J. Louis Giddings, Ward H. Goodenough, A. Irving Hallowell, Alfred V. Kidder II, Wilton M. Krogman, Froelich Rainey, Ruben Reina, and Linton Saterthwaite. They may not always recognize the final product, but they all contributed to it in important ways.

A similar debt is owed to all of those anthropologists with whom I have worked or discussed research interests and the field in general. There are too many of them to list here, but surely they have had an important impact on my own thinking, and so on this book. Finally, the influence of all of those who assisted in the preparation of the first three editions must linger on in this new edition. They are all listed in the prefaces to the earlier editions, and the fourth edition benefits from their influence.

In the course of this revision, as with the last two, I asked my colleagues at the University of Vermont for sources and advice in their areas of expertise, as well as for critical review of rewritten material. I consider myself fortunate to have such colleagues and wish to thank them: Robert Gordon, William E. Mitchell, Stephen and Carrol Pastner, Marjory Power, Peter A. Thomas, and A. Peter Woolfson.

This revision has also benefited from the comments of a number of anthropologists who made suggestions for this edition based on their review of the third edition: Elvio Angeloni, Pasadena City College; Donald J. Metzger, University of Akron; James Myers, California State University, Chico; John Poggie, University of Rhode Island; Ruben Reina, University of Pennsylvania; Dennis Shaw, Miami-Dade Community College, and Aminal Islam, Wright State University. In addition, Richard Emerick, University of Maine, Orono; Al Hansen, Westchester Community College; Greg Truex, California State University, Northridge; Martha Ward, University of New Orleans; and Michael Whiteford, Iowa State University, made valuable comments on the first draft manuscript of this revision. All of their comments were carefully considered; how I have made use of them has been determined by my own perspective of anthropology as well as my experience with undergraduate students. Therefore, neither they nor any of the other anthropologists mentioned here should be held responsible for any defects in this book.

I also wish to acknowledge my debt to a number of nonanthropologists who helped with this book. David Bynton of Holt, Rinehart and Winston talked me into this project in the first place. I have always valued his friendly advice and his broad knowledge of anthropology and anthropologists when working on the various editions of this book, the present one included. I am saddened that his retirement makes this edition our last together. The whole field of anthropology will feel the loss of its great friend in commercial publishing. This time around editorial assistance was provided by Ruth Stark. Robert Kopelman was design supervisor, and Annette Mayeski guided the production process. I am also grateful that they allowed me such a free hand with this, as with the previous, revisions, though of course it means that I cannot "pass the buck" so far as defects in the book are concerned.

I have been teaching introductory cultural anthropology since 1965, and I must acknowledge the contribution made by the students who have enrolled in the course over the years. My experience with them, and their reaction to previous editions of this text, as well as to others, have been important in determining what has and what has not gone into this book. One of those students, Sarah Burke, deserves special thanks for helping me this time around with the "cut and paste" process, and for her honest and perceptive comments about what particularly excited her about the book.

Again the greatest debt of all is owed my wife and children. Not only did they have to put up with my preoccupation with this book when it was first written, as well as revised, but they had to attend to the needs of various sheep, pigs, chickens, and geese on those occasions when my preoccupation kept me late in my office.

Burlington, Vt.   W.A.H.

Contents

TO David P. Boynton

*The kind of editor every
author would like to have,
and whose confidence in
this author is greatly
appreciated.*

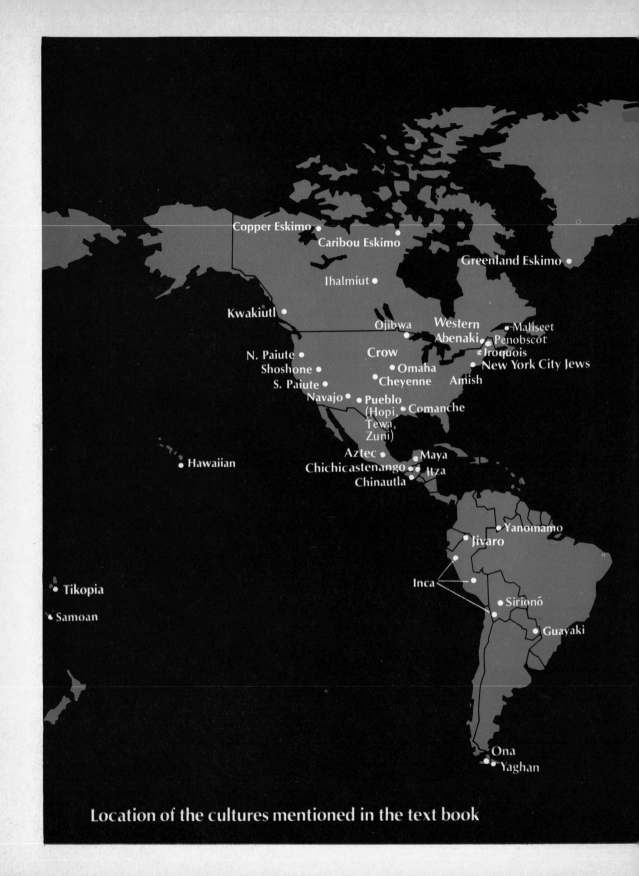

Copper Eskimo
Caribou Eskimo
Greenland Eskimo
Ihalmiut
Kwakiutl
Ojibwa
Western Abenaki
Maliseet
Penobscot
Iroquois
Crow
New York City Jews
N. Paiute
Omaha
Shoshone
Cheyenne
Amish
S. Paiute
Navajo
Pueblo (Hopi, Tewa, Zuni)
Comanche
Hawaiian
Aztec
Maya
Chichicastenango
Itza
Chinautla
Tikopia
Samoan
Yanomamo
Jivaro
Inca
Sirionó
Guayaki
Ona
Yaghan

Location of the cultures mentioned in the text book

Anthropologists, like all social and behavioral scientists, attempt to understand and explain human behavior. Such an undertaking requires a knowledge of human behavior in non-Western as well as Western societies. Because non-Western peoples have been relatively neglected by other social and behavioral scientists, anthropologists have devoted much attention to such peoples. Here a Hopi potter paints a design on a jar. In North America, the rise of anthropology as a field of study was closely linked with the study of North American Indians.

PART ONE

ANTHROPOLOGY AND THE STUDY OF CULTURE

INTRODUCTION

nthropology is the most liberating of all the sciences. Not only has it exposed the fallacies of racial and cultural superiority, but its devotion to the study of all peoples, regardless of where and when they lived, has cast more light on human nature than all the reflections of sages or the studies of laboratory scientists. If this sounds like the assertion of an overly enthusiastic anthropologist, it is not; it was all said by the philosopher Grace de Laguna in her 1941 presidential address to the Eastern Division of the American Philosophical Association.

The subject matter of anthropology is vast, as we shall see in the first three chapters of this book: it includes everything that has to do with human beings, past and present. Of course, many other disciplines are concerned in one way or another with human beings. Some, such as anatomy and physiology, study humans as biological organisms. The social sciences are concerned with the distinctive forms of human relationships, while the humanities examine the great achievements of human culture. Anthropologists are interested in all of these things too, but they try to deal with them all together, in all places and times. It is this unique, broad perspective which equips anthropologists so well to deal with that elusive thing called human nature.

Needless to say, no single anthropologist is able to investigate personally everything that has to do with human beings. For practical purposes, the discipline is divided into various subfields, and individual anthropologists specialize in one or more of these. Whatever their specialization, though, they retain a commitment to a broader, overall perspective on humankind. For example, cultural anthropologists specialize in the study of human behavior, while physical anthropologists specialize in the study of humans as biological organisms. Yet neither can afford to ignore the work of the other, for human behavior and biology are inextricably intertwined, with each affecting the other in important ways. We can see, for example, how biology affects a cultural practice, color-naming behavior. Human populations differ in the density of pigmentation within the eye itself, which in turn affects people's ability to distinguish the color blue from green, black, or both. For this reason, a number of cultures identify blue with green, black, or both. We can see also how a cultural practice may affect human biology, as exemplified by the sickle-cell trait and related conditions. In certain parts of the Old World, when humans took up the practice of farming, they altered the ecology in a way that, by chance, created ideal conditions for the breeding of mosquitoes. As a result, malaria became a serious problem, and a biological response to this was the spread of certain genes that, in substantial numbers of people living in malarial areas, produced a built-in resistance to the disease.

To begin our introduction to the study of cultural anthropology, we will look closely at the nature of the discipline. In Chapter 1, we will see how the field of anthropology is subdivided, how the subdivisions relate to one another, and how they relate to other disciplines, particularly the other sciences. Following this, we will turn our attention to the core concept of anthropology, the concept of culture. In Chapter 2, we will discuss the nature of culture and its significance for human individuals and human societies. We will conclude this part of the book with a chapter that gives us a look at how human culture began and gained primacy over biological change as the human mechanism for solving the problems of existence. We will see, also, how cultural evolution has its roots in biological evolution, and how it has played a significant role in making human beings what they are today. With these things done, we will have set the stage for a detailed look at the subject matter of cultural anthropology.

1 The Nature of Anthropology

The landing of Columbus, as depicted in a print that accompanied a 1493 Italian printing of Columbus' first letter. The discovery of the Americas with their previously unknown peoples was a major stimulus to new and revolutionary thinking about humanity on the part of Europeans.

PREVIEW

WHAT IS ANTHROPOLOGY?

Anthropology, the study of humankind, seeks to produce useful generalizations about people and their behavior and to arrive at an unbiased understanding of human diversity.

WHAT DO ANTHROPOLOGISTS DO?

Physical anthropologists study humans as biological organisms, tracing the evolutionary development of the human animal and looking at the biological variations within the species. Cultural anthropologists are concerned with human cultures, or the ways of life in societies. Within the field of cultural anthropology are archeologists, who seek to explain human behavior by studying material objects, usually from past cultures; linguists, who study languages, by which cultures are maintained and passed on to succeeding generations; and ethnologists, who study cultures as they can be experienced and discussed with persons whose culture is to be understood.

HOW DO ANTHROPOLOGISTS DO WHAT THEY DO?

Anthropologists, in common with other scientists, are concerned with the formulation and testing of hypotheses, or tentative explanations of observed phenomena. In so doing, they hope to arrive at a system of validated hypotheses or theory, although they recognize that no theory is ever completely beyond challenge. In order to frame hypotheses that are as objective and free of cultural bias as possible, anthropologists typically develop them through a kind of total immersion in the field, becoming so familiar with the minute details of the situation that they can begin to recognize patterns inherent in the data. It is also through fieldwork that anthropologists test existing hypotheses.

For as long as they have been on earth, people have wondered about who they are, where they came from, and why they act the way they do. Throughout most of their history, though, people were unable to accumulate an extensive and reliable body of data concerning their own behavior and background, and so they relied on bodies of myth and folklore to answer these questions. Anthropology, over the last 200 years, has emerged as a more scientific approach to answering the questions people ask about themselves. Simply stated, anthropology is the study of humankind. The anthropologist is concerned primarily with a single species—*Homo sapiens*—the human species, its ancestors, and near relatives. Because the anthropologist is a member of the species being studied, it is difficult, if not impossible, to be completely objective. However, anthropologists have found that the use of the scientific approach produces useful generalizations about humans and their behavior. With the scientific approach, anthropologists are better able to arrive at a reasonably reliable understanding of human diversity.

DEVELOPMENT OF ANTHROPOLOGY

The discipline of anthropology, as we know it, is a relatively recent product of Western civilization. In the United States, for example, the first course in general anthropology to carry credit in a college or university,

Drawing of a Hottentot community from a British publication of 1731. The widespread availability of written accounts and pictures of diverse non-European peoples led Europeans to question traditional explanations of human origins.

In the United States, anthropology began in the nine-teenth century as a number of dedicated amateurs, many of whom were women, went into the field to find out for themselves whether prevailing ideas about so-called savage and barbarian peoples had any validity. Shown here are Alice Fletcher, who spent the better part of 30 years documenting the ways of the Omaha Indians, and Frank Hamilton Cushing, who lived for 4½ years in a Zuni pueblo in New Mexico.

which was offered at the University of Vermont, was not offered until 1886.[1] If people have always wondered about themselves and their origins, why then did it take such a long time for a systematic discipline of anthropology to appear?

The answer to this is as complex as human history. In part, the question of anthropology's slow growth may be answered by reference to the limits of human technol-

ogy. Throughout most of history, people have been restricted in their geographical horizons. Without the means of traveling to distant parts of the world, observation of cultures and peoples far from one's own was a difficult—if not impossible—venture. Extensive travel was usually the exclusive prerogative of a few; the study of foreign peoples and cultures was not likely to flourish until adequate modes of transportation and communication could be developed.

This is not to say that people have always been unaware of the existence of other people in the world who look and act differ-

---

[1] William A. Haviland and Louise A. Basa, "Anthropology and the Academy: George Perkins and the Nineteenth Century," *Man in the Northeast* (Fall 1974), 8:120.

ently from themselves. The Judeo-Christian Bible, for example, is full of references to diverse peoples, among them Jews, Egyptians, Hittites, Babylonians, Ethiopians, Romans, and so forth. But different though they may have been, these peoples were at least familiar to one another, and familiar differences are one thing while unfamiliar differences are another. It was the massive encounter with hitherto unknown peoples, which came with the Age of Exploration, that focused attention on human differences in all their glory.

Another significant element that contributed to the slow growth of anthropology was the failure of Europeans to recognize the common humanity that they share with people everywhere. Those societies that did not subscribe to the fundamental cultural values of the European were regarded as "savage" or "barbarian." It was not until the late eighteenth century that a significant number of Europeans considered the behavior of foreigners to be at all relevant to an understanding of themselves.

This awareness of human diversity, coming at a time when there were increasing efforts to explain things in terms of natural laws, cast doubts on the traditional biblical mythology, which no longer adequately "explained" human diversity. From the reexamination that followed came the awareness that the study of "savages" is a study of all humankind.

ANTHROPOLOGY AND THE OTHER SCIENCES

It would be incorrect to infer from the foregoing that serious attempts were not made to analyze human diversity before the eighteenth century. Anthropology is not the only discipline that studies people. In this respect, it shares its objectives with the other social and natural sciences. Anthropologists do not think of their findings as something quite apart from those of psychologists, economists, sociologists, or biologists; rather, they welcome the contribu-

Sociologists have respondents who are interviewed and to whom questionnaires are administered, and psychologists have subjects with whom they experiment. Anthropologists, by contrast, have informants from whom they learn.

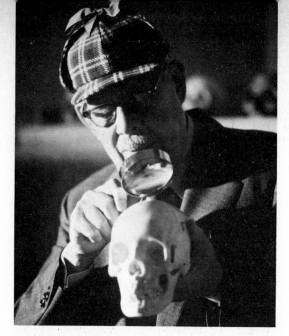

Physical anthropologists do not necessarily spend all of their time, or even the better part of it, studying human fossils. Wilton M. Krogman, one of this country's foremost physical anthropologists (and a member of the Baker Street Irregulars), does a considerable amount of detective work: identifying human remains found under suspicious circumstances.

> **Physical anthropology: The systematic study of humans as biological organisms.**

> **Cultural anthropology: The branch of anthropology that focuses on the patterns of life of a society.**

THE DISCIPLINE OF ANTHROPOLOGY

Anthropology is traditionally divided into four branches: physical anthropology and the three branches of cultural anthropology, which are archeology, linguistics, and ethnology. **Physical anthropology** is concerned primarily with humans as biological organisms, while **cultural anthropology** deals with humans as cultural animals. Both, of course, are closely related, and each contributes significantly to our knowledge of the other; we want to know how biology does and does not influence culture, and how culture can and does affect biology.

Physical Anthropology

Physical anthropology is that branch of anthropology which focuses on humans as biological organisms, and one of its concerns is human evolution. Whatever distinctions people may claim for themselves, they are mammals—specifically, primates—and, as such, they share a common ancestry with other primates, most specifically apes and monkeys. Through the analysis of fossils and the observation of living primates, the physical anthropologist tries to trace the ancestry of the human species in order to understand how, when, and why we became the kind of animal we are today.

Another concern of physical anthropology is the study of human variation. Although we are all members of a single spe-

tions these other disciplines have to make to the common goal of understanding humanity, and they gladly offer their own findings for the benefit of these other disciplines. Anthropologists do not expect, for example, to know as much about the structure of the human eye as anatomists, or as much about the perception of color as psychologists. But as synthesizers, they are better prepared to understand these things in analyzing color-naming behavior in different human societies than any of their fellow scientists. Because they look for the broad basis of human behavior without limiting themselves to any single social or biological aspect of that behavior, anthropologists are especially able to acquire an extensive overview of the complex biological and cultural organism that is the human being.

cies, we differ from each other in many obvious and not so obvious ways. We differ not only in such visible traits as the color of our skin or the shape of our noses, but also in such biochemical factors as our blood types and our susceptibility to certain diseases. The modern physical anthropologist applies a knowledge of genetics and biochemistry to achieve a fuller understanding of human variation and the ways in which people have adapted to their various environments.

Cultural Anthropology

Because there is no culture without the human animal, the work of the physical anthropologist provides a necessary framework for the cultural anthropologist. In order to understand the work of the cultural anthropologist, we must clarify what we mean when we refer to culture. The subject will be taken up in more detail in Chapter 2, but for our purposes here, we may think of culture as the rules or standards by which societies—groups of people—operate. These standards are learned rather than acquired through biological inheritance. Since they determine, or at least guide, the day-to-day behavior of the members of a society, human behavior is above all cultural behavior. The manifestations of culture may vary considerably from place to place, but no person is "more cultured" in the anthropological sense than any other.

Just as physical anthropology is closely related to the other biological sciences, cultural anthropology is closely related to the other social sciences. The one to which cultural anthropology has most often been compared is sociology, since both are concerned with the description and explanation of behavior of people within a social context. However, sociologists have concentrated so heavily on studies of people living in modern, or at least recent, North American and European societies that their theories of human behavior tend to be **culture-bound;** that is, they are based on assumptions about the world and reality which are part of their own Western culture, usually the middle-class version most typical of professional people. Cultural anthropologists, by contrast, seek to minimize the problem of culture-bound theory by studying the whole of humanity and do not limit themselves to the study of Western peoples: anthropologists have concluded that to fully understand human behavior, *all* humans must be studied. Perhaps more than any other feature, a concern with non-Western societies has distinguished cultural anthropology from the other social sciences.

The emphasis cultural anthropology places on studies of prehistoric or more recent non-Western cultures has often led to findings that dispute existing beliefs arrived at on the basis of Western studies. For example, Margaret Mead's work in Samoa in the 1920s disputed the generally accepted theory that the biological changes of adolescence are inevitably accompanied by a good deal of social and psychological storm and stress. Similarly, the anthropologist Bronislaw Malinowski was one of the first to cast doubt upon the supposed uni-

The subfields of anthropology.

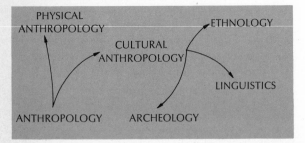

PHYSICAL ANTHROPOLOGY

CULTURAL ANTHROPOLOGY

ETHNOLOGY

LINGUISTICS

ANTHROPOLOGY   ARCHEOLOGY

versality of the **Oedipus complex**—the strong sexual attachment of a boy to his mother, coupled with hostility toward his father—which Freud had observed and named. Because the findings of the cultural anthropologist have often challenged the conclusions of the sociologist, the psychologist, and the economist, anthropology has traditionally played the constructive role of "devil's advocate" to the social sciences.

Cultural anthropology may be divided into the areas of archeology, linguistic anthropology, and ethnology. Although each of these areas has its own special interests and methods, all deal with cultural data. The archeologist, the linguist, and the ethnologist may take different approaches to the subject, but each is primarily concerned with gathering and analyzing data that may be useful in explaining the various human cultures and the ways that cultures everywhere develop, adapt, and continue to change.

ARCHEOLOGY **Archeology** is the branch of cultural anthropology that studies material objects in order to describe and explain human behavior. For the most part, it has focused on the human past, for things rather than ideas are often all that survive of that past. The archeologist studies the tools, pottery, and other enduring relics that remain as the legacy of extinct cultures, some of them as much as 2.5 million years old. Unlike the historian, the archeologist is not restricted to the past 5000 years of human history during which written records have been left of human accomplishments.

Although archeologists have concentrated on the human past, there are some who are concerned with the study of material objects in contemporary settings. This is one of the concerns of the University of Arizona's "Garbage Project," which, by a

> **Culture-bound:** Based on assumptions about the world and reality which are part of one's own culture.

> **Oedipus complex:** Freud's theory that a boy feels a sexual desire for his mother, but hostility toward his father.

> **Archeology:** The study of material objects, usually from the past, to describe and explain human behavior.

carefully controlled study of household waste, is producing much information about contemporary social issues.[2] One of the several aims of this project is to test the validity of interview-survey techniques, upon which sociologists, economists, and other social scientists rely heavily for their data. The tests clearly show a significant difference between what people think, or at least say, they do and what garbage analysis shows they actually do. For example, in 1973, conventional sociological techniques were used to construct and administer a questionnaire to find out about the rate of alcoholic consumption in Tucson. In one part of town, 15 percent of respondent households admitted consuming beer, and no household reported consumption of more than eight cans a week. Analysis of garbage from the same area, however, demonstrated that some beer was consumed in over 80 percent of households, and 50 percent discarded more than eight empty cans a week. Another interesting finding of the Garbage Project is that when beef prices reached an all-time high in 1973, so did the

_____

[2] David H. Thomas, *Archaeology* (New York: Holt, Rinehart and Winston, 1979), pp. 416, 421.

Archeologists study material remains in order to learn about human behavior. Shown here is the author, who is investigating the remains of an eighteenth-century charcoal manufacturing operation. The investigation of remains dating to periods for which historic records are available is known as historic archeology.

Archeologist William Rathje, director of the Garbage Project, with an array of choice "artifacts."

amount of beef wasted by households. The same thing happened with sugar, when it was scarce in 1975. Although economic theory, not to mention common sense, would lead us to suppose just the opposite, high prices and scarcity seem to result in more, rather than less, waste. Obviously, such findings are important, for they suggest that ideas about human behavior based on conventional interview-survey techniques alone may be seriously in error.

LINGUISTIC ANTHROPOLOGY   Perhaps the most distinctive human feature is the ability to speak. Humans are not alone in the use of symbolic communication. Studies have shown that the sounds and gestures made by some other animals—especially by apes—may serve functions comparable to those of human speech; yet no other animal has developed so complex a system of symbolic communication as have humans. Ultimately, it is languages that allow people to preserve and transmit their culture from generation to generation.

The branch of cultural anthropology that studies human languages is called **linguistic anthropology.** Linguistics may deal with the description of a language (the way it forms a sentence or conjugates a verb) or with the history of languages (the way languages develop and influence each other with the passage of time). Both approaches yield valuable information, not only about the ways in which people communicate but about the ways in which they understand the external world as well. The colloquial language of most North Americans, for example, includes a number of slang words, such as "dough," "greenback," "dust," "loot," and "bread," to identify what a Papuan would recognize only as "money." Such situations help identify things that are considered of special importance to a culture. Through the study of linguistics, the anthropologist is better able to understand how people perceive themselves and the world around them.

Anthropological linguists may also make a significant contribution to our understanding of the human past. By working out the genealogical relationships among languages, and studying the distributions of those languages, they may estimate how long the speakers of those languages have lived where they do. By identifying those words in related languages that go back to an ancient ancestral tongue, they can also suggest where the speakers of the ancestral language lived, as well as how they lived.

ETHNOLOGY As the archeologist has traditionally concentrated on cultures of the past, so the **ethnologist** concentrates on cultures of the present. While the archeologist focuses on the study of material objects to learn about human behavior, the ethnologist concentrates on the study of human behavior as it can be seen, experienced, and discussed with those whose culture is to be understood.

Fundamental to the ethnologist's approach is descriptive **ethnography.** It has been observed with some validity that "the ethnographer is an archeologist who catches his archeology alive."[3] Whenever possible the ethnologist becomes ethnographer by going into the field to live among the people under study. By eating their food, speaking their language, and personally observing their habits and customs, the ethnographer is able to understand a society's way of life to a far greater extent than any "armchair anthropologist" ever could; one learns a culture best by learning how to behave acceptably oneself in the society in

Linguistic anthropology: The branch of cultural anthropology that studies human language.

Ethnologist: An anthropologist who studies cultures from a comparative or historical point of view.

Ethnography: The systematic description of a culture based on firsthand observation.

Holistic perspective: In anthropology, the attempt to view things in the broadest possible context, in order to understand their interconnections and interdependence.

which one is doing fieldwork. The ethnographer tries to become a participant-observer in the culture under study. This does not mean that one must join in a people's battles in order to study a culture in which warfare is prominent. But by living among a warlike people, the ethnographer should be able to understand the role of warfare in the overall cultural scheme. He or she must be a meticulous observer in order to be able to get a broad overview of a culture without placing undue stress on any of its component parts. Only by discovering how all cultural institutions—social, political, economic, religious—fit together can the ethnographer begin to understand the cultural system. Anthropologists refer to this as the **holistic perspective,** and it is one of the distinguishing features of anthropology. Robert Gordon, an anthropologist from Namibia, speaks of it in this way: "Whereas the sociologist or the political scientist might examine the beauty of a flower petal by petal, the anthropologist is

[3]Clyde Kluckhohn, *Mirror for Man: A Survey of Human Behavior and Social Attitudes* (Greenwich, Conn.: Fawcett Publications, 1970).

Cultural anthropologists often study a society by trying to live as its people do. Here, Dr. Napoleon Chagnon is eating a sweet fruit, known as the Surinam cherry, with Yanomamö Indian tribes-people.

the person that stands on the top of the mountain and looks at the beauty of the field. In other words, we try and go for the wider perspective."[4]

So basic is ethnographic fieldwork to ethnology that the well-known British anthropologist C. G. Seligman once asserted, "Field research in anthropology is what the blood of the martyrs is to the church."[5] Although undertaken to improve our understanding of human behavior, fieldwork has at the same time an important effect on the emotional and intellectual growth of the individual who undertakes it. Something of this is conveyed by the following brief Original Study in which Frederica de Laguna discusses her first field trip, to Greenland, in 1929.

[4] Robert Gordon, Interview for KOCE-TV in Los Angeles, December 4, 1981.

[5] I. M. Lewis, *Social Anthropology in Perspective* (Harmondsworth, Eng.: Penguin, 1976), p. 27.

Frederica de Laguna, Therkel Mathiassen, and two Greenland Eskimos examine an ancient sealskin mitten.

ORIGINAL STUDY

A Voyage to Greenland[6]

The journey really began that spring when I went from London to Copenhagen for a few weeks to study the famous Danish Eskimo collections. Unexpectedly, the trip led on to a great voyage across the North Atlantic to Arctic Greenland (and ultimately to a Ph.D. in anthropology). But, more important, it was a journey into a new life, and for me a new way of looking at the world.

Here began my association with the Danish anthropologists Therkel Mathiassen and Kaj Birket-Smith, later both expedition comrades. It was their influence and example, almost more than my training at Columbia under Franz Boas, Ruth Benedict, and Gladys Reichard (or one term in 1929 at London under Malinowski), that made me an anthropologist. At least, my first week's contact with the Danish scholars in the National Museum of Denmark in Co-

---

[6] Frederica de Laguna, *Voyage to Greenland: A Personal Initiation into Anthropology.* Copyright © 1977 by Frederica de Laguna. Reprinted by permission of W. W. Norton & Company, Inc., pp. 11–12.

penhagen convinced me that anthropology was what I wanted most in the world. Having once set foot in Greenland for a stay of almost half a year, I could not turn aside from that long journey or that vocation, even though I had to give up the man I loved.

The first field trip of an anthropologist is probably the most momentous occurrence in his or her professional life—more than the Ph.D., this marks the real initiation, and the true beginning of a professional career. The experience can be traumatic, exhausting, disgusting, frustrating, or terrifying, so much so that the budding anthropologist may be frightened away. Or this revulsion can occur even on a later field trip and doom him to a merely academic or museum profession. How fortunate I have been that my first field experience was so happy, and that it led to so many more. I knew, from the beginning, that this Greenland summer was to be glorious, no matter how strange, and because I was so sure of this, that made it so.

Anthropology is a way of life—not just another academic discipline in which one tries to pass on to students what one has learned. In the deepest sense this is perhaps impossible, for what one learns in living with and studying others in that alien world is not only those others but, ultimately, oneself. The first field trip is therefore truly an initiation, for it effects a transformation and, like all field experiences, by offering new opportunities for self-expression and living, demanding new adaptation to the queer and the uncomfortable and the alien, forces one to develop potentialities that might never have found fulfillment in ordinary life. In discovering and remaking oneself, of course, one discovers the world of man, where alien thoughts and feelings mask common humanity. Having become a citizen of that world, however humble or ignorant, one never returns as the same person to one's own native country.

The popular image of ethnographic fieldwork is that it takes place among far-off, exotic peoples. To be sure, a lot of ethnographic work has been done in places like Africa, the islands of the Pacific Ocean, the deserts of Australia, and so on. Yet anthropologists have recognized from the start that an understanding of human behavior depends upon a knowledge of all cultures and peoples, including their own. Hence, there have always been ethnographers working "in their own back yards," so to speak. A case in point is the work of the anthropologist W. Lloyd Warner, whose studies of "Yankee City" have become recognized as classics in their field by U.S. sociologists. It is true that in the past studies of non-Western peoples have been dominant in ethnography, in part because they were largely ignored by other social scientists. But more and more, ethnographers are finding that the same research techniques which served them so well in the study of cultures of non-Western peoples are equally well suited to the study of subcultures in our own society, be they the subcultures of street gangs, ethnic minorities, hospitals, or factories. Moreover, the knowledge gained usually does not emerge from the kinds of research done by other social scientists, such as sociologists. James Spradley, who has made a specialty of this kind of work, provides a nice illustration:

Take, for example, the theory of cultural deprivation. This idea arose in concrete form during the 1960s to explain the educational failure of many children. In order to account for their lack of achievement, it was proposed that they were "culturally deprived." Studies of cultural deprivation were undertaken, mostly focusing on Indians, Blacks, Chicanos, and other cultural groups. This theory can be confirmed by studying children from these cultures through the protective screen of this theory. However, ethnographic research on the cultures of "culturally deprived children" reveals a different story. They have elaborate, sophisticated, and adaptive cultures which are simply different from the ones espoused by the educational system. Although still supported in some quarters, this theory is culture-bound. Cultural deprivation is merely a way of saying that people are deprived of "my culture." Certainly no one would argue that such children do not speak adequate Spanish or Black English, that they do not do well the things that are considered rewarding in *their* cultures.[7]

Although ethnographic fieldwork is basic to ethnology, it is not the sole occupation of the ethnologist. Working with his or her own ethnographic data as well as those gathered by others, the ethnologist may choose to study one particular aspect of culture by comparing it with that same aspect in others.

Anthropologists constantly make such cross-cultural comparisons, and this is another hallmark of the discipline. Interesting insights into our own practices may come from cross-cultural comparisons, as when Arthur Kleinman compared Western with

non-Western (Taiwanese) approaches to curing.[8] From this he argues that the technological emphasis of Western medicine has led to a concern with the treatment of kidneys and gallbladders rather than people, who happen to be more than the sum of their organs. Non-Western approaches to curing, by contrast, deal with people's experiences of their illness, as well as their diseases, and Western physicians have much to learn from these. Cross-cultural comparisons highlight alternative ways of doing things, and so have much to offer North Americans, who, opinion polls show,

[8] Arthur Kleinman, "The Failure of Western Medicine," in David Hunter and Phillip Whitten, eds., *Anthropology: Contemporary Perspectives*, 3rd ed. (Boston: Little, Brown, 1982).

Rerebawä, a Yanomamö Indian, looks on as Dr. Chagnon records some of his observations.

[7] James P. Spradley, *The Ethnographic Interview* (New York: Holt, Rinehart and Winston, 1979), p. 11.

are becoming increasingly pessimistic about the effectiveness of their own ways of doing things. In this sense, one may think of ethnology as the study of alternative cultures. At the same time, by making systematic cross-cultural comparisons of cultures, ethnologists seek to arrive at valid conclusions concerning the nature of culture in all times and places.

ANTHROPOLOGY AND SCIENCE

The chief concern of all anthropologists is the careful and systematic study of humankind. If anthropologists were to pursue their work in an entirely subjective or even haphazard fashion, we might classify them along with poets or philosophers as serious but unscientific investigators of the human condition. However, this is not the case. Anthropology has been called a social or a behavioral science by some, a life science by others, and one of the humanities by still others. Can the work of the anthropologist properly be labeled scientific? What exactly do we mean by the term "science"?

Science is a powerful and elegant way people have hit upon to understand the workings of the visible world and universe. Science seeks testable explanations for observed phenomena in terms of the workings of hidden but universal and immutable principles or laws. Two basic ingredients are required for this: imagination and skepticism. Imagination, though capable of leading us astray, is required in order that we may imagine the ways in which phenomena might be ordered, and think of old things in new ways. Without it, there can be no science. Skepticism is what allows us to distinguish fact from fancy, to test our speculations, and to prevent our imaginations from running away with us.

In their search for explanations, scientists do not assume that things are always as they appear on the surface. After all, what could be more obvious than that the earth is a stable entity, around which the sun travels every day? And yet, it isn't so. Supernatural explanations are rejected, as are all explanations which are not supported by strong observational evidence. Because explanations are constantly challenged by new observations and novel ideas, science is self-correcting; that is, inadequate explanations are sooner or later shown up as such, and are replaced by more adequate explanations.

The scientist begins with a **hypothesis,** or tentative explanation of the relationship between certain phenomena. By gathering various kinds of data which seem to support such generalizations, and, equally important, by showing why alternative hypotheses may be falsified, or eliminated from consideration, the scientist arrives at a system of validated hypotheses, or **theory.** Although a theory may be accepted as true, no theory is thought to be beyond challenge. Truth, in science, is not considered to be absolute, but rather a matter of varying degrees of probability; what is considered to be true is what is most probable. This is true of anthropology, just as it is true of biology or physics. As our knowledge expands, the odds in favor of some theories over others are generally increased, but sometimes old "truths" must be discarded as alternative theories are shown to be more probable.

Difficulties of the Scientific Approach

Straightforward though the scientific approach may appear to be, there are serious difficulties in its application in anthropology. One of them is that once one has stated a hypothesis, one is strongly motivated to verify it, and this can cause one unwittingly to overlook negative evidence, not to mention all sorts of other unexpected things. In the fields of cultural anthropology, there is a further difficulty: in order to arrive at useful theories concerning human behavior, one must begin with hypotheses that are as objective and culture-free as possible. And here lies a major—some people would say insurmountable—problem: it is difficult for someone who has grown up in one culture to frame objective and culture-free hypotheses about another culture.

As our example of this sort of problem, we may look at attempts by archeologists to understand the nature of settlement in the Classic period of Maya civilization. This civilization flourished between A.D. 250 and 950 in what is now northern Guatemala, Belize, and adjacent portions of Mexico and Honduras. Today, much of this region is covered by a dense tropical forest of the sort that people of European background find difficult to deal with. In recent times, this forest has been inhabited by few people, who eke out an existence on the basis of slash-and-burn farming. Yet numerous archeological sites, featuring temples sometimes as tall as a modern 20-story building, other sorts of monumental architecture, and carved monuments are to be found there. Because of their cultural bias against tropical forests as places to live, and against slash-and-burn farming as a means of raising food, North American and European archeologists asked the question: How could the Maya have maintained large, permanent settlements on the basis of slash-and-burn farming? The answer seemed self-evident—they couldn't; therefore, the great archeological sites must have been ceremonial centers inhabited by few, if any, people. Periodically a rural peasantry liv-

> **Hypothesis:** A tentative explanation of the relation between certain phenomena.
>
> **Theory:** A system of validated hypotheses that explains phenomena systematically.

ing scattered in small hamlets over the countryside would gather in these centers for rituals, or to provide labor for their construction and maintenance.

This view was the dominant one for several decades, and it was not until 1960 that archeologists working at Tikal, one of the largest of all Maya sites, decided to ask the simplest and least biased questions they could think of: Did anyone live at this particular site on a permanent basis, and if so, how many; and how were they supported? Working intensively over the next several years, with as few preconceived notions as possible, the archeologists were able to establish that Tikal was a huge settlement inhabited by tens of thousands of people, who were supported by intensive forms of agriculture. It was this work at Tikal that paved the way for a new understanding of Classic Maya civilization totally at odds with the older, culture-bound ideas.

Recognizing the problem of framing culture-free hypotheses, anthropologists have relied heavily on a technique that has proved successful in other fields of the natural sciences. As did the archeologists working at Tikal, they massively soak themselves in the data, in naturalism as uncontaminated by the examiner as humanly possible. By doing so, they become so thoroughly familiar with the minute details that they can begin to recognize patterns inherent in the data, many of which might otherwise have been overlooked. It is these patterns that allow the anthropologist to frame hypotheses, which then may be subjected to further testing.

This approach is most easily seen in ethnographic fieldwork, but it is just as important in archeology. Unlike the sociologist, the ethnographer usually does not go into the field armed with prefigured questionnaires, which have a tendency to find only what they were designed to find. Rather, the ethnographer recognizes that there are probably all sorts of unguessed things to be found only by maintaining as open a mind as one can. This is not to say that anthropologists never use questionnaires, for sometimes they do. Generally, though, they are used as a means of supplementing or elucidating information gained through some other means. As the field-

work proceeds, the ethnographer sorts his or her complex observations into a meaningful whole, sometimes by formulating and testing limited, or low-level, hypotheses, but as often as not by making use of intuition and playing hunches. What is more important is that the results are constantly scrutinized for consistency, for if the parts fail to fit together in a manner that is internally consistent, then the ethnographer knows that a mistake has been made and that further work is necessary.

The end result of archeological or ethnographic fieldwork is a coherent account of a culture which provides an explanatory framework for understanding the behavior of the people who have been studied. And this, in turn, is what permits the anthropologist to frame broader hypotheses about human behavior. Plausible though such

The excavation of ancient house sites at Tikal, Guatemala.

hypotheses may be, however, the consideration of a single society is generally insufficient for their testing. Without some basis for comparison, the hypothesis grounded on a single case may be no more than an historical coincidence. A single case may be adequate, however, to cast doubt on, if not refute, a theory that had previously been held to be valid. Margaret Mead's discovery in 1928 that Samoan adolescents grow up virtually free from stress was sufficient ground for questioning the theory that adolescence is invariably, in all societies, accompanied by psychological stress.

Hypothetical explanations of cultural phenomena may be tested by the comparison of archeological and/or ethnographic data for several societies found in a particular region. Nonhistorical, controlled comparison provides a broader context for understanding cultural phenomena than does the study of a single culture. The anthropologist who undertakes such a comparison may be more confident that the conditions believed to be related really are related, at least within the region which is under investigation; however, an explanation that is valid in one region is not necessarily valid in another.

Ideally, theories in cultural anthropology are generated from worldwide comparisons. The cross-cultural researcher examines a worldwide sample of societies in order to discover whether or not hypotheses proposed to explain cultural phenomena seem to be universally applicable. Because the sample is selected at random, it is probable that the conclusions of the cross-cultural researcher will be valid; however, the greater the number of societies that are being examined, the less likely it is that the investigator will have a detailed understanding of all the societies encompassed by the study. The cross-cultural researcher depends upon the ethnographer for data. It

> **Ethnohistory: The study of cultures of the recent past through accounts left by explorers, missionaries, and traders, and through the analysis of such records as land titles, birth and death records, and other archival materials.**

is difficult for any single individual personally to perform in-depth analyses of a broad sampling of human cultures throughout the world.

In anthropology, cultural comparisons need not be restricted to ethnographic data. Anthropologists can, for example, turn to archeological data for the testing of hypotheses about culture change. Cultural characteristics thought to be caused by certain specified conditions can be tested archeologically by investigating situations where such conditions actually occurred. Also useful are data provided by the ethnohistorian. **Ethnohistory** is a kind of historic ethnography which studies cultures of the recent past through the accounts of explorers, missionaries, and traders and through the analysis of such records as land titles, birth and death records, and other archival materials. The ethnohistorical analysis of cultures, like archeology, is a valuable approach to understanding the phenomenon of change. By examining the conditions believed to have caused certain phenomena, we can discover whether or not those conditions truly predate those phenomena.

Ethnohistorical research, like the field studies of archeologists, is valuable for testing and confirming hypotheses about culture. And like much of anthropology, it has practical utility as well. In the United States, ethnohistorical research has flourished, for it often provides the key evidence necessary for deciding legal cases involving American Indian land claims.

Charles Darwin   Herbert Spencer   Edward Tylor

The emergence of anthropology in the late nineteenth century as a recognized field of inquiry owes a great deal to the three men pictured above. Darwin's ideas on biological evolution gave impetus to concepts of cultural evolution being developed at the same time by social theorists such as Herbert Spencer. Sir Edward B. Tylor, the first anthropologist to hold a chair at a British university, formulated the first well-known definition of culture.

Anthropology and Contemporary Life

Anthropology has come a long way in the past 200 years, and is anything but a static discipline. To the contrary, new discoveries are constantly being made, and anthropological phenomena are in a constant state of flux. Looking at our own culture, we can easily see the alteration of traditional values and institutions. Changing sexual roles, new attitudes toward the wedding ritual, and new alternatives to the traditional forms of marriage and the family are just a few examples of the fundamental changes readily apparent in our own culture. New areas of research are being opened to the anthropologist all the time; yet, at the same time, many opportunities seem to be rapidly disappearing. The plundering of valuable archeological sites for financial or political gain, for example,

casts a veil of urgency over the work of the anthropologist. Modern anthropology is a demanding and fulltime discipline requiring concerned and well-trained individuals. Anthropology is the systematic study of the human species and its works, past and present. Younger than most of the social sciences, anthropology is rapidly gaining in sophistication and importance. It intends not to replace the work of the economist, the historian, the political scientist, the psychologist, and the sociologist, but rather to supplement, expand, and synthesize that work. Above all, it intends to avoid allowing a "coldly" scientific approach to blind it to the fact that the human species is made up of individuals with rich assortments of emotions and aspirations which demand respect. Anthropology has sometimes been called the most humanistic of the sciences, a designation in which anthropologists take considerable pride.

CHAPTER SUMMARY

Throughout human history, people have asked questions about who they are, where they came from, and why they behave as they do. Folklore was the method traditionally relied upon to answer these questions. Anthropology, as it has emerged over the last 200 years, offers another approach to answering the questions people ask about themselves.

Anthropology is the study of humankind. In employing a scientific approach, anthropologists seek to produce useful generalizations about humans and their behavior and to arrive at an unbiased understanding of human diversity. The two major fields of anthropology are physical anthropology and cultural anthropology. Physical anthropology focuses on humans as biological organisms. Particular emphasis is given by physical anthropologists to tracing the evolutionary development of the human animal and studying biological variation within the species. Cultural anthropologists study humans in terms of their cultures. Culture is the rules or standards by which societies operate, and it has to do with all the learned behavior passed on from one generation to the next.

Three areas of cultural anthropology are archeology, linguistics, and ethnology. Archeologists study material objects from past cultures in order to explain human behavior. Linguists, who study human languages, may deal with the description of a language or with the history of languages. Ethnologists concentrate on cultures of the present or recent past; in doing comparative studies of culture, they may also focus on a particular aspect of culture, such as religious or economic practices, or as ethnographers, they may go into the field to observe and describe human behavior as it can be seen, experienced, and discussed with persons whose culture is to be understood.

Anthropology is unique among the social and natural sciences in that it is concerned with formulating explanations of human diversity based on a study of all aspects of human biology and behavior in all known societies, rather than in European and North American societies alone. Thus anthropologists have devoted much attention to the study of non-Western peoples.

Anthropologists are concerned with the objective and systematic study of humankind. The anthropologist employs the methods of other scientists by developing a hypothesis, or assumed explanation, using other data to test the hypothesis, and ultimately arriving at a theory—a system of validated hypotheses. The data used by the anthropologist may be field data of one society or comparative studies of numerous societies.

The subject matter of anthropology is ever-changing because new discoveries are being made, and cultures themselves are in a constant state of flux. Changing sexual roles and new attitudes toward marriage and the family are examples of changes that are readily apparent in our own culture. As new areas of anthropological research are opened up, as tools and methods of study become more efficient, and as anthropologists continue to maintain their commitment to sharing in the humanity of others, anthropology grows ever more successful as a genuinely humanistic science of humankind.

SUGGESTED READINGS

Fried, Morton H. *The Study of Anthropology*. New York: Crowell, 1972.
This is a nuts-and-bolts discussion of anthropology as a way of life and study; a modest, how-to-volume addressed to undergraduates and potential graduate students. Fried delineates the character of anthropology in the United States, as well as how to get into the profession.

Harris, Marvin. *The Rise of Anthropological Theory: A History of Theories of Culture*. New York: Crowell, 1968.
One of the most provocative histories of anthropological theory, this book traces the development of the profession as a science. Harris takes a very definite stand in support of the cultural-materialist approach and criticizes his colleagues from this point of view. Because of the opinionated nature of the book, it has been the focus of much controversy in the field, but still stands as one of the most exciting histories of the field ever written.

Oliver, Douglas Z. *Invitation to Anthropology*. Garden City, N.Y.: Natural History Press, 1964.
This guide to the basic concepts of anthropology is seen by the author as an outline of what ideally he would like all high school graduates to know about the anthropological profession. This slim volume is neither a textbook nor a substantive introduction, but a brief overview of the field.

Spradley, James P. *The Ethnographic Interview*. New York: Holt, Rinehart and Winston, 1979.
This contains one of the best discussions of the nature and value of ethnographic research to be found. The bulk of the book is devoted to a step-by-step, easy-to-understand account of how one carries out ethnographic research with the assistance of "native" informants. Numerous examples drawn from the author's own research conducted in such diverse settings as skid row, courtrooms, and bars make for interesting reading.

Spradley, James P. *Participant Observation*. New York: Holt, Rinehart and Winston, 1980.
This companion volume to *The Ethnographic Interview* focuses on ethnographic research through participant observation.

Voget, Fred W. *A History of Ethnology*. New York: Holt, Rinehart and Winston, 1975.
This history of cultural anthropology attempts to describe and to interpret the major intellectual strands, in their cultural and historical contexts, which influenced the development of the field. The author tries for a balanced view of his subject, rather than one that would support a particular theoretical position.

2 | The Nature of Culture

Peruvian peasants as seen from the train from Cuzco to Machu Picchu. All over the world people have worked out their own cultural solutions to particular problems of existence—solutions that persist in modern terms. Although sometimes construed as "old-fashioned," traditional ways may offer more in the way of human satisfaction than so-called modern ways.

PREVIEW

WHAT IS CULTURE?

Culture consists of the abstract values, beliefs, and perceptions of the world that lie behind people's behavior, and which that behavior reflects. These are shared by the members of a society, and when acted upon they produce behavior considered acceptable within that society. Cultures are learned, through the medium of language, rather than inherited biologically, and the parts of a culture function as an integrated whole.

HOW IS CULTURE STUDIED?

Anthropologists, like children, learn about a culture by experiencing it and talking about it with those who live by its rules. Of course, anthropologists have less time to learn, but are more systematic in the way that they learn. Through careful observation and discussion with informants who are particularly knowledgeable in the ways of their culture, the anthropologist abstracts a set of rules in order to explain how people behave in a particular society.

WHY DO CULTURES EXIST?

People maintain cultures to deal with problems or matters that concern them. To survive, a culture must satisfy the basic needs of those who live by its rules, provide for its own continuity, and provide an orderly existence for the members of a society. In doing so, a culture must strike a balance between the self-interests of individuals and the needs of society as a whole. And finally, a culture must have the capacity to change in order to adapt to new circumstances or to changed perceptions of existing circumstances.

Students of anthropology are bound to find themselves studying a seemingly endless variety of human societies, each with its own distinctive system of politics, economics, and religion. Yet for all this variation, these societies have one thing in common. Each is a collection of people cooperating to ensure their collective survival and well-being. In order for this to work, some degree of predictable behavior is required of each individual within the society, for group living and cooperation are impossible unless individuals know how each other will behave in any given situation. In humans, this predictability is achieved through culture.

THE CONCEPT OF CULTURE

The **culture** concept was first developed by anthropologists toward the end of the nineteenth century. The first really clear and comprehensive definition was that of the British anthropologist Sir Edward Burnett Tylor. Writing in 1871, Tylor defined culture as "that complex whole which includes knowledge, belief, art, law, morals, custom and any other capabilities and habits acquired by man as a member of society." Since Tylor's time, definitions of culture have proliferated. In the 1950s, the late A. L. Kroeber and Clyde Kluckhohn combed the literature and collected over a hundred definitions of culture. Recent definitions tend to distinguish more clearly between actual behavior on the one hand and the abstract values, beliefs, and perceptions of the world that lie behind that behavior on the other. To put it another way, culture is not observable behavior but rather the values and beliefs that people use to interpret experience and generate behavior, and which that behavior reflects. An acceptable modern definition of culture,

A. R. Radcliffe-Brown (1881–1955)

This British anthropologist was the originator of the structural-functionalist school of thought. He and his followers maintained that each custom and belief of a society has a specific function that serves to perpetuate the structure of that society—its ordered arrangement of parts—so that the society's continued existence is possible. The work of the anthropologist, then, was to study the ways in which customs and beliefs function to solve the problem of maintaining the system. From such studies should emerge universal laws of human behavior.

The value of the structural-functionalist approach is that it resulted in much fieldwork carried out by observers who were trained in anthropological theory as well as methods of scientific observation. This not only produced valuable ethnographic information, it also set high standards for future fieldwork. It also gave a new dimension to comparative studies, as present-day societies were compared in terms of structural-functional similarities and differences, rather than their presumed historical connections. But Radcliffe-Brown's universal laws have not emerged, and the questions remain: why do particular customs arise in the first place, and how do cultures change?

then, runs as follows: culture is a set of rules or standards that, when acted upon by the members of a society, produce behavior that falls within a range of variance the members consider proper and acceptable.

CHARACTERISTICS OF CULTURE

Through the comparative study of many different cultures, anthropologists have arrived at an understanding of the basic characteristics that all cultures share. A careful study of these helps us to see the importance and the function of culture itself.

> **Culture:** A set of rules or standards shared by members of a society that when acted upon by the members, produce behavior that falls within a range the members consider proper and acceptable.

> **Society:** A group of people who occupy a specific locality and who share the same cultural traditions.

> **Social structure or social organization:** The relationships of groups within a society which hold it together.

Culture Is Shared

Culture is a set of shared ideals, values, and standards of behavior; it is the common denominator that makes the actions of individuals intelligible to the group. Because they share a common culture, people can predict each other's actions in a given circumstance and react accordingly. A group of people from many cultures stranded over a period of time on a desert island might appear to become a society of sorts. The members would have a common interest—survival—and would develop techniques for living and working together. Each of the members of this group, however, would retain his or her own identity and cultural background, and the group would disintegrate without further ado as soon as its members were rescued from the island. The group would have been merely an aggregate in time and not a cultural entity. **Society** may be defined as a group of people occupying a specific locality who are dependent on each other for survival, and who share a common culture. The way in which these people depend upon each other can be seen in their economic systems and in their family relationships; moreover, members of a society are held together by a sense of group identity. The relationships that hold a society together are known as **social structure** or **social organization.**

British and North American anthropologists have debated the relative importance of culture and society for understanding human behavior. A. R. Radcliffe-Brown, a leading exponent of the British viewpoint, was more interested in observable social relationships than in the rules that lay behind them. Essentially the conflict is a difference of emphasis. Culture and society are two closely related concepts, and an anthropologist must study both.

Obviously, there can be no culture without society, just as there can be no society without individuals. Conversely, there are no known human societies that do not exhibit culture. However, some other species of animals lead a social existence. Ants and bees, for example, instinctively cooperate in a manner that clearly indicates a degree of social organization; yet this instinctual behavior is not culture. One can, therefore, have society without culture, even though one cannot have culture without society. Whether or not there exist animals other than humans that are capable of culture is a question which will be dealt with shortly.

While culture is shared by the members of society, it is important to realize that all is not uniformity. In any human society, at the very least there is some difference between male and female roles. This means that there are some things that women must be concerned with that men are not, and vice versa. So, there is bound to be some difference between men's culture and women's culture in any society. In addition, there will be some age variation. In any society, children are not expected to behave as adults, and the reverse is equally true. Besides age and sex variation, there may be variation among subgroups in societies. This may involve occupational groups, where there is a complex division of labor, or social classes in a stratified society, or ethnic groups in some other societies. When such groups exist within a society, each functioning by its own distinctive standards of behavior, we speak of **subcultural variation.** The degree to which subcultures are tolerated varies greatly from one society to another. Consider, for example, the following case from the *Minneapolis Tribune:*

CROWD MISTAKES RESCUE ATTEMPT, ATTACKS POLICE

Nov. 23, 1973. HARTFORD, Connecticut—Three policemen giving a heart massage and oxygen to a heart attack victim Friday were attacked by a crowd of 75 to 100 persons who apparently did not realize what the policemen were doing.

Other policemen fended off the crowd of mostly Spanish-speaking residents until an ambulance arrived. Police said they tried to ex-

plain to the crowd what they were doing, but the crowd apparently thought they were beating the woman.

Despite the policemen's efforts the victim, Evangelica Echevarria, 59, died.

Anthropologist James Spradley has explained this incident as follows:

Members of two different groups observed the same event but their *interpretations* were drastically different. The crowd used their cultural knowledge to (a) interpret the behavior of the policemen as cruel, and, (b) to act on the woman's behalf to put a stop to what they saw as brutality. They had acquired the cultural principles for acting and interpreting things in this way through a particular shared experience.

The policemen, on the other hand, used their culture (a) to interpret the woman's condition as heart failure and their own behavior as a life-saving effort, and (b) to give cardiac massage and oxygen to the woman. They used artifacts like an oxygen mask and an ambulance. Furthermore, they interpreted the actions of the crowd in a manner entirely different from how the crowd saw their own behavior. These two groups of people each had elaborate cultural rules for interpreting their experience and for acting in emergency situations. The conflict arose, at least in part, because these cultural rules were so different.[1]

The last example raises the issue of so-called **pluralistic societies.** Such societies

---

[1] James P. Spradley, *The Ethnographic Interview* (New York: Holt, Rinehart and Winston, 1979), pp. 5–6.

Amish children, in their distinctive plain clothing. Because of a religious prohibition against mechanized vehicles, the children must walk to school even in near-zero weather, although the schoolhouse may be several miles away. Upon arriving at the schoolhouse, they must clean their shoes before entering. An important part of Amish training is learning how to manage horses and produce crops.

> **Subcultural variation: A distinctive set of standards and behavior patterns by which a group within a larger society operates.**
>
> **Pluralistic societies: Societies in which there exist a diversity of subcultural patterns.**

are those in which subcultural variation is particularly marked. They are characterized by a particular problem: the groups within them, by virtue of the marked degree of subcultural variation, are all essentially operating by different sets of rules. This can create problems, given the fact that social living demands predictable behavior. In a culturally plural society, it may become difficult to comprehend the different standards by which the various subgroups operate.

An example of a subculture in the United States can be seen in the Amish.[2] The Old Order Amish originated in Austria and Moravia during the Reformation; today members of this order number about 60,000 and live mainly in Pennsylvania, Ohio, and Indiana. They are pacifistic, agrarian people whose lives focus on their religious beliefs. They value simplicity, hard work, and a high degree of neighborly cooperation. They dress in a distinctive, plain garb, and even today rely on the horse for transportation as well as agricultural work. They rarely mingle with non-Amish.

The goal of Amish education is to teach reading, writing, and arithmetic and to instill Amish values in their children. They

---

[2] John Hostetler and Gertrude Huntington, *Children in Amish Society* (New York: Holt, Rinehart and Winston, 1971).

reject "worldly" knowledge and the idea of schools producing good citizens for the state. The Amish insist that their children attend school near home and that teachers be committed to Amish values. Their nonconformity to the standards of the larger culture has caused the Amish frequent conflict with state authorities, as well as legal and personal harassment. They have resisted all attempts to force their children to attend regular public schools. Some compromise has been necessary, and "vocational training" has been introduced beyond the elementary school level to fulfill state requirements. The Amish have succeeded in gaining control of their schools and maintaining their way of life. In return, they are a beleaguered, defensive culture, more distrustful than ever of the larger culture around them.

The experience of the Amish is one example of the way a subculture is tolerated by the larger culture within which it functions. As different as they are, the Amish actually practice many values that our nation respects in the abstract: thrift, hard work, independence, a close family life. The degree of tolerance accorded to them may also be due in part to the fact that the Amish are white Europeans, of the same race as the dominant culture. American Indian subcultures have been treated differently by whites. There was a racial difference; the whites came as conquerors, and Indian values were not as easily understood or sympathized with by the larger culture. The nation was less willing to tolerate the differences of the Indians, with results that are both a matter of history and very much a current concern.

In every culture, there are persons whose idiosyncratic behavior has earned them the terms of "eccentric," "crazy," or "queer." Such persons are looked upon suspiciously by society and are sooner or later excluded from participating in the activities of the group if their behavior becomes too idiosyncratic. Such exclusion acts to keep deviant behavior outside the group. Most societies have cultural mechanisms whereby some forms of deviant behavior are incorporated into the group in an acceptable way. In traditional Mohave Indian culture, for example, transvestitism was accepted so long as the transvestite underwent an initiation ceremony; the person then assumed for life the role of someone of the opposite sex and was permitted to marry.[3]

Because individuals who share a culture tend to marry within their society and thus to share certain physical characteristics, some people mistakenly believe that there is a direct relationship between culture and race. Research has shown that racial characteristics represent biological adaptations to climate and have nothing to do with differences in intelligence or cultural superiority. Some North American blacks have concluded that they have more in common with black Africans than they do with their fellow North Americans who are light-skinned and straight-haired. Yet if they suddenly had to live with Bantu tribesmen, they would find themselves lacking the cultural adaptations to be successful members of this group. The culture they share with white North Americans is more significant than the physical traits they share with the Bantu.

Culture Is Learned

All culture is learned rather than biologically inherited. One learns one's culture by growing up in it. Ralph Linton referred

[3] George Devereux. "Institutionalized Homosexuality of the Mohave Indians," in Hendrik M. Ruitenbeek, ed., *The Problem of Homosexuality in Modern Society* (New York: Dutton, 1963).

Humans are not the only primates for whom learned behavior is important. Here, two chimpanzees use twigs as tools to extract termites from a nest, a feat which the animals learn and pass on to others.

Enculturation: The process by which a society's culture is transmitted from one generation to the next.

The biological needs of humans are the same as those of other animals: food, shelter, companionship, self-defense, and sexual gratification. Each culture determines how these needs will be met.

Not all learned behavior is cultural. A dog may learn tricks, but this behavior is reflexive, the result of conditioning by repeated training, not the product of enculturation. On the other hand, nonhuman primates are capable of forms of cultural behavior. A chimpanzee, for example, will take a twig and strip it of all leaves in order to make a tool that will extract termites from a hole. Such toolmaking, learned through imitation, is unquestionably a form of cultural behavior until recently thought to be exclusively human. The cultural capacity of apes, however, is obviously limited compared to that of humans. It is the superior learning ability of the human species that makes it distinctive as a cultural animal.

to culture as humanity's "social heredity." The process whereby culture is transmitted from one generation to the next is called **enculturation.**

Most animals eat and drink whenever the urge arises. Humans, however, do most of their eating and drinking at certain culturally prescribed times and feel hungry as those times approach. These eating times vary from culture to culture. Similarly, a North American's idea of a comfortable way to sleep will vary greatly from that of a Japanese or an African. The need to sleep is determined by biology; the way it is satisfied is cultural.

Through enculturation one learns the socially appropriate way of satisfying one's biologically determined needs. It is important to distinguish between the needs themselves, which are not learned, and the learned ways in which they are satisfied.

Culture Is Based on Symbols

The anthropologist Leslie White considered that all human behavior originates in the use of symbols. Art, religion, and money involve the use of symbols. We are all familiar with the fervor and devotion that religion can elicit from a believer; a cross, an image, any object of worship may bring to mind centuries of struggle and persecution or may stand for a whole philosophy or creed. The most important symbolic aspect of culture is language—the substitution of words for objects. Stanley Salthe

Leslie A. White (1900–1975)

Leslie White was a major theoretician in North American anthropology who saw culture as consisting of three essential components. He referred to these components as the techno-economic, the social, and the ideological. White defined the techno-economic aspect of a culture as the way in which the members of the culture deal with their environment, and it is this aspect which then determines the social and ideological aspects of the culture. Because White considered the manner in which a culture adapts to its environment to be the most significant factor in its development, his approach has been labeled the cultural materialist approach. In *The Evolution of Culture* (1959), White stated his basic law of evolution, that culture evolves in proportion to the increased output of energy on the part of each individual, or to the increased efficiency with which that energy is put to work. In other words, culture develops in direct response to technological progress. A problem with White's position is his failure to account for the fact that technological "progress" may occur in response to purely cultural stimuli. In this respect, his theories were heavily influenced by eighteenth-century notions of human progress.

points out, "Symbolic language is the foundation upon which human cultures are built. The institutions of these cultures (political structures, religions, arts, economic organization) could not possibly exist without symbols. . . ."[4]

It is through language—defined by Edward Sapir as the "purely human and noninstinctive method of communicating ideas, emotions, and desires by means of a system of voluntarily produced symbols"[5]—that humans are able to transmit culture from one generation to another. We shall consider the important relationship between language and culture in greater detail in Chapter 4.

Culture Is Integrated

For purposes of comparison and analysis, anthropologists customarily break a culture down into many seemingly discrete parts, but such distinctions are arbitrary. The anthropologist who examines one aspect of a culture, invariably finds it necessary to examine others as well. This tendency for all aspects of a culture to function as an interrelated whole is called **integration.**

The integration of the economic, political, and social aspects of a society can be illustrated by the Kapauku Papuans, a mountain people of western New Guinea studied in 1955 by the North American anthropologist Leopold Pospisil.[6] Their economy relies on plant cultivation, along with pig breeding, hunting, and fishing. Al-

---

[4] Stanley N. Salthe, *Evolutionary Biology* (New York: Holt, Rinehart and Winston, 1972), p. 402.

[5] Edward Sapir, *Language* (New York: Harcourt Brace Jovanovich, 1949), p. 8.

[6] Leopold Pospisil, *The Kapauku Papuans of New Guinea* (New York: Holt, Rinehart and Winston, 1963).

A group of young unmarried women takes time out for a chat during the long festivities that attend the killing of a pig among the Kapauku.

Cultural materialist: The approach to anthropology that regards the manner in which a culture adapts to its environment as the most significant factor in its development.

Integration: The tendency for all aspects of a culture to function as an interrelated whole.

though plant cultivation provides most of the people's food, it is through pig breeding that one achieves political power and positions of legal authority.

Among the Kapauku, pig breeding is a complex business. Raising lots of pigs, obviously, requires lots of food to feed them. This consists primarily of sweet potatoes, grown in garden plots. But some essential gardening activities can be performed only by women. Not only this, but pigs must be cared for by women. So, to raise lots of pigs, one has to have lots of women in the household. The way one gets them is by marrying them; in Kapauku society, multiple wives (polygyny) are not only permitted, they are highly desired. To get them, however, requires payment of bride prices, which can be expensive. In addition, wives have to be compensated for their care of pigs. Put simply, it takes pigs, by which wealth is measured, to get wives, which are necessary to

raise pigs in the first place. Needless to say, this requires considerable entrepreneurship. It is this ability that produces leaders in Kapauku society.

The interrelatedness of the various parts of Kapauku culture is even more complex than this. For example, the practice of polygyny works best if there are considerably more adult women than men. In the Kapauku case, warfare is endemic, regarded as a necessary evil. By the rules of Kapauku warfare, men get killed but women do not. This system works to promote the kind of imbalance of sexes necessary for polygyny. Polygyny also tends to work best if wives come to live in their husband's village, rather than the other way around, and that is the case among the Kapauku. Thus, the men of a village are "blood" relatives of one another. Given this, a patrilineal (descent reckoned through men) emphasis in Kapauku culture is not unexpected. And so it goes. These examples by no means exhaust the interrelationships to be found in Kapauku culture. They are sufficient, though, to illustrate the point.

From all of this, one might suppose that the various aspects of a culture must operate in perfect harmony at all times. The analogy would be that of a machine; the parts must all be adjusted to one an-

Describing another culture is like trying to describe a new game. The people in this picture may look as though they are playing baseball—but they are playing cricket. To describe cricket in the language of baseball would be at best a caricature of the game as the British know it. The problem in anthropology is how to describe another culture for an audience unfamiliar with it so that the description is not a caricature.

other or it won't run. Try putting diesel fuel in the tank of a car that runs on gasoline and you've got a problem; one part of the system is no longer consistent with the rest. To a degree, this is true of all cultures. A change in any part of a culture frequently will affect the other parts to varying degrees. For example, suppose that an attempt is made to eliminate warfare in the New Guinea highlands. Laudable though we might think this to be, it surely would alter the ratio of males to females among the Kapauku. This would certainly create problems for the further practice of polygyny, which functions best if there are more women than men in a society. Or suppose, for a moment, that a direct attempt is made to eliminate polygyny among the Kapauku. Obviously, this could have serious political and economic consequences. Or suppose that outside "experts" succeed in introducing new methods of agriculture, which must be carried out by men. This could well lead to changes in household composition and, again, political structure. Granted that these are hypothetical situations, the principle involved is an important one at a time when "experts," primarily from Western countries, are introducing all sorts of changes into societies around the world.

At the same time that we must recognize that a degree of harmony is necessary in any properly functioning culture, we should not assume that complete harmony is required. Because no two individuals experience the enculturation process in precisely the same way, no two individuals perceive their culture in exactly the same way, and so there is always some potential for change in any culture. So we should speak, instead, of a strain to consistency in culture. So long as the parts are reasonably consistent, a culture will operate reasonably well. If, however, that strain to consistency breaks down, a situation of cultural crisis ensues.

STUDYING CULTURE IN THE FIELD

Armed, now, with some understanding of what culture is, the question arises, How does an anthropologist study culture in the field? Culture, being a set of rules or standards, cannot itself be directly observed; only actual behavior is observable. In order to understand the problems of an anthropologist doing fieldwork in a strange culture, it may be helpful to imagine the unlikely situation in which someone from the interior of New Guinea is brought for the first time into a modern urban hospital, free to explore at will. Our tribesman would find rooms containing one, two, four, or six very odd-looking hammocks occupied by resting or sleeping persons. Men and women in white would be seen going to and from the hammocks, as well as pausing at little sites in the corridors. There would be strange moving rooms that go from floor to floor. Eerily masked figures might be found probing inside an apparently lifeless body. Elsewhere there would be offices, restaurants, shops, kitchens, a laundry, a pharmacy, voices filling the air from nowhere saying "Dr. Wilson, Dr. Jones, Dr. Shapiro, Dr. Anderson." The visitor would have no way of understanding any of this, and would be unable to fit any two parts together. How would the main purpose of the place be discovered? How would the visitor know which, of all the people seen, are the beneficiaries of this main purpose and which its agents? How could the rooms and activities devoted to primary tasks be distinguished from those devoted to secondary, supportive tasks? If our tribesman were to decide that the cafeteria or the laundry was the center of this place, this would be wrong. If our tribesman concluded that there was no relation among any of the things seen, this would be wrong again.

The anthropologist is not really in the same position as this imaginary visitor. The anthropologist goes into the field with the most advanced tools and methods of investigation available. Nonetheless, he or she will be confronted by a series of interrelated activities that at first may be difficult to understand. What is seen may be as foreign to the anthropologist as an urban hospital may be to a tribesman from New Guinea. Moreover, what is seen will in reality be as cohesive and interconnected to the insider as the various departments of a hospital are to an intern. The anthropologist must try to abstract a set of rules from what is observed and heard in order to explain social behavior, much as a linguist, from the way people speak a language, tries to develop a set of rules to account for the ways those speakers combine sounds into meaningful phrases.

To pursue this further, consider the following discussion of exogamy—marriage outside one's own group—among the Trobriand Islanders as described by Bronislaw Malinowski.

If you were to inquire into the matter among the Trobrianders, you would find that . . . the natives show horror at the idea of violating the rules of exogamy and that they believe that sores, diseases, even death might follow clan incest. [But] from the viewpoint of the native libertine, *suvasova* (the breach of exogamy) is indeed a specially interesting and spicy form of erotic experience. Most of my informants would not only admit but did actually boast about having committed this offense. . . .[7]

Malinowski himself determined that although such breaches did occasionally occur, they were much less frequent than gossip would have it. Had Malinowski re-

_____
[7] Bronislaw Malinowski, *Argonauts of the Western Pacific* (New York: Dutton, 1922).

lied solely on what the Trobrianders told him, his description of their culture would have been inaccurate. The same sort of discrepancy between cultural ideals and the way people really do behave can be found in any culture. In Chapter 1 we saw an example from contemporary North America in our discussion of the Garbage Project.

From these examples, it is obvious that an anthropologist must be cautious if a realistic description of a culture is to be given. To play it safe, data drawn in three different ways ought to be considered. First, the people's own understanding of the rules they share—that is, their notion of the way their society *ought* to be—must be examined. Second, the extent to which people believe they are observing those rules—that is, how they think they actually do behave—needs to be examined. Third, the behavior that can be directly observed should be considered—in the example of the Trobrianders, whether or not the rule of *suvasova* is actually violated. As we see here, and as we saw in our discussion of the Garbage Project, the way people think they should behave, the way in which they think they do behave, and the way in which they

Bronislaw Malinowski (1884–1942)

The Polish-born anthropologist Bronislaw Malinowski argued that people everywhere share certain biological and psychological needs and that the ultimate function of all cultural institutions is to fulfill those needs. Everyone, for example, needs to feel secure in relation to the physical universe. Therefore, when science and technology are inadequate to explain certain natural phenomena—such as eclipses or earthquakes—people develop religion and magic to account for those phenomena and to restore a feeling of security. The nature of the institution, according to Malinowski, is determined by its function.

Malinowski outlined three fundamental levels of needs which he claimed had to be resolved by all cultures.

1. A culture must provide for biological needs, such as the need for food and procreation.
2. A culture must provide for instrumental needs, such as the need for law and education.
3. A culture must provide for integrative needs, such as religion and art.

If anthropologists could analyze the ways in which a culture fills these needs for its members, Malinowski believed that they could also deduce the origin of cultural traits. Although this belief was never justified, Malinowski's functionalist approach played an important role in emphasizing the interrelationships within cultures and the ways cultures function to fill the needs of those who live by their rules.

actually behave may be three distinctly different things. By carefully evaluating these elements, the anthropologist may draw up a set of rules which actually may explain the acceptable behavior within a culture.

Of course, the anthropologist is only human. One cannot completely cast aside one's own personal feelings and biases, which have been shaped by one's own culture. The best that can be done is to be as aware of these as possible, so that they can be kept under control. A nice illustration of all this is provided by Napoleon Chagnon's account of an incident that occurred in 1971, when he was doing fieldwork among South America's Yanomamö Indians.

ORIGINAL STUDY
The Anthropologist in the Field[8]

A thousand previous days concluded with the same melodic incantations, pierced irregularly by a half-scream, half-growl as the shaman struck a powerful blow with his arm or arrow at one of a multitude of humanoid spirits (hekura) radiant in their fiery halos, bearing incandescent names, and partaking of the substance of human souls. I did not have to look up to know that the score of glistening men, streaked with green, ebene-laden nasal mucus, were growing more aggressive and violent as the effect of the magical powder hit them, and their foreboding preoccupation with sickness and death became more complete. They were growing surly, and I made a mental note to avoid that area as I methodically went through my IBM printout of village residents and photographed people, moving unobtrusively from house to house. I had run out of film and returned to my house—a section of the roof I shared with the headman and his family—to fumble another roll of Tri-X into my Pentax, attempting to keep my sweaty hands from fouling the pressure plate and focal plane. Droplets formed on my forehead, tickling as they coalesced and ran down my nose, stinging as they seeped into the corners of my eyes.

Dedeheiwä, the accomplished shaman, and Möawä, his son-in-law and the man whose house I shared, were leading the afternoon session in front of Yoinakuwä's place, some 40 yards off to my left. I could recognize their somber droning above the voices of the others, for I had gotten to know these two men quite well over the past three years. The village waiteri—"fierce ones"—were assembled to drive out the perceived, but mostly imagined, sickness that Dedeheiwä diagnosed as the effects of hekura sent by his enemies in Yeisikorowä-teri, a village far to the south. Dedeheiwä, as was his style, led the attack—very vigorously for a man his age. I remember taking periodic glances in their direction, unconsciously aware that the mood was volatile and a few of

---

[8] From *Studying the Yanomamö* by Napoleon A. Chagnon. Copyright © 1974 by Holt, Rinehart and Winston, Inc. Reprinted by permission of Holt, Rinehart and Winston, pp. 1–4.

A Yanomamö shaman has hallucinogenic *ebene* powder blown into his nose.

the men were becoming uncontrollable. I was concerned about what the head-man's younger brother, Yahohoiwä, might do. Living in the shadow of the headman's renown, he had every reason to be concerned about his status and ferocity. He was, however, an unpredictable character and quite capable of violent expressions. Earlier in the day he expounded about his ferocity to me at considerable length and named the men he had killed on various raids—just before demanding a machete. He was piqued when I didn't give it to him, annoyed because I was seemingly oblivious to the status he had and had developed so carefully in his exposition. Later, he openly insulted me as I passed before his house taking identification photographs and making sketches of the hammock positions and sleeping arrangements there. When I paid his remark no attention and passed his hammock in silence, he became more irate. I didn't see him coming and realized the degree of his anger only when I felt the sharp blow of his clenched fist on my chest. I could let his verbal insult bounce off unattended, but I could not take a smart thump on my pectoral that lightly. Why? Two reasons. First, it invites more of the same—or escalation. Second, after three years of that kind of thing I was reaching a saturation point and beginning to despise the pecking system within which I had to conduct my fieldwork. In this particular case, I retained enough of my wits and cultural relativism to measure my response. He was an edgy, unpredictable, and boisterous man, and very concerned about his personal status. Yanomamö men do not tell you how fierce they are unless there seems to be some question about the validity of their claims.

I dropped my field books and pencils when he hit me, and pretentiously mimed, in the most grotesque manner, the kinesthetic prancings of Yanomamö ferocity incarnate. The observing women and children giggled and squirmed, as I expected they would. The scene, potentially explosive, was now one of the subhuman buffoon fieldworker exhibiting agonistic stances of the least convincing kind; clearly aware that the provocation called for a reaction, but seemingly incapable of pulling it off in the appropriate fashion. But the reaction was recognizably Yanomamö for all its ribaldry. In the midst of the chuckles I smacked him back on the chest. To the observer, it was one of those slow-motion, fake blows. But I put a little ''English'' on the tail of it and I knew from his surprised look that it stung, just enough to communicate to him that I might not be teasing as much as my antics implied. It was a joke with a grain of kinetic truth.

For the time being I had made a public farce out of something that I knew was gnawing at him, and went about my work as if there were nothing amiss. I knew him well enough to avoid him for the time being, and when he and the others assembled for their daily *ebene* party, I was well advised to stay at a distance.

I closed my camera and began putting my notebooks and tape measure back into my side pack to resume my work. The din of the chanters suddenly gave way to the alarmed screams of women and children who scrambled in terror for the safety of the backside of the *shabono* roof. Men shouted and tried to disarm Yahohoiwä, who had, in the ecstasy of his high, taken up his bow and arrows and was now running back and forth, eluding his pursuers and intimidating the women and children. I watched briefly as the men approached him cautiously and attempted to disarm him. They stayed at a comfortable distance, and he kept them at bay by ominously pointing his arrow at them. I had seen this, too, on many other occasions. The rules of the ''game'' are to permit the man to display his ferocity (chasing women and children), even to the point of letting him discharge an arrow or two wildly into the roof. The general panic he creates strokes his ego, and the concern that the men show for him, their attempts—often very delicate, flattering entreaties to disarm—reinforce the feeling that *here is a man to be feared and respected.* They usually succeed in taking the weapons away and then devote their attention to the man to ''cool'' him down. Rarely do these displays lead to actual violence, although I recorded a few incidents that did. My reaction was: they are 40 yards from me and the men are already attempting to disarm him, so I can ignore it.

I congratulated myself at the wisdom of having decided to avoid that area of the village and continued putting my cameras and notebooks into my side pack. Then the women and children in the house next to me shrieked in unison and scattered. Most of them escaped by diving out the back of the house. I looked up to see Yahohoiwä staggering toward me with a wild, glazed look on his face. His nocked arrow was aimed right at my chest. Yanomamö, like most people, resent being stared at. I looked into his eyes and knew that the glint was not altogether chemically induced. I decided I was not going to play this stupid game with him and do what he obviously wanted me to do: turn tail and dive out the back of the house as the women and children had done. I also suspected that if I *did* play the game he might not be compelled, because of the earlier incident, to play the game according to the rules and shoot to miss. The thought of his barbed arrow in my retreating rear did not appeal to me, and quite frankly, I was getting angry. I decided to make a stand and stare him down. He was about to shoot when he realized that I was not going to run, and this startled him enough that he temporarily "lost" the nock in his arrow. I could tell he was annoyed, but by the time he had recovered his nock he was at a poor angle to get a good shot at me: he had run almost past me and had to turn slightly to shoot. His arrow whizzed past my ear and imbedded itself in the roof behind me. The men caught up to him and dragged him back to the chanting arena in front of Yoinakuwä's house and soothed him. I went about my work, but with diminished enthusiasm.

CULTURE AND PROCESS

In the course of their evolution humans, like all animals, have been continually faced with the problem of adapting to their environment. The term **adaptation** refers to a process by which organisms achieve a beneficial adjustment to an available environment, and the results of that process, the possession of characteristics that permit organisms to overcome the hazards, and secure the resources that they need, in the particular environments in which they live. With the exception of humans, organisms have generally adapted by developing advantageous anatomical and physiological characteristics. For example, a body covering of hair, coupled with certain other physiological mechanisms, protects mammals from extremes of temperature; specialized teeth help them to procure the kinds of food they need; and so on. Humans, however, have come to depend more and more on cultural adaptation. For example,

they have not relied on biology to provide them with built-in fur coats to protect them in cold climates. Instead, they make their own coats, build fires, and erect shelters to protect themselves against the cold. More than this, culture enables people to exploit a wide diversity of environments; by manipulating environments through cultural means, people have been able to move into the Arctic, the Sahara, and have even gotten to the moon. Through culture the human species has secured not just its survival but its expansion as well.

This is not to say that everything that humans do they do *because* it is adaptive to a particular environment. For one thing, people don't just react to an environment as given; rather, they react to it as they perceive it, and different groups of people may perceive the same environment in radically different ways. They also react to things other than the environment: their own biological natures, for one, and their beliefs, attitudes, and the consequences of their

own behavior, for others. All of these things present them with problems, and people maintain cultures to deal with problems, or matters that concern them. To be sure, their cultures must produce behavior that is generally adaptive, or at least not maladaptive, but this is not the same as saying that cultural practices necessarily arise because they are adaptive in a given environment.

A further complication is the relativity of any given adaptation: what is adaptive in one context may be seriously maladaptive in another. For example, the sanitation practices of hunters and gatherers are appropriate to contexts of low population levels and some degree of residential mobility, but become serious health hazards in the context of large, fully sedentary populations. Similarly, behavior that is adaptive in the short run may be maladaptive over the long run. For example, successful stock breeding by pastoralists over the short run may result in overgrazing, as in the desertification of much of coastal North Africa. Or in our own case the "development" of prime farmland in places like the

The Yanomamö are a people who live in the tropical forest of South America. The top photo shows one of their villages, on the edge of cleared land that has been planted with a crop of plantains. The other photos show living quarters within the village, with plantains hanging from the beams, and a group of men about to depart for a raid on another village.

45

eastern United States for purposes other than food production makes us increasingly dependent on food raised in marginal environments. High yields are presently possible through the application of expensive technology, but continuing loss of topsoil, increasing salinity of soils through evaporation of irrigation waters, and silting of irrigation works, not to mention increasing shortages of water and fossil fuels, make continuing high yields over the long term unlikely.

Cultural Adaptation

A good example of the way cultural factors are involved in a people's adaptation is afforded by the Yanomamö people of Venezuela and Brazil, who were just cited in connection with the difficulties of fieldwork.[9] Their adaptation to their sociopolitical environment is as important as their adaptation to nature, and their adjustment to it affects the way they are distributed over the land, their patterns of migration, and the kinds of relationships they maintain with their neighbors.

The Yanomamö are a fiercely combative people who inhabit tropical forest villages numbering 40 to 250 persons. Village life revolves around the cultivation of a plantain garden and warring against other villages. Because peace is so uncertain, a village must be prepared to evacuate, either to a new location or to the parent village, on very short notice. But since the garden is of such economic importance, abandoning it to start a new one elsewhere is seen as a formidable task, and is resisted except in the most extreme situations. Alliances are therefore made with neighboring villages, so that one village joins another's

---

[9] Napoleon A. Chagnon, *Yanomamö: The Fierce People* (New York: Holt, Rinehart and Winston, 1968).

war parties, or takes in the inhabitants of another village during times of need.

The Yanomamö are so combative that in a village of 100 people there is bound to be feuding and bloodshed, necessitating a split, with the dissident faction going off to establish a new garden. Although Yanomamö try to avoid the establishment of a new garden because of the labor and uncertainty of the first harvest, their political way of life forces them to this decision frequently. While they are a gardening people, their choice of a garden site is based on political considerations.

Functions of Culture

A culture cannot survive if it does not satisfy certain basic needs of its members. The extent to which a culture achieves the fulfillment of these needs will determine its ultimate success. "Success" is measured by the values of the culture itself rather than by those of an outsider. A culture must provide for the production and distribution of goods and services considered necessary for life. It must provide for biological continuity through the reproduction of its members. It must enculturate new members so that they can become functioning adults. It must maintain order among its members. It must likewise maintain order between its members and outsiders. Finally, it must motivate its members to survive and engage in those activities necessary for survival.

Culture and Change

All cultures change over a period of time in response to such things as the intrusion of outsiders, or modification of behavior and values within the culture. Within our own culture, clothing fashions change frequently. In recent decades, it has become

In the United States, clothing fashions change frequently, as illustrated by this series of photos. The tennis dress worn by Billy Jean King at Wimbledon in 1964 contrasts markedly with that worn by Mary K. Brown at Forest Hills in the 1920s, which contrasts with the tennis dresses worn by these earlier players.

culturally permissible for us to bare more of our bodies not just in swimming, but in dress as well. Along with this has come greater permissiveness about the body in photographs and movies. Finally, the sexual attitudes and practices of North Americans have become more permissive in recent years. Obviously these changes are interrelated, reflecting an underlying change in attitudes toward cultural rules regarding sex.

Culture change can bring unexpected and often disastrous results. For the Yir-Yoront people of Australia, the stone ax was the main technological tool as well as one of the most important mythical symbols.[10] The ax was a tribal totem and a symbol of masculinity. As such, it had an important place in the cosmology of the Yir-Yoront. Moreover, ax heads were important objects of trade acquired annually at ceremonial tribal gatherings. Because they were scarce, stone axes were owned only by senior men. Several decades ago, some well-intentioned missionaries provided the Yir-Yoront with steel axes. These then became so plentiful that even women and children had their own. The steel axes eliminated the need for the traditional stone ones. As a result, the stone ax as a symbol of masculinity was destroyed; and as the steel ax could not be related to the tribal totem, the whole ideological system of the Yir-Yoront began to disintegrate. The annual tribal gatherings dwindled, as there was no need to obtain stone ax heads through trade. The introduction of steel axes undermined the whole structure of Yir-Yoront society, and no substitute for the old order has yet been found.

---

[10]Lauriston-Sharp, "Steel Axes for Stone Age Australians," in Edward H. Spicer, ed., *Human Problems in Technological Change* (New York: Russell Sage Foundation, 1952).

Culture, Society, and the Individual

Ultimately, a society is no more than a union of individuals, all of whom have their own special needs and interests. If a society is to survive, it must succeed in balancing the self-interest of its members against the demands of the society as a whole. To accomplish this, a society offers rewards for adherence to its cultural standards. In most cases, these rewards assume the form of social acceptance. In contemporary North American society, a man who holds a good job, is faithful to his wife, and goes to church, for example, may be elected "Model Citizen" by his neighbors. In order to ensure the survival of the group, each individual must learn to postpone certain immediate satisfactions. Yet the needs of the individual cannot be suppressed too far, lest levels of stress become too much to bear. Hence, a delicate balance always exists between an individual's personal interests and the demands made upon each individual by the group. Take, for example, the matter of sex. Sex is important in any society, for it helps to solidify cooperative bonds between men and women, as well as to ensure the perpetuation of the society itself. Yet sex can be disruptive to social living if it is not controlled. If who has sexual access to whom is not clearly spelled out, competition for sexual privileges can destroy the cooperative bonds on which human survival depends. Hence, every culture controls sex for the good of society, but this must be balanced against the need for sufficient individual gratification lest frustration build up to the point of being disruptive in its own right.

So it is, then, that all cultures must strike a fine balance between the needs of individuals and those of society. Should those of society take precedence, then individuals experience excessive stress. Mani-

Revitalization movements: Social movements, often of a religious nature, with the purpose of totally reforming a society.

festations of this may involve all sorts of antisocial activities, including crime, drug abuse, or simply alienation. If this proceeds too far, the end result can be cultural breakdown, with violent change. Very often **revitalization movements** develop in such a situation. Such movements, which we will discuss in Chapter 14, are deliberate attempts to construct a more satisfying culture.

Just as problems develop if the needs of society take precedence over those of the individual, so they develop if the balance is upset in the other direction. Then it may become impossible to maintain integration of large populations, or to maintain much in the way of cultural complexity.

Evaluation of Culture

We have knowledge of diverse cultural solutions to the problems of human existence. The question often arises, Which is best? In the nineteenth century, Western peoples had no doubts about the answer— Western civilization was obviously the peak of human development. There were, though, some anthropologists who were intrigued to find that all cultures with which they had any familiarity saw themselves as the best of all possible worlds. Often this was reflected in a name for the society, which roughly translated meant "we human beings" as opposed to "you subhumans." Now it is recognized that any culture that is functioning adequately regards itself as the best, a view reflecting the

Failure of a culture to adequately satisfy the needs of the individuals who live by its rules may ultimately erupt in violence. Yet, the violence itself will be structured by the culture. In North America, violent protestors frequently burn property, as in the explosion that ripped La Guardia Airport in 1975. In southeast Asia, like this Buddhist monk, protestors may burn themselves.

phenomenon known as **ethnocentrism.** Hence, the nineteenth-century Westerners were merely displaying their own ethnocentrism.

Anthropology's reaction against ethnocentrism began when anthropologists started to live among so-called "savage" peoples and discovered that they were really just as human as anyone else. They have had a strong commitment to vigorously counter ethnocentrism ever since. In reaction against ethnocentrism, anthropologists began to examine each culture on its own terms. They questioned whether or not the culture satisfied the needs and expectations of the people themselves. If the people were cannibals, for example, they asked whether or not the eating of human flesh was acceptable according to native values. The idea that a culture must be evaluated according to its own standards, and those alone, is called **cultural relativism.** One could say, for instance, that the eating of other human beings may be acceptable to cannibals, yet it is a custom North Americans and other peoples would not wish to emulate, no matter how functional it may be to some other group of people.

While cultural relativism is vastly preferable to the ethnocentric approach, both positions represent extreme viewpoints. Cultural relativism replaces one set of subjective standards—those of the anthropologist's culture—for another—those of the culture that is studied. To be truly objective, the anthropologist needs a criterion for evaluation which is not derived from anyone's cultural values. Since science itself is a product of culture, it is not entirely value free, but it does offer a useful criterion for evaluation. This is the ability to survive, which is the ultimate criterion of success in biological evolution.

A culture is essentially a system to ensure the continued existence of a group of people; therefore, the ultimate test of a culture is its capability to adapt to new circumstances. In other words, a culture may be termed successful if it can secure the survival of a society and is reasonably fulfilling for its members. Of course, only the members of a culture can indicate what "reasonably fulfilling" means. An existence that seems fulfilling to one group may not be seen as tolerable to another. In evaluating a culture on this basis, the anthropologist avoids the worst pitfalls of ethnocentrism and relativism and arrives at a reasonably meaningful evaluation.

CHAPTER SUMMARY

The first important definition of culture was given by the British anthropologist Sir Edward B. Tylor in 1871. Tylor defined culture as "that complex whole which includes knowledge, belief, art, law, morals, customs, and any other capabilities and habits acquired by man as a member of society." Recent definitions have tended to emphasize abstract values and beliefs which lie behind observable behavior, rather than the behavior itself.

All cultures share certain basic characteristics; study of these can shed light on the nature and function of culture itself. Culture is a set of shared ideals, values, and standards of behavior. It cannot exist without society: a group of people occupying a specific locality who are dependent on each

> **Ethnocentrism:** The belief that one's own culture is superior in every way to all others.

> **Cultural relativism:** The thesis that because cultures are unique, they can be evaluated only according to their own standards and values.

other for survival. Society is held together by relationships determined by social structure or social organization. Culture cannot exist without society, although one can have society without culture. All is not uniformity within a culture. In any human society there is some difference between male and female roles; there is also age variation; and in some cultures there is also subcultural variation. A subculture is a group functioning within the general confines of the larger culture while observing a set of rules that is somewhat different from the standard. Pluralistic societies are those in which subcultural variation is particularly marked. They are characterized by a number of groups operating under different sets of rules. A subculture in the United States can be seen in the Amish.

A second basic characteristic of all cultures is that they are learned. Individual members of a society learn the accepted norms of social behavior through the process of enculturation.

A third characteristic is that culture is based on symbols. It is transmitted through the communication of ideas, emotions, and desires expressed in language.

Finally, culture is integrated, so that all aspects of a culture function as an integrated whole. In a properly functioning culture, though, complete harmony of all elements is not required.

The job of the anthropologist is to abstract a set of rules from what he or she observes in order to explain the social behavior of people. To arrive at a realistic description of a culture free from personal and cultural biases, the anthropologist must (1) examine a people's notion of the way their society ought to function; (2) determine how a people think they behave; and (3) describe how a people actually do behave.

Cultural adaptation has enabled humans, in the course of evolution, to survive and expand in a variety of environments. Sometimes, though, what is adaptive in one set of circumstances, or over the short run, is maladaptive in another set of circumstances, or over the long run.

To survive a culture must satisfy the basic biological needs of its members, provide for their continuity, and maintain order among its members and between its members and outsiders.

All cultures change over time, sometimes as the result of the intrusion of outsiders or because values within the culture have undergone modification. Sometimes the unforeseen consequence is the undermining of the entire social structure.

A society must strike a balance between the self-interest of individuals and the needs of the group. If one or the other becomes paramount, the result may be cultural breakdown.

A recurring question asked by nonanthropologists has been, Which culture is best? Ethnocentrism is the tendency to regard one's own culture as better than all others. One concept anthropologists use to counter ethnocentrism is cultural relativism, which involves examining each culture on its own terms, according to its own standards. Both the ethnocentric approach and cultural relativism apply subjective measures; to achieve a measure of objectivity the anthropologist must employ a criterion derived from science and examine each culture in terms of its success in surviving.

SUGGESTED READINGS

Gamst, Frederick C., and Edward Norbeck. *Ideas of Culture: Sources and Uses.* New York: Holt, Rinehart and Winston, 1976.

This is a book of selected writings, with editorial comments, about the culture concept. From these selections one can see how the concept has grown, as well as how it has given rise to narrow specializations within the field of anthropology.

Goodenough, Ward H. *Description and Comparison in Cultural Anthropology.* Chicago: Aldine, 1970.

The major question to which Goodenough addresses himself is how the anthropologist is to avoid ethnocentric bias when studying culture. His approach relies on models of descriptive linguistics. A large part of the book is concerned with kinship and terminology, with a discussion of the problems of a universal definition of marriage and the family. This is a particularly lucid discussion of culture, its relation to society, and the problem of individual variance.

Keesing, Roger M. *Cultural Anthropology: A Contemporary Perspective.* New York: Holt, Rinehart and Winston, 1976.

This book approaches anthropology by tackling the important problems of cultural anthropology, discussing them through ethnographic examples and theoretical considerations. In the process the author takes a critical stance toward conventional anthropological thinking and practice.

Kluckhohn, Clyde, and Alfred L. Kroeber, "Culture: A Critical Review of Concepts and Definitions," in *Papers of the Peabody Museum of Archaeology and Ethnology,* 1952, 47(1). Cambridge, Mass.: Peabody Museum.

This paper presents varying definitions of the concept of culture. There is a semantic history of the word "culture" and its related word, "civilization," analyses of various definitions according to anthropological concepts, and indexes of the definitions categorized by author and conceptual components. In addition, Kluckhohn presents definitions of "culture" as employed in other countries.

Kroeber, Alfred L. *Anthropology: Culture Processes and Patterns.* New York: Harcourt, 1963. This volume consists of chapters dealing specifically with matters of culture patterns and processes. The chapters are selected from Kroeber's major work, *Anthropology.*

Linton, Ralph. *The Study of Man: An Introduction.* New York: Appleton, 1964. Linton wrote this book in 1936 with the intention of providing a general survey of the field of anthropology. His study of social structure is illuminating. This book is regarded as a classic and is an important source historically.

3 | The Beginnings of Human Culture

A mature male gorilla keeps his eye on two juveniles. From the study of those primates most closely related to us, we can discover which characteristics we share with them and which we do not. The former characteristics we presumably owe to a common ancestry, while the latter are what make us distinctively human.

PREVIEW

FROM WHAT GROUP OF ANIMALS DID HUMANS EVOLVE?

Humans are classified by biologists as belonging to the Primate Order, a group that also includes lemurs, lorises, tarsiers, monkeys, and apes. By studying the anatomy and behavior of monkeys and apes, the primates most closely related to us, we draw closer to understanding how and why humans developed as they did.

WHEN AND HOW DID HUMANS EVOLVE?

Present evidence suggests that humans evolved from the small, apelike Ramapithecines, which lived about 12 million years ago. By 4 million years ago *Australopithecus,* apparently a descendant of Ramapithecines, had become fully adapted for moving about on the open savanna on its hind legs in the distinctive human manner. But otherwise, the behavior of this human ancestor probably was comparable to that of modern-day chimpanzees and gorillas.

WHEN AND HOW DID HUMAN CULTURE EVOLVE?

Human culture appears to have developed as some populations of *Australopithecus* began making stone tools with which they could butcher animals for their meat. Actually, the earliest stone tools and evidence of significant meat eating date to about 2 million years ago, along with the appearance of the genus *Homo,* whose brain was significantly advanced over that of *Australopithecus.* From then on the increasing importance of culture in human survival favored the evolution of a better brain, which in turn made possible improvement in culture as the vehicle through which humans secured their survival. By about 100,000 years ago the human brain had reached its modern size, but culture has continued to evolve and change down to the present time.

Early forerunners of humanity, like all other creatures, depended mostly on physical attributes for survival. Their behavior was to a large extent biologically inherited rather than learned; and their legacy to each succeeding generation was that of favorable genes rather than accumulated knowledge and skills. In the course of evolution, however, humans were to take a significant departure toward a more rapid and more flexible way of adapting to the environment. They learned to manufacture and utilize tools; they organized into social units more proficient at hunting and gathering than their ancestors had ever been; and eventually they learned to preserve their traditions and knowledge to bridge past and present, through the use of symbols. In other words, humans acquired the ability to produce culture.

This ability has made humans the most influential creatures on this planet. Humans do not merely adapt to the environment; they attempt to mold and manipulate it to suit needs and desires which they themselves define. If they manage to avoid self-destructing through misuse of their technology, their medical technology may eventually enable them to control genetic inheritance and thus the future course of their biological evolution. Space technology may enable them to propagate their species in extraterrestrial environments. And computer technology enables them to correlate and organize an ever-increasing amount of knowledge as they attempt to keep pace with the changes they themselves have brought about.

At this stage in their development, however, humans are also concerned with the implications of this remarkable culture-creating ability. Survival is threatened less by the environment than by people themselves. Atomic and hydrogen bombs, pollution, and population explosion—all these products of modern human civiliza-tion have triggered questions concerning the direction of human progress, as we shall see in Chapter 15. On the verge of a civilization even more highly organized and automated than our present urban environments, many people are attempting a "return to nature," to a simpler existence in which modern humans, like their ancestors, must rely more heavily on their own individual efforts and physical prowess. Others, bewildered and frightened by the complexity and pace of life, have escaped not to nature but into madness. And still others, who feel excluded and uncertain of their roles in our increasingly complex culture, have resorted to violence and aggression.

Yet the desire to get back to "simpler" times is a difficult one. The simplicity of bygone days is somewhat of an illusion, a sentimental attitude that fails to take into account the harsh realities of a time when survival was everyone's primary occupation. How hard the "simpler" life of only 100 years ago could be is easily appreciated by reading the inscriptions and vital statistics on gravestones in cemeteries of the time. And even if we did wish to live without the live-saving benefits of modern medicine, a literal return to the past would still be impossible, for conditions in the last quarter of the twentieth century are far different than they have ever been in the past. Among other things, there are now something like four times as many people living in the world than there were 100 years ago. If too many of today's city dwellers tried to live the kind of semirural existence that was characteristic of North America in the late nineteenth century, they couldn't do it—there simply wouldn't be enough space for them to do so.

In evolution there is no going back, at least in a literal sense, but we may be more capable of clarifying, adjusting to, and even controlling the direction of, present and future cultural transformations by simply *looking* back. Behaviorally and biologically, we are still in many ways similar to our prehistoric forebears. By studying the evolution of the hominid line and the physiological and cultural adjustments our ancestors have made, we may gain greater insight into the problems of adaptation that all humans are facing today.

HUMANS AND THE OTHER PRIMATES

Humans are classified by biologists as belonging to the **Primate Order,** a group of mammals which also includes lemurs, lorises, tarsiers, monkeys, and apes. One might properly question the value of studying primates other than humans when it is humans and their distinctive cultural capacities that concern us. But humans did not start out as cultural beings—they did not even start out as humans. Their roots, like those of the other living primates, lie in ancient times and in less specialized biological creatures; their development was influenced by the same evolutionary processes. By studying the environment of those times, the anatomical features which evolved in response to that environment, and the rudimentary cultural adaptations of those primates who share in the human ancestral heritage, we may draw closer to an understanding of how and why humans developed as they did.

A new, mild climate favored the spread of dense tropical and subtropical forests over much of the earth, including North and South America, Southeast Asia, the Middle East, and most of Africa. This led to an increase in the numbers and spread of grasses, ivies, shrubs, and other flowering plants, such as the trees that are found in forests. Forestation set the stage for the evolutionary development from a rodentlike ground existence to tree living.

> **Primate Order:** That group of mammals including lemurs, lorises, tarsiers, monkeys, apes and humans.

Evolution through Adaptation

The term adaptation refers to both a process by which organisms achieve a beneficial adjustment to an available environment, and the results of that process, the characteristics of organisms that fit them to the particular set of conditions of the environment in which they are generally found. The process of natural selection favors not just the survival of well-adapted individuals, but the propagation of their genetic traits. Although some individuals less suited to the environment may in fact survive, they often do not reproduce; they may be incapable of attracting mates, or they may be sterile, or they may produce offspring that do not survive after birth.

By chance, the ancestral primates possessed certain characteristics that allowed them to adapt to life in the forests. Their relatively small size allowed them to exploit the smaller branches of trees; larger and heavier competitors and predators could not follow. The move to the smaller branches also opened up an abundant new food supply. The primates were able to gather leaves, flowers, fruits, insects, birds' eggs, and even nesting birds, rather than having to wait for them to fall to the ground.

The move to an arboreal existence brought a combination of the problems of earthbound existence and those of flight. In their exploitation of space, birds developed a highly stereotyped behavior pattern, keyed to the problems of flight. Animals living on the ground developed a slower-paced, more flexible relationship to the environment.

The tree-dwelling primates, however, were obliged to develop both flexible behavior as well as virtually automatic mechanisms for moving through the trees; for if they were no longer limited to roaming around on the ground, they also no longer had the certainty of a substantial surface directly beneath their feet. Initial forays into the trees must have included many errors in judgment and coordination, leading to falls that injured or killed those who were poorly adapted to arboreal life. Natural selection favored those who judged depth correctly and gripped the branches tightly. Although it is likely that the early primates who took to the trees were in some measure preadapted—that is, they already possessed certain rudimentary features useful to tree-dwellers while still living on the ground—the transition to life in the trees required important physical adjustments. The way in which early primates anatomically adapted has considerable relevance for their human descendants.

Anatomical Adaptation

Based on the study of both ancient and modern primates, anthropologsts have worked out a list of characteristics common to them all.

PRIMATE DENTITION The diet available to arboreal primates—shoots, leaves, insects, and soft fruits—required less specialized teeth than those found in other mammals. On the evidence of comparative anatomy and the fossil record, the mammals ancestral to the primates possessed three incisors, one canine, four premolars, and three molars on each side of the jaw, top and bottom, for a total of 44 teeth. The incisors (in the front of the mouth) were used for gripping, canines (behind the incisors) for tearing and shredding, and molars and premolars (the "cheek teeth") for grinding and chewing food.

The evolutionary trend for primate dentition has generally been toward economy, with fewer, smaller, more efficient teeth doing more work. In the early stages, one incisor on each side of the upper and lower jaws was lost, further differentiating primates from other mammals. The canines of most of the primates grew longer, forming daggerlike teeth that enabled them to rip open tough husks of fruit and other foods. Over the millennia, the first and second premolars became smaller and eventually disappeared altogether; the third and fourth premolars grew larger and more efficient by adding a second pointed projection, or cusp, thus becoming "bicuspid." The molars also evolved from a three-cusp to a more efficient four-cusp pattern. Thus the functions of grasping, cutting, and grinding were served by different kinds of teeth.

SENSE ORGANS The primates' adaptation to life in the trees involved changes in the form and function of their sensory apparatus. To mammals living on the ground, the sense of smell is of great importance, for it enables them to operate at night, as well as to sense what is out of sight—to "see around corners," as it were. Not only can they sniff out their food, but they can be warned of the presence of hidden predators. Up in the trees, though, primates are out of the way of most predators, and good vision is a better guide than a good sense of smell in judging correctly where the next branch is. Accordingly, the sense of smell declined in primates, while the sense of sight became highly developed.

Traveling through trees demands judgments concerning depth, direction, distance, and the relationships of objects hanging in space, such as vines or branches.

In tarsiers, monkeys, apes, and humans, this is achieved through stereoscopic color vision, or the ability to see the world in the three dimensions of height, width, and depth. It requires two eyes set next to one another on the same plane so that the visual fields of the two eyes overlap. Stereoscopic vision is one of the most important factors in primate evolution, for it appears to have led to increased brain size in the visual area and a greater complexity at nerve connections.

A more acute sense of touch also characterized the arboreal primates. An effective feeling and grasping mechanism helped prevent them from falling and tumbling while speeding through the trees. The primitive mammals from which primates evolved possessed tiny hairs that gave them extremely sensitive tactile capacities. In primates these hairs were replaced by the more informative pads on the tips of the animals' fingers and toes.

THE PRIMATE BRAIN By far the most outstanding characteristic of primate evolution has been the great increase in size of the brain. The cerebral hemispheres—the areas of conscious thought—have grown dramatically, and in monkeys, apes, and humans they completely cover the cerebellum, the part of the brain that coordinates the muscles and maintains body equilibrium.

One of the main reasons for this change is probably the primates' arboreal existence. An animal living in the trees is constantly acting and reacting to the environment. Messages from the hands and feet, eyes and ears, as well as from the sensors of balance, movement, heat, touch, and pain, are simultaneously relayed to the cortex. Obviously the cortex had to develop considerably in order to receive, analyze, and coordinate these impressions and transmit

The primate skeleton—in this case an adult male orangutan. Note where the skull and spinal column are joined; the spinal column is well down beneath the skull, rather than at the back. While the jaws of the orangutan are large, there is no actual muzzle, and the eyes are together in a frontal position.

the appropriate response back down the motor nerves to the proper receptor. The enlarged cortex not only made the primates more efficient in the daily struggle for survival, but also prepared the way for cerebration, or thought—an ability that probably played a decisive role in the primate evolution that led to the emergence of humanity.

THE PRIMATE SKELETON The skeleton gives an animal its basic shape or silhouette, supports the soft tissues, and helps protect the vital internal organs. The opening of the skull through which the spinal cord passes and connects to the brain is an important clue to evolutionary relationships. In primates, the trend is for this opening to shift forward, toward the center of the skull's base, so that it faces downward, rather than directly backward as in dogs and other mammals. This shift enables the backbone to join the skull at the center of its base, a more advantageous arrangement for an animal that assumes an upright posture, at least occasionally. The head is thus balanced on the vertebral column, instead of projecting forward from it.

In most primates, the snout, or muzzle portion of the skull, was reduced as the sense of smell declined. The smaller snout offers less interference with stereoscopic vision and enables the eyes to be placed in a more frontal position. A solid partition exists in most primate species between the eye and the temple, protecting the eyes in their vulnerable position.

Below the primate skull and neck is the clavicle, or collarbone. It acts as a strut, placing the arms at the side rather than in front of the body and thus permitting them to swing sideways and outwards from the trunk of the body. Apes and humans especially are able to move their arms with great freedom. In the case of apes, this enables them to swing and hang vertically among the trees.

The limbs end in hands and feet with five extremely flexible digits. At the tips of these are sensitive pads protected by flat nails which provide an excellent grasping device for use when moving from branch to branch. The thumb and great toe are opposable to varying degrees, so food can easily be handled and branches grasped.

Hindsight indicates that the flexible unspecialized primate hand was to prove a valuable asset to late primates. It was, in part, the generalized grasping hand which enabled hominids to manufacture and utilize tools and thus speed their evolutionary change.

The relationships among the various Old World anthropoids, as revealed by molecular similarities and differences, are shown in this diagram. Its authors, V. M. Sarich and A. C. Wilson, have stated that it is difficult to consider seriously any date in excess of 10 million years for the origin of the separate lineages for chimpanzees, gorillas, and humans. Adapted from V. M. Sarich and A. C. Wilson, "Immunological Time Scale for Hominid Evolution," *Science,* 1967, 158:1201.

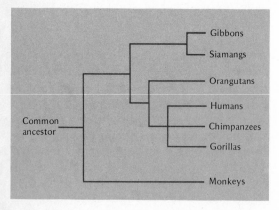

Adaptation through Behavior

Important though anatomical adaptation has been to the primates, it has not been the only way of coping with the environment. Studies of monkeys and apes living today—particularly the gorilla and chimpanzee, which are the closest living relatives of humans—indicate that learned social behavior plays an important role in adaptation. Admittedly, much of this behavior is inextricably woven with instinctual imperatives. Furthermore, modern chimp and gorilla communities have in their own ways changed from earlier times, and undoubtedly certain forms of behavior that they now exhibit were not found among their primate ancestors. But by studying their behavior, we may discover clues to fundamental patterns that contributed to primate adaptation and the evolution of human cultural behavior.

CHIMPANZEE BEHAVIOR   Studies in genetics, biochemistry, and anatomy indicate the chimpanzee is our closest relative. At the genetic level, we are at least 98 percent identical. Among chimps, there is some behavioral variation from one group to another, but the group social structure tends to be rather loose, and considerable independence is tolerated among individuals.[1] There is, however, a group leader (usually a mature male) who signals the group when it is time to move from one foraging area to another. In the absence of the dominant male, or in the case of subgroups that have formed for the day, a senior male becomes the leader.

One of the most notable activities is grooming, the ritual cleaning of another chimp's coat to remove parasites and other matter. This seems to be a gesture of friendliness, submission, appeasement, or closeness. Group sociability, an important behavioral trait probably found among human precursors, is also expressed in embracing, touching, and the joyous welcoming of chimps from the same or other neighboring groups. Group protection and coordination of group efforts is facilitated by visual and vocal communication. Apparently, there are warning calls, threat calls, and gathering calls.

The sexes intermingle continually and, as with humans, there is apparently no breeding season. However, sexual activity—initiated by either the male or the female—occurs only during the period each month when the female is receptive to impregnation. Once impregnated, females are not sexually receptive until their offspring is weaned. When chimps are born, they are given much attention and protection. The mother-infant bond is especially strong and

[1] Jane van Lawick-Goodall, *In the Shadow of Man* (New York: Dell, 1972).

lasts about five years. A close association between mother and child normally continues after this, even for the lifetime of the mother. Unlike humans, the chimp baby must be ready at birth to go everywhere with its mother, for its survival depends on the ability to remain close to her. As among groups of human hunters and gatherers, males wander widely; the females and children provide stability in the group. However, the males are attentive and may share in parental responsibilities. At the least, they provide both mother and infant with protection from other animals. This kind of grouping of adult male (or males), often several adult females, and children may have been the forerunner of human family groupings.

Chimpanzees show a remarkable ability to learn from, and thus adapt to, the environment. Jane Goodall has seen an infant chimp intently watch its mother building her nest, then build a play nest of its own. One infant watched its mother copulate, and explored with its hands the genitals of the copulating pair. Primates raised in captivity often have difficulty in copulating successfully, apparently as a result of limited learning experience in an artificial environment.

Along with the ability to learn, chimpanzees possess the ability to make and use tools, and will often teach toolmaking to the young. Admittedly, the trait is elementary in its exhibited form; but it may reflect one of the preliminary adaptations that led to human cultural achievements. Chimps have been observed using grass stalks, branches they have stripped of leaves, and sticks up to three feet long to catch termites. If the end of the stick becomes bent or unusable, the chimp breaks it off and discards it. Chimps are equally deliberate in their nest-building, and will test vines and branches to make sure they are usable.

Among nonhuman primates, the few examples of food sharing that have been observed involve meat eating among chimpanzees. Food sharing on a regular basis among humans may have developed out of such beginnings, as early *Homo* became more of a hunter as well as a gatherer of wild foods.

Termites, plants, and fruits form the usual diet. But occasionally, as several fieldworkers have observed, chimpanzees will kill and eat monkeys and other small animals. For example, one chimp was seen climbing tree A, where it caught the eye of a small monkey sitting opposite in tree B. While the monkey was thus distracted, a second chimpanzee climbed tree B, sprang on the monkey, and broke its neck. Several chimpanzees then ate the monkey. This one "scene" contains several interesting features which may have been significant in human evolutionary development: teamwork in order to trap and kill prey; group sharing of the spoils (though this is not always observed among chimps); and meat-

eating, an activity which eventually established itself among the hominids and which significantly affected their biological and technological development. Modern-day chimps may be recent meat-eaters; living at the edge of the savanna, they may be just starting to exploit a food source that hominids tapped in similar circumstances millions of years earlier.

GORILLA BEHAVIOR   The gorilla is the largest of the apes, with some adult males weighing over 400 pounds.[2] They live and travel in groups led by a mature, silver-backed male, which include younger, black-backed males, females, and infant gorillas. As among chimps, there is considerable tolerance of independent behavior. Individual males may join or leave the group for a day, several days, or even months. Large groups may split up for the day and keep in touch by periodic calling (some 20 distinct calls have been recorded for gorillas). But on the whole, gorilla groups are much less transitory than those of the chimps.

Gorillas are gentle and remarkably self-controlled toward the behavior of others, especially their physical inferiors; they may try to intimidate with a chest-beating show of strength, but will not actually attack unless protecting their home and food supply. They are aloof and independent, and there is little personal interaction among them. Gestures of friendship between adults are rare, and usually quite restrained. Grooming is mainly a hygienic activity. Furthermore, while one band of gorillas may associate with another, the visiting group is not accorded the excited and joyous welcome shown among bands of chimps.

[2] George B. Schaller, *The Year of the Gorilla* (New York: Ballantine, 1964).

Some gestures by which other primates communicate resemble those used by humans. The chimpanzee is using a facial expression which, with his overall posture, communicates confident threat on the part of a dominant male. Heads of state are in a sense dominant males, and may use similar facial gestures.

Sex does not appear to be very significant in the gorilla lifestyle; in almost a year of investigating mountain gorillas, zoologist George Schaller witnessed only two copulations. As with chimps, breeding may occur whenever the female is ready for fertilization, and both menstruation and pregnancy are of nearly the same length as among humans. Gorilla infants and young juveniles share their mother's nests and have been seen sharing nests with mature childless females. Schaller observed such a relationship as well as one in which a gorilla infant went "visiting" another infant its own age and the infant's mother daily for weeks.

Unlike chimps, gorillas do not appear to be even occasional meat-eaters, and neither make nor use tools in any significant way. These facts are not meant to imply a lesser degree of intelligence, for studies of a young captive gorilla named Koko indicate a degree of intelligence and capacity for conceptual thought hitherto unsuspected for any nonhuman primate (we shall have more to say about such studies near the end of Chapter 4).

ORIGINAL STUDY

Intelligence in a Captive Gorilla[3]

With Koko's physical well-being provided for, we have every opportunity to promote and observe her mental and social progress. From the start I monitored Koko's performance on human intelligence tests. In February 1975 Koko's intelligence quotient was 84 on the Stanford-Binet Intelligence Scale. Five months later, at the age of 4, her IQ rose to 95, only slightly below the average for a human child. By January 1976 the IQ was back to 85, which is not an uncommon fluctuation. Her scores on other tests confirmed the general range established by the Stanford-Binet scale.

Testing Koko's IQ has not been easy. There is, for instance, a cultural bias toward humans that shows up when tests are administered to a gorilla. One quiz asked the child, "Point to the two things that are good to eat." The depicted objects were a block, an apple, a shoe, a flower, and an ice-cream sundae. Koko, reflecting her gorilla tastes, picked the apple and the flower. Another asked the child to pick where he would run to shelter from the rain. The choices were a hat, a spoon, a tree, and a house. Koko naturally chose the tree. Rules for the scoring required that I record these responses as errors.

Koko has made numerous other "errors" that offer insight into the personality of an adolescent gorilla. One day my associate Barbara Hiller saw Koko signing, "That red," as she built a nest out of a white towel. Barbara said, "You know better, Koko. What color is it?" Koko insisted that it was red—"red, Red, RED"—and finally held up a minute speck of red lint that had been clinging to the towel. Koko was grinning.

Another time, after persistent efforts on Barbara's part to get Koko to sign, "Drink," our mischievous charge finally leaned back on the counter and executed a perfect drink sign—in her ear. Again she was grinning. Sometimes Koko will respond negatively, but without a grin—leading me to believe her intent is not to joke but to be disobedient.

She seems to relish the effects of her practical jokes, often responding exactly opposite to what I ask her to do. One day, during a videotaping session, I asked Koko to place a toy animal under a bag, and she responded by taking the toy and stretching to hold it up to the ceiling.

With Koko in a contrary mood I can almost program her actions. For example, Ron Cohen got her to stop breaking plastic spoons by signing, "Good, break them," whereupon Koko stopped bending them and started kissing them. On such occasions Koko knows that she is misbehaving, and once when I became irritated with her negativity, she quite accurately described herself as a "stubborn devil."

---

[3] Francine Patterson and Ronald Cohen, "Conversations with a Gorilla," *National Geographic,* 1978, 154(4):454–462.

Remembrance of Events and Emotions

A cardinal characteristic of human language is displacement, the ability to refer to events removed in time and place from the act of communication. To learn whether another animal has this ability, we try to find out if the animal uses its sign vocabulary merely to label the events of its world, or if it is framing propositions that re-create a particular event. Does the animal use its symbols to refer to events earlier or later in time?

Koko and I had a revealing conversation about a biting incident. My try at cross examination—three days after the event—went much as follows:

Me: "What did you do to Penny?"

Koko: "Bite." (Koko, at the time of the incident, called it a scratch.)

Me: "You admit it?"

Koko: "Sorry bite scratch."

(At this point I showed Koko the mark on my hand—it really did look like a scratch.)

Koko: "Wrong bite."

Me: "Why bite?"

Koko: "Because mad."

Me: "Why mad?"

Koko: "Don't know."

The entire conversation concerns a past event and, equally significant, a past emotional state. It is not a discussion one would expect to have with an animal whose memories were dim, unsorted recollections of pain and pleasure.

Koko Learns To Lie

Perhaps the most telling, yet elusive, evidence that a creature can displace events is lying. When someone tells a lie, he is using language to distort the listener's perception of reality. He is using symbols to describe something that never happened, or won't happen. Evidence I have been accumulating strongly suggests that Koko expresses a make-believe capacity similar to humans'.

At about the age of 5 Koko discovered the value of the lie to get herself out of a jam. After numerous repeat performances I'm convinced that Koko really is lying in these circumstances and not merely making mistakes. One of her first lies also involved the reconstruction of an earlier happening. My assistant Kate Mann was with Koko, then tipping the scales at 90 pounds, when the gorilla plumped down on the kitchen sink in the trailer and it separated from its frame and dropped out of alignment. Later, when I asked Koko if she broke the sink, she signed, "Kate there bad," pointing to the sink. Koko couldn't know, of course, that I would never accept the idea that Kate would go around breaking sinks.

Some of Koko's lies are startlingly ingenious. Once, while I was busy writing, she snatched up a red crayon and began chewing on it. A moment later I noticed and said, "You're not eating that crayon are you?" Koko signed, "Lip," and began moving the crayon first across her upper, then her lower lip as if applying lipstick.

A Sense of Past and Future

Gradually Koko is acquiring signs that make reference to past and future. One day during a filming session she signed, "First pour that," as I was preparing milk for her. "First that yes!" I exclaimed, delighted that she had used the sign "first." Just as I began to sign, "Then you drink," Koko signed, "Later Koko drink."

More recently she has begun to use the sign "later" to postpone discussion of possibly unpleasant subjects. "Tell me about what you did," I demanded one day. "Later. Me drink," was Koko's reply. She understands other words referring to the future. One bright morning that followed weeks of rain, I told Koko that if it was still sunny during the afternoon, I would take her out. When I arrived at three o'clock, she looked out at the still-bright weather and collected her gear to go outside.

In sign-language experiments with chimps, the animals learned to draw on different gestures to describe a new object or event. Dr. Roger Fouts, at the University of Oklahoma, noted that chimps could describe objects for which they had no sign: Washoe, for example, once called swans "water birds." Koko, too, has generated compound names to describe novelties. She referred to a zebra as a "white tiger," a Pinocchio doll as an "elephant baby," and a mask as an "eye hat."

A memorable joke turned on one of Koko's cleverer associations. Last winter, Cindy Duggan was holding a jelly container when Koko signed, "Do food."

"Do where, in your mouth?"

"Nose."

"Nose?"

"Fake mouth," said Koko, opening her mouth and then licking the jelly container.

"Where's your fake mouth?" asked Cindy.

"Nose," repeated Koko.

The next day I asked Koko what was a fake mouth, and she said, "Nose."

Koko displays remarkable mental gymnastics in merging different signs to create compound or composite words. For instance, she has made the sign for "Coke" superimposed on the sign for "love." For grapefruit—which she doesn't like—Koko simultaneously made the signs for "frown" and "drink," executing "drink" in the position of the sign for "fruit."

HUMAN ANCESTORS

On the basis of molecular similarities and differences, it is estimated that the evolutionary lines leading to humans, chimpanzees, and gorillas could not have separated from a common ancestral stock more than 10 million years ago.[4] Fossils, on the other hand, tell us that humans were going their separate evolutionary way by at least 4 million, if not 5.5 million years ago. Quite possibly, our ancestry lies among a group of apelike animals that lived in parts of Asia, Africa, and Europe between 15 and 8 million years ago. Some of these animals are called **Ramapithecus** and some are called **Sivapithecus.** In form, size, and function, the differences between them seem to be a good deal less than between modern chimpanzees and gorillas, but about equivalent to those between the pygmy and common chimpanzee.[5] Because we are dealing with essentially one kind of animal, there are those who feel that the two separate names *Ramapithecus* and *Sivapithecus* are not justified, but there is not yet complete agreement about this. Until some agreement is reached, a number of anthropologists have chosen to use some less formal designation, such as "ramamorphs" or **"ramapithecines,"** to refer to what in the past were called *Ramapithecus* and *Sivapithecus.*

The Ramapithecines

The teeth and jaws of the ramapithecines, by which these animals are best known, are clearly apelike overall. Still, the

> *Ramapithecus* and *Sivapithecus:* Small apes, some of which were probably ancestral to the hominids.
>
> Ramapithecines: A designation embracing both *Ramapithecus* and *Sivapithecus* apes.
>
> Hominid: A member of the human family.
>
> *Australopithecus:* The first undoubted hominid; lived between 1 and 4 or 5 million years ago, and included one (or two) robust species and one (or two) smaller, lightly built species.

incisors are a bit more vertically placed in the mouth, the canines are smaller relative to the molars and premolars, the molar enamel is noticeably thicker, and the tooth row tends to be slightly more V-shaped than is usual in apes. The interesting thing about these features is that they seem to point in a somewhat human direction.

For a long time, teeth and jaws were all we had of the ramapithecines, but over the past few years, a number of skull and limb bone fragments of this primate have been found in China, Hungary, and Pakistan. In many respects, these are remarkably orangutan-like, which is interesting, since ramapithecine teeth, while not quite like those of any living ape, are more like those of orangs than they are like those of African apes. It is interesting, too, because there are some resemblances between the shoulder girdle of the earliest-known **hominid, Australopithecus,** and that of orangs. This suggests that hominids evolved from a primate capable of arm movements like those of orangs, and the ramapithecines were capable of just such arm movements.

---

[4] A. C. Wilson and V. M. Sarich, "A Molecular Time Scale for Human Evolution," *Proceedings of the National Academy of Sciences*, 1969, 63:1092.

[5] Leonard Owen Greenfield, "On the Adaptive Pattern of 'Ramapithecus,'" *American Journal of Physical Anthropology*, 1979, 50:527–547.

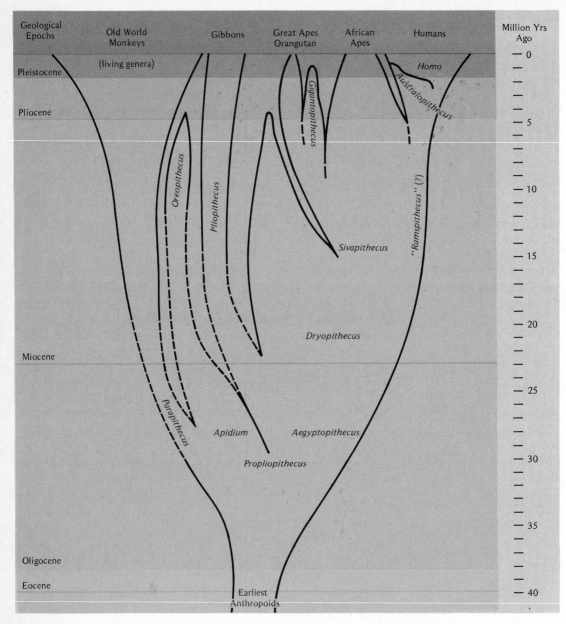

Possible evolutionary relationships of the Old World monkeys, apes, and humans. Debate continues over some of the details; for example, there are some who see the
African apes as direct descendants of *Dryopithecus,* and there are some who would
place the divergence of hominids from apes earlier in the Miocene.

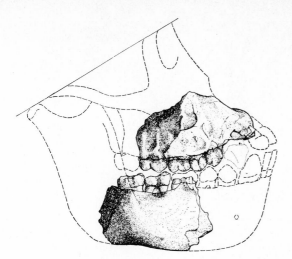

Reconstructed face of a ramapithecine, based on existing fragments of upper and lower jaws. Although apelike, the canine teeth are less massive than in most apes.

Molar teeth like those of the ramapithecines, having low crown relief, thick enamel, and surfaces poorly developed for cutting, are found in a number of modern primates.[6] Some of these species are terrestrial and some are aboreal, but all have one thing in common: they eat very hard nuts, fruits with very tough rinds, and some seeds. This provides them with a rich source of easily digested nutrients that are not accessible to species with thin molar enamel that is incapable of standing up to the stresses of tough rind removal or nut-cracking. Thus the ramapithecines probably ate food similar to that eaten by these latter-day nut crackers.

Analysis of other materials from deposits in which ramapithecine fossils have been found suggests utilization of a broad range of habitats, including tropical rainforests as well as drier bush country. Of particular interest to us, from the standpoint of human origins, are those populations that lived on the edge of open country, where food could be obtained through foraging on the ground out in the open, as well as in the trees of the forests. As it happened, there was a climatic shift underway, causing a gradual but persistent breaking up of forested areas with a consequent expansion of open savanna country. Under such circumstances, it seems likely that those populations of ramapithecines living at the edge of the forests were obliged to supplement food from the forest more and more with seeds and other foods readily available on the open savannas. Consistent with this theory, late ramapithecine fossils are typically found in association with greater numbers of the remains of animals adapted to grasslands than are earlier ramapithecine fossils.

Because ramapithecines already had large, thickly enameled molars, those populations that had to were capable of dealing with the tough and abrasive foods available on the savanna. What these populations lacked, however, were canine teeth of sufficient size to have served as effective "weapons" of defense. By contrast, most modern ground-dwelling species of monkeys and apes rely heavily for defense on the massive, fang-like canines possessed by the males. Ramapithecines were not very big (no species was bigger than a modern pygmy chimpanzee, and some were smaller), and since there was a proliferation of catlike predators on the savanna at the time, ramapithecines would seem to have been very vulnerable primates indeed. Probably the forest fringe was more than just a source of foods different from those of the savanna; its trees would have provided refuge when danger threatened. Yet, with continued expansion of savanna country, trees for refuge would have become fewer and farther apart.

[6]Richard F. Kay, "The Nut-crackers—A New Theory of the Adaptations of the Ramapithecinae," *American Journal of Physical Anthropology*, 1981, 55:141–151.

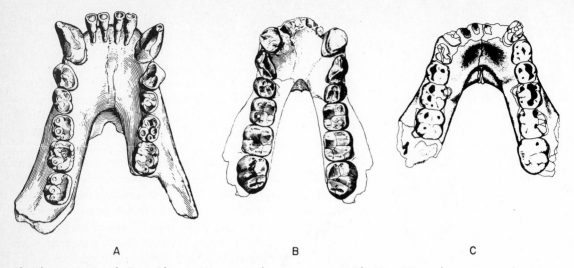

A   B   C

The lower jaws of *Dryopithecus* (A), an early ape, a ramapithecine (B) and *Australopithecus* (C) from Laetoli, east Africa. The latter is a hominid who lived nearly 4 million years ago. Relative to the cheek teeth, all have comparably small teeth at the very front of the jaw. There is a general similarity between (A) and (B), as well as between (B) and (C). The major difference between the ramapithecine and *Australopithecus* is that the rows of cheek teeth are further apart in the hominid.

Slowly, however, physical and behavioral changes must have improved these primates' chances for survival on the savanna. For one thing, those that were able to gather food on the ground and then carry it to the safety of a tree probably had a better rate of survival than those who did not. Although many species of monkeys have cheek pouches in which to carry food, apes do not. Occasionally, modern apes will assume a bipedal stance in order to transport food in their arms, but they are quite awkward about it. However, the center of gravity is higher in the body of modern apes than it seems to have been in their earlier ancestors, so that bipedal food transport may not have been quite so awkward for the ramapithecines.

Food may not have been the only thing transported. Among modern primates, infants must be able to cling to their mother in order to be transported; since the mother is using her forelimbs in locomotion, either to walk or swing by, she can't very well carry her infant. Chimpanzee infants, for example, must cling for themselves to their mother, and even at the age of four, they make long journeys on their mother's back. Injuries caused by falling from the mother are a significant cause of infant mortality.[7] Thus, mothers able to carry their infants would have made a significant contribution to the survivorship of their offspring, and the ramapithecines may have been capable of doing just this.

Other advantages of at least the occasional assumption of a bipedal stance would have been the ability to scan the savanna, so that predators could be seen be-

---

[7] C. Owen Lovejoy, "The Origin of Man," *Science*, 1981, 211(4480):344, 349.

fore they got too close. Such scanning can be seen from time to time among baboons today when out on the savanna, even though their anatomy is less suited for this than we presume the ramapithecines' to have been. One final advantage of bipedalism would have been the ability to use the hands to throw available objects at predators. Among primates, "threat gestures" typically involve shaking branches and throwing things, and on the ground, chimpanzees have been observed throwing rocks at leopards. There is every reason to suppose that, lacking the large body size and formidable canines of chimpanzees, the ramapithecines when away from the trees and faced by a predator indulged in the same kind of behavior.

Although the ramapithecines display a number of features pointing in a somewhat human direction, and may occasionally have walked bipedally, they were still too apelike to be considered a hominid—a member of the human family. The first undoubted hominid and one who walked about in a fully human manner is *Australopithecus*, who appeared on the scene by 4 million if not by 5.5 million years ago.

Australopithecus

We know much more about *Australopithecus* than we do about the ramapithecines, for we have hundreds of fossils from eastern Africa, from South Africa as far north as Ethiopia's Afar depression. The intermediate stages of development between the non-hominid ramapithecines and the hominid *Australopithecus* are open to debate, since no fossil remains from the gap separating the appearance of these two forms have as yet been discovered. The transformation was indeed significant: *Australopithecus* was primitive by hominid

> **Gracile: Small and lightly built.**

standards, but was well within the hominid line, physically if not yet culturally.

There has been considerable debate about *Australopithecus*. Most anthropologists recognize at least two distinct species: *A. africanus* and *A. robustus*. Some refer to this latter as *A. boisei*, while others would reserve this name for a third, super-robust species. Finally, a fourth species, *A. afarensis*, has recently been proposed for the earliest *Australopithecus* fossils from the Afar depression and Laetoli, in Tanzania.

In spite of the difference of opinion over the exact number of species, it is generally agreed that there were basically just two kinds of *Australopithecus*. One, represented by *A. africanus* and *A. afarensis*, was small and lightly built, or **gracile.** The other, represented by *A. robustus* and *A. boisei*, was heavier, with a more robust frame and jaws which are large, relative to the size of the brain case. Perhaps they represent two differing lines of hominid evolution, with the robust form ultimately becoming extinct and the gracile form giving rise to more modern hominids. Recently, however, Pilbeam and Gould have argued that the robust form is simply an enlarged version of the earlier gracile form which had diverged from the line of evolution to more modern hominids.[8] This view has not yet been generally accepted, but it is consistent with the even more recently expressed view of Johanson and White that two lines of evolution, to robust *Australopithecus* and modern hominids, emerged from a common ancestral stock represented by the earliest gracile form, which they call

---

[8] D. Pilbeam and S. J. Gould, "Size and Scaling in Human Evolution," *Science*, 1974, 186:892–901.

The skeletal remains of "Lucy," a female *Australopithecus* that lived between 2.6 and 3.3 million years ago in Ethiopia. The hip and leg bones reveal that "Lucy" walked about in a fully human manner.

A. afarensis.[9] The slightly later gracile form, *A. africanus*, already shows the first steps in the evolution of the robust form, though it differs only slightly from *A. afarensis.*

All these hominids were generally not as large as most modern people. The structure and size of the teeth are more like those of modern people than they are like those of apes, and the condition of the molars suggests that food was chewed in hominid fashion. Unlike the apes, no gap exists between the canines and the teeth next to them on the lower jaw, except occasionally in the case of *A. afarensis.* The large mandible is very similar to the more advanced hominid *Homo erectus,* although some apelike features are still apparent in the mandible of *A. afarensis.* The brain-body ratio, which permits a very rough estimate of intelligence, suggests that the information-processing capacity of *Australopithecus* was about that of a modern chimpanzee or gorilla.

Australopithecus fossils have also provided anthropology with two striking facts. First, by at least 4 million years ago, this hominid was fully bipedal, walking erect. Second, despite traditional emphasis on the importance of the brain in evolutionary development, hominids acquired their erect bipedal posture long before they acquired their highly developed and enlarged brain. Bipedalism was an important adaptive feature in the savanna environment. A biped couldn't run as fast as a quadruped, but could travel long distances in search of

[9]D. C. Johanson and T. D. White, "A Systematic Assessment of Early African Hominids," *Science*, 1979, 203:328.

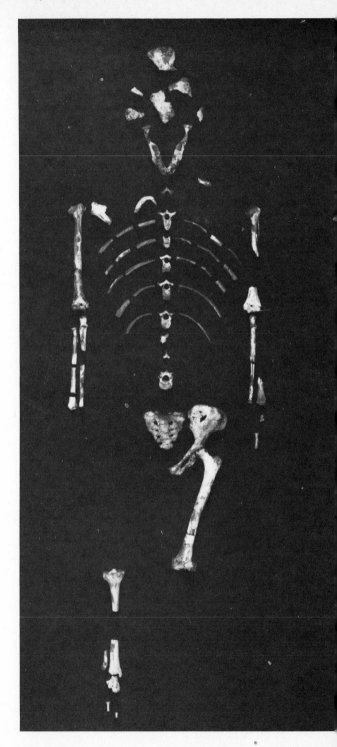

The footprints of *Australopithecus* from Laetoli, Tanzania.

food without tiring. It could carry food to places where it could be eaten in relative safety, and it could carry infants, rather than relying on the latter to hang on for themselves. And, standing erect on the open savanna, it could see farther and spot both food and predators.

Although vegetable food probably continued to account for the bulk of *Australopithecus'* diet, there is evidence that at least some of them may have been eating more meat than is usual for most primates. The evidence, however, suggests that meat was scavenged rather than hunted.[10]

EARLY HOMO

This new interest in meat on the part of evolving hominids is a point of major importance. Much of a popular nature has been written about this, often with numerous colorful references to "killer apes." Such references are quite misleading, not only because hominids are not apes but also because killing has been greatly overemphasized. Meat can be obtained, after all, by scavenging, or even by stealing it from other predators. What is significant is that teeth such as those possessed by *Australopithecus* are not very well suited for meat-eating. What is needed for really efficient utilization of meat, in the absence of teeth like those possessed by carnivorous animals, are sharp tools for butchering. The earliest identifiable tools are about 2.5 million years old and are found in Ethiopia.

---

[10]Catherine E. Read-Martin and Dwight W. Read, "Australopithecine Scavenging and Human Evolution: A Faunal Analysis," *Current Anthropology*, 1975, 16(3):363–364.

Their appearance marks the beginning of the **Paleolithic,** or Old Stone Age. The earliest Paleolithic tools consist of a number of crude implements made of stones of a size easily held in a human hand which bear evidence of being shaped by the human hand. Certain tools appear to have been produced by percussion flaking, removing a few flakes from a stone core by striking its surface, leaving either a one- or two-faced tool. Such tools could be used for cutting meat, scraping hides, or cracking bones to extract marrow. This represents an important technological advance for early hominids that not only saved labor and time but also made possible the exploitation of a whole new food source. The existence of these tools led scientists to define a "pebble tool culture," which they named **Oldowan.** But what people were responsible for this culture?

Since the late 1960s, a number of the same deposits in South and East Africa which have produced Oldowan tools have also produced the fossil remains of a lightly built hominid with a number of features reminiscent of gracile *Australopithecus,* but with hands more modern in appearance, teeth that are smaller both absolutely and relatively, and brains that are significantly larger relative to body size. This latter means that there was a marked advance in information-processing capacity over that of *Australopithecus.* Since major brain-size increase and tooth-size reduction are important trends in the evolution of the genus *Homo,* but not of *Australopithecus,* it looks as if these hominids were evolving in a more human direction. It is probably significant that the earliest fossils to exhibit this trend appeared 2 million years ago, not long after the earliest evidence for stone

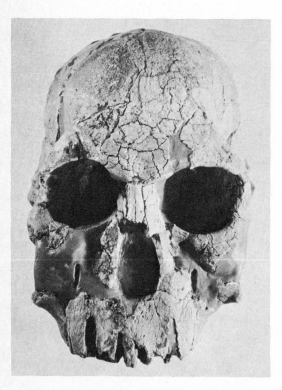

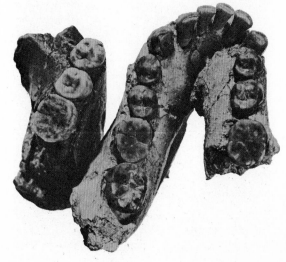

Earliest remains of the genus *Homo.* At left is a 2 million-year-old skull found in the early 1970s near Lake Turkana in Kenya. At right is a jaw fragment about 1.8 million years old from Olduvai Gorge, Tanzania (right) compared with a similar jaw fragment from Java (left). Apparently, early *Homo* did not live exclusively in Africa.

toolmaking and hunting, as opposed to scavenging.

Although these early members of the genus *Homo* lived at the same time as did later robust forms of *Australopithecus*, the resemblances they have to the earliest gracile form suggest an ancestor-descendant relationship. Present thinking postulates a line of evolution to the genus *Homo*, branching off from that of early gracile *Australopithecus*.

The significance of meat-eating and toolmaking for future human evolution was enormous. While early hominids may have scavenged for their first meat, this soon was supplemented, if not replaced, by hunting. Since they lacked size and strength to overpower prey, speed to run it down, and the built-in killing apparatus of other carnivores, they must have had to rely on their wit and cunning for success. Indeed, from watching modern hunting peoples in action, such as the Bushmen of South Africa, it is apparent that their minds are constantly in action as they analyze the movement of the game, predict what it will do next, and devise strategies for outwitting it.

For reasons that will be discussed in Chapter 6, it was probably the early hominid males, rather than females, who became the hunters. The females, for their part, continued to gather the same kinds of foods that their ancestors had been eating all along. But instead of consuming all this food themselves as they gathered it, as other primates do, they provided some to the males who, in turn, provided the females with meat. In order for this sharing to work, the females, like the males, had to "sharpen their wits." They had to plan ahead so as to know where food would be found in sufficient quantities, see to its transport to some agreed upon location for division, while at the same time ensuring

> **Paleolithic:** The Old Stone Age, characterized by chipped stone tools.
>
> **Oldowan tools:** The earliest identifiable stone tools; first appear 2.5 million years ago.

that it did not spoil. So it seems that female gathering played as important a role in the development of better brains as did male hunting.

Another way in which the addition of meat to the hominid diet was important for the development of larger brains has to do with its nutritive value. The nutritive demands of nervous tissue, of which the brain is made, are high—higher, in fact, than the demands of the other types of tissue in the human body. One can meet these demands on a vegetarian diet, but the overall nutritive value of a given amount of vegetable food is less than that of the same amount of meat. Thus, the use of meat as well as vegetable foods ensured that a reliable source of high quality nutrition would be available to support a more highly developed brain, once it evolved. But more than this, animals that live on plant foods must eat large quantities of vegetation, and this consumes much of their time. Meat eaters, by contrast, have no need to eat so much, or so often. Consequently, meat-eating hominids may have had more leisure time available to explore and exploit their environment; like lions and leopards, they would have time to spend lying around and playing.

Finally, toolmaking itself seems to have played a role in the evolution of the human brain, by putting a premium on manual dexterity and fine manipulation, as opposed to hand use emphasizing power rather than precision. Presumably, this put

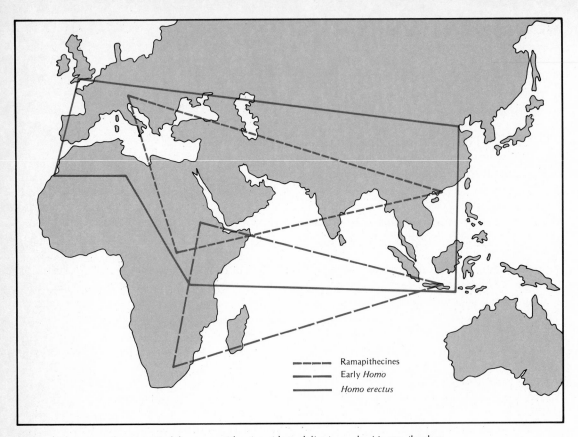

- - - - -	Ramapithecines
─ ─ ─ ─	Early *Homo*
────────	*Homo erectus*

The areas apparently occupied by ramapithecine (dotted line), early *Homo* (broken line), and *Homo erectus* (solid line), based on fossil finds. Apparently, there has been a steady expansion of human populations into new areas as the efficiency of cultural adaptation has increased.

a premium on improved organization of the nervous system. In sum, a combination of factors, all associated in one way or another with the addition of more meat into the human diet, seems to have imposed strong selective pressures on both males and females for better brains in early *Homo.* From this point on, the record is one of increasing brain size and increasing cultural development, each presumably acting to promote the other.

Although early *Homo* is best known from fossils found in South Africa, Tanzania, and Kenya, similar fossils are known from Java, suggesting that these early ancestors of ours were widespread in the Old World Tropics. Even more widespread, however, was the next figure in human evolution, **Homo erectus,** whose remains have been found not only in Africa and Southeast Asia but up into Europe and China as well.

Homo erectus

In spite of their broad distribution, fossils of *H. erectus* reveal no more significant physical variations than are to be seen in modern human populations. These fossils indicate that *H. erectus* had a larger brain than earlier members of the genus *Homo*, one that was well within the lower range of modern brain size. The dentition was fully human, though large by modern standards. The leg and foot bones were also fully human and indicate that *H. erectus* could walk and run as well as modern people. Some small changes in the pelvis from *Australopithecus* probably relate to changes

Homo erectus: **Species of** *Homo* **preceding, and ancestral to,** *Homo sapiens.*

required for the birth of larger-brained infants, rather than improvements in bipedal locomotion.

As one might expect given the larger brain, *H. erectus* had outstripped its predecessors in cultural development. From sites in China and Europe, we have the first clear evidence for the use of fire for protection, warmth, and cooking. For example, at Choukoutien, a fossil site about 30 miles from Peking, thousands of broken and charred bones of deer, sheep, antelope, roebuck, small hares, camels, bison, and elephants indicate that *H. erectus* was an accomplished hunter who cooked food.

It is likely that *H. erectus* used fire that was originally started by lightning or through spontaneous combustion, rather than by instruments developed for kindling fire. But the use of fire in itself represents a

Reconstructed skull of *Homo erectus* from Peking, and the excavation site where the Peking skulls were found. A numbered grid system was used to locate the fossil finds.

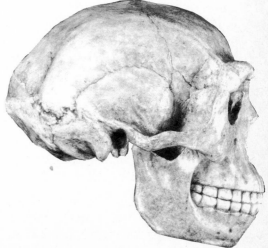

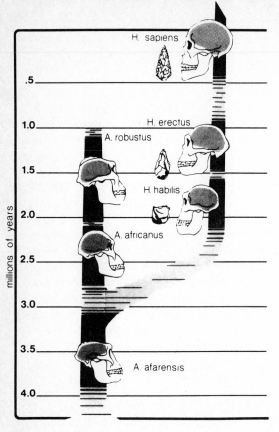

A plausible view of early human evolution.

sion of day and night, perhaps encouraging *H. erectus* to stay up after dark to review the day's events, and plan the next day's activities.

The cultural advance represented by Chinese *H. erectus'* use of fire, however, was not complemented by any significant development of stone tools. Chopper tools were made, but they reveal a lesser concern with technological matters than those being produced by western *H. erectus*.

Unlike their eastern counterparts, western populations of *H. erectus* were refining the tradition begun by the pebble toolmakers in East Africa. While Asians were satisfied with chopper tools, *H. erectus* in Africa was transforming the Oldowan chopper into the more sophisticated hand ax (the Stone Age equivalent of "building a better mousetrap"). In marginal parts of Europe, pebble tools continued to be made,

very significant step in human cultural adaptation. It may have altered the forces of natural selection which previously favored individuals with heavy jaws and large, sharp teeth (needed for chewing and ripping uncooked meat), thus paving the way for reduction in tooth size as well as supportive facial architecture. Like tools and intelligence, fire gave people more control over their environment. It may have been used, if not by *H. erectus,* then by subsequent hominids, to frighten away cave-dwelling predators so that they might live in the caves themselves; and it could then be used to provide warmth and light in these cold and dark habitations. Even more, it also modified the natural succes-

The methods of manufacture shown are: (A) direct percussion with a hammerstone (N.E. Australia); (B) indirect percussion (North America); (C) pressure flaking (North America); (D) pressure flaking (N.W. Australia). The tools were used chiefly for butchering and defense.

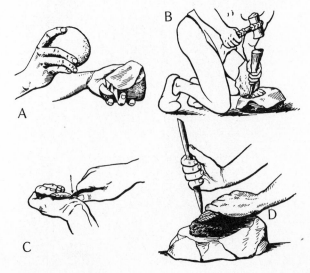

but later, in both Africa and Europe, the hand ax appears further refined and developed.

During this time, tool cultures also began to diversify, indicating the increased efficiency of *H. erectus* in adapting to diverse environments. At first the hand axes—shaped by regular blows that gave them a larger and finer cutting edge than pebble tools—were probably all-purpose tools, useful in food processing, hide scraping, and defense. But *H. erectus* then developed cleavers (U-shaped chopping tools) which could be used for killing and butchering; several different types of flint-core scrapers, which would be used for processing hides for "blankets" and clothing; and flake tools to cut meat and process certain vegetables. Adaptation to specific regions is also indicated: there is a greater prominence of flake tools in north and east Europe than in the south and west, and cleavers have been found only in Africa.

The superior technological efficiency of *H. erectus* is also evident in the selection of raw materials. Instead of making a few large tools out of large pieces of stone, smaller tools, more economical of raw materials, began to be made.

Later, western *H. erectus* developed two toolmaking techniques to produce thinner, straighter, and sharper axes. The use of a hard wooden baton for flaking produced shallow flake scars, rather than the crushed edge found on the older axes. By first preparing a flat platform on the core, from which flakes could be struck off, even sharper and thinner axes could be made.

The Acheulean hand ax (left) seen in front view and profile, was an all-purpose tool, slim enough to fit easily into the hand as can be seen in the detail (right) of an aborigine holding a similar type of hand ax.

The toolmaker could also shape the core so that flake points 3 to 6 inches long could be struck off all ready to use.

Advanced toolmaking in the west and knowledge of fire in both east and west enabled *H. erectus* to become a better hunter than earlier members of the genus *Homo*. However, the sophistication of hunting techniques suggests more than just greater technological capability; it also reflects an increased organizational ability. For example, excavations in Spain at Torralba and Ambrona indicate group hunting techniques were used to kill a large amount of game; fire was used by *H. erectus* to drive elephants into a bog, where the trapped creatures could easily be slaughtered.

With *H. erectus*, then, we find a clearer manifestation of the interplay among cultural, physical, and environmental factors than ever before. Social organization and technology developed concomitantly with an increase in brain size and complexity. Cultural adaptations such as cooking and more complex tool kits facilitated dental reduction; and dental reduction in turn encouraged an even heavier reliance upon tool development and facilitated the development of language. Improvements in communication and social organization brought about by language undoubtedly contributed to the use of improved hunting methods, a population increase, and territorial expansion. Evidence from tools and fossils indicates that just as *H. erectus* was able to move into areas previously uninhabited by hominids (Europe and northern China), **Homo sapiens**—the subject of our next discussion—was able to live in areas previously uninhabited by *H. erectus*.

So-called classic Neanderthal skulls have often been taken to indicate an excessively primitive look on the part of European Neanderthals; actually, they could probably pass almost unnoticed among living human populations.

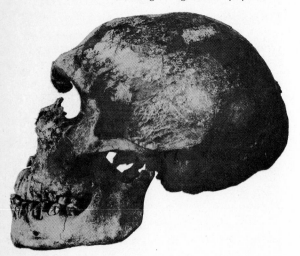

HOMO SAPIENS

At various sites in Europe and Africa, a number of hominid fossils have been found which seem to date roughly between 300,000 and 200,000 years ago. Some of these—most commonly the African fossils, but also a skull from southern France— have been called *Homo erectus;* others— most commonly skulls from Steinheim, Germany, and Swanscombe, England— have been called *Homo sapiens.* In fact, most of them show a mixture of characteristics of both forms, which is what one would expect of remains transitional between the two. For example, skulls from Ethiopia, Steinheim, and Swanscombe had rather large brains for *Homo erectus.* Their overall appearance, however, is different from skulls like ours: they are large and robust with their maximum breadth lower on the skull, and they had more prominent brow ridges, larger faces, and bigger teeth. Even a skull from Morocco, which had a rather small brain for *Homo sapiens,* looks surprisingly modern from the back. Finally, the various jaws from Morocco and France seem to combine features of *Homo erectus* with those of the European Neanderthals.

Whether one chooses to call these early humans "primitive" *H. sapiens* or "advanced" *H. erectus* seems to be a matter of taste; whichever one calls them does not alter their apparently transitional status.

Neanderthals

The discovery of **Neanderthal** remains in 1851 was greeted with incredulity and distrust by those who protested that humans were descended from humans— Adam and Eve—and not from primitive primates. Even today some scholars persist in excluding Neanderthals from our ancestry, though for reasons other than biblical

> *Homo sapiens:* The modern human species.

> Neanderthal: Representative of "archaic" *Homo sapiens* in Europe and the Middle East, living from about 100,000 years ago to about 35,000 years ago.

transgression. But the sum total of investigations has proven that Neanderthal was truly *H. sapiens* and not, as had once been thought, a deformed or aberrant specimen unrelated to modern humans.

It has been argued there are two types of Neanderthal: Classic (so called because this was the first type to be found), and Generalized. Classic Neanderthal was typically heavier and lived in Europe; the generalized type was lighter and more modern in form and facial features and lived in the Middle East. Despite this classification, several "classic" remains are known from the Middle East, and some "generalized" remains are known from Europe. What we seem to have are two varied populations in neighboring regions which show considerable overlap with one another. The most economical explanation of such a situation is that both populations shared genes in common, although gene frequencies probably differed in the two regions. Roughly contemporary with the Neanderthals, and showing some similarities to them, are human fossils from some other parts of the world. In 1931, for example, a number of interesting fossils were found in Java, near the Solo River, that suggest a being with features common to *H. erectus,* Neanderthal, and more modern *H. sapiens.* These Solo fossils seem to represent a southeast Asian equivalent of the Neanderthals, and their singular features probably reflect genetic continuity with earlier populations.

Reconstruction of a Middle Paleolithic "house" at Malodova, Russia. Shelters like these were built by Mousterian hunters of mammoths, who utilized the bones and tusks in their housing.

"Rhodesian man," an individual represented by fossil remains in southern Africa, also manifested a combination of Neanderthal and modern traits. Like the Solo fossils, the Rhodesian remains probably represent an African equivalent of Neanderthal. Finally, Neanderthal-like remains have been found in China, in a cave north of Canton.

Adaptations to the environment for the Neanderthals were, of course, both physical and cultural, but the capacity for cultural adaptation was predictably superior to what it had been. Neanderthal's extensive use of fire was essential to survival in an arctic climate like that of Europe at the time. They lived in small bands or single family units both in the open and in caves, and undoubtedly communicated by speech (see Chapter 4). Evidence of deliberate burials suggest a belief in some kind of afterlife, and other remains indicate ritualistic or religious behavior in the form of animal cults (especially cave bear cults). Moreover, the remains of an amputee discovered in Iraq and an arthritic man unearthed in France imply that Neanderthals cared for the disabled, an unprecedented example of social concern.

Hunting techniques improved with improved social organization and an advanced technology in weapon and toolmaking. The toolmaking tradition of the Neanderthals, called **Mousterian** after a site (Le Mousier) in France, dates from 100,000 to 40,000 B.C. and characterized this period in Europe, North Africa, and western Asia.

Mousterian tools are generally lighter and smaller than those of previous traditions. Whereas previously only two or three flakes could be obtained from the entire core, Neanderthal toolmakers obtained many more smaller flakes, which they skillfully retouched and sharpened. Their tool kits also contained a greater variety of tool types than the previous traditions: hand axes, flakes, scrapers, borers, notched flakes for shaving wood, and many types of points that could be attached to shafts of wood to form spears. This variety of tools facilitated a greater exploitation of food resources and improved the quality of clothing and shelter.

This improved ability at cultural adaptation no doubt is related to the fact that, with the Neanderthals, the human brain had become fully modern. Such a brain

Mousterian: Toolmaking tradition of the Neanderthals of Europe, Southwest Asia, and North Africa.

made possible not only sophisticated technology; it also made possible conceptual thought of considerable sophistication. Evidence for this is provided by the remains of magico-religious ceremonies and manufac-

Mousterian tools are far more varied and specialized than the tools made by *Homo erectus.* This collection includes scrapers (A and B), a disc core (C), a point (D), an anvil or hammer stone (E), hand axes (F and G), and an oval flake tool (H).

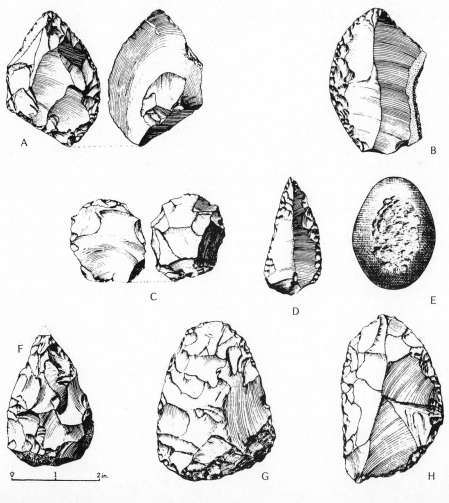

tured objects of apparently symbolic significance. The ceremonial evidence has already been mentioned; the other objects consist of nonutilitarian items, such as pendants, and carved and engraved markings on objects that are likely to have required some form of linguistic explanation.[11] Some of these are reminiscent of the churingas made by Australian aborigines, which have symbolic significance.

The question that continues to perplex some scientists is, What happened to the Neanderthals? In the Middle East and south-central Europe, fossil remains show transitional forms between Neanderthal and more modern types. Only in western Europe is there a 10,000-year gap in the fossil record. While some anthropologists hold that Neanderthals disappeared, there is evidence to suggest that they and others like them in Asia and Africa simply evolved into modern humans.[12] The basic difference between earlier and later *H. sapiens* is that the modern face is less massive, as is the bony architecture at the rear of the skull which would act as a counterbalance for a massive face.

Upper Paleolithic Peoples

In what is called **Upper Paleolithic** times, about 35,000–40,000 years ago, the Neanderthals and others like them were succeeded by a people who possessed a physical appearance similar to our own. These more modern representatives of *Homo sapiens* are often referred to as **Cro-Magnons,** after the French rock shelter in which their bones were first found. Since the name really refers to Upper Paleolithic remains from Europe, it is best to refer to human remains from other parts of the world as those of **Upper Paleolithic peoples.**

Cro-Magnon and other Upper Paleolithic remains reveal considerable physical variability, as is usual in human populations. Generally speaking, however, these people had characteristically modern-looking faces. As suggested in our discussion of *H. erectus*, specialized tools and cooking helped achieve this modernization by gradually assuming the chewing and softening functions once served by large teeth and heavy jaws. Selection seems to have favored diminished muscles for chewing, and consequently the bones to which these muscles were attached became smaller and finer.

At this point in human evolution, culture has become a more potent force than biology. As the smaller features of Upper Paleolithic peoples suggest, physical bulk was no longer required for survival. Fast technological developments had contributed to the increasing complexity of the brain by the time of the Neanderthals, and this complexity now enabled people to create an even more sophisticated technology. Similarly, conceptual thought and symbolic behavior seem to have developed beyond what we saw in the case of the Neanderthals. Intelligence henceforth provides the key to humanity's increased reliance on cultural rather than physical adaptation.

In Upper Paleolithic times, human intelligence enabled people to manufacture tools that surpassed the physical equipment of predators and to develop more efficient means of social organization and cooperation—all of which made them extremely proficient hunters as well as

[11] Alexander Marshack, "Some Implications of the Paleolithic Symbolic Evidence for the Origin of Language," *Current Anthropology*, 1976, 17(2):277–278.

[12] C. Loring Brace, "Tales of the Phylogenetic Woods: The Evolution and Significance of Phylogenetic Trees," *American Journal of Physical Anthropology*, 1981, 56:424.

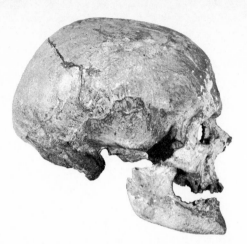

The Cro-Magnon skull, above, differs little from our own. Below, an enterprising French businessman has built a hotel on the site of the excavation in which the first Cro-Magnon remains were found. The open door of the garage leads to the excavation; the back wall of the hotel is the cliff that sheltered early hotel-less people.

gatherers. Cultural adaptation also became highly specific and regional, thus increasing human chances for survival under a variety of environmental conditions. Instead of manufacturing crude all-purpose tools, Upper Paleolithic populations of the savanna, forest, and shore each developed specialized devices suited to exploiting their particular environment, and the dif-

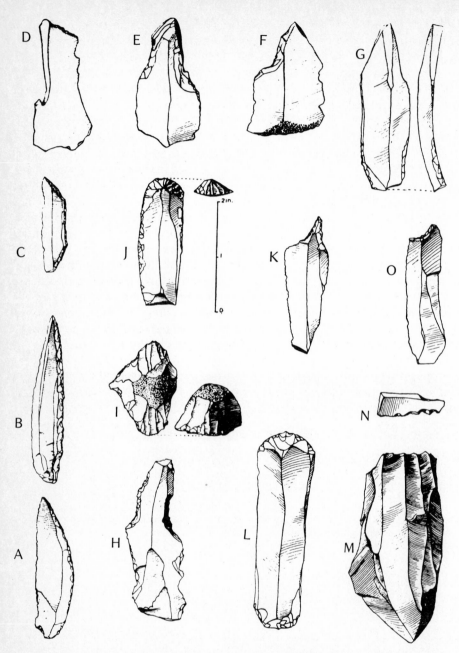

Tools made by the Cro-Magnons are even more specialized and efficient than those of the Neanderthals. This collection includes knife points (A and B), truncated blade (C), gravers (D, E, F, and G), scrapers (I, J, L, and O), a strangulated blade (H), a piercer (K), a blade core (M), and a miscellaneous notched piece (N).

ferent seasons, in which they were being used. It also permitted human habitation of new areas, such as Australia and the Americas.

This degree of specialization naturally required improved manufacturing techniques. The blade method of manufacture, used widely in Europe and western Asia, used less raw material than was needed before, and resulted in smaller and lighter tools with a better ratio between weight of flint and length of cutting edge. The pressure-flaking technique—which used bone, antler, or a wooden tool to press off small flakes from a flint core—gave the toolmaker greater control over the shape of the tool than was possible with percussion flaking.

Although invented by Mousterian toolmakers, the burin—a stone tool with chisel-like edges—came into common use in the Upper Paleolithic. The burin provided an excellent means of carving bone and antler, used for such tools as fishhooks and harpoons. The atlatl, which consisted of a piece of wood and a groove in it for holding and throwing a spear, also appeared at this time. By using the atlatl, a hunter increased the force behind the spear throw. The bow and arrow worked on the same principle. The bowstring increased the force on the arrow, enabling it to travel farther and with greater effectiveness than if it had been thrown by hand.

One important aspect of Upper Paleolithic culture in the west is the art of this period. As far as we know, humans had not produced art work of this caliber before this time; therefore, the level of artistic proficiency is certainly amazing. Tools and weapons were decorated with engravings of animal figures; pendants made of bone and ivory were created; and there was sculpting in clay. More spectacular, and quite unlike anything undertaken by the earlier Neanderthals, are the cave paintings in Spain and France. Made with mineral oxide pigments, these skillfully executed paintings almost exclusively depict animals that were hunted by Upper Paleolithic peoples. It is not known for certain why other subject matter was not chosen, nor composi-

The intellectual capabilities of Upper Paleolithic peoples, whose skeletons differ in no significant ways from those of modern humans, are reflected in the efficiency with which some of them hunted animals far larger and more powerful than themselves, as well as the sophistication of some of their art. Shown here is an engraving of a woolly mammoth—one of the animals hunted—by an artist who was not only a master of the medium, but who knew intimately the anatomy of the animal depicted.

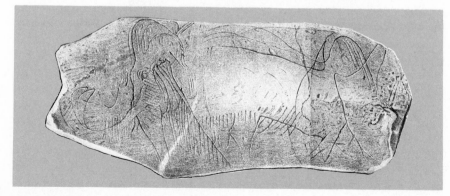

tional background provided for the animals portrayed. It is also curious that later paintings were found in the darkest recesses of the caves, suggesting that they served other than a decorative function. Some anthropologists suggest that these paintings served a magico-religious function having to do with control over the animals thus represented, or a symbolic function having to do with male initiation ceremonies. In any case, they reflect a remarkably developed aesthetic sensibility.

OVERVIEW

By the Upper Paleolithic, we have reached the end of the Paleolithic. With biologically modern varieties of humans on the scene, as well as hunting and gathering cultures comparable to those known for recent hunting and gathering peoples, we have reached a convenient place to end our examination of the beginnings of human culture. What we have seen is a close interrelation between developing culture and developing humanity. The critical importance of culture as the human adaptive mechanism

seems to have imposed selective pressures favoring a better brain, and a better brain, in turn, made possible improved cultural adaptation. Indeed, it seems fair to say that modern humans look the way they do today because cultural adaptation came to play such an important role in the survival of our ancient ancestors. Because cultural adaptation worked so well, human populations were able to grow, probably very slowly, with a consequent expansion into previously uninhabited parts of the world. And this, too, affected cultural adaptation, as adjustments were made to meet new conditions.

Ending our examination of human cultural development here should not be taken to mean that human evolution stopped at the end of the Paleolithic. Since then, the human species has continued to change biologically, even though it remains the same species now as then. Culture, too, has continued to change, and revolutionary developments in cultural evolution, such as the development of food production and, later, civilization, came after the Paleolithic. These developments will be touched upon in subsequent chapters, especially Chapters 6 and 14.

CHAPTER SUMMARY

Anthropology includes the study of primates other than humans in order to explain why and how humans developed as they did. As the early primates became tree dwelling, various modifications took place in dental characteristics, sense organs, the brain, and skeletal structure that helped them to adapt to their environment. At the same time, learned social behavior became increasingly important to them. Through the study of the behavior of present-day primates, such as the chimpanzee and gorilla, anthropologists seek clues with which to reconstruct behavior patterns that may have characterized those apelike primates ancestral to both humans and present-day apes.

Chimpanzees live in structured social groups and express their sociability through communication by visual and vocal signals. They also exhibit an ability to learn from experience and can make and use tools. Gorillas also live and travel in groups and communicate visually and by calling. At least one gorilla raised in captivity shows a capacity for conceptual thought hitherto unsuspected in any nonhuman primate.

The earliest undoubted member of the human family was *Australopithecus,* who was living in Africa by 4 million years ago. Anthropologists recognize two kinds of *Australopithecus,* a gracile (small, lightly built) and a robust form. This hominid, fully bipedal and able to walk and run erect, was well equipped for generalized food gathering in the savanna environment. Although still strikingly apelike from the waist up, *Australopithecus* had a fully human dentition, many features of which are foreshadowed in the earlier ramapithecines. Some of these early apes lived in situations where they had to spend considerable time on the ground, and they appear to have had the capacity for at least occasional bipedal locomotion.

It appears that an early form of gracile *Australopithecus* gave rise to an early form of the genus *Homo.* It is of major significance that members of this new genus were both meat eaters and toolmakers. Toolmaking enabled early *Homo* to process meat so that it could be eaten; because toolmaking depended on fine manipulation of the hands, it put a premium on more developed brains. So too did the analytic and planning abilities required to hunt, and to gather the surplus of other wild foods for sharing.

Homo erectus exhibited a brain close in size to the modern human brain, and the dental characteristics were fully human. The possession of fire by *H. erectus* gave them a further means of controlling their environment. The technological efficiency of *H. erectus* is evidenced in a refined toolmaking, with the development of the hand axe and, later, specialized tools for hunting, butchering, food processing, hide-scraping, and defense. In addition, the improved hunting techniques of *H. erectus* reflected a considerable advance in organizational ability.

The Neanderthals possessed the brain capacity to be considered true *Homo sapiens.* It is likely that several local variations of Neanderthals and others like them existed, within which there was considerable individual variation. Their capacity for cultural adaptation was considerable, doubtless because their fully modern brain made possible not only sophisticated technology but sophisticated conceptual thought as well. Those who lived in Europe used fire extensively in their arctic climate, lived in small bands, and communicated by speech. Remains indicate that they believed in some form of afterlife and that religious belief played a part in their lives.

Evidence suggests that Neanderthal-like populations evolved into modern humans. Cro-Magnons and other Upper Paleolithic peoples possessed physical features similar to those of modern human populations. With these Upper Paleolithic peoples, the future of humans began to lie with culture rather than with biology as sheer physical bulk gave way to smaller features and intelligence became the means to advance cultural adaptation. The art work of Cro-Magnon cultures surpasses any undertaken by previous humans. Cave paintings found in Spain and France, which most anthropologists believe served a religious purpose, attest to a highly sophisticated aesthetic sensibility.

SUGGESTED READINGS

Brace, C. Loring, Harry Nelson, and Noel Korn. *Atlas of Human Evolution*, 2d ed. New York: Holt, Rinehart and Winston, 1979.

The core of this atlas consists of a series of drawings which provide a pictorial survey of all the key fossils that form the basis of our knowledge of human evolution. Each drawing highlights the diagnostic character of the fossil find to facilitate comparison and is accompanied by notes on date, geological age, place of discovery, and interpretations. Maps showing the distribution of important sites and stone tool distributions are included for each stage.

Jolly, Alison. *The Evolution of Primate Behavior*. New York: Macmillan, 1972.

In this book, Jolly attempts a survey of current knowledge about primate behavior and its relevance to human behavior. Part 1, entitled "Ecology," deals with habitat and locomotion, food, predation, interspecific relations, reasons for sociability and group range, size, and structure. "Society," Part 2, discusses learning and instinct, communication, status, affiliation and sex, mothers and infants, growing up in a troop, and violence and warfare. The volume concludes with "Intelligence," with sections on primate psychology, manipulation and tools, cognition, language, social learning, and the evolution of intelligence. The bibliography is also very useful.

Johanson, Donald, and Maitland Edey. *Lucy: The Beginnings of Humankind*. New York: Simon and Schuster, 1981.

This book tells the story of the discovery of "Lucy" and the other fossils of *Australopithecus afarensis*, and why they have enhanced our understanding of the early stages of human evolution. It reads like a first-rate detective story, at the same time giving one of the best descriptions of *Australopithecus*, one of the best discussions of the issues involved and the arguments over when *Homo* appeared, and one of the best accounts of how paleoanthropologists analyze their fossils to be found in literature.

Pfeiffer, John E. *The Emergence of Man*, 3d ed. New York: Harper & Row, 1978.

This is a revision of a widely read survey of human biological and cultural evolution through the Paleolithic. The author writes for a general audience rather than for specialists, and this makes for good reading.

Schaller, George B. *The Year of the Gorilla*. New York: Ballantine, 1971.

Schaller, who has written a scientific monograph on the mountain gorilla, describes here in popular form some of the results of his work in Africa. This is a personal book about gorillas and the way they behave. The author's simple line drawings and clear prose make this book a fine introduction to primate behavior, as well as a book which can be read for pure pleasure.

Van Lawick-Goodall, Jane. *In the Shadow of Man*. New York: Dell, 1972.

Jane van Lawick-Goodall's account of her 10 years of study of wild chimpanzees in Tanzania is written in a readable, informative style. The "family life," sex, infant, and child-mother relations of chimps are discussed thoroughly. The correspondence of primate behavior to human life is stressed. One problem is her artificial feeding of the chimps she studied, which may have distorted normal behavior patterns in significant ways.

In the Maya Indian community of Chichicastenango, children accompany their parents on market day. The childhood years are critical years for all cultures. Children must learn a language, which permits them to be given their basic orientation to the world, and appropriate patterns of behavior. By the time they reach adulthood, they are expected not only to have developed their personalities in ways consistent with the standards of their culture, but also to have learned the acceptable ways of making a living.

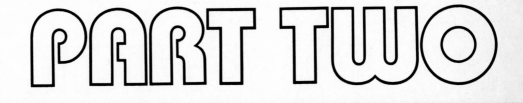

PART TWO

CULTURE AND SURVIVAL

Communicating, Raising Children, and Staying Alive

INTRODUCTION

All living creatures, be they great or small, fierce or timid, active or inactive, face a fundamental problem in common, the problem of survival. Simply put, unless they are able to adapt themselves to some available environment, they cannot survive. Adaptation requires the development of behavior patterns that will help an organism to utilize the environment to its advantage—to find food and sustenance, avoid hazards, and, if the species is to survive, reproduce its own kind. In turn, organisms need to have the biological equipment that makes possible the development of appropriate patterns of behavior. For the hundreds of millions of years that life has existed on earth, biological adaptation has been the primary means by which the problem of survival has been solved. This is accomplished as those organisms of a particular kind, whose biological equipment is best suited to a particular way of life, produce more offspring than those whose equipment is not. In this way, advantageous characteristics become more common in succeeding generations, while less advantageous ones become less common.

About 2 million years ago, some time after the line of human evolution had branched off from that of the apes, a new means of dealing with the problems of existence came into being. Early hominids began to rely for survival more and more on what their minds could invent rather than on what their bodies were capable of. Although the human species has not freed itself entirely, even today, from the forces of biological adaptation, it has come to rely primarily on culture—a body of learned traditions that, in essence, tells people how to live—as the medium through which the problems of human existence are to be solved. The consequences of this are profound. As evolving hominids developed cultural rather than biological solutions to their problems, their chances of survival generally improved. For example, when hunting and gathering as means of subsistence developed roughly 2 million years ago, the resources available to evolving hominids increased substantially. Moreover, the tools and cooperative techniques that made possible this new way of life made hominids somewhat less vulnerable to predators than they had been before. Thus life became a bit easier, and with humans, as with other animals, this generally makes for easier reproduction, and with more offspring surviving than before, populations grow. As the archeological record clearly shows, a slow but steady growth of human populations followed the development of hunting and gathering.

Among most mammals, population growth frequently leads to the dispersal of fringe populations into regions previously uninhabited by the particular species. There, they find new environments to which they must adapt or face extinction. This pattern of dispersal seems to have been followed by the evolving human species, for following the invention of hunting and gathering, humans began to spread geographically, inhabiting new and even harsh environments. But as they did so they devised cultural rather than biological solutions to the new problems of existence which they met. This is illustrated by human habitation of the cold regions of the world, which was not dependent on the evolution of humans capable of growing heavy coats of fur, as do other mammals that live in such regions. Instead, humans devised forms of clothing and shelter that, coupled with the use of fire, enabled them to overcome the cold. Moreover, this "cold adaptation," unlike most biological adaptations, could be rapidly changed in the face of different circumstances. The fact is that cultural equipment and techniques can be changed drastically in less than a single generation, whereas biological change takes many generations to accomplish.

As the medium through which humans handle the problems of existence, culture has become basic to human survival. It cannot do its job, though, unless it deals successfully with certain basic problems to ensure its own continued existence. Because culture is learned, and not inherited biologically, its transmission from one person to another, and from one generation to the next, depends upon an effective system of communication that must be far more complex than that of any other animal. Thus, a first requirement for any culture is that it provides a means of communication among the individuals who live by its rules. All cultures do this through some form of language. Although humans may communicate in other ways as well, it is language that makes possible the efficient transmission from one person to another of new techniques for dealing with the problems of existence as they are perceived by a culture. In Chapter 4, we shall look at language, its relation to other systems of communication, and its relation to culture itself.

In human societies each generation must learn its culture anew. The learning process itself is thus crucial to a culture's survival. A second requirement of culture, then, is the development of reliable means by which individuals learn to behave as the members of their community expect them to behave. Whether the role of educating children remains with the family, is taken over by professionals, as in the United States and other industrialized countries, or is played by age associations, how children learn appears to be as important as what they learn. Since to a large extent adult personality is the product of life experiences, the ways children are raised and educated play a major part in the shaping of their later selves. Indeed, the ability of individuals to function properly as adults depends, to a degree, upon how effectively their personalities have been shaped to fit their culture. As we shall see in Chapter 5, some findings have emerged from anthropological investigations in these areas which have implications for human behavior that go beyond anthropology. For example, it has been suggested that because a great deal of behavior is learned rather than biologically induced, by changing child-rearing practices it might be possible to alleviate some of the tensions and antisocial behavior that are frequently associated with the period of adolescence in industrialized societies.

Important as effective communication and education are for the survival of a culture, they are to no avail unless the culture is able to satisfy the basic needs of the individuals who live by its rules. A third requirement of culture, therefore, is the ability to provide its members with food, water, and protection from the elements. Without these, people cannot survive, and if the people who carry a culture cannot live, neither can the culture itself. Every culture, then, must develop procedures and equipment that enable people to survive in the environment in which they live. In Chapter 6, we discuss the ways by which cultures handle people's basic needs and the ways societies adapt through culture to the environment. Since this leads to the production, distribution, and consumption of goods—the subject matter of economic anthropology—we conclude this section with a chapter (Chapter 7) on economic systems.

4 | Language and Communication

Although humans rely primarily on language for communication, it is by no means the only system used. This child is communicating through a combination of facial expressions and nonlinguistic noises (crying). Her clothes too communicate. In Guatemala, such clothes say that the wearer is Indian.

PREVIEW

WHAT IS LANGUAGE?

Language is a system of sounds that, when put together according to certain rules, result in meanings that are intelligible to all speakers. Although humans rely primarily on language to communicate with one another, it is not their sole means of communication. Other means are paralanguage, a system of extralinguistic noises that accompany language, and kinesics, a system of body motions used to convey messages.

HOW IS LANGUAGE RELATED TO CULTURE?

Languages are spoken by people, who are members of societies, each of which has its own distinctive culture. Social variables such as class and status of the speaker will influence people's use of language. Moreover, people communicate what is meaningful to them, and what is or is not meaningful is defined by their particular culture. In fact, our use of language affects, and is affected by, our culture.

HOW DID LANGUAGE BEGIN?

Many theories have been proposed to account for the origin of language, several of them quite farfetched. One theory held by some anthropologists today is that human language began as a system of gestures. Various factors in the environment, together with biological changes in early hominids, set the stage for speech, with mouth gestures perhaps playing an important role in this transformation.

All normal humans have the ability to talk, and in many societies they may spend a considerable part of each day doing so. Indeed, so involved with our lives is **language** that it permeates everything we do, and everything we do permeates language. There is no doubt that our ability to speak rests squarely upon our biological organization. We are "programmed" to speak, although only in a general sort of way. Beyond the cries of babies, which are not learned but which do communicate, humans must learn how to speak. We must be taught to speak a particular language, and any normal child who begins early enough can learn any particular language.

Language is a system for the communication, in **symbols,** of any kind of information. Since nonhuman animals also communicate certain kinds of information systematically, we may also speak of animal language. But symbol in our definition means any kind of sound or gesture to which we ourselves have given meaning as standing for something, and not one that has a natural or biological meaning, which we call a **signal.** A tear is a signal of crying, and crying is a signal of some kind of emotional or physical state; the word "crying," however, is a symbol, a group of sounds to which we have learned to assign the meaning of a particular action, and which we can use to communicate that meaning whether or not anyone around us is actually crying.

At the moment language experts are not certain whether to give credit to animals—bees, dolphins, or chimpanzees—for the ability to use symbols as well as signals, even though these animals and many others have been found to communicate in remarkable ways. Some apes have been taught the American Sign Language for the Deaf with results such as those described in the Original Study for Chapter 2. What are the implications of this for our understanding of the nature and evolution of language? No certain answer can be given until we have a better understanding of animal communication than we now have. What we can be sure of is that human culture, as we know it, is ultimately dependent on a system of communication far more complex than that of any other animal. The reason for this is that culture must be learned; each individual has to be taught by other individuals the knowledge and rules for behavior which are appropriate for full participation in his or her society. While learning can and does take place in the absence of language by observation and imitation, guided by just a few signs or symbols, all known cultures are so rich in their content that they require systems of communication which not only can give precise labels to various classes of phenomena, but which also permit people to range over their experiences in the past and future, as well as the present. The central, and most highly developed, human system of communication is language. A knowledge of the workings of language, then, is essential to any kind of work in anthropology.

THE NATURE OF LANGUAGE

Any human language—English, Chinese, Swahili—is obviously a means of transmitting information and sharing with others both cultural and individual experiences. Because we tend to take language for granted, it is perhaps not so obvious that language is also a system that enables us to translate our concerns, beliefs, and perceptions into symbols that can be understood and interpreted by others. This is done by taking a few sounds—no language uses more than about 50—and developing rules for putting them together in meaningful ways. The many such languages presently in existence all over the world—an estimated 3000 different languages—may well astound and mystify us by their great variety and complexity; but basically languages are all orderly systems, invented, developed, and perpetuated by humans, and we should be able to figure them out, if only we have the right methods and the time.

Linguistics, the modern scientific study of language, began as early as the seventeenth century, in the age of exploration and discovery, with the accumulation of facts: the collecting of sounds, words, and sentences from as many different languages as possible, chiefly those encountered in exotic lands by European explorers, invaders, and missionaries. The great contribution of the nineteenth century was the discovery of system, regularity, and relationships in the data and the tentative formulation of some laws and regular principles. In the twentieth century, while we are still collecting data, we have made considerable progress in the reasoning process, testing and working from new and improved theories. Insofar as theories and facts of language are verifiable by independent researchers looking at the same materials, there may be said now to be a science of linguistics.

The Sound and Shape of Language

How can an anthropologst, a missionary, a social worker, or a medical worker approach and make sense of a language that has not already been analyzed and described, or for which there are no immediately available materials? There are hundreds of such languages in the world; fortunately, some fairly efficient methods have been developed to help with the task.

Language: A system of communication using sounds that are put together in meaningful ways according to a set of rules.

Symbols: Sounds or gestures that stand for meanings among a group of people.

Signal: A sound or gesture that has a natural or biological meaning.

Linguistics: The modern scientific study of all aspects of language.

Phonetics: The study of the production, transmission, and reception of speech sounds.

It is a painstaking process to unravel a language, but it is ultimately rewarding and often even fascinating for its own sake.

The process requires first a trained ear and a thorough understanding of the way speech sounds are produced. Otherwise it will be extremely difficult to write out or make intelligent use of any data. To satisfy this preliminary requirement, most people need special training in **phonetics,** or the systematic study of the production, transmission, and reception of speech sounds.

PHONOLOGY In order to analyze and describe any new language, an inventory of all of its sounds and an accurate way of writing them down are needed. Some sounds of other languages may be very much like the sounds of English, others may be sounds that we have never consciously produced; but since we all have the same vocal equipment, there is no reason why we should not be able, with practice, to reproduce all the sounds that anyone else

Yanomamö speak into anthropologist Napoleon Chagnon's tape recorder as he carries out studies in field linguistics. Such studies require accurate collections of sounds, words, and sentences, so that the language may be adequately described and analyzed.

makes. Once this is accomplished, the sound patterns of language can be studied to discover the abstract rules which tell us which combinations of sounds are permissible and which are not. This study is known as **phonology.**

The first step in studying any particular language, once a number of utterances have been collected, is to isolate the smallest classes of sound that make a difference in meaning, called **phonemes,** and to analyze the actual sounds which belong to each of these classes, called **allophones.** This isolation and analysis may be done by a process called the minimal pair test: the linguist tries to find two short words that appear to be exactly alike except for one sound, such as *bat* and *pat* in English. If the substitution of [b] for [p] in this minimal pair makes a difference in meaning, which it does in English, then those two sounds have been identified as members of distinct phonemes of the language and will require

Table 4.1 Phonetic Vowel Symbols (Sapir System)*

i (Fr. *fini*)	*ü* (Fr. *lune*)	*ɨ*	*u̇* (Swed. *hus*)	*ï*	*u* (Ger. *gut*)
ι (Eng. *bit*)	*ϋ* (Ger. *Mütze*)	*ι*	*v̇*	*ï*	*ʋ* (Eng. *put*)
e (Fr. *été*)	*ö* (Fr. *peu*)	—	*ȯ*	*α* (Eng. *but*)	*o* (Ger. *so*)
ε (Eng. *men*)	*ɔ̈* (Ger. *Götter*)	—	*ɔ̇*	*a* (Ger. *Mann*)	*ɔ* (Ger. *Volk*)
—	*ω̈* (Fr. *peur*)	—	*ω̇*	—	*ω* (Eng. *law*)
ä (Eng. *man*)	—	*ȧ* (Fr. *patte*)	—	—	—

*The symbol *ə* is used for an "indeterminate" vowel.

Source: George L. Trager, *Language and Languages* (San Francisco: Chandler Publishing Company, 1972), p. 304.

two different symbols to record. If, however, the linguist finds two different pronunciations, and then finds that there is no difference in their meaning for a native speaker, the sounds represented will be considered allophones of the same phoneme, and for economy of representation only one of the two symbols will be used to record that sound wherever it is found. For greater accuracy and to avoid confusion with the various sounds of our own language, the symbols of a phonetic alphabet, such as was developed by Edward Sapir for the American Anthropological Association (Table 4.1), can be used to distinguish between the sounds of most languages in a way comprehensible to anyone who knows the system.

MORPHOLOGY   The process of making and studying an inventory of sounds may of course be a long task; concurrently, the **morphologist** may begin to work out all groups or combinations of sounds that seem to have meaning. These are called **morphemes,** and they are the smallest units that have meaning in the language. They may consist of words or parts of words. A field linguist can abstract morphemes and their meanings from speakers of a language by means of pointing or gesturing to elicit words and their meanings, but the ideal situation is to have an informant, a person who knows enough of a common second language, so that approximate translations can be made more efficiently and confidently. It is pointless to write down data without any suggestion of meaning for them. *Cat* and *dog* would, of course, turn out to be morphemes, or meaningful combinations of sounds, in English. By pointing to two of either of them, the linguist could elicit *cats* and *dogs*. This indicates that there is another meaningful unit, an *-s*, that may be added to the original morpheme to mean "plural." When the linguist finds that

---

Phonology: The study of the sound patterns of language.

Phonemes: In linguistics, the smallest classes of sound that make a difference in meaning.

Allophones: In linguistics, different sounds belonging to the same sound class, or phoneme.

Morphologist: In linguistics, a person who studies sound combinations.

Morphemes: In linguistics, the smallest units of sounds that carry a meaning.

Bound morpheme: A sound that can occur in a language only in combination with other sounds, as *s* in English to signify the plural.

Free morphemes: Morphemes that can occur unattached in a language; for example, *dog* and *cat* are free morphemes in English.

Allomorphs: Variants of a single morpheme.

---

this *-s* cannot occur in the language unattached, it will be identified as a **bound morpheme;** because *dog* and *cat* can occur unattached to anything, they are called **free morphemes.** Because the sound represented as *s* is actually different in the two words (*s* in *cats* and *z* in *dogs*), the linguist will conclude that the sounds *s* and *z* are **allomorphs** of the plural morpheme; that is, they are two varieties of the same morpheme (even though they may be two different phonemes), occurring in different contexts but with no difference in meaning.

GRAMMAR AND SYNTAX The next step is to put morphemes together to form phrases or sentences. This process is known as identifying the syntactic units of the language, or the meaningful combination of morphemes in larger chains or strings. One way to do this is to use a method called **frame substitution.** By proceeding slowly at first, and relying on pointing or gestures, the field linguist can elicit such strings as *my cat, your cat,* or *her cat,* and *I see your cat, she sees my cat.* This begins to establish the rules or principles of phrase and sentence making, the **syntax** of the language.

Further success of this linguistic study depends greatly on individual ingenuity, tact, logic, and experience with language. A language may make extensive use of kinds of utterances that are not found at all in English, and which the English-speaking linguist may not therefore even think of asking for. Furthermore, certain speakers may pretend not to be able to say (or may truly not be able to say) certain things they consider to be impolite, taboo, or inappropriate for mention to outsiders. It may even be culturally unacceptable to point, in which case the linguist will have to devise roundabout ways of eliciting words for objects.

The **grammar** of the language will ultimately consist of all observations about the morphemes and the syntax. Further work may include the establishment by means of substitution frames of all the **form classes** of the language: that is, the parts of speech or categories of words that work the same way in any sentence. For example, we may establish a category we call "nouns" defined as anything that will fit the substitution frame, "I see a ____." We simply make the frame, try out a number of words in it, and have a native speaker indicate "yes" or "no" for whether the words work. In English, the words *house* and *cat* will fit this frame and will be said to belong to the same form class, but the word *think* will not. Another possible substitution frame for nouns might be "The ____ died," in which the word *cat* will fit, but not the word *house.* Thus we can identify subclasses of our nouns: in this case what we can call "animate" or "inanimate" subclasses. The same procedure may be followed for all the words of the language, using as many different frames as necessary, until we have a lexicon, or dictionary, that accurately describes the possible uses of all the words in the language.

One of the strengths of modern descriptive linguistics is the scientific objectivity of its methods. A descriptive linguist will not approach a language with the idea that it must have nouns, verbs, prepositions, or any other of the form classes identifiable in English. The linguist instead sees what turns up in the language and makes an attempt to describe it in terms of its own inner workings. For convenience, morphemes that behave approximately like English nouns and verbs may be labeled as such, but if it is thought that the terms are misleading, the linguist may instead call them "x-words" and "y-words," or "form class A" and "form class B."

The methods of descriptive linguistics are important tools for the cultural anthropologist, even when working with a language that has already been described. No analysis of any language is ever complete, and improvements, fresh insights, and new interpretations are always possible.

Paralanguage

VOICE QUALITIES Although humans rely primarily on language for their communication, it is by no means the only system used. How often has it been remarked:

"It's not what he said so much as how he said it"? What the speaker is concerned with in this phrase is **paralanguage,** a less developed system of communication than langauge which always accompanies it. Paralanguage may most easily be defined as a system of extralinguistic noises which generally accompany language. While it is not always easy for the linguist to distinguish between the sounds of language and paralinguistic noises, two different kinds of the latter have been identified. The first has to do with **voice qualities,** which operate as the background characteristics of a speaker's voice. These involve pitch range, or spread upward or downward; vocal lip control, ranging from hoarseness to openness; glottis control, or sharp to smooth transitions in pitch; articulation control, or forceful and relaxed speech; rhythm control, or smooth and jerky setting off of portions of vocal activity; resonance, ranging from resonant to thin; and tempo, an increase or decrease from the norm.

Voice qualities are capable of communicating much about the state of being of the person who is speaking, quite apart from what is being said. An obvious example of this is slurred speech, which may indicate that the speaker is intoxicated. Or, if someone says with a drawl, coupled with a restricted pitch range, that they are delighted with something, it probably indicates that they aren't delighted at all. The same thing said more rapidly, with increasing pitch, might indicate that the speaker really is genuinely excited about the matter. While the speaker's state of being is affected by his or her anatomical and physiological status, it is also markedly affected by the individual's overall self-image in the given situation. If he or she is made to feel anxious by being crowded in some way, or by some aspects of the social situation, for example, this anxiety will probably be conveyed by certain voice qualities.

> **Frame substitution:** A method used to identify the syntactic units of language. For example, a category called "nouns" may be established as anything that will fit the substitution frame "I see a _____."

> **Syntax:** In linguistics, the rules or principles of phrase and sentence making.

> **Grammar:** The entire formal structure of a language consisting of all observations about the morphemes and syntax.

> **Form classes:** The parts of speech or categories of words that work the same way in any sentence.

> **Paralanguage:** The extralinguistic noises that accompany language, for example, those of crying or laughing.

> **Voice qualities:** In paralanguage, the background characteristics of a speaker's voice.

> **Vocalizations:** Identifiable paralinguistic noises which are turned on and off at perceivable and relatively short intervals.

> **Vocal characterizers:** In paralanguage, sound productions such as laughing or crying which humans "speak through."

VOCALIZATIONS The second kind of paralinguistic noises consists of **vocalizations.** Instead of being background characteristics, these are actual identifiable noises that, unlike voice qualities, are turned on and off at perceivable and relatively short intervals. They are, nonetheless, separate from language sounds. One category of vocalizations are **vocal characterizers:** laughing or crying, yelling or whispering, yawning or belching, and the like. One "talks through" vocal characterizers, and they are generally indicative of the speaker's attitude. If one yawns while speaking to someone, for example, this may indicate an attitude of boredom on the part of the speaker. Breaking, an intermittent tensing and relaxing of the vocal musculature producing a tremulousness while speaking, may indicate great emotion on the part of the speaker.

Another category of vocalizations consists of **vocal qualifiers.** These are of briefer duration than vocal characterizers, being limited generally to the space of a single intonation pattern of language. They modify utterances in terms of intensity—loud versus soft; pitch—high versus low; and

extent—drawl versus clipping. These indicate the speaker's attitude to specific phrases such as "get out." The third category consists of **vocal segregates.** These are somewhat like the actual sounds of language, but they don't appear in the kinds of sequences that can be called words. Examples of vocal segregates familiar to English-speaking peoples are such substitutes for language as *shh, uh, uh,* or *uh huh.*

Kinesics

Kinesics may be thought of as a system for communication through motion. Familiar to many through the phrase "body language," kinesics is a system of postures, facial expressions, and bodily motions which convey messages. These messages may be

There is a great deal of similarity around the world in basic expressions such as smiling, laughing, crying, and the facial expressions of anger. Shown here are smiling people from the Great Nicobar Island (top right), Tanzania (bottom right), and Bali (below).

> **Vocal qualifiers:** In paralanguage, sound productions of brief duration that modify utterances in terms of intensity.

> **Vocal segregates:** In paralanguage, sound productions similar to the sounds of language but that do not appear in sequences which can properly be called words.

> **Kinesics:** A system of postures, facial expressions, and body motions that convey messages.

communicated directly, as in the case of gestures. For example, in North America scratching one's scalp, biting one's lip, or knitting one's brows are ways of conveying doubt. A more complex example is afforded by the gender signals sent by North Ameri-

While there is some similarity around the world in kinesic gestures, there are also marked differences. This sequence of four photos shows two Yanomamö men from different villages engaging in a ritual chest-pounding duel with closed fists. The intention is at once both friendly and threatening—a reminder that they might hurt one another but are refraining from doing so.

can men and women.[1] Although there is some regional and class variation, women generally bring their legs together, at times to the point that the upper legs cross, either in a full leg cross with feet still together, the outer sides of the feet parallel to one another, or in standing knee over knee. The pelvis is carried rolled slightly forward. The upper arms are held close to the body, and in movement, the entire body from neck to ankle is presented as a moving whole. Men, by contrast, hold their legs apart, with the upper legs at a 10 or 15 degree angle. Their pelvis is carried in a slightly rolled back position. The arms are held out at 10 to 15 degrees from the body, and they are moved independently of the body. Finally, a man may subtly wag his hips with a slight right and left presentation, with a movement involving a twist at the base of the rib cage and at the ankles.

Such gender signals are not the same as invitations to sexual activity, although, in the proper context, they do play a role. For example, men are less likely to respond sexually to women who send out masculine gender signals. On the other hand, changing sex roles in North American society are causing a good deal of confusion in the learning of traditional gender-identifying postures and movements.

Kinesic messages may also complement spoken messages. This is what is done by nodding the head while affirming something verbally at the same time. Other examples are punching the palm of the hand for emphasis, raising the head and brows when asking a question, or using the hands to illustrate what is being talked about. Such gestures are rather like bound morphemes—they have meaning but don't

stand alone except in certain situations, such as a nodded response to a question.

Although little scientific notice was taken of kinesics prior to the 1950s, there has since been exhaustive research, particularly involving North Americans. Cross-cultural research has shown, however, that there is a good deal of similarity around the world in such basic expressions as smiling, laughing, crying, and the facial expressions of anger. More specifically, there is great similarity in the routine for greeting over a distance around the world. Europeans, Balinese, Papuans, Samoans, Bushmen, and at least some South American Indians all smile and nod, and if the individuals are especially friendly, they will raise their eyebrows with a rapid movement, keeping them raised for a fraction of a second. All of this signals a readiness for contact. The Japanese, however, suppress the eyebrow flash, regarding it as indecent, which goes to show that there are differences, as well as similarities, cross-culturally. This can be seen in kinesic expressions for "yes" and "no." In our culture, one nods the head for "yes" or shakes it for "no." The Ceylonese, like us, will nod to answer "yes" to a factual question, but if asked to do something, a slow sideways movement of the head means "yes." In Greece, the nodded head means "yes," but "no" is indicated by jerking the head back so as to lift the face; at the same time, the eyes are often closed and the eyebrows lifted.

Linguistic Change

In our discussion of the sound and shape of language, we looked briefly at the internal organization of language—its phonology, morphology, syntax, and grammar. It is the descriptive approach to language that is concerned with registering and explaining all the features of any one given

[1]Ray L. Birdwhistell, *Kinesics and Context* (Philadelphia: University of Pennsylvania Press, 1970), p. 44.

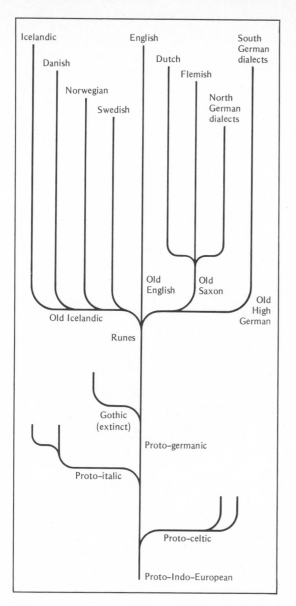

English is one of a group of languages in the Germanic subgroup of the Indo-European family; this diagram shows its relationship to other languages in the same subgroup. The root was Proto-Indo-European, a language spoken by a people who spread westward over Europe, bringing both their customs and their language with them.

Descriptive linguistics: The study of language concerned with registering and explaining all the features of a language at one point in history.

Historical linguistics: The study of relationships between earlier and later forms of a language, antecedents in older languages of developments in modern languages, and relationships among older languages.

language at any one time in its history. **Descriptive linguistics** concentrates, for example, on the way modern French or Spanish function now, as if they were closed systems, consistent within themselves, without any appeal to historical reasons for their development. Yet languages, like cultures, have histories. The Latin *ille* ("that") is identifiable as the origin of both French *le* ("the") and Spanish *el* ("the"), even though the descriptive linguist treats *le* and *el* only as they function in the modern language, where the meaning "that" is no longer relevant and very few people are aware that they are speaking a modern development of Latin. **Historical linguistics,** by contrast, investigates relationships between earlier and later forms of the same language, antecedents in older languages for developments in modern languages, and questions of relationships between older languages. Historical linguists, for example, attempt to identify and explain the development of early medieval spoken Latin into later medieval French and Spanish by investigating both natural change in the original language and the influence of contacts with the barbarian invaders from the north. There is no conflict between historical and descriptive linguists, the two approaches being recognized as interde-

INDO–EUROPEAN

AFRO–ASIATIC

SINO–TIBETAN

ALTAIC

DRAVIDIAN

AUSTRO–ASIATIC

FINNO–UGRIC

The principal language families of the world.

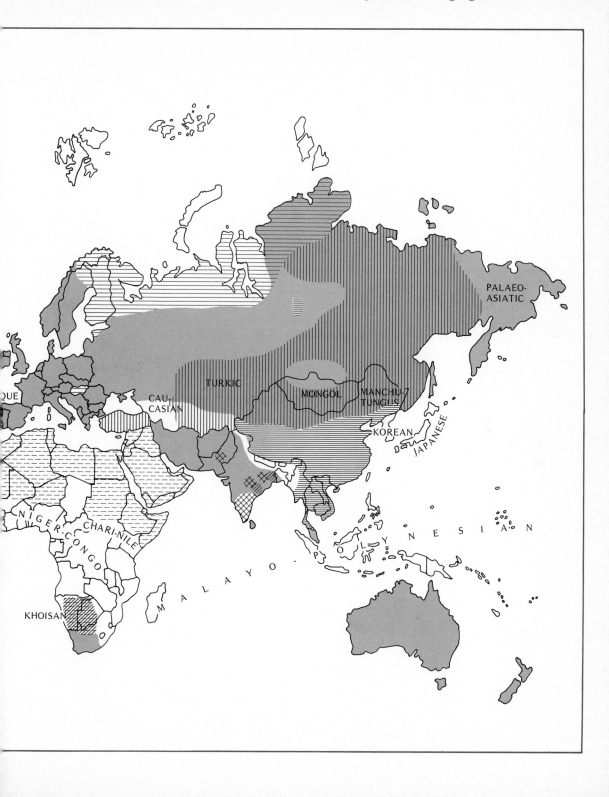

pendent. Even a modern language is constantly changing, and it changes according to principles that can only be established historically.

Historical linguists have achieved considerable success in working out the genealogical relationships between different languages, and these are reflected in genealogical schemes of classification. For example, English is one of a number of languages classified in the Indo-European **language family.** This family is subdivided into some 11 **language subgroups,** which reflect the fact that there has been a long period of **linguistic divergence** from an ancient unified language, referred to as a Proto-Indo-European, into separate languages. English is one of a number of languages in the Germanic subgroup. These languages are the result of further linguistic divergence, but they are all more closely related to one another than they are to the languages of other subgroups of the Indo-European family.

Historical linguists have also been successful in describing the changes that have taken place as languages have diverged from more ancient parent languages. They have also developed means of estimating when certain migrations, invasions, and contacts of peoples have taken place on the basis of linguistic similarities and differences. The concept of linguistic divergence, for example, is used to suggest the time at which one group of speakers of a language separated from another group. A more complicated technique, known as **glottochronology,** was developed by Swadesh and Lees in the early 1950s to try to date the divergence of related languages, such as Latin and Greek, from an earlier common language. The technique is based on the assumption that changes in a language's **core vocabulary,** pronouns, lower numerals, and names for parts of the body and natural objects, change at a more or less constant rate. By applying a logarithmic formula to two related core vocabularies, one should be able to determine how many years the languages have been separated. Actually, glottochronology lacks the precision it was originally thought to possess, but it is useful in estimating when languages may have separated.

If many of the changes that have taken place in the course of linguistic divergence are well known, the causes of these changes are not. One force for linguistic change is borrowing by one language from another, and languages do readily borrow from one another. But if borrowing were the sole force for change, linguistic differences would be expected to become less pronounced through time. It is by studying modern languages in their cultural settings that one can begin to understand the forces for change. One such force is novelty, pure and simple. There seems to be a human tendency to admire the person who comes up with a new and clever idiom, a new and useful word, or a particularly stylish pronunciation, so long as these do not seriously interfere with communication. Indeed, in linguistic matters, complexity tends to be admired while simplicity seems dull. Hence, about as fast as a language may be simplified, purged of needlessly complex constructions or phrases, new ones will arise.

Group membership also plays a role in linguistic change. Part of this is functional: professions, sects, or other groups in a society often have need of special vocabularies to be able to communicate effectively about their special interests. Beyond this, special vocabularies may serve as labeling devices; those who use such vocabularies are set off as a group from those who do not, and this helps to create a strong sense of group identity.

. . . when a linguist writes of "morphophonic alteration in the verb paradigm" or an anthropologist writes of "the structural implications of matrilateral cross-cousin marriage," they express, in part at least, their membership in a profession and their ability to use its language. To those on the inside, professional terminology may connote the comforting security of their familiar ingroup; to those on the outside it may seem an unneeded and pretentious use of mumbo-jumbo where perfectly adequate and simple words would do as well. But whether needed or not, professional terminology does serve to differentiate language and to set the speech of one group apart from that of others. To that degree it is a force for stylistic divergence.[2]

Phonological differences between groups may be regarded in the same light as vocabulary differences. In a class-structured society, for example, members of the upper class may try to keep their pronunciation distinct from that of lower classes. An example of a different sort is afforded by coastal communities in the state of Maine, in particular, though it may be seen to varying degrees elsewhere along the New England coast. In the past, people in these communities have had a style of pronunciation quite distinct from the styles of "inlanders." More recently, as outsiders have moved into these coastal communities, either as summer people or as permanent residents, the traditional coastal style has come to identify those who adhere to traditional coastal values, as opposed to those who do not.

One other, far-reaching, force for linguistic change is **linguistic nationalism,** where whole nations attempt to proclaim their independence by purging their vocabularies of "foreign" terms. This phenome-

---

Language family: A group of languages which are ultimately descended from a single ancestral language.

Language subgroups: Languages of a family that are more closely related to one another than they are to other languages of the same family.

Linguistic divergence: The development of different languages from a single ancestral language.

Glottochronology: In linguistics, a method of dating divergence in branches of language families.

Core vocabulary: In language, pronouns, lower numerals, and names for body parts and natural objects.

Linguistic nationalism: The attempt by nations to proclaim independence by purging their languages of foreign terms.

---

non is particularly characteristic of the former colonial countries of Africa and Asia today. It is by no means limited to those countries, however, as one can see by recent French attempts to purge their language of such americanisms as *le hamburger*. Also in the category of linguistic nationalism are attempts to resurrect languages no longer in common use, such as Gaelic and Hebrew.

LANGUAGE IN ITS CULTURAL SETTING

Rewarding though it is to analyze language as a system in which linguistic variables operate which depend upon other linguistic phenomena, it is important to realize that

---

[2]Robbins Burling, *Man's Many Voices: Language in Its Cultural Context* (New York: Holt, Rinehart and Winston, 1970), p. 192.

languages are spoken by people, who are members of societies, each of which has its own distinctive culture. Individuals tend to vary in the ways they use language, and as the preceding discussion suggests, social variables such as class and status of the speaker will also influence their use of language. Moreover, people choose words and sentences so as to communicate meaning, and what is meaningful in one culture may differ from what is meaningful in another. The fact is that our use of language affects, and is affected by, our culture.

The whole question of the relationships between language and culture is the province of **ethnolinguistics,** a field that has grown out of both ethnology and descriptive linguistics to become almost a separate area of inquiry. Ethnolinguistics is concerned with every aspect of the structure and use of language that has anything to do with society, culture, and human behavior.

Language and Thought

An important ethnolinguistic concern of the 1930s and 1940s was the question of whether language might indeed determine culture. Do we see and react differently to the colors blue and green, with different cultural symbolism for the two different colors, only because our language has different names for these two neighboring sections of the unbroken color spectrum? When anthropologists noticed that some cultures lump together blue and green with one name, they began to wonder about this question. The American linguist Edward Sapir first formulated the problem, and his student, Benjamin Lee Whorf, drawing on his experience with the language of the Hopi Indians, developed a full-fledged theory, sometimes called the **Whorfian hypothesis.** Whorf proposed that a language is not simply an encoding process for voicing

our ideas and needs but is rather a shaping force that, by providing habitual grooves of expression which predispose people to see the world in a certain way, guides their thinking and behavior. The problem is a little like the old question of the chicken or the egg, and some later formulations of Whorf's theory about which came first, thinking and behavior or language, have since been generally criticized as both logically unsound and not amenable to any experimentation or proof. Its primary value is that it did begin to focus attention on the relationships between language and culture.

The opposite point of view is that language reflects reality. In this view, language mirrors cultural reality, and as the latter changes, so too will language. Some support for this point of view comes from recent studies of blue-green color terms.[3] It has been shown that eye pigmentation acts to filter out the shorter wavelengths of solar radiation. Color vision is thus limited through a reduced sensitivity to blue and confusion between the short visible wavelengths. The effect shows up in color-naming behavior, where green may be identified with blue, blue with black, and green and blue with black. Both the severity of visual limitation and the extent of lumping of color terms depends on the density of eye pigmentation characteristic of the people in a given society.

These findings do not mean that language is only a reflection of reality, any more than thinking and behavior are determined by language. The truth of the matter is probably as anthropologist Peter Woolfson has put it:

---

[3] Marc H. Bornstein, "The Influence of Visual Perception on Culture," *American Anthropologist*, 1975, 77(4):774–798.

Reality should be the same for us all. Our nervous systems, however, are being bombarded by a continual flow of sensations of different kinds, intensities, and durations. It is obvious that all of these sensations do not reach our consciousness; some kind of filtering system reduces them to manageable propositions. The Whorfian hypothesis suggests that the filtering system is one's language. Our language, in effect, provides us with a special pair of glasses that heightens certain perceptions and dims others. Thus, while all sensations are received by the nervous system, only some are brought to the level of consciousness.[4]

Linguists are finding that although language is generally flexible and adaptable, once a terminology is established it tends to perpetuate itself and to reflect and reveal the social structure and the common perceptions and concerns of a group. For example, the English words for war and the tactics of war and the hierarchy of officers and men who fight, reflect what is obviously a reality for our culture. An observer from an entirely different and perhaps warless culture could understand a great deal about our institution of war and its conventions simply from what we have found necessary to name and talk about in our military terminology. Similarly, anthropologists have noted that in the Arabic dialects of Bedouin tribes in the Middle East there is an elaborate system of terminology for everything having to do with camels; with a certain amount of study we can determine from the naming system alone the importance of camels to the culture, attitudes toward camels (which are often treated with more care than people), and the whole etiquette of human and

---

[4]Peter Woolfson, "Language, Thought, and Culture," in Virginia P. Clark, Paul A. Escholz, and Alfred F. Rosa, eds., *Language* (New York: St. Martin's, 1972), p. 4.

> **Ethnolinguistics: The study of the relation between language and culture.**
>
> **Whorfian hypothesis: The hypothesis, proposed by the linguist B. L. Whorf, which states that language, by providing habitual grooves of expression, predisposes people to see the world in a certain way and so guides their thinking and behavior.**

camel relationships. But a people's language does not prevent them from thinking in new and novel ways. If this leads to important changes in common perceptions and concerns of a group, then langauge can be expected to change accordingly.

KINSHIP TERMS In the same connection, anthropologists have paid considerable attention to the way people name their relatives in various societies: further observations on the question of kinship terms will be found in Chapter 9. In English we have terms to identify brother, sister, mother, father, grandmother, grandfather, granddaughter, grandson, niece, nephew, mother-in-law, father-in-law, sister-in-law, and brother-in-law. Some people also distinguish first and second cousin and great-aunt and great-uncle. Is this the only possible system for naming relatives and identifying relationships? Obviously not. We could have separate and individual words, as some cultures do, for younger brother and older brother, for mother's sister and father's sister, and so on. What we can describe in English with a phrase, if pressed to do so, other languages make explicit from the outset, and vice versa: some West African languages use the same word to denote both a brother and a cousin, and a

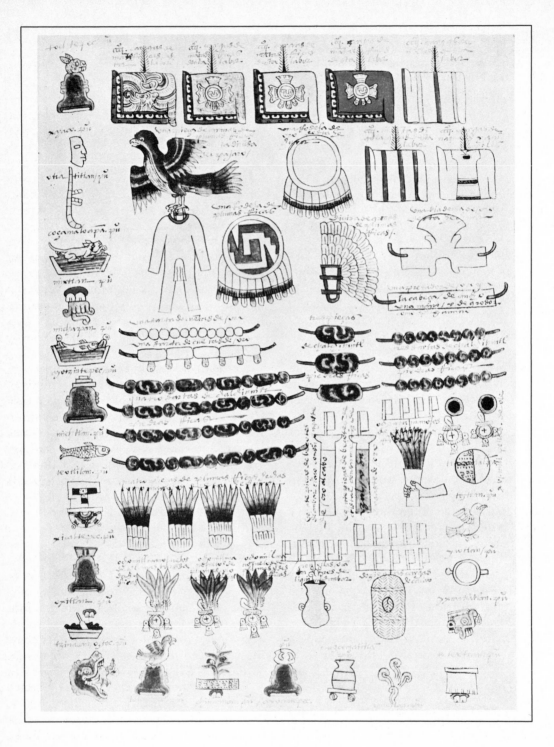

The impermanence of spoken words contrasts with the relative permanence of written records. Opposite is a page from the Codex Mendoza, an early Spanish attempt to decipher Mexican writing, which was pictographic rather than syllabic. Below is a Sumerian cylinder seal. When rolled over tablets of wet clay, it produced a pictographic record like that shown above, which was then baked to ensure permanence.

mother's sister may also be called by the same term as one's mother.

What do kinship terms reveal? From them we can certainly gain a good idea of how the family is structured, what relationships are considered close or distant, and sometimes what attitudes toward relationships may prevail. Caution is required, however, in drawing conclusions from kinship terms. Just because we do not distinguish linguistically in English between our mother's parents and our father's parents (both are simply grandmother and grandfather), does that mean that in our culture we lump them all together as faceless old people or that we treat old people badly? Some people have argued that it is so. But in France, where there is reputedly considerably more respect and concern for older relatives, perhaps even exaggeratedly so by our standards, there is no more linguistic difference between a mother's mother and a father's mother than there is in English-speaking cultures. Kinship terms can establish the limits of so-called extended families in certain cultures, and they can define the cultural relationships between families brought together by a marriage. Other implications are still uncertain, but the area is a rich one for investigation.

Taboo Words

Another interesting concern of ethnolinguistics is the matter of taboo words, obscenities, and acceptable and unacceptable language in general. Consider, for example, the question of whether this textbook should supply here an example of an obscenity common in American English, such as "bullshit," to illustrate the point. The answer, obviously, is that it may, though this would certainly not be permissible in a textbook intended for use in an

SE-QUO-YAH

The symbols used in writing a language are, at best, only approximations of those used in speaking a language. In this somewhat idealized portrait, the Cherokee Indian Sequoia points to the alphabet which he invented to write the Cherokee language. Of the 86 characters, about a third were freely invented while the rest are derived from English, in which Sequoia was illiterate.

elementary school. What makes words socially unacceptable or inappropriate in certain contexts in certain languages? There is no universal taboo about words related to sex and excrement, as there supposedly is in our culture, and some cultures find our obscenities to be only a little foolish or peculiar, as we do theirs. For example, consider the English obscenity "bloody" or the French one *sacre bleu* ("blue rite"); both sound odd to American ears. By determining what may or may not be said, and when and where, we can understand a great deal about beliefs and social relationships. An

interesting study has been made recently by the British anthropologist Edmund Leach of the striking relationships among animal names, verbal abuse, and cultural taboos. Leach finds a relation, for example, between a long-standing cultural belief in the dirtiness of a dog—it is insulting in English to call someone a dog—and the fact that we may not and do not eat the dog for meat (though some cultures do). What is meat and what is not, what is insult and what is not, what is dirty and what is not: all of these are important questions that may be answered in part in language, and they are likewise matters for investigation in ethnolinguistics.

Social Dialects

In our previous discussion of linguistic change, phonological and vocabulary differences between groups were noted as important forces for linguistic change. Varying forms of a language that are similar enough to be mutually intelligible are known as **dialects,** and the study of dialects is a concern of **sociolinguistics.** Technically all dialects are languages—there is nothing partial or sublinguistic about them—and the point at which two different dialects become distinctly different languages is roughly the point at which speakers of one are almost totally unable to communicate with speakers of the other. Boundaries may be psychological, geographical, social, or economic, and they are not always very clear. There is usually a transitional territory, or perhaps a buffer zone, where features of both are found and understood, as between central and southern China. The fact is that if you learn the Chinese of Peking you cannot communicate with the waiter in your local Chinese restaurant who comes from Canton or Hong Kong, although both languages—or dialects—are conventionally called Chinese.

A classic example of the kind of dialect that may set one group apart from others within a single society is afforded by the following study of nonstandard English. It illustrates as well how culture-bound theories may lead to serious misunderstanding of such differences.

> **Dialects:** Varying forms of a language that reflect particular regions or social classes and that are similar enough to be mutually intelligible.
>
> **Sociolinguistics:** The study of the structure and use of language as it relates to its social setting.

ORIGINAL STUDY

The Logic of Nonstandard English[5]

The verbal behavior which is shown by the child in the situation quoted above [a black child's verbal ability was "tested" by an adult white interviewer in a New York City school] is not the result of the ineptness of the interviewer. It is rather the result of regular sociolinguistic factors operating upon adult and child in this asymmetrical situation. In our work in urban ghetto areas, we have often encountered such behavior. Ordinarily we worked with boys ten to seventeen years old, and whenever we extended our approach downward to eight- or nine-year-olds, we began to see the need for different techniques to explore the verbal capacity of the child. At one point we began a series of interviews with younger brothers of the Thunderbirds in 1390 Fifth Avenue (Ed. Note: a preadolescent group studied in this research). Clarence Robins (CR) returned after an interview with eight-year-old Leon L., who showed the following minimal response to topics which arouse intense interest in other interviews with older boys.

> CR: What if you saw somebody kickin' somebody else on the ground, or was using a stick, what would you do if you saw that?
> LEON: Mmmm.
> CR: If it was supposed to be a fair fight—
> LEON: I don' know.
> CR: You don't know? Would you do anything? . . . huh? I can't hear you.
> LEON: No.
> CR: Did you ever see somebody got beat up real bad?
> LEON: . . . Nope. . .
> CR: Well—uh—did you ever get into a fight with a guy?
> LEON: Nope.

---

[5] William Labov, "The Logic of Nonstandard English," in Frederick Williams, ed., *Language and Poverty: Perspectives of a Theme* (New York, N.Y.: Academic Press, 1970), pp. 94–97. Copyright by William Labov.

CR: That was bigger than you?
LEON: Nope . . .
CR: You never been in a fight?
LEON: Nope . . .
CR: Nobody ever pick on you?
LEON: Nope.
CR: Nobody ever hit you?
LEON: Nope.
CR: How come?
LEON: Ah 'on' know.
CR: Didn't you ever hit somebody?
LEON: Nope.
CR: (incredulously) You never hit nobody?
LEON: Mhm.
CR: Aww, ba-a-a-be, you ain't gonna tell me that!

It may be that Leon is here defending himself against accusations of wrongdoing, since Clarence knows that Leon has been in fights, that he has been taking pencils away from little boys, and so on. But if we turn to a more neutral subject, we find the same pattern:

CR: You watch—you like to watch television? . . . Hey, Leon . . . you like to watch television? (Leon nods) What's your favorite program?
LEON: Uhhmmmm . . . I look at cartoons.
CR: Well, what's your favorite one? What's your favorite program?
LEON: Superman . . .
CR: Yeah? Did you see Superman—ah—yesterday, or day before yesterday? When's the last time you saw Superman?
LEON: Sa-aturday . . .
CR: You rem—you saw it Saturday? What was the story all about? You remember the story?
LEON: M-m.
CR: You don't remember the story of what—that you saw of Superman?
LEON: Nope.
CR: You don't remember what happened, huh?
LEON: Hm-m.
CR: I see—ah—what other stories do you like to watch on TV?
LEON: Mmmm? . . . umm . . . (glottalization)
CR: Hmm? (four seconds)
LEON: Hh?
CR: What's th' other stories that you like to watch?
LEON: Mi-ighty Mouse . . .
CR: and what else?
LEON: Ummmm . . . ahm . . .

This nonverbal behavior occurs in a relatively favorable context for adult-child interaction. The adult is a Negro man raised in Harlem, who knows this particular neighborhood and these boys very well. He is a skilled interviewer who has obtained a very high level of verbal response with techniques developed for a different age level, and he has an extraordinary advantage over most teachers or experimenters in these respects. But even his skills and personality are ineffective in breaking down the social constraints that prevail here.

When we reviewed the record of this interview with Leon, we decided to use it as a test of our own knowledge of the sociolinguistic factors which control speech. In the next interview with Leon we made the following changes in the social situation:

1. Clarence brought along a supply of potato chips, changing the interview into something more in the nature of a party.

2. He brought along Leon's best friend, eight-year-old Gregory.

3. We reduced the height by having Clarence get down on the floor of Leon's room; he dropped from six feet, two inches to three feet, six inches.

4. Clarence introduced taboo words and taboo topics, and proved, to Leon's surprise, that one can say anything into our microphone without any fear of retaliation. The result of these changes is a striking difference in the volume and style of speech. (The tape is punctuated throughout by the sound of potato chips.)

CR: Is there anybody who says *your momma drink pee?*
{ LEON: (rapidly and breathlessly) Yee-ah!
{ GREG: Yup!
LEON: And *your father eat doo-doo for breakfas'!*
CR: Ohhh! ! (laughs)
LEON: And they say your father—*your father eat doo-doo for dinner!*
GREG: When they sound on me, I say *C.B.S. C.B.M.*
CR: What that mean?
{ (LEON: Congo booger-snatch! (laughs)
{ (GREG: Congo booger-snatcher! (laughs)
GREG: And sometimes I'll curse with *B.B.*
CR: What that?
GREG: Black boy! (Leon crunching on potato chips) Oh that's a *M.B.B.*
CR: *M.B.B.* What's that?
GREG: 'Merican Black Boy.
CR: Ohh . . .
GREG: Anyway, 'Mericans is same like white people, right?
LEON: And they talk about Allah.
CR: Oh yeah?
GREG: Yeah.
CR: What they say about Allah?
{ (LEON: Allah—Allah is God.
{ (GREG: Allah—
CR: And what else?
LEON: I don' know the res'.
GREG: Allah i—Allah is God, Allah is the only God, Allah . . .
LEON: Allah is the *son* of God.
GREG: But can he make magic?
LEON: Nope.
GREG: I know who can make magic.
CR: Who can?
LEON: The God, the *real* one.
CR: Who can make magic?

GREG: The son of po'—(CR: Hm?) I'm sayin' the po'k chop God!* He only a po'k chop God! (Leon chuckles).

(The "nonverbal" Leon is now competing actively for the floor; Gregory and Leon talk to each other as much as they do to the interviewer.)

We can make a more direct comparison of the two interviews by examining the section on fighting. Leon persists in denying that he fights, but he can no longer use monosyllabic answers, and Gregory cuts through his facade in a way that Clarence Robins alone was unable to do.

CR: Now, you said you had this fight now; but I wanted you to tell me about the fight that you had.
LEON: I ain't had no fight.
{ (GREG: Yes you did! He said Barry . . .
{ (CR: You said you had one! you had a fight with Butchie.
{ (GREG: An he say Garland! . . . an' Michael!
{ (CR: an' Barry . . .
{ (LEON: I di'n'; you said that, Gregory!
{ (GREG: You did!
{ (LEON: You know you said that!
{ (GREG: You said Garland, remember that?
{ (GREG: You said Garland! Yes you did!
{ (CR: You said Garland, that's right.
GREG: He said Mich—an' I say Michael.
{ (CR: Did you have a fight with Garland?
{ (LEON: Uh-Uh.
CR: You had one, and he beat you up, too!
GREG: Yes he did!
LEON: No, I di—I never had a fight with Butch! . . .

The same pattern can be seen on other local topics, where the interviewer brings neighborhood gossip to bear on Leon, and Gregory acts as a witness.

CR: . . . Hey Gregory! I heard that around here . . . and I'm 'on' tell you who said it, too . . .
LEON: Who?
CR: about you . . .
{ (LEON: Who?
{ (GREG: I'd say it!
CR: They said that—they say that the only person you play with is David Gilbert.
{ (LEON: Yee-ah! yee-ah! yee-ah! . . .
{ (GREG: That's who you play with!

---

*The reference to the *pork chop God* condenses several concepts of black nationalism current in the Harlem community. A *pork chop* is a Negro who has not lost the traditional subservient ideology of the South, who has no knowledge of himself in Muslim terms, and the *pork chop God* would be the traditional God of Southern Baptists. He and His followers may be pork chops, but He still holds the power in Leon and Gregory's world.

  { (LEON: I 'on' play with him no more!
  { (GREG: Yes you do!
    LEON: I 'on' play with him no more!
    GREG: But remember, about me and Robbie?
    LEON: So that's not—
    GREG: and you went to Petey and Gilbert's house, 'member? *Ah haaah!!*
    LEON: So that's—so—but I would—I had came back out, an' I ain't go to his house no more . . .

The observer must now draw a very different conclusion about the verbal capacity of Leon. The monosyllabic speaker who had nothing to say about anything and cannot remember what he did yesterday has disappeared. Instead, we have two boys who have so much to say they keep interrupting each other, and who seem to have no difficulty in using the English language to express themselves. In turn we obtain the volume of speech and the rich array of grammatical devices which we need for analyzing the structure of nonstandard Negro English; for example: negative concord ("I 'on' play with him no more"), the pluperfect ("had came back out"), negative perfect ("I ain't had"), the negative preterite ("I ain't go"), and so on.

We can now transfer this demonstration of the sociolinguistic control of speech to other test situations, including IQ and reading tests in school. It should be immediately apparent that none of the standard tests will come anywhere near measuring Leon's verbal capacity. On these tests he will show up as very much the monosyllabic, inept, ignorant, bumbling child of our first interview. The teacher has far less ability than Clarence Robins to elicit speech from this child. Clarence knows the community, the things that Leon has been doing, and the things that Leon would like to talk about. But the power relationships in a one-to-one confrontation between adult and child are too asymmetrical. This does not mean that some Negro child will not talk a great deal when alone with an adult, or that an adult cannot get close to any child. It means that the social situation is the most powerful determinant of verbal behavior and that an adult must enter into the right social relation with a child if he wants to find out what a child can do. This is just what many teachers cannot do.

The view of the Negro speech community which we obtain from our work in the ghetto areas is precisely the opposite from that reported by Deutsch or by Bereiter and Englemann. We see a child bathed in verbal stimulation from morning to night. We see many speech events which depend upon the competitive exhibition of verbal skills—sounding, singing, toasts, rifting, louding—a whole range of activities in which the individual gains status through his use of language (see Labov, et al. 1968, section 4.2). We see the younger child trying to acquire these skills from older children, hanging around on the outskirts of older peer groups, and imitating this behavior to the best of his ability. We see no connection between verbal skill in the speech events characteristic of the street culture and success in the schoolroom.

CODE SWITCHING In addition to the larger problem of determining dialect boundaries, and trying to determine whether linguistic differences in any given case also reflect cultural differences, there is also the problem in dialect studies of why and how people in the same community, whether a large North American city or a small African town, can and do speak the same language in different ways. Some people are able to speak one social dialect in one situation and a different one in another situation. As a rather extreme example, in New York City presently some second-generation immigrant children from Puerto Rico are able to speak the language of their parents at home, a dialect known as Puerto Rican "Spanglish" with their contemporaries, and New York English with their teachers. The process of changing from one level of language to another, whether from one language to another or from one dialect of a language to another, is known as **code switching,** and it has been the subject of a number of sociolinguistic studies. Almost all of us can switch from formality to informality in our speech, and the question of why and when such things are done in various cultures is only beginning to be investigated.

OTHER SOCIOLINGUISTIC CONCERNS Of the many other concerns of sociolinguistics today we can only mention that we also find investigations of children's languages and word games, the structure of folktales and folk songs, bilingualism and multilingualism, pidgin languages and creoles, linguistic borrowing and innovation, formulas of address and politeness, secret languages, magic languages, and myth. The list increases and has begun to duplicate many of the concerns of other fields or disciplines. Almost every aspect of anthropology and sociology has a linguistic side or a relevance to linguistics. This new field of sociolinguistics proves to be not one field but many, and it is providing an opportunity for some productive cooperation and sharing between disciplines. The practical value of such cooperation is illustrated by the Original Study of nonstandard English presented earlier in this chapter.

THEORETICAL LINGUISTICS

Having surveyed the sound and shape of language, linguistic change, and language in its cultural setting, we may now turn to the question of how language works. This is the primary concern of **theoretical linguistics.** A theoretical linguist, such as the well-known Noam Chomsky of the Massachusetts Institute of Technology, develops a framework and a system for describing what happens in the whole encoding and sentence-making process. He hopes that his system will hold for all languages, though he may develop it in detail for only one.

Transformational-Generative Grammar

What happens when we talk? How do we make sentences? One theory is that each individual speaker of a language possesses an innate, deeply buried knowledge of what that language will allow in the construction of a sentence and what is not possible. This innate base generates **deep structures,** which are underlying grammatical forms of sentences that are transformed by a set of rules into actual utterances. The finished product, the complete utterance or sentence, is said to display **surface structure,** a complex web of transformed and integrated units from the deep structure. The principle is assumed to be the same for all languages, but the deep structure will differ, and the processes of getting from deep structure to surface structure should vary according to the habits, conventions, and social adaptations of different cultures. Understanding or explaining any language, according to this theory, should amount to identifying the rules used to move from general innate language structure to an actual speaking and hearing ability. A complete set of rules should then be capable of generating or producing all possible sentences speakers of a language have used, could use, or will use.

Chomsky's theory has been widely acclaimed for bringing about a revolution in our thinking about language. **Transformational-generative** studies of various languages have suggested that there is a basic similarity between them in their rules, and even their deep structures are not all that different. Through such studies, theoretical linguists hope to learn more about the general features of grammatical structure common to all languages, which they see as reflecting certain fundamental properties of the human mind.

THE ORIGINS OF LANGUAGE

A realization of the central importance of language for human culture leads inevitably to speculation about how language might have started in the first place. The question of the origin of language has long been a popular subject, and some reasonable and many not so reasonable theories have been proposed: exclamations became words, sounds in nature were imitated, or people simply got together and assigned sounds to objects and actions. The main trouble with past theories is that there was so little in the way of evidence that theorizing often reached the point of wild speculation. The result was a reaction against such

> **Code switching:** The process of changing from one level of language to another.
>
> **Theoretical linguistics:** An approach to descriptive linguistics that makes a framework and a system for describing what happens in the whole encoding and sentence-making process for all languages.
>
> **Deep structures:** In the theoretical linguistics of Noam Chomsky, underlying grammatical forms of sentences that convey meaning from which all utterances are built.
>
> **Surface structure:** In theoretical linguistics, a complete utterance or sentence that is built up unconsciously from the underlying deep structure.
>
> **Transformational-generative grammar:** The theoretical linguistic theory of Noam Chomsky that attempts to find the complete set of rules capable of generating or producing all possible sentences in a language.

theorizing, exemplified by the ban imposed in 1866 by the Société de Linguistique de Paris against papers on linguistic origins. Now there is more evidence to work with—better knowledge of primate brains, new studies of primate communication, more human fossils which can be used to tentatively reconstruct vocal tracts, and a better understanding of early hominid ways of life. We still can't prove how and when human language developed, but we can speculate much less wildly than was once the case.

Humans talk, but other primates communicate largely through gestures. Still, humans have not abandoned gestural communication altogether, as we see here. The human and the rhesus monkey are using the same open-mouth threat.

Attempts to teach other primates to talk like humans have not been successful. In a lengthy experiment in communication, the chimpanzee Viki learned to voice only a few words, such as "up," "mama," and "papa." The problem of speech in other primates seems to be twofold: a lack of connection in the nonhuman primate brain between auditory and motor speech areas and a difference in construction between the human and nonhuman primate vocal apparatus.

Better results have been achieved through nonvocal methods. Chimpanzees and gorillas in the wild make a variety of vocalizations, but these are mainly emotional rather than propositional. In this sense, they are equivalent to human paralanguage. Much of their communication takes place by kinesic means—the use of specific gestures and postures. Indeed, some of these, such as kissing and embracing, are in virtually universal use today among humans, as well as apes. Allen and Beatrice Gardner began teaching the American Sign Language, used by the deaf, to their young chimpanzee Washoe in 1966. After 22 months, Washoe had a vocabulary of 30 signs, and her rate of acquisition was accelerating. By the time she was four years old, she had a vocabulary of 132 signs. The first signs she learned were for nouns. She was able to transfer each sign from its original referent to other appropriate objects, and even pictures of objects. Her vocabulary includes verbs, adjectives, and words like "sorry," and "please." Washoe can string signs together properly to produce original sentences.

The chimpanzee Sarah has learned to converse by means of pictographs—designs such as squares and triangles—on brightly colored plastic chips. Each pictograph stands for a noun or a verb. Sarah can also produce new sentences of her own. Another chimpanzee, Lana, converses by means of a computer with a keyboard somewhat like that of a typewriter, but with symbols rather than letters.

One of the most recent, and fascinating, experiments has been the teaching of the American Sign Language to the young gorilla, Koko, who was the subject of the Original Study in Chapter 3. Koko's working vocabulary—those signs used regularly and appropriately—consists of 375 signs. But she has used as many as 645 signs correctly, and as many as 251 of them in a single hour. She not only responds to and asks questions, but she refers to events removed in time and space. This last characteristic, **displacement,** is one of the distinctive characteristics of human speech. Koko has now been joined by a young gorilla named Michael, and the two regularly converse with one another.

Washoe, Sarah, Lana, and Koko are only a few of the apes whose abilities to communicate have been investigated in recent years. Not everyone is convinced that they are capable of true language. The basic question seems to be: Do they *know* that a sign can stand for an object in time and space, and that a name can be used to convey information to other animal beings?

> **Displacement: The ability to refer to things and events removed in time and space.**

After all, say the critics, even pigeons can be taught to peck selectively at red keys to obtain food and green keys to obtain water. Might not the apes be doing a very clever version of this?

Part of the problem here seems to be an "either-or" aspect of the debate: either apes have language capabilities comparable to those of humans or they do not. What gets lost in the arguments is the possibility that apes may have *some* language capabilities though not necessarily on a par with those of humans. Certainly, studies such as that of Koko strongly support the proposition that apes have more than no language capabilities at all.

One can argue reasonably that the early hominids, who share a common ancestry with the African apes, probably had a system of communication not unlike what we see among modern chimpanzees and gorillas, and that human paralanguage and kinesics are altered survivals of that system. The experiments with Washoe, Koko, and other apes show the potential represented by this kind of system. Working from information such as this, Gordon W. Hewes has revived and refined the hypothesis that human language began as a gestural, rather than vocal, system.[6] That the earliest representatives of the genus *Homo* were making stone tools and exhibited the beginnings of human culture (Chapter 3) suggests that their communicative abilities surpassed those of wild apes and may have

[6] Gordon W. Hewes, "Primate Communication and the Gestural Origin of Language," *Current Anthropology*, 1973, 14(1–2):5–24.

been comparable to Koko's. Such a sign language would probably have sufficed for their purposes, and their skulls and mouth parts suggest that they were incapable of human speech sounds. Hewes argues that the growing importance of precise hand movements associated with toolmaking and use, coupled with the importance of analyzing sounds in hunting—animal calls, rustlings in the underbrush, and so on—set the stage for speech. These two developments favored cerebral lateralization (right-handedness with left-hemisphere dominance) and cross-modal transfer of learning, making for easy integration of vocal-auditory and visual-tactile experience, which is necessary for spoken language. Once these biological changes had developed sufficiently, the change from purely gestural to spoken language could have taken place, with mouth gestures perhaps playing an important role.

Just when such a switch from gestural to spoken language might have taken place is unknown. Many anthropologists believe that *Homo erectus'* use of more complex tools, control of fire, and effective hunting of big game through strategies such as co-operative fire drives would have required some sort of spoken language. Others do not feel that the vocal apparatus of *H. erectus* was adequate for speech. Indeed, much publicity has been given to the argument that the Neanderthals lacked the physical features necessary for spoken language. It has been shown, however, that the reconstruction of the Neanderthal larynx, on which this argument is partially based, is faulty.[7] Moreover, the brain as reflected by endocranial casts suggests the Neanderthals had the neural development neces-

sary for language.[8] Finally, modern adults with as much flattening of the skull base and facial protrusion as some Neanderthals have no trouble talking. Talking Neanderthals make a good deal of sense when it is realized that their way of life (described in Chapter 3) seems to have been comparable to those of some hunting and gathering peoples known from historic times. In short, we can be reasonably sure that Neanderthals had some sort of spoken language. But we know nothing about that language, nor do we know how primitive it may have been.

The search for a truly primitive language spoken by a living people that might show the processes of language just beginning or developing has been abandoned, no doubt permanently. Is there such a thing as a primitive language? So far, all the natural languages that have been described and studied, even among people with something approximating a Stone Age culture, appear to be highly developed, complex, and capable of expressing an immense range of experience, belief, and perceptions. At one time linguists thought they had found a truly primitive or archaic language, that of the central Australian tribe called the Arunta, described in 1930 when the tribe seemed to be on the point of extinction. This language was found to have only three vowel sounds (*a*, *i*, and *u*), very few consonant sounds (*p, t, k, m, n, l, r, ch*), no names for objects but only for states or actions, and no connective words like our prepositions or conjunctions. On the other hand, the Arunta made use of at least 400 different gestures to supplement the spoken language. What was "missing" verbally seems to have been supplied visually. In

[7] Dean Falk, "Comparative Anatomy of the Larynx in Man and the Chimpanzee: Implications for Language in Neanderthal," *American Journal of Physical Anthropology*, 1975, 43(1):123–132.

[8] Marjorie LeMay, "The Language Capability of Neanderthal Man," *American Journal of Physical Anthropology*, 1975, 43(1):9–14.

spite of the apparent simplicity of the language, it proved to be no less difficult to learn properly, or even to describe accurately, than any other language. The truth is that people have been talking in this world for an extremely long time, and every known language, wherever it is, now has a long history and has developed subtleties and complexities that strongly resist any label of "primitivism." What a language may or may not express is no measure of its age, but of the kind of life of its speakers, reflecting what they want or need to share and communicate with others.

CHAPTER SUMMARY

Anthropologists need to understand the workings of language, because it is through language that people in every culture are able to share their experiences, concerns, and beliefs, over the past and present, and to communicate these to the next generation. Language makes communication possible by employing a few sounds that, when put together according to certain rules, result in meanings that are intelligible to all speakers.

Linguistics is the modern scientific study of all aspects of language. Phonetics focuses on the production, transmission, and reception of speech sounds. Phonology studies the sound patterns of language in order to extract the rules that govern the way sounds are combined. Morphology is concerned with the smallest units of meaningful combinations of sounds—morphemes—in a language. Syntax refers to the principles according to which phrases and sentences are built. The entire formal structure of a language, consisting of all observations about the morphemes and syntax, constitutes the grammar of a language.

Paralanguage, which always accompanies language, is a less developed means of communication than language and involves such noises as voice qualities and vocalizations. Another means of communication is kinesics, a system of body motions used to convey messages.

Descriptive linguistics registers and explains the features of a language at any time in history. Historical linguistics investigates relationships between earlier and later forms of the same language. A primary concern of historical linguists is to identify the forces behind the changes that have taken place in languages in the course of linguistic divergence. Historical linguistics also provides a means of roughly dating certain migrations, invasions, and contacts of people.

Ethnolinguistics deals with language as it relates to society, culture, and human behavior. Some linguists, such as Benjamin Lee Whorf, have proposed that language shapes the way people think and behave. Others believe that language reflects reality. Although linguists find language flexible and adaptable, they have found that once a terminology is established, it tends to perpetuate itself and to reflect the social structure of the group.

Anthropologists are interested in the way different societies name their relatives. Kinship terms help reveal how a family is structured, what relationships are considered close or distant, and what attitudes toward relationships are held. Anthropologists are also interested in taboo words, social dialects, and code switching. A taboo word can reveal much about a society's beliefs and social relationships. A social dialect is the language of a group of people within a larger group of people, all of whom may speak more or less the same language. Sociolinguists are concerned with whether dialect differences reflect cultural differences. They also study code switching—the process of changing from one level of language to another—for much the same reason.

The way language works is the province of the theoretical linguist. The well-known linguist Noam Chomsky developed the first logical and consistent model for scientifically describing what happens in the whole sentence-making process. His theory is called transformational-generative grammar. Chomsky holds that a series of rules generates underlying grammatical forms of sentences called deep structures, which are transformed into actual utterances that display surface structure. The principle is assumed to be the same for all languages, but the deep structures differ. Understanding a language involves identifying deep structure and establishing the rules by which the deep structure is transformed into surface structure.

Some anthropologists believe that human language began as a gestural rather than a vocal system. Various factors in the environment, together with biological changes that took place in early hominids, set the stage for speech, with mouth gestures perhaps playing an important role in this transformation.

For some time linguists searched for a truly primitive language spoken by a living group that would reveal language in its very early state. This search has been abandoned, however. All natural languages that have been studied, including those of people with "primitive" cultures, are complex, sophisticated, and able to express a wide range of experiences. What a language is capable of expressing has nothing to do with its age but with the kind of culture its speakers share and wish to communicate.

SUGGESTED READINGS

Birdwhistell, Ray L. *Kinesics and Context*. Philadelphia: University of Pennsylvania Press, 1970.
    Kinesics was first delineated as an area for anthropological research by Birdwhistell, so this book is particularly appropriate for those who wish to know more about the phenomenon.

Burling, Robbins. *Man's Many Voices: Language in Its Cultural Context*. New York: Holt, Rinehart and Winston, 1970.
    An investigation into the nonlinguistic factors that affect the use of language, such as kinship systems and the wider cultural context. It relies heavily on examples from South and Southeast Asia.

Gelb, Ignace J. *A Study of Writing.* London: Routledge, 1952.
> The aim of this study is to lay a foundation for a new science of writing, grammatology. It attempts to establish general principles governing the use and evolution of writing on a comparative basis, and is the first systematic presentation of the history of writing based on these principles.

Gleason, H. A., Jr. *An Introduction to Descriptive Linguistics*, rev. ed. New York: Holt, Rinehart and Winston, 1966.
> This book focuses on the descriptive approach, studying languages in terms of their internal structures. It is a lucid, well-written introduction to the study of language.

Lehmann, Winifred P. *Historical Linguistics, An Introduction*, 2d ed. New York: Holt, Rinehart and Winston, 1973.
> In recent years, historical linguistics has tended to be overshadowed by descriptive linguistics. Historical linguistics, however, remains an active and changing field, and this book is a good introduction to it.

Hickerson, Nancy Parrot. *Linguistic Anthropology.* New York: Holt, Rinehart and Winston, 1980.
> A description and explanation of what anthropological linguistics is all about, written so as to be understood by beginning students.

Premack, Ann James, and David Premack. "Teaching Language to an Ape," *Scientific American*, 1972, 227(4):92–99.
> This interesting article tests the hypothesis that language is unique to the human species. It concludes that certain gestures of human speech belong to a more general system and are capable of being understood by other primates. The program that was used to teach the chimpanzee Sarah to communicate has been successfully applied to people suffering certain types of brain damage.

Trager, George L. "Paralanguage: A First Approximation," in *Language in Culture and Society*, Dell Hymes, ed. New York: Harper & Row, 1964. Pp. 274–279.
> The author is the pioneer in paralinguistic research, and in this article he discusses what paralanguage is, why it should be studied, and how.

5 | Culture and Personality

A North American father playfully boxing with his son. Anthropologists have long been interested in how techniques of child-rearing, which differ from one culture to another, affect adult personalities. In the United States, we have traditionally admired men who are strong and able to defend themselves, and play activity of the sort shown here plays an important role in the development of these characteristics.

PREVIEW

WHAT IS ENCULTURATION?

Enculturation is the process by which culture is passed from one generation to the next. It begins soon after birth as self-awareness—the ability
to perceive oneself as an object in time and space and to judge one's own
actions—starts to develop. For self-awareness to function, the individual
must be provided with a behavioral environment. First, one learns about a
world of objects other than self, and these are always perceived in terms
of the values of the culture in which one grows up. Along with this, one
is provided with spatial, temporal, and normative orientations.

WHAT IS THE EFFECT OF ENCULTURATION ON ADULT PERSONALITY?

Studies have shown that there is some kind of nonrandom relationship
between enculturation and personality development, although it is also
clear that each individual begins with certain broad potentials and limitations which are genetically inherited. In some cultures certain child-rearing practices seem to promote the development of compliant personalities,
while in others different practices seem to promote more independent,
self-reliant personalities.

ARE DIFFERENT PERSONALITIES CHARACTERISTIC OF DIFFERENT CULTURES?

Although cultures vary a great deal in terms of the personality traits that
are looked upon with admiration or disapproval, it is difficult to characterize cultures in terms of particular personalities. Of the several attempts
that have been made, the concept of modal personality is the most satisfactory. This recognizes that in any human society there will be a range of
individual personalities, but that some will be more "typical" than others.

DO CULTURES DIFFER IN WHAT THEY REGARD AS ABNORMAL PERSONALITIES?

A normal personality may be thought of as one that approximates the
modal personality of a particular culture. Since modal personalities may
differ from one culture to another, and since cultures may differ in the
range of variation they will accept, it is clear that abnormal personality is
a relative concept. A particular personality regarded as abnormal in one
culture may not be so regarded in another.

In 1690, John Locke presented his *tabula rasa* theory in his book *An Essay Concerning Human Understanding*. This notion held that the newborn human was like a blank slate, and what the individual became in life was written on the slate by his or her life experiences. The implication is that all individuals are biologically identical in their potential for personality development at birth and that their adult personalities are exclusively the products of their postnatal experiences, which will differ from culture to culture. Stated in these terms, the theory is not acceptable, for we know that each person is born with unique inherited tendencies which will influence the adult personality. But it is also known that genetic inheritance sets only the broadest potentials and limitations and that life experiences, particularly in the early years, are critically important in the shaping of individual personalities. Since different cultures handle the raising and education of children in different ways, such practices and their effects on personalities are important subjects of anthropological inquiry. Traditionally, they have been the core of the subfield of psychological anthropology, and are the subjects of the present chapter.

THE SELF AND ITS BEHAVIORAL ENVIRONMENT

Since culture is created and learned rather than biologically inherited, all societies must somehow ensure that culture is adequately transmitted from one generation to the next. This process of transmission is known as **enculturation,** and it begins soon after birth. The first agents of enculturation in all societies are the members of the family into which a person is born. At first, the most important members of the family are the newborn's mother and—frequently but not invariably—father, but whatever other members are present will soon come to play roles in the process. These may include siblings and grandparents, other wives of the father, or other husbands of the mother, depending on family structure in the particular society. As the individual matures, individuals outside the family are brought into the process. These may include other kin, such as a mother's brother, and will surely include the individual's peers. The latter may be included informally in the form of play groups or formally in age associations, where children actually teach other children. In some societies, and our own is a good example, professionals take over the job of enculturation when the child is considered old enough. In the United States, six years has traditionally been regarded as the appropriate age for this formal learning to begin. In recent years, though, there has developed a realization that chronological age is only a rough guide to the biological and developmental "age" of the child, and that some children may be ready for the professionals earlier than others.

The Self

Enculturation begins with the development of **self-awareness**—the ability to identify oneself as an object, to react to oneself, and to appraise or evaluate oneself. Humans do not have this ability at birth, even though it is essential for existence in human societies. It is self-awareness that permits one to assume responsibility for one's conduct, to learn how to react to others, and to assume a variety of roles. An important aspect of self-awareness is the attachment of positive value to the self. This is necessary in order to motivate an individual to act to his or her advantage rather than disadvantage. Self-identification by itself is not sufficient for this.

Self-awareness does not come all at once. In our own society, for example, self and nonself are not clearly distinguished until about two years of age.[1] But then, the development of self-awareness in our society may lag somewhat, since the neuromotor development of infants, which proceeds in concert with it, has been shown to lag in our society behind that of infants in many, perhaps even most, non-Western societies. The reasons for this are not yet clear, although the amount of human contact and stimulation that infants receive probably plays an important role. For example, at 15 weeks of age, the home-reared infant in North America is in contact with its mother for about 20 percent of the time on the average. At the same age, infants in traditional Bushman society of South Africa's Kalahari Desert are in close contact with their mothers about 70 percent of the time. Moreover, their contacts are not usually limited to their mothers; they include numerous other adults and children of virtually all ages. Other factors that may also affect the rate of neuromotor development include nutrition before and after pregnancy, parental attitudes toward pregnancy and children, and perhaps even differing frequencies of certain genes between human populations.

In the development of self-awareness, perception, or a kind of vague awareness of one's existence precedes conception, or more specific knowledge of what one is, and this involves a cultural definition of self. In this definition language plays a crucial role. So it is that in all cultures individuals master personal and possessive pronouns at an early age. Personal names, too, are important devices for self-identification in all cultures.

---

[1] A. I. Hallowell, *Culture and Experience* (Philadelphia: University of Pennsylvania Press, 1955), p. 90.

> **Enculturation:** The process by which a society's culture is transmitted from one generation to the next.

> **Self-awareness:** The ability to identify oneself as an object, to react to oneself, and to appraise oneself.

The neuromotor development of !Kung children, who live in South Africa's Kalahari Desert, is advanced compared with that of children of equivalent age in North American society.

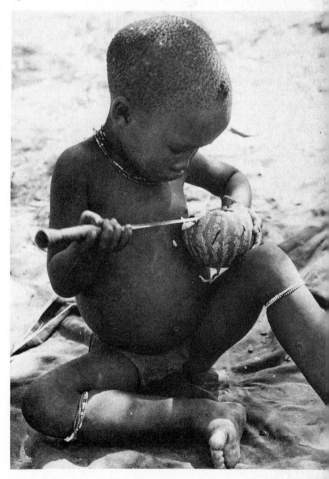

Two different cultures may perceive the same environment in entirely different ways. To most North Americans today, Mount Katahdin is impressive and fun to climb, but that is about it. To Penobscot Indians, however, it was the home of Pemúle, an awesome supernatural creature, and no one in his or her right mind would think of climbing it.

Among sedentary peoples, ancestors are a major force in the culturally constituted behavioral environment. A Haitian cemetery: tombs have spaces for candles and offerings of food.

The Behavioral Environment

In order for self-awareness to emerge and function, basic orientations which structure the psychological field in which the self is prepared to act are necessary. Thus each individual must learn about a world of objects other than self. The basis of this world of other than self is what we would think of as the objective environment of things. The objective environment, though, is organized culturally and mediated symbolically through language. Putting this another way, we might say that the objective world is perceived through cultural glasses. Those attributes of the environment that are culturally significant are singled out for attention and labeled; those that are not may be ignored or lumped together in broad categories. But culture also explains the perceived environment. This is important, for it provides the individual with an orderly, rather than chaotic, universe within which to act. Suffice it to say, such an orderly universe seems essential as a setting for orderly behavior. In non-Western, traditional societies, which lack the scientific approach of recent Western culture, such explanations are apt to be quite subjective in nature. For that matter, there are large numbers of peoples in Western Societies who still subscribe to nonscientific explanations of the universe. The proponents of what is ironically referred to as "scientific creationism" constitute a recent case in point.

The behavioral environment in which the self acts involves more than object orientation alone. Action requires spatial orientation, or the ability to get from one object, or place, to another. In all societies, names and significant features of places are important means of discriminating and representing points of reference for spatial orientation. Individuals must also know where they have been and will be in order to get from one place to another. They also need to maintain a sense of self-continuity, so that past actions are connected with those in the present and future. Hence, temporal orientation is also part of the behavioral environment. Just as the perceived environment is organized in cultural terms, so too are time and space.

A final aspect of the behavioral environment is what might best be called the normative orientation. Values, ideals, and standards, which are purely cultural in origin, are as much a part of the individual's behavioral environment as are trees, rivers, and mountains. Without them one would have no standard by which to judge either one's own actions or those of others. In short, the self-appraisal aspect of self-awareness could not be made functional.

Like any aspects of culture, conceptions of the self may vary considerably from one society to another. In many societies today, particularly those of Europe and North America, the concept tends to be more or less scientific, but it has not always been this way. Two hundred years ago the conception was quite different, and still is today in a number of the world's more traditional societies. The Penobscot Indians, a one-time hunting and gathering people whose descendants still live today in the woodlands of northeastern North America, serve as an example.[2]

THE PENOBSCOT   In the seventeenth century the Penobscot conceived of each individual as being made up of two parts—the body and what may be called the "vital self." The latter was dependent on the body, yet was able to disengage itself from

---

[2] Frank G. Speck, "Penobscot Shamanism," *Memoirs of the American Anthropological Association*, 1920, 6(3):239–288.

the body and travel about for short periods of time, to perform overt acts and to interact with other "selves." It was activity on the part of the vital self that was thought to occur in dreams. So long as the vital self returned to the body in a reasonable period of time, the individual remained in good health. But if the vital self was prevented from returning to the body, then the individual sickened and died. Along with this dual nature of the self went a potential for every individual to work magic. Theoretically, it was possible to send one's vital self out to work mischief on others, just as it was possible for others to lure one's vital self away from the body, resulting in sickness and eventual death.

To many people today, the seventeenth-century Penobscot concept of self may seem strange. To the British colonists of New England, such ideas were regarded as false and shot through with superstition, even though their own concept of self at the time was no less supernaturalistic. To the Indians their concept made sense, for in the absence of scientific knowledge, it adequately accounted for their experience regardless of its rightness or wrongness in any objective sense. Furthermore, the Penobscot view of self is relevant for anyone who might wish to understand Penobscot behavior in the days when the British and French first tried to settle in North America. For one thing, it was responsible for an undercurrent of suspicion and distrust of strangers as well as the individual secretiveness that characterized traditional Penobscot society. This propensity for individual secretiveness made it difficult for a potentially malevolent stranger to gain control of an individual's vital self. Also, the belief that dreams are real experiences, rather than expressions of unconscious desires, could impose burdens of guilt and anxiety on individuals who dreamed of doing things not accepted as proper. Finally, individuals indulged in acts that would strike many people today as quite mad. A case in point is the Penobscot Indian who spent the night literally fighting for his life with a fallen tree. To the Indian, this was a metamorphosed magician who was out to get him, and it would have been unthinkable not to try to overcome his adversary.

The behavioral environment in which the Penobscot self operated consisted of a flat world, which these people conceived as being surrounded on all sides by salt water. They could actually see the latter downriver, where the Penobscot River reached the sea. The river itself was the spatial reference point and was as well the main artery for canoe travel in the region. The largest of a number of watercourses, it flowed through forests abounding with game. Like humans, these animals were also composed of a body and a vital self. Along with the animals were various quasi-human supernatural beings which inhabited bodies of water and mountains or roamed freely through the forest. One of these, Gluskabe, created the all-important Penobscot River by killing a greedy giant frog which had monopolized the world's water supply. Gluskabe was also responsible for a number of other natural features of the world, often as a by-product of punishment such as that of the giant frog for transgressions of the moral code. Indeed, individuals had to worry about their behavior vis-à-vis both animals and these quasi-human beings or they too would come to various kinds of grief. Hence, these supernaturals not only "explained" many otherwise unexplainable natural phenomena to the Penobscot but they also were important in structuring the Penobscot moral order. To the Penobscot, all of this was quite believable; the lone hunter, for example, off for extended periods in the forest, knew he would hear in the night the cry of Pskedemus, the swamp woman. And a Penobscot accepted the fact that his or her vital self routinely traveled about while the body slept, interacting with various of these supernatural beings.

Penobscot concepts of the self and behavioral environment have changed considerably since the seventeenth century, just as have those of the descendants of the early Europeans who first came to New England. Both groups may now be said to hold modern beliefs about the nature of their selves and the world they live in. But the old beliefs were associated with **patterns of affect**—how people *feel* about themselves and others—which differed considerably between Indian and European culture. This is significant, for as the Chinese-born anthropologist Francis L. K. Hsu has pointed out, patterns of affect are likely to persist over thousands of years, even in the face of far-reaching changes in all other aspects of culture.[3] A failure to understand this point seems to be at least partially responsible for the generally negative attitude on the part of many non-Indians to the Land Claims Suit which the Penobscots recently pressed (and won) against the State of Maine, the largest ever brought by an Indian tribe in the 48 contiguous states.

✓PERSONALITY

In the process of enculturation, we have seen that each individual is introduced to the concepts of self and the behavioral environment characteristic of his or her culture. The result is that a kind of cognitive map of the operating world is built up, in terms of which the individual will think and act. This cognitive map is an integrated, dynamic system of perceptual assemblages,

Patterns of affect: How people feel about themselves and others.
Personality: The distinctive way a person thinks, feels, and behaves.

including the self and its behavioral environment. When we speak of an individual's **personality,** we are generalizing about that individual's cognitive map over time. Hence, personalities are products of enculturation, as experienced by individuals, each with a particular genetic makeup. "Personality" does not lend itself to a formal definition, but for our purposes we may take it as the distinctive way a person thinks, feels, and behaves.

The Development of Personality

Although what one learns is important to personality development, most anthropologists assume that how one learns is no less important. With the psychoanalytic theorists, they view adult personality as strongly influenced by early childhood experiences. Indeed, many anthropologists have been strongly attracted by psychoanalytic theory, but with a difference. The psychoanalytic literature tends to be long on concepts, speculation, and clinical data, but short on less culture-bound studies.[4] Anthropologists, for their part, are most interested in studies that seek to prove, modify, or at least shed light on this assumption. For example, in Western society, adolescence is a period of tension and stress. The young person must come to terms with biological changes and sexual

---

[3] Francis L. K. Hsu, "Role, Affect, and Anthropology," *American Anthropologist*, 1977, 79:807.

[4] Raoul Naroll, "Holocultural Theory Tests," in Raoul Naroll and Frada Naroll, eds., *Main Currents in Cultural Anthropology* (New York: Appleton-Century-Crofts, 1973), p. 342.

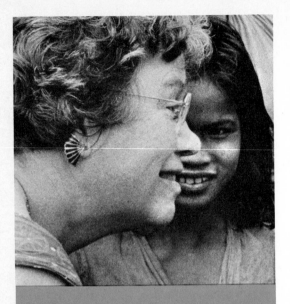

Margaret Mead (1901–1978)

Although all of the natural and social sciences are able to look back and pay homage to certain "founding fathers," anthropologists take pride in the fact that they have a number of "founding mothers" to whom they pay homage. One is Margaret Mead, who was encouraged by her teacher, Franz Boas, to pursue a career in anthropology at a time when most other academic disciplines were not exactly welcoming women into their ranks. The publication in 1928 of *Coming of Age in Samoa: a Psychological Study of Primitive Youth for Western Civilization* is generally credited as marking the beginning of the field of culture and personality. The book is a landmark for several reasons: not only was it a deliberate test of a Western psychological hypothesis, it also showed psychologists the value of modifying intelligence tests so as to be appropriate for the population under study; and by emphasizing the lesson to be drawn for Mead's own society, it laid the groundwork for the popularization of anthropology and advanced the cause of applied anthropology.

desire and with the social demands surrounding sexual initiation. Children may begin to question the "truths" they have been brought up with; they may come to see that injustices in the world do not correspond to the ideals they were raised to revere. Some writers believe that these conflicts arise out of the very nature of adolescence and therefore are universal. But are they? In 1925, a young anthropologist named Margaret Mead went to Samoa to try to find the answer.

SAMOANS As Mead describes them in her book *Coming of Age in Samoa,* Samoan children learn that they can have their own way if they are quiet and obedient. Preference is given not to the arrogant, the flippant, or the courageous, but to the quiet and demure boy or girl who "speaks softly and treads lightly." Standards of conduct dictate that small children should keep quiet, wake up early, obey, work hard and cheerfully, and play with children of their own sex; young people should work industriously and skillfully, not be presuming, marry discretely, be loyal to their relatives, and not carry tales or be troublemakers; adults should be wise, peaceable, serene, generous, and anxious for the prestige of their village and conduct their lives with good form.

Little girls move and play together, reacting to boys with antagonism or avoidance. As they grow up, however, these groups slowly begin to break up, and boys and girls begin to play and banter together good-naturedly during parties and torch-fishing excursions. A few years after puberty, a girl may take the first of a series of lovers. Liaisons may last for some time, or adolescents may slip away together into the bush. As long as there is no breach of customs, such as incest or a boy's aspiring to love an older woman, society considers these premarital relations completely natural and pays little attention to them.

Samoans grow up with minimal sexual or social stress in a society characterized by peaceful conformity and tolerant attitude toward sex. The transition from childhood to adulthood is relatively smooth. From her study of the Samoans, Mead generalized that "adolescence is not necessarily a time of stress and strain, but that cultural conditions make it so."[5]

Although Mead's work on *Samoa* strongly suggested that childhood training was important in the formation of the adult personality, it also demonstrated that there are alternatives to Western practices of child training. This stimulated an interest in child rearing not only as an anthropological problem but also as a practical one. If a great deal of adolescent behavior is learned rather than biologically induced, then in our own culture it might be possible to minimize the anxiety and antisocial behavior associated with adolescence by changing the culture. The converse might also be possible: by changing child-rearing practices, we may be able to change the structure of society. However, Mead cautioned against thinking we can accomplish anything by simply copying Samoans, because "unfortunately, the conditions which vex our adolescents are the flesh and bone of our society, no more subject to straightforward manipulation upon our part than is the language we speak."[6]

THE OEDIPUS COMPLEX Another example of anthropological testing of psychoanalytical concepts concerns Freud's Oedipus complex. In *Totem and Taboo* (1913) he used

---

> **Oedipus complex:** Freud's theory that a boy feels a sexual desire for his mother, but hostility toward his father.

> **Incest taboo:** The prohibition of sexual relations between immediate kin, such as parent and child or siblings.

> **Exogamy:** The rule that marriage must be outside the group.

---

the **Oedipus complex**—the sexual desire of a boy for his mother, which Freud saw as the most important factor in individual personality development—to explain the origins of culture and society. According to this scheme, early societies were strongly patriarchal (ruled by men), with the father possessing exclusive sexual rights over his sisters and daughters. The sexually deprived sons rebelled, killed their father, and ate him. Overcome with guilt, the brothers then repressed their sexual desires toward their mother, sisters, and daughters. Thus came into being the **incest taboo** and **exogamy,** the requirement that one must seek a sexual partner outside one's own family or group. Through what Freud called the "racial unconscious," the sons inherited the primal guilt over the killing of the father.[7]

Almost no anthropologist would accept this theory in its original form, because there is no evidence to substantiate it. However, one need not accept Freud's hypothesis concerning the origins of society in order to find in the Oedipus complex a possible basis for significant cultural norms and values. Some followers of Freud, such as Hungarian anthropologist Géza Róheim,

---

[5] Margaret Mead, *Coming of Age in Samoa* (New York: Morrow, 1928), p. 234.

[6] Mead, p. 234.

[7] Marvin Harris, *The Rise of Anthropological Theory* (New York: Crowell, 1968), p. 425.

This picture is symbolic of dependence training, in which individuals are brought up to be dependent on the group. This Maya Indian woman is showing great warmth and affection for her child, a major feature of dependence training.

believe that tensions rising from the Oedipal family situation, in which the boy feels antagonistic toward his father and has to suppress his incestual desires toward his mother, are to be found in all societies, and are indeed the source of such cultural phenomena as the incest taboo and exogamy. According to Róheim, any anthropologist who denies this is simply repressing his own Oedipus complex.[8]

Bronislaw Malinowski was one of the first to challenge the universality of the Oedipus complex required by Freud's theory with careful field research.[9] The people of the Trobriand Islands, he pointed out, do not think of a child as belonging to the father's family. Because Trobriand society emphasizes **matrilineal descent,** group membership based on descent traced exclusively through the female line, the mother's elder brother functions as a child's disciplinarian and authority figure, while the father assumes the role of friend and companion to the child. Whereas the Oedipus complex is based on the triangular relationship of mother, father, and son, the true complex of relationships for the Trobriands is brother, sister, and sister's son. The Trobriand boy's hostility is directed not against his mother's sex partner (the boy's father) but against the man who has disciplinary authority over him. At the same time, the boy has an interest in his sister's sexual activity, for she will ultimately bear sons over whom he will have authority (he will be their mother's brother). This sexual interest in sisters must be repressed, however, for it conflicts with the incest taboo.

DEPENDENCE TRAINING While the early anthropological studies of the effects of child-rearing experience on personality were primarily case studies of particular societies, more recent work has emphasized cross-cultural comparisons. The pioneers here have been John and Beatrice Whiting and Irvin L. Child, who, with their various associates, have carried out almost all of the studies of this sort. Their work has demonstrated a number of apparent regularities. For example, it is possible to distinguish at a broad level of generalization between two different patterns of child

---

[8]Harris, p. 428.

[9]Annemarie deWaal Malefijt, *Images of Man* (New York: Knopf, 1974), p. 296.

rearing, which we may label for convenience dependence training and independence training.[10]

Dependence training tends to ensure compliance in the performance of assigned tasks and to keep individuals within the group. This pattern is typically associated with **extended families,** which consist of several husband-wife-children groups, and which are most apt to be found in societies in which the economy is based on subsistence farming. Such families are important, for they provide the large labor force necessary to till the soil, tend whatever flocks are kept, and carry out other part-time economic pursuits considered necessary for existence. Such large families, however, have built into them certain stressful situations which are potentially disruptive. For example, one of the adults typically makes the important family decisions, which must be followed by the other family members. In addition, the in-marrying spouses—husbands and/or wives—must subordinate themselves to the will of the group, which may not be easy. Dependence training helps to manage these potential problems and involves both positive and negative aspects. On the positive side, indulgence is shown to children, particularly in the form of prolonged oral gratification. Nursing continues for several years and is virtually on demand. This may be interpreted as rewarding the child for seeking support within the family, the main agent in meeting the child's needs. Also on the positive side, children at a relatively early age are assigned a number of child-care and domestic tasks, all of which make significant and obvious contributions to the family's welfare. Thus, family members all actively work to help and support one another. On the negative side, behavior that is inter-

> **Matrilineal descent:** A system according to which descent is traced exclusively through the female line for purposes of group membership.

> **Dependence training:** Child-rearing practices that foster compliance in the performance of assigned tasks and dependence on the family rather than reliance on oneself.

> **Extended families:** Collections of nuclear families, related by ties of blood, that live together.

> **Independence training:** Child-rearing practices that promote independence, self-reliance, and personal achievement on the part of the child.

> **Nuclear families:** Family units consisting of a mother, father, and dependent children.

preted by the adults as aggressive or sexual is apt to be actively discouraged. Moreover, the adults tend to be quite insistent on overall obedience. This is seen as rendering the individual subordinate to the group. This combination of positive and negative actions ideally produces individuals who are obedient, supportive, noncompetitive, and generally responsible, who will stay within the fold and not do anything potentially disruptive.

INDEPENDENCE TRAINING   By contrast, **independence training** emphasizes individual independence, self-reliance, and personal achievement. It is typically associated with societies in which **nuclear families,** consisting of a husband, wife, and their offspring, are independent rather than a part of some larger family group. Inde-

---

[10] Eric Wolf, *Peasants* (Englewood Cliffs, N.J.: Prentice-Hall, 1966), pp. 69–70.

pendence training is particularly characteristic of industrial societies such as our own, where self-reliance and personal achievement are important traits for survival. Again, there are positive as well as negative aspects to this pattern of training. On the negative side, little emphasis is placed on prolonged oral gratification, and feeding is more by schedule than on demand. In the United States, for example, we like to establish a schedule as soon as possible. Moreover, it is not long before we start feeding infants baby food, and even trying to get them to feed themselves. Indeed, this has reached the point where many parents are delighted if they can prop their infants up in the crib or playpen so that they can hold their own bottles. In fact, infants do not receive the amount of attention they so often do in nonindustrialized societies. In the United States, a mother may be very affectionate with her 15-week-old infant during the 20 percent of the time she is in contact with it, but for the other 80 percent of the time the infant is more or less on its own. Nor is collective responsibility encouraged in children; they are not given responsible tasks to perform until later in childhood, and these are generally few in number. Moreover, their contribution to the welfare of the family is often not immediately apparent to the child, to whom the tasks appear arbitrary as a result.

On the positive side, displays of aggression and sexuality, if not encouraged, are at least tolerated to a greater degree than where dependence training is the rule. In schools, and even in the family, competition is emphasized. Such training generally encourages individuals to seek help and attention, rather than to give it, and to try to exert individual dominance. Such qualities are useful in societies with social structures that emphasize personal achievement and where the prevailing rule is "every man for himself."

Anthropologists have pondered the significance of differing child-rearing customs in the formation of adult personalities. This picture symbolizes the ultimate in independence training. A mechanically controlled environment keeps temperature and humidity constant in a sterile atmosphere, but it doesn't provide much in the way of human companionship. This contrasts with dependence training, which encourages the individual to seek gratification as a member of the family.

In hunting and gathering societies, child-rearing practices combine elements of independence and dependence training. In such societies, those individuals most capable of personal achievement, independence, and self-reliance are apt to be the most successful in the food quest, and as in modern industrial societies, these characteristics are developed in children in the context of small, nuclear families. But the pattern is not the same, for infants receive much more in the way of positive, affectionate attention from adults, along with prolonged oral gratification. This, as well as low pressure for compliance and a lack of emphasis on competition, encourages individuals to be more supportive of one another than is often the case in modern industrial societies. At the same time, personal achievement and independence are encouraged as they are in industrial societies, along with an even higher degree of self-reliance.

Having spoken in general terms about differences in child-rearing practices, let us now look at a particular situation that combines elements of modern industrial society with those of nonindustrial, agrarian society. In the following Original Study, we turn to an example from contemporary United States society.

ORIGINAL STUDY

Child-Rearing Practices among Migratory Workers[11]

Children in migrant labor camps are raised by many people. The group living pattern affects child-rearing practices as it does every other aspect of life. Men and women work, and children wander around in the camp or in the fields with relatively little parental supervision. They are protected and disciplined by whoever is around at the moment. This is a point of confusion, both for adults and children. On the one hand, there is a tendency to discipline other people's children since they are underfoot much more than in other circumstances. On the other hand, this is often considered by parents to be interference and is resented. Similarly, children waver between defying and accepting the supervision of adults other than their parents. This is an ambiguous area with few normative rules.

There are other ambiguities in child-rearing practices. The model of comportment held by many mothers includes a gentility out of place in the migrant setting. Should one encourage children to display the toughness requisite in migrant society, or does this include behavior that is upsetting to other, more middle-class values? Parents often despair of the language used by their young and the difficulties in controlling them. They complain that the camp is ruining their children, but at the same time are proud of demonstrations of toughness and precocity. This ambiguity leads to alternating approval and harsh, spontaneous discipline. For the most part, however, attitudes are permissive. The following selections focus on these ambiguities: first, with respect to the problem of authority, and second, in the definitions of appropriate behavior.

---

[11]From *Migrant: Agricultural Workers in America's Northeast* by William H. Friedland and Dorothy Helkin. Copyright © 1971 by Holt, Rinehart and Winston, Inc. Reprinted by permission of Holt, Rinehart and Winston, pp. 249–252.

Everybody in our camp tends to correct the children. If there has been a conflict with a child's parents, however, this becomes a point of sensitivity. Larry had an argument with Spaceman and his wife. The next day Spaceman's kids were around our side of the building, playing in front of Larry's door. When the little boy put his bottles and trash up by the door, Larry asked me to tell the kid to leave—although in the past he has never hesitated to correct the children. I asked him why he didn't tell the child to go away himself. "He's playing in front of your door not mine." Larry replied, "No, I don't want any trouble from his mother." People who are married and have children of their own discipline other children more than those who are single. The older women, also, give the children the most attention.

When women go out to work, they leave their babies in the nursery if it is open. Otherwise a group of children from many families will be left with one adult in the camp, or the children will be brought to the field. The bus often waits for the nursery to open; otherwise I have seen women just leave telling whoever is around to see to it that the child gets to the nursery later in the morning. (GP)

Early one morning, a three-year-old was sitting outside, eating a hot dog on a slice of bread. Raymond, one of the older men, noticed that she was just licking it and told her to eat it up. She ate the bread and defiantly tossed the hot dog over the fence. Adults often tell children who are not their own what to do. They scold children for making too much noise. Sometimes, as in this case, the children ignore or defy adults other than their parents, but at other times, they accept the word of any adult at all. (IM)

A little boy, age three, threw some tomatoes at Bertha, so she gave him a slap. When he cried, his father came in and said, "You leave this boy alone. When he cries I have to come in and see what's wrong. Don't touch him." Bertha said that the father was stupid. The boy ought to be punished when he does something wrong or he'll grow up to be a hoodlum. Sugarmama then told a story about a man convicted to die. His final wish was to see his mother. When she came, he said to her, "If you had spanked me when I was little, I wouldn't be here. Now I'm about to lose my life." Then he leaned over as if to whisper something in his mother's ear and he bit her ear off. Bertha and Honey agreed, "If you don't spank them now, you'll be sorry later." (DG)

When we go out picking, two little children, about three years old, come regularly to the fields. They are objects of community attention. They know all the adults well. When Sugarmama said, "I'm going to hit you, I'll wop you on the head," they laughed, knowing that she didn't mean it. The kids are looked after by the entire crew. Longo warned them to get off the road. Sugarmama gave them some food and Bertha gave them water and wiped their noses. Longo and his wife often bring along their three young boys, all under ten. The family works together, although the boys are often more interested in running around. Once in a while, Longo yells at one of them to get busy, but they don't pay much attention. (DG)

The women talked about a children's summer school program near the camp. They said that even the parents couldn't control the children from the camp, and they could hardly blame teachers for not wanting to teach the kids. "They'll do anything and say anything to you." One of the women, a mother of seven children, criticized them for swearing; although she curses a great deal herself, she did not connect this with the children cursing. She talked about a little girl who stood in the back of the bus "just twisting her behind." She had "never seen anything like it before," again ignoring the activities observed by the children in the jukes each day. The women agreed and thought the children's behavior was terrible. "It seems to me that those kids are around white people enough so that they would learn how to act decent. I don't know why they do the things they do. It seems that kids just don't want to learn today." (GP)

Roy was playing with his baby son. He spotted an older kid playing with a knife and shouted at him to put it down. Then, holding the baby out precariously at arms' length as he often does while playing with him, Roy looked him in the

Although children are not supposed to work, it adds to family income.

face and said, "When you grow up, you're not going to have a knife to play with are you? If someone messes with you, you're gonna get a motherfucking pistol and shoot him. This boy's not gonna be a knife man, he's going to have a gun." Roy's wife said something about getting their baby off to a wrong start, but she was smiling and both she, Roy, and the baby enjoyed the scene. (CL)

Honey and her grandchild are very close. The baby calls her "Mumma" and is always coming up to her and punching her affectionately. Honey says she loves the baby more than her own child. She talked about how children must learn to fight. She claims she forced the child to "get out there and fight," but then she had to pay a lot of money in hospital bills. "She is always getting messed up." Honey said all this seriously, but was exaggerating. The baby will be only three years old in October. (DG)

There is usually little adult supervision over the children, but if a parent sees his child do something wrong, he will often take off his belt or shoe and hit him. Yesterday, Checker Bill saw his little boy standing at the ballgame when he was supposed to be doing a job for him. Saying nothing, he took off his shoe and slapped the kid on the leg. This prompted a discussion among those who saw the incident concerning how to raise children. Someone had seen Checker Bill's little girl drinking leftover beer in the juke that morning, and Checker Bill went into a tirade about how the camp was ruining his children. People felt the children were spoiled by having so many people around so that the kids didn't listen any more. Checker Bill's children are afraid of him; he feels the only way to handle them is to hit them. Sara told a story about her ten-year-old. One day in the barbershop, the barber accidently nipped the boy with the scissors. The kid turned around and said, "If you do that again, I'm going to break your black ass." His mother thought this was funny, but Miss Bea said it was bad to have them use that language when they're so young. (LR)

In the Original Study just presented, a certain ambiguity was noted in child-rearing practices such that certain behaviors may be encouraged and regarded with pride in some instances, but discouraged and deplored in others. Part of the problem is that at least some of the parents aspire to middle-class values, which conflict somewhat with the realities of life in migrant society. But it would be a mistake to suppose that such ambiguities are confined to special cases such as this. As we have seen, independence training generally tends to be stressed in the United States as a whole, and we tend to speak in glowing terms of the worth of personal independence, the dignity of the individual, and so on. But our pronouncements do not always suit our actions. In spite of our professed desire for personal independence, there seems to be a strong underlying desire for compliance. This is reflected, for example, in the decisions handed down over the past ten years or so by the Supreme Court, which generally favor the rights of authority over those of individuals. It is reflected as well by the way the federal government in the early 1980s, at a time when it was working to ease up on enforcement and legislation dealing with civil rights, aggressively sought to prosecute to the fullest extent young men who, for whatever reason, did not register for the draft. Finally, it is reflected by the fate of "whistle blowers" in government bureaus, who, if they don't lose their jobs, are at least shunted to one side and passed by when the rewards are handed out. In business and in government, there is a tendency for the rewards to be given to those who go along with the system, while criticism, no matter how constructive, is a risky business. Yet, in spite of pressures for compliance, which would be most effectively served by dependence training, we continue to raise our children to be independent, and then wonder why they so often refuse to behave the way adults would have them behave.

Group Personality

From studies such as those reviewed here, it is clear that personality, child-rearing practices, and other aspects of culture are interrelated in some kind of nonrandom way. Whiting and Child have argued that child-rearing practices originate in the basic customs of a society surrounding nourishment, shelter, and protection and that these child-rearing practices in turn produce particular kinds of adult personalities.[12] The trouble is that correlations do not prove cause and effect. We are still left with the fact that, however logical it may seem, such a causal chain remains an unproved hypothesis.

The existence of a close, if not causal, interrelationship between child-rearing practices and personality, coupled with the variation in child-rearing practices from

---

[12] John W. M. Whiting and Irvin L. Child, *Child Training and Personality: A Cross-cultural Study* (New Haven, Conn.: Yale University Press, 1953).

> **Basic personality structures: Personality traits shared by nearly all members of a society.**

one society to another, have led to a number of attempts to characterize groups in terms of particular kinds of personalities. Indeed, common sense suggests that personalities appropriate for one culture may be less appropriate for some others. For example, a dependent personality would be out of place where independence is held in great esteem. Or, in the context of traditional Penobscot Indian culture which we examined briefly earlier in this chapter, an open and extroverted personality would seem inappropriate, for it would be inconsistent with the traditional Penobscot conception of the self. Unfortunately, common sense, like conventional wisdom in general, isn't always true. But the question is worth asking: Can we describe a group personality without falling into stereotyping? The answer appears to be yes, though there are all sorts of pitfalls along the way.

This question has been approached in various ways, some of which have achieved widespread popularity at one time or another. One of these is the approach of Ruth Benedict, which is briefly described in the box on p. 150. Another is that taken by Abram Kardiner (1939), a trained psychoanalyst whose interest was to lift Freud's theories from their ethnocentric European matrix. Rather than ascribing certain personality types to given cultures, Kardiner discussed the range of personalities to be found within a culture. According to this scheme, the personality "types" described by Benedict are replaced by **basic personality structures,** or traits shared by nearly all group members. The analyst determines these by inference from an ethnographic description, which ideally includes all the

Ruth Fulton Benedict (1887–1947)

Ruth Benedict came late to anthropology; upon her graduation from Vassar College, she taught high school English, published poetry, studied dancing, and tried her hand at social work. In anthropology, she developed the idea that culture was a projection of the personality of those who created it. In her most famous book, *Patterns of Culture* (1934), she compared the cultures of three peoples—the Kwakiutl of western Canada, the Zuni of the southwestern United States, and the Dobuans of Melanesia. She held that each was comparable to a great work of art, with an internal coherence and consistency of its own. Seeing the Kwakiutl as egocentric, individualistic, and ecstatic in their rituals, she labeled their cultural configuration "Dionysian"; the Zuni, whom she saw as living by the golden mean, wanting no part of excess or disruptive psychological states, and distrusting of individualism, she characterized as "Apollonian." The Dobuans, whose culture seemed magic-ridden, with everyone fearing and hating everyone else, she characterized as "Paranoid."

Although *Patterns of Culture* still enjoys popularity in some nonanthropological circles, anthropologists have long since abandoned its approach as impressionistic and not susceptible to replication. To compound the problem, Benedict's characterizations of cul-

tures are misleading (the supposedly "Apollonian" Zunis, for example, sometimes indulge in such seemingly "Dionysian" practices as sword swallowing and walking over hot coals), and the use of such value-laden terms as "Paranoid" prejudices others toward it. Nonetheless, the book did have an enormous and valuable influence in focusing attention on the problem of the interrelation between culture and personality, and in popularizing the reality of cultural variation.

seemingly trivial details of social behavior which fieldworkers might ordinarily notice but not report.

The most complete source of ethnopsychological data analyzed by Kardiner came from Cora Dubois' study of the Alorese culture of the South Pacific.[13] From her data, an aggressive, egocentric basic personality is inferred. The problem, though, is relating the personality structures of individuals to

basic personality traits. At one point, Kardiner speaks of the difficulty of deciding how typical a particular Alorese individual is, but later refers to the same individual as "the most typical," with his personality corresponding most closely to the basic personality structure. The fatal flaw of both the basic personality approach and the cultural configuration approach of Ruth Benedict is well summed up by the anthropologist Paul Bohannan: "In their effort to see the exotic groups different from ourselves, anthropologists have sometimes underem-

---

[13] Cora Dubois, *The People of Alor* (Minneapolis: University of Minnesota Press, 1944).

phasized the fact that there is likely to be as great a difference in the personalities of an exotic society as there is among members of western society."[14]

As an example of the fact that individual personalities in traditional societies are far from uniform, consider the case of the Yanomamö, whom we discussed in Chapter 2. Among them, individual men strive to achieve a reputation for fierceness and aggressiveness that they are willing to defend at the risk of serious personal injury and death. And yet there are men among the Yanomamö who are quiet and somewhat retiring. In any gathering of these people, the quiet ones are all too easily overlooked by outsiders when almost everyone else is in the front row pushing and demanding attention.[15] Not only do traditional societies include a range of personalities, but some of those personalities may differ in no important way from those of some individuals in our own society. For example, Ruth Landes reports that an Ojibwa Indian shaman she knew at Emo, Ontario, had exactly Richard Nixon's "cold, moralistic, driven personality."[16]

Modal Personality

Obviously, any fruitful approach to the problem of group personality must recognize that each individual is unique to a degree in both inheritance and life experiences, and that we should expect a range of personality types in any society. Given this, we may focus our attention on the **modal personality** of a group. We may define this

---

[14] Paul Bohannan, *Social Anthropology* (New York: Holt, Rinehart and Winston, 1963), p. 22.

[15] Napoleon Chagnon, *Yanomamö: The Fierce People*, 3d ed. (New York: Holt, Rinehart and Winston, 1983).

[16] Ruth Landes, "Comment," *Current Anthropology*, 1982, 23:401.

> **Modal personality:** The personality typical of a society as indicated by the central tendency of a defined frequency distribution.

as the personality typical of a culturally bounded population as indicated by the central tendency of a defined frequency distribution.[17] Modal personality is, then, a statistical concept. As such, it opens up for investigation the questions of how societies organize diversity and how diversity can facilitate culture change. Such questions

---

[17] Anthony F. C. Wallace, *Culture and Personality*, 2d ed. (New York: Random House, 1970), p. 152.

Two Yanomamö men show their fierceness in a chest-pounding duel. While flamboyant, belligerent personalities are especially compatible with the Yanomamö ideal that men should be fierce, some are quiet and retiring.

are easily overlooked if one assumes the uniformity of personality of the Benedict or Kardiner approach. At the same time, modal personalities of different groups can be compared.

Data on modal personality are best gathered by means of psychological tests administered to a sample of the population in question. Those most often used include the Rorschach, or "ink-blot" test, and the Thematic Apperception Test (TAT). The latter consists of pictures which the individual tested is asked to explain, or tell what is going on. There are as well other sorts of projective tests which have been used at one time or another; all have in common a purposeful ambiguity, so that the individual tested has to structure the situation before responding. The idea is that his or her personality is projected into the ambiguous situation. Along with the use of such tests, observations recording the frequency of certain behaviors, the collection and analysis of life histories and dreams, and the analysis of oral literature are also helpful in eliciting data on modal personality. For example, in her study of the Alorese, Cora Dubois did not rely on Kardiner's analysis of basic personality alone; she also administered projective tests and submitted children's drawings for expert analysis in an attempt to elicit modal personality.

It is clear that the concept of modal personality as a means of dealing with group personality has more to recommend it than other concepts like basic personality. But it too presents difficulties. One of these is the complexity of the measurement techniques themselves, which may be difficult to carry out in the field. For one thing, an adequate representative sample of subjects is necessary. The problem here is twofold: making sure that the sample is genuinely representative and having the time and personnel necessary to administer the tests, conduct interviews, and so on, all of which can be lengthy proceedings. Too, the tests themselves may constitute a problem, for tests devised in one cultural setting may not be appropriate in another. This is more of a problem with the TAT than with some other tests, but different pictures have been devised for other cultures. Still, to minimize any hidden cultural bias, it is best not to rely on projective tests alone. In addition to all this, there may be language problems which may lead to misinterpretation. Then, too, the field investigator may be in conflict with cultural values. A people like the Penobscot, whose concept of self we surveyed earlier, might not take kindly to revealing their dreams to strangers. Finally, there is the question of what is being measured. Just what, for example, is aggression? Does everyone define it the same way? Is it a legitimate entity, or does it involve other variables?

National Character

No discussion of group personality would be complete without a consideration of national character, which popular thought all too often ascribes to the citizens of many different countries. Henry Miller epitomizes this view when he says, "Madmen are logical—as are the French," suggesting that Frenchmen, in general, are overly rational. A Parisian, on the other hand, might view North Americans as maudlin and unsophisticated. Similarly, we all have in mind some image, perhaps not well defined, of the typical Russian or Japanese or Englishman. Essentially, these are simply stereotypes. But we might well ask if these stereotypes have any basis in fact. Is there, in reality, such a thing as national character?

Some anthropologists thought that maybe the answer was yes. Accordingly, national character studies were begun which have much in common with Kardiner's basic personality approach. Essentially, they have sought to discover basic personality characteristics of the peoples of modern nations. Along with this has been emphasis on child-rearing practices and education as the factors that theoretically produce such characteristics. Margaret Mead, Ruth Benedict, and Geoffrey Gorer conducted national character studies using relatively small samples of informants. During World War II, techniques were developed for studying "culture at a distance" through the analysis of newspapers, books, and photographs. By investigating memories of childhood and cultural attitudes, and by examining graphic material for the appearance of recurrent themes and values, researchers attempted to portray national character.

THE JAPANESE At the height of World War II, Geoffrey Gorer attempted to determine the underlying reasons for the "contrast between the all-pervasive gentleness of Japanese family life in Japan, which has charmed nearly every visitor, and the overwhelming brutality and sadism of the Japanese at War." Strongly under the influence of Freud, Gorer sought his causes in the toilet-training practices of the Japanese, which he believed were severe and threatening. He suggested that because Japanese infants were forced to control their sphincters before they had acquired the necessary muscular or intellectual development, they grew up filled with repressed rage. As adults, the Japanese were able to express this rage in their brutality in war.[18] Another anthropologist, Weston La Barre, independently came to the same conclusions after studying U.S. citizens of Japanese descent who had been placed in concentration camps at Topaz, Utah, during World War II.[19]

Neither Gorer nor La Barre was able to do fieldwork in Japan. When, after the war, the toilet-training hypothesis could be tested, it was found that the severity of Japanese toilet training was a myth. Children were not subject to severe threats or punishment. Nor were all Japanese soldiers brutal and sadistic in war; some were, but then so were some North Americans. Also, the fact that the postwar Japanese took the lead in the peace movements in the Far East hardly conformed to the wartime image of brutality.

This study was most important, not in revealing the importance of Japanese sphincters on the national character but in pointing out the dangers of generalizing from minimal evidence and employing simplistic individual psychology to explain complex social phenomena.

THE RUSSIANS Despite severe criticism from some of their colleagues, a few anthropologists have continued their interest in the question of national character. They have tried to refine their techniques and expanded their samples, with some interesting results.

One example of this newer approach is the Harvard Project on the Soviet social system.[20] Nearly 3000 Soviet citizens, who were displaced by World War II and who had decided not to return to the U.S.S.R., completed a long questionnaire. A few hundred of these people were also extensively

---

[18] Geoffrey Gorer, "Themes in Japanese Culture," *Transactions of the New York Academy of Sciences*, 1943, Series II, 5(5).

[19] Weston La Barre, "Some Observations on Character Structure in the Orient: The Japanese," *Psychiatry*, 1945, 8.

[20] Alex Inkeles, Eugenia Hanfmann, and Helen Beier, "Modal Personality and Adjustment to the Soviet Sociopolitical System," in Bert Kaplan, ed., *Studying Personality Cross-culturally* (New York: Harper & Row, 1961).

These photos rather amusingly depict some of the stereotypes North Americans hold of the national character of other countries. The Japanese tea ceremony, the French lovers and gendarmes, the subway crowds, and the Englishman with his umbrella, bowler, and pipe are part of our mythology about these foreign countries. Yet we would surely protest foreign views of the typical American and protest the error of the stereotype.

interviewed, and 51 were clinically studied in depth. What emerged from this study was a portrait of the modal personality of a particular nation at a particular point in time.

The strongest and most pervasive quality of the Russian personality is affiliation, or the need for interaction with other people in direct personal relationship. Unlike the average North American, the Russian is likely to have a relatively small drive to achieve. Surprisingly, there are few pronounced differences between the basic attitudes of Russians and North Americans in relation to authority, except that the Russians seem to have greater fear of their authority figures and fewer positive expectations of them. Both Russians and North Americans feel guilt and shame, but these emotions are aroused under different circumstances. A North American feels guilty when he or she has failed to meet the formal rules of etiquette or procedural forms; the Russian does not care about formal rules, but feels guilt and shame for defects of character in interpersonal relations. In sum, the Russian personality is characterized by emotional aliveness, expressiveness, spontaneity, gregariousness, and a certain need for dependence on authority.

OBJECTIONS TO NATIONAL CHARACTER STUDIES Critics of national character theories have emphasized the tendency for such work to be based on unscientific and overgeneralized data. The concept of modal personality has a certain statistical validity, they argue, but to generalize the qualities of a complex nation on the basis of such limited data is to lend insufficient recognition to the countless individuals who vary from the generalization. Further, such studies tend to be highly subjective; for example, the tendency during the late 1930s and 1940s for anthropologists to characterize the German people as aggressive paranoids was obviously a reflection of wartime hostilities and not of scientific objectivity.

It has also been pointed out that occupational and social status tends to cut across national boundaries. A French farmer may have less in common with a French factory worker than he does with a German farmer. Yet in spite of all the difficulties, and the valid criticisms of past studies, Francis Hsu, in his presidential address to the American Anthropological Association in 1978, stated that there is a new urgency to studies of national character.[21] Without them, we will probably never really understand what motivates the leaders and civil servants of modern nations.

ABNORMAL PERSONALITY

The concept of modal personality holds that a range of personalities will exist in any society. The modal personality itself may be thought of as normal for that society, but may be shared by less than half the population.[22] What of those personalities which differ from this? The Dobuans of New Guinea and certain Plains Indian tribes furnish striking examples of normal and abnormal behavior radically different from our own.

Normal and Abnormal Behavior

The individual man in Dobu whom the other villagers considered neurotic and thoroughly disoriented was a man who was naturally friendly and found activity an

end in itself. He was a pleasant fellow who did not seek to overthrow his fellows or to punish them. He worked for anyone who asked him, and he was tireless in carrying out their commands. In any other Dobuan, this would have been scandalous behavior, but in him it was regarded as merely silly. The village treated him in a kindly fashion, not taking advantage of him, nor making sport of or ridiculing him, but he was definitely regarded as one who stood outside the normal conventions of behavior.

Among certain Plains Indians, a man, compelled by supernatural spirits, could assume woman's attire, perform woman's work, and even marry another man. Under the institution of the "berdache," such an individual would find himself living in a dramatically different manner from most men; yet, although the berdache was rare among Indians, it was not looked upon as the behavior of an abnormal individual. Quite the contrary, for the berdache was often sought out as a curer, artist, matchmaker, and companion of warriors because of the great spiritual power he was thought to possess.

The standards that define normal behavior for any culture are determined by that culture itself. Obviously, no society could survive if murdering one's neighbor was looked upon as normal behavior; yet each culture determines for itself the circumstances under which murdering one's neighbor may be acceptable. What is judged to be murder in one society may be treated as justifiable homicide in another. Moral acts are those that conform to certain cultural standards of good and evil, and each society determines those standards for itself. Morality is thus based on culturally determined ideals.

Is this to suggest that "normalcy" is a meaningless concept as it is applied to personality? Within the context of a given culture, the concept of normal personality is

---

[21] Francis L. K. Hsu, "The Cultural Problem of the Cultural Anthropologist," *American Anthropologist*, 1979, 81:528.

[22] Wallace, p. 153.

quite meaningful. A. I. Hallowell somewhat ironically observed that it is normal to share the delusions traditionally accepted by one's society. Abnormality involves the development of a delusional system not sanctioned by culture. The individual who is disturbed because he or she cannot adequately measure up to the norms of society, and yet be happy, may be termed neurotic. When one's delusional system is significantly different from that of one's society and in no way reflects its norms, the individual may be termed psychotic.

Culturally induced conflicts can not only produce psychosis, but can determine the form of the psychosis as well. In a culture that encourages aggressiveness and suspicion, the madman is that individual who is passive and trusting. In a culture that encourages passivity and trust, the madman is that individual who is aggressive and suspicious. Just as each society establishes its own norms, each individual is unique in his or her perceptions. Many anthropologists see the only meaningful criterion for personality evaluation as the correlation between personality and social conformity.

While it is true that culture defines what is and what is not normal behavior, the situation is complicated by findings suggesting that major categories of mental disorders may be universal types of human affliction. Take, for example, the case of schizophrenia, probably the most common of all psychoses. Individuals afflicted by schizophrenia experience distortions of reality which impair their ability to function adequately, and so they withdraw from the social world into their own psychological shell, from which they do not emerge. Although environmental factors play a role, there is evidence that schizophrenia is caused by a biochemical disorder for which there is an inherited tendency. One of the more severe forms of this disorder is para-

> **Ethnic psychoses:** Mental disorders peculiar to particular ethnic groups.

noid schizophrenia. Those suffering from it fear and mistrust almost everyone; they hear voices that whisper dreadful things to them and they are convinced that someone is "out to get them." Acting on this conviction, they engage in bizarre types of behavior, which leads to their removal from society, usually to a mental institution.

A precise image of paranoid schizophrenia is one of the so-called **ethnic psychoses** known as *Windigo*.[23] Such psychoses involve symptoms of mental disorder peculiar to certain ethnic groups. Windigo psychosis is limited to northern Algonkian Indian groups such as the Chippewa, Cree, and Ojibwa. There is considerable argument in anthropological circles as to whether or not Windigo psychosis ever really existed, but the problem may be that Europeans who have written about it have given us a highly distorted view of the actual situation. In their traditional belief systems, these northern Indians recognized the existence of cannibalistic monsters called Windigos. Those individuals afflicted by the psychosis developed the delusion that, falling under control of these monsters themselves, they were being transformed into Windigos, with a craving for human flesh. At the same time, they saw people around them turning into various edible animals. Although the victim of Windigo psychosis developed the exaggerated fear of actually indulging in cannibalism, there are no known instances where victims actually indulged in this as the result of the psychosis alone. This is a major reason why some anthropologists have

---

[23] Wallace, p. 218.

An ethnic psychosis that has been observed widely among native peoples of circumpolar regions is Arctic hysteria. These photos show a Greenland Eskimo woman in the throes of this disorder. Among Eskimos, Arctic hysteria seems to be caused by a unique combination of factors including calcium deficiency, absence of a regular twenty-four hour alternation of light and dark, and an almost total lack of privacy.

doubted the existence of the psychosis, but the fear of cannibalism seems to have been real enough.

At first, Windigo psychosis seems quite different from Western clinical cases of paranoid schizophrenia, but a closer look suggests otherwise; the disorder was merely being expressed in ways compatible with traditional northern Algonkian culture. Ideas of persecution, instead of being directed toward other humans, are directed

toward supernatural beings (the Windigo monsters), cannibalistic panic replaces homosexual panic, and the like. The northern Algonkian Indian, like the Westerner, expresses his or her problem in terms compatible with the appropriate view of the self and its behavioral environment. The northern Algonkian, though, was removed from society not by being committed to a mental institution, but by being killed.

Windigo behavior has seemed exotic and dramatic to the Westerner. But the effect of culture, in this case subcultural differences, may be seen in Western society as well. For example, male Irish schizophrenics direct their strongly repressed anxieties and hostilities against female figures. Male Italians, on the other hand, direct their less strongly repressed hostilities against their fathers.

CURRENT TRENDS IN PSYCHOLOGICAL ANTHROPOLOGY

Although they may now be criticized for being impressionistic and not susceptible to replication, rather than scientific, the classic studies of Benedict, Mead, and other pioneers in the investigation of culture and personality remain important for their contribution to the realization that human behavior is relative. The theory of cultural relativity resulting from the study of many societies undermined the ethnocentrism common to all social groups. Anthropologists have established that cultures are indeed different and that these differences are associated with personality differences.

By 1960, however, there was a sense that a point of diminishing returns had been reached in the study of personality differences between cultures. Instead of looking at individual differences within cultures as annoying distortions of norms, many culture and personality specialists began to look more closely at such differences in order to understand better such behavior as the altered states of consciousness employed by religious practitioners in many of the world's societies. Others began to devote more attention to the study of cognitive processes—how people think and perceive the world in which they live. By observing how individual members of particular societies segment, interpret, and express reality through language, anthropologists should be able to draw general conclusions about the implicit mental representations of reality in the minds of these individual culture bearers—their cognitive "models" of the world around them. This, of course, continues an interest in the self and its behavioral environment, as discussed earlier in this chapter.

An interest in psychoanalytical theory has always characterized culture and personality studies, but current investigators are combining psychoanalytically based theories with biological and social variables to discover, analyze, and explain the laws of cultural dynamics. Thus, current studies are examining human genetic and ecological processes that are entirely independent of culture, but that cause change in the human biological system upon which culture depends.

Studies of child-rearing practices, a central concern of culture and personality studies from their earliest days, have burgeoned into a specialized field in their own right. Today the emphasis is on cross-cultural studies of physiological maturation, interpersonal contacts, group composition, and the like, often to test the theories developed in the other social and behavioral sciences. But they have been broadened to embrace the new subfield of educational anthropology. Similarly, the old interest in abnormal personality has given birth to numerous cross-cultural studies of mental health and illness, which are now part of the new specialty called medical anthropology.

In sum, the field of culture and personality has expanded and become a highly varied field. As a reflection of this, specialists began in the 1960s to refer to their field as psychological anthropology. This anthropological specialty is flourishing today, and we shall deal with some of its findings in later chapters of this book, as in our discussion of revitalization movements in Chapters 12 and 15.

CHAPTER SUMMARY

Enculturation, the process by which culture is passed from one generation to the next, begins soon after birth. Its first agents are an individual's family members, but later, in some societies, this role is assumed by professionals. For enculturation to proceed, individuals must possess self-awareness, or the ability to perceive themselves as objects in time and space and to judge their own actions. A major facet of self-awareness is a positive view of the self, for it is this which motivates persons to act to their advantage rather than disadvantage.

Several requirements involving one's behavioral environment need to be met in order for emerging self-awareness to function. The individual first needs to learn about a world of objects other than self; this environment is perceived in terms of the cultural values into which one is born. Also required is a sense of both spatial and temporal orientation. Finally, the growing individual needs a normative orientation, or an understanding of the values, ideals, and standards that constitute the behavioral environment.

Personality is a product of enculturation and refers to the distinctive ways a person thinks, feels, and behaves. With the psychoanalysts, most anthropologists believe that adult personality is shaped by early childhood experiences. A prime goal of anthropologists has been to produce objective studies that test this theory, such as Margaret Mead's classic investigation of adolescence among Samoans. These studies indicate that a great deal of adolescent behavior is learned.

Anthropologists John and Beatrice Whiting, and Irvin Child, on the basis of cross-cultural studies, have established the interrelation of personality, child-rearing practices, and other aspects of culture. One may speak, for example, of dependence training. Usually associated with traditional farming societies, it tends to guarantee that members of society will willingly and routinely perform the jobs assigned to them. At the opposite extreme, independence training, typical of societies characterized by independent nuclear families, puts a premium on self-reliance and independent behavior. Whiting and Child believe that child-rearing practices have their roots in a society's customs surrounding the meeting of the basic physical needs of its members; these practices, in turn, are responsible for the development of particular kinds of adult personalities.

Anthropologists have long worked on the problem of whether it is possible to delineate a group personality without falling into stereotyping. Ruth Benedict believed that each culture chooses, from the vast array of human traits, those that it sees as normative or ideal. Individuals who conform to these norms are rewarded; the rest are punished. From this more or less homogenized world view a group personality emerges. Another approach to group personality is that of Abram Kardiner, who considered the range of personalities found within a culture. He sought to identify basic personality structures, or traits, shared by nearly all members of a society. The modal personality of a group is the personality typical of a culturally bounded population. Although a more valid approach to group personality than other methods, the concept of modal personality is not without difficulties.

National character studies have focused on the modal characteristics of modern nations. They have then attempted to determine the child-rearing practices and education which shape such a personality. Investigators during World War II interviewed foreign-born nationals and analyzed other sources in an effort to depict national character. Many anthropologists believe that national character theories are based on unscientific and overgeneralized data. Others believe that new studies, without the flaws of past studies, are needed of national character if we are really to understand what motivates the leaders and civil servants of modern nations.

What defines normal behavior in any culture is determined by the culture itself, and morality is defined by culturally determined ideals. Abnormality involves developing a delusional system not accepted by culture. Culturally induced conflicts cannot only produce psychosis but can determine the form of the psychosis as well.

Current studies in psychological anthropology are combining traditional psychoanalytically based theories with biological and social factors to explain culture and cultural dynamics. Attention is also being given to cognitive processes of the mind, which are the basic mechanisms responsible for such cultural expression as language, myth, and art. At the same time, cross-cultural studies of child-rearing and mental health have become established as anthropological subfields in their own right.

SUGGESTED READINGS

Bourguignon, Erika. *Psychological Anthropology: An Introduction to Human Nature and Cultural Differences.* New York: Holt, Rinehart and Winston, 1979.
This book is designed to introduce students to the diverse subjects and problems of psychological anthropology as it exists today. Therefore, it covers not only the traditional subject matter of culture and personality, but new topics as well, such as altered states of consciousness. Throughout the book the author is concerned with practical applications of the findings of psychological anthropology.

Hunt, Robert C., ed. *Personalities and Cultures: Readings in Psychological Anthropology.* Garden City, N.Y.: Natural History Press, 1967.
The eighteen articles included in this book focus on various aspects of culture and personality. Attention is given to psychological and sociocultural variables and the relationships between them.

Norbeck, Edward, Douglas Price Williams, and William McCord, eds. *The Study of Personality: An Interdisciplinary Appraisal.* New York: Holt, Rinehart and Winston, 1968.
The volume contains addresses given at Rice University in 1966. Its objective is to review and appraise knowledge and theories concerning personality in several scholarly fields (psychology, anthropology, sociology, philosophy of science, etc.). It also discusses factors that influence the formation of personality, and the personalities of social and psychiatric deviates.

Wallace, Anthony F. *Culture and Personality,* 2d ed. New York: Random House, 1970.
The logical and methodological foundations of culture and personality as a science form the basis of this book. The study is guided by the assumptions that anthropology should develop a scientific theory about culture, and that a theory pretending to explain or predict cultural phenomena must reckon with noncultural phenomena (such as personality) as well.

Whiting, John W. M., and I. Child. *Child Training and Personality: A Crosscultural Study.* New Haven, Conn.: Yale University Press, 1953.
How culture is integrated through the medium of personality processes is the main concern of this study. It covers both the influence of culture on personality and personality on culture. It is oriented toward testing general hypotheses about human behavior in any and all societies, rather than toward a detailed analysis of a particular society.

6 | Patterns of Subsistence

In southern Africa's Kalahari Desert, a !Kung man sets out on a hunt. Securing the survival of those who live by its rules is always the basic business of a culture, and so the study of subsistence patterns is an important aspect of anthropological study.

PREVIEW

WHAT IS ADAPTATION?

Adaptation refers to the process of interaction between changes made by an organism on its environment and changes made by the environment on the organism. This kind of two-way adjustment is necessary for the survival of all life forms, including human beings.

HOW DO HUMANS ADAPT?

Humans adapt through the medium of culture as they develop ways of doing things that are compatible with the resources they have available to them as well as within the limitations of the environment in which they live. Within a particular region people living in similar environments tend to borrow from one another customs that seem to work well in those environments.

WHAT SORTS OF ADAPTATIONS HAVE HUMANS ACHIEVED THROUGH THE AGES?

Hunting and gathering is the oldest and most basic type of human adaptation. To it we owe such important elements of social organization as the sexual division of labor, food-sharing, and a home base as the center of daily activity and where food-sharing is accomplished. Quite different adaptations, involving farming and animal husbandry, began to develop in some parts of the world between nine and eleven thousand years ago. Horticulture—the cultivation of domestic plants by means of simple hand tools—made possible more permanent settlements and a reorganization of the division of labor. Under pastoralism—reliance on raising herds of domestic animals—nomadism continued, but new modes of interaction with other peoples were developed. Urbanism began to develop as early as five thousand years ago in some places as intensive agriculture produced sufficient food to support full-time specialists of various sorts. With this went a further transformation of the social fabric.

Several times today you will interrupt your activities to eat or drink. You may take this very much for granted, but if you went totally without food for as long as a day, you would begin to feel the symptoms of starvation: weakness, fatigue, headache. After a month of starvation, your body would probably never repair the damage. A mere week to ten days without water would be enough to kill you.

All living beings, and people are obviously no exception, must satisfy certain basic needs in order to stay alive. Among these needs are food, water, and shelter. Humans may not live by bread alone, but nobody can live long without any bread at all; and no creature could long survive if its relations with its environment were random and chaotic. Living beings must have regular access to a supply of food and water and a reliable means of obtaining and using it. A lion might die if all its prey disappeared, if its teeth and claws grew soft, or if its digestive system failed. Although people face these same problems, they have an overwhelming advantage over their fellow creatures; people have culture. If our meat supply dwindles, we can turn to some vegetable, like the soybean, and process it to taste like meat. When our tools fail, we replace them or invent better ones. Even when our stomachs are incapable of digesting food, we can predigest food by boiling or pureeing. However, we are subject to the same needs and pressures as all living creatures, and it is important to understand human behavior from this point of view. The crucial concept that underlies such a perspective is **adaptation,** that is, how humans manage to deal with the contingencies of daily life. Dealing with these contingencies is the basic business of all cultures.

ADAPTATION

The process of adaptation establishes a moving balance between the needs of a population and the potential of its environment. One illustration of this process can be seen in the case of the Tsembaga, New

The men of the Big Namba tribe turn out in their most elaborate costumes for a pig festival. Among many New Guinea peoples, such festivals function to keep pig populations from becoming so large as to put a strain on agricultural land, and ensure that everyone gets some high-quality animal protein to eat from time to time.

Guinea, highlanders who support themselves chiefly through **horticulture**—the cultivation of crops carried out with simple hand tools.[1] Although they also raise pigs, they eat them only under conditions of illness, injury, warfare, or celebration. At such times the pigs are sacrificed to ancestor spirits, and their flesh is ritually consumed by those people involved in the crisis. (This guarantees a supply of high-quality protein when it is most needed.)

In precolonial times, the Tsembaga and their neighbors were bound together in a unique cycle of pig sacrifices that served to mark the end of hostilities between groups. Frequent hostilities were set off by a number of ecological pressures in which pigs were a significant factor. Since very few pigs were normally slaughtered and their food requirements were great, they could

—————————

[1] Roy A. Rappaport, "Ritual Regulation of Environmental Relations among a New Guinea People," in Andrew P. Vayda, ed., *Environment and Cultural Behavior* (Garden City, N.Y.: Natural History Press, 1969), pp. 181–201.

> **Adaptation:** The possession of anatomical, physiological, and/or behavioral characteristics that foster the survival of organisms in the special environmental conditions in which they are generally found.

> **Horticulture:** Cultivation of crops carried out with hand tools such as digging sticks or hoes.

very quickly literally eat a local group out of house and home. The need to expand food production in order to support the prestigious but hungry pigs put a strain on the land best suited for farming. Therefore, when one group had driven another off its land, hostilities ended and the new residents celebrated their victory with a pig festival. Many pigs were slaughtered, and the pork was widely shared among allied groups. Even without hostilities, festivals were held whenever the pig population became unmanageable, every 5 to 10 years,

depending on the groups' success at farming. Thus the cycle of fighting and feasting kept the balance among humans, land, and animals.

The term "adaptation" also refers to the process of interaction between changes made by an organism on its environment and changes made by the environment on the organism. The spread of the gene for sickle-cell anemia is a case in point.[2] Long ago, in the Old World tropics west of India, a genetic mutation appeared in human populations, causing the manufacture of red blood cells that take on a sickle shape under conditions of low oxygen pressure. Since persons who receive a gene for this trait from each parent usually develop severe anemia and die in childhood, there was a selective pressure exerted against the spread of this gene in the local gene pool.

Then slash-and-burn horticulture was introduced into this tropical region, creating a change in the natural environment by removal—through cutting ("slashing") and burning—of the natural vegetative cover. This was conducive to the breeding of mosquitos that carry the parasite causing falciparum malaria. When transmitted to humans, the parasites live in the red blood cells and cause a disease that is always debilitating and very often fatal. However, individuals who received the gene for the sickle-cell trait from only one parent, while receiving one "normal" gene from the other, turned out to have a specific natural defense against the parasite. Its presence in any red blood cell caused that cell to sickle; when that cell circulated through the spleen, which routinely screens out all damaged or worn red blood cells, the infected cell and the parasite along with it

were destroyed. Since heterozygotes were therefore resistant to malaria, they were selected, and the sickling trait became more and more frequent in the population. Thus, while people changed their environment, their environment also changed them.

The case of sickle-cell anemia is a neat illustration of the relativity of any adaptation. In malarial areas, the gene responsible for this condition is adaptive for human populations, even though some individuals suffer as a result of its presence. In nonmalarial regions, however, it is positively maladaptive, for it confers no advantage at all on human populations living under such conditions, while some individuals die as a result of its presence.

The Unit of Adaptation

The unit of adaptation includes both organisms and environment. Organisms exist as members of populations, which as populations must have the flexibility to cope with variability and change within the environment. In biological terms, this means that different organisms within the population have somewhat differing genetic endowments. In cultural terms, it means that there is variation among individual skills, knowledge, and personalities. Organisms and environments form interacting systems. People might as easily be farmers as fishermen; but we do not expect to find farmers north of the Arctic Circle or fishermen in the Sahara Desert.

We might consider the example of a group of lakeside fishermen. The people live off fish, which, in turn, live off smaller organisms. Those animals, in turn, consume green plants; plants liberate minerals from water and mud, and, with energy from sunlight, transform them into proteins and carbohydrates. Dead plant and animal matter is decomposed by bacteria,

---

[2] Frank B. Livingstone, "The Distribution of Abnormal Hemoglobin Genes and Their Significance for Human Evolution," in C. Loring Brace and James Metress, eds., *Man in Evolutionary Perspective* (New York: Wiley, 1973), pp. 373–386.

and chemicals are returned to the soil and water. Some energy escapes from this system in the form of heat. Evaporation and rainfall constantly recirculate the water. People add chemicals to the system in the form of their wastes, and, if they are judicious, they may help to regulate the balance of animals and plants.

Some anthropologists have borrowed the ecologists' term **ecosystem**. An ecosystem is composed of both the physical environment and the organisms living within it. The system is bound by the activities of the organisms as well as by such physical processes as erosion and evaporation.

Human ecologists are generally concerned with detailed microstudies of particular human ecosystems; they emphasize that all aspects of human culture must be considered, not only the most obvious technological ones. The Tsembaga's attitude toward pigs and the cycle of sacrifices have important economic functions; we see them in this way, but the Tsembaga do not. They are motivated by their belief in the power and needs of their ancestral spirits. Although the pigs are consumed *by* the living, they are sacrificed *for* ancestors. Human ecosystems must often be interpreted in cultural terms.

Evolutionary Adaptation

Adaptation must also be understood from a historical point of view. In order for an organism to fit into an ecosystem, it must have the potential ability to adjust to or become a part of it. The Comanche, whose tribal history began in the harsh, arid country of southern Idaho, provide a good example.[3] In their original home, they subsisted on wild plants, small animals,

---

[3] Ernest Wallace and E. Adamson Hoebel, *The Comanches* (Norman: University of Oklahoma Press, 1952).

Ecosystem: A system, or a functioning whole, composed of both the physical environment and the organisms living within it.

Preadaptations: In culture, existing customs with the potential for a new cultural adaptation.

and occasionally large game. Their material equipment was simple and limited to what could be transported by the women of the tribe. The size of their groups was restricted, and what little social power could develop was in the hands of the shaman, who was a combination of medicine man and spiritual guide.

At some point in their nomadic history, the Comanche entered the Great Plains, where buffalo were abundant and the Indians' potential as hunters could be fully developed. As larger groups could be supported by the new food supply, the need arose for a more complex political organization. Hunting ability thus became a means to acquire political power.

Eventually the Comanche acquired the "white man's" horse and gun, which greatly extended their hunting prowess, and the great hunting chiefs became powerful indeed. The Comanche became raiders in order to get horses, for they were not horse breeders, and their hunting chiefs evolved into war chiefs. The once "poor" and peaceful hunter-gatherers of the Great Basin became wealthy pirates, dominating the Southwest from the borders of New Spain (Mexico) in the south to those of new France (Louisiana) and the fledgling United States in the east and north. In passing from one environment to another, and in evolving from one way of life to a second, the Comanche made the best advantage of their developing potentials, or cultural **preadaptations**.

Many different societies develop independently, and some find similar solutions to similar problems. For example, another group that moved out onto the Great Plains and took up a form of Plains Indian culture similar in many ways to that of the Comanche were the Cheyenne. Yet their cultural background was quite different; formerly, they were settled farmers with social, political, and religious institutions quite different from those of the Comanche back in their ancestral homeland. The development of similar cultural adaptations to similar environmental conditions by peoples of quite different cultural backgrounds is called **convergent evolution.**

Somewhat similar to the phenomenon of convergent evolution is **parallel evolution,** the difference being that similar adaptations are achieved by peoples of somewhat similar cultural backgrounds. To a large extent, the rise of great civilizations in such widely separated areas as China, northwest Mesopotamia, and Peru was made possible by the apparent independent invention of irrigation agriculture in each of these areas. The problems of applying irrigation agriculture to making a living in riverine environments—problems of labor and distribution—played an important role in the development of a number of parallels in the social and cultural development of those societies.

Culture Areas

The Great Plains was an aboriginal **culture area,** a geographic region in which there existed a number of societies following similar patterns of life. Thirty-one politically independent tribes faced a common environment, in which the buffalo was the most obvious and practical source of food and materials for clothing and shelter. Living close by each other, they were able to share new inventions and discoveries. They reached a common and shared adaptation to a particular ecological zone.

The Indians of the Great Plains were, at the time of contact with Europeans, invariably buffalo hunters, dependent upon this animal for food, clothing, shelter, and bone tools. Each tribe was generally organized into a number of warrior societies, and prestige came from hunting and fighting skills. Their camps were typically arranged in a distinctive circular pattern. Many religious rituals, such as the Sun Dance, were practiced throughout the plains region.

Sometimes geographic regions are not uniform in climate and topography, and so new discoveries do not always spread from one group to another. Moreover, within a culture area, there are variations between local environments, and these variations favor variations in adaptation. The Great Basin of the western United States—an area embracing the states of Nevada and Utah, with adjacent portions of California, Oregon, Wyoming, and Idaho—is a case in point.[4] The Great Basin Shoshone Indians were divided into a northern and a western group, both primarily migratory hunters and gatherers. In the north, a relative abundance of game animals provided for the maintenance of larger populations, requiring a great degree of cooperation among local groups. The western Shoshone, on the other hand, were almost entirely dependent upon the gathering of wild crops for a living, and as these varied considerably in their seasonal and local availability, the western Shoshone were forced to cover vast distances in search of food. Under such conditions, it was most efficient to travel in groups of only a few families, only occa-

---

[4]Julian H. Steward, *Theory of Culture Change: The Methodology of Multilinear Evolution* (Urbana: University of Illinois Press, 1972).

sionally coming together with other groups, and not always with the same ones.

The Shoshone were not the only inhabitants of the Great Basin. To the south lived another closely related tribe, the Paiutes. They were also hunter-gatherers living under the same environmental conditions as the Shoshone, but the Paiute more actively managed their wild food resources by diverting small streams to irrigate wild crops. They did not plant and cultivate crops, but even so, the Paiute were able to secure a steadier food supply than their northern neighbors. Hence, their populations were larger than those of the Shoshone and they led a more settled existence.

Convergent evolution: In cultural evolution, the development of similar adaptations to similar environmental conditions by peoples of quite different cultural backgrounds.

Parallel evolution: In cultural evolution, the development of similar adaptations to similar environmental conditions by peoples of similar cultural backgrounds.

Culture area: A geographic region in which a number of different societies follow a similar pattern of life.

Indian tribes of the North American Plains, such as the Sioux, Crow, and Comanche, show a great deal of cultural similarity because they have had to adapt to similar environmental conditions. For a map of native American culture areas, see page 172.

PORTFOLIO 1

Seasons of the Eskimo

Of all the earth's regions, the Eskimo live in the harshest and most forbidding. Summers are short, cool, and mosquito-plagued; winters long, dark, and cold. Yet despite the murderous climate and ever-present threat of famine, the Eskimo are gay, gregarious, good-natured, and amazingly contented. Innuit, the people, the Eskimo proudly call themselves. Men, pre-eminent, the Original Men to whom earth herself gave birth.

Eskimo society in the past was one of equals. They acknowledged neither chiefs nor superiors; their language lacks the terms. The closest they can come is to call a man "ishumata"—he who had none. What power there was lay within the community, in the rule of public opinion. The approval and esteem of other members of his group were a man's highest reward, ostracism his worst punishment.

The advent of the white culture destroyed the fragile fabric of this ancient way of life. Its concepts of master and servant, of material wealth as a measure of a person's worth, subordinated one individual's wishes to another's will and thus were alien and mystifying to the Eskimo mind. And as the Eskimo settled in permanent communities and adopted the white culture, they lost touch with the cycle of the seasons. Their children no longer learn the lore of hunting and the ice and even sometimes do not learn their grandparents' language. In some smaller communities, however, the hunting-trapping life of the camps persists according to the immutable rules of old: to take from each season what each season brings; to share your food with all members of the group, as they will share theirs with you; to rise to superhuman efforts when the hunt requires it, and to live in quiet harmony with yourself and others when bad weather imprisons you in your tent; to do as you like and let others do as they like.

One of the last and largest camp areas in Canada (pictured on

Winter camp in drifting snow.

Hunter wears slit-type bone goggles to protect his eyes from the intense glare of spring ice and snow.

Igloo for the night, built during a hunting trip.

Hunters with polar bear.

A hunter readies his harpoon; he has killed two seals already.

Eskimos gaff halibut that have floated up into a lead—a break in the thawing spring ice.

Hunter in a kayak.

Grandmother.

Drying caribou sinew; later it will be slit and used as thread to sew fur clothing.

Hanging split char (fish) to dry for preservation.

Women sew the sealskin cover onto a kayak frame.

Summer migration across the tundra with pack dogs.

the preceding pages) is Bathhurst Inlet in the Central Arctic, inhabited by fewer than 90 people living in 11 widely scattered camps. In winter they hunt seal at the breathing holes and fish through the ice. In spring, the caribou come from the taiga in the south across the vastness of the tundra to the Arctic shores. In summer, the men fish; in fall, the seals are fat and float when shot, the new clove-brown fur of the caribou is short and strong, ideal for winter clothes, and the animals are heavy after pasturing all summer on the Arctic meadows. Fat char ascend the rivers, and ground squirrels, ready for their eight-month winter sleep, look like plump, furred sausages with feet. It is the time to collect meat and fish for the dark, lean months of winter ahead.

Camp life is hard. It is an unpredictable life. One year spring comes, but the caribou do not. The people travel far, work hard, and find nothing. They may have to trap ground squirrels to subsist. The dogs become weak; traveling is curtailed. Another year, large numbers of caribou stay near the camps all year, seals are plentiful, life is relatively easy. To endure and succeed in such a life, a hunter must be resourceful and hardy, he must have faith in himself, a lot of optimism, a certain fatalism, and the ability to live each day and enjoy the good it brings and not spoil it with worry about the morrow. In the words of an Eskimo song:

And yet, there is only
One great thing,
The only thing:
To live;
To see in huts and on journeys
The great day that dawns,
And the light that fills the world.

Photographs by Fred Breummer
Text adapted from "Seasons of the Eskimo" by Fred Breummer

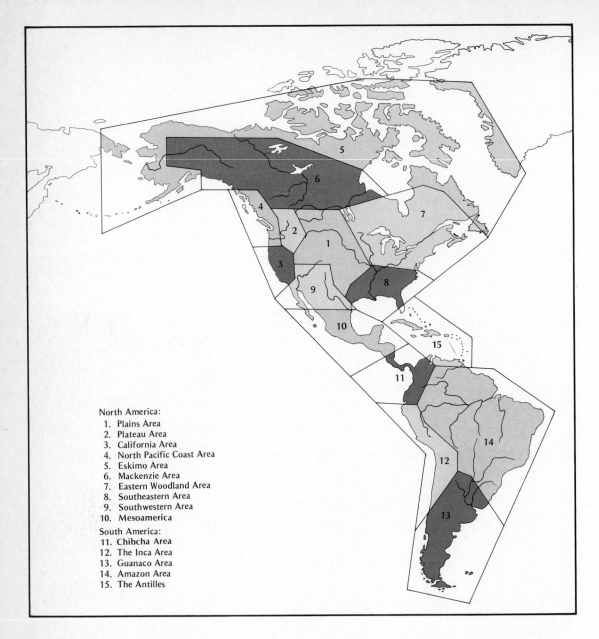

North America:
1. Plains Area
2. Plateau Area
3. California Area
4. North Pacific Coast Area
5. Eskimo Area
6. Mackenzie Area
7. Eastern Woodland Area
8. Southeastern Area
9. Southwestern Area
10. Mesoamerica

South America:
11. Chibcha Area
12. The Inca Area
13. Guanaco Area
14. Amazon Area
15. The Antilles

The culture-area concept was developed by North American anthropologists in the early part of this century. This map shows culture areas that have been defined for the Americas; within each numbered area, there is an overall similarity of native cultures which is not as apparent when the native cultures of one area are compared with those of another.

In order to explain variations within a given region, Julian Steward proposed the concept of **culture type,** a culture considered in terms of a particular technology and its relationship with the particular environmental features that technology is equipped to deal with. The example of the Great Plains shows how technology helps decide just which environmental features will be useful. Those same prairies that once supported tribes of buffalo hunters now support grain farmers. The Indians were prevented from farming the plains not for environmental reasons, nor for lack of knowledge about farming, since some of the plains tribes had been farmers before they

> **Culture type:** The view of a culture in terms of the relation of its particular technology to the environment exploited by that technology.

> **Cultural ecology:** The study of the interaction of specific human cultures with their environment.

moved on to the plains. They did not farm because the buffalo herds provided abundant food without farming, and because farming would have been difficult without the steel-tipped plow that was needed to

Julian H. Steward (1902–1972)

This North American acted as pioneer of an approach which he called **cultural ecology**—that is, the interaction of specific cultures with their environments. Initially, Steward was struck by a number of similarities in the development of urban civilizations in both Peru and Mesoamerica and noted that certain developments were paralleled in the urban civilizations of the Old World. He identified the constants and abstracted from them his laws of cultural development. Steward proposed three fundamental procedures for cultural ecology:

1. The interrelationship of a culture's technology and its environment must be analyzed. How effectively does the culture exploit available resources to provide food and housing for its members?

2. The pattern of behavior associated with a culture's technology must be analyzed. How do members of the culture go about performing the work that must be performed for their survival?

3. The relation between those behavior patterns and the rest of the cultural system must be determined. How does the work they do to survive affect the people's attitudes and outlooks? How is their survival behavior linked to their social activities and their personal relationships?

break up the compacted prairie sod. The farming potential of the Great Plains was simply not a relevant feature of the environment, given the available resources and technology before the coming of the Europeans.

Culture Core

Environment and technology are not the only factors that determine a society's way of subsistence; social and political organization also affect the application of technology to the problem of staying alive. In order to understand the rise of irrigation agriculture in the great centers of ancient civilization, such as China, Mesopotamia, and Mesoamerica, it is important to note not only the technological and environmental factors that made possible the building of huge irrigation works but also the social and political organization needed to mobil-

ize large groups of workers to build and maintain the systems. It is necessary to examine the monarchies and priesthoods that organized the work and decided where the water would be used and how the agricultural products of this joint venture would be distributed.

Those features of a culture that play a part in the society's way of making its living are called its **culture core.** This includes the society's productive techniques and its knowledge of the resources available to it. It encompasses the patterns of labor involved in applying those techniques to the local environment. For example, do people work every day for a fixed number of hours, or is most work concentrated during certain times of the year? The culture core also includes other aspects of culture that bear on the production and distribution of food. An example of the way ideology can indirectly affect subsistence can be seen in a

Locations of major early civilizations. Those of North and South America developed wholly independently of those in Africa and Asia; Chinese civilization may well have developed independently of Southwest Asian (including the Nile and Indus) civilization.

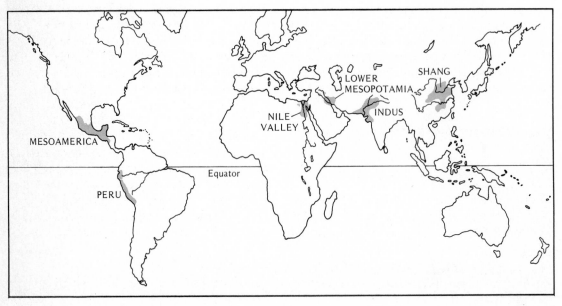

number of cultures where religion may lead to failure to utilize foods that are both locally available and nutritionally valuable. One reported example of this is the taboo that some Eskimos follow, which forbids the hunting of seals in the summer. It has been said that if land game fails, a whole group will starve, even though seals are available to them.[5]

A number of anthropologists, known as **ethnoscientists,** are actively attempting to understand the principles behind folk ideologies and the way those principles usually help keep a people alive. The Tsembaga, for example, avoid certain low-lying, marshy areas because they believe those areas are inhabited by red spirits who punish trespassers. Western science, by contrast, interprets those areas as the home of mosquitos, and the "punishment" as malaria. Whatever Westerners may think of the Tsembaga's belief in red spirits, it is a perfectly useful and reasonable one; it keeps them away from marshy areas just as surely as does a belief in malaria. If we want to understand why people in other cultures behave the way they do, we must understand their system of thought from their point of view as well as our own. Not all such beliefs are as easy to translate into our terms as are those of the Tsembaga red spirits.

THE HUNTING-GATHERING LIFE

At the present time, a scant quarter of a million people—only 0.003 percent of a world population of over four billion—support themselves chiefly through hunting, fishing, and the gathering of wild fruits and

> **Culture core:** The features of a culture that play a part in matters relating to the society's way of making a living.

> **Ethnoscientists:** Anthropologists who seek to understand how natives understand their universe.

vegetables.[6] Yet, before the domestication of plants and animals, over the last 10,000 years, all people supported themselves through some combination of plant gathering, hunting, and fishing. Of all the people who have *ever* lived, 90 percent have been hunter-gatherers, and it was as hunters and gatherers that human beings acquired the basic habits of dealing with one another and with the world around them which still guide the behavior of individuals, communities, and nations. Thus, if we would know who we are and how we came to be, if we would understand the relationship between environment and culture, and if we would comprehend the institutions of the food-producing societies that have arisen since the development of farming and pastoralism, we should turn first to the oldest and most basic of fully human life-styles, the hunter-gatherer adaptation. The beginnings of this we examined in Chapter 3.

When hunter-gatherers had the world to themselves some 10,000 years ago, they had their pick of the best environments. These have long since been appropriated by farming and, more recently, by industrial societies. Today, most hunter-gatherers have been left to their traditional life only in the world's marginal areas—frozen arctic tundra, deserts, inaccessible forests.

---

[5] Annemarie deWaal Malefijt, *Religion and Culture: An Introduction to Anthropology of Religion* (London: Macmillan, 1969), pp. 326–327.

[6] Carleton S. Coon, *The Hunting Peoples* (Boston: Little, Brown, 1971), p. xvii.

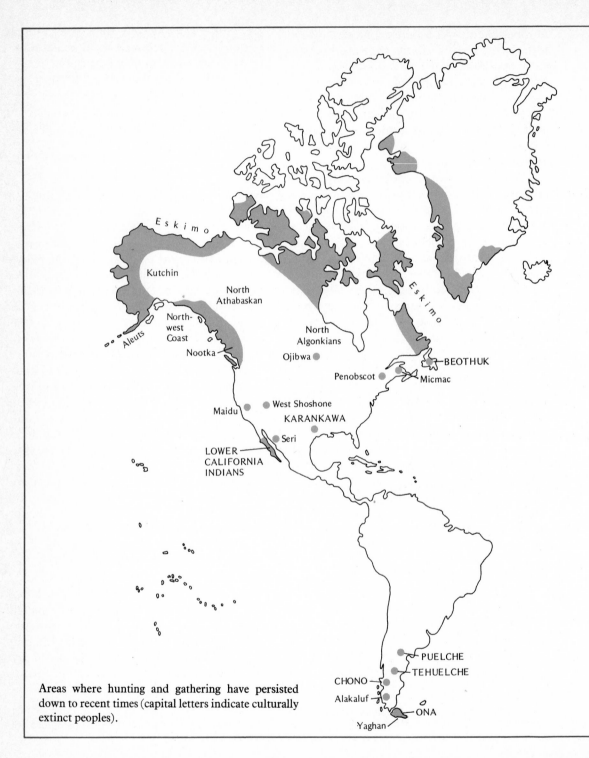

Areas where hunting and gathering have persisted down to recent times (capital letters indicate culturally extinct peoples).

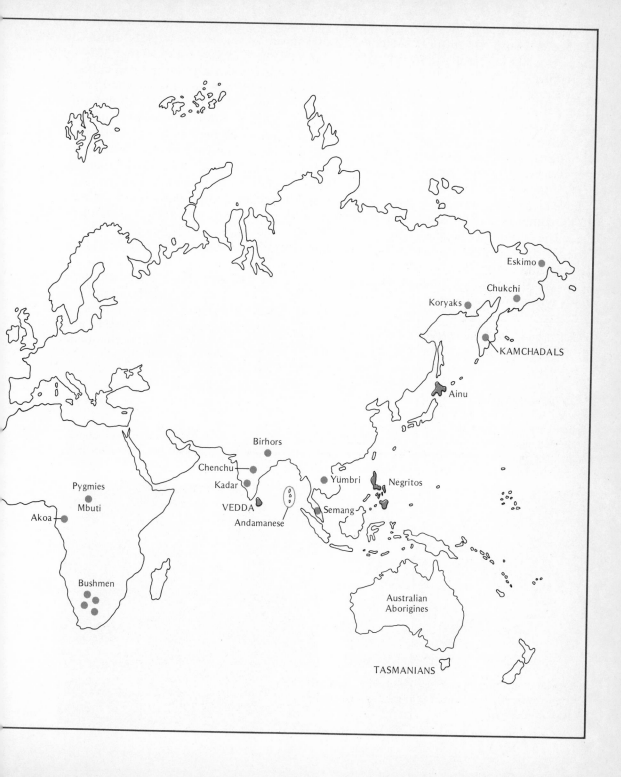

Eskimo

Chukchi

Koryaks

KAMCHADALS

Ainu

Birhors

Chenchu

Kadar

Yümbri

Negritos

VEDDA

Semang

Andamanese

Pygmies

Mbuti

Akoa

Bushmen

Australian
Aborigines

TASMANIANS

These habitats, although they may not support large or dense agricultural societies, provide a good living for hunting and gathering peoples.

Until recently, it was assumed that a hunting-gathering life in these areas was difficult, and that one had to work hard just to stay alive. But one anthropologist, Marshall Sahlins, has gone so far as to describe hunter-gatherers as the "original affluent society."[7] In his view, their diets are ample, they have plenty of leisure time, and if their material comforts are limited, so are their desires. The !Kung (the ! refers to a click—the tongue tip is pressed against the roof of the mouth and drawn sharply away) Bushmen of South Africa's Kalahari Desert, scarcely what one would call a "lush" envi-

ronment, obtain a better than subsistence diet in an average work week of about 20 hours. Others have observed that this is clearly not true for all hunting and gathering societies. Some people, like the Birhor of India, work very hard indeed and still often go hungry. But it is probably true that the majority of ancient hunter-gatherers lived in better environments with more secure and plentiful sources of food than do most of their modern counterparts.

All modern hunter-gatherers have had some degree of exposure to more technologically "advanced" neighbors. Modern hunter-gatherers often have metal and firearms, and some do a little farming on the side. Even the Kalahari Bushmen have been known to plant corn when rainfall has been especially good. Contact with other peoples has fundamentally altered, and sometimes completely disrupted, the social

---

[7] Marshall Sahlins, *Stone Age Economics* (Chicago: Aldine, 1972), p. 1.

Huts in a dry season camp of the !Kung Bushmen of southwest Africa. Since hunter-gatherers usually must abandon camps periodically, their shelters must be easily portable or, as here, built of easy to find materials. The thatched walls cut the cold winter winds, and the open roofs let in the warm sunshine.

Hunter-gatherers always have a division of labor in which men hunt and women gather. Here, two Bushmen women dig for bulbs.

Bushman hut built for the rainy season. Like the dry season hut, the materials for its construction are easy to find; unlike the dry season hut, it is roofed to keep out rain, but the sides are open since the winds are not strong.

These two Bushmen hunters carry with them the tools of their trade, virtually the only possessions they have or need—bow, arrow, digging stick, club, and spear.

A small band of Bushmen on the move to a new locale. Because they have to carry with them everything they own, personal belongings are few.

Two Bushmen carefully fasten down with wooden stakes the hide of a hartebeest; when it is dried, the hide will be scraped and tanned.

organizations of some hunting and gathering societies. The Mbuti Pygmies of the Congolese Ituri rain forest live in a complex patron-client relationship with their neighbors, some Bantu and Sudani peoples who are farmers. They exchange meat and military service for farm produce and manufactured goods. During part of the year, they live in their patron's village and are incorporated into his kin group, even to the point of allowing him to arrange their marriages.

There are also some hunter-gatherers, such as the Sirionos of South America and the Veddas of Sri Lanka, who seem to have reverted to this way of life after giving up farming. Indeed, as the current deteriorating world economic situation has led to the abandonment of many sheep stations in the Australian "Out Back," a number of Australian aborigines have returned to a hunting-gathering way of life, thereby emancipating themselves from the dependency on the government into which they had been forced.

Characteristics of the Hunting-Gathering Life

Hunter-gatherers are by definition people who do not farm or practice animal husbandry. Hence, they must accommodate their places of residence to naturally available food sources. This being the case, it is no wonder that they move about a great deal. Such movement is not aimless wandering but is done within a fixed territory or home range. Some, like the !Kung Bushmen who depend on the reliable and highly drought-resistant Mongongo nut, may keep to fairly fixed annual routes and cover only a restricted territory. Others, such as the Great Basin Shoshone, must cover a wider territory; their course is determined by the local availability of the erratically productive pine nut. A crucial factor in this mobility is the availability of water. The distance between the food supply and water must not be so great that more energy is required to fetch water than can be obtained from the food.

Another characteristic of the hunter-gatherer adaptation is the small size of local groups, 25 to 50 being the average number. Although no completely satisfactory explanation of group size has yet been offered, it seems certain that both ecological and social factors are involved. Among those suggested are the **carrying capacity** of the land, the number of people who can be supported by the available resources at a given level of food-getting techniques, and the **density of social relations,** roughly the number and intensity of interactions between camp members. More people means a higher social density, which, in turn, means more opportunities for conflict.

Both carrying capacity and social density are complex variables. Carrying capacity involves not only the immediate presence of food and water but the tools and work necessary to secure them, as well as short- and long-term fluctuations in their availability. Social density involves not only the number of people and their interactions but also the circumstances and quality of those interactions and the mechanisms for regulating them. A mob of a hundred angry strangers has a different social density than the same number of neighbors enjoying themselves at a block party.

Among hunter-gatherer populations, social density seems always to be in a state of flux, as people spend more or less time away from camp and as they move to other camps, either on visits or more permanently. This redistribution of people is an important mechanism for regulating social density as well as for assuring that the size and composition of local groups is suited to local variations in resources. Thus, cultural adaptations serve to help transcend the limitations of the physical environment.

How this redistribution of people takes place is nicely illustrated in the following Original Study by Richard Lee, who carried out intensive ethnographic studies of the !Kung in the 1960s.

> **Carrying capacity:** The number of people who can be supported by the available resources at a given level of technology.

> **Density of social relations:** Roughly, the number and intensity of interactions among the members of a camp or other residential unit.

ORIGINAL STUDY

The Changing Composition of Camps among the !Kung[8]

What makes camps change in numbers and composition? Short-term processes are of three kinds: exhaustion of local food resources, visiting trips and receiving visitors, and conflict within the group. In actual practice it is often difficult to distinguish between each of these causes. When an argument breaks out in a camp suddenly the food resources of another area become more attractive. The !Kung love to go visiting and the practice acts as a safety valve when tempers get frayed. In fact the !Kung usually move, not when their food is exhausted, but rather when only their patience is exhausted.

In the longer run, processes that affect group composition include residential shifts at marriage, the adjustment of sex and dependency ratios, and the adjustment of overall numbers. In the first instance the marriage of a boy to a girl usually results in the boy taking up residence in his in-laws' village [a practice known as bride-service]. But frequently the boy's brother or sister and their spouses may also join him for weeks or months, and occasionally his parents as well. Thus entire families may come together at the time of a marriage and not just the bride and groom.

When a group's dependency ratio—the proportion of dependents per 100 able-bodied producers—gets too high or too low, steps may be taken to bring this ratio back into line. For example, if a camp has many young children to feed this creates a burden on the working adults. One or more of the young families may be encouraged to join other camps where the dependency ratios are more favorable. Similarly, a group with few or no young children may see its future in jeopardy and take steps to recruit a related family with young

---

[8] From Richard Lee, *The Dobe !Kung.* © 1984 by CBS College Publishing. Reprinted by permission of Holt, Rinehart and Winston.

children to take up the n!ore. By these means the reproduction of the groups is perpetuated and the burden of work effort is evenly allocated throughout the area.

In spite of these mechanisms, however, groups don't survive indefinitely. Each decade some disband and their members distribute themselves among their kin in other camps. For example, of the 16 Dobe Area camps in 1964, ten were intact in 1973 while six had disbanded, and six new camps had come into being.

All this visiting, shifting, and adjusting of numbers will make sense to us when we realize that the !Kung camp is a unit of sharing. The food brought into a camp each day is distributed widely so that each member receives an equitable share. Thus it is crucial that the people in the camp get on well together. If arguments break out, then sharing breaks down and when that happens the basis for camp life is lost. Only when one or both of the feuding parties leave or when they settle their differences can the sharing be restored.

The dynamic of !Kung camp life is thus composed of work and leisure, harmony and conflict, and group solidarity interspersed with periods of group fission.

In addition to seasonal or local adjustments, long-term adjustments to resources must be made. Most hunter-gatherer populations seem to stabilize in numbers well below the carrying capacity of their land. In fact, the home ranges of most hunter-gatherers can support from three to five times as many people as they typically do. In the long run, it may be more adaptive for a group to keep its numbers low, rather than to expand indefinitely and risk being cut down by a sudden and unexpected natural reduction in food resources. The population density of hunter-gatherer groups rarely exceeds one person per square mile, a very low density; yet their resources could support greater numbers.

Just how hunting and gathering peoples regulate population size is not entirely certain, but infanticide, abortion, and the use of various herbal drugs which may interfere with fertility or conception have been mentioned at one time or another. A fascinating new possibility has been suggested by Bushmen who have recently taken up farming.[9] Such a switch leads to a dramatic upsurge in the birth rate. The reason for this seems to be that farmers have available a variety of foods which can be used as baby foods, which hunters and gatherers lack. Hence, instead of nursing children for three or four years, mothers wean them earlier. Prolonged nursing of children does not completely eliminate ovulation, but it does have a significant dampening effect. Moreover, prolonged nursing is often found in association with a taboo against sexual intercourse. The combination of the two, then, leads to wide spacing between children, so that each woman bears fewer children than the number she is ultimately capable of bearing. In

---

[9]Gina Bari Kolata, "!Kung Hunter-Gatherers: Feminism, Diet, and Birth Control," *Science*, 1974, 185:932–934.

some societies, if by accident a child is born to a woman who is still nursing another child, the newly born child may be put to death so as not to jeopardize the first child's milk supply.

The Impact of Hunting and Gathering on Human Society

Recently much has been written on the supposed importance of hunting in shaping the supposedly competitive and aggressive nature of the human species. Most anthropologists are unconvinced by these arguments, since most known hunting and gathering peoples are remarkably unaggressive and place more emphasis on cooperation than they do on competition. It does seem likely that three crucial elements of human social organization did develop along with hunting. The first of these is the sexual division of labor. Some form of division of labor by sex, however modified, has been observed in all human societies. There is some tendency in contemporary Western society to do away with such division, as we shall see in the next chapter. One may ask what the implications are for future cooperative relationships between men and women. We will discuss this problem further in Chapter 8.

SEXUAL DIVISION OF LABOR Hunting is universally a male occupation. There seem to be several reasons for this, and some of them appear to be rooted in the biological differences between men and women. In the absence of modern contraceptive devices and formulas which can be bottle-fed to infants, women in their prime are apt to be either pregnant or nursing mothers. In either case, their ability to travel long distances on foot, something that is essential to successful hunting, is significantly restricted. In addition to wide-ranging mobil-

ity, the successful hunter must also be able to mobilize rapidly high bursts of energy. Although some women can certainly run faster than some men, it is a fact that in general men can run faster than women, even if the latter are not pregnant or encumbered with infants to be nursed. Because human females must be able to give birth to infants with relatively large heads, their pelvic structure differs from that of human males to a greater degree than among most other species of mammals. Because of this, the human female is not as well equipped as is the human male where rapid and prolonged mobility are required.[10] Finally, there is a higher risk attached to hunting than to the tasks that usually occupy women in hunting and gathering societies. To place women at risk is to place their offspring, actual and potential, at risk as well. Men, on the other hand, are relatively expendable for, to put the matter bluntly, a very few men are capable of impregnating a large number of women. In evolutionary terms, the group that places its men at risk is less likely to jeopardize its chances for reproductive success than is the group that places its women at risk.

The tasks of women in hunting and gathering societies are generally less dangerous and require less in the way of rapid and prolonged mobility than those of men. Neither do they require a woman's complete and undivided attention, and they are readily resumed after interruption. Such tasks typically involve the gathering and preparation of wild plant foods. Although the work is frequently no less arduous than hunting, it does not require long-distnce travel and can be done while taking care of

[10] Susan Brandt Graham, "Biology and Human Social Behavior: A Response to van den Berghe and Barash," *American Anthropologist*, 1979, 81:358.

children. It can also be done in company with other women, which may alleviate somewhat the monotony of the work.

In the past, there has been a tendency to underestimate the contribution made by the food-gathering activities of women to the survival of hunting and gathering peoples. Most modern hunters and gatherers actually obtain 60 to 70 percent of their diets from the vegetable foods, with perhaps some fish and shellfish provided by women. This diet, it may be noted, is similar to that of many nonhuman primates in that it includes some bits of animal protein along with a wide variety of plant foods. But nonhuman primates gather only what is sufficient to satisfy their own individual appetites of the moment. The human female, by contrast, gathers more than is needed for herself at the moment, and so she must plan ahead for both food transport, preservation, and storage.

Although women in hunting and gathering societies may spend a good deal of their time gathering food, men do not spend all or even the greatest part of their time in hunting. The amount of energy expended in hunting, especially in hot climates, is often greater than the energy return from the kill. Too much time spent at hunting might actually be counterproductive. Energy itself is derived primarily from plant carbohydrates; it is the female gatherer who brings in the bulk of the calories. A certain amount of meat in the diet, though, guarantees high-quality protein that is less easily obtained from vegetable sources, for meat contains all of the amino acids, the building blocks of protein, and in exactly the right balance, that are required by the human body. This is important, for the entire spectrum must be provided in the proper balance at the same meal if their full value is to be realized, and the lack of just one prevents full utilization of the oth-

ers. No one plant food does this by itself, and in order to get by without meat, one must hit on exactly the right combination of plants together to provide the essential amino acids in the right proportions.

FOOD-SHARING A second element of human social organization is that hunting, whether cooperative or not, seems to be correlated with food-sharing among adults, a very rare occurrence among nonhuman primates. Food-sharing on a regular basis is the second key feature of human social organization. It is easy enough to see why sharing would be necessary if game is hunted cooperatively; but even individual hunters find it in their interest to share what they cannot consume. Among the Hadza of northern Tanzania, a man will eat his fill at his killsite, then carry what he can back to camp. If the kill has been especially good, the camp may move to him. For the individual hunter, food-sharing is really a way of storing food for the future; his generosity gives him a claim on the future surpluses of other hunters. As a cultural trait, food-sharing has the obvious survival value of distributing resources needed for subsistence.

Although carnivorous animals often share food, the few examples of food-sharing among nonhuman primates all involve groups of male chimpanzees cooperating in a hunt and later sharing the spoils and even offering some to females and infants. It is difficult to say how typical this behavior is for chimpanzees uninfluenced by human intruders, but it does suggest that the origins of food-sharing and the division of labor are related to a shift in food habits from infrequent meat-eating to more of a balance between hunting and gathering. This seems to have occurred with the appearance of the earliest members of the genus *Homo*, by 2 million years ago.

A final distinctive feature of the hunting-gathering economy is the importance of the camp as the center of daily activity and the place where food-sharing actually occurs. Among nonhuman primates, activities tend to be divided between feeding areas and sleeping areas, and the latter tend to be shifted each evening. Hunting and gathering people, however, live in camps of some permanence, ranging from the dry-season camps of the Bushmen that serve for the entire winter to the dry-season camps of the Hadza, oriented to the hunt and serving for several days or a week or two. Moreover, human camps are more than sleeping areas; people are in and out all day, eating, working, and socializing in camps to a greater extent than any other primates. It is thought that the first camps were primarily places where food was shared and the spoils of the hunt were butchered, then being consumed over a period of several days. It would seem that it is to these earliest hunters that we owe the very concept of home.

CULTURAL ADAPTATIONS AND MATERIAL TECHNOLOGY The mobility of hunter-gatherer groups may depend on the availability of water, as in the case of the !Kung; of pine nuts, as in the Shoshone example; or of game animals, as in the Hadza example. Hunting styles and equipment may also play a role in determining population size and movement. Some Mbuti Pygmies hunt with nets. This requires the cooperation of 7 to 30 families; consequently, their camps are relatively large. The camps of those who hunt with bow and arrow number from three to six families. Too many archers in the same locale means that each must travel a great distance daily to keep out of the other's way. Only during mid-summer do the archers collect into larger camps for religious ceremonies, matrimonial bar-

gains, and social exchange. At this time the bowmen turn to communal beat-hunts. Without nets they are less effective than their neighbors, so it is only when the net-hunters are widely dispersed in the pursuit of honey that the archers can come together.

EGALITARIAN SOCIETY An important characteristic of the hunter-gatherer society is its egalitarianism. Hunter-gatherers are usually highly mobile and, lacking animal or mechanical means of transportation, they must be able to travel without many encumbrances, especially on food-getting expeditions. Their material goods must be limited to the barest essentials, which include weapons that serve for hunting, fighting, building, and toolmaking and cooking utensils, traps, and nets. There is little chance for the accumulation of luxuries or surplus goods, and the fact that no one owns significantly more than another helps to limit status differences. Age and sex are usually the only sources of important status differences in hunter-gatherer societies.

Hunter-gatherers make no attempt to accumulate surplus foodstuffs, often an important source of status in agricultural societies. To say that hunters do not accumulate food surpluses, however, is not to say that they live constantly on the verge of starvation. Their environment is their storehouse, and, except in the coldest climates (where a surplus is put by to see people through the lean season), or in times of acute ecological disaster, there is always some food to be found in a group's territory. Because food resources are typically distributed equally throughout the group, no one achieves the wealth or status that hoarding might bring. In such a society, wealth is a sign of deviance rather than a desirable characteristic.

The hunter-gatherer's concept of territory contributes as much to social equality as it does to the equal distribution of resources. Most groups have home ranges which they exploit and within which access to resources is open to all members. If a Mbuti hunter discovers a honey tree, he has first rights; but when he has taken his share, others have a turn. In the unlikely possibility that he does not take advantage of his discovery, others will. No one owns the tree; the system is first come, first served. Therefore knowledge of the existence of food resources circulates quickly throughout the entire group.

Families move easily from one group to another, settling in any group where they have a previous kinship tie. The composition of groups is always shifting. This loose attitude toward group membership promotes the widest access to resources and, at the same time, is a leveling device that promotes social equality.

The hunter-gatherer pattern of generalized exchange, or sharing without any expectation of a direct return, also serves the ends of resource distribution and social equality. A !Kung Bushman spends as much as two thirds of his day visiting others or receiving guests; during this time, many exchanges of gifts take place. To refuse to share—to hoard—would be morally wrong. By sharing whatever is at hand, the !Kung achieve social leveling and assure their right to share in the windfalls of others.

FOOD-PRODUCING SOCIETY

As we saw in Chapter 3, it was the invention of toolmaking that made humans successful hunters and gatherers. The next momentous event in human history, an event that also led to rapid cultural evolution, was the domestication of plants and animals. The transition from hunter and gatherer to food producer (the available evidence suggests this change began 9000 to 11,000 years ago) has been termed revolutionary. After this revolution, much of human society no longer depended on a capricious nature for food; by planting and harvesting crops and keeping domestic animals, people could choose the time and the place of their next meal. But more than this, they could change the nature of human society itself.

Just why this change came about is one of the important questions in anthropology, and the answer is not yet in. In some parts of the world, such as southwest Asia and highland Mexico, food production may have developed as an almost accidental byproduct of increased management of wild food resources. As a result of this human intervention, new strains developed, which, by chance, were useful to humans and so were subjected to further management techniques. The result was more and more emphasis on the new strains, with a gradual lessening of reliance on wild foods.

Recently, some anthropologists have gone so far as to argue that farming is a subsistence practice of last resort, which hunting and gathering peoples will take up only if they have no real choice.[11] On the coast of Peru, for example, the transition from hunting and gathering may have been caused by an increasing shortage of the wild subsistence resources on which people depended. The shortage may have been the result of climatic change, growing populations, or both. The latter does not conflict with the tendency of hunter-gatherers to

---

[11] Mark N. Cohen, *The Food Crisis in Prehistory: Overpopulation and the Origins of Agriculture* (New Haven, Conn.: Yale University Press, 1977).

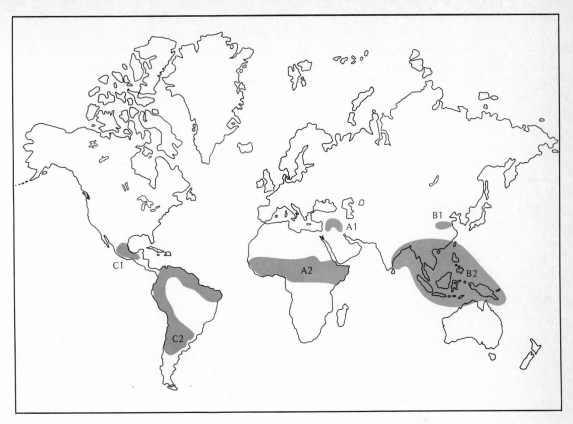

Areas of early plant and animal domestication: A1, Southwest Asia; A2, Central Africa; B1, China; B2, Southeast Asia; C1, Mesoamerica; C2, South America.

stabilize populations below carrying capacity, for their populations do not remain absolutely static, and success at achieving stability may fluctuate considerably.

THE SETTLED LIFE OF FARMERS Whatever the causes, one of the most significant correlates of this new way of life was the development of permanent settlements, in which families of farmers lived together. The task of food production lent itself to a different kind of social organization; the hard work of some members of the group could provide food for all, thus freeing certain people to devote their time to inventing and manu-facturing the equipment needed for a new way of life. Harvesting and digging tools, pottery for storage and cooking, clothing made of woven textiles, and housing made of stone, wood, or sun-dried bricks were some of the results of this combination of new needs and altered division of labor.

The transition also brought important changes in social structure. At first, social relations were egalitarian and hardly different from those that prevailed among hunters and gatherers. However, as settlements grew and large numbers of people began to share the same important resources, such as land and water, society became more structured. Kinship groups such as lineages, which do not commonly play a large part in the social order of hunter-gatherers, were probably the organizing units for this kind of work; as will be discussed in Chapter 9, they provide a convenient way to handle the problems of land use and ownership that arise in a food-producing society.

Humans adapted to this new settled life in a number of ways. For example, some societies became horticultural—small communities of gardeners working with simple hand tools and using neither irrigation nor the plow. Horticulturists typically cultivate several varieties of crops together in small gardens they have cleared by hand. Technologically more complex than the horticulturists are the intensive agriculturalists, who employ such techniques as irrigation, fertilizers, and the wooden or metal plow pulled by harnessed draft animals to produce food on larger plots of land. The distinction between horticulturalist and agriculturalist is not always an easy one to make. For example, the Hopi Indians of the North American Southwest traditionally employed irrigation in their farming, while at the same time using simple hand tools.

As food producers, people have developed several major crop complexes: two adapted to seasonal uplands and two to tropical wetlands. In the dry uplands of southwest Asia, for example, they time their agricultural activities with the rhythm of the changing seasons, cultivating wheat, barley, flax, rye and millet. In the tropical wetlands of the Old World, rice and tubers such as yams and taro are cultivated. In the New World, people have adapted to environments similar to those of the Old World, but have cultivated different plants. Maize, beans, squash, and the potato are typically grown in drier areas, whereas manioc is extensively grown in the tropical wetlands.

Horticulture: The Gururumba

A good example of a horticultural society that has exploited its environment successfully is the Gururumba, a tribe of 1121

Gururumba men carrying away gifts from a food distribution. A complex system of gift exchange helps to knit Gururumba society together.

people who live in six villages spread over 30 square miles in the Upper Asaro valley of New Guinea. Because of the elevation, the climate is cool and damp, and the area receives about 100 inches of rain a year.[12]

Each Gururumba village has a number of gardens separated by fences; several nuclear families may have plots inside each fenced area. Every adult is involved in food production, with a strict division of labor according to sex. Men plant and tend sugarcane, bananas, taro, and yams, while women cultivate sweet potatoes and a variety of green vegetables. A family's social prestige is partially based on the neatness and productivity of its garden. Crops are rotated, but fertilizers are not used. Each gardener maintains more than one plot and uses different soils and different ecological zones for different crops; thus, the gardens are ready for harvesting at different times of the year, assuring a constant food supply. (Another technologically simple cultivating technique used by many horticultural societies, but not the Gururumba, is the slash-and-burn method, in which trees are toppled, allowed to season several months, then set afire. The ashes provide nutrients for the soil, which is then seeded and cultivated.) Since rainfall is plentiful, the Gururumba do not irrigate their gardens, and although some plots are planted on slopes with angles of 45 degrees, terracing is not practiced. Simple hand tools, such as digging sticks made of wood or ground stone, are used by the men to break the soil.

Like many such societies in this culture area, Gururumba society is knit together through a complex system of gift exchange, in which men lavish gifts on one another and so accumulate a host of debtors. The

---

[12] Most of the following information is taken from Philip L. Newman, *Knowing the Gururumba* (New York: Holt, Rinehart and Winston, 1965).

> **Pastoralist:** One who practices a type of subsistence pattern in which food production is based largely upon the maintenance of animal herds.

more a man gives away, the more is owed him, and hence the more prestige he has. For this reason every man keeps two gardens, one with crops to fulfill his everyday needs and one with "prestige" crops for his exchange needs. Although the crops planted in the latter gardens are not special, particular care is given to this garden to assure crops of the finest quality. A man anticipates a major occasion when he will have to give a feast, such as a daughter's wedding or a son's initiation, by planting his prestige garden a year in advance.

The second major feature of the Gururumba subsistence pattern, also common throughout this culture area, is the keeping of pigs. Pigs are raised not primarily for food but as gift-exchange items to raise social prestige. Every five to seven years, a huge pig feast, called an *idzi namo* ("pig flute") is held. Hundreds of pigs are killed, cooked, and distributed, simultaneously abolishing old obligations and creating new ones for the clan that gives the feast. As was the case among the Tsembaga whom we met earlier in this chapter, the pig feast helps the Gururumba get rid of a pig population that has grown too large to continue feeding; it also provides occasional animal protein in their diet.

Pastoralism: The Bakhtiari

One of the more striking examples of human adaptation to the environment is the **pastoralist,** who keeps domesticated animals such as cattle, sheep, horses, and camels. Pastoralism is usually an adaptation to heavy grasslands, mountains, deserts, or other regions not amenable to horti-culture or agriculture. In addition, pastoral societies are seasonally nomadic, moving with their herds over large territories in response to the annual weather cycle.

In the south Zagros mountains of west-ern Iran dwell a fiercely independent tribe of some 50,000 to 150,000 pastoral nomads who tend herds of goats and fat-tailed sheep; they are the Bakhtiari.[13] Although some of the tribesmen own horses and most own donkeys, these are used only for trans-port; the animals around which Bakhtiari life revolves are the sheep and goat.

The harsh, bleak environment domi-nates the lives of these people: it deter-mines when and where they move their flocks, the clothes they wear, the food they eat, and even their dispositions—they have been called "mountain bears" by Iranian townspeople. In the Zagros are ridges which reach altitudes of 12,000 to 14,000 feet. Their steep, rocky trails and escarp-ments challenge the hardiest and ablest climbers; jagged peaks, deep chasms, and watercourses with thunderous torrents also make living and traveling hazardous.

The pastoral life of the Bakhtiari re-volves around two seasonal migrations to find better grazing lands for the flocks. Twice yearly the tribe moves: in the fall, from their *sardsin*, or summer quarters in the mountains, and in the spring, from their *garmsin*, or winter quarters in the lowlands. In the fall, before the harsh win-ter comes to the mountains, the nomads

load their tents, women, and children on donkeys and drive their flocks down to the warm plains that border Iraq in the west; grazing land here is excellent and well wa-tered in the winter. In the spring, when the low-lying pastures dry up, the Bakhtiari return to the mountain valleys, where a new crop of grass is sprouting. For this trek, they split into five groups, each containing about 5000 individuals and 50,000 animals.

The return trip north is the more dan-gerous because the mountain snows are melting and the gorges are full of turbulent, ice-cold water rushing down from the mountain peaks. This long trek is further impeded by the kids that are born in spring, just before migration. Where the water courses are not very deep, the nomads ford them. Deeper channels, including one river which is a half mile wide, are crossed with the help of inflatable goatskin rafts, on which are placed infants, the elderly and infirm, and lambs and kids; the rafts are then pushed by the men swimming along-side in the icy water. If they work from dawn to dusk, the nomads can get the en-tire 5000 people and 50,000 animals across the river in five days. Not surprisingly, doz-ens of sheep are drowned each day at the river crossing.

In the mountain passes, where a biting wind numbs the skin and brings tears to the eyes, the Bakhtiari must make their way through slippery unmelted snow. Climbing the steep escarpments is dangerous, and the stronger men must often carry their own children and the newborn kids on their shoulders as they make their way over the ice and snow to the lush mountain valley that is their goal. During each migration, the tribe may cover as many as 200 miles, and the trek can take weeks because the flocks travel slowly and require constant attention. The nomads have fixed routes and a somewhat definite itinerary; gener-

[13] Material on the Bakhtiari is drawn mainly from Frederik Barth, "Nomadism in the Mountain and Pla-teau Areas of South West Asia," *The Problems of the Arid Zone* (Unesco, 1960), pp. 341–355; Carleton S. Coon, *Caravan: The Story of the Middle East*, 2d ed. (New York: Holt, Rinehart and Winston, 1958), Chap. 13; Philip C. Salzman, "Political Organization among Nomadic Peoples," *Proceedings of the American Philosophical Society*, 1967, 111(2):115–131.

ally, they know where they should be and when they should be there. On the drive, the men and boys herd the sheep and goats, while the women and children ride the donkeys along with the tents and other equipment.

When they reach their destination, the Bakhtiari live in black tents of goat's hair cloth woven by the women. The tents have sloping tops and vertical sides, held up by wooden poles. Inside, the furnishings are sparse: rugs woven by the women or heavy felt pads cover the floor. Against one side of the tent are blankets; containers made of goat skin, copper utensils, clay jugs, and bags of grain line the opposite side. Bakhtiari tents provide an excellent example of adaptation to a changing environment. The goat's hair cloth retains heat and repels water during the winter, and keeps out heat during the summer. These portable homes are very easy to erect, take down, and transport.

Sheep and goats are central to Bakhtiari subsistence. The animals provide milk, cheese, butter, meat, hides, and wool, which is woven into clothes, tents, storage bags, and other essentials by the women or sold in towns. The tribe also engages in very limited horticulture; it owns lands that contain orchards, and the fruit is consumed by the nomads or sold to townspeople. The division of labor is according to sex. The men, who take great pride in their marksmanship and horsemanship, engage in a limited amount of hunting on horseback, but their chief task is the tending of the flocks. The women cook, sew, weave, care for the children, and carry fuel and water.

The Bakhtiari have their own system of justice, including laws and a penal code. They are governed by tribal leaders, or *khans*, who are elected or inherit their office. Most of the *khans* grew wealthy when oil was discovered on tribal lands around the turn of the last century, and many of them are well educated, having attended Iranian or foreign universities. Despite this, and although some of them own houses in cities, the *khans* spend much of their lives among their people.

Urban Life among Nonindustrial Peoples

As improved agricultural techniques lead to higher crop yields and increased population—or perhaps the sequence is the reverse, we are not sure—an agricultural settlement may grow into a city. This goes with an entirely new way of life, involving intense specialization of labor. Individuals who had previously been engaged in agriculture were freed to specialize in other activities. Thus, such craftsmen as carpenters, blacksmiths, sculptors, basketmakers, and stonecutters contribute to the vibrant, diversified life of the city.

Unlike horticulturalists and pastoralists, city dwellers are only indirectly concerned with adapting to their natural environment. Far more important is the fact that they must adapt to living and getting along with their fellow urbanites. Urbanization brings with it a new social order: society becomes stratified and people are ranked according to the kind of work they do, or the family they are born into. As social institutions cease to operate in simple, face-to-face groups of acquaintances and friends, they become more formal and bureaucratic, with specialized political institutions.

With urbanization came a sharp increase in the tempo of human cultural evolution. Writing was invented, trade intensified and expanded, and the wheel, the sail, metallurgy, and other crafts were invented. In many early cities, monumental buildings, such as royal palaces and temples, were built by thousands of men, often slaves taken in war; these feats of engineering still amaze modern architects and engineers. The inhabitants of these buildings—the ruling class composed of nobles and priests—formed a central government that dictated social and religious rules; in turn, the rules were carried out by the merchants, soldiers, artisans, farmers, and other citizens.

Aztec City Life

The Aztec empire, which flourished in Mexico in the sixteenth century, is a good example of a highly developed urban society among non-Western peoples.[14] The capital city of the empire, Tenochtitlán (modern-day Mexico City), was located in a fertile valley 7000 feet above sea level. It is thought that the population of Tenochtitlán, and its sister city, Tlatelolco, was about 200,000 in 1519, when Cortes first saw it. Thus, this Aztec city was five times more populous than the city of London at the same time. The city sat on an island in the middle of a salt lake which has since dried up, and two aqueducts brought in fresh water from springs on the mainland. A 10-mile dike rimmed the eastern end of the city to ward off floodwaters originating in the neighboring lakes during the rainy season.

As in the early cities of southwest Asia, the foundation of Aztec society was agriculture. Corn was the principal crop. Each family, alloted a plot of land by its lineage, cultivated any of a number of crops, including beans, squash, gourds, peppers, tomatoes, cotton, and tobacco. Unlike Old World

---

[14]Most of the following information is taken from Frances F. Berdan, *The Aztecs of Central Mexico* (New York: Holt, Rinehart and Winston, 1982).

societies, however, only a few animals were domesticated; these included dogs and turkeys (both for eating).

As Tenochtitlán grew and land became scarce, Aztec farmers made use of an ingenious method to cope with this situation: they created *chinampas*, or reed-walled gardens, out of the marsh that surrounded the capital. Each *chinampa*, actually a small, man-made island whose soil was as fertile as that of the Nile Delta, was tended by farmers who paddled around the interconnecting canals in small dugout canoes. Even today, *chinampas* can be found at Xochimilco, a few miles outside Mexico City.

Aztec agricultural success provided for an increasingly large population and the diversification of labor. Skilled artisans, such as sculptors, silversmiths, stone workers, potters, weavers, feather workers, and painters were able to make good livings by pursuing these crafts exclusively. Since religion was central to the operation of the Aztec social order, these craftsmen were continuously engaged in the manufacture of religious artifacts, clothing, and decorations for buildings and temples. Other nonagricultural specialists included some of the warriors, the traveling merchants or *pochteca*, the priests, and the government bureaucracy of nobles.

As specialization, both among individuals and cities of the Aztec empire increased, the market became an extremely important economic and social institution. In addition to the daily markets in each city, there were larger markets in the various cities held at different times of year. Buyers and sellers traveled to these from the far reaches of the empire. The market at the city of Tlatelolco was so huge that the Spanish compared it to those of Rome and Constantinople. At the Aztec markets, barter was the primary means of exchange.

However, at times, cacao beans, gold dust, crescent-shaped knives, and copper were used. In addition to its obvious economic use, the market served social functions: people went there not only to buy or to sell, but to meet other people and to hear the latest news. A law actually required that each person go to market at least once within a specified number of days; this ensured that the citizenry was kept informed of all important news. The other major economic institution, trade networks between the capital and other Aztec cities, brought goods such as chocolate, vanilla beans, and pineapples into Tenochtitlán.

Aztec social order was stratified into three main classes: nobles, commoners, and serfs. The nobles operated outside the lineage system on the basis of land and serfs alloted them by the ruler from conquered peoples. The commoners were divided into lineages, on which they were dependent for land. Within each of these, individual status depended on the degree of descent from the founder: those more closely related to the lineage founder had higher status than those whose kinship was more distant. The third class in Aztec society consisted of serfs bound to the land and porters employed as carriers by merchants. Lowest of this class were the slaves. Some had voluntarily sold themselves into bondage; others were captives taken in war.

The Aztecs were governed by a semidivine king, who was chosen by a council of nobles, priests, and leaders from among candidates of royal lineage. Although the king was an absolute monarch, the councilors advised him on affairs of state. A vast number of government officials oversaw various functions, such as the maintenance of the tax system, the courts of justice, management of government storehouses, and control of military training.

As in a modern city, housing in Tenochtitlán ranged from squalid to magnificent. On the outskirts of the city, on *chinampas*, were the farmers' hovels, huts of thatched straw and wattle smeared with mud. In the city proper were the houses of the middle

A model of the center of Tenochtitlán, the Aztec capital city.

class—graceful, multi-roomed, single- and two-story stone and mortar buildings, each of which surrounded a flower-filled patio and rested on a stone platform for protection against floods. It is estimated that

Scenes of Aztec life from the Florentine Codex, dating early after the Spanish conquest.

there were about 60,000 houses in Tenochtitlán. The focal points of the city were the *teocallis*, or pyramidal temples, at which religious ceremonies, including human sacrifice, were held. The 100-foot-high double temple dedicated to the war god and the rain god was made of stone and featured a steep staircase which led to a platform con-

The modern industrial city is a very recent human invention, although its roots lie in the so-called preindustrial city. The widespread belief that preindustrial cities are things of the past, industrial cities things of the future is based on culture-bound assumptions rather than established fact.

taining an altar, a chamber containing shrines, and an antechamber for the priests.

The typical Aztec city was rectangular and reflected the way the land was divided among the lineages. In the center was a large plaza containing the temple and the house of the city's chief. At Tenochtitlán, with a total area of about 20 square miles, a huge temple and two lavish palaces stood in the central plaza, also called the Sacred Precinct. Surrounding this area were other ceremonial buildings belonging to each lineage.

The palace of the emperor Montezuma boasted numerous rooms for attendants and concubines, a menagerie, hanging gardens, and a swimming pool. Since Tenochtitlán sat in the middle of a lake, it was unfortified and connected to the mainland by three causeways. Communication among different parts of the city was easy, and one could travel either by land or by water. A series of canals, with footpaths running beside them, ran throughout the city. The Spaniards who came to this city reported that thousands of canoes plied the canals, carrying passengers and cargo around the city; these Europeans were so impressed by the communication network that they

> **Preindustrial cities:** The kinds of urban settlements that are characteristic of nonindustrial civilizations.

called Tenochtitlán the Venice of the New World.

PREINDUSTRIAL CITIES IN THE MODERN WORLD

Tenochtitlán is a good example of the kind of urban settlement that was characteristic of most ancient, nonindustrial civilizations. Commonly termed **preindustrial cities**, they are apt to be thought of as things of the past, or as little more than stages in some sort of inevitable progression toward the kinds of industrial cities one finds today in places like Europe and North America. This essentially ethnocentric view obscures the fact that "preindustrial" cities are far from uncommon in the world today—especially in the so-called Third World countries. Furthermore, industrial cities have not yet come close to demonstrating that they have the long-term viability shown by preindustrial cities, which in some parts of the world have been around for not just hundreds but thousands of years.

CHAPTER SUMMARY

Needs and pressures force people to alter their behavior to suit their environment. This adjustment is a part of adaptation. Adaptation means that there is a moving balance between a society's needs and its environmental potential. Adaptation also refers to the interaction of an organism and its environment, with each causing changes in the other. The unit of adaptation includes both the organism and its environment. Adaptation takes place over long periods of time, and it is essential for survival. An ecosystem is bound by the activities of organisms and by physical forces such as erosion. Human ecosystems must be considered in terms of all aspects of culture.

To fit into an ecosystem an organism must be able to adapt, or become a part of it. To survive societies too must be flexible and be able to move from one environment or from one way of life to another.

A culture area is a geographical region in which various societies follow similar patterns of life. Since geographical regions are not always uniform in climate and topography, new discoveries do not always filter out to every group. Environmental variation also favors variation in technology, since needs may be quite different from area to area.

Julian Steward used the concept of culture type to explain variations within geographical regions. In this view a culture is considered in terms of a particular technology and of the particular environmental features that technology is best suited to exploit.

The social and political organization of a society are other factors that influence how technology is to be used to ensure survival. Those features of a culture that play a part in the way the society makes a living are its culture core. Anthropologists can trace direct relationships between types of culture cores and types of environments.

The hunting-gathering life, the oldest and most basic type of human adaptation, requires that people move their residence according to changing food sources. In addition, for as yet unknown ecological and social factors, local group size is kept small. One explanation contends that small sizes fit land capacity to sustain the groups. Another states that the fewer the people, the less the chance of social conflict. How hunter-gatherers regulate population size is not certain, but late weaning, prolonged post-partum sex taboos, infanticide, abortion, and the use of contraceptive herbal drugs probably play a part.

Three important elements of human social organization probably developed along with hunting. These are a sexual division of labor, food-sharing, and the camp as the center of daily activity and the place where food-sharing takes place.

A characteristic of hunting-gathering societies is their egalitarianism. Since the hunting-gathering life requires mobility, people accumulate only the material goods necessary for survival, so that status differences are limited to those based on age and sex. Food resources are distributed equally throughout the groups and thus no individual can achieve the wealth or status that hoarding might bring.

The reason for the transition from hunting and gathering to food producing, which began about eleven to nine thousand years ago, has not been established with certainty. Some anthropologists believe it was caused by a shortage of wild subsistence foods, which might have been the unforeseen result of increased management of wild food resources, or perhaps it was caused by climatic change, growing populations, or even all three. One correlate of the food-producing revolution was the development of permanent settlements, as people practiced simple horticulture, using neither the plow nor irrigation or intensive agriculture, a more complex activity that requires irrigation, fertilizers, and draft animals. Pastoralism is a means of subsistence which relies on raising herds of domesticated animals such as cattle, sheep, and goats. Pastoralists are usually nomads, moving to higher ground in the summer.

Cities developed when improved agricultural techniques created a surplus, freeing individuals to specialize in other activities. The social structure becomes increasingly stratified with the development of cities, and people are ranked according to the work they do and the family they are born into. Social relationships grow more formal and political institutions are formed. In some parts of the world, so-called preindustrial cities have been around for hundreds, and even thousands, of years. Industrial cities, by contrast, are a relatively recent development. Whether or not they will ever fully supplant preindustrial cities in the Third World remains to be seen, as does their long-term viability.

SUGGESTED READINGS

Bicchieri, M. G., ed. *Hunters and Gatherers Today: A Socioeconomic Study of Eleven Such Cultures in the Twentieth Century.* New York: Holt, Rinehart and Winston, 1972.
Both ecological-historial reconstruction and participant-observer ethnographies are contained in this volume. Each chapter is preceded by a short introduction pointing out the specific character and basic features of each of the studies.

Lustig-Arecco, Vera. *Technology: Strategies for Survival.* New York: Holt, Rinehart and Winston, 1975.
Although the early anthropologists devoted a good deal of attention to technology, the subject fell into neglect early in the twentieth century. This is one of the few recent studies of the subject. The author's particular interest is the technoeconomic adaptation of hunters, pastoralists, and farmers.

Oswalt, Wendell H. *Habitat and Technology.* New York: Holt, Rinehart and Winston, 1972.
The author develops a taxonomy which permits precise cross-cultural comparisons of the complexity of manufactures. The research is based on a systematic analysis of the known manufactures of non-Western peoples. Shelters, tools, clothing, implements, and cultivated foodstuffs are considered.

Sjoberg, Gideon. *The Preindustrial City.* New York: Free Press, 1960.
In this important study, the author draws on cross-cultural research to discuss the nature of preindustrial cities everywhere.

Vayda, Andrew, ed. *Environment and Cultural Behavior: Ecological Studies in Cultural Anthropology.* New York: Natural History Press, 1969.
The focus of the studies collected here is the interrelationship between cultural behavior and environmental phenomena. The writers attempt to make cultural behavior intelligible by relating it to the material world in which it develops. This volume includes articles concerning population, divination, ritual, warfare, food production, climate, and diseases.

7 | Economic Systems

The first and most basic characteristic of the market in non-Western societies is that it always means a marketplace, a specific site where the actual goods are exchanged. This market is in the Maya Indian community of Chichicastenango, Guatemala. On market day, Indians and non-Indians alike are able to exchange things they have produced for themselves for things that they need but can get only from others.

PREVIEW

HOW DO ANTHROPOLOGISTS STUDY ECONOMIC SYSTEMS?

Anthropologists study the means by which goods are produced, distributed, and consumed in the context of the total culture of particular societies. Although they have borrowed theories and concepts from economists, many anthropologists feel that principles derived from the study of Western market economies are not applicable to economic systems where people do not produce and exchange goods for profit.

HOW DO THE ECONOMIES OF NONINDUSTRIAL PEOPLES WORK?

In non-Western, nonindustrial societies there is always a division of labor by age and sex, with some additional craft specialization. Land and other valuable resources are usually controlled by groups of relatives, such as bands or lineages, and individual ownership is rare. Production is dependent upon the natural environment, and most goods are consumed by the group that produces them.

HOW AND WHY ARE GOODS EXCHANGED IN NONINDUSTRIAL SOCIETIES?

Nonindustrial peoples exchange goods through the processes of reciprocity, redistribution, and market exchange. Reciprocity involves the exchange of goods and services of roughly equivalent value, and it is often undertaken for ritual purposes or in order to gain prestige. Redistribution requires some sort of government and/or religious elite to collect and then reallocate resources, in the form of either goods or services. Market exchange, which in nonindustrial societies means going to a specific place for direct exchange of goods, also serves as entertainment and as a means of exchanging important information. The latter are frequently primary motivating forces bringing people into the marketplace.

An economic system may be defined as one by which goods are produced, distributed, and consumed. Since a people, in pursuing a particular means of subsistence necessarily produce, distribute, and consume things, it is obvious that our earlier discussion of patterns of subsistence (Chapter 6) involved us with economic matters. Yet there is much more to economic systems than we have so far covered. In this chapter, we shall look at aspects of economic systems—specifically systems of production, exchange, and redistribution—that require more discussion than we were able to give them in the last chapter.

ECONOMIC ANTHROPOLOGY

It is perhaps in the study of the economy of nonliterate peoples that we are most apt to fall prey to interpreting anthropological data in terms of our own technologies, our own values of work and property, and our own determination of what is rational. Such ethnocentrism has been responsible for statements, for example, that certain West African people act like children in their seeming inability to plan ahead. These people conventionally and traditionally use up so much of their food feasting during the dry season that, when the wet season comes and they must break up the land for new planting, they do not have enough food. Similarly, ethnocentrism has sometimes led to the Kogi Indians being termed "superstitious" because of the way they use their land. The Kogi, who inhabit the Sierra Nevada range of Colombia, are faced with a scarcity of land. In these mountain ranges, however, there are many terraces built by earlier inhabitants; using them as farmland would save the Kogi much moving from one place to another. Yet the Kogi will not use these terraces.

"There are many spirits of the dead there," they say.[1]

In order to understand how the schedule of wants or demands of a given society is balanced against the supply of goods and services available it is necessary to introduce a third variable—the anthropological variable of culture. In any given economic system, economic processes cannot be interpreted without culturally defining the demands and understanding the conventions that dictate how and when they are satisfied.

In the last 30 years, anthropologists have borrowed theory and concepts from the discipline of economics in an attempt to understand certain relationships of nonliterate people. Since the field of economics has concentrated its attention on the study of the allocation of scarce goods and services in industrial society, it is a matter of controversy as to what modifications must be made in order for economic theory to be applicable to nonindustrial societies. Can we speak of the profit motive, savings, capital goods, and all the other concepts that economists use, in relation to nonindustrial societies?

Some anthropologists adhere to the point of view that there is little to be learned from the study of market economies, where the principal motivation is profit, in studying people who do not exchange goods for gain. This position is called **substantivism.**

Other scholars, who adhere to the school of thought known as **formalism,** take a different view. Formalists claim that economic theory really has to do with the ways people get the greatest personal satisfaction in saving things and in distributing

---

[1] Melville Herskovits, *Economic Anthropology: A Study in Comparative Economics*, 2d ed. (New York: Knopf, 1952).

Among the Tiwi of North Australia, women gather the everyday staple foods, which the men supplement with meat. Here, we see a woman collecting wild honeycomb from a tree she has felled, and men returning from a hunt. Among the Tiwi, a well-fed household is one with several wives to provide the staples.

Substantivism: The view that the principles of market economics cannot be applied in the study of societies that do not exchange goods for gain.

Formalism: A school of thought which holds that the principles of economics are general enough to be applied usefully to all societies.

scarce resources. If this is true, then economic theory is certainly general enough to apply to all societies.

RESOURCES

In every society there are customs and rules governing the kinds of work that are done, who does the work, who owns the resources and tools, and how the work is accomplished. Resources, labor, capital, and technology are the productive resources that a social group may use to produce desired goods and services. The rules surrounding the use of these things are embedded in the culture and determine the way the economy operates.

Patterns of Labor

In every human society, there has always been a division of labor along sex and age categories; such division is simply a further development of the patterns found in all higher primates.

SEXUAL DIVISION OF LABOR Whether men or women do a particular job varies from group to group, but much work has been set apart as the work of either one sex or the other. The sexual division of labor in human societies of all sorts has been studied extensively by anthropologists, and we discussed some aspects of it in the preceding chapter. For example, we have seen that it has its roots in biology, and that the tasks most often regarded as "women's work" tend to be those that can be carried out near home and that are easily resumed after interruption. Those tasks most often regarded as "men's work" tend to be those that require physical strength, rapid mobilization of high bursts of energy, frequent travel at some distance from home, and assumption of high levels of risk and danger. Beyond all this, though, a study of the work done by men and women in particular groups soon shows that "the specific forms taken by sex division of labor must be referred to the historical development of the particular body of traditions by which a particular people order their lives."[2] Therefore, each society must be studied to see how it goes about dividing the work load between men and women.

In modern industrial societies the biological factors underlying the sexual division of labor have largely been overcome by a variety of technological and organizational innovations. These include such things as contraceptive devices, synthetic infant formulas which can be fed from a bottle, day care centers, new forms of transportation, and ways and means by which occupational hazards have been reduced, if not eliminated. Thus, there is no longer any compelling reason why women should not be able to hold jobs once reserved for men, nor is there any reason why men should not perform tasks once exclusively performed by women; the only thing men cannot do is give birth to children.

AGE DIVISION OF LABOR There may also be a division of labor according to age. Among the Tiwi of North Australia, for ex-

[2]Herskovits, p. 132.

In modern industrial societies, as these two pictures illustrate, culture has overidden most of the biological factors underlying the traditional sexual division of labor, and sex roles are changing accordingly.

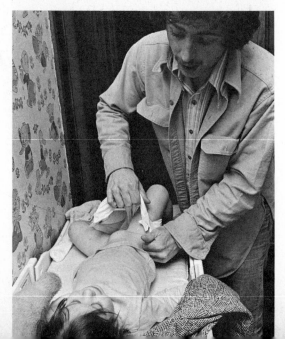

ample, the men who were too old to hunt manufactured the tools and artifacts of the tribe.[3] The older men, those with multiple wives and therefore large households with a large labor force, had leisure time to develop skills in the manufacture of canoes, baskets, digging sticks, and beautifully made artistic creations, such as grave posts and ceremonial spears. These men also composed songs and dances. Their wives, meanwhile, provided their households with abundant vegetables, grubs, and worms so that all were well fed.

Among the Ihalmiut of Northern Canada's "Barren Grounds," old age was a difficult time because the harsh climate and the migratory life of these Caribou hunters posed special hardships for the old.[4] The cold and damp accelerated aging, apparently, and the old suffered the most during famines. There was little work easy enough for the old of either sex to accomplish, although old people were the repositories of wisdom—the "libraries" of a nonliterate people. So, old people constituted more of a burden for the Ihalmiut than for people for whom subsistence activities are less difficult. The same was true of children, who made little of an economic contribution until they were in their teens.

In many nonindustrial societies, both children and older people make a greater contribution to the economy in terms of work and responsibility than is common in our own. In South Vietnam, for example, young children not only look after their younger brothers and sisters but help with housework as well. "An American would be horrified to see a child, four or five years

old, handling a chopping knife or lighting an oil lamp, but in Vietnam it is common."[5] Unlike the elderly Eskimos, old people in South Vietnam retain economic responsibilities. The grandmother, for example, holds the purse strings, markets, cooks, and cleans the house. A similar allocation of responsibility used to be common in rural North American households, where the work load was heavy and the labor pool small.

COOPERATION Cooperative work groups can be found everywhere in nonliterate as well as literate and in nonindustrial as well as industrial societies. Often, if the effort involves the whole community, there is a festive spirit to the work. Jomo Kenyatta, the anthropologist who went on to become a respected statesman as well as "father" of an independent Kenya, described the time of enjoyment after a day's labor in his country:

If a stranger happens to pass by, he will have no idea that these people who are singing and dancing have completed their day's work. This is why most Europeans have erred by not realizing that the African in his own environment does not count hours or work by the movement of the clock, but works with good spirit and enthusiasm to complete the tasks before him.[6]

In Dahomey, the iron workers cooperate in the operation of their forges. Each man owns his own iron, and the members of the forge work on the iron of one man at a time. The product belongs to the man who provided the iron, and he is free to sell it in the market for personal gain, reinvesting this return in more iron. Meanwhile, he works

[3] C. W. M. Hart and Arnold R. Pilling, *The Tiwi of North Australia* (New York: Holt, Rinehart and Winston, 1960).

[4] Farley Mowat, *People of the Deer* (Toronto: Bantam Books, 1981).

[5] Randy Gellerman in the *New York Times*, July 24, 1973, p. 40.

[6] Herskovits, p. 103.

at the forge for each other man until his turn comes again.[7]

Cooperative work is not necessarily voluntary. It may be part of fulfilling duties to inlaws; it may be performed for chiefs or priests, by command. The institutions of family, kinship, religion, and the state all may act as organizing elements that define the nature and condition of each worker's cooperative obligations.

CRAFT SPECIALIZATION In nonindustrial societies, where division of labor occurs along lines of age and sex, each person in the society has knowledge and competence in all aspects of work appropriate to his or her age and sex. In modern industrial societies, by contrast, there exists a greater diversity of more specialized tasks to be performed, and no individual can even begin to have knowledge of all those appropriate for his or her age and sex. Yet even in nonindustrial societies there is some specialization of craft. This is often minimal in hunting and gathering societies, but even here the arrow points of one man may be in some demand because of his particular skill in making them. Among people who produce their own food, there is apt to be more in the way of specialization. Among Trobriand Islanders, for example, the artisans of one village specialize in stone blades for adzes, whereas their neighbors may specialize in decorating pots or carving wooden handles for the stone blades.

An example of specialization can be seen among Afar tribesmen of the Ethiopian Danakil depression: they are miners of salt, which since ancient times has been widely traded in East Africa. It is mined from the crust of an extensive salt plain in the north part of the depression, and to get it is a risky and difficult business. L. M.

Nesbitt, the first European to successfully traverse the depression, labeled it "the hell hole of creation."[8] The heat is extreme during the day, with shade temperatures between 140 and 156 degrees F not unusual. Shade is not to be found on the salt plain,

_____
[7] Herskovits, p. 108.

_____
[8] L. M. Nesbitt, *Hell-Hole of Creation* (New York: Knopf, 1935).

The Afar tribesmen of Ethiopia's Danakil depression have a narrow economic specialization; they mine and sell salt to neighboring peoples. This requires cooperative effort on the part of the men, who are shown (above) prying loose slabs of solid salt. Once a crew of men has pried up and removed salt, another crew cuts it into standard-sized blocks, and a third crew smooths these down. These blocks are then loaded on animals, usually camels because they stand up best under the desert conditions, and transported to the coast and highlands for sale.

however, unless a shelter of salt blocks is built. Nor is there food or water for man or beast. To add to the difficulty, until recently the Muslim Afars and the Christian Tegreans, highlanders who also mine salt, were mortal enemies.

Successful mining, then, requires skill at planning and organization, as well as physical strength and the will to work under the most trying conditions.[9] Pack animals to carry the salt have to be fed in advance, for to carry sufficient fodder for them interferes with their ability to carry out salt. Food and water must be carried for the miners, who usually number 30 to 40 per group. Travel is planned to take place at night to avoid the intense heat of day. In the past, measures to protect against attack had to be taken. Finally, timing is critical; a party has to get back to sources of food and water before their own supplies are too long exhausted, and before their animals are unable to continue farther.

Control of Land

All societies have regulations that determine the way that valuable land resources will be allocated. Hunter-gatherer societies must determine who can hunt game and gather plants and where these activities take place. Horticulturists must decide how their farmland is to be acquired, worked, and passed on. Pastoralists require a system that determines rights to watering places and grazing land, as well as the right of access to land over which they move their herds. Full-time or intensive agriculturists must have some means of determining title to land and access to

[9] Haile Michael Mesghinua, "Salt Mining in Enderta," *Journal of Ethiopian Studies*, 1966, 4(2); Kevin O'Mahoney, "The Salt Trade," *Journal of Ethiopian Studies*, 1970, 8(2).

water supplies for irrigation purposes. In our own industrialized Western society, a system of private ownership of land and rights to natural resources prevails. Actually, it is closer to the truth to say that we pretend that private ownership prevails. The fact is that in the United States more land and resources are in the hands of the federal and state governments than are privately owned. Moreover, elaborate laws have been established to regulate the buying, owning, and selling of land and water resources. Nevertheless, if individuals wish to reallocate valuable farm land, for instance, for another purpose, they are generally able to do so.

In nonindustrial societies individual ownership of land is rare; generally it is controlled by kinship groups such as the lineage (discussed in Chapter 9) or band. For example, among the Tiwi, all land is owned by one of nine bands. Each band of about 200 to 300 people lived on roughly 200 square miles of land which they considered to be their territory—their own country. The territorial boundaries between bands were well known, although they might strike Westerners as vague and imprecise. Anthropologists Charles Hart and Arnold Pilling comment:

All pieces of country—clumps of jungle, stretches of grassland, sections of thick woods—had names. A thickly wooded area belonged to one band, while the more open country that began where the woods thinned out belonged to another; thus the boundary was not a sharp line but a transitional zone—perhaps several miles—where the change from trees to savannah became noticeable. The Tiwi thought of the landscape as a sort of spectrum where a man moved gradually out of one district into another as he passed from one type of landscape into another.[10]

----

[10]Hart and Pilling, p. 12.

The adaptive value of this attitude toward land ownership is clear; the size of the band territories, as well as the size of the bands themselves, can change in size to adjust to change in amount of resources in any given place. Such adjustment would be more difficult under a system of individual ownership of land.

Among some West African horticultural peoples, a feudal system of land ownership prevails, by which all land belongs to the head chief. He allocates it to various subchiefs, who in turn distribute it to lineages; lineage leaders then assign individual plots to each farmer. Just as in medieval Europe, the African people owe allegiance to the subchiefs (or nobles) and the principal chief (or king). The people who work the land must pay taxes and fight for the king when necessary. The people, in a sense, "own" the land and transmit their ownership to their heirs. However, an individual cannot give away, sell, or otherwise dispose of a plot of land without approval from the elder of the lineage. When an individual no longer needs the land which has been allocated, the lineage head rescinds title to it and reallocates it to someone else in the lineage. The important operative principle among such farmers is that such a system extends the right of the individual to use land for a certain period of time, and the land is not "owned" outright. This serves to maintain the integrity of valuable farmland as such, preventing its loss through subdivision and conversion to other uses.

Capital

Economists use the term **capital** to describe any resource that is not used up in the process of producing goods. In our society, capital means steel furnaces, drill presses, and jigsaws, as well as the money that will buy such tools. But even nonindustrial societies have means of creating and allocating the tools and other artifacts used in the production of goods and passed on to succeeding generations. The number and kinds of tools that a society uses are limited by the life-styles of its members. Hunter-gatherers and nomads, who are frequently on the move, have fewer and simpler tools than the more sedentary farmer, because a great number of complex tools would decrease their mobility.

Hunters and gatherers make and use a variety of weapons, many of which are ingenious in their effectiveness. (For a look at some of the tools of such a society, see the Color Portfolio on the Eskimo, p. 170.) They usually make the tools they need and so have first rights to their use. They may give or lend tools to others in exchange for the products resulting from their use. For example, a Bushman who gives his arrow to another hunter has a right to a share in any animals that the hunter may kill. Game is thought to "belong" to the man whose arrow killed it.

Among horticulturists, the slashing knife and the digging stick or hoe are the primary tools. Since these are relatively easy to produce, every person can make them. Although the maker has first rights to their use, when that person is not using them, any member of the family may ask to use them and usually is granted permission to do so. To refuse would mean the tool owner would be treated with scorn for this singular lack of concern for others. If another relative helps raise the crop that is traded for a particular tool, that relative becomes part owner of the implement, and it may not be traded or given away without his or her permission.

As tools and other productive goods become more complex and more difficult and costlier to make, individual ownership in them usually becomes more absolute, as

> **Capital:** Any resource that is not used up in the process of producing goods.

do the conditions under which persons may borrow and use such equipment. It is easy to replace a knife lost by a relative during palm cultivation, but much more difficult to replace an iron plow or a power-driven threshing machine. Rights to the ownership of complex tools are more rigidly applied; generally the person who has supplied the capital for the purchase of a complex piece of machinery is considered the sole owner and may decide how and by whom it will be used.

Technology

The economy of any society is related to the level of technological knowledge. In literate societies, this knowledge is preserved in books; in nonliterate societies it is retained in the minds of the living members of the group.

The division of labor is a method by which much of the technology can be apportioned among the members so that it will not be lost and can even be improved. Knowledge of various plants—when they can be harvested, where they are found, which parts are edible, and how they should be prepared and cooked—is acquired by children as they watch adults. Lévi-Strauss reports that small children may know the names and uses of hundreds of plants.[11] The behavior and habits of animals, how to track them, how to use their bones and skin, how to make arrows or spears for the hunt, all are bits and pieces of the technology of nonindustrial people. It is on this technology that their livelihood

---

[11] Claude Lévi-Strauss, *The Savage Mind* (Chicago: University of Chicago Press, 1966).

rests, and all of it must be learned and passed on to the next generation in order for the group to survive.

PRODUCTION—THE YEARLY ECONOMIC CYCLE

In an agricultural society, the patterns of work involved in the production of farm goods follow the seasons. The yearly economic cycle in a small village in modern Greece is a good illustration of production in an economic system.[12]

The crops of the village are grown both for home consumption and for the market. The first event of the agricultural year is the pruning of the grape vines, which is commenced at the end of the winter rains. Pruning, followed by deep hand hoeing, is considered a man's occupation and must be completed quickly so that the men can turn to plowing the cotton fields. Cotton is a commercial crop, whereas the grapes are grown for the wine made and consumed by the household. Cotton is usually plowed by rented tractors; the planting is done by hand.

Once the cotton starts to grow, the hoeing begins. This arduous labor is performed by the girls and women of the household. Other women from the village or even from neighboring villages may be hired if the crop is a large one. This work takes place in addition to, rather than instead of, everyday housework.

In June the wheat which was planted in the late fall is harvested by machines that are owned and operated by people outside the village. Payment is in kind, 8 percent of the amount of wheat threshed. The wheat, made into bread and consumed at

Women of Vasilika, a village in Greece, hoeing. This arduous labor is considered women's work, but it does not excuse them from their regular household work.

home, is still, literally, the staff of life, the basic food for the people of the village. The chaff and straw are used for the animals.

In late June and early July the tobacco, which was planted at about the same time as the wheat, is ready to be picked and strung for drying—a task welcomed by the women after the hot, back-breaking work of hoeing the cotton. They can sit in the shade near their houses.

Irrigation work in the cotton fields starts for the men in July. Each field is irrigated about three times. In October and November the cotton is picked, which requires prolonged work by many hands as the cotton does not ripen uniformly. Women do this job and again may be hired if necessary. The farmer's problem is to get

---

[12] Ernestine Friedl, *Vasilika, a Village in Modern Greece* (New York: Holt, Rinehart and Winston, 1962).

the cotton picked before the winter rains set in.

Meanwhile, the vines have ripened, and winemaking takes place in October. This is an occasion much enjoyed, for the men, women, and children all pick the grapes together, talk and joke, and eat a little of the produce.

The round of productive activities starts again for the next year. The Greek farmer, like any peasant, really runs a household rather than a commercial enterprise. The men are motivated by a desire to provide for the welfare of their own families; each family, as an economic unit, works as a group to maintain or improve its common position. The villagers measure prestige and honor by the degree to which a family succeeds in fulfilling its obligations. The natural environment, the technology, and the work roles of the family members all influence the success from year to year of the family efforts.

Plowing and dragging the wheat fields is the work of men. For motive power, a horse or two are used if weather conditions are normal. Otherwise, a tractor may be hired to be sure the job gets done before the winter rains set in.

> Reciprocity: The exchange of goods and services, of approximately equal value, between two parties.

DISTRIBUTION AND EXCHANGE

In our own money economy, there is a two-step process between labor and consumption. The money received for labor must be translated into something else before it is directly consumable. In societies with no medium of exchange, the rewards for labor are usually direct. The workers in a family group consume what they harvest; they eat what the hunter brings home; they use the tools that they themselves make. But even where there is no formal medium of exchange, some distribution of goods takes place. Karl Polanyi, an economist, classified the cultural systems of distributing material goods into three modes: reciprocity, redistribution, and market exchange.[13]

Reciprocity

Reciprocity refers to a transaction between two parties whereby goods and services of roughly equivalent value are exchanged. This may involve gift giving, but in non-Western societies, pure altruism in gift giving is as rare as it is in our own society. The overriding motive is to fulfill social obligations and perhaps to gain a bit of social prestige in the process. It might best be compared in our society to a hostess who gives a dinner party. She may compete within her social circle in the gourmet food

[13] Karl Polanyi, "The Economy as Instituted Process," in Edward E. LeClair, Jr., and Harold K. Schneider, eds., *Economic Anthropology: Readings in Theory and Analysis* (New York: Holt, Rinehart and Winston, 1968), pp. 122–143.

she prepares, the originality of her decorations, and the quality of wit and conversation of her guests. Her expectation is that she will be invited to similar parties by some, although perhaps not all, of the guests.

Social customs dictate the nature and occasion of exchange. When an animal is killed by a group of hunters in Australia, the meat is divided among the families of the hunters and other relatives. Each person in the camp gets a share, the size depending on the nature of the person's kinship tie to the hunters. The least desirable parts may be kept by the hunters themselves. When a kangaroo was killed, the left hind leg went to the brother of the hunter, the tail to his father's brother's son, the loins and the fat to his father-in-law, the ribs to his mother-in-law, the forelegs to his father's younger sister, the head to his wife, and the entrails and the blood to the hunter. If there were arguments over the apportionment, it was because the principles of distribution were not being followed properly. The hunter and his family would seem to fare badly according to this arrangement, but they would have their turn when another man made the kill. The giving and receiving was obligatory, as was the particularity of the distribution. Such sharing of food reinforces community bonds and ensures that everyone eats. It might also be viewed as a way of saving perishable goods. By giving away part of his kill, the hunter gets a social IOU for a similar amount of food in the future. It is quite similar to putting money in a time-deposit savings account.

The food-distribution practices just described for Australian hunters constitute an example of **generalized reciprocity.** This may be defined as exchange in which neither the value of what is given is calculated nor the time of repayment specified. Gift giving, in the altruistic sense, also falls in this category. Most commonly, generalized reciprocity occurs among close kin or people who otherwise have very close ties with one another.

Balanced reciprocity is not part of a long-term process. The giving and receiving, as well as the time involved, are more specific. Examples of balanced reciprocity among the Crow Indians are related by Robert Lowie.[14] A woman skilled in the tanning of buffalo hides might offer her services to a neighbor who needed a new cover for her tepee. It took an expert to design a tepee cover, which required from 14 to 20 skins. The designer might need as many as 20 collaborators, whom she instructed in the sewing together of the skins and whom the tepee owner might remunerate with a feast. The designer herself would be given some kind of property by the tepee owner. In another example from the Crow, Lowie relates that if a married woman brought her brother a present of food, he might reciprocate with a present of 10 arrows for her husband, which rated as the equivalent of a horse.

Giving, receiving, and sharing as so far described constitute a form of social security or insurance. A family contributes to others when they have the means and can count on receiving from others in time of need. A **leveling mechanism** is at work in the process of generalized or balanced reciprocity. Social obligations compel a family to distribute their goods, and no one is permitted to accumulate too much more than the others. Greater wealth simply brings a greater obligation to give.

Leveling mechanisms may also be found in traditional farming communities that are egalitarian in nature, as in many of

---

[14]Robert Lowie, *Crow Indians* (New York: Holt, Rinehart and Winston, 1956; original edition, 1935), p. 75.

the Indian villages and towns of highland Mexico. In these communities, cargo systems function to siphon off any excess wealth that people may accumulate. A cargo system is a civil-religious hierarchy which, on a revolving basis, combines most of the civic and ceremonial offices of a community in a hierarchial sequence with each office being occupied for one year. All offices are open to all men, and eventually virtually everyone has at least one term in office. The scale is pyramidal, which is to say that more offices exist at the lower levels, with progressively fewer at the top. For example, in a community of about 8000 people, there may be four levels of offices with 32 on the lowest, 12 on the next one up, 6 on the next, and 2 at the top. Offices at the lower level include those for the performance of various menial chores such as sweeping and carrying messages. The higher offices are those of councilmen, judges, mayors, and ceremonial positions. These positions demand expenditures on the part of the office holder, either in the form of sponsorship of festivals or for banquets associated with the transmission of office. After holding a cargo position, a man usually has a period of rest during which he may accumulate sufficient resources to campaign for a higher office. Each male citizen of the community is socially obligated to serve in the system at least once, and social pressure to do so is such that it drives individuals who have once again accumulated excess wealth to apply for higher offices in order to raise their social status. Thus, while some individuals have appreciably more prestige than others in their community, no one has appreciably more wealth in a material sense than anyone else.

Negative reciprocity is a third form of exchange, in which the giver tries to get the better of the exchange. The parties involved

> **Generalized reciprocity: A mode of exchange in which neither the value of the gift is calculated nor the time of repayment specified.**
>
> **Balanced reciprocity: A mode of exchange in which the giving and the receiving are specific as to the value of the goods and the time of their delivery.**
>
> **Leveling mechanism: A social obligation compelling a family to distribute goods so that no one accumulates more wealth than anyone else.**
>
> **Negative reciprocity: A form of exchange in which the giver tries to get the better of the exchange.**

have opposed interests, usually live at some distance from one another, and are not closely related. The ultimate form of negative reciprocity is to take something by force. Less extreme forms involve the use of guile and deception, or at the least hard bargaining. Among the Navajo, according to the anthropologist Clyde Kluckhohn, "to deceive when trading with foreign tribes is morally accepted."[15]

BARTER AND TRADE Exchange that takes place within a group of people generally takes the form of generalized or balanced reciprocity. When it takes place between two groups, there is apt to be at least a potential for hostility and competition. Therefore, such exchange may well be in the form of negative reciprocity unless some sort of arrangement has been made to ensure at

---

[15]Clyde Kluckhohn, quoted in Marshall Sahlins, *Stone Age Economics* (Chicago: Aldine, 1972), p. 200.

least an approach to balance. Barter is one form of negative reciprocity by which scarce items from one group are exchanged for desirable goods from another group. Relative value is calculated, and despite an outward show of indifference, sharp trading is more the rule when compared to the reciprocal nature of the exchanges within a group.

An arrangement that partook partly of balanced reciprocity and partly of barter existed between the Kota, in India, and three neighboring tribes who traded their surplus goods and certain services with the Kota. The Kota were the musicians and artisans for the area. They exchanged iron tools with the other three groups and provided the music essential for ceremonial occasions. The Toda furnished to the Kota ghee (a kind of butter) for certain ceremonies and buffalo for funerals; relations between the Kota and the Toda were friendly. The Badaga were agricultural and traded their grain for music and tools. Between the Kota and Badaga there was a feeling of great competition, which sometimes led to some one-sided trading practices; it was usually the Kota who procured the advantage. The forest-dwelling Kurumba, who were dreaded sorcerers, had honey, canes, and occasionally fruits to offer, but their main contribution was protection against the supernatural. The Kota feared the Kurumba, and the Kurumba took advantage of this fact in their trade dealings, so that they always got more than they gave. Thus there was great latent hostility between these two tribes.

Silent trade is a specialized form of barter in which no verbal communication takes place. The earliest description that we know of was given by Herodotus, who told of silent trade between the Carthaginians and the people who lived on the western coast of Africa, beyond the Pillars of Hercules. In California, an instance of silent trade occurred between the Tubatulabel and the other tribes with whom they had peaceful relations. They would trade piñon nuts and tobacco for lengths of white clamshell disks which passed for currency among all the tribes of that region.

Silent trade need not involve actual face-to-face contact. Such is the case with many forest-dwelling people in the world. Carleton Coon has described how this system works:

The forest people creep through the lianas to the trading place, and leave a neat pile of jungle products, such as wax, camphor, monkeys' gall bladders, birds' nests for Chinese soup. They creep back a certain distance, and wait in a safe place. The partners to the exchange, who are usually agriculturalists with a more elaborate and extensive set of material possessions but who cannot be bothered stumbling through the jungle after wax when they have someone else to do it for them, discover the little pile, and lay down beside it what they consider its equivalent in metal cutting tools, cheap cloth, bananas, and the like. They too discreetly retire. The shy folk then reappear, inspect the two piles, and if they are satisfied, take the second one away. Then the opposite group comes back and takes pile number one, and the exchange is completed. If the forest people are dissatisfied, they can retire once more, and if the other people want to increase their offering they may, time and again, until everyone is happy.[16]

The reasons for silent trade can only be postulated, but in some situations trade may be silent for lack of a common language. More often it may serve to control hostility so as to keep relations peaceful. In a very real sense, good relations are maintained by preventing relations. Another possibility, which does not exclude the others, is that it makes exchange possible where

---

[16]Carleton S. Coon, *A Reader in General Anthropology* (New York: Holt, Rinehart and Winston, 1948), p. 594.

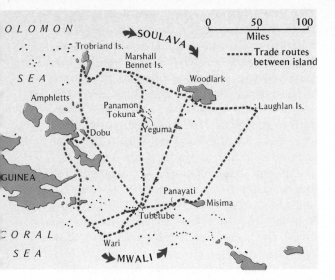

The ceremonial trading of necklaces and armbands in the Kula ring encourages trade throughout Melanesia.

The Kula Ring

Silent trade is one means by which the potential dangers of negative reciprocity may be controlled. But there are other means of accomplishing this as well. One is to find ways to make relations more sociable than they would otherwise be, in order to achieve a more balanced reciprocity. An example of this is the Kula of the Trobriand Islanders, first described by Malinowski.[17] The Kula is a trading system that involves the exchange of scarce goods, competition for prestige, and the all-important ceremonial exchange of highly valued necklaces and arm shells. Some of the first-class neck-

_____
[17] Bronislaw Malinowski, *Argonauts of the Western Pacific* (New York: Dutton, 1922).

> **Silent trade: A form of barter in which no verbal communication takes place.**

laces and arm shells have names and histories, analogous to Stradivarius violins, and, as Malinowski said, "always create a sensation when they appear in a district." The trade takes place throughout the islands, with the necklaces traveling in a clockwise fashion from island to island and the arm shells traveling counterclockwise. No one man holds these valuables very long, and each employs strategies to improve his position. It is the Trobriand Island version of how to win without actually cheating. But a man cannot be too crafty or no one will trade with him.

A few men on each island participate in the Kula and have trading partners on the other islands. An important man may have as many as 100 trading partners. These partnerships are lifetime relationships. Much ceremony and magic are attached to the Kula.

The Kula involves ocean voyages of 50 miles or more, and, as might be expected, more than necklaces and arm shells are exchanged. A man may simply exchange necklaces and arm shells with his Kula partner, but he is free to haggle and barter over other goods he has brought along on the trip for trading. In this way these island people have access to a whole range of material goods not found on their own islands.

The Kula is a most elaborate complex of ceremony, social relationships, economic exchange, travel, magic, and social integration. To see it only in its economic aspects is to misunderstand it completely. The Kula demonstrates once more the close interrelationship of cultural factors that is especially characteristic of non-Western societies.

problems of status might make verbal communication unthinkable. In any event, it provides for the exchange of goods between groups in spite of potential barriers.

Redistribution

In nonindustrial societies, where there is a sufficient surplus to support a government, income will flow into the public coffers in the form of gifts, taxes, and the spoils of war; then it will be distributed again. The chief or king has three motives in disposing of this income: the first is to maintain his position of superiority by a display of wealth; the second is to assure those who support him an adequate standard of living; and the third is to establish alliances outside of his territory.

The administration of the Inca empire in Peru was one of the most efficient the world has ever known, both in the collection of taxes and methods of control.[18] A census was kept of the population and resources. Tributes in goods and, more important, in services were levied. Each craftsman had to produce a specific quota

_____

[18] J. Alden Mason, *The Ancient Civilizations of Peru* (Baltimore, Md.: Penguin, 1957).

of goods from materials supplied by overseers. Forced labor might be used for agricultural work or work in the mines. Forced labor was also employed in a program of public works, which included a remarkable system of roads and bridges throughout the mountainous terrain, aqueducts that guaranteed a supply of water, and storehouses that held surplus food for use in times of famine. Careful accounts were kept of income and expenditures. A governmental bureaucracy had the responsibility for seeing that production was maintained and that commodities were distributed according to the regulations set forth by the ruling powers.

Through the activities of the government, **redistribution** took place. The ruling class lived in great luxury, but goods were redistributed to the common people when necessary. Redistribution is a pattern of distribution by which the exchange is not between individuals or between groups, but, rather, by which a proportion of the products of labor is funneled into one

This frieze from the staircase of Persepolis illustrates wealthy Persians bringing goods and livestock in tribute to the king; he redistributes the wealth to others.

source and is parceled out again as directed by a central administration. Taxes are a form of redistribution in the United States; people pay taxes to the government, some of which support the government itself while the rest are redistributed either in the form of cash, as in the case of welfare payments or the recent government loan to keep the Chrysler Corporation in business, or in the form of services, as in the case of food and drug inspection, construction of freeways, and the like. For a process of redistribution to be possible, a society must have a complex system of political organization as well as an economic surplus over and above people's immediate needs.

Distribution of Wealth

In societies in which people devote most of their time to subsistence activities, gradations of wealth are small, and systems

Conspicuous consumption: fur coats do not keep one any warmer than other kinds of coats which are far less expensive, easier to care for, and less wasteful of the world's wildlife resources. Furthermore, they would be more comfortable to wear with the fur inside rather than outside.

> **Redistribution:** A form of exchange in which goods flow into a central place, such as a market, and are distributed again.

> **Conspicuous consumption:** A term coined by Thorstein Veblen to describe the display of wealth for social prestige.

of reciprocity serve to distribute in a fairly equitable fashion what little wealth exists.

Display for social prestige, what economist Thorstein Veblen called **conspicuous consumption,** is a strong motivating force for the distribution of wealth in societies where some substantial surplus is produced. It has, of course, long been recognized that conspicuous consumption plays a prominent role in our own society as individuals compete with one another for prestige. Indeed, many North Americans spend much of their lives trying to impress others, and this requires the display of items symbolic of prestigious positions in life. The ultimate in prestigious statuses is that of someone who doesn't have to work for a living, and here lies the irony: people may work long and hard in order to acquire the things that will make it appear as if they belong to a nonworking class of society. This all fits very nicely into an economy based on consumer wants:

In an expanding economy based on consumer wants, every effort must be made to place the standard of living in the center of public and private consideration, and every effort must therefore be lent to remove material and psychological impediments to consumption. Hence, rather than feelings of restraint, feelings of letting-go must be in the ascendant, and the institutions supporting restraint must recede into the background and give way to their opposite.[19]

A form of conspicuous consumption may occur in nonindustrial societies, and a case in point is the potlatch, an important ceremony among the Indians of the northwest coast of North America. In traditional northwest coast society, potlatches were held when new high-ranking individuals assumed the office of chief; later they became a means by which persons of high status might compete for even higher status through the grandiose display, and even destruction, of wealth. Although outlawed for a while by the Canadian government, potlatching is again legal, and is alive and well today among peoples such as the Kwakiutl Indians, who are the subject of the following Original Study.

[19] Jules Henry, "A Theory for an Anthropological Analysis of American Culture," in Joseph G. Jorgensen and Marcello Truzzi, eds., *Anthropology and American Life* (Englewood Cliffs, N. J.: Prentice-Hall, 1974), p. 14.

ORIGINAL STUDY

The Potlatch[20]

Among the Kwakiutl Indians of British Columbia, the potlatch is the most important public ceremony for the announcement of significant events and the claiming of hierarchical names, hereditary rights, and privileges. Such announcements or claims are always accompanied by the giving of gifts from a host to all guests. The guests are invited to witness, and later to validate, a host's claims, and each receives gifts of varying worth according to his rank.

Potlatches are held to celebrate births, marriages, deaths, adoptions, or the coming of age of young people. They may also be given as a penalty for breaking a taboo, such as behaving frivolously or performing ineptly during a sacred winter dance. A potlatch to save face can be prompted by an accident even as trivial as the capsizing of a canoe or the birth of a deformed child. Among the most extravagant potlatches are those given for rivalry or vengeance.

All potlatches are public. The host, with the support of his family, numima (the next largest tribal subdivision), or tribe invites other families, numimas, or tribes. The size of the gathering reveals the affluence and prestige of the host. At the ceremony, he traces his line of descent and his rights to the claims he is making. Every name, dance or song used by the host must be acknowledged and legitimized by the guests. No announcement or claim is made without

[20] From *The Kwakiutl: Indians of British Columbia* by Ronald P. Rohner and Evelyn C. Rohner. Copyright © 1970 by Holt, Rinehart and Winston, Inc. Adapted and reprinted by permission of Holt, Rinehart and Winston, pp. 95, 97–98, 103–104.

feasting and the distribution of gifts. Gifts are given to guests in the order of their tribal importance and of a value relative to this prestige. Clearly high-ranking chiefs receive more gifts than lesser men. But the value and quantity of gifts distributed at a potlatch reflect less on the recipients than on the donor. The gifts he gives away—or in some cases the property he publicly destroys—are marks of his wealth, rank, generosity, and self-esteem. Over a period of time, they also measure the power and prestige that he will be able to maintain over others of high status. For, at a later potlatch, each high-ranking guest will try to return as much, or preferably more, than he received. To keep track of the gifts distributed and the precise hierarchy of guests, each donor has the assistance of a "potlatch secretary" whose records are needed to maintain correct social form and avoid offense.

Potlatch gifts vary widely, from money to property. They include boats, blankets, flour, kettles, fish oil, and, in former times, slaves. More recently, gifts have included sewing machines, furniture, even pool tables. Probably the most valuable potlatch material has little intrinsic worth but enormous symbolic value. These are coppers—large pieces of beaten sheet copper shaped like shields with a ridge running down the center of the lower half. They are painted with black lead and a design is incised through the paint. Each copper has a name and its potlatch history determines its value. One copper, called "All other coppers are ashamed to look at it," had been paid for with 7500 blankets; another known as "Making the house empty of wealth" was worth 5000 blankets.

During a potlatch, which can last several days and long into each night, speeches, songs, and dances are mixed with the giving of gifts, snacks and more lavish feasting. The host is not the only speaker; usually high-ranking guests also speak or supervise the singing, dancing, and drumming. Elaborate ceremonial costumes are worn by the speaker—who holds a "speaker's staff"—by dancers and musicians; the hall where the potlatch is held is decorated with painted hangings and tribal insignia.

All potlatch ceremonies are marked by exacting standards of etiquette and behavior. Impropriety, whether intentional or accidental, requires an immediate response. Mistakes in procedure, public quarreling, or an accident witnessed by others brings a sense of shame and indignity on its perpetrator, who must immediately "cover (or wipe off) the shame," making a payment to reestablish his self-esteem. Often, blankets are torn into strips and each witness is given a piece.

The Kwakiutl respond similarly to insults. Potlatchers sometimes deliberately insult a guest by calling his name out of order, by spilling oil on him, by throwing him his gift, or by presenting him with an inappropriate portion of food. The offended guest retaliates immediately by giving gifts himself, or by destroying something valuable of his own while denouncing the potlatcher. Violence sometimes erupts. On some occasions the host ignores a face-saving gesture of a guest and this may precipitate a rivalry potlatch. If a host mistakenly offends, a guest restores his pride by giving the host a reprimand gift.

Embarrassed by his carelessness, the correct host will make restitution in double the amount of the reprimand gift.

Rivalries also develop when two men compete for the same name, song, or other privilege. Each contestant recites his closest genealogical connection with the claim and tries to outdo his rival in the amount of property he can give away. In the heat of such rivalries, contestants sometimes break off a piece of copper, thereby destroying its value, and give the piece to their rival. The rival might then bring out his own copper of at least equal value, break it, and give both pieces back to the opponent. Great merit came to the man who threw his copper into the sea, "drowning it," thus showing his utter contempt for property and implying that his importance was such that what he destroyed was of little concern to him. At times this ostentatious destruction of property included canoes, house planks, blankets, and even slaves, in former days.

A Chilkat blanket from the Northwest Coast of North America. Because of their rarity, such blankets were valuable, and to display them was to demonstrate one's prosperity and power to others.

Among the Indians of the Northwest Coast of North America, a potlatch was necessary to validate the assumption of an important title or status. In the process, the necessary giving of gifts ensured the widespread distribution of goods. These pictures show an episode in a Kwakiutl potlatch, and a Kwakiutl chief holding a "copper." The value of coppers depended on how many times they were involved in potlatches; this one was worth 5000 blankets.

The witnesses to these dramatic acts of the potlatch act as judges to the claims; ultimately, they decide the victor. A powerful and prestigious man can sway public opinion by recognizing the claim of one contestant over another at a subsequent potlatch. Indeed, this is a basic principle of the potlatch; a successful potlatch in itself cannot legitimize a claim. It is the behavior of other hosts at later potlatches that validates a claim for once and for all.

In the case of the potlatch, a surplus is created for the express purpose of gaining prestige through a display of wealth and generous giving of gifts. But, unlike conspicuous consumption in our own society, the emphasis is not so much on the hoarding of goods which would make them unavailable to others. Instead, the emphasis is on giving away, or at least getting rid of one's wealth goods. Thus, potlatch serves as a leveling mechanism, preventing some individuals from accumulating too much wealth at the expense of other members of society.

Market Exchange

The flow of goods passing from owner to owner in the marketplace, as a form of exchange, is familiar to North Americans and is readily observable in foreign places. In fact, in the United States, there has been a revival and proliferation of "flea markets" where anyone, for a small fee, may display and sell handicrafts, secondhand items, farm produce, and paintings. There is excitement in the search for bargains and an opportunity for haggling. A carnival atmosphere prevails with eating, laughing, and conversation, and items may even be bartered without any cash passing hands. These flea markets, or farmers' markets, are similar to the markets of non-Western societies.

The first and most basic characteristic of the market in non-Western societies is that it always means a marketplace, a specific site where the actual goods are exchanged. (For a vivid example of a market, see the Color Portfolio on the Quiché Maya of Chichicastenango, p. 362). In non-Western societies, the marketplace is totally different from what is known in modern economics as the principle of market exchange. The market principle involves the system of establishing prices by the powers of supply and demand, no matter where the transactions are made. Although some of our market transactions do take place in a specific identifiable location— much of the trade in cotton, for example, takes place in New Orleans' Cotton Exchange—it is also quite possible for a North American to buy and sell goods without ever being on the same side of the continent.

This difference between "principle" and "place" clearly separates the market economy of modern industrial societies from the kind of marketing that prevails in traditional non-Western societies. When people talk about a market in today's world, the particular place where something is sold is often not important at all. For example, think of the way people speak of a "market" for certain types of automobiles, or for mouthwash.

The chief goods exchanged in non-Western markets are material items produced by the people, who bring to the mar-

In nearly every society, the market is an important focus of social as well as economic activity. In our own society, going shopping is a popular weekend social occasion for groups of family and friends. The fact that many shoppers dress up in their best clothes emphasizes the social aspect of the excursion. This photo shows a Spanish market.

A flea market in the United States—a common week-end event in many areas of the country.

The Chicago Commodities Exchange—where people are buying and selling even though no goods are present on the spot.

This muddy food market is located in a Hong Kong slum.

ket the produce and animals they have grown and raised and the handicrafts they have made. These they sell or exchange for items they want and cannot produce themselves. Land, labor, and occupations are not bought and sold as they are through the Western market economy. In other words, what happens in the marketplace has nothing to do with the price of land, the amount paid for labor, or the cost of services. The market is local, specific, and contained. Some noneconomic aspects of market-places in nonindustrial societies over-shadow the strictly economic aspects. Social relationships are as important in the marketplace as they are in other aspects of the economy. For example, dancers and other entertainers perform in the market-place. It is customary for people to gather there to hear news. In ancient Mexico, under the Aztecs, people were required by law to go to market at specific intervals, in order to be informed as to what was going on. Chiefs held court and settled judicial disputes at the market. Above all, the market is a gathering place where people renew friendships, see relatives, gossip, and keep up with the world.

CHAPTER SUMMARY

An economic system is the means by which goods are produced, distributed, and consumed. The study of the economics of nonliterate, nonindustrial societies can be undertaken only in the context of the total culture of each society. Each society solves the problem of getting its living within the limitations of its resources, land, capital, and technology and distributes goods according to its own priorities.

The work people do is a major productive resource, and the allotment of work is always governed by rules according to sex and age. Only a few broad generalizations can be made covering the kinds of work performed by men and women. The cooperation of many people working together is a typical feature of both nonliterate and literate societies. Specialization of craft is important even in societies with a very simple technology.

All societies regulate the way that the valuable resources of land will be allocated. In nonindustrial societies, individual ownership of land is rare; generally land is controlled by kinship groups such as the lineage or band. This system provides for greater flexibility of land use, since the size of the band territories, or of the bands themselves, can be adjusted according to change in land resources in any particular place. The technology of a people in the form of the tools they use, their knowledge of plants and animals, and their ability to control the environment determines their livelihood. The division of labor is a means of apportioning the technology among the members of a society so that it will not be lost and can be improved.

Production is dependent upon the natural environment. Hunters and gatherers follow the migrations of animals and the seasonal occurrence of fruits and vegetables. The yearly cycle of planting and harvesting circumscribes the productive activities of horticulturalists and agriculturalists.

Nonliterate people consume most of what they produce themselves. But there is an exchange of goods. The processes of distribution which may be distinguished are reciprocity, redistribution, and market exchange. Reciprocity is a transaction between individuals or groups involving the exchange of goods and services of roughly equivalent value. Usually it is prescribed by ritual and ceremony.

Barter and trade take place between groups. There are elements of reciprocity in trading exchanges, but there is a greater calculation of the relative value of goods exchanged. Barter is one form of negative reciprocity by which scarce goods from one group are exchanged for desirable goods from another group. Silent trade, which need not involve face-to-face contact, is a specialized form of barter in which no verbal communication takes place. It is one means by which the potential dangers of negative reciprocity may be controlled. A classic example of exchange between groups which partook of both reciprocity and sharp trading was the Kula ring of the Trobriand Islanders.

A complex economic and political organization is necessary for redistribution to take place. The government assesses each citizen a tax or tribute, uses the proceeds to support the governmental and religious elite, and redistributes the rest in the form of public services. The collection of taxes and delivery of government services in United States is a form of redistribution.

Display for social prestige is a motivating force in societies including our own where there is some surplus of goods produced. In our society, goods which are accumulated for display generally remain in the hands of those who accumulated them, whereas in other societies they are generally given away; the prestige comes from publicly divesting oneself of valuables.

Exchange in the marketplace serves to distribute goods in a district. In nonindustrial societies, the marketplace is always a specific site where material items produced by the people are exchanged. It also functions as a social gathering place and a news medium. The marketplace is in sharp contrast to the principle of market exchange that prevails in industrialized countries, where prices are set by supply and demand.

SUGGESTED READINGS

Bohannan, Paul, and George Dalton, eds. *Markets in Africa*. Evanston, Ill.: Northwestern University Press, 1962.
  Essays on the market system of African economic life. Studies economic activities ranging in complexity from aboriginal to present-day marketing systems. Discusses the noneconomic function of African markets. One article deals with current changes in Africa as they affect markets.
Heilbroner, Robert L. *The Making of Economic Society*, 4th ed. Englewood Cliffs, N.J.: Prentice-Hall, 1972.
  This book attempts to present some of the basic content of economics in the light of theory and history. Emphasis is on the rise and development of the market system, the central theme of Western economic heritage. It begins with the premarket economy of antiquity and carries the study through the market society, industrial revolution and technology, to capitalism and modern economic society.
Leclair, Edward E., Jr., and Harold K. Schneider. *Economic Anthropology: Readings in Theory and Analysis*. New York: Holt, Rinehart and Winston, 1968.
  A selection of significant writings in economic anthropology from the past 50 years. In the first section are theoretical papers covering the major points of view, and in the second are case materials selected to show the practical application of the various theoretical positions.
Nash, Manning. *Primitive and Peasant Economic Systems*. San Francisco: Chandler, 1966.
  This book studies the problems of economic anthropology, especially the dynamics of social and economic change, in terms of primitive and peasant economic systems. The book is heavily theoretical, but draws on the author's fieldwork in Guatemala, Mexico, and Burma.

Without cooperation, these high steel workers would
not get far with their task, any more than would hunters and gatherers in their food quest, farmers in the
growing of their crops, or pastoralists in the care of
their herds. The fact is that cooperation is basic to
human survival, and the formation of groups is what
makes human cooperation work.

PART THREE

THE FORMATION OF GROUPS

Solving the Problem of Cooperation

INTRODUCTION

One of the really important things to emerge from anthropological study is the realization of just how fundamental cooperation is to human survival. Through cooperation, all known humans handle even the most basic problems of existence, the need for food and protection—not only from the elements but from predatory animals and even each other. To some extent, this is true for all the higher primates. A baboon troop, for example, relies on its dominant males for defense and the maintenance of internal order. No matter how social they may be, though, cooperation in subsistence activities is not customary among nonhuman primates. Chimpanzees, for example, may share meat, but they don't have meat very often, and they don't normally share other kinds of food. By contrast, all humans show some form of cooperation in subsistence activities on a regular basis. At the least, this takes the form of the sexual division of labor as seen among hunting and gathering peoples, and this is probably as old as human hunting.

Just as cooperation seems to be basic to human nature, so the organization of groups is basic to effective cooperation. Humans form many kinds of groups, and each is geared to solving different kinds of problems with which people must cope. Social groups are important to humans also because they give identity and support to their members. Stemming from the parent-child bond and the interdependency of men and women, the family has traditionally been the starting point for people to collaborate in handling problems faced by all human groups. The central importance of the family is that it provides for economic cooperation between men and women while providing at the same time a proper setting within which child-rearing may take place. Another problem faced by all human societies is the need to control sexual activity, and this is the job of marriage. Given the close connection between sexual activity and the production of children, which must then be nurtured, a close interconnection between marriage and family structure is to be expected.

Many different marriage and family patterns exist the world over, but all societies have some form of marriage and some form of family organization. As we shall see in Chapter 8, the form of family and marriage organization is to a large extent shaped by the specific kinds of problems people must solve in particular environments.

The solutions to some organizational challenges are beyond the scope of the family. These include such matters as defense, allocation of resources, and provision of work forces for tasks too large to be undertaken by a family. Some societies develop formal political systems to perform these functions. Nonindustrial societies frequently meet these challenges through kinship groups, which we discuss in Chapter 9. These large, cohesive groups of individuals base their loyalty to one another on descent from a common ancestor or their relationship to a living individual. In societies where a great number of people are linked by kinship, these groups serve the important function of precisely defining the social roles of their members. In this way, they reduce the potential for tension that might arise from the sudden and unexpected behavior of an individual. They also provide their members with material security and moral support through religious and ceremonial activities.

Other important forms of human social groups are the subjects of Chapter 10. Where kinship ties do not provide for all of the organizational needs of a society, age grouping is one force that may be used to create social groups. In North America, as well as in many non-Western countries, today and in the past, the organization of persons by age is common. In many areas of the world, too, social groups based on the common interests of their members serve a vital function. In industrializing countries, they may help to ease the transition of rural individuals into the urban setting. Finally, groups based on social rank are characteristic of the world's civilizations, past and present. Such groups are referred to as social classes, and they are always ranked high versus low relative to one another. Class structure involves inequalities between classes and frequently is the means by which one group may dominate large numbers of other people. To the extent that social class membership cuts across lines of kinship, residence, age, or other group membership, it may work to counteract tendencies for a society to fragment into discrete special interest groups.

8 | Marriage and the Family

A Greenland Eskimo mother and her children. Caring for children is one of the basic functions of the human family.

PREVIEW

WHAT IS THE FAMILY?

The human family is a group composed of a woman, her dependent children, and at least one adult male joined through marriage or blood relationship. The family may take many forms, ranging all the way from a husband and wife with their children, as in our society, to a large group composed of several brothers and sisters with the sisters' children, as in southwest India among the Nayar. The particular form taken by the family is related to the specific problems with which it must deal.

WHY IS THE FAMILY UNIVERSAL?

Certain problems are universal in all human societies: the need to provide for the nurturance of children, the need to provide children with adult role models of the same sex, the need for cooperation between the sexes, and the need to control sexual relations. Because these are all interrelated, it is logical that they should be dealt with in the context of a single institution, the family.

WHAT ARE SOME OF THE PROBLEMS OF FAMILY ORGANIZATION?

Although the family exists to solve in various ways problems with which all peoples must deal, the different forms that the family may take are all accompanied by their own characteristic problems. Where families are small and relatively independent, as they are in our society, individuals are isolated from the aid and support of kin and must fend for themselves in many situations. By contrast, families that include several adults within the same large household must find ways of resolving various kinds of conflicts that may easily arise between their members.

The family, long regarded as a critically necessary, core social institution, today has become a matter for controversy and discussion. Women going outside the home to take jobs rather than staying home with children, young couples living together without the formality of marriage, and soaring divorce and delinquency rates have raised questions about the functions of the family in North American society and its ability to survive in a period of rapid social change. Evidence of the widespread interest in these questions can be seen in the convening, in 1980, of a White House Conference on Families.

Does the family, as presently constituted in North America, offer the best environment for bringing up children? Does it impose an inferior status on the woman, confined and isolated in the home, performing household and child-raising chores? Does the man, locked into an authoritarian role, suffer unduly in his personal development from bearing the sole responsibility of supporting the family? Are there adequate substitutes for people who have no family to care for them, such as old people and orphans? If the family as we know it today is found wanting, what are the alternatives?

Historical and cross-cultural studies of the family offer as many different family patterns as the fertile human imagination can invent. These different family patterns are not just interesting products of human inventiveness; they are solutions to the different sorts of problems with which people must cope. Different family forms, at the same time, themselves present certain sets of problems which somehow must be dealt with. How men and women in other societies live together in families can be studied, not as bizarre and exotic forms of human behavior, but as evidence of the potential of culture to find solutions to a variety of problems.

FUNCTIONS OF THE FAMILY

We may begin our discussion of the family by noting that reliance on group living for survival is a basic human characteristic. Humans appear to have inherited this from their primate ancestors, though they have developed it in their own distinctively human ways. Even among monkeys and apes, group living requires the participation of adults of both sexes. Because adult males tend to be larger and stronger than females, and because their teeth are usually more efficient for fighting, they are essential for the group's defense. Moreover, the close relationship between infants and their mothers renders the adult primate female less well suited than the males to handle defense.

Nurturance of Children

Taking care of the young is primarily the job of the adult primate female. Primate babies are born relatively helpless, and remain dependent upon their parents for a longer time than any other animals. This dependence is not only for food and physical care, but, as a number of studies have shown, primate infants deprived of normal maternal attention will not grow and develop normally. The protective presence of adult males makes it possible for the mothers to devote the necessary attention to their infants.

Among humans, the sexual division of labor has been developed beyond that of other primates. Until the recent advent of efficient contraceptive methods and synthetic infant formulas, the human female has for the most part been occupied much of the time with child-rearing. And human infants need no less active mothering than do the young of other primates. For one thing, they are even more helpless at birth, and for another, the period of infant dependency is longer in humans. Besides all this, studies have shown that human infants, no less than other primates, need more than just food and physical care if they are to develop normally. In fact, the cross-cultural research that we discussed in Chapter 5 suggests that the rate at which human infants develop in the first few years is directly related to the amount of contact they have with their mothers. But human females are always responsible for more than child-rearing alone. In the past, they have generally been engaged in economic activities which are compatible with their child-rearing role, which generally will not place them or their offspring at risk, and which complement the activities of men. Thus, men and women could share the results of their labors on a regular basis, as was discussed in Chapters 6 and 7.

An effective way to facilitate both economic cooperation between the sexes, as well as to provide for the necessary close bond between mother and child, is through the establishment of residential groups which include adults of both sexes. The differing nature of male and female roles, as these are defined by different cultures, requires a child to be closely associated with an adult of the same sex to serve as a proper model for the appropriate adult role. The presence of adult men and women in the same residential group provides for this.

This is not to say that the family is the only unit capable of providing these conditions. Theoretically, other arrangements might be possible. For example, groups of children might be raised by paired teams of trained male and female specialists as they are on the Israeli kibbutz. So the child-rear-

Group living among monkeys and apes requires the presence of adult males as well as adult females. This typical gorilla group is led by a silver-backed male (yawning). In the right foreground is a female, behind her is a black-backed male, and then another female. Facing the camera in front of the silver-backed male is a juvenile.

ing function alone cannot account for the observed universality of the human family, even though the function itself is universal. Obviously, other factors must be involved, as we shall see.

Control of Sexual Relations

A second distinctively human characteristic is the tendency for the human female, like the human male, to be more or less constantly receptive sexually. While this is not unusual on the part of male mammals in general, it is not usual on the part of females. Although frequent receptivity is characteristic of all female primates whose offspring have been weaned but who have not yet become pregnant again, only the human female is continually receptive. On the basis of clues from the behavior of other primates, anthropologists have speculated about the evolutionary significance of this trait. The best current explanation is that it arose as a side effect of persistent bipedal locomotion in early hominids.[1] The energetic requirements of this form of locomotion are such that endurance is impossible without a hormone output that is significantly greater than that of other primates. These hormones catalyze the steady release of energy in muscles that is required for endurance; at the same time, they make us the "sexiest" of all primates.

Although developed as an accidental by-product of something else, a common phenomenon in evolution, constant sexual receptivity on the part of females would have been advantageous to early hominids to the extent that it acted, not alone but with other factors, to tie members of both

sexes more firmly to the social groups so crucial to their survival. But at the same time that sexual activity can reinforce group ties, it can also be disruptive. This stems from the basic primate characteristic of male dominance. It is based on the fact that, on the average, males are bigger and more muscular than females, although this differentiation is less noticeable in modern *Homo sapiens* than it was in the earliest hominids. The males' larger size allows them to dominate females when the latter are at the height of their sexuality; this trait can be seen among baboons, gorillas, and, though less obviously, chimpanzees. With the continual sexual receptiveness of early hominid females, the dominant males may have attempted to monopolize females; an added inducement could have been the prowess of the female at food gathering. In hunting-gathering societies, the bulk of the food is usually provided by the gathering activities of women. Such a tendency to monopolize would introduce a competitive, combative element into hominid groupings—one that cannot be allowed to disrupt harmonious social relationships.

RULES OF SEXUAL ACCESS   We find that everywhere societies have cultural rules controlling sexual relations. In modern North American society, there is a blanket taboo on sexual activity outside of wedlock. One is supposed to establish a family, which we do through marriage. With this, a person establishes a continuing claim to the right of sexual access to another person. Actually, the United States is among a very small minority—about 5 percent—of all known societies whose formal codes of behavior prohibit any sexual involvement outside of marriage.[2] In other societies,

---

[1] James N. Spubler, "Continuities and Discontinuities in Anthropoid-Hominid Behavioral Evolution: Bipedal Locomotion and Sexual Reception," in N. A. Chagnon and William Irons, eds., *Evolutionary Biology and Human Social Behavior* (North Scituate, Mass.: Duxbury Press, 1979), pp. 454–461.

[2] F. Ivan Nye and Felix M. Berardo, *The Family: Its Structure and Interaction* (New York: Macmillan, 1973), p. 173.

things are often done quite differently. By way of example, we may look at the way things are done among the Nayar peoples of India.[3]

The Nayar peoples constitute a land-owning, warrior caste from southwest India. Among them, estates are held by corporations of sorts which are made up of kinsmen related in the female line. These kinsmen all live together in a large household, with the eldest male serving as manager.

Three transactions which take place among the Nayar are of concern to us here. The first occurs shortly before a girl undergoes her first menstruation. It involves a ceremony that joins together in a temporary union the girl with a young man. This union, which may or may not involve sexual relations, lasts for a few days and then breaks up. There is no further obligation on the part of either individual, although the woman and her future children will probably mourn for the man when he dies. What this transaction does is to establish the girl's eligibility for sexual activity with men who are approved by her household. With this, she is officially an adult.

The second transaction takes place when a girl enters into a sexual liaison with an approved man. This is a formal relationship, which requires the man to present her with gifts three times each year until such time as the relationship may be terminated. In return, the man may spend the nights with her. In spite of continuing sexual privileges, however, the man has no obligation to support his sex partner economically, nor is her home regarded as his home. In fact, she may have such an arrangement with more than one man at a time. Regardless of how many men are in-

> **Marriage:** A transaction and resulting contract in which a woman and man establish a continuing claim to the right of sexual access to one another, and in which the woman involved is eligible to bear children.

volved with a single woman, this second Nayar transaction, which is their version of marriage, clearly specifies who has sexual access to whom, so as to avoid conflict. We may define **marriage** as a transaction and resulting contract in which a woman and man establish a continuing claim to the right of sexual access to one another, and in which the woman involved is eligible to bear children.[4] Thus defined, marriage is universal, presumably because the problems with which it deals are universal.

In the absence of effective birth control devices, the usual result of sexual activity is that, sooner or later, the woman becomes pregnant. When this happens among the Nayar, some man must formally acknowledge paternity. This is done by his making gifts to the woman and the midwife. Though he may continue to take much interest in the child, he has no further obligations, for the education and support of the child are the obligation of the child's mother's brothers, with whom the child and its mother live. What we have in this third transaction is one that establishes the legitimacy of the child. In this sense, it is the counterpart of the registration of birth in our own culture, in which motherhood and fatherhood are spelled out. In our society, the father is supposed to be the mother's husband, but in numerous other societies, there is no such necessity.

Before leaving the Nayar, it is important to note that there is nothing here comparable to the family as we know it in our

---

[3] My interpretation of the Nayar follows Ward H. Goodenough, *Description and Comparison in Cultural Anthropology* (Chicago: Aldine, 1970), pp. 6–11.

[4] Goodenough, pp. 12–13.

own society. The group that forms the household does not include **affinal kin,** or those individuals joined by a **conjugal bond** established by marriage. The fact is, a household doesn't have to be a family as we know it. Among the Nayar, the household is composed wholly of what we often call "blood" relatives, but which are technically known as **consanguineal kin.** Sexual relations are with those who are not consanguineal kin, and so live in other households. And this brings us to another human universal, the incest taboo.

THE INCEST TABOO All societies at all times in history have formulated a rule, called the **incest taboo,** that prohibits sexual relations between certain close relatives. The universality of the rule has fascinated anthropologists and other students of human behavior. In all known societies sexual relations are prohibited between parent and child and (with few exceptions) between siblings as well. It has become a matter of serious import for anthropologists to explain why incest should always be regarded as such a loathsome thing.

Many explanations have been given. Of those that have gained some popularity at one time or another, the simplest and least satisfactory is based on "human nature"—that is, some instinctive horror of incest. It is also documented that human beings raised together have less sexual attraction for one another, but by itself this argument may simply substitute the result for the cause. The incest taboo ensures that children and their parents, who are constantly in intimate contact, avoid regarding one another as sexual objects. Besides this, if there were an instinctive horror of incest, we would be hard pressed to account for the not infrequent violations of the incest taboo, such as occur in our own society, or for cases of institutionalized incest, such as

that which required the head of the Inca empire in Peru to marry his own sister.

Various psychological explanations of the incest taboo have been advanced at one time or another. Sigmund Freud tried to account for it in his psychoanalytic theory of the unconscious. The son desires the mother, creating a rivalry with the father. (Freud called this the Oedipus complex; see Chapter 5.) He must suppress these feelings or earn the wrath of the father, who is far more powerful than he. The attraction of the daughter to the father, or the Electra complex, places her in rivalry with her mother. Freud's theory can be viewed as an elaboration of the reasons for a deep-seated aversion to sexual relations within the family. Some other psychologists have endorsed the belief that young children can be emotionally scarred by sexual experiences, which they may have interpreted as violent and frightening acts of aggression. The incest taboo thus protects children against sexual advances by older members of the family. A closely related theory is that the incest taboo helps prevent girls who are socially and emotionally too young for motherhood from becoming pregnant.

Early students of genetics thought that the incest taboo precluded the deleterious effects of inbreeding. While this is true, it is also true that as with domestic animals, inbreeding can increase desired characteristics as well as deleterious ones. Furthermore, deleterious effects will show up sooner than would otherwise be the case, so that whatever genes are responsible for them may be more quickly eliminated from the population. On the other hand, preference for a genetically different mate does tend to maintain a higher level of genetic diversity within a population, and in evolution this generally works to a species' advantage. Without genetic diversity a species cannot adapt biologically to a changed environment should this become necessary.

A truly convincing explanation of the incest taboo has yet to be advanced. Yet there are persistent hints that it may be a cultural elaboration of an underlying biological tendency toward avoidance of inbreeding. Studies of animal behavior have shown such a tendency to be common among those species that are relatively large, long-lived, slow to mature, and intelligent. Humans qualify for membership in this group on all counts. So do a number of other primates, including those most closely related to humans—chimpanzees. Although they exhibit few sexual inhibitions, chimpanzees do tend to avoid inbreeding between siblings and between females and their male offspring. So perhaps the tendency for human children to look outside the group in which they have been raised for sex partners is not just the result of the incest taboo after all. Support for this is often said to come from studies that show that children raised together on an Israeli kibbutz, although not required or even encouraged to do so, almost invariably marry outside their group. But then, most Israeli youths leave their kibbutz in their late teens for service in the armed forces, and are most likely to be involved with outsiders of the opposite sex at about the time they are ready to consider marriage. An even greater problem, however, comes from detailed census records made in Roman Egypt that conclusively demonstrate that brother-sister marriages were an entirely normal occurrence among ordinary members of the farming class.[5]

If indeed there is a biological basis for inbreeding avoidance among humans, it clearly is far from being completely effective in its operation, nor is its mechanism

---

[5] Edmund Leach, *Social Anthropology* (Glasgow: Fontana Paperbacks, 1982), p. 51.

Affinal kin: Relatives by marriage.

Conjugal bond: The bond between a man and a woman who are married.

Consanguineal kin: Relatives by birth; that is, "blood" relatives.

Incest taboo: The prohibition of sexual relations between immediate kin, such as parent and child or siblings.

Endogamy: Marriage within a particular group or category of individuals.

Exogamy: Marriage outside the group.

understood. To say that certain genes program specifically for inbreeding avoidance, as some have claimed, is not warranted on the basis of existing evidence, nor is it likely based upon what we do know about the workings of human genes.

ENDOGAMY AND EXOGAMY Whatever its cause, the utility of the incest taboo can be seen by examining its effects on social structure. Closely related to prohibitions against incest are rules against **endogamy,** or marriage within a group of related individuals. If the group is defined as just one immediate family, then almost all societies prohibit endogamy and practice **exogamy,** or marriage outside the group. However, if the group of relatives covered by the incest taboo is enlarged to include more members—second and third cousins, for example—then we find that endogamy may be a common practice. For example, Scottish Highlanders traditionally married within the network of alliances of the family clan,

Claude Lévi-Strauss (1908–   )

Claude Lévi-Strauss is the leading exponent of French Structuralism, which sees culture as a surface representation of underlying mental structures that have been affected by a group's physical and social environment, as well as its history. Thus, cultures may vary considerably from one another, even though the structure of the human thought processes responsible for them is the same everywhere.

Human thought processes are structured, according to Lévi-Strauss, into contrastive pairs of polar opposites such as light versus dark, good versus evil, nature versus culture, raw versus cooked. The ultimate contrastive pair is that of "self" versus "others," which is necessary for true symbolic communication to take place, and upon which culture depends. Communication is reciprocal exchange, which is extended to include goods and women. Hence, the incest taboo stems from this fundamental contrastive pair. From this universal taboo stem the many and varied marriage rules which have been described by ethnographers.

strengthening its political and economic position.

Sir Edward Tylor, in fact, advanced the proposition that alternatives to inbreeding were either "marrying out or being killed out."[6] Our ancestors, he suggested, discovered the advantage of intermarriage to create bonds of friendship. Claude Lévi-Strauss elaborated on this premise. He saw exogamy as the basis of a distinction between early hominid life in isolated endogamous groups and the life of *Homo sapiens* in a supportive society with an accumulating culture. Alliances with other groups, established and strengthened by marriage ties, make possible a sharing of culture.

In a roundabout way, exogamy also helps to explain some exceptions to the incest taboo, such as that of brother and sister marriage within the royal families of ancient Egyptians, Incans, and Hawaiians. Members of such royal families were considered semidivine, and their very sacredness usually kept them from marrying mere mortals. The brother and sister married to keep intact the godliness and purity of the royal line.[7] Of course, this is of no help in explaining the brother-sister marriages that were common among farmers of Roman Egypt, which remain an enigma.

FORM OF THE FAMILY

In our discussion of the Nayar, we saw that their household was not at all like the family as we know it in our society. If we define the family in terms with which we are familiar as requiring fathers, mothers, and children, then the Nayar do not have fami-

---

[6] Quoted in Roger M. Keesing, *Cultural Anthropology: A Contemporary Perspective* (New York: Holt, Rinehart and Winston, 1976), p. 286.

[7] Keesing, p. 285.

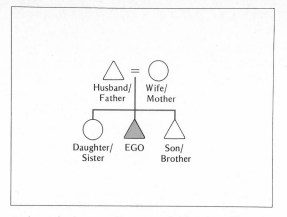

Anthropologists use diagrams of this sort to illustrate the relationships formed through marriage. The diagram always begins with a hypothetical individual, called Ego, and then demonstrates the kinship and marital ties in Ego's immediate family. This diagram shows the relationships in a nuclear family such as is found in our own society. Only two generations are represented, but all possible relationships between the individuals can be determined from the diagram.

A typical North American nuclear family today, shown together in their backyard.

Family: A group composed of a woman, her dependent children, and at least one adult male joined through marriage or blood relationship.
Nuclear family: A family unit consisting of husband, wife, and dependent children.
Consanguine family: A family consisting of related women, their brothers, and the offspring of the women.

lies. A somewhat less ethnocentric definition of the **family** sees it as a group composed of a woman and her dependent children and at least one adult male joined through marriage or blood relationship.[8] The North American family is a conjugal one, formed on the basis of marital ties between husband and wife. The basic unit of mother, father, and dependent children is referred to as the **nuclear family;** other forms of conjugal families are polygynous and polyandrous families, which may be thought of as aggregates of nuclear families with one spouse in common. A polygynous family includes the multiple wives of a single husband, while a polyandrous family includes the multiple husbands of a single wife.

An alternative to the conjugal family is the **consanguine family,** which consists of women and their brothers and the dependent offspring of the women. In such societies, men and women get married, but do not live together as husbands and mates. Rather, they spend their lives in the households in which they grew up, with the men "commuting" for sexual activity with their wives.

[8] Goodenough, p. 19.

Consanguine families are not common; the classic case is the Nayar household group. But consanguine families are found elsewhere, as among the Tory Islanders, a Roman Catholic, Gaelic-speaking fisher folk living off the coast of Ireland. These people do not marry until they are in their late twenties or early thirties, by which time there is tremendous resistance to breaking up existing household arrangements. The Tory Islanders look at it this way:

"Oh well, you get married at that age it's too late to break up arrangements that you have already known for a long time. . . . You know, I have my sisters and brothers to look after, why should I leave home to go live with a husband? After all, he's got his sisters and his brothers looking after him."[9]

Because the community numbers only a few hundred people, husbands and wives are within easy commuting distance of one another.

The Nuclear Family

In North American society, the nuclear family, a form of conjugal family, has become the ideal. It is not considered desirable for young people to live with their parents beyond a certain age, nor is it considered a moral responsibility for a couple to take their aged parents into their home when the old people are no longer able to care for themselves. Additional family members are no longer an economic asset but an expense.

The nuclear family as the usual family form is also found in societies that live in harsh environments, such as the Eskimos. The Eskimo husband and wife each have

their work to do. In the winter, these little families roam the vast arctic wilderness in search of food. The husband hunts and makes shelters. The wife cooks, is responsible for the children, and makes and keeps the clothing in good repair. One of her chores is to chew her husband's boots to soften the leather for the next day, so that he can resume his search for game. The wife and her children could not survive without the husband, and life for a man is unimaginable without a wife.

Certain parallels can be drawn between the contemporary nuclear family in industrial societies and families living on

Co-wives in a West African (Kpelle) society hull rice together. Polygyny is one device that facilitates cooperation among women where women's work is hard.

---

[9] Robin Fox, Interview for KOCE-TV in Los Angeles, December 3, 1981.

the bare edge of survival. In both cases, the family is an independent unit that must fend for itself; this creates a strong dependence of individual members on one another. There is little help from outside in the event of emergencies or catastrophes. When their usefulness is at an end, the elderly are cared for only if it is feasible. In the event of death of the mother or father, life becomes precarious for the child. Yet this form of family is well adapted to a life that requires a high degree of mobility. For the Eskimo, this mobility permits the hunt for food; for North Americans, it is the hunt for jobs and improved social status that requires a mobile form of family unit.

MARRIAGE

Although, as we saw in our discussion of the Nayar, marriage does not have to result in the formation of a new family, it can easily serve this purpose, in addition to its main function of indicating who has continuing sexual access to whom. This is precisely what is done in the case of conjugal families, including nuclear families.

Monogamy, Polygyny, and Group Marriage

Monogamy, or the taking of a single spouse, is the form of marriage with which we are most familiar. It is also the most common, primarily for economic rather than moral reasons. A man must be fairly wealthy to be able to afford **polygyny,** or marriage to more than one wife. Among the Kapauku of western New Guinea,[10] the ideal is to have as many wives as possible, and a woman actually urges her husband to

---

[10] Leopold Pospisil, *The Kapauku Papuans of West New Guinea* (New York: Holt, Rinehart and Winston, 1963).

> **Monogamy: Marriage in which an individual has a single spouse.**

> **Polygyny: The marriage custom of a man having several wives at the same time; a form of polygamy.**

spend money on acquiring additional wives. She even has the legal right to divorce him if she can prove that he has money for bride-price and refuses to remarry. Wives are desirable because they work in the fields and care for pigs, by which wealth is measured. But not all men are wealthy enough to afford bride-price for multiple wives.

Although most marriages around the world tend to be monogamous, polygyny is the preferred form in by far a majority of the world's societies. Furthermore, the vast majority of primate species are not "monogamous" in their mating patterns. Although some smaller species of South American monkeys, a few island-dwelling populations of leaf-eating Old World monkeys, and all of the smaller apes (gibbons and siamangs) do mate for life with a single individual of the opposite sex, none of these are closely related to human beings, nor do "monogamous" primate species ever display the degree of anatomical differences between males and females that is characteristic of our closest primate relatives, or that was characteristic of our own ancient ancestors. Thus, it is not likely that the human species began its career as a monogamous species. More likely, monogamy developed as economic circumstances made other forms of marriage impractical or less useful.

Although monogamy and polygyny are the most common forms of marriage in the world today, other forms do occur, however rarely. **Polyandry,** the marriage of a woman to several men at the same time, is known in only a few societies, perhaps in part because a man's life expectancy is shorter than a woman's, and male infant mortality is high, so a surplus of men in a society is unlikely. Another reason is that it limits a man's descendants more than any other pattern. **Group marriage,** in which several men and women have sexual access to one another, also occurs but rarely. Even in communal groups today, among young people seeking alternatives to modern marriage forms, group marriage seems to be a transitory phenomenon, despite the publicity it may receive.

The Levirate and the Sororate

If a husband dies, leaving a wife and children, it is often the custom that the wife marry one of the brothers of the dead man. This custom, called the **levirate,** not only provides social security for the widow and her children but also is a way for the husband's family to maintain their rights over her sexuality and her future children: it acts to preserve the bonds established. When a man marries the sister of his dead wife, it is called the **sororate.** In societies that have the levirate and sororate, the relationship between the two families is maintained even after the death of a spouse; in essence, the family supplies another spouse to take the place of the member who died. And in such societies, an adequate supply of brothers and sisters is generally ensured by the structure of the kinship system (discussed in Chapter 9).

Serial Marriage

Perhaps the most exotic and bizarre of marriage forms is our own **serial marriage.**

In this form, the man or the woman either marries or lives with a series of partners in succession. The term was used in the recent past by sociologists and anthropologists to describe the marital patterns of West Indians and lower-class urban blacks. A series of men fathered the children, who remained with the mother. An adult man's loyalties might be to his mother rather than his present wife, and he, too, might bring his children to his mother to care for. Usually, the grandmother was the head of the household (which amounted to a consanguine family); it was she who cared for all the children, while the daughters worked to support the whole group.

Middle-class white North Americans have taken up a variant of this pattern. The children, born out of a series of marriages, remain with the mother. In a society such as ours, in which a major value is the well-being and happiness of each individual, divorce may not necessarily signal social disorganization, but a liberating of the individual. Serial marriage may be evolving as an alternative to the extreme form of the nuclear family as it has existed in the United States.

Choice of Mate

The Western egalitarian ideal that an individual should be free to marry whomever he or she chooses is an unusual arrangement, certainly not one that is universally embraced. However, desirable such an ideal may be in the abstract, it is fraught with difficulties, and certainly contributes to the apparent instability of the family in modern North American society. An interesting light is cast on these difficulties in the following Original Study, written by Jules Henry in 1966.

The idea of "romantic love" is medieval in origin. Only aristocrats could afford it.

Polyandry: The marriage custom of a woman having several husbands at one time; a form of polygamy.

Group marriage: Marriage in which several men and women have sexual access to one another.

Levirate: A marriage custom according to which a widow marries a brother of her dead husband.

Sororate: A marriage custom according to which a widower marries his dead wife's sister.

Serial marriage: A marriage form in which a man or a woman marries or lives with a series of partners in succession.

ORIGINAL STUDY

The Metaphysic of Youth, Beauty, and Romantic Love[11]

The emphasis on youth, beauty and romantic love is a sustaining force in our economy. While it is ancient, having roots in the Judeo-Christian and Greek traditions—this emphasis, amounting to an implied metaphysic, has reached unparalleled expansive significance in our economy, which must monetize everything in order to remain viable. Without the pecuniary exploitation of romantic love and female youth and beauty the women's wear, cosmetics and beauty-parlour industries would largely disappear and the movies, TV and phonograph-record businesses would on the whole cease to be economically functional, degenerating, perhaps, to the relative economic insignificance of education. It is true that women would still need clothes to protect themselves from the elements, and that civilization demands that they cover their bodies

[11] Jules Henry, "The Metaphysic of Youth, Beauty, and Romantic Love," in Seymour Farber and Roger Wilson, eds., *The Challenge to Women* (New York: Basic Books, 1966).

even in hot weather; but the billions spent on women's wear these days is more in the interest of making women attractive than in protecting them from the cold. Furthermore, without the erotizing effects of the metaphysic of youth, beauty and romantic love, cigarettes, hard and soft drinks, beer, automobiles and so on would not sell nearly as well. As a matter of fact, even men's wear and toiletries could not be marketed as efficiently without an adoring, pretty woman (well under thirty-five years of age) looking at a man wearing a stylish shirt or sniffing at a man wearing a deodorant.

While the saturation of the pecuniary media with the metaphysic of youth, beauty and romantic love should not be attacked, lest the economy collapse—just as if we suddenly attacked the profit motive; and while the metaphysic speeds up courtship and the birthrate, thus adding further to expenditures and to the gross national product, obsession with youth, beauty and romantic love punishes the woman who, having reached thirty-five, begins to see in the mirror the fact that the metaphysic and its implied defences no longer exist for her. We have a metaphysic for beauty and youth but none for the years when these are gone. In this sense the West is probably unique; for while throughout history culture has provided a set of principles for guidance through every stage of life, in the contemporary West ageing hangs in nothingness. For many a woman of thirty-five and beyond therefore it is as if the universe had physically withdrawn and left her hurtling into nothingness. And thus, deprived of the youth, beauty and romantic love, which once made them feel safe, many women feel they have no place to go but down.

Since a metaphysic is a system of first principles underlying a subject of inquiry, since our subject of inquiry is urban woman, and since she is without a metaphysic after forty, we are bound to state what the metaphysic was in the first place. It should be mentioned, in passing, that it is not necessary that a metaphysic be 'true,' for it can just as well be a system of principles supporting a false position; and the history of thought has shown that this is usually the case.

The metaphysic of which I speak embodies the following principles: (1) A man validates himself by working and supporting; a woman validates herself by getting a man. (2) A man does, a woman is. Man performs; woman attracts. Behind this principle lies the fact that urban woman has lost most of her productive economic functions; and even when she does productive labour, the money she earns is used largely to expand the family's life style rather than to create fundamental conditions for living. (3) Existence must be made aesthetically pleasing. (4) Since man's province is that of action, it is up to the woman to make life aesthetically attractive to him, and to display his masculinity by being attractive. (5) From all this it follows that women must be beautiful. (6) Since beauty is by definition physical and since the body loses its freshness even before the end of the child-bearing years, a woman is in danger of losing her husband in this period. To these principles, deriving from the metaphysic of youth and beauty, add the following from romantic love. (7) Since in our culture marriage is not arranged by parents and the spouse is not determined by

> **Affines: Relatives by marriage.**

highly specific social rules, every woman must find and attract a husband for herself. Often in traditional peasant China a girl did not see her husband before the wedding day, for the marriage was arranged by the parents. In many tribal cultures, on the other hand, a girl's husband is selected for her, even before birth, because she has to marry a specific person according to rules prescribed by tradition. (8) Romantic love is based on obsession with the beloved, to the exclusion of all others, and requires the idealization of the object. It is clear meanwhile that grand obsession and idealization can rarely withstand the rigours of marriage. It follows from principles (7) and (8) that as youth and beauty wane and as the realities of marriage erode obsession and idealization, urban woman in our culture is bound to become uneasy, for what once seemed to protect her from nothingness seems to be going away.

Summing up, in a somewhat oversimplified way: as long as a woman has little to offer but her physical person, love as obsession and idealization will fade as she gets old and as the daily collisions of marriage make living together difficult or merely routine.

Since in our urban culture marriage is not consolidated through cooperative work but through a complicated hallucination of intangibles based on obsession and idealization, the loss of youth and beauty may appear to threaten a woman whose youth and beauty are passing. Meanwhile, since she probably knows many cases in which an older man has deserted his wife for a younger and more attractive woman, a wife cannot but ask, "When will it happen to me?"

Now, we should not conclude that all North Americans subscribe or succumb to the metaphysic of youth, beauty, and romantic love. On the other hand, we can see how North Americans are nudged by their culture in such a way that marriages may all too easily be based on trivial and transient characteristics. In no other part of the world are such chances taken with something as important as marriage.

AFFINES AND ALLIES. Among the Arapesh, as described by Margaret Mead, the father chooses his son's wife, who must be from another clan. Her brothers and her male cousins, who will be his son's brothers-in-law and his grandchildren's maternal uncles, must be "good hunters, successful gardeners, slow to anger, and wise in making decisions."[12] Rather than a necessary evil, the Arapesh regard marriage primarily as an opportunity to acquire **affines,** or relatives by marriage, and thereby increase the warm family circle within which one's descendants may then live.

_____

[12] Margaret Mead, *Sex and Temperament in Three Primitive Societies*, 3d ed. (New York: Morrow, 1963), p. 67.

In Gopalpur, a small village in southern India, marriage to any person related through the paternal line is regarded as incest.[13] Marriage to relatives of a sister or a mother is looked for. Brides are usually brought in from another village and must be in the same caste.

In societies where the family is the most powerful institution exercising social control over individuals, marriages tend to be arranged for the economic and political advantage of the family unit, as, for example, in feudal Europe, traditional China and

India, and until most recent times, in Japan. The marriage of two individuals who must spend their whole lives together and raise their children together is only incidental to the serious matter of making allies of two families by means of the marriage bond. Marriage involves a transfer of rights between families, including rights to property and rights over the children, as well as sexual rights.

In many societies, marriage and the establishment of a family are considered far too important to be left to the whims of young people. The function of marriage in such cases is often economic in nature and, for wealthy and powerful families, politi-

---

[13] Alan R. Beals, *Gopalpur: A South Indian Village* (New York: Holt, Rinehart and Winston, 1972), p. 25.

Marriage is a means of creating alliances between groups of people—the relatives of the bride and those of the groom. Since such alliances have important economic and political implications, the decision to marry cannot be left in the hands of two young and inexperienced people. Below, a ceremony takes place in a Philippine community in which the relatives of a boy and girl seal plans for the marriage. The picture at right was taken at the wedding of Princess (now Queen) Elizabeth of England and Prince Philip of Greece.

cal. Even in our own society, the children of wealthy and powerful families are segregated in private schools and carefully steered toward a "proper" marriage. A careful reading of announced engagements in the society pages of the *New York Times* provides clear evidence of such family alliances.

Divorce

Like marriage, divorce in non-Western societies is a matter of great concern to the families of the couple. Since marriage is primarily not a religious but an economic matter, divorce arrangements can be made for a variety of reasons and with varying degrees of difficulty.

Among the Gusii of Kenya, sterility or impotence were grounds for a divorce. Among the Chenchu of Hyderabad and the Caribou Indians of Canada, divorce was discouraged after children were born, and a couple were usually urged by their families to adjust their differences. A Zuni woman, on the other hand, might divorce her husband at any time by placing his belongings outside the door to indicate he was no longer welcome in the household. Divorce was fairly common among the Yahgan, who lived at the southernmost tip of South America, and was seen as justified if the husband was considered cruel or failed as a provider.

Divorce in these societies seems familiar and even sensible, considered in the light of our own entangled arrangements. In one way or another, the children are taken care of. An adult unmarried woman is almost unheard of in most non-Western societies; a divorced woman will soon remarry. In many societies, economic consid-

erations are often the strongest motivation to marry. A man of New Guinea does not marry because of sexual needs, which he can readily satisfy out of wedlock, but because he needs a woman to make pots and cook his meals, to fabricate nets and weed his plantings.[14] A man without a wife among the Australian aborigines is in an unsatisfactory position, since he has no one to supply him regularly with food or firewood.[15] In all societies, the smallest economic unit is the family.

It is of interest to note that divorce rates in Western societies are low when compared to those in some societies, notably matrilineal societies such as that of the Zuni. Yet they are high enough to cause many North Americans to worry about the future of marriage and the family in the contemporary world. Undoubtedly, the causes of divorce in our society are many and varied. Among them are the trivial and transient characteristics that we have already discussed on which marriages may all too easily be based. Then, too, the stresses and strains inherent in the family organization typical of our society may result in the breakup of some marriages. We will discuss the nature of these at the end of this chapter.

Another contributing factor may relate to the demise of sex-role stereotypes. Although the sexual division of labor served humanity well in the past, the demise of sex-role stereotypes is generally considered a good thing. In modern complex societies, they waste talents and abilities needed by society and greatly restrict a woman's

[14] Robert Lowie, cited by Leslie White, *The Science of Culture: A Study of Man and Civilization* (Garden City, N.Y.: Doubleday, 1969).

[15] Charles W. Hart and Arnold R. Pilling, *Tiwi of North Australia* (New York: Holt, Rinehart and Winston, 1960).

chance for personal fulfillment. It is, of course, perfectly possible to do away with the stereotypes without at the same time doing away with the opportunity for individual men and women to cooperate in tasks that complement each other, so as to ensure relatively stable pair bonds. Unfortunately, in societies such as ours, which place high values on individual competitiveness, it is all too easy for this cooperative arrangement, one of the essential bases for family life, to break down.

As if these disruptive forces were not enough to contend with, a weakening of the taboo on all sexual activity out of wedlock further diminishes the need for a stable pair bond between individual men and women. With modern contraceptive devices, sexual activity need not lead to the birth of children, and even if it does, the important child-rearing functions once handled by the family are now easily met by other institutional arrangements. When all is said and done, we should perhaps not be dismayed that divorce is as common as it is in our society. The wonder of it is that divorce rates are not higher.

The Extended Family

The small nuclear family of industrialized societies has evolved from the larger **extended family** of the farm, a combination of conjugal and consanguine families, which might include grandparents, mother and father, unmarried brothers and sisters, perhaps a spinster aunt, and a stray cousin or two. All these people, related by various ties of blood or marriage, lived and worked together. Because members of the younger generation brought their spouses (husbands or wives) to live in the family, extended families, like consanguine families, had continuity through time. As older members died off, new members were being born into the family.

Such families still survive in some communities along the Maine coast.[16] They developed in response to a unique economy featuring a mix of farming and seafaring, coupled with an ideal of self-sufficiency. Because family farms were incapable of providing self-sufficiency, seafaring was taken up as an economic alternative. Since periodic depression afflicted seagoing com-

> **Extended family: A collection of nuclear families, related by ties of blood, that live together.**

merce, family farming remained important as a cushion against hard times. The need for sufficient manpower to tend the farm, while at the same time furnishing officers, crew, or both for locally owned vessels, was satisfied by the custom of a couple, when they married, of settling on the farm of either the bride's or the groom's parents. Thus, most people spent their lives cooperating on a day-to-day basis in economic ac-

---

[16]William A. Haviland, "Farming, Seafaring and Bilocal Residence on the Coast of Maine," *Man in the Northeast*, No. 6 (Fall 1973), pp. 31–44.

Divorce rates, selected countries 1955–1975.

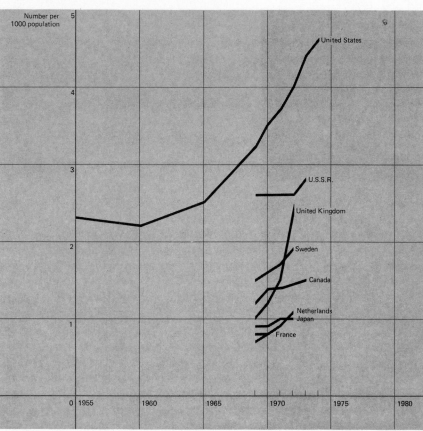

Extended families are still found in some parts of rural North America. All the members of this Kentucky family are descended from the couple at the back of the photo.

tivities with close relatives, all of whom lived together on the same farm.

The Tanala of Madagascar also formed extended families.[17] When the sons grew up and married, they brought their wives to live in houses close to the parental home. The head of the family was the father, who made the important decisions concerning the agricultural activities of the family. If the sons worked on the outside, they gave their earnings to the father for the purchase

of new cattle or for other family needs. The family worked together as a group and dealt with outsiders as a single unit.

Extended families living together in a single household were the most important social unit among the Zuni Pueblo Indians of New Mexico.[18] Ideally, the head of the household was an old woman; her married daughters, their husbands, and their children lived with her. The women of the household owned land, but it was tilled by

[17] E. Adamson Hoebel, *Anthropology: The Study of Man,* 3d ed. (New York: McGraw-Hill, 1966), p. 434.

[18] Wendell H. Oswalt, *Other Peoples, Other Customs* (New York: Holt, Rinehart and Winston, 1972), p. 294.

the men (usually their husbands). When extra help was needed during the harvest, for example, other male relatives, or friends, or persons designated by local religious organizations, formed work groups and turned the hard work into a party. The women performed household tasks, such as the making of pottery, together. Over the past decade or so, there have been various attempts on the part of young people in our own society to reinvent a form of extended family living. Their families are groups of nuclear families that own property in common and live together. It is further noteworthy that the life-style of these modern families often emphasizes the kinds of co-operative family ties to be found in the rural North American extended family of old, where this family pattern provided a labor pool for the many tasks required for economic survival.

RESIDENCE PATTERNS Where some form of conjugal or extended family is the norm, incest taboos require that at least the husband or wife must move to a new household upon marriage. There are five common patterns of residence that a newly married couple may adopt:

1. A woman may live with the family in which her husband grew up. This is called **patrilocal residence.**

2. A man may live with the family in which his wife grew up. This is called **matrilocal residence.**

3. A married couple may have the choice of living with the family in which either the husband or the wife grew up. This arrangement is called **ambilocal** or **bilocal residence.**

4. A married couple may form a household in an independent location. This arrangement is referred to as **neolocal residence.**

Patrilocal residence: A residence pattern in which a married couple lives in the locality associated with the husband's father's relatives.

Matrilocal residence: A residence pattern in which a married couple lives in the locality associated with the wife's relatives.

Ambilocal or bilocal residence: A pattern in which a married couple may choose either matrilocal or patrilocal residence.

Neolocal residence: A residence pattern in which a married couple form a household in a location that has no connection with either the husband or the wife.

Avunculocal residence: Residence of a married couple with the husband's mother's brother.

5. The final pattern is far less common than any of the others: a married couple may live with the husband's mother's brother. This is called **avunculocal residence.**

There are variations of these patterns, but they need not concern us here.

Why do different societies practice different patterns of residence? Briefly, the prime determinants of residence are ecological circumstances, although other factors enter in as well.[19] If these make the role of the man predominant in subsistence, patrilocal residence is the likely result. This is even more likely if in addition men own

[19] Raoul Naroll, "Holocultural Theory Tests," in Raoul Naroll and Frada Naroll, eds., *Main Currents in Cultural Anthropology* (New York: Appleton-Century-Crofts, 1973), p. 320.

property that can be accumulated, if polygyny is customary, if warfare is prominent enough to make cooperation among men important, and if there is elaborate political organization, in which men wield authority. Where patrilocal residence is customary, it is often the case that the bride must move to a different band or community. In such cases, her parents' family is not only losing the services of a useful family member, they are losing her potential offspring as well. Hence, some kind of compensation to her family is usual. The most common form is the **bride price**, where money or other valuables are paid to her close kin. Other forms are an exchange

The Jie are an East African pastoral people who live in homesteads such as the one shown in the photograph (left). As the plan below shows, a homestead is typically the residence of an extended family, ideally patrilocal, which controls a herd of animals. It is divided into yards, one for each wife and her children.

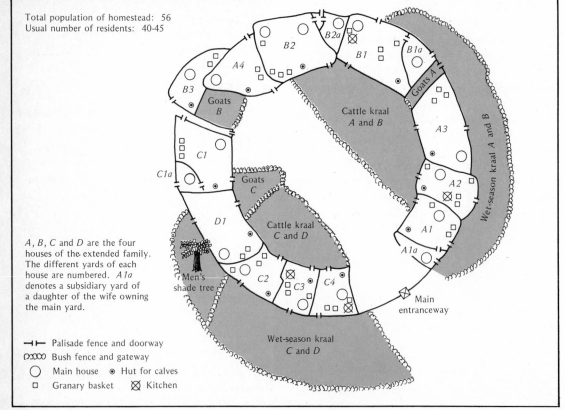

Total population of homestead: 56
Usual number of residents: 40-45

A, *B*, *C* and *D* are the four houses of the extended family. The different yards of each house are numbered. *A1a* denotes a subsidiary yard of a daughter of the wife owning the main yard.

⊣⊢   Palisade fence and doorway
ᴐᴊᴊᴊ Bush fence and gateway
◯   Main house   ⊙ Hut for calves
▢   Granary basket   ⊗ Kitchen

B2, B2a, B1, B1a, A4, B3, Goats B, Goats A, Cattle kraal A and B, A3, Wet-season kraal A and B, C1, C1a, Goats C, A2, D1, Cattle kraal C and D, A1, A1a, Men's shade tree, C2, C3, C4, Main entranceway, Wet-season kraal C and D of women between families—my son will marry your daughter if your son will marry my daughter—or **bride service,** a period of time during which the groom works for the bride's family.

Matrilocal residence is a likely result if ecological circumstances make the role of the woman predominant in subsistence. It is found most often in horticultural societies where political complexity is relatively undeveloped, and where cooperation among women is important. Under matrilocal residence, men usually do not move very far from the family in which they were raised, and so they are available to help out there from time to time. Therefore, marriage usually does not involve compensation to the groom's family.

Ambilocal residence is particularly well suited to situations where cooperation of more people than are available in the nuclear family is needed, but where resources are limited. Because one can join either the bride's or the groom's family, family membership is flexible, and one can go where the resources look best. The example of the !Kung Bushmen illustrates the way in which a hunting and gathering group can adjust itself to fluctuating resources.[20] The Bushmen typically live in one place for a few days until they have exhausted all available food resources. They then move as separate family units into camps where relatives with more abundant food resources are to be found. Ambilocality greatly enhances the Bushmen's opportunity to find food. For a people of low population density, ambilocality can be a crucial factor for survival.

Neolocal residence occurs where the independence of the nuclear family is emphasized. In our own society, where most

---

[20] Lorna Marshall, "Sharing, Talking and Giving Relief of Social Tensions among !Kung Bushmen," *Africa*, 1961, 31.

> **Bride price:** Compensation paid by the groom or his family to the bride's family upon marriage.

> **Bride service:** A designated period of time after marriage during which the groom works for the bride's family.

economic activity occurs outside the family, and where it is important for individuals to be able to move where jobs are to be found, neolocal residence is better suited than any of the other patterns.

PROBLEMS OF FAMILY ORGANIZATION

We may conclude this chapter by noting that the family strengthens the bonds of an individual to a society. The web of relationships and the social control that is exerted by families over the individual is an important force in integrating a society and making it cohesive. The problems of child-rearing, the regulation of sex, the need for cooperation between the sexes, the formation of political and economic alliances need not all be performed by the same institution. But they are interrelated functions. Child-rearing follows from sexual activity, and it requires cooperation between man and woman, who cooperate in other ways as well. At the same time that economic cooperation takes place between adult men and women, it also takes place between adults and children, as well as between larger bands of adults who form an extended family group. A reasonable and logical approach to this network of social needs is to deal with them together in the context of a single institution, the family, and that is the way that most societies function.

POLYGAMY While the family is a convenient and effective organizational device for dealing with these problems, different forms of family organization are accompanied by their own problems, which also must be solved. Polygamous families, for example, have within them the potential for conflict between the multiple spouses of the one individual to whom they are married. Under polygyny, the most common form of polygamy, the several wives of a man must be able to get along with a minimum of bickering and jealousy. One way to handle this is through sororal polygyny, or marriage to women who are sisters. Presumably, women who have grown up together can get along as co-wives of a man

more easily than women who grew up in different households and have never had to live together before. Another mechanism is to provide each wife with a separate apartment or house within a household compound, and require the husband to adhere to a system of rotation for sleeping purposes. This at least prevents the husband from playing obvious favorites among his wives. It should not be assumed, though, that polygyny is necessarily a difficult situation for the women involved. In societies where women's work is hard and boring, polygyny provides a means of sharing the work load and alleviating boredom through sociability.

EXTENDED FAMILIES Extended families have their own potential areas of stress. Decision-making in such families usually rests with an older individual, and other family members are obliged to abide by the elders' decisions. Among a group of siblings, an older sibling usually has the authority. Then there is the problem of in-marrying spouses, who must adjust their ways to those of the family in which they now live. To try to ensure that these potential problems do not become serious, dependence training of children, as discussed in Chapter 5, tends to be characteristic where extended families are important. This helps ensure that individuals are rendered dependent on the group, and that they will do nothing potentially disruptive.

Independence training is more characteristic of societies where nuclear families are not merely component parts of polyga-

The bride price may take many forms. In the case of the pastoral Jie of East Africa, it consists of cattle, which are shown here being driven to the bride's homestead. Among Kaoka speakers on Guadalcanal, it consists of discs, dogs' teeth and porpoise teeth, shown here on display at a wedding.

mous or extended families. This is certainly true in the case of our own society, and herein lies one of the problems faced by the young people who have experimented with extended family living. Most of these young people have been trained to be independent individuals. Given this, it is scarcely surprising that they frequently encounter serious difficulties trying to make their new extended families work. This is not to say that this is the only problem they face, but because it is unexpected, it may be more difficult to handle than more obvious problems such as the disapproval expressed by more conventional parents and members of other nuclear families who live nearby.

NUCLEAR FAMILIES   If extended families have built into them certain potentially serious problems, so too do nuclear families, especially in modern industrial societies where neolocal residence tends to isolate husbands and wives from both sets of kin. Because there are no clearly established patterns of responsibility between hus-

bands and wives, each couple must work them out for themselves. This may be particularly difficult if they grew up in families with widely divergent practices. Being isolated from their kin, there is no one on hand to help stabilize the new marriage; for that matter, intervention of kin would likely be regarded as interference.

Isolation from kin also means that a young mother-to-be must face pregnancy and childbirth without the aid and support of female kin with whom she already has a relationship, and who have been through pregnancy and childbirth themselves. Instead, she must turn for advice and guidance to physicians (who are more often men than women), books, and friends and neighbors who themselves are likely to be inexperienced. The problem continues through motherhood, in the absence of experienced women within the family, as well as a clear model for child-rearing. So reliance on physicians, books, and mostly inexperienced friends for advice and support continues. The problems are exacerbated, for families

Some young North Americans have attempted to recreate the extended family in the formation of communes. These attempts sometimes run into trouble as young people cope with the stresses associated with extended family organization for which they are unprepared.

differ widely in the ways in which they deal with their children. The children themselves recognize this and often use such differences against their parents to their own ends.

A further problem connected with the raising of children confronts the woman who has devoted herself entirely to this task: what will she do when the children are gone? One answer to this, of course, is to pursue some sort of career. But this, too, may present problems. She may have a husband who thinks "a woman's place is in the home." Or, it may be difficult to begin a career in middle age. To begin a career earlier may involve difficult choices: should she have her career at the expense of having children, or should she have both simultaneously? If the latter, there are not likely to be kin available to look after the children, as there would be in an extended family, and so arrangements must be made with people who are nonkin. And, of course, all of these thorny decisions must be made without the aid and support of kin.

The impermanence of the nuclear family itself may constitute a problem, in the form of anxieties over old age. Once the children are gone, who will care for the parents in their old age? The problem does not arise in an extended family, where one is cared for from womb to tomb.

At the start of this chapter, we posed a number of questions relating in one way or another to the effectiveness of the family as we know it today in North America in meeting human needs. From what we have just discussed, it is obvious that neolocal nuclear families impose considerable stress upon the individuals in such families. On the other hand, it is also obvious that alternative forms of family organization come complete with their own distinctive stresses and strains. To the question, Which of the alternatives is preferable?, one must answer: it depends on what problems one wishes to overcome, and what price one is willing to pay.

CHAPTER SUMMARY

Dependence on group living for survival is a basic human characteristic. Nurturance of children has traditionally been the job of the adult female, while carrying out economic tasks compatible with the child-rearing role. Economic tasks complementary to those of the females are undertaken by the males. The presence of adults of both sexes in a residential group is required to provide the child with an adult model of the same sex from whom can be learned the appropriate adult role.

Among primates, only the human female is continually receptive sexually. While such activity may reinforce social bonds among people, it can also be disruptive, so that in every society there are rules that govern sexual access. The near universality of the incest taboo, which forbids sexual relations between close relatives, has long interested anthropologists, but a truly convincing explanation of the taboo has yet to be advanced. Endogamy is marriage within a group of related individuals; exogamy is marriage outside the group. If the group is limited to the immediate family, all societies can be said to prohibit endogamy and practice exogamy. If more members are included in the group—say second cousins—one then finds endogamy to be a fairly common practice. Exogamy may help to explain the exceptions to the incest taboo, as in certain cases in which royalty kept marriage within the family in order to preserve intact the purity of the royal line.

A definition that avoids Western ethnocentrism sees the family as a group composed of a woman and her dependent children, with at least one adult male joined through marriage or blood relationship. Conjugal families are those formed on the basis of marital ties. The smallest conjugal unit of mother, father, and their children is called the nuclear family. The consanguine family, an alternative to the conjugal family, consists of women, their brothers, and the dependent children of the women. The nuclear family, which has become the ideal in North American society, is also found in societies that live in harsh environments, such as the Eskimos. In both modern industrial societies and societies that exist in particularly harsh environments, the nuclear family is an independent unit that must look after itself. The result is that individual members are strongly dependent on each other. This form of family is well suited to the mobility required in hunting and gathering groups and in the United States as well, where frequent job changes on the part of the breadwinner necessitate family mobility.

Monogamy, or the taking of a single spouse, is the most common form of marriage, primarily for economic reasons. A man must have a certain amount of wealth to be able to afford polygyny, or marriage to more than one wife at the same time. Since few societies have a surplus of men, polyandry, or the custom of a woman having several husbands, is uncommon. Also rare is group marriage, in which several men and several women have sexual access to one another. The levirate ensures the security of a woman by providing that a widow marry her husband's brother; the sororate provides that a widower marry his wife's sister.

Serial marriage is a form in which a man or woman marries or lives with a series of partners. Middle-class Americans have taken up a variant of this pattern as individuals divorce and remarry.

In the United States and many of the other industrialized countries of the West, marriages run the risk of being based on a metaphysic of youth, beauty, and romantic love. In no other parts of the world would marriages based on such trivial and transitory characteristics be expected to work. In most non-Western societies economic considerations strongly motivate an individual to marry. The family arranges marriages in societies in which it is the most powerful social institution. Marriage serves to bind two families as allies. The family serves to supply a society with new members, ensuring its survival.

Divorce, though generally frowned upon, is possible in all societies, though reasons for divorce as well as its frequency vary widely from one society to another. In the United States, factors contributing to the breakup of marriages include the trivial and transitory characteristics on which many marriages are based, the breakdown in the complementary relationship between roles filled by married men and women, a weakening of the taboo on sex out of wedlock, and the stresses inherent in neolocal, nuclear family organization. Given all of these, it is a wonder that divorce rates in our society are as low as they are.

Industrial society evolved the small nuclear family from the larger extended family, a combination conjugal-consanguineal family. Ideally, an extended family's members are related by blood or marriage, and all live and work together. The family follows five basic residence patterns: patrilocal, matrilocal, ambilocal, neolocal, and avunculocal.

Different forms of family organization are accompanied by their own problems. In polygamous families there is the potential for conflict among the several spouses of the one individual to whom they are married. One solution to this problem is sororal polygyny. In extended families, the matter of decision-making may be the source of stress, resting as it does with an older individual whose views may not coincide with those of the younger family members.

In neolocal, nuclear families, individuals are isolated from the aid and support of kin, and so husbands and wives must work out on their own solutions to the problems of living together and having children. The problems are especially difficult owing to an absence of clearly understood patterns of responsibility between husbands and wives, as well as a clear model for child-rearing.

SUGGESTED READINGS

Fox, Robin. *Kinship and Marriage in an Anthropological Perspective.* New York: Penguin, 1968.
    Professor Fox starts his argument with the universal biological bond between mother and child and imagines a process in which the husband intrudes into the basic group.
Friedl, Ernestine. *Women and Men: An Anthropologist's View.* New York: Holt, Rinehart and Winston, 1975.
    A subject closely related to marriage, the family, and postmarital residence choice is sex roles, and this is a good introduction to the topic. In this book, the author offers a series of hypotheses about the determinants and expressions of sex roles based on cross-cultural data.
Goodenough, Ward H. *Description and Comparison in Cultural Anthropology.* Chicago: Aldine, 1970.
    The book illustrates the difficulties anthropologists confront in describing and comparing social organization cross-culturally. The author begins with an examination of marriage and family, clarifying these and related concepts in important ways.

Mair, Lucy. *Marriage*. New York: Penguin, 1972.

Dr. Mair traces the evolution of marriage and such alternative relationships as surrogates and protectors. Commenting upon marriage as an institution and drawing her examples from tribal cultures, Dr. Mair deals with the function, rules, symbolic rituals, and economic factors of marriage. She also cites the inferior status of women and discusses the self-determining behavior of "serious free women" as an important factor in social change.

Needham, Rodney, ed. *Rethinking Kinship and Marriage*. London: Tavistock, 1972.

This collection of essays is concerned with a definition of kinship and the marriage procedure. It deals cross-culturally with the practices and rituals, and the relationship of marriage to the entire social structure. Contributors include Edmund Leach, Francis Korn, David McKnight.

2 | Kinship and Descent

On the Northwest Coast of North America, a distinctive art style developed, based on representative carving in wood. Primarily heraldic in nature, much of this art had to do with the histories of family lines and ancestors, all of which were important for Northwest Coast social organization.

PREVIEW

WHAT ARE DESCENT GROUPS?

A descent group is a kind of kinship group in which being a lineal descendant of a particular real or mythical ancestor is a criterion of membership. Descent may be reckoned exclusively through men, exclusively through women, or through either at the discretion of the individual. In some cases, two different means of reckoning descent are used at the same time, to assign individuals to different groups for different purposes.

WHAT FUNCTIONS DO DESCENT GROUPS SERVE?

Descent groups of various kinds—lineages, clans, phratries, and moieties—are convenient devices for solving a number of problems that commonly confront human societies: the need to maintain the integrity of resources that cannot be divided without being destroyed; the need to provide work forces for tasks that require a labor pool larger than families can provide; the need for members of one sovereign local group to be able to claim support and protection from members of another. Not all societies have descent groups; in many hunting and gathering, and industrial, societies some of these problems are commonly handled by the kindred, a group of people with a living relative in common. But the kindred does not exist in perpetuity, as does the descent group, nor is its membership as clearly and explicitly defined. Hence, it is generally a weaker unit than the descent group.

HOW DO DESCENT GROUPS EVOLVE?

Descent groups arise from extended family organization, so long as there are problems of organization that such groups help to solve. This is most apt to happen in food-producing, as opposed to food-gathering, societies. First to develop are localized lineages, followed by larger dispersed groups such as clans and phratries. With the passage of time kinship terminology itself is affected by and adjusts to the kinds of descent or other kinship groups that are important in a society.

All societies have found some form of family organization a convenient way to deal with problems faced by all human groups: the need to facilitate economic cooperation between the sexes, the need to provide a proper setting within which child-rearing may take place, and the need to control sexual activity. Efficient and flexible though family organization may be in rising to challenges connected with such problems, the fact is that many societies confront problems that are beyond the ability of family organization to deal with. For one, there is often a need for some means by which members of one sovereign local group can claim support and protection from individuals in another. This can be important for defense against natural or man-made disasters; if people have the right of entry into local groups other than their own, they are able to secure protection or critical resources when their own group cannot provide them. For another, there frequently is a need for a way to share rights in some means of production which cannot be divided without its destruction. This frequently is the case in horticultural societies, where division of land is impractical beyond a certain point. This can be avoided if ownership of land is vested in a corporate group. Finally, there is often a need for some means of providing cooperative work forces for tasks that require more participants than can be provided by families alone.

There are many ways to deal with these sorts of problems. One way is through the development of a formal political system with personnel to make and enforce laws, keep the peace, allocate resources, and perform other regulatory and societal functions. A more common way in nonindustrial societies—especially horticultural and pastoral societies—is through the development of kinship groups. The importance of kinship groups in a non-Western society

Lewis Henry Morgan 1818–1881

This major theoretician of nineteenth-century North American anthropology has been regarded as the founder of kinship studies. In *Systems of Consanguinity and Affinity of the Human Family* (1871), he classified and compared the kinship systems of peoples around the world in an attempt to prove the Asiatic origin of American Indians. In doing so, he developed the idea that the human family had evolved through a series of evolutionary stages from primitive promiscuity on the one hand to the monogamous, patriarchal family on the other. Although subsequent work showed Morgan to be wrong about this and a number of other things, his work showed the potential value of studying the distribution of different kinship systems in order to frame hypotheses of a developmental or historical nature and, by noting the connection between terminology and behavior, showed the value of kinship for sociological study. Besides his contributions to kinship and evolutionary studies, he produced an ethnography of the Iroquois which still stands as a major source of information.

may be illustrated by the Ifugao of the Philippines.[1] Among the Ifugaos, the kin group consists of the descendants of an individual's four pairs of great-grandparents. It may include as many as 2000 persons. In this case, practically the entire village is related in one way or another. In such a society, where the net of kinship, social, and political ties is very tight, it is extremely important that individuals know the exact nature of their relationship to each of their relatives—that one know, for example, who has the strongest claim on one's loyalties, and to whom one may turn in time of need. This sorting-out process is achieved through the society's kinship system, which lets an individual know exactly how he or she is related to others and what they can thus expect of each other. The kinship system structures the obligations and interests of its members: it dictates sharing economic and religious undertakings, provides psychological support in time of crisis, and legal help and defense when required. Among the Ila, a cattle-breeding people of Zambia, for example, one's descent determines one's rights in the use of farmland, one's share in the distribution of grain and other goods, one's place in the work force, and one's treatment in disputes and quarrels.[2]

DESCENT GROUPS

A frequently encountered kind of kinship group is the **descent group:** any publicly recognized social entity in which being a

---

[1] R. F. Barton, *Ifugao Law* (Berkeley: University of California Publications in American Archaeology and Ethnology, Vol. XV, 1919).

[2] Arthur Tuden, "Slavery and Stratification among the Ila of Central Africa," in Arthur Tuden and Leonard Plotnicov, eds., *Social Stratification in Africa* (New York: Free Press, 1970), pp. 47–58.

> **Descent group:** Any publicly recognized social entity such that being a lineal descendant of a particular real or mythical ancestor is a criterion of membership.

lineal descendant of a particular real or mythical ancestor is a criterion of membership. Members of a descent group, then, trace their connections back to a common ancestor through a chain of parent-child links. In this feature, we may have an answer to why descent groups are so common in human societies. They appear to stem from the parent-child bond, which is built upon as the basis for a structured social group. This is a convenient thing to seize upon, and the addition of a few nonburdensome obligations and avoidances acts as a kind of "glue" to help hold the group together.

To operate most efficiently, membership in a descent group ought to be clearly defined. Otherwise, membership overlaps and it is not always clear where one's primary loyalty belongs. There are a number of means by which membership can be restricted. It can be done on the basis of where you live; for example, if your parents live patrilocally, you might automatically be assigned to your father's descent group. Another way is through choice; each individual might be presented with a number of options, among which he or she may choose. This, though, introduces a possibility of competition and conflict as groups vie for members and may not be desirable. The most common way to restrict membership is by making sex jurally relevant. Instead of tracing membership back to the common ancestor, sometimes through men and sometimes through women, one does it exclusively through one sex. In this way, each individual is automatically assigned to his or her mother's or father's group, and that group only.

Unilineal Descent

Unilineal descent (sometimes called unisexual or unilateral descent) establishes descent group membership exclusively through the male or the female line. In non-Western societies, unilineal descent groups are the most common form. The individual is assigned at birth to membership in a specific descent group which may be traced either by **matrilineal descent,** through the female line, or by **patrilineal descent,** through the male line. In patrilineal societies the males are far more important than the females, for it is they who are considered to be responsible for the perpetuation of the group. In matrilineal societies, this responsibility falls on the female members of the group.

There seems to be a close relation between the descent system and the economy of a society. Generally, patrilineal descent predominates where the man is the breadwinner, as among pastoralists and intensive agriculturalists, where male labor is a prime factor. Matrilineal descent is important mainly among horticulturalists with societies where women are the breadwinners. Numerous matrilineal societies are found in South Asia, one of the cradles of agriculture in the Old World. Matrilineal systems exist in India, Ceylon, Indonesia, Sumatra, Tibet, South China, and many Indonesian islands. They were also prominent in parts of aboriginal North America and still are in parts of Africa.

It is now recognized that in all societies, the kin of both mother and father are important components of the social structure. Just because descent may be recognized patrilineally, for example, does not mean that maternal relatives are necessarily unimportant. It simply means that, for purposes of group membership, the mother's relatives are being excluded. Similarly, under matrilineal descent, the father's relatives are being excluded for purposes of group membership.

PATRILINEAL DESCENT AND ORGANIZATION Patrilineal descent (sometimes called agnatic, or male, descent) is the more widespread of the two basic systems of unilineal descent. The male members of a patrilineal descent group trace through the males their descent from a common ancestor. Brothers and sisters belong to the descent group of their father's father, their father, their father's siblings, and their father's brother's children. A man's son and daughter also trace their descent back through the male line to their common ancestor. In the typical patrilineal group, the power for training the children rests with the father or his

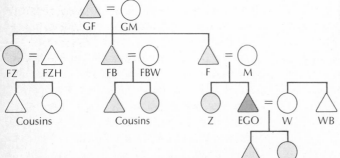

How patrilineal descent is traced. Only the individuals symbolized by a colored circle or triangle are in the same descent group as Ego. The abbreviation F stands for father, B for brother, H for husband, S for son, Z for sister, D for daughter, and W for wife.

elder brother. A woman belongs to the same descent group as her father and his brothers, but her children cannot trace their descent through them. A person's paternal aunt's children, for example, trace their descent through the patrilineal group of her husband.

THE TIKOPIA: A TYPICAL PATRILINEAL SOCIETY Among the Tikopia, a people of the western Pacific islands of Polynesia, studied extensively by Raymond Firth, a patrilineal system prevails.[3] The family, consisting of the father, mother, children, and usually the father's sister (if unmarried), lives near the house of the father's father. Residence, therefore, is patrilocal, as defined in Chapter 8. As in most patrilineal societies, the father's brother and his sons are important in the life of the father's male children. The children look upon their paternal uncle as a second father and behave toward him accordingly. The father's sister has a unique position toward her brother's children. She is looked upon as a secondary mother, acting as nurse, protector, and mentor; her authority and ritual powers are akin to those of her brother.

Every individual Tikopian family belongs to a larger group known as a *paito* (which means "house"). Each *paito* is composed of a number of families, the core members of which trace their descent through the male line to a common ancestor. The head of the *paito* is the senior living male descendant of this ancestor. A number of *paitos* combine to form the *kainana*, or clan, the largest social group on the island.

The position of an individual within the *paito* determines his or her social status. The kind of instruction a person will receive as a child and his or her rights to

---

[3] Raymond Firth, *We the Tikopia* (Boston: Beacon Press, 1963).

Unilineal descent: Descent that establishes group membership exclusively through either the mother's or the father's line.

Matrilineal descent: Descent traced exclusively through the female line for purposes of group membership.

Patrilineal descent: Descent traced exclusively through the male line for purposes of group membership.

the produce of the land depend on this. As an adult, a man will be entitled to a share in the land and other property, a house site, and a given name when he marries. Membership in his family *paito* also entitles him to economic and ritual assistance when required, as well as use of religious formulas and certain prerogatives when he appeals to his principal ancestral deities. Too, the *paito* determines the person's rank in the *kainana*.

The patrilineal system reaches throughout Tikopian social relations and determines legal matters of succession and inheritance. Succession to the position of *paito* head is solely in the male line; under no circumstances can a person belong to the *paito* of the mother rather than that of the father. On the death of an elder or chief, the kin group goes to the farthest limits of male descent and explores the collateral lines to the utmost to find an heir. The immediate sister's son is never even considered; he is excluded because his mother married into another patrilineage.

Each *paito* has its own economic organization. Its members are responsible for the production and consumption of food, the exchange of property, or ownership. Political activities of the paito involve the transmission of cultural goods, tradition, rank, and property as well as judicial matters such as the settling of disputes, both internal and external. The *paito* meets also on social and religious occasions, such as marriages, births, and initiation ceremonies. The patrilineal kinship group is indeed the backbone of Tikopian society.

MATRILINEAL DESCENT AND ORGANIZATION
In one respect, matrilineal descent is the opposite of patrilineal descent: descent is reckoned through the female line. The matrilineal pattern differs from the patrilineal in that descent does not confer authority. Thus, while patrilineal societies are patriarchal, matrilineal societies are not matriarchal. Although descent passes through the female line, and women may be important in many ways, they do not actually exercise authority in the descent group; the males do. These males are the brothers, rather than the husbands, of the women through whom descent is reckoned. Apparently, the adaptive purpose of the matrilineal system is to provide continuous female solidarity within the female work group. Matrilineal systems are usually found in farming societies in which women perform much of the productive work. Because women's work is regarded as so important to the society, matrilineal descent prevails.

In the matrilineal system, brothers and sisters belong to the descent group of the mother's mother, the mother, the mother's siblings, and the mother's sister's children. Males belong to the same descent group as their mother and sister, but their children cannot trace their descent through them. For example, the children of a man's maternal uncle are considered members of the uncle's wife's matrilineal descent group. Similarly, a man's own children belong to his wife's, but not his, descent group.

A common feature of matrilineal systems is the weakness of the tie between husband and wife. The wife's brother, and not the husband-father, distributes goods, organizes work, settles disputes, administers inheritance and succession rules, and supervises rituals. The husband has legal authority not in his own household but in that of his sister. He is strongly tied to his natal household even though he and his wife may live elsewhere. Thus, brother-sister bonds are strengthened at the expense of husband-wife bonds. They are further strengthened by the fact that the father's property and status are not inherited by his own son but by his sister's son. It is not surprising that divorce, even though frowned upon, is often common in matrilineal societies.

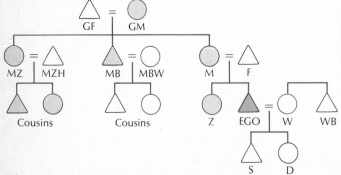

This diagram, which traces descent matrilineally, can be compared with that on page 262, showing patrilineal descent. The two patterns are virtually mirror images. Note that a male Ego cannot transmit descent to his own children.

ORIGINAL STUDY

Matrilineal Descent and Residence Choice in Truk[4]

In my published report on Truk, I indicated that the cornerstone of its social structure is the property-owning corporation, which, because it perpetuates its membership by a principle of matrilineal descent and is a segment of the community rather than widely extended across community lines, I chose to call a lineage. No individual can exist independent of some lineage affiliation. If he goes to another community he must either affiliate with one of its lineages or remain outside the community pale without food, shelter, or protection. If it has enough adult members and access to a suitable site, a lineage has its own dwelling house (or cluster of houses) which is regarded as the place where it is physically located. A large lineage may contain two or even three separately localized sublineages. Lineages may move from one site to another as they gain right of access to different plots of land; house sites are not regarded as permanent. There are several ways in which a lineage may have right of access. It may itself own the ground under full or provisional title; one of its members may hold personal title to the ground; or a sublineage may be the owner. A lineage may also be localized on land which belongs to a man who has married into it. When this happens, the understanding is invariably that the man's children, who are members of the lineage, have received the land in gift from their father, so that in localizing here the lineage has moved, in effect, to land belonging to one of its members. With the tendency nowadays for the lineage to be localized in a cluster of smaller houses instead of a single large one as in former times, the site may consist of several adjacent plots under separate ownership; but each case will conform to the pattern above—three adjacent plots, for example, being held by the lineage, one of its members, and one of its husbands respectively. The need for juggling of this kind has also been increased on Romonum Island with the movement of all house sites to the beach, during the decade before World War II. The point of importance to note, however, is that a man who is living on land which he got from his father is in all probability not living in the extended family associated with his father's lineage, but in that associated with his or his wife's. Let us now see what are the possible choices of residence open to a married couple within this setting.

The first thing to note is that the choice is always between extended family households. Couples do not go off and set up in isolation by themselves. The only exceptions to this are native pastors and catechists whose residence is determined by their occupation. (They find it necessary, however, to try to make some arrangements for domestic cooperation with a neighboring household.) The important question for a married couple, then, is: to what extended

---

[4]Ward H. Goodenough, "Residence Rules," *Southwestern Journal of Anthropology,* 1956, 12:30–32. By permission of the author and *Journal of Anthropological Research.*

families does it have access? It has access by right to the extended family associated with the lineage of either the bride or the groom. A member of a lineage which is not localized becomes a dependent of his or her father's lineage for purposes of shelter. The extended families associated with the wife's father's lineage and husband's father's lineage form, therefore, a pair of secondary possibilities for choice of residence. At any one time, however, a couple has but two alternatives: on the one hand the wife's lineage or, if it is not localized, then her father's lineage, and on the other hand the husband's lineage or, if it is not localized, then his father's. Other things being equal, as long as one party to the marriage belongs to a lineage which is localized, this lineage will be chosen before joining the other's father's lineage. Resort to a father's lineage of either spouse is, therefore, a fairly rare occurrence. Other things being equal, moreover, a couple will regularly choose to live with the extended family associated with the wife's lineage rather than that associated with the husband's. It is regarded as proper for one's children to grow up in the bosom of their own lineage in close association with their lineage "brothers" and "sisters," with whom they are expected to maintain absolute solidarity, no matter what the circumstances, for the rest of their lives. Given matrilineal descent as the principle of lineage membership, regular residence with the extended family associated with the husband's lineage would keep lineage brothers separated from one another until adulthood and lineage sisters would not normally live and work together, either as children or adults. Choosing to reside with the wife's localized lineage, therefore, is consistent with the high value placed on lineage solidarity.

But what are the considerations which make other things unequal? Under what circumstances do people regularly choose in favor of the husband's localized lineage even though the wife's lineage is localized? And under what circumstances do couples prefer to reside with a wife's father's lineage household rather than the household associated directly with the husband's lineage? What are the factors, in short, which favor a husband instead of his wife and a secondary instead of a primary affiliation?

Most instances of residence with the husband's lineage household occur in cases where the wife's lineage is not localized because it does not have enough adult women to run a separate household or lacks access to suitable land. But there are other circumstances favoring such residence. Ultimate responsibility and authority in a lineage is vested in its adult men. If residence with the wife's kin would take the husband too far away from where his own lineage house is located, it may appear advisable for him to bring his wife to live at the latter place. As the physical distance between the husband's and wife's lineage households increases and as the importance of the husband in his lineage affairs increases, the greater the likelihood that residence will be with the husband's kin. Where the husband or his lineage is in a position to provide the children with far more land than the wife's lineage, and at the same time the husband and wife come from communities too widely separated to make it possible to reside in one and maintain the land in the other, residence will be with the husband's kin. If the husband's lineage will soon die out, so

> **Double descent:** A system according to which descent is reckoned matrilineally for some purposes and patrilineally for others.

that his children will take over its lands, these children may organize as a new lineage temporarily operating jointly with the survivors of their father's lineage. Such of these children as are women may bring their husbands into what may be regarded either as the wife's or wife's father's localized lineage (the former as one looks to the future, the latter as one looks to the past).

Finally, it may happen that a young couple may be requested to reside with elder relatives in a household in which they do not have any "right" to live. In Fischer's census, for example, I note the case of an elderly man residing with his wife's localized kin group. He and his wife have no children. Nor are there junior kin in his wife's lineage who do not have greater responsibilities to others in the household (judging from my genealogical data). Living with them are this old man's sister's daughter and her newly acquired husband. As head of her lineage, the old man has obviously pulled her into this household with the consent of his wife and her kin (who are thus relieved of undue responsibility). She has no other reason for being there, and the arrangement will terminate when either the old man or his wife dies. Temporary arrangements like this one, made for mutual convenience and with the consent of those concerned, may be on the increase today. I suspect, however, that one hundred years ago they would also have accounted for the residence of up to five percent of the married couples.

Double Descent

Double descent, or double unilineal descent, whereby descent is reckoned both patrilineally and matrilineally, is very rare. In this system, descent is matrilineal for some purposes and patrilineal for others. Generally, where double descent is reckoned, the matrilineal and patrilineal groups take action in different spheres of society.

For example, among the Yakö of eastern Nigeria, property is divided between patrilineal line possessions and matrilineal line possessions.[5] The patrilineage owns

[5] C. Daryll Forde, "Double Descent among the Yako," in Paul Bohannan and John Middleton, eds., *Kinship and Social Organization* (Garden City, N.Y.: Natural History Press, 1968), pp. 179–191.

perpetual productive resources, such as land, whereas the matrilineage owns consumable property, such as livestock. The legally weaker matrilineal line is somewhat more important in religious matters than the patrilineal line. Because of the existence of double descent, a Yakö individual might inherit grazing lands from the father's patrilineal group and certain ritual privileges from the mother's matrilineal line.

Ambilineal Descent

Unilineal descent provides an easy way of restricting descent group membership, so as to avoid problems of divided loyalty and the like. A number of societies, many of them in the Pacific and Southeast Asia, ac-

This photo shows three generations of a Jewish family. Close family ties have always been important in eastern European Jewish culture. In order to maintain such ties in the United States, the descendants of eastern European Jews developed ambilineal descent groups.

complish the same thing in other ways, though perhaps not quite so neatly. The resultant descent groups are known as ambilineal, nonunilineal, or cognatic, descent groups. **Ambilineal descent** provides a measure of flexibility not normally found under unilineal descent; each individual has the option of affiliating with either the mother's or the father's descent group. In many of these societies an individual may belong to only one group at any one time, regardless of how many groups one may be eligible to join. Thus, the society may be divided into the same sorts of discrete and separate groups of kin as in a patrilineal or matrilineal society. But there are other cognatic societies, such as the Samoans of the South Pacific and the Bella Coola and the southern branch of the Kwakiutl of the Pacific Northwest Coast, which allow overlapping membership in a number of descent groups. As George Murdock notes, too great a range of individual choice interferes with the orderly functioning of any kin-oriented society:

An individual's plural membership almost inevitably becomes segregated into one primary membership, which is strongly activated by residence, and one or more secondary memberships in which participation is only partial or occasional.[6]

---

[6] George P. Murdock, "Cognatic Forms of Social Organization," in G. P. Murdock, ed., *Social Structure in Southeast Asia* (Chicago: Quadrangle, 1960), p. 11.

AMBILINEAL DESCENT AMONG NEW YORK CITY JEWS For an example of ambilineal organization we might easily turn to a traditional, non-Western society, as we have for patrilineal and matrilineal organization. But instead, we shall turn to our contemporary North American society, in order to dispel the common notion that descent groups are necessarily incompatible in structure and function with the demands of modern, industrial society. In fact, large corporate descent groups are to be found in New York City, as well as in every other large city in the United States where a substantial Jewish population of eastern European background is to be found.[7] Furthermore, these descent groups are not survivals of an old eastern European, descent-based organization. Rather, they represent a social innovation designed to restructure and preserve the traditionally close affective family ties of the old eastern European Jewish culture in the face of continuing immigration to the United States, subsequent dispersal from New York City, and the development of significant social and even temperamental differences among their descendants. The earliest of these descent groups developed at the end of the first decade of the 1900s, some 40 years after the immigration of eastern European Jews began in earnest. Although some groups have disbanded, they generally have remained alive and vital right down to the present day.

The original Jewish descent groups in New York City are known as *family circles*. The potential members of a family circle consist of all living descendants, with their spouses, of an ancestral pair. In actuality, not all who are eligible actually join, so there is an element of voluntarism. But eli-

---

[7] William E. Mitchell, *Mishpokhe: A Study of New York City Jewish Family Clubs* (The Hague: Mouton, 1978).

> **Ambilineal descent:** Descent in which the individual may affiliate with either the mother's or the father's descent group.

gibility is explicitly determined by descent, using both male and female links without set order to establish the connection with the ancestral pair. Thus, individuals are normally eligible for membership in more than one group. To activate one's membership, one simply pays the required dues, attends meetings, and participates in the affairs of the group. Individuals can, and frequently do, belong to two or three groups for which they are eligible at the same time. Each family circle bears a name, usually including the surname of the male ancestor, each has elected officers, and each meets regularly throughout the year rather than just once or twice. At the least, the family circle as a corporation holds funds in common, and some hold title to burial plots for the use of members. Originally, they functioned as mutual aid societies, as well as for the purpose of maintaining family solidarity. Now, as the mutual aid functions have been taken over by outside agencies, the promotion of solidarity has become their primary goal. It will be interesting to see if reduced government funding for these agencies leads to a resurgence of the mutual aid function of family circles.

In the years just prior to World War II, an interesting variant of the ambilineal descent group developed among younger-generation descendants of east European Jewish immigrants. Being more assimilated into North American culture, some of them sought to separate themselves somewhat from members of older generations who were perceived as being a bit old-fashioned. Yet, they still wished to maintain the traditional Jewish ethic of family solidarity. The result was the *cousins club*, which consists of a group of first cousins who themselves share a common ancestry, their spouses, and their descendants. Excluded are parents and grandparents of the cousins, with their older views and life-styles. Ambilineal descent remains the primary organizing principle, but it has been modified by a generational principle. Otherwise, cousins clubs are organized and function in many of the same ways as family circles.

FORMS AND FUNCTIONS OF DESCENT GROUPS

Descent groups with restricted membership, regardless of how descent is reckoned, are usually more than just groups of relatives providing warmth and a sense of belonging; in nonindustrial societies they are tightly organized working units providing security and services in the course of what can be a difficult, uncertain life. The tasks performed by descent groups are manifold. Besides acting as economic units providing mutual aid to their members, they may act to support the aged and infirm or help in the case of marriage or death. Often, they play a role in determining whom an individual may or may not marry. The descent group may also act as a repository of religious traditions. Ancestor worship, for example, is a powerful force acting to reinforce group solidarity.

Lineage

A **lineage** is a corporate descent group composed of consanguineal kin who claim descent from a common ancestor and who are able to trace descent genealogically through known links. The term is usually employed where some form of unilineal descent is the rule, but there are similar ambilineal groups, such as the Jewish family circles just discussed.

The lineage is ancestor-oriented; membership in the group is recognized only if relationship to a common ancestor can be traced and proved. In many societies, an individual has no legal or political status except as a member of a lineage. We have already seen an example of this, in the Original Study earlier in this chapter. Since "citizenship" is derived from lineage membership and legal status depends on it, political and religious power are thus derived from it as well. Important religious and magical powers, such as those associated with the cults of gods and ancestors, may also be bound to the lineage.

The lineage, like General Motors or Polaroid, is a corporate group. Because it continues after the death of members as new members are continually being born into it, it has a perpetual existence which enables a lineage to take corporate actions such as owning property, organizing productive activities, distributing goods and manpower, assigning status, and regulating relations with other groups. The lineage is a strong, effective base of social organization.

A common feature of lineages is that they are exogamous. This means that members of a lineage must find their marriage partners in other lineages. One advantage of lineage exogamy is that potential sexual competition within the group is curbed, promoting the group's solidarity. Lineage exogamy also means that each marriage is more than an arrangement between two individuals; it amounts as well to a new alliance between lineages. This helps to maintain them as components of larger social systems. Finally, lineage exogamy maintains open communication within a society, promoting the diffusion of knowledge from one lineage to another.

Clan

In the course of time, as generation succeeds generation and new members are born into the lineage, its membership may become too large to be manageable, or too much for the lineage's resources to support. When this happens, **fission** will take place; that is, the lineage will split up into new, smaller lineages. When fission occurs, it is usual for the members of the new lineages to continue to recognize their ultimate relationship to one another. The result of this process is the appearance of a second kind of descent group, the **clan.** The term "clan," and its close relative, the term "sib," have been used differently by different anthropologists, and a certain amount of confusion exists about their meaning. The clan (or sib) will here be defined as a noncorporate descent group in which each member assumes descent from a common ancestor (who may be real or fictive), but is unable to trace the actual genealogical links back to the ancestor. This stems from the great genealogical depth of the clan, whose

> **Lineage:** A corporate descent group whose members claim descent from a common ancestor and can trace their genealogical links to that ancestor.
>
> **Fission:** The splitting of a descent group into two or more new descent groups.
>
> **Clan:** A noncorporate descent group with each member claiming descent from a common ancestor without actually knowing the genealogical links to that ancestor.

founding ancestor lived so far in the past that the links to that ancestor are assumed rather than known in detail. A clan differs from a lineage in another respect: it lacks the residential unity that is generally—though not invariably—characteristic of the lineage. As with the lineage, descent may be patrilineal, matrilineal, or ambilineal.

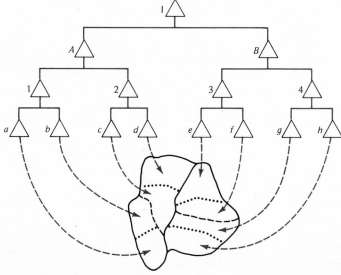

Lineage organization among the Tiv of West Africa. In this case, the geographical distribution of lineages corresponds to their genealogical relationships.

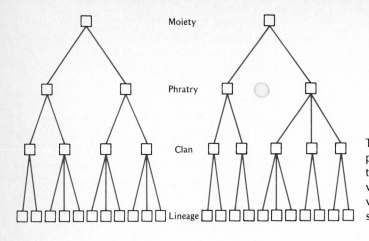

This diagram shows how lineages, clans, phratries, and moieties form an organizational hierarchy. Each moiety is subdivided into phratries, each phratry is subdivided into clans, and each clan is subdivided into lineages.

Because clan membership is dispersed rather than localized, it usually does not hold tangible property corporately. Instead, it tends to be more of a unit for ceremonial matters. Only on special occasions will the membership gather together for specific purposes. Clans, however, may handle important integrative functions. Like lineages, they may regulate marriage through exogamy. Because of their dispersed membership, they give individuals the right of entry into local groups other than their own. One is usually expected to give protection and hospitality to one's fellow clan members. Hence, these can be expected in any local group which includes members of one's own clan.

Clans, lacking the residential unity of lineages, depend on symbols—of animals, plants, natural forces, and objects—to provide members with solidarity and a ready means of identification. These symbols, called **totems,** are often associated with the clan's mythical origin and provide clan members with a means of reinforcing the awareness of their common descent. The word "totem" comes from the Ojibwa American Indian word *ototeman*, meaning "he is a relative of mine." **Totemism** has

been defined by A. R. Radcliffe-Brown as a set of "customs and beliefs by which there is set up a special system of relations between the society and the plants, animals, and other natural objects that are important in the social life."[8] Creek Indian matriclans bear such totemic names as Alligator, Arrow, Bird, Corn, Deer, Red Paint, Spanish Moss, and Wind.

Totemism is a changing concept that varies from clan to clan. A kind of "watered-down" totemism may even be found in our own society where baseball and football teams are given the names of such powerful wild animals as Bears, Tigers, and Wildcats. This extends to the Democratic Party's donkey and the Republican Party's elephant, to the Elks, the Lions, and other fraternal and social organizations. Our animal emblems, however, do not involve the same notions of descent and strong sense of kinship, nor are they associated with the various ritual observances associated with clan totems.

---

[8] A. R. Radcliffe-Brown, "Social Organization of Australian Tribes," *Oceania Monographs*, No. 1 (Melbourne: Macmillan, 1931), p. 29.

Phratries and Moieties

Other kinds of descent group are phratries and moieties. A **phratry** is a unilineal descent group composed of two or more clans which are supposedly related, whether or not they really are. Like individuals of the clan, members of the phratry are unable to trace accurately their descent links to a common ancestor, though they believe such an ancestor exists.

If the entire society is divided into two and only two major descent groups, be they equivalent to clans or phratries, each group is called a **moiety** (after the French word for "half"). Members of the moiety believe themselves to share a common ancestor, but are unable to prove it through definite genealogical links. As a rule, the feeling of kinship among members of lineages and clans is stronger than that felt among members of phratries and moieties. This may be due to the larger size and more diffuse nature of the latter groups.

Bilateral Kinship and the Kindred

Important though descent groups are in many societies, they are not found in all societies, nor are they the only kinds of nonfamilial kinship group to be found. Bilateral kinship, a characteristic of Western society, relates a person to other close relatives through both sexes; in other words, the individual traces descent through both parents simultaneously and recognizes multiple ancestors. Theoretically, one is affiliated equally with all relatives on both the mother's and father's sides of the family. Thus, this principle relates an individual lineally to all eight great-grandparents and laterally to all third and fourth cousins. Since such a huge group is too big to be socially practical, the group is usually reduced to a small circle of paternal and ma-

Totems: Symbols with religious significance, usually animals but sometimes plants, natural forces, or objects, used by a clan as means of identification.

Totemism: The belief that people are descended from animals, plants, or natural objects.

Phratry: A unilineal descent group composed of two or more clans that claim to be related by kinship. If there are only two such groups, each is a moiety.

Moiety: Each group that results from a division of a society into two halves on the basis of descent.

Kindred: A group of people closely related to one living individual through both parents.

ternal relatives, called the **kindred.** The kindred may be defined as a group of people closely related to one living individual through both parents. Unlike unilineal descent groups, the kindred is laterally rather than lineally organized. That is, ego, or the focal person from whom the degree of each relationship is reckoned, is the center of the group. We are all familiar with the kindred; we simply call them relatives. It includes the relatives on both sides of the family whom we see on important occasions, such as family reunions and funerals. Most of us can identify the members of our kindred up to second cousins and grandparents. In our society, the limits of the kindred are variable and indefinite; no one can ever be absolutely certain which relatives to invite to every important function and which to exclude. Inevitably, situations arise which require some debate about whether or not to invite certain, usually distant, relatives. The kindred is thus somewhat vaguely defined, lacking the distinctiveness of the unilineal or ambilineal descent group. (It is also temporary, lasting only as long as the function it has been assembled to attend.)

The kindred possesses one feature that sets it apart from all other descent groups: because of its bilateral structure, a kindred is never the same for any two persons except siblings (brothers and sisters). Thus, no two people (except siblings) belong to the same kindred. Ego's father's kindred, for example, ranges lineally to the father's grandparents and laterally to cousins too distant for ego to know; the same is true of ego's mother, maternal and paternal aunts, and uncles. Thus, the kindred is not composed of people with an ancestor in common, but of people with a living relative in common—ego.

THE EGO: CENTER OF THE KINDRED Kindreds are referred to as ego-centered or ego-focused groups because ego, or the person viewing the group, is at its center. Even in relation to ego, the membership of the group is constantly changing as ego moves through life. When one is young, it consists of one's parents, siblings, and other close consanguineal relatives, most of whom are usually older than ego is. As ego grows older and has children, the composition of the kindred changes; it consists of one's descendants and the remaining relatives of one's own generation. Thus, because of its vagueness, temporary nature, and changeableness, the kindred is a weaker social unit than descent groups. For example, it cannot function as a group except in relation to ego. Unlike descent groups, it is not a self-perpetuating group—it ceases with ego's death. It has no constant leader, nor can it hold, administer, or pass on property. In most cases, it cannot organize work, nor can it easily administer justice or assign

Modern versions of the kindred. In the left photo, a French kindred attends a wedding of one of its members; the right photo shows the kindred of Magnus McDonald in Marion, Illinois, enjoying their annual family reunion.

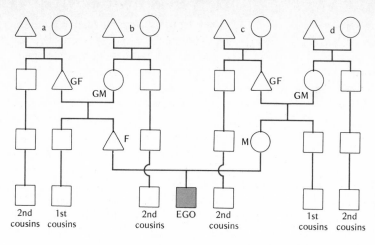

The kinship pattern of the kindred. These people are related not to a common ancestor but to a living relative, Ego. The squares represent persons of either sex; sex is not relevant in determining relationship.

status. But it can be turned to for aid. In non-Western societies, for example, head-hunting and trading parties may be composed of kindred groups. The group is assembled, goes on the hunt, shares the spoils, then disbands. It can also act as a ceremonial group for rites of passage: initiation ceremonies and the like. Thus, kindreds assemble only for a specific purpose. Finally, they can also regulate marriage through exogamy.

Because of its shortcomings, the non-Western bilateral group usually exists side by side with more useful descent groups. Kindreds are found mostly in industrial societies, such as our own, where mobility weakens contact with relatives. Individuality is emphasized in such societies, and a strong kinship system is usually not as important as it is among non-Western peoples.

Evolution of the Descent Group

Just as different types of families occur in different societies, so do different kinds of descent systems. Descent groups, for example, are not a common feature of hunting and gathering societies, where mar-

riage acts as the social mechanism for integrating individuals within the society. In horticultural, pastoral, or many intensive agricultural societies, however, the descent group usually provides the structural framework upon which the fabric of the society rests.

It is generally agreed that lineages arise from extended family organization, so long as there are problems of organization which such groups help solve.[9] All that is required, really, is that as members of existing extended families find it necessary to split off and establish new families elsewhere, they not move too far away, that the core members of such related families (men in patrilocal, women in matrilocal, members of both sexes in ambilocal extended families) explicitly acknowledge their descent from a common ancestor, and that they continue to participate in common activities in an organized way. As this proceeds, lineages will develop, and these may with time give rise to clans and ultimately phratries.

---

[9] Raoul Naroll, "Holocultural Theory Tests," in Raoul Naroll and Frada Naroll, eds., *Main Currents in Cultural Anthropology* (New York: Appleton, 1973), p. 329.

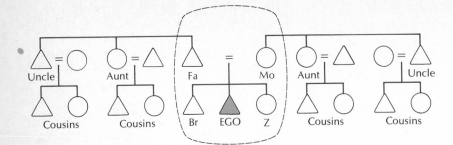

The Eskimo system of kinship terminology emphasizes the nuclear family (indicated by the broken line). Ego's father and mother are distinguished from his aunts and uncles, and his siblings are distinguished from his cousins.

As larger, dispersed descent groups develop, the conditions that gave rise to extended families and lineages may change. For example, economic diversity and the availability of alternative occupations among which individuals may choose may conflict with the residential unity of extended families and (usually) lineages. Or lineages may lose their economic bases if control of resources is taken over by developing political institutions. In such circumstances, lineages would be expected to disappear as important organizational units. Clans, however, might survive if they continued to provide an important integrative function. In this sense, the Jewish family circles and cousins clubs that we discussed earlier have become essentially clanlike in their function. This helps explain their continued strength and vitality in the United States today: they perform an integrative function among kin who are geographically dispersed as well as socially diverse, but in a way that does not conflict with the mobility that is characteristic of our society.

In societies where the small domestic unit—nuclear families—is of primary importance, bilateral kinship and kindred organization are apt to be the result. This can be seen in our own industrial society, as well as in many hunting and gathering societies throughout the world.

KINSHIP TERMINOLOGY AND KINSHIP GROUPS

Any system of organizing people who are relatives into different kinds of groups, be they descent-based or ego-oriented, is bound to have an important effect upon the ways in which relatives are labeled in any given society. The fact is, the kinship terminologies of other peoples are far from being the arbitrary, and even capricious, ways of labeling relatives that Westerners all too often take them to be. Rather, they reflect the positions individuals occupy within their society. In particular, kinship terminology is affected by, and adjusts to, the kinds of kinship groups which exist in a society. But there are other factors also at work as well in each system of kinship terminology that help differentiate one kin from another. These factors may be sex, generational differences, or genealogical differences. In the various systems of kinship terminology, any one of these factors may be emphasized at the expense of others. But regardless of the factors emphasized, all kinship terminologies accomplish two important tasks. First, they classify particular kinds of persons into single specific categories; second, they separate different kinds of persons into distinct categories. Generally, two or more kin are merged under the same term when similarity of status exists between the individuals. These similarities are then emphasized by the application of one term to both individuals.

Six different systems of kinship terminology result from the application of the above principles: the Eskimo, Hawaiian, Iroquois, Omaha, Crow, and Descriptive systems. Each of these six systems can be identified according to the way cousins are classified.

Eskimo System

The **Eskimo system** of kinship terminology, comparatively rare among all the systems of the world, is the system used by Anglo-American cultures. It is also used by a number of hunting and gathering peoples. The Eskimo system, or lineal system, of terminology emphasizes the nuclear family by specifically identifying mother, father, brother, and sister, while merging together all other relatives such as maternal and paternal aunts, uncles, and cousins, without differentiating among them. For example, one's father is distinguished from one's father's brother (uncle); but one's father's brother is not distinguished from the mother's brother (both are called uncle). In addition, one calls all the sons and daughters of

> **Eskimo system:** System of kinship terminology, also called lineal system, which emphasizes the nuclear family by specifically identifying mother, father, brother, and sister, while merging together all other relatives.

> **Hawaiian system:** A mode of kinship reckoning in which all relatives of the same sex and generation are referred to by the same term.

aunts and uncles cousin, without distinguishing their sex or the side of the family to which they belong.

Unlike other terminologies, the Eskimo system provides separate and distinct terms for each member of the nuclear family. This is probably because the Eskimo system is generally found in societies where the dominant kin group is the bilateral kindred, in which only the closest members of the family are important in day-to-day affairs. This is especially true of our own society, in which the family is independent, living apart from, and not directly involved with, other kin except on ceremonial occasions. Thus, we distinguish between our closest kin (our parents and siblings), but use the same terms (aunt, uncle, cousin) for other kin on both sides of the family.

Hawaiian System

The **Hawaiian system** of kinship terminology, common in Hawaii and other Malayo-Polynesian-speaking areas, but found

The Hawaiian kinship system. The men numbered 2 and 6 are all called by the same term as father (3) by Ego; the women numbered 1 and 5 are all called by the same term as mother (4). All cousins of Ego's own generation (7–16) are considered brothers and sisters.

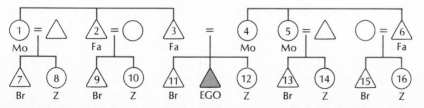

elsewhere as well, is the least complex system in that it uses the least number of terms. The Hawaiian system is also called the generational system, since all relatives of the same generation and sex are referred to by the same term. For example, in one's father's generation, one's father, his brother, and one's mother's brother are all referred to by the same term as "father." Similarly, one's mother, her sister, and one's father's sister are all called by the same term as "mother." In ego's generation, male and female cousins are distinguished by sex and are equated with brothers and sisters.

The Hawaiian system reflects the absence of strong unilineal descent and is usually associated with ambilineal descent. Because ambilineal descent rules allow one to trace descent through either side of the family, and members on both father's and mother's side of the family are looked upon as being more or less equal, a certain degree of similarity is created among the father's and the mother's siblings. Thus, they are all simultaneously recognized as being similar relations and are merged together under a single term. In like manner, the children of the mother's and father's siblings are related to oneself in the same way as one's brother and sister are.

Iroquois System

In the **Iroquois system** of kinship terminology, one's father and father's brother are referred to by a single term, as are one's mother and mother's sister; however, one's father's sister and one's mother's brother are given separate terms. In one's own generation, brothers, sisters, and parallel cousins (offspring of parental siblings of the same sex, i.e., the children of mother's sister or father's brother) of the same sex are referred to by the same terms, which is logical enough considering that they are the offspring of people who are classified in the same category as ego's actual mother and father. Cross cousins (offspring of parental siblings of opposite sex, i.e. the children of mother's brother or father's sister) are distinguished by separate terms. Such a method of differentiating is called a **bifurcate merging.** The Omaha and the Crow systems are also examples of bifurcate-merging terminology.

Iroquois terminology is very widespread and is usually found with unilineal descent groups, particularly in weak matrilineal systems of social organization.

Omaha System

In the preceding systems of terminology, some relatives were grouped under common terms, while others of the same generation were separated and given different labels or terms. In the Omaha and Crow systems, another variable enters the pic-

According to the Iroquois system of kinship terminology, father's brother (2) is called by the same term as father (3); mother's sister (5) is called by the same term as mother (4); but the people 1 and 6 have separate terms for themselves. Those numbered 9–14 are all considered siblings, but 7, 8, 15, and 16 are cousins.

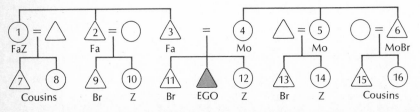

ture: both systems ignore the distinction that occurs between generations among certain kinsmen.

The **Omaha system,** found in many parts of the world, is associated with a pattern of strong patrilineal descent group organization and thus groups differently relations on the father's side and mother's side. Cross cousins on the maternal side are merged with the parental generation (mother's sister or mother's brother), while those on the paternal side are merged with the generation of ego's children. Otherwise, the system is much like the Iroquois system.

From our point of view, such a system seems terribly complex and illogical. Why does it exist? The Omaha system is found where strong patrilineal descent groups exist. Thus, maternal cross cousins are terminologically merged with the lineage of ego's mother, the lineage that, figuratively speaking, gave birth to ego. Ego's lineage, in turn, stands in the same relationship to the children of father's sister and ego's own sister; they are given birth by ego's lineage.

Crow System

The **Crow system,** named after the North American Indian tribe, is the matrilineal equivalent of the patrilineal Omaha

In the Omaha system, 2 is called by the same term as father (3); 5 is called by the same term as mother (4); but 1 and 6 have separate terms. In Ego's generation, 9–14 are all considered siblings, but 7 and 8 are equated with the generation of Ego's children, while 15 and 16 are equated with the generation of Ego's parents.

Iroquois system: System of kinship terminology wherein one's father and father's brother are referred to by a single term, as are one's mother and mother's sister, but one's father's sister and one's mother's brother are given separate terms; parallel cousins are classified with brothers and sisters, but not with cross cousins.

Bifurcate merging: A system of kinship terminology in which maternal and paternal relatives of the parental generation are separated (or bifurcated) and given different names, while others are combined (or merged) under a common term (father with father's brother, mother with mother's sister).

Omaha system: A mode of kinship classification usually but not always associated with patrilineal descent in which a line of mother's patrilineal kin are terminologically equated across generations.

Crow system: System of kinship terminology that is the matrilineal equivalent of the patrilineal Omaha system. Thus, one's mother and one's mother's sister are called by the same term, whereas one's father and father's brother are merged under another, while one's father's sister and father's sister's daughter are merged under a third.

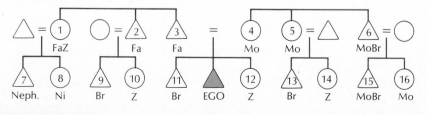

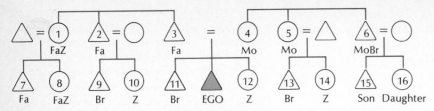

The Crow system is the obverse of the Omaha system. Those numbered 4 and 5 are merged under a single term, as are 2, 3, and 7. Ego's parallel cousins (9, 10, 13, 14) are considered siblings, while mother's brother's children (15, 16) are equated with Ego's own children.

system. Thus, one's mother and one's mother's sister are designated by a single term, whereas one's father and father's brother are merged together under another, while one's father's sister and father's sister's daughter are merged together under a third. The term "father's sister" serves to mark out the line of matrilineal descent in ego's father's lineage. One's male parallel cousins receive the same term as one's

brother; one's female parallel cousins receive the same term as one's sister.

Descriptive System

In the relatively rare **descriptive system,** one's mother's brother is distinguished from one's father's brother, as is one's mother's sister from one's father's sister. Each cousin is distinguished from each other, as well as from siblings. It is therefore more precise than any of the other systems, including our own. This may be one reason it is so rare. In few societies are all one's aunts, uncles, cousins, and siblings treated differently from one another.

CHAPTER SUMMARY

In all societies, family organization is the principal means for dealing with the basic problems faced by all human groups. But some problems are beyond the scope of the family, such as those involving defense or the allocation of resources. In nonindustrial societies kinship groups commonly serve these functions. As societies become larger and more complex, formal political systems take over many of these matters.

A common form of kinship group is the descent group, which has as its criterion of membership descent from a common ancestor through a series of parent-child links. Unilineal descent establishes kinship exclusively through the male or female line. Matrilineal descent is traced through the female line; patrilineal, through the male.

The descent system is closely tied to the economic base of a society. Generally, patrilineal descent predominates where the male is the breadwinner, matrilineal where the female is the breadwinner. Anthropologists now recognize that in all societies the kin of both mother and father are important

> **Descriptive system:** System of kinship terminology wherein one's father, father's brother, and mother's brother are distinguished from one another as are mother, mother's sister, and father's sister; and cousins are distinguished from each other as well as from siblings.

elements in the social structure, regardless of how descent group membership is defined.

The male members of a patrilineage trace their descent from a common male ancestor. A female belongs to the same descent group as her father and his brother; but her children cannot trace their descent through him. Typically, responsibility for training the children lies with the father or his elder brother.

In one respect, matrilineal descent is the opposite of patrilineal descent, with descent being traced through the female line. Unlike the patrilineal pattern, which confers authority on men, matrilineal descent does not confer authority on women. The matrilineal system is common in societies in which women perform much of the productive work. This system is often the source of family tension, since the husband's authority is not in his own household but in that of his sister. Divorce is often common in matrilineal societies.

Double descent is matrilineal for some purposes and patrilineal for others. Ambilineal descent provides a measure of flexibility in that an individual has the option of affiliating with either the mother's or the father's descent group.

Descent groups are often highly structured economic units that provide aid and security to their members. They may also be repositories of religious tradition, with group solidarity enhanced by worship of a common ancestor. A lineage is a corporate descent group made up of consanguineal kin who are able to trace their genealogical links to a common ancestor. Since lineages are commonly exogamous, sexual competition within the group is largely avoided. In addition, marriage of a member of the group represents an alliance of two lineages. Lineage exogamy also serves to maintain open communication within a society and fosters the exchange of information among lineages.

Fission is the splitting up of a large lineage group into new, smaller lineages, with the original lineage becoming a clan. Clan members claim descent from a common ancestor but without actually knowing the genealogical links to that ancestor. Unlike lineages, clan residence is usually dispersed rather than localized. In the absence of residential unity, clan identification is reinforced by totems, usually symbols from nature, that remind members of their common ancestry. A phratry or moiety is a unilineal descent group of two or more clans which are supposedly related.

Bilateral kinship, characteristic of Western society, is traced through both parents simultaneously and recognizes several ancestors. An individual is affiliated equally with all relatives on both the mother's and father's sides. Such a large group is socially impractical and is usually reduced to a small circle of paternal and maternal relatives called the kindred. A kindred is never the same for any two persons except siblings. Because of its vagueness, temporary nature, and changeableness, the kindred is a weaker social unit than the descent group.

Different types of descent systems appear in different societies. In industrial societies as well as among hunting and gathering peoples, where the nuclear family is paramount, bilateral kinship and kindred organization are likely to prevail.

In any society, cultural rules dictate the way kinship relationships are defined. Factors such as sex, generational differences, or genealogical differences help distinguish one kin from another. The Hawaiian system is the simplest kinship system. All relatives of the same generation and sex are referred to by the same name. The Eskimo system, used by Anglo-American cultures, emphasizes the nuclear family and merges all other relatives without differentiating among them. In the Iroquois system, the same term is used for an individual's father and father's brother, as well as for one's mother and mother's sister. In the Omaha and Crow systems no distinction is made between generations among certain kinsmen. The relatively rare descriptive system treats all one's aunts, uncles, cousins, and siblings as different from one another.

SUGGESTED READINGS

Fox, Robin. *Kinship and Marriage in an Anthropological Perspective*. Baltimore: Penguin, 1968.

An excellent introduction to the concepts of kinship and marriage, outlining some of the methods of analysis used in the anthropological treatment of kinship and marriage. Updates Radcliffe-Brown's *African Systems of Kinship and Marriage* and features a perspective focused on kinship groups and social organization.

Goodenough, Ward H. *Description and Comparison in Cultural Anthropology*. Chicago: Aldine, 1970.

This is an important contribution to the study of social organization which confronts the problem of describing kinship organization—kindred and clan, sibling and cousin—in such a way that meaningful cross-cultural comparisons can be made.

Keesing, Roger M. *Kin Groups and Social Structure*. New York: Holt, Rinehart and Winston, 1975.

This is a high-level introduction to kinship theory suitable for advanced undergraduate students. A strong point of the work is the attention given to nonunilineal, as well as unilineal, systems.

Needham, Rodney, ed. *Rethinking Kinship and Marriage*. New York: Barnes & Noble, 1972.
    This is a collection of papers dealing with various aspects of the concept of kinship and marriage. Although fairly technical, it provides an introduction by the editor on present issues in theory and practice in the field of social anthropology.
Schusky, Ernest L. *Variation in Kinship*. New York: Holt, Rinehart and Winston, 1975.
    This book is an introduction to kinship, descent, and residence for the beginner. A reliance on a case study approach leads the reader from basic data to generalizations, a strategy that helps remove some of the abstraction students of kinship organization sometimes find confusing.

10 | Age, Common Interest, and Stratification

These North American women are members of a church group holding its annual Christmas bazaar to raise funds. Such groups constitute examples of common-interest associations. Groups based on common interest are particularly prominent in modern industrial societies, but are found in many of the world's traditional societies as well.

PREVIEW

WHAT IS AGE GRADING?

Age grading—the formation of groups on the basis of age—is a means of organizing people without recourse to kinship or descent. The principle is widely used in human societies, including our own. In industrial societies or nonindustrial societies in which populations are relatively large, age grades may be broken down in age sets—groups of people of approximately the same age who move as groups through the series of age grades.

WHAT ARE COMMON-INTEREST ASSOCIATIONS?

Common-interest associations are formed to deal with specific problems. They acquire their members through an act of joining on the part of individuals. This act may range all the way from fully voluntary to compulsory. Common-interest associations have been a feature of human societies since the advent of the first farming villages several thousand years ago, but have become especially prominent in modern industrial or industrializing societies.

WHAT IS SOCIAL STRATIFICATION?

Stratification is the division of society into two or more classes of people that do not share equally in basic resources, influence, or prestige. Such class structure is characteristic of all of the world's societies in which one finds large and heterogeneous populations with centralized political control. Among others, these include the ancient civilizations of the Middle East, Asia, Mexico, and Peru, as well as modern industrial societies, including our own.

WHAT DO SUCH GROUPS DO IN HUMAN SOCIETIES?

Age grades and sets, common-interest associations, and social classes are organizing devices that societies may use to deal with problems not conveniently handled by the family, descent group, or kindred. While by no means unimportant in the world's more traditional societies, they tend to become more prominent as traditional ways give way to new ones, with new problems to solve.

Social organization based on kinship and marriage has received an extraordinary amount of attention from anthropologists, and the subject usually is quite prominent in anthropological writing. There are several reasons for this: in one way or another, kinship and marriage operate as organizing principles in all societies, and in the tribal and band societies traditionally studied by anthropologists, they are usually the most important organizational principles. There is, too, a certain fascination in the almost mathematical way in which kinship systems at least appear to work. To the unwary, all this attention to kinship and marriage may convey the impression that these are the only principles of social organization that really count. Yet, it is obvious from the case of our own society that other principles of social organization not only exist but may be quite important.

While kinship and marriage seem to be sufficient to handle most of the organizational problems there may be in some societies, they frequently are supplemented by other principles. Beyond this, as traditional ways are forced to vie with new ones, the importance of kinship diminishes to a great degree. One or more members of a family may be forced to leave their village for work in the cities or the mines, or are drawn away from home by a desire for adventure and excitement. In the United States, there has been some movement out of the cities back to the farm on the part of young people in recent years, but elsewhere in the world, movement of young people in search of both opportunity and excitement, to cities such as Caracas, Nairobi, or Port Moresby continues. Old ways may be abruptly dropped in such a move, or they may be snatched away, as under colonial rule or the coming of the missionaries. As kinship serves less and less the organizational needs of societies in such circumstances, other forms of association arise to take its place. Among these forms of nonkinship social organization we will examine age grouping, common-interest associations, and stratification.

AGE GROUPING

Age grouping is so familiar and so important that it and sex have sometimes been called the only universal factors in the determination of one's position in society. In our own society, our first friends generally are children our own age. Together we are sent off to school where together we remain until our late teens. At a certain age we become "legally adult," meaning that we can vote, should support ourselves, and must, if required, go off to war. Until that time we are not supposed to drink liquor, drive a car, or do any number of things reserved for our elders. Ultimately, we retire from our jobs and, more and more, live out the final years of our lives with others of our own age in "retirement communities," segregated

Age grading in modern North American society is exemplified by the educational system, which specifies that at 6 years of age all children must enter the first grade.

from the rest of society. We are "teenagers," "middle-aged," "senior citizens," whether we like it or not, and for no other reason than our age.

The pervasiveness of age grouping in our own society is further illustrated by its effects on the Jewish descent groups that we discussed in Chapter 9. Until well into the 1930s, these always took on a more or less conventional ambilineal structure, which united relatives of all generations from the very old to the very young, with no age restrictions. But by the late 1930s, younger generations of Jews of eastern European background were becoming assimilated into North American culture to the degree that some of them began to form new descent groups that deliberately excluded any kin of the parental and grandparental generations. In these new cousins clubs, as they are called, descendants of the cousins are eligible for membership, but not until they reach legal majority or are married, whichever comes first. Here again, these newer descent groups contrast with the older family circles, in which membership can be activated at any age, no matter how young.

Age classification also plays a significant role in non-Western societies, where at least a distinction is made among the immature, mature, and older people whose physical powers are waning. Old age often has profound significance, bringing with it the period of greatest respect (for women it may mean the first social equality with men), although it may also in some cases mean abandonment—psychological, as in the United States, or literal, as in certain Eskimo societies when the physical survival of the group is at stake. The ultimate irony is that in the United States, all of the ingenuity of modern science is used to keep alive the bodies of individuals who, in virtually every other way, have been shunted aside by society.

> **Age grade:** A category of people based on age; every individual passes through a series of such categories in the course of a lifetime.

> **Age class:** A collection of people occupying an age grade.

One thing that may contribute to the frequent "casting away" of the elderly in our society is that we rely on the written word for our long-term memory. In nonliterate societies, by contrast, the elders are the repository of accumulated wisdom; they are the "living libraries" for their people. To cast them aside would be analogous to closing down all the archives and libraries in our society.

The institutionalization of age, as P. Gulliver points out, makes it clear that cultural rather than biological factors are of prime importance in determining social status.[1] All human societies recognize a number of life stages; precisely how they are defined will vary from one culture to another. Out of this recognition they establish patterns of activity, attitudes, prohibitions, and obligations. In some instances, they are designed to help the transition from one age to another, to teach needed skills, or to lend economic assistance. Often they are taken as the basis for the formation of organized groups.

Institutions of Age Grouping

An organized group of people with membership on the basis of age is known as an **age grade.** The actual individuals currently occupying an age grade form an **age class.** Theoretically speaking, membership in an age grade ought to be automatic: one

---

[1] P. Gulliver, "Age Differentiation," *International Encyclopedia of the Social Sciences,* 1968, 1:157–162.

In many societies, it is common for children of the same age to play, eat, and learn together, like this group of African boys. Such a group may form the basis of age-set organization.

age-grade members may have much in common, engage in similar activities, cooperate with one another, and share the same orientation and aspirations, their membership may not be entirely parallel with physiological age. A specific time is often ritually established for moving from a younger to an older grade. Although members of senior groups commonly expect deference from and acknowledge certain responsibilities to their juniors, this does not necessarily mean that one grade is "better" or "worse" or even more important than another. There can be standardized competition (opposition) between age grades, such as between sophomores and freshmen on U.S. college campuses. One can, comparably, accept the realities of being a teenager without feeling the need to "prove anything."

Some forms of age-set organizations are found in North American society, as illustrated here by the annual tug of war between the freshman and sophomore classes at Dartmouth College.

reaches the appropriate age, and so one is included, without question, in the particular age grade. Just such situations do exist, as among the East African Tiriki, who are the subject of the Original Study later in this chapter. Sometimes, though, one has to buy one's way into the age grade for which one is eligible. For example, among some of the Indian tribes of the North American plains, boys had to purchase the appropriate costumes, dances, and songs for age-grade membership. In societies where entrance fees are expensive, not all people eligible for membership in a particular age grade may actually be able to join.

Entry into and transfer out of age grades may be accomplished individually, either by a biological distinction, such as puberty, or by a socially recognized status, such as marriage or childbirth. Whereas

In some societies, age grades are subdivided into **age sets.** An age set is a group of persons initiated into an age grade who will move through the system together. For example, among the Tiriki of East Africa, the age group consisting of those initiated into an age grade over a 15-year period amounts to an age set. Age sets, unlike age grades, do not cease to exist after a specified number of years; the members of an age set usually remain closely associated throughout their lives, or at least through much of their lives.

> **Age sets:** Groups of persons initiated into age grades at the same time and who move through the series of categories together.

A certain amount of controversy has arisen over the relative strength, cohesiveness, and stability that go into an age grouping. The age-set notion implies strong feelings of loyalty and mutual support. Because such groups may possess property, songs, shield designs, and rituals, and are internally organized for collective decision-making and leadership, a distinction is called for between them and simple age-grade groupings. We may also distinguish between transitory age grades—which initially concern younger men (sometimes women too), but become less important and disintegrate as the members grow older—and the comprehensive systems that affect people through the whole of their lives.

Age Groupings in African Societies

While age is used as a criterion for group membership in many parts of the world, its most varied and elaborate use is found in Africa south of the Sahara. An example of a simple, traditionally defined age class is the Nuer of East Africa, as described by E. E. Evans-Pritchard.[2] Among the Nuer, the position of every male in relation to every other male Nuer is defined only in terms of seniority, equality, or juniority. Initiation has no educational or moral purpose. At initiation a boy receives a spear from his father or uncle and becomes a warrior; he is given an ox and becomes a herdsman. Once initiated, he remains in this grade for the rest of his life. His new status implies no administrative, judicial, or other political or military functions other than a taboo against milking, and his domestic duties remain largely unstructured until marriage. His membership does have certain definite ritual observations and avoidances; for example, a man may not marry or have sexual relations with the daughter of an age mate, for she is regarded as his "daughter" and he as her "father." In matters of etiquette and division of food, his behavior is carefully structured according to seniority. These distinctions have no connotation of privilege but only of stratification and are superseded only by kinship.

More elaborate age groupings are to be seen among the Afikpo Ibo of Eastern Nigeria.[3] A village men's society, the *Ogo*, is found in every Afikpo village. All initiated males perform religious, moral, and recreational functions involving the overall society, including the establishment of rules of conduct for all villagers. Also influential to a certain degree are age sets, which consist of persons living in one village born within

[2] E. E. Evans-Pritchard, *The Nuer: A Description of the Modes of Livelihood and Political Institutions of a Nilotic People* (London: Oxford University Press, 1968).

[3] Phoebe Ottenberg, "The Afikpo Ibo of Eastern Nigeria," in James L. Gibbs, Jr., ed., *Peoples of Africa* (New York: Holt, Rinehart and Winston, 1965), pp. 3–39.

approximately three years of one another. Men's and women's sets are paired and support one another in feasting and ceremonial activities. Age grades, composed of several contiguous age sets, form a larger body with important social and economic functions, strong feelings of loyalty, and mutual support. Age sets are formed on a village basis; age grades are organized on the basis of both the village and village group. Women's age sets and age grades exist at less highly organized levels and are subject to rulings of the men's age grades. Since the 1940s, village improvement associations and village group unions have also arisen.

Among the Afikpo, age grouping applies primarily to males. Girls' age groups sometimes occur, but the rights and obligations individually acquired in marriage and motherhood effectively curtail further relationships by age. Affairs purely for women are often organized by married women's groups, but age is an infrequent criterion, and the groups are weakly developed. Men's age grades determine the relationships for both men and women.

ORIGINAL STUDY

Changing Age-Group Organization among the Tiriki of Kenya[4]

The Tiriki age group organization is directly borrowed from the Nilo-Hamitic Terik who border the Tiriki to the south. There are seven named age groups (Kabalach, Golongolo, Jiminigayi, Nyonje, Mayina, Juma, and Sawe), each embracing approximately a fifteen-year age span. In addition, each age group passes successively through four distinctive age grades. The system is cyclical, each age group being reinstated with new initiates approximately every 105 years.

Perhaps the easiest way to grasp the difference in age groups and age grades is to review the nature of our college class system. Freshmen entering college in the autumn of 1958, for example, immediately become known as the Class of 1962—the year when they are due to graduate. Thenceforth, for as long as they live, they are known as the Class of 1962. While in college, however, members of the Class of 1962 must pass in successive years through four ranked grades: freshman, sophomore, junior, and senior.

In Tiriki each age group contains those men who were initiated over a fifteen-year age span, not simply during one year. The initiation rites . . . traditionally extend over a six months' period, and are held every four years; thus each age group receives recruits from three or four successive initiations. The four traditional Tiriki age grades are "bandu bi lihe," "balulu" (the warriors),

---

[4] From "The Bantu Tiriki of Western Kenya," by Walter H. Sangree, in *Peoples of Africa,* edited by James Gibbs, Jr. Copyright © 1965 by Holt, Rinehart and Winston, Inc. Reprinted by permission of Holt, Rinehart and Winston, pp. 69–72.

"balulu basaxulu" (the elder warriors), "basaxulu bi bilina," "basaxulu bu luhya" (the judicial elders), and "basaxulu basaalisi" (the ritual elders). Before they were prohibited by the British about 1900, handing-over ceremonies were held at about fifteen-year intervals in conjunction with the closing of an age group to more initiates. At this time the age group just closed to initiates became formally instated in the warriors age grade, the age group that had just been the warriors' moved on to the elder warrior grade, the former elder warriors moved on to the judicial elder grade, and the former judicial elders moved on to the ritual eldership.

The cyclical aspect of Tiriki age groups can also be readily compared with the system of college classes, if one substitutes the Tiriki age group name for "Class of ___," and remembers that each Tiriki age group embraces fifteen years. The Class of '62 at Harvard, for example, has been reinstated every 100 years for several centuries with a new group of college men, and thus can be viewed as part of a cyclical process. In Tiriki each cycle lasts 105 years instead of a century, because the seven age groups, "each" embracing fifteen years, cover a total span of 105 years. The Sawe age group, for example, open for initiates from 1948 to 1963, was previously instated and open to initiates from roughly 1843 to 1858.

The "warriors" were formally given the responsibility of guarding the country. They were said "to hold the land." An age group's lasting reputation was principally earned while it was occupying the warrior age grade. Similarly

The Tiriki initiates are shown wearing initiation garb.

the reputation accompanying a man throughout the remainder of his life and then remembered by his posterity was primarily based on the leadership, courage, and good fortune he exhibited while a warrior.

The duties and prerogatives of the "elder warriors" were neither as glorious nor as well defined as those of the warriors. They had relatively few specialized social tasks, but they gradually assumed an increasing share of administrative type activities in areas that were basically the responsibility of the elder age groups. For example, at public post-funeral gatherings held to settle property claims, usually a man of the elder warrior group was called upon to serve as chairman. His duty was to maintain order, to see that all the claims and counterclaims were heard, to initiate compromises, but always to seek and defer to the judgment of the elders in matters that were equivocal or a departure from tradition. Members of this age grade also served as couriers and envoys when important news needed to be transmitted between elders of different subtribes.

The age group occupying the "judicial elder" age grade fulfilled most of the tasks connected with the arbitration and settlement of local disputes. This included everything from delinquent or contested bridewealth payments to cases of assault or accidental injury. Any major disturbance or legitimate complaint by the head of a household served as sufficient reason for the community judicial elders to gather at the local meeting ground to hear the plaintiff and defendant, question witnesses, and give a judgment.

The "ritual elders" presided over the priestly functions of the homestead ancestral shrine observances, at subclan meetings concerning inheritance and the like, at semiannual community supplications, and at the initiation rites. Also, the ritual elders were accredited with having access to magical powers. They were the group who expelled or killed witches, or at least who were counted on to neutralize their evil powers, and they also were the group who underwrote the death through sorcery of anyone cursed by the community for violating the initiation secrets or for committing some other heinous crime. The advice of the ritual elders was sought in all situations that seemed to hold danger for or entail the general well-being of the community or the tribe. For example, the warriors solicited the auguries of the ritual elders before embarking on a major raid, and postponed the raid if the omens were bad.

Today, over sixty years after the last formal handing-over ceremony, the age group cycle still continues, kept alive by the regular performance of the initiation rites. The four graded statuses are still manifest in informal social behavior and in current social ideology and action, albeit in relatively informal and altered form. Young men whose age group according to traditional reckoning would now be warriors, are still occasionally called, or referred to as "warriors," but only in a spirit of friendliness and flattery. Today, instead of fighting, young men of this age grade find a modicum of excitement and adventure through extended employment away from the tribe. A fortunate few are pursuing secondary or advanced studies, teaching school, or holding clerical jobs; but in most cases they, too, are employed or are studying off-tribe. Members of the warrior age grade are no longer held in such esteem as formerly, and no one ever speaks of them as "holding the land." Their active participation, however, in the new and rapidly changing world beyond tribal boundaries still lends the warrior age grade a bit of glamour.

In contrast to that of the warriors, the relative status of those occupying the elder warrior age grade has increased dramatically during the last fifty years. Men of this age grade have assumed nearly all the new administrative and executive roles created by the advent and growth of a centralized tribal administrative bureaucracy. With few exceptions they hold all the salaried offices in the tribal administration. It is quite in keeping with traditional age grade expectations that members of this age grade should occupy the executive and administrative positions, but pre-European conditions provided only a minimal number of such roles.

The judicial elders still serve as the local judiciary body, although their authority was somewhat altered and curtailed by the British colonial administration.

The ritual elders have suffered a severe diminution of their functions and powers. During the last twenty years, ancestor worship has declined until today the formal aspects of the cult are virtually extinct. They, like the warriors, have been deprived of a major part of their traditional age grade activity; but unlike the warriors, they have not found any substitute activity. The positions of leadership in the Christian church have been assumed by a small number of men, mostly of the elder warrior age grade. The ritual elders continue, however, to hold the most important positions in the initiation ceremonies, and their power as sorcerers and witchcraft expungers remains almost universally feared and respected.

The role of age groups varies considerably as these examples show; yet they are always of great importance in maintaining social continuity, in providing "performers" for various social roles from generation to generation, and in transmitting the social and cultural heritage of a society. This importance tends to increase in societies in which kinship is insufficient to provide workable solutions to all of a society's need for functional divisions among its members. This may be because age is a criterion that can be applied to all members of a society in the allocation of roles. Moreover, since age relationships have no contractual bond to begin with, there is no obstruction to setting up standards of behavior based on age. So strong is the force of age grouping that it is capable of cutting across and conflicting with both political and kinship ties, and with the possibilities of specialization and the achievement of privilege by effort and good fortune in a stratified society. In such instances, kinship dominates only where conflict might arise through antipathetic age roles.

Age, therefore, must be accepted as a force creating social units. Yet it may play only an indirect role in grouping; its influence is limited by sex division, and systems for social organization exist outside age and kinship grouping.

COMMON-INTEREST ASSOCIATIONS

The rise of **common-interest associations,** whether out of individual predilection or community need, is a theme intimately associated with world urbanization and its attendant social upheavals; our own society's fondness for joining is incontestably related to its complexity. This phenomenon poses a major threat to the inviolability of age and kinship grouping. Individuals are often separated from their brothers, sisters, or age mates; they obviously cannot obtain their help in learning to cope with life in a new and bewildering environment, in learning a new language or mannerisms necessary for the change from village to city if they are not present. But such functions must somehow be met. Because common-interest associations are by nature quite flexible, they are increasingly, both in the cities and in tribal villages, filling this gap in the social structure. But common-interest associations are not restricted to modernizing societies alone; they are to be found in many traditional societies as well. There is reason to believe that they may have arisen with the emergence of the first horticultural villages.[5]

Common-interest associations have traditionally been referred to in the anthropological literature as voluntary associations, but this term is misleading. The act of joining may range from being fully voluntary to being required by law. For example, in our society, under the draft laws one sometimes became a member of the armed forces without choosing to join. It is not really compulsory to join a labor union, but unless one does, one can't work in a union shop. What really is meant by the term

This pair of pictures furnishes implicit evidence of the value of common-interest associations in bringing benefit to the group members. Above is a turn-of-the-century factory scene; below is a meeting of a powerful modern labor union.

[5] James N. Kerri, "Studying Voluntary Associations as Adaptive Mechanisms: A Review of Anthropological Perspectives," *Current Anthropology*, 1976, 17(1):25.

"voluntary association" are those associations not based on age, kinship, marriage, or territory that result from an act of joining. The act may often be voluntary, but it doesn't have to be.

> **Common-interest associations: Associations not based on age, kinship, marriage, or territory that result from an act of joining.**

Kinds of Common-Interest Associations

The diversity of common-interest associations is astonishing. Their goals may include the pursuit of friendship, recreation, and the expression and distinction of rank as well as governing function and the pursuit or defense of economic interests. Traditionally, associations have served for the preservation of tribal songs, history, language, and moral beliefs; the Tribal Unions of West Africa, for example, continue to serve this purpose. Similar organizations, often operating clandestinely, have kept traditions alive among North American Indians who are undergoing a resurgence of ethnic pride despite generations of reservation schooling. Also a significant force in the formation of associations is the supernatural experience common to all members; the Crow Indian Tobacco Society, the secret associations of the Kwakiutl Indians of British Columbia with their cycles of secret rituals, and the Katchina Cults of the Pueblo Indians are well-known examples. Among other traditional forms of association are military, occupational, political, and entertainment groups that parallel such familiar groups as the American Legion, labor unions, block associations, and "co-ops" of every kind.

Such organizations are frequently exclusive, but a prevailing characteristic is their concern for the general well-being of an entire village or village group. The rain that falls as a result of the work of Pueblo rainmakers nourishes the crops of members and nonmembers alike.

The diversity of common-interest associations is astonishing. Shown here are a street gang, and Ralph Nader with members of his organization testifying on behalf of consumer interests.

MEN'S AND WOMEN'S ASSOCIATIONS Until recently, women's contributions to common-interest associations have been regarded by social scientists as less significant than men's. The reason is that men's associations generally have been more noticeable around the world than women's. Heinrich Schurtz's theory, published in 1902, that underlying the differentiation between kinship and associational groups is a profound difference in the psychology of the sexes was widely accepted for years.[6] To Schurtz, women were eminently unsocial beings who preferred to remain in kinship groups based on sexual relations and the reproductive function rather than form units on the basis of commonly held interests. Men, on the other hand, were said to view sexual relations as isolated episodes, an attitude that fostered the purely social factor that makes "birds of a feather flock together."

Today, needless to say, this kind of thinking is being heatedly challenged by scholars of both sexes. It is suggested that women have not formed associations to the extent that men have because of the demands of raising a family and their daily activities, and because men have frequently not encouraged them to do so. But given the plethora of women's clubs of all kinds in the United States for several generations, one wonders how this belief of women as unsocial survived as long as it did. Earlier, of course, when women had to stay at home in rural situations, with no near neighbors, they had little chance to participate in com-

[6]Dorothy Hammond, *Associations* (Reading, Mass.: Addison-Wesley, Modular Publications, 14, 1972), p. 8.

Common-interest associations are not limited to modern industrial societies. This 1833 picture shows a Mandan Indian Bull Dance. The Bulls were one of several common-interest groups which were at once concerned with social and military affairs.

mon-interest associations. Moreover, some functions of men's associations—like military duties—may be culturally defined as purely for men or simply repugnant to women. Finally, in a number of the world's traditional societies, the opportunities for female sociability are so great that there may be little need for women's associations. Among the Indians of northern New England and Canada south of the St. Lawrence River, the men spent extended periods off in the woods hunting, either by themselves or with a single companion. The women, by contrast, spent most of their time in their village, in close, everyday contact with all the other women of the group. Not only were there lots of people to talk to but there was always someone available to help with whatever tasks required assistance.

But, as Robert Lowie and others clearly point out, women do play important roles in associations of their own and even in those in which men predominate. Among the Crow, women participated even in the secret Tobacco Society as well as in their own exclusive groups. Throughout Africa, women's social clubs complement the men's and are concerned with educating women and with crafts and charitable activities. In Sierra Leone, where once-simple dancing societies have developed under urban conditions into complex organizations with a set of modern objectives, the dancing *compin* is made up of young women as well as men, who together perform plays based on traditional music and dancing and raise money for various mutual benefit causes. The Kpelle of Liberia maintain initiation or "bush" schools for both young men and women; women also alternate with men in ritual supremacy of a chiefdom. The cycle of instruction and rule (four years for males, three for females) that marks these periods derives from the

Kpelle's association of the number four with maleness and three with femaleness rather than from a notion of sexual superiority.

Women's liberation organizations, consciousness-raising groups, and professional organizations for women are examples of some of the associations arising directly or indirectly out of today's social climate. These groups cover the entire range of association forming, from simple friendship and support groups to political, guildlike, and economic (the publication of magazines, groups designed to influence advertising) associations on a national scale. If an unresolved point does exist in the matter of women's participation, it is in determining why women are excluded from associations in some societies, whereas in others their participation is essentially equal with that of men.

Associations in the Urban World

The importance of common-interest associations in areas of rapid social change is considerable. Increasingly such organizations assume the roles and functions formerly held by kinship or age groups; in many areas, they hold the key both to individual adaptation to new circumstances and to group survival. Where once groups were organized to preserve traditional ways and structure against the intrusion of the modern world, urban associations accept the reality of such intrusions and help their members to cope both socially and economically. Members may turn to associations for support and sympathy while unemployed or sick; the groups may also provide education or socialization. An important need met by many of these associations is economic survival; to achieve such ends they may help raise capital, regu-

Political parties are a frequent form of common-interest association, and their formation is characteristic of Third World countries in the throes of modernization. These pictures were taken at the 1976 U.S. Democratic and Republican conventions.

late prices, discourage competition, and organize cooperative activities.

Always the keynote of these groups is adaptation. As Kenneth Little observes, adaptation implies not only the modification of institutions but also the development of new ones to meet the demands of an industrial economy and urban way of life.[7] Modern urbanism involves the rapid diffusion of entirely new ideas, habits, and technical procedures, as well as a considerable reconstruction of social relationships as a consequence of new technical roles and groups created. Age-old conventions yield to necessity, as women and young people in general gain new status in the urban economy. Women's participation, especially in associations with mixed membership, involves them in new kinds of social relationships with men, including companionship and the chance to choose a mate by oneself. Young persons on the whole become leaders for their less Westernized counterparts. Even in rural areas, such associations thrive, reflecting the increasing consciousness of the outer world. With an irony implicit in many former colonial situations, the European contact that so frequently shattered permanent age and kinship groups has, partly through the influence of education, helped remove restrictions in association membership both in age and sex.

In our own culture, common-interest associations such as women's clubs, Boy and Girl Scouts, Kiwanis, Rotary, and PTA abound. Elements of secret initiatory cults survive, to some extent, in the Masonic lodges and fraternity and sorority initiations. Women's associations recently seem to have proliferated. Although we may

[7] Kenneth Little, "The Role of Voluntary Associations in West African Urbanization," in Pierre Van den Berghe, ed., *Africa: Social Problems of Change and Conflict* (San Francisco: Chandler, 1964).

think of our own groups as more complex and highly organized than those of traditional non-Western societies, many of the new urban voluntary associations in Africa, for example, are elaborately structured and rival many of our secular and religious organizations. Such traditional groups, with their antecedents reaching far back in history, may have served as models for associations familiar to us; now, in becoming Westernized, they promise to outstrip our own in complexity, an interesting phenomenon to watch as the non-Western countries become "modernized."

SOCIAL STRATIFICATION

The study of social stratification involves the examination of distinctions that may seem unfair or even outrageous. But social stratification is a common and powerful phenomenon in some of the world's societies. Civilizations in particular, with their large and heterogeneous populations, are invariably stratified.

Basically, a **stratified society** is one that is divided into two or more groups of people, and these groups are ranked high and low relative to one another. When the people in one such group or stratum are compared with those in another, marked differences in privileges, rewards, restrictions, and obligations become apparent. Members of low-ranked groups will tend to have fewer privileges than those in higher-ranked groups. In addition, they tend not to be rewarded to the same degree, and their restrictions and obligations are apt to be a bit more onerous, although members of high-ranked groups will usually have their own distinctive restrictions and obligations to attend to. In short, social stratification amounts to institutionalized inequality. Without ranking—high versus low—there

> **Stratified society:** A class-structured society in which all members do not share equally in the basic resources that support life or in influence and social prestige.
>
> **Egalitarian societies:** Political systems in which as many valued positions exist as there are persons capable of filling them.
>
> **Social class:** A set of families that enjoy equal, or nearly equal, prestige according to the system of evaluation.

is no stratification; social differences without this do not constitute stratification.

Stratified societies stand in sharp contrast to **egalitarian societies.** As we saw in Chapter 6, hunting and gathering societies are characteristically egalitarian, although there are some exceptions. In such societies, there are as many valued positions as there are people capable of filling them. Hence, individuals' positions in society depend pretty much on their own abilities alone. A poor hunter may become a good hunter if he has the ability; he is not excluded from such a prestigious position because he comes from a group of poor hunters. Poor hunters do not constitute a social stratum. Furthermore, they have as much right to the resources of their society as any other of its members. No one can deny a poor hunter a fair share of food, the right to be heard when important decisions are to be made, or anything else to which a man is entitled.

Class and Caste

The basic unit of stratification is known as a **social class.** A class may be de-

India's caste system is one of the most rigid known, though it has now changed considerably. Still, low-caste people are barred from many kinds of social opportunities. Rapid change in the system may bring benefits to such individuals, but it also creates much social confusion.

fined as a set of families that show equal, or nearly equal, prestige according to the system of evaluation.[8] The qualification "nearly equal" is important, for there may be a certain amount of inequality within a given class. If this is so, to an outside observer low-ranking individuals in an upper class may not look much different from the highest-ranking members of a lower class. Yet there will be marked differences when the classes are compared as wholes with one another. The point here is that class distinctions will not be clear-cut and obvious in societies such as our own where there is a continuous range of differential privileges, for example, from virtually none to several. Such a continuum can be divided up into classes in a variety of ways. If fine distinctions are made, then many classes may be recognized. If, however, only a few gross distinctions are made, then only a few classes will be recognized. Thus, some speak of our society as divided into three classes: lower, middle, and upper. Others speak of several classes: lower-lower, middle-lower, upper-lower, lower-middle, and so forth.

A **caste** is a particular kind of social class, one in which membership is fairly fixed or impermeable. Castes are strongly endogamous, and offspring are automatically members of their parents' caste. The classic case of social castes is the caste structure of India. Coupled with strict endogamy and membership by descent in Indian castes is an association of specific castes with specific occupations and notions of ritual purity and impurity. Indeed, there are some who would restrict use of the term "caste" to the Indian situation. Others find this much too restricted a usage, since castelike situations are known elsewhere in the world. Some people have

[8] Bernard Barber, *Social Stratification* (New York: Harcourt, 1957), p. 73.

argued that in our own society, as automation reduces the need for unskilled workers, a castelike "under class" consisting of unemployed, unemployable, or considerably underemployed people is emerging.[9] Lacking both economic and political power, they are forced to live in both urban and rural slums, where they do not have access to the kinds of educational facilities that would enable them and their children to improve their lot.

---

[9]Gunnar Myrdal, "Challenge to Affluence: The Emergence of an 'Under-class,'" in Joseph O. Jorgensen and Marcello Truzzi, eds., *Anthropology and American Life* (Englewood Cliffs, N.J.: Prentice-Hall, 1974).

> **Caste:** A special form of social class in which membership is determined by birth and remains fixed for life.

The basis of social class structure is role differentiation. There is, of course, always some role differentiation in any society, at least along the lines of sex and age. Furthermore, any necessary role will always be valued to some degree. In a hunting and gathering society, the role of "good hunter" will be valued. However, the fact that one man may already play that role doesn't prevent another man from playing

One indicator of class standing in stratified societies is how people behave toward one another. Here, a village chief in Nigeria has lower standing than the turbaned king, to whom he must pay homage.

Symbolic indicators of class or caste standing include factors of life-style, as illustrated here by ways of enjoying oneself on a hot day, and contrasting neighborhoods.

it too in an egalitarian society. Therefore, role differentiation by itself is not sufficient for stratification. What is necessary are two more ingredients: formalized evaluation of roles involving attitudes such as like-dislike, attraction-revulsion, and restricted access to the more highly valued ones. Obviously, the greater the diversity of roles in a society, the more complex can evaluation and restriction become. Since great role diversity is most characteristic of civilizations, it is not surprising that stratification is one of the usual features of civilization.

Social classes are manifest in several ways. One way is through **verbal evaluation**—what people say about other people in their own society. For this, anything can be singled out for attention and spoken of favorably or unfavorably: political, military, religious, economic, or professional roles; wealth and property; kinship; personal qualities; community activity; and a host of other things. Different cultures do this differently, and what may be spoken of favorably in one may be spoken of unfavorably in another and ignored in a third. Furthermore, cultural values may change, so that something regarded favorably at one point in time may not be at another. This is one reason why a researcher may be misled by verbal evaluation, for what people say may not correspond completely with reality.

Social classes are also manifest through patterns of association; not just who interacts with whom, but in what context, and how do those who are interacting treat one another. In Western society, informal, friendly relations take place mostly within one's own class. Relations with members of other classes tend to be less informal and occur in the context of specific situations. For example, a corporation executive and a janitor normally are members of different social classes. They may

> **Verbal evaluation:** The way people in a stratified society evaluate other members of their own society.

> **Symbolic indicators:** In a stratified society, activities and possessions that are indicative of social class.

have frequent contact with one another, but it occurs in the setting of the corporation offices and usually requires certain stereotyped behavior patterns.

A third way social classes are manifest is through **symbolic indicators.** Included here are activities and possessions indicative of class; for example, in our society, occupation—a garbage collector has different class status than a physician; wealth—rich people generally are in a higher social class than poor people; dress—we have all heard the expression "white collar" versus "blue collar"; form of recreation—upper-class people are expected to play golf rather than shoot pool down at the pool hall (but they can do it at home); residential location—upper-class people do not ordinarily live in slums; kind of car; and so on. The fact is there are all sorts of status symbols indicative of class position, including such things as how many bathrooms one's house has. At the same time, symbolic indicators may be cruder indicators of class position than verbal indicators or patterns of association. One reason is that access to wealth may not be wholly restricted to upper classes, so that individuals can buy status symbols suggestive of upper-class status, whether or not this really is their status. Conversely, a member of an upper class may deliberately choose a more simple life-style than is customary. Instead of driving a Mercedes, he may drive a beat-up Volkswagen.

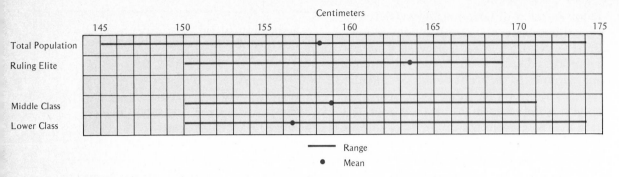

Centimeters

| | 145 | 150 | 155 | 160 | 165 | 170 | 175 |

Total Population

Ruling Elite

Middle Class

Lower Class

——— Range
● Mean

In a stratified society, better food and an easier life usually go with upper-class standing. This may result in greater physical stature in upper-class members of society, as here. The graph shows class-related stature differences in the men of Tikal, an ancient Maya site in Guatemala, between A.D. 700 and 830.

Symbolic indicators involve not only factors of life-style but also differences in life chances. Generally, life is apt to be less hard for members of an upper class as opposed to a lower class. This will show up in a tendency for lower infant mortality and longer life expectancy for the upper class. One may also see a tendency to greater physical stature and robustness on the part of upper-class people, the result of better diet and less hardship.

Mobility

Mobility is present in all stratified societies. Even in the Indian caste system, probably the most restrictive known, there is some mobility. Some of this is associated with the recent changes which "modernization" has brought to India, but there seems to have been some mobility even before this. For example, it was possible for a woman to marry into the next highest subcaste—one notch up—a practice known as **hypergamy.** But the amount of mobility is not great in a caste type of society. Still, there is enough to help ease the strains that exist in any system of inequality.

Those societies that permit a great deal in the way of mobility are referred to as **open class societies.** Even here, though, mobility is apt to be more limited than one might suppose. In the United States, in spite of our "rags to riches" ideology, most mobility involves a move up or down only a notch, although if this continues over several generations, it may add up to a major

Although as a general rule people with high incomes can move up to a higher social class, income is not a foolproof indicator of class standing. These prostitutes have high incomes, but their profession gives them low prestige.

change. Generally, our culture makes much of those relatively rare examples of great mobility which are consistent with our cultural values and tends not to notice the numerous cases of little or no mobility.

The degree of mobility in a stratified society is related to the prevailing kind of family organization. Where the family usually takes the form of an extended family, mobility usually is difficult. The reason is that each individual is strongly tied to the large family group. Hence, for the individual to move up to a higher social class, his or her family must move up too. Mobility is easier where the usual family is the nuclear family. Then, the individual is closely tied to fewer individuals. Moreover, under neolocal residence, individuals normally leave the family into which they were born. So it is, then, that through careful marriage, occupational success, and by severing one's tie to a lower-class family in which one was raised, all of which are based on residential mobility, one can more easily "move up" in society.

Development of Stratification

The evils in social stratification of any kind may tend to overshadow the good; they at least appear to make life oppressive for large segments of a population. Often, the lower classes are placated by means of religion, which offers them a tolerable existence in the hereafter. If they have this to look forward to, they are more likely to accept the "here and now." In considering social stratification, we must, however, reckon with such common tendencies as the desire for prestige, either for oneself or one's group. Although the impulse need not result inevitably in the ranking of individuals or groups relative to one another, it sometimes may.

Mobility: The ability to change one's class position.

Hypergamy: In a caste-structured society, the practice of allowing marriage into the next higher caste.

Open class societies: Stratified societies that permit a great deal of social mobility.

Among the Winebago and Hopi Indians, the Sherente and Ugandan peoples, clan superiority and kinship lineages are recognized in electing chiefs, performing sacred rituals, and other special tasks, whether or not membership entails any economic advantages.

This sort of situation could easily develop into full-fledged stratification. Just such a development may have taken place among the Maya of Central America.[10] There is some indication that these people began as horticulturalists with a relatively egalitarian, kinship-based organization. In the last centuries B.C., a strong religion developed as a way of dealing with the very serious problems of agriculture, such as uncertain rains, vulnerability of crops to a variety of pests, and periodic devastation from hurricanes. As this took place, a priesthood arose, along with some craft specialization in the service of religion. Out of the priesthood developed, in the last century B.C., hereditary ruling dynasties. As all of this took place, certain lineages seem to have monopolized the important civic and ceremonial positions, and these were

[10]William A. Haviland, "The Ancient Maya and the Evolution of Urban Society," *University of Colorado Museum of Anthropology Miscellaneous Series*, 37, 1975; and "A New Look at Classic Maya Social Organization at Tikal," *Ceramica de Cultura Maya*, 1972, 8:1–16.

ranked above other lineages, forming the basis of an upper class.

Just as lineages may come to be ranked differentially relative to one another, so may ethnic groups. One theory on the origin of the Indian caste system is that it was instituted some time after 1500 B.C. by conquerors, who spoke an Indo-European language. The caste system was a means by which they could maintain their favored position in society. Even without conquest, though, ethnic differences often lead to diverse classes and even castes, as members of our own society have experienced through the racial stereotyping that leads to social and economic disadvantages.

Classes perform an integrative function in society. They may cut across some or all lines of kinship, residence, occupation, and age group, depending on the particular society, thus counteracting potential tendencies for society to fragment into discrete entities. Stratification may also provide a means for an alien group to dominate large numbers of people. Those who dominate are aided by their acknowledged "upper-class" status. They try to convert this into respect on the part of the lower classes, who will then "know their place" and so not contest this domination.

CHAPTER SUMMARY

As traditional ways give way to new ones, kinship comes to serve less and less the organizational needs of societies. Age grouping is one form of association that may augment or replace kinship grouping. An age grade is a category of persons, usually of the same sex, organized on the basis of age. The people who occupy an age grade form an age class. Age grades in some societies are broken up into age sets, which include individuals who are initiated into an age grade at the same time and move together through a series of life stages. A specific time is often ritually established for moving from a younger to an older age grade.

The most varied use of grouping by age is found in African societies south of the Sahara. An example of a simple, traditionally defined age class is found among the Nuer of East Africa. Here the position of each male is defined only in terms of seniority, equality, or juniority. More elaborate age groupings are seen among the Afikpo Ibo of eastern Nigeria and the Tiriki of western Kenya. Among the Afikpo Ibo, age grading is well developed among both sexes, although women's age sets and age groups are far less important than those for males. A men's society in every village oversees most village functions. Age sets consist of persons from the same village who are born within three years of one another.

Common-interest associations are linked with rapid social change and urbanization. They are increasingly assuming the roles formerly played by kinship or age groups. In urban areas, they help new arrivals cope with the changes demanded by the move from the village to the city. Common-interest associations are also seen in traditional societies, and some anthropologists believe their roots are to be found in the first horticultural villages. Membership may range from being voluntary to required by law.

Until recently, social scientists have mistakenly viewed women's contributions to common-interest associations as less important than men's, largely because male associations have been more visible. A question that remains to be resolved is why women are barred from associations in some societies, while in others they participate on an equal basis with men.

A stratified society is one that is divided into two or more groups of people which do not share equally in basic resources or in influence and prestige. This form contrasts with the egalitarian society, in which as many valued positions exist as there are persons capable of filling them. Social class is the basic unit of stratification. Members of a class enjoy equal or nearly equal prestige according to the way this is defined. Class differences are not always clear-cut and obvious. Where fine distinctions are made in privileges, the result is a multiplicity of classes. In societies where only gross distinctions are made, there are only a few social classes.

Caste is a special form of social class in which membership is determined by birth and fixed for life. Endogamy is particularly marked within castes, and children automatically belong to their parents' caste. Social class structure is based on role differentiation, although role differentiation by itself is not sufficient for stratification. Also necessary are formalized evaluation of roles involving attitudes and restricted access to the valued roles.

Social classes are given expression in several ways. One is through verbal evaluation, or what people say about other people in their society. Another is through patterns of association—who interacts with whom, how, and in what context. Social classes are also manifest through symbolic indicators. These include activities and possessions indicative of class position.

Mobility is inherent to a greater or lesser extent in all stratified societies. Open-class societies are those that allow a great deal of mobility. In most cases, however, the move is limited to one notch up or down the social ladder. The degree of mobility is related to the type of family organization that prevails in a society. Where the extended family is the pattern, mobility tends to be severely limited. The independent nuclear family provides a situation in which mobility is easier.

Social stratification can be based on many criteria, such as wealth, cultural level, legal status, birth, personal qualities, and ideology. A rigidly stratified society in which mobility is limited can make life oppressive for large segments of a population.

SUGGESTED READINGS

Bradfield, Richard M. *A Natural History of Associations.* New York: International Universities, 1973.

This two-volume work is the first major anthropological study of common-interest associations since 1902. It attempts to provide a comprehensive theory of the origin of associations and their role in kin-based societies.

Eisenstadt, S. N. *From Generation to Generation: Age Groups and Social Structure.* New York: Free Press, 1956.

Various social phenomena known as age-group and youth movements are analyzed to ascertain whether it is possible to specify the social conditions in which they occur. The analysis is based on a study of various societies: "primitive," historical, and modern. The basic hypothesis of the book is that age groups exist in universalistic societies in which the family is not the basic unit of the social division of labor.

Hammond, Dorothy. *Associations.* Reading, Mass.: Addison-Wesley Modular Publications, 14, 1972.

This is a brief, first-rate review of anthropological thinking and the literature on common-interest associations and age groups.

Lenski, Gerhard E. *Power and Privilege: A Theory of Social Stratification.* New York: McGraw-Hill, 1966.

Who gets what and why is explained by the distributive process and systems of social stratification in industrial nations: U.S., U.S.S.R., Sweden, and Britain. Using a broadly comparative approach, the author makes heavy use of anthropological and historical material as well as the usual sociological materials on modern industrial societies. The basic approach is theoretical and analytical; the book builds on certain postulates about the nature of humans and society, seeking to develop in a systematic manner an explanation of a variety of patterns of stratification. The theory presented is a synthesis of the two dominant theoretical traditions of the past and present, currently represented in both Marxian and functionalist theory.

Lowie, Robert H. *Social Organization.* New York: Holt, Rinehart and Winston, 1948.

This is a classic, though somewhat dated, study of social organization. The author discusses social organization on a cross-cultural basis, including age grading and common-interest associations.

Machu Picchu, Peru, an ancient ceremonial and administrative center inhabited by members of the Incan bureaucracy. The integration of the vast empire over which the Incas ruled was achieved through centralized political control in the hands of a ruling elite, an interdependence for goods which were collected and redistributed by the government, and participation in religious ceremonies directed by a strong full-time priesthood. Economics, politics, and religion serve as integrative forces in different ways and to varying degrees in human society.

PART FOUR

SOCIAL INTEGRATION

Solving the Problems of Social Living

INTRODUCTION

I t is an irony of human life that something as fundamental to our existence as cooperation should contain within it the seeds of its own destruction. It is nonetheless true that the groups that people form to take care of important organizational needs do not just facilitate cooperation among the members of those groups, they also create conditions that may lead to the fragmentation of society. The attitude that "my group is better than your group" is not confined to any one of the world's cultures, and it not infrequently takes the form of a sense of rivalry between groups: descent group against descent group, age grade against age grade, social class against social class, and so forth. This is not to say that such rivalry has to be disruptive; indeed, it may function to ensure that the members of groups perform their jobs well so as not to "lose face" or be subject to ridicule. But rivalry can become a serious problem if it develops into conflict. In Western culture, much attention has been given to the subject of social class conflict, which may erupt in revolution. Similarly, relatively unstratified communities in the non-Western world have sometimes split apart along kinship lines because of conflicts between descent groups.

In order to counter the forces that would fragment society, every culture must devise ways by which some kind of overall integration may be achieved. We have already touched upon some of these in previous chapters. One way is through an interdependence between groups of people for goods and services which can be a powerful force for binding those groups together. Another way is through marriage alliances. Under a rule of exogamy, individuals must seek spouses among members of groups other than their own. In such circumstances, the marriage amounts to an alliance between the two groups. Another way is through group memberships which cross-cut one another. If, for instance, members of common-interest associations are drawn from several different descent groups, then one's loyalty to one's own descent group, as opposed to others, is counteracted by loyalty to one's common-interest association, which includes members of other descent groups. Effective though such integrative techniques may be, they are not sufficient by themselves to prevent fragmentation, particularly in those societies with a diversity of roles for people to play.

In the three chapters that follow, we shall look at other cultural mechanisms by which societies seek to overcome the forces for fragmentation and

312

achieve wider integration. As we shall see, some of these have integration as their primary function, while some do not.

Regardless of how interdependent individuals and groups may be upon one another for economic goods and services or marriage partners, and no matter how effectively group memberships may crosscut one another, conflicts inevitably arise. Every society, therefore, must have means by which conflicts can be resolved and decisions can be made which are acceptable to the people who must live by them. Political systems and social control, which have integration as their primary function, are the subjects of Chapter 11.

Effective though a culture may be in equipping, organizing, and integrating a society to provide for the needs of its members, there are always certain problems that defy solution through existing technological or organizational means. The response of every culture is to devise a set of rituals, with a set of beliefs to explain them, aimed at solving these problems through the manipulation of supernatural beings and powers. In short, religion and magic exist to transform the uncertainties of life into certainties. At the same time, they may serve as powerful integrative forces through commonly held values, beliefs, and practices. Important as well is religion's rationalization of the existing social order, which thereby becomes a moral order as well. Thus, there is a link between religion and magic on the one hand, and political organization and social control on the other. Religion and magic are, then, appropriate subjects for discussion in Chapter 12 of this section on social integration.

Like religion and magic, the arts also contribute to human well-being and help give shape and significance to life. They too help promote the integration of human societies. Indeed, the relationship between art and religion goes deeper than this, for much of what we call art has come into being in the service of religion: myths to explain ritual practices, objects to portray important deities, music and dances for ceremonial use, and the like. For that matter, it has sometimes been observed that a religion, like a fine drama, is itself a work of art. Accordingly, a chapter on the arts follows our chapter on religion and concludes this section.

11 | Political Organization and Social Control

Social control may be accomplished in a variety of ways. Here, a formal council of Ethiopian Qemant elders is shown conferring on a two-year-old dispute over some land.

PREVIEW

WHAT IS POLITICAL ORGANIZATION?

Political organization refers to the means by which a society maintains order internally and manages its affairs with other societies externally. Such organization may be relatively decentralized and informal, as in bands and tribes, or centralized and formal, as in chiefdoms and states.

HOW IS ORDER MAINTAINED INTERNALLY?

Social controls may be internalized—"built into" individuals—or externalized, in the form of sanctions. Built-in controls rely on such deterrents as personal shame and fear of supernatural punishment. Sanctions, by contrast, rely on actions taken by other members of society towards behavior that is specifically approved or disapproved. Positive sanctions encourage approved behavior, while negative sanctions discourage behavior that is disapproved. Sanctions that are formalized and enforced by an authorized political body are called laws. Consequently, we may say that laws are sanctions, but not all sanctions are laws. Similarly, societies do not maintain order through law alone.

HOW ARE EXTERNAL AFFAIRS MANAGED?

Just as the threatened or actual use of force may be employed to maintain order within a society, so may it be used to manage affairs among bands, lineages, clans, or whatever the largest autonomous political units may be. However, not all societies rely on force, because societies exist that do not practice warfare as we know it. Such societies generally have a view of themselves and their place in the world that has not been characteristic of centrally organized states.

HOW DO POLITICAL SYSTEMS OBTAIN PEOPLE'S ALLEGIANCE?

No form of political organization can function without the loyalty and support of those it governs. To a greater or lesser extent, political organizations the world over use religion to legitimize their power. In decentralized systems loyalty and cooperation are freely given also because everyone participates in making decisions. Centralized systems, by contrast, rely more heavily on force and coercion, although in the long run these may lessen the effectiveness of the system.

Louis XIV proclaimed: "I am the state." With this sweeping statement, the king declared absolute rule over France; he believed himself to be the law, the lawmaker, the courts, the judge, jailer and executioner—in short, the seat of all political organization in France.

Louis took a great deal of responsibility on his royal shoulders; had he actually performed each of these functions, he would have done the work of thousands of people, the number required to keep the machinery of a large political organization such as a state running at full steam. As a form of political organization, the state of seventeenth-century France was not much different from many that exist in modern times, including our own. All large states require elaborate, centralized structures involving hierarchies of executives, legislators, and judges who initiate, pass, and enforce laws for large numbers of people.

But such complex structures have not always been in existence, and even today, there are societies that depend on far less formal means of organization. In some societies, flexible and informal kinship systems with leaders who lack real power prevail. Social problems such as homicide and theft are perceived as serious "family quarrels" rather than affairs that affect the entire community. Between these two polarities of political organization lies a world of variety, including societies with chiefs, Big Men, or charismatic leaders, and segmented tribal societies with multicentric authority systems. Such disparity prompts the question, What is political organization?

The term "political organization" refers to those aspects of social organization specifically concerned with the management of the affairs of public policy of a society, whether it be organizing a giraffe hunt or raising an army. In other words, political organization is the system of social relationships that provides for the coordination and regulation of behavior insofar as that behavior is related to the maintenance of public order. Government, on the other hand, consists of an administrative system having specialized personnel which may or may not form a part of the political organization, depending on the complexity of the society. Some form of political organization exists in all societies, but it is not always a government.

KINDS OF POLITICAL SYSTEMS

Political organization is the means through which a society maintains social order and reduces social disorder. Such organization assumes a variety of forms among the peoples of the world, but scholars have simplified this complex subject by identifying four basic kinds of political systems. These are (in order of complexity) bands, tribes, chiefdoms, and states. The first two forms are uncentralized socio-political systems; the latter two are centralized systems.

Decentralized Political Systems

Until recently, many non-Western peoples have had neither chiefs with established rights and duties nor any fixed form of government as we understand the term. Instead, kinship and descent form the chief means of social organization among such peoples. The economies of these societies are of a subsistence type, and populations are typically very small. Leaders do not have real authority to enforce the society's customs or laws, but if individual members do not conform, they may be ostracized or made the target of scorn and gossip. Important decisions are usually made in a demo-

316

cratic manner by a consensus of adult males; dissenting members may decide to act with the majority, or they may choose to adopt some other course of action if they are willing to risk the social consequences. This form of political organization provides great flexibility, which in many situations confers an adaptive advantage.

BAND ORGANIZATION The **band** is a small autonomous group; it is the least complicated form of political organization. Bands are usually found among hunter-gatherers and other nomadic societies in which there are factors that limit the size of the group. Bands are kin groups, composed of related men and/or women and their spouses and unmarried children; the closeness of the group is indicated by the usual presence of rules that prohibit marriage between band members. Bands may be characterized as associations of related families who occupy a common territory and who live together on it so long as environmental and subsistence circumstances are favorable. The band is probably the oldest form of political organization, since all humans were once hunters and gatherers, and remained so until the development of farming and pastoralism over the last 10,000 years.

Since band members are typically hunter-gatherers who often must range far and wide to search for food sources, they are generally on the move most of the year, following herds and harvests. This nomadic mode of existence is correlated with a second important feature of the band: its small size. Population density of the band is quite low, varying from a handful to usually no more than about 500 individuals; its size depends on the methods employed in gathering food. The more food the group has available to it, the more individuals it can support, and the larger the band. During seasons when food is scarce, the band may

> **Band: A small group of related people occupying a single region.**

disperse over a broad area, perhaps dividing into several smaller groups.

Bands are generally quite democratic: no band member may tell another individual what to do, how to hunt, or whom to marry. There is no private ownership (except in the case of a few weapons or tools), and game and other foods are shared by all members of the group. Rank (other than age and sex-status differentiation), the specialization of labor, and formal political organization are not found in this kind of society. Generally, the band lacks the social techniques that would be necessary to integrate its members into larger political groups. Decisions are usually made by a consensus of all adult members of the band, and so they require little formal implementation. The decision to undertake a hunting expedition or to begin a ritual celebration is reached after a meeting of the band's senior adult males.

Bands are usually led by older men whose courage, success in hunting, or ability to placate supernatural forces is recognized and admired by other members. A man is followed not because he has coercive power but because in the past he has demonstrated good sense, skill, and success; when he fails to lead well and make the right decisions, members will choose to follow another man. The leader is simply the first among equals, a leader with personal authority that stems from his abilities.

An example of the informal nature of leadership in the band is found among the !Kung of the Kalahari Desert, whom we met in Chapter 6. Each !Kung band is composed of a group of families who live together, linked to one another and to the headman through kinship. Although each

hts to the territory which it
the resources within it, two or
bands may range over the
same territory. The headman, called the
kxau or "owner," is the focal point for the
band's theoretical ownership of the territory. The headman does not really own the
land or resources, but he symbolically per-
sonifies the rights of band members to
them. If the headman leaves a territory to
live elsewhere, he ceases to be headman,
and some other member of the band takes
his place.

The headman coordinates the band's
movements when resources are no longer
adequate for subsistence in a particular territory. His chief duty is to plan when and
where the group will move; when the band
moves, the headman's position is at the
head of the line. He chooses the site for the
new settlement, and he has the first choice
of a spot for his own fire. He has no other
rewards or duties. For example, the headman does not organize hunting parties,
trading expeditions, the making of artifacts, or gift giving; nor does he make marriage arrangements. Individual band members instigate their own activities. The
headman is not a judge, nor is he obligated
to punish other band members. Wrong-
doers are judged and regulated by public
opinion, usually expressed by gossip among
band members. If a headman is too young
or too old or loses the desired qualities of
leadership, band members will turn to another man to lead them.

TRIBAL ORGANIZATION The second type
of decentralized or multicentric authority
system is the **tribe,** in which separate bands
or other social units are integrated by a
number of pantribal factors. For example,
such integration can be provided by kinship groups such as clans that unite people
in separate bands or communities, or age

grades or associations that cross-cut kinship or territorial boundaries.

Typically, though not invariably, a
tribe produces its goods through some form
of farming or herding. Since these methods
of production usually yield more food than
those of the hunter-gatherer band, tribal
membership is usually greater than band
membership. Greater population density in
tribes than bands brings a new set of problems to be solved at the same time that it
permits new kinds of solutions.

Each tribe consists of one or more
small autonomous units; these may then
form alliances with one another for various
purposes. As in the band, political organization in the tribe is informal and of a temporary nature. Whenever a situation requiring political integration of all or
several tribal groups arises, they join to
deal with the situation in a cooperative
manner. When the problem is satisfactorily
solved, each group then returns to its autonomous state.

Band organization is characteristic of hunting and
gathering peoples. This is a picture of the leader of a
band of Bushmen from South Africa. Such leaders
work through their powers of persuasion, since they
have no power to coerce.

Leadership among tribes is also informal. Among the Navajo Indians, for example, the individual did not think of government as something fixed and all-powerful, and leadership was not vested in a central authority. A local leader was a man respected for his age, integrity, and wisdom. His advice was therefore sought frequently, but he had no formal means of control and could not enforce any decision on those who asked for his help. Group decisions were made on the basis of public consensus, with the most influential man usually somewhat more responsible than others for the final decision. Among the social mechanisms that induced members to abide by group decisions were withdrawal of cooperation, gossip, criticism, and the belief that disease was caused by antisocial actions.[1]

KINSHIP ORGANIZATION   In many tribal societies, the organizing unit and seat of political authority is the clan, an association of people who consider themselves to be descended from a common ancestor. Within the clan, elders or headmen are responsible for regulating the affairs of members and represent their clan in relations with other clans. As a group, the elders of all the clans may form a council that acts within the tribe or for the tribe in dealings with outsiders. In some societies, the strategic and tactical planning for warfare rests in the hands of the clan.

Another form of tribal kinship bond that provides political organization is the **segmentary lineage system.** This system is similar in operation to the clan, but it is less extensive and is a relatively rare form of political organization. The economy of the segmentary tribe is generally just above subsistence level. Production is small scale,

Tribe: A group of bands that speak a common language, share a common culture, and occupy a specific region.

Segmentary lineage system: A form of political organization in which a larger group is broken up into clans, which are divided into lineages.

and the tribe probably has a labor pool just large enough to provide necessities. Since each lineage in the tribe produces the same goods, none depends on another for goods or services. Political organization among segmentary lineage societies is usually informal: there are neither political offices nor chiefs, although older tribal members may exercise some personal authority. In his study of the Tiv and the Nuer, Marshall Sahlins describes the way that the segmentary lineage form of political organization works.[2] According to Sahlins, segmentation is the normal process of tribal growth. It is also the social means of temporary unification of a fragmented tribal society to join in particular action. The segmentary lineage may be viewed as a substitute for the fixed political structure which a tribe cannot maintain.

Among the Nuer, who number some 200,000 people living in the swampland and savanna of East Africa, there are at least 20 clans. Each clan is patrilineal and is segmented into lineages which are further segmented. A clan is separated into maximal lineages; maximal lineages are segmented into major lineages, which are segmented into minor lineages, which in turn are segmented into minimal lineages. The minimal lineage is a group descended

[1] Elman Service, *Profiles in Ethnology* (New York: Harper & Row, 1958).

[2] Marshall Sahlins, "The Segmentary Lineage: An Organization of Predatory Expansion," *American Anthropologist, 1961, 63:322–343.*

from one great grandfather or a great great grandfather.

The lineage segments among the Nuer are all equal, and no real leadership or political organization at all exists above the level of the autonomous minimal or primary segments. The entire superstructure of the lineage is nothing more than an alliance, active only during conflicts between any of the minimal segments. In any serious dispute between members of different minimal lineage segments, members of all other segments take the side of the contestant to whom they are most closely related, and the issue is then joined between the higher-order lineages involved. Such a system of political organization is known as complementary or balanced opposition.

Disputes among the Nuer are frequent, and under the segmentary lineage system, they can lead to widespread feuds. This possible source of social disruption is minimized by the actions of the "leopard skin chief," or holder of a ritual office of conciliation. The leopard skin chief has no political power and is looked on as standing outside the lineage network. All he can do is try to persuade feuding lineages to accept payment in "blood cattle" rather than taking another life. His mediation gives each side the chance to back down gracefully before too many people are killed; but if the participants are for some reason unwilling to compromise, the leopard skin chief has no authority to enforce a settlement.

AGE-GRADE ORGANIZATION Age-grade systems provide a tribal society with the means of political organization beyond the kin group. Under this system, youths, usually at puberty, are initiated into an age grade. They then pass as a set from one age grade to another when they reach the proper age (see Chapter 10). Age grades and sets cut across territorial and kin groupings

and are an important means of political organization.

Political matters of the tribe are in the hands of the age grades and their officers. An example of the age-grade system as a form of political organization is found among the Kipsigis of East Africa, where there are two principal age grades: that of *murenik,* or warrior, and that of *poysiek,* or senior elder.[3] Secondary age grades are the junior warriors (males below the age of puberty), junior elders, and retired elders. Young men are initiated into the warrior-age class at puberty, at which time they are taught tribal customs and religious codes. The tasks of the warriors are military and economic: they must defend the country and enrich and strengthen the tribe by begetting many children and capturing many cattle. The principal tasks of the elders are military, administrative, judicial, and religious. They may fight in defensive battles, and certain of them serve as chiefs of staff, organizing and advising the army.

Most political authority among the Kipsigis is vested in the age set of the elders who serve in the hamlet, village, and territorial group. In the hamlet, an elder versed in law mediates disputes. If the case cannot be resolved at the hamlet level, it is sent up to the village level, where a council of elders judges the case. Certain elders also preside at initiation ceremonies and at those ceremonies where one age set is retiring and another rising to take its place.

ASSOCIATION ORGANIZATION Common-interest associations that function as politically integrative systems within tribes are found in many areas of the world, including Africa, Melanesia, and India. A good example of association organization functioned

[3]A. H. J. Prins, *East African Age Systems* (Gronigen, The Netherlands: J. B. Walters, 1953).

A Kapauku Big Man delivering a political speech. Verbal eloquence is one of the skills necessary for leadership in this society.

during the nineteenth century among the Indians of the western plains of the United States, such as the Cheyenne, whom we'll talk about again later in this chapter. The basic territorial and political unit of the Cheyenne was the band, but seven military societies, or warriors' clubs, were common to the entire tribe; the clubs functioned in several areas. A boy might be invited to join one of these societies when he achieved warrior status, whereupon he became familiar with the society's particular insignia, songs, and rituals. In addition to their military functions, the warriors' societies also had ceremonial and social functions.

The Cheyenne warriors' routine daily tasks consisted of overseeing movements in the camp, protecting a moving column, and enforcing rules against individual hunting when the whole tribe was on a buffalo hunt. In addition, each warrior society had its own repertoire of dances that the members performed on special ceremonial occasions. Since identical military societies bearing identical names existed in each Cheyenne band, the societies thus served to integrate the entire tribe for military and political purposes.[4]

THE MELANESIAN BIG MAN Throughout much of Melanesia there appears a type of leader called the Big Man. The Big Man combines a small amount of interest in his tribe's welfare with a great deal of self-interested cunning and calculation for his own personal gain. His authority is personal; he does not come to office nor is he elected. His status is the result of acts that raise him above most other tribe members and attract to him a band of loyal followers.

An example of this form of political organization can be seen among the Kapauku of West New Guinea. There the Big Man is called the *tonowi*, or "rich one." To achieve this status, one must be male, wealthy, generous, and eloquent; physical bravery and skills in dealing with the supernatural are also frequent characteristics of a *tonowi*, but they are not essential. The *tonowi* functions as the headman of the village unit.

Kapauku culture places a high value on wealth, so it is not surprising that a wealthy individual is considered to be a successful and admirable man. Yet the possession of wealth must be coupled with the trait of generosity, which in this society means not gift giving but the willingness to make loans. Wealthy men who refuse to

---

[4] E. A. Hoebel, *The Cheyennes: Indians of the Great Plains* (New York: Holt, Rinehart and Winston, 1960).

lend money to other villagers may be ostracized, ridiculed, and in extreme cases, actually executed by a group of warriors. This social pressure ensures that economic wealth is rarely hoarded, but is distributed throughout the group.

It is through the loans he makes that the *tonowi* acquires his political power. Other villagers comply with his requests because they are in his debt (often without paying interest), and they do not want to have to repay their loans. Those who have not yet borrowed money from the *tonowi* probably hope to do so in the future, and so they too want to keep his goodwill.

Other sources of support for the *tonowi* are the apprentices whom he has taken into his household for training. They are fed, housed, given a chance to learn the *tonowi's* business wisdom, and given a loan to buy a wife when they leave; in return, they act as messengers and bodyguards. Even after they leave his household, these men are tied to the *tonowi* by bonds of affection and gratitude. Political support also comes from the *tonowi's* kinsmen, whose relationship brings with it varying obligations.

The *tonowi* functions as a leader in a wide variety of situations. He represents the group in dealing with outsiders and other villages; he acts as negotiator and/or judge when disputes break out among his followers. Leopold Pospisil, who studied the Kapauku extensively, notes:

The multiple functions of a *tonowi* are not limited to the political and legal fields only. His word also carries weight in economic and social matters. He is especially influential in determining proper dates for pig feasts and pig markets, in inducing specific individuals to become co-sponsors at feasts, in sponsoring communal dance expeditions to other villages, and in initiating large projects, such as extensive drainage ditches and main fences or bridges, the comple-

tion of which requires a joint effort of the whole community.[5]

The *tonowi's* wealth comes from his success at pig breeding (an activity we discussed in Chapter 2), for pigs are the focus of the entire Kapauku economy. Like all kinds of cultivation and domestication, raising pigs requires a combination of strength, skill, and luck. It is not uncommon for a *tonowi* to lose his fortune rapidly, due to bad management or bad luck with his pigs. Thus the political structure of the Kapauku shifts frequently; as one man loses wealth and consequently power, another gains it and becomes a *tonowi*. These changes confer a degree of flexibility on the political organization, but prevent long-range planning and thus limit the scope of any one *tonowi's* political power over the rest of the villagers.

Centralized Political Systems

Among bands and tribes, authority is uncentralized, and each group is economically and politically autonomous. Political organization is vested in kinship, age, and common-interest groups. Populations are small and relatively homogeneous, and people are engaged for the most part in the same sorts of activities throughout their lives. But as a society's social life becomes more complex, as population rises and technology becomes more complex, as the specialization of labor and trade networks produces surpluses of goods, the need for formal, stable, permanent leadership becomes greater. In such societies, political authority and power are concentrated in a

---

[5] Leopold Pospisil, *The Kapauku Papuans of West New Guinea* (New York: Holt, Rinehart and Winston, 1963), pp. 51–52.

single individual—the chief—or in numerous groups of individuals—the state. The state is a form of organization best suited to a heterogeneous society where each individual must interact on a regular basis with large numbers of people with diversified interests who are neither kin nor close acquaintances.

CHIEFDOMS   A **chiefdom** is a ranked society in which every member has a position in the hierarchy. An individual's status in such a community is determined by membership in a descent group: those in the uppermost levels, closest to the chief, are officially superior and receive deferential treatment from those in lower ranks.

The Hawaiian King Kamehameha was able, through conquest, to transform several independent chiefdoms into a single kingdom, or state. Competition between chiefs for supremacy is typical of chiefdoms.

> **Chiefdom: A ranked society in which every member has a position in the hierarchy.**

The office of the chief may or may not be hereditary. Unlike the headmen of bands and lineages, the chief is generally a true authority figure, and his authority serves to unite his community in all affairs and at all times. For example, a chief can distribute land among his community and recruit members into his military service. In chiefdoms, there is a recognized hierarchy consisting of major and minor authorities who control major and minor subdivisions of the chiefdom. Such an arrangement is, in effect, a chain of command linking leaders at every level. It serves to bind tribal groups in the heartland to the chief's headquarters, be it a mud and dung hut or a marble palace.

On the economic level, a chief controls the productive activities of his people. Chiefdoms are typically redistributive economic systems; the chief has control over surplus goods and perhaps even the labor force of his community. Thus, the chief may demand a quota of rice from farmers which he will redistribute to the entire community. Similarly, he may recruit laborers to build irrigation works, a palace, or a temple.

The chief may also amass a great amount of personal wealth and pass it on to his heirs. Land, cattle, and luxury goods produced by specialists can be collected by the chief and become part of his power base. Moreover, high-ranking families of the chiefdom may engage in the same practice and use their possessions as evidence of status.

An example of this form of political organization was found in traditional Hawaiian society. There was a class of nobles, rigidly differentiated in rank and specialized in occupation; they led the army and served as religious and political officials. Status was hereditary, and the gradations of status were so distinct that even children of the same parents were ranked in the order of their birth. The nobles near the top of the hierarchy were so important and powerful that ordinary people were required to throw themselves face down on the ground whenever one passed.

At the top of the hierarchy of nobles was the chief. It was believed that he was given the right to rule by the gods, to whom he was related. Around each chief was gathered a group of loyal nobles, who administered the affairs of politics, warfare, and religion. The nobles all paid some kind of tribute—goods and money—to the chief; they in turn collected tributes from inferior nobles, who collected tribute from the commoners. The chief's wealth gave him additional power and permitted him to undertake large-scale projects, such as wars of conquest. The chief had the right of life and death over all his subjects; he could also take away their property.

Although such a system would seem very stable, political power in Hawaiian society changed frequently. War was the way to gain territory and maintain power; great chiefs set out to conquer one another in an effort to become paramount chief of all the islands. When one chief conquered another, the loser and all his nobles were dispossessed of all property and were lucky if they escaped alive. The new chief then appointed his own supporters to positions of political power. So there was very little continuity of governmental or religious administration.

STATE SYSTEMS The **state,** the most formal of political organizations, is one of the hallmarks of civilization. Inherent in the concept of the state is the idea of perma-

nent government, public and sovereign, by which the state can use legitimized force to regulate the affairs of its citizens as well as its relations with other states. The state has a central power and a formal code of law administered by the central power.

An important aspect of the state is its delegation of authority to maintain order within and without its borders. Police, foreign ministries, war ministries, and other branches of the government function to control and punish such disruptive acts as crime, terror, and rebellion. By such agencies, authority is asserted impersonally and (ideally) objectively in the state.

The state is found only in societies with numerous diverse groups, social classes, and associations; it brings together under a common rule many kinds of people. Typically, state society is divided into social classes, and economic functions and wealth are distributed unequally. A market economy is an integral part of the state, as are vast surpluses of goods and services and the intense specialization of labor.[6]

Our own form of government, of course, is a state government, and its organization and workings are undoubtedly familiar to everyone. An example of a not so familiar state is afforded by the Swazi of Swaziland, a Bantu-speaking people who live in Southeast Africa.[7] They are primarily farmers, but cattle raising is more highly valued than farming: the ritual, wealth, and power of their authority system are all intricately linked with cattle. In addition to farming and cattle raising, there is some specialization of labor; certain people become specialists in ritual, smithing, woodcarving, and pottery. Their

---

[6] L. Krader, *Formation of the State* (Englewood Cliffs, N.J.: Prentice-Hall, 1968).

[7] Hilda Kuper, "The Swazi of Swaziland," in James L. Gibbs, Jr., ed., *Peoples of Africa* (New York: Holt, Rinehart and Winston, 1965), pp. 479–512.

goods and services are traded, but the Swazi do not have elaborate markets.

The Swazi authority system is characterized by a highly developed dual monarchy, a hereditary aristocracy, and elaborate rituals of kinship as well as by state-wide age sets. The king and his mother are the central figures of all national activity, linking all the people of the Swazi state: they preside over higher courts, summon national gatherings, control age classes, allocate land, disburse national wealth, take precedence in ritual, and help organize important social events.

Advising the king are the senior princes, who are usually his uncles and

> **State:** In anthropology, a centralized political system with the power to coerce.

half-brothers. Between the king and the princes are two specially created *tinsila*, or "blood brothers," who are chosen from certain common clans. These men are his shields, protecting him from evildoers and serving him in intimate personal situations. In addition, the king is guided by two *tindvuna*, or counselors, one civil and one military. The people of the state make their opinions known through two councils: the *liqoqo*, or privy council composed of senior

Symbolic of the state's authority over its citizens is the power to order executions, whether by electrocution, as in the United States, by sacrifice, as in Aztec society, or some other means.

princes, and the *libanda,* or council of state, composed of chiefs and headmen and open to all adult males of the state. The *liqoqo* may advise the king, make decisions, and execute them. For example, they may rule on such questions as land, education, traditional ritual, court procedure, and transport.

Government extends from the smallest local unit—the homestead—upward to the central administration. The head of a homestead has legal and administrative powers: he is responsible for the crimes of those under him, controls their property, and speaks for them before his superiors. On the district level, political organization is similar to that of the central government. However the relationship between a district chief and his subjects is personal and familiar; he knows all the families in his district. The main check on any autocratic tendencies he may exhibit rests in his subjects' ability to transfer their allegiance to a more responsive chief. Swazi officials hold their positions for life and are dismissed only for treason or witchcraft. Incompetence, drunkenness, and stupidity are frowned upon, but they are not considered to be sufficient grounds for dismissal.

POLITICAL ORGANIZATION AND SOCIAL CONTROL

Whatever form the political organization of a society may take, and whatever else it may do, it is always involved in one way or another with social control. Always, it seeks to ensure that people behave in acceptable ways, and defines the proper action to take when they don't. In the case of chiefdoms and states, some sort of centralized authority has the power to regulate the affairs of society. But, in bands and tribes, people behave generally as they are expected to without the direct intervention of any centralized political authority. To a large degree, gossip, criticism, fear of supernatural forces, and the like, serve as effective deterrents to antisocial behavior. In order to see how such seemingly informal considerations serve to keep people in line, we will now look at a specific example. It comes from contemporary New Guinea—where we have already looked at examples of tribal organization—and is of particular interest because it shows how traditional means of social control may continue to function even in societies that have been heavily influenced by Western culture.

ORIGINAL STUDY

A New Weapon Stirs Up Old Ghosts[8]

The hamlet now had its own gun and hunting could begin in earnest. The first step was an annunciation feast called, in Pidgin, a "kapti" ("cup of tea"). Its purpose was to inform the villagers' dead ancestors about the new gun. This was important because ancestral ghosts roam the forest land of their lineage, protecting it from intruders and driving game to their hunting descendants. The

---

[8] William E. Mitchell, "A New Weapon Stirs Up Old Ghosts," adapted and reprinted, with permission, from *Natural History Magazine,* December 1973, pp. 77–84. Copyright © The American Museum of Natural History, 1973.

hunter's most important hunting aide is his dead male relatives, to whom he prays for game upon entering his hunting lands. The dead remain active in the affairs of the living by protecting them from harm, providing them with meat, and punishing those who have wronged them.

The small sacrificial feast was held in front of Auwe's house. Placing the upright gun on a makeshift table in the midst of the food, Auwe rubbed it with sacred ginger. One of Auwe's elderly clansmen, standing and facing his land, called out to his ancestors by name and told them about the new gun. He implored them to send wild pigs and cassowaries to Auwe.

Several men spoke of the new morality that was to accompany hunting with a gun. The villagers should not argue or quarrel among themselves; problems must be settled quietly and without bitterness; malicious gossip and stealing were forbidden. If these rules were not obeyed, Auwe would not find game.

In traditional Wape culture there is no feast analogous to the "kapti." Indeed, there are no general community-wide feasts. The "kapti" is apparently modeled on a European social gathering.

For the remainder of my stay in Taute, I followed closely the fortunes of the Taute guns and of guns in nearby villages as well. All seemed to be faced with the same two problems: game was rarely seen; and when seen, was rarely killed. Considering that a cartridge belongs to a villager, not the gunman, how was this economic loss handled? This presented a most intriguing and novel problem for there were no analogs to this type of predicament within the traditional culture. By Wape standards, the pecuniary implications of such a loss, although but a few Australian shillings, could not graciously be ignored by the loser. At the very least the loss had to be explained even if the money for the cartridges could not be retrieved.

Now I understood the concern about the ancestral ghosts. If the hunter shot and missed, the owner of the fired shells was being punished by being denied meat. Either he or a close family member had quarreled or wronged another person whose ghost-relative was securing revenge by causing the hunter to miss. This, then, was the functional meaning of the proscription against quarreling. By avoiding disputes, the villagers were trying to prevent the intervention of ancestral ghosts in human affairs. In a peaceful village without quarrels, the gunman could hunt undisturbed by vengeful ghosts chasing away game or misrouting costly shells.

Although a number of factors in European culture have influenced the shotgun cult, the cult's basic premise of a positive correlation between quarreling and bad hunting is derived directly from traditional Wape culture. In bow and arrow hunting, an individual who feels he was not given his fair share of a hunter's kill may punish the hunter by gossiping about him or quarreling openly with him. The aggrieved person's ancestral ghosts revenge the slight by chasing the game away from the offending hunter or misdirecting his arrows. But this is a private affair between the hunter and the angered person; their quarrel has no influence upon the hunting of others. And it is rare for an issue other than distribution of game to cause a ghost to hinder a bowman's success.

The hunter's prowess is restored only when the angered person performs a brief supplication rite over the hunter.

This, then, is the conceptual basis for the tie between quarreling and bad hunting. Originally relevant only to bow and arrow hunting, it was then broadened to accommodate the government's pronouncements about the shotgun and keeping the village peace. And it applies perfectly to the special circumstances of shotgun hunting. Because the shotgun is community owned and many villagers buy cartridges for it, the villagers are identified with both the gun and the gunman. As a proxy hunter for the villagers, the gunman is potentially subject to the ghostly sanctions resulting from their collective wrongs. Thus gun hunting, unlike bow and arrow hunting, is a community affair and the community-wide taboo against quarrels and personal transgressions is the only effective way to prevent spiteful ghosts from wrecking the hunt.

No village, however, even if populated by people as disciplined and well behaved as the Wape, can constantly live in the state of pious peace considered necessary for continuous good gun hunting. When the hunting is poor,

A feast held to appease ghosts who might have been causing game to flee; the upright shotgun, center, is placed near the offerings. Auwe is the gunman or *sutboi* who is standing by the gun. The food left, consisting of sago dumplings and boiled tulip leaves, is later consumed by the villagers.

the gunman must discover the quarrels and wrongs within the village. After having identified the individuals whose ancestral ghosts are sabotaging the hunting, the gunman must also see to it that they implore the ghosts to stop. Embarrassed by the public disclosure, they will quickly comply.

The common method for detecting points of friction within the village is to bring the villagers together for a special meeting. The gunman will then document in detail his misfortunes and call on the villagers to find out what is ruining the hunting. If confessions of wrongdoing are not forthcoming, questioning accusations result. The meeting, beginning in Pidgin, moves into Wape as the discussion becomes more complex and voluble. It may last up to three hours; but even if there is no resolution, it always ends amiably—at least on the surface. For it is important to create no new antagonisms.

The other technique for locating the source of the hunting problem is to call in a professional clairvoyant. As the villagers must pay for his services, he is usually consulted only after a series of unsuccessful meetings. Clairvoyants have replaced the shamans, who were outlawed by the government and the mission because they practiced sorcery and ritual murders. The Wape do not consider a clairvoyant a sorcerer; he is a man with second sight who is experienced in discovering and treating the hidden causes of intractable problems. As such, shotguns are among his best patients.

Mewau, a clairvoyant from a neighboring village, held a "shotgun clinic" in Taute to examine the Mifu and Kafiere guns. For about an hour he examined the two guns and questioned the villagers. Then he declared the reasons for their misfortune.

Kapul, a dead Mifu shaman, was preventing the Mifu gun from killing game because a close relative of the gunman had allegedly stolen valuables from Kapul's daughter. Because of the family ties between the gunman and the thief, Kapul's ghost was punishing the gunman.

The Kafiere gun, Mewau declared, was not able to find game because a widow in the village felt that her dead husband's clan had not previously distributed game to her in a fair way. By interfering with the Kafiere gun, her husband's ghost was punishing his clan for the neglect of his family.

Once the source of trouble is named, there are several possible types of remedial ritual depending upon the seriousness of the situation. For example, the circumstances surrounding the naming of the husband's ghost were considered serious, and a "kapti" was held to placate him. Another, simpler ritual involves the preparation of taro soup, which the gunman consumes. But the simplest, commonest remedial rite is the supplication ritual without sacrificial food offerings, a ritual in which I became involved.

Mifu's gunman had shot a pig with one of his own cartridges but did not give me the small portion due me as a part owner of the gun. Partly as a test to see if my ancestors counted for anything in Taute and partly because I did not want to let this calculated slight go unchallenged, I, in typical Wape fashion, said nothing to the gunman but gossiped discreetly about his selfishness. The gunman continued to hunt but had no further success. When his bad luck persisted, a meeting was called to find out the reason. The gunman asked me if I was angry because I had not been given my portion of the pig. When I acknowledged my anger, he handed the shotgun to me and I dutifully spoke out to my ancestors to stop turning the game away from the gun.

But the gunman still had no success in the hunt, and the villagers decided there were other wrongs as well. The search for the offending ghosts continued. Eventually the villagers became so discouraged with the Mifu gun that they stopped giving cartridges to the gunman. The consensus was that a major undetected wrong existed in the hamlet, and until it was uncovered and the guilty ghost called off, hunting with the gun was senseless and extravagant. Thus the propriety of a remedial rite is established if there is success on the next hunt. The system is completely empirical; if no game is seen or if seen, is not killed, then the search for the wrong must continue.

Wape people are generally even tempered, and their villages, in contrast to many in New Guinea, strike the newcomer as almost serene. But the social impact of the guns at this time was pervasive, and life in Taute literally revolved around the guns and their hunting fortunes. Whereas the villagers previously had kept to their own affairs, they now became embroiled in meeting after meeting, seeking out transgressions, quarrels, and wrongdoing. As the gunman continued to have bad luck, his efforts to discover the cause became more zealous. A certain amount of polarization resulted: the gunman accused the villagers, the men accused the women, and the adults accused the young people of hiding their wrongs. And a few who had lost many cartridges wondered if the "sutboi" was keeping the game for himself. But no one ever suggested that he was an inexperienced shotgun hunter. The gunman was generally considered to be blameless; in fact, the more game he missed, the more self-righteous he became and the more miscreant the villagers.

Internalized Controls

The Wape concern about ancestral ghosts is a good example of internalized controls—beliefs that are so thoroughly ingrained in each person that each becomes personally responsible for his or her own good conduct. Examples of this can also be found in our own society; for instance, people refrain from committing incest not so much from fear of legal punishment as from a deep abhorrence of the act and the shame they would feel in performing it. Built-in or internalized controls rely on such deterrents as the fear of supernatural punishment—such as ancestral ghosts sabotaging the hunting—and magical retaliation. The individual expects to be punished, even though no one in the community may be aware of the wrongdoing.

Externalized Controls

Because internalized controls are not wholly sufficient even in bands and tribes, every society develops institutions designed to encourage conformity to social norms. These institutions are referred to as **sanctions;** they are externalized social controls. According to Radcliffe-Brown, "a sanction is a reaction on the part of a society or of a considerable number of its members to a mode of behavior which is thereby approved (positive sanctions) or disapproved (negative sanctions)."[9] Furthermore, sanctions may be either formal or informal and may vary significantly within a given society.

Each group and subgroup within a society tends to develop its own distinctive pattern or usages and the means of maintaining them without necessary recourse to the municipal law. Sanctions there come to operate within every conceivable set of group relationships: they include not only the organized sanctions of the law but also the gossip of neighbors or the customs regulating norms of production that are spontaneously generated among workers on the factory floor. In small scale communities . . . informal sanctions may become more drastic than the penalties provided for in the legal code. . . .[10]

Sanctions, then, operate within social groups of all sizes. Moreover, they need not be enacted into law in order to play a significant role in social control. If a sanction is to be effective, it cannot be arbitrary. Quite the opposite: sanctions must be consistently applied, and their existence must be generally known by the members of the society.

NEGATIVE AND POSITIVE SANCTIONS Social sanctions may be categorized as either positive or negative. Positive sanctions consist of such incentives to conformity as awards, titles, and recognition by one's neighbors. Negative sanctions consist of such threats as imprisonment, corporal punishment, or ostracism from the community for viola-

---

[9] A. R. Radcliffe-Brown, *Structure and Function in Primitive Society* (New York: Free Press, 1952), p. 205.

[10] A. L. Epstein, "Sanctions," *International Encyclopedia of Social Sciences*, 1968, 14:3.

> **Sanctions: Externalized social controls designed to encourage conformity to social norms.**

tion of social norms. If some individuals do not recognize the advantages of social conformity, they are still likely to be more willing to conform to society's rules than to accept the consequences of not doing so.

FORMAL AND INFORMAL SANCTIONS Sanctions may also be categorized as either formal or informal, depending on whether or not a legal statute is involved. In our society the man who wears tennis shorts to a church service may be subject to a variety

Negative sanctions may involve some form of regulated combat, as seen here in a picture of Mexican schoolboys settling a quarrel with boxing gloves.

of informal sanctions, ranging from the glances of the clergyman to the chuckling of other parishioners. But if he were to show up without any trousers at all, he would be subject to the formal sanction of arrest for indecent exposure. Only in the second instance would he have been guilty of breaking the **law.**

Formal sanctions, like laws, are always organized because they attempt to precisely and explicitly regulate people's behavior. Other examples of organized sanctions include, on the positive side, such things as military decorations and monetary rewards. On the negative side are such things as loss of status or rank, exclusion from social life and its privileges, seizure of property, imprisonment, and even bodily mutilation or death.

The effectiveness of positive sanctions in promoting certain kinds of behavior is suggested by this picture. These Portuguese army officers seem satisfied with the positive sanctions—medals, honor, wealth—they have won.

Informal sanctions are diffuse in nature, involving spontaneous expressions of approval or disapproval by members of the group or community. Such sanctions are very effective in enforcing a large number of seemingly unimportant customs. Because most people want to be accepted, they are willing to acquiesce to the rules that govern dress, eating, conversation, even in the absence of actual laws.

Witchcraft beliefs may act as a powerful agent of social control in societies, whether or not they possess centralized political systems. An individual would naturally hesitate to offend one's neighbor when that neighbor might retaliate by resorting to black magic. Similarly, individuals may not wish to be accused of practicing witchcraft themselves, and so they will behave with greater circumspection. Among the Azande of the Sudan, people who think they have been bewitched may consult an oracle who, after performing the appropriate mystical rites, may then establish or confirm the identity of the offending witch.[11] Confronted with this evidence, the "witch" will usually agree to cooperate in order to avoid any additional trouble. Should the victim die, the relatives of the deceased may choose to make magic against the witch, ultimately accepting the death of some villager both as evidence of guilt and the efficacy of their magic. For the Azande, witchcraft provides not only a sanction against antisocial behavior but also a means of dealing with natural hostilities and death. No one wishes to be thought of as a witch, and surely no one wishes to be victimized by one. By institutionalizing their emotional responses, the Azande successfully maintain social order.

[11] E. E. Evans-Pritchard, *Witchcraft, Oracles and Magic among the Azande* (London: Oxford University Press, 1937).

Another important social control, and one that is likely to be internalized, is the religious sanction. Just as a devout Christian may avoid sinning for fear of hell, so may other worshippers tend to behave in a manner intended not to offend their powerful supernatural beings. The threat of punishment—either in this life or in the next—by gods, ancestral spirits, or ghosts is a strong incentive for proper behavior. In some societies, it is believed that ancestral spirits are very much concerned with the maintenance of good relations among the living members of their lineage. Death or illness in the lineage may be explained by reference to some violation of tradition or custom. Religious sanctions may thus serve not only to regulate behavior but to explain unexplainable phenomena as well.

LAW IN NON-WESTERN SOCIETIES

The Ifugao are a tribe of head-hunters living in the mountains of Luzon. Among the Ifugao, an individual who is unable to settle a dispute with someone else through personal negotiations may enlist the aid of a professional go-between known as a *monkalun*. If a settlement cannot be agreed upon with the assistance of the *monkalun*, the plaintiff, with the aid of relatives, may attempt to kill the defendant or relatives of the defendant. Among the Ifugao, the alternative to peaceful negotiation is feud. Ultimately, there is no binding legal authority.

In Western society, on the other hand, someone who commits an offense against another person is subject to a series of complex legal proceedings. The offender will be arrested by the police; tried before a judge and, perhaps, a jury; and, if the crime is serious enough, may be fined, imprisoned, or even executed. Throughout this chain of events, the accused party is dealt with by

> **Law:** A social norm, the neglect or infraction of which is regularly met, in threat or in fact, by the application of physical force on the part of an individual or group possessing the socially recognized privilege of so acting.

presumably disinterested police, judges, jurors, and jailers who may have no personal acquaintance whatsoever with the plaintiff or the defendant. How strange this would seem to the Ifugao! Clearly, the Westerner and the Ifugao operate under distinctly different assumptions.

Each society establishes institutions to encourage conformity to its rules and to define proper action in the event of breach of those rules. Through its sanctions, a society exercises a degree of control over the behavior of its members. An important part of a society's total system of social controls is that aspect referred to as law.

Definition of Law

When two Eskimos settle a dispute by engaging in a song contest, the result of the contest is binding; that is, the affair is closed. No further action need be expected. Would we choose to describe the outcome of such a contest as a legal decision? If every law is a sanction, but not every sanction is a law, how are we to distinguish between social sanctions in general and those to which we will apply the label law?

The definition of law has been a lively point of contention among anthropologists in the twentieth century. In 1926, Malinowski argued that the rules of law are distinguished from the rules of custom in that "they are regarded as the obligation of one person and the rightful claim of another, sanctioned not by mere psychological motive, but by a definite social machinery of binding force based . . . upon mutual dependence."[12] An example of one rule of custom in our own society might be seen in the dictate that guests at a dinner party should repay the person who gave the party with entertainment in the future. A host or hostess who does not receive a return invitation may feel cheated of something thought to be owed, but there is no legal claim against the ungrateful guest for the $22.67 spent on food. However, if an individual was cheated of the same sum by the grocer when shopping, the law could be invoked. Although Malinowski's definition introduced several important elements of law, his failure to distinguish adequately between legal and nonlegal sanctions left the problem of form-

ulating a workable definition of law in the hands of later anthropologists.

An important pioneer in the anthropological study of law was E. Adamson Hoebel. According to Hoebel, "a social norm is legal if its neglect or infraction is regularly met, in threat or in fact, by the application of physical force by an individual or group possessing the socially recognized privilege of so acting."[13] In stressing the legitimate use of physical coercion, Hoebel deemphasized the traditional association of law with a centralized court system. Although judge and jury are fundamental features of Western jurisprudence, they are not the universal backbone of human law.

---

[12] Bronislaw Malinowski, *Crime and Custom in Savage Society* (London: Routledge, 1951), p. 55.

[13] E. Adamson Hoebel, *The Law of Primitive Man: A Study in Comparative Legal Dynamics* (Cambridge, Mass.: Harvard University Press, 1954), p. 28.

At a Kapauku legal trial, the headman (the judge), with his hand on his head, is contemplating the argument of the "defense counsel" (on the headman's right.)

In his study of the Kapauku Papuans, Leopold Pospisil defined law in terms of four basic attributes:[14]

1. A legal decision is backed by authority. Some individual or group of individuals must possess sufficient influence to insure the conformity of disputing parties to its decisions.
2. A legal decision is intended to have universal applicability; that is, it is expected that a legal decision made today will apply to comparable situations in the future.
3. A legal decision determines the rights of one party and the duties of the other. Law recognizes the two-sided nature of every dispute.
4. A legal decision determines the nature and degree of sanctions. Legal sanction may be physical—such as imprisonment or confiscation of property—or psychological—such as public ridicule or avoidance.

Some anthropologists have proposed that a precise definition of law is an impossible—and perhaps even undesirable—undertaking. When we speak of "the law," are we not inclined to fall back on our familiar Western conception of rules enacted by an authorized legislative body and enforced by the judicial mechanisms of the state? Can any concept of law be applied to such societies as the Nuer or the Ifugao for whom the notion of a centralized judiciary is virtually meaningless? How shall we categorize duels, song contests, and other socially condoned forms of self-help which seem to meet some but not all of the criteria of law?

Ultimately, it seems of greatest value to consider each case within its cultural context. That each society exercises a degree of control over its members by means of rules and sanctions, and that some of these sanctions are more formalized than others, is indisputable; yet, in distinguishing between legal and nonlegal sanctions, we should be careful not to allow questions of terminology to overshadow our efforts to understand individual situations as they arise.

Functions of Law

In *The Law of Primitive Man* (1954), Hoebel writes of a time when the notion that private property should be generously shared was a fundamental precept of Cheyenne Indian life. Subsequently, however, some men assumed the privilege of borrowing other men's horses without bothering to obtain permission. When Wolf Lies Down complained of such unauthorized borrowing to the members of the Elk Soldier Society, the Elk Soldiers not only had his horse returned to him but also secured an award for damages from the offender. The Elk Soldiers then announced that, to avoid such difficulties in the future, horses were no longer to be borrowed without permission. Furthermore, they declared their intention of retrieving any such property and administering a whipping to anyone who resisted their efforts to return improperly borrowed goods.

The case of Wolf Lies Down and the Elk Soldier Society clearly illustrates three basic functions of law. First, it defines relationships among the members of society, determining proper behavior under specified circumstances. Knowledge of the law permits each person to know his or her rights and duties in respect to every other member of society. Second, law allocates the authority to employ coercion in the enforcement of sanctions. In societies with centralized political systems, such authority is generally vested in the government and its court system. In societies that lack

---

[14] Leopold Pospisil, *Anthropology of Law* (New York: Harper & Row, 1971), pp. 39–96.

centralized political control, the authority to employ force may be allocated directly to the injured party. Third, law functions to redefine social relations and to ensure social flexibility. As new situations arise, law must determine whether old rules and assumptions retain their validity and to what extent they must be altered. Law, if it is to operate efficiently, must allow room for change.

In actual practice, law is rarely the smooth and well-integrated system described above. In any given society, various legal sanctions may apply at various levels of society. Because each individual in a society is usually a member of numerous subgroups, he or she is subject to the various dictates of these diverse groups. The Kapauku individual is, simultaneously, a member of a family, a household, a sublineage, and a confederacy, and is subject to all the laws of each. In some cases, it may be impossible for an individual to submit to contradictory legal indications:

In one of the confederacy's lineages, incestuous relations between members of the same sib were punished by execution of the culprits, and in another by severe beating, in the third constituent lineage such a relationship was not punishable and . . . was not regarded as incest at all. In one of the sublineages, it became even a preferred type of marriage.[15]

Furthermore, the power to employ sanctions may vary from level to level within a given society. The head of a Kapauku household may punish a member of his household by means of slapping or beating, but the authority to confiscate property is vested exclusively in the headman of the lineage. An example of a similar dilemma in our own society occurred a few years ago in Oklahoma, a state in which the sale of liquor by the drink is illegal. State officials arrested several passengers and workers on an Amtrak train passing through the state; these people knew their actions were legal under federal law but were unaware that they could be prosecuted under state law. The complexity of legal jurisdiction within each society casts a shadow of doubt over any easy generalization about law.

Crime

As we have observed, an important function of sanctions, legal or otherwise, is to discourage the breach of social norms. A person contemplating theft is aware of the possibility of being captured and punished; yet, even in the face of severe sanctions, individuals in every society sometimes violate the norms and subject themselves to the consequences of their behavior. What is the nature of crime in non-Western societies?

In Western society, a clear distinction can be made between offenses against the state and offenses against an individual. Henry Campbell Black said:

The distinction between a crime and a tort or civil injury is that the former is a breach and violation of the public right and of duties due to the whole community considered as such, and in its social and aggregate capacity; whereas the latter is an infringement or privation of the civil rights of individuals merely.[16]

Thus a reckless driver who crashes into another car may be guilty of a crime in endangering public safety. The same driver may also be guilty of a tort, in causing damages to the other car, and can be sued for their cost by the other driver.

---

[15] Pospisil, p. 36.

[16] Henry Campbell Black, *Black's Law Dictionary* (St. Paul, Minn.: West, 1968).

In many non-Western societies, however, there is no conception of a central state. Consequently, all offenses are conceived of as offenses against individuals, rendering the distinction between crime and tort of little value. Indeed, a dispute between individuals may seriously disrupt the social order, especially in small groups where the number of disputants may be a relatively large proportion of the total population. Although the Mbuti Pygmies have no effective domestic or economic unit beyond the family, a dispute between two people will disrupt the effectiveness of the hunt by interfering with the necessary cooperation and is consequently a matter of community concern. The goal of judicial proceedings in most cases is to restore social harmony rather than punish an offender. In distinguishing between offenses of concern to the community as a whole and those of concern only to a few individuals, we may refer to offenses as public or private rather than distinguishing between criminal and civil law. In this way, we may avoid values and assumptions which are irrelevant to a discussion of non-Western systems of law.

Perhaps the most fruitful path to understanding the nature of law lies in the thorough analysis of individual dispute cases, each within its own unique social context. Basically, a dispute may be settled in either of two ways. On the one hand, disputing parties may, by means of argument and compromise, voluntarily arrive at a mutually satisfactory agreement. This form of settlement, which may or may not involve the mediation of a third party, is referred to as **negotiation** or **mediation.** In bands and tribes, a third-party mediator has no coercive power, and so cannot force disputants to abide by his decision. But as a person who commands great personal respect, he may frequently effect a settlement

Negotiation: The use of direct argument and compromise by the parties to a dispute to arrive voluntarily at a mutually satisfactory agreement.

Mediation: Settlement of a dispute through negotiation assisted by an unbiased third party.

Adjudication: Mediation, with the ultimate decision made by an unbiased third party.

through his judgments.

In chiefdoms and states, an authorized third party may issue a binding decision which the disputing parties will be obligated to respect. This process is referred to as **adjudication.** The difference between negotiation and adjudication is basically a difference in authorization. In a dispute settled by adjudication, the disputing parties present their positions as convincingly as they can, but they do not participate in the ultimate decision-making.

Although the adjudication process is not characteristic of all societies, every society employs some form of negotiation in the settlement of disputes. Often, negotiation acts as a prerequisite or an alternative to adjudication. For example, in the resolution of U.S. labor disputes, striking workers may first negotiate with management, often with the mediation of a third party. If the state decides that the strike constitutes a threat to the public welfare, the disputing parties may be forced to submit to adjudication. In this case, the responsibility for resolving the dispute is transferred to a presumably impartial judge.

The work of the judge is difficult and complex. Not only must evidence which is presented be sifted through, but the judge must consider a wide range of norms, values, and earlier rulings in order to arrive at a decision which is intended to be considered just not only by the disputing parties but by the public and other judges as well. In most tribal societies, a greater value is placed on reconciling disputing parties and resuming tribal harmony than on administering awards and punishments. Thus, "tribal courts may . . . work in ways more akin to Western marriage conciliators, lawyers, arbitrators, and industrial conciliators than to Western judges in court."[17]

In many societies, judgment is thought to be made by incorruptible supernatural powers, through a trial by ordeal. An example of such a trial was described by James L. Gibbs, Jr., who studied the Kpelle in Liberia:

When there is some reason to doubt the testimony of a witness, or where the testimony of witnesses is in conflict, . . . a messenger is ordered to administer a spoonful of *katu* to the witness(es): *Katu* is a colorless liquid kept in a stoppered whiskey or wine bottle and is believed to have supernatural potency. In taking it, the witness swears over it, "If I bear false witness, then the *sale* [spirits] should kill me." It is believed that a person who breaks such an oath will be "caught" by the *katu*. His stomach will swell and he will die, or some other sickness will eventually strike. In the tropics, such a misfortune often occurs fairly soon, thereby supporting the belief in the efficacy of the liquid.[18]

Although trial by ordeal is not part of our own legal system, the principle is not altogether absent: each individual who gives testimony in court is made to swear an oath

involving the supernatural powers of the Judeo-Christian tradition.

POLITICAL ORGANIZATION AND EXTERNAL AFFAIRS

Although the regulation of internal affairs is an important function of any political system, it is by no means the sole function. Another is the management of external affairs—what we would call international relations, but which in the case of bands and tribes amounts to relations among different bands, lineages, clans, or whatever the largest autonomous political unit may be. And just as the threatened or actual use of force may be used to maintain order within a society, so may it be used in the conduct of external affairs.

War

One of the responsibilities of the state is the organization and execution of the activities of war. Throughout the last few thousand years of history, people have engaged in a seemingly endless chain of wars and intergroup hostilities. Why do wars occur? Is the need to wage war an instinctive feature of the human personality? What are the alternatives to violence as a means of settling disputes between societies?

Everyone shares certain fundamental needs. In order to survive, each of us requires sufficient food, water, and living space. Because these resources are available only in limited quantities, every society is faced with the problem of securing them for its members. Therefore, it is believed that a significant factor in human aggression is the stress related to population pressures. In societies with relatively efficient means of food production, it often happens

[17] Max Gluckman, *The Judicial Process among the Barotse of Northern Rhodesia* (New York: Free Press, 1975).

[18] James L. Gibbs, Jr., "The Kpelle of Liberia," in *Peoples of Africa* (New York: Holt, Rinehart and Winston, 1965), pp. 224–225.

A paramount chief among the Kpelle of Liberia settling a dispute. The defendant's mother pleads for her son in a case heard on the porch of the chief's house.

New Guinea, and the Hopi of North America. Among those societies where warfare is practiced, levels of violence may differ dramatically. Of warfare in New Guinea, for example, the anthropologist Robert Gordon notes:

. . . it's slightly more civilized than the violence of warfare which we practice insofar as it's strictly between two groups. And as an outsider, you can go up and interview people and talk to them while they're fighting and the arrows will miss you. It's quite safe and you can take photographs. Now, of course, the problem with modern warfare is precisely that it kills indiscriminately and you can't do much research on it, but at the same time, you can learn a lot talking to these people about the dynamics of how violence escalates into full-blown warfare.[19]

There is reason to suppose that war has become a serious problem only in the last 10,000 years, since the invention of food-production techniques, the rise of the city, and the invention of centralized states. Among hunters and gatherers, with their decentralized political systems, warfare is not a common method of relieving population pressures; some sort of voluntary redistribution is much more likely. Because territorial boundaries and membership among hunting and gathering bands are usually fluid and loosely defined, a man who hunts with one band today may hunt with a neighboring band tomorrow. Warfare is further rendered impractical by the systematic interchange of women among hunting and gathering groups—it is likely that someone in each band will have a sister, a brother, or a cousin in a neighboring band. Where property ownership is minimal and no state organization exists, the likelihood of warfare is greatly diminished.

that population increases faster than living standards improve. Obviously, a large population will need more food, water, and space than a small one. As population density rises, stress rises not only within a society, but between societies as well. War is one method of regulating and redistributing population.

War is not a universal phenomenon, for in various parts of the world, societies exist in which warfare as we know it is not practiced. Examples include people as diverse as the Bushmen of Africa, the Arapesh of

[19] Robert J. Gordon, Interview for KOCE-TV, held in Los Angeles, Dec. 4, 1981.

Despite the traditional view of the farmer as a gentle tiller of the soil, it is among farming and pastoral populations that warfare is most prominent. As a result of the commitment to the land inherent in farming, agricultural societies tend to be far more centralized and less fluid in their membership than hunting and gathering societies. Because these societies are often rigidly matrilocal or patrilocal, each new generation is thus bound to the same territory, no matter how small it may be or how large the group trying to live within it.

The availability of virgin land may not serve as a sufficient detriment to the outbreak of war. Among slash-and-burn horticulturalists, for example, competition for land cleared of virgin forest frequently leads to hostility and armed conflict. The centralization of political control and the possession of valuable property among farming people provide many more stimuli for warfare. It is among such peoples, especially those organized into states, that the violence of warfare is most apt to result in indiscriminant killing.

On a broader scale, the difference between food gathering and food producing populations may be viewed as a difference in **world view.** As a general rule, hunters and gatherers tend to conceive of themselves as a part of the natural world and in some sort of balance with it. This is reflected in their attitudes toward the animals they kill. Western Abenaki hunters, for example, thought that animals, like humans, were composed of a body and vital self. Although Abenakis hunted and killed animals to sustain their own lives, they clearly recognized that animals were entitled to proper respect. Thus, when beaver, muskrat, or waterfowl were killed, one couldn't just toss their bones into the nearest garbage pit. Proper respect required that their bones be returned to the water,

with a request that the species be continued. Such attitudes may be referred to as a naturalistic world view.

The Abenaki's respect for nature contrasts sharply with the kind of world view prevalent among farmers and pastoralists, who do not find their food in nature but take steps to produce it. The attitude that nature exists only to be used by humans may be referred to as an exploitative world view. By extension, a society which adopts such a world view may find nothing wrong with manipulating other societies in order to assure its own survival. The exploitative world view, prevalent among food-producing peoples, is an important contributor to intersocietal warfare.

Generally, a naturalistic world view has not been characteristic of modern industrial societies, although there are increasing numbers of people who would like to see this change. Although technology and contraception have the potential to greatly reduce population pressures, the large populations of Western societies have created a great deal of stress both internal and external. Through the systematic exploitation of underdeveloped lands, European and North American societies in particular have largely overcome the need to fight for food and water; now they fight for power and influence. Despite the ability to control population, the elimination of war has yet to be achieved; value systems would therefore seem to be a crucial element in the existence of warfare.

POLITICAL SYSTEMS AND THE QUESTION OF LEGITIMACY

Whatever form the political system of a society may take, and however it may go about its business, it must always first find some way to obtain the people's allegiance.

In decentralized systems, in which everyone participates in the making of all decisions, loyalty and cooperation are freely given, since each person is considered to be a part of the political system. But as the group grows larger, and the organization becomes more formal, the problems of obtaining and keeping public support become greater.

In centralized political systems increased reliance is placed upon coercion as a means of social control. This, however, tends to lessen the effectiveness of a political system. For example, the staff needed to apply force must often be large and may it-

> **World view:** The conceptions, explicit and implicit, of a society or an individual of the limits and workings of its world.

self grow to be a political force. The emphasis on force may also create resentment on the part of those to whom it is applied and so lessens cooperation. Thus police states are generally short-lived; most societies choose less extreme forms of social coercion.

Also basic to the political process is the concept of legitimacy, or the right of political leaders to rule. Like force, legitimacy is a form of support for a political system; unlike force, legitimacy is based on the values a particular society believes most important. Thus among the Kapauku, the legitimacy of the *tonowi's* power comes from his wealth; the kings of Hawaii, and England and France before their revolutions, were thought to have a divine right to rule; the head of the Dahomey state of West Africa acquires legitimacy through his age, as he is always the oldest living male of the people.

Legitimacy grants the right to hold, use, and allocate power. Power based on legitimacy may be distinguished from power based on force: obedience to the former results from the belief that obedience is "right"; compliance to power based on force is the result of fear of the deprivation of liberty, physical well-being, life, material property. Thus, power based on legitimacy is symbolic and depends not upon any intrinsic value, but upon the positive expectations of those who recognize and accede to it. If the expectations are not met regularly (if the shaman fails too many times or the leader is continuously unsuccessful in preventing horse or camel theft),

At the opening of the Democratic National Convention in Kansas City in August 1976 a Cherokee-Ojibwa Indian girl sings the national anthem. As societies become larger and more formally organized, the problems of obtaining and keeping public support become greater.

The legitimacy of any government rests ultimately on the consent of those governed. Consequently, not even his "divine right to rule" could save Louis XVI when he lost the consent of his people.

the legitimacy of the recognized power figure is minimized and may collapse altogether.

RELIGION AND POLITICS

Religion is intricately connected with politics. Religious beliefs may influence laws: acts that people believe to be sinful, such as sodomy and incest, are often illegal. Frequently, it is religion that legitimizes government.

In both industrial and nonindustrial societies, belief in the supernatural is important and is reflected in the governments of the people. The effect of religion on poli-

tics is perhaps best exemplified by medieval Europe. Holy wars were fought over the smallest matter; immense cathedrals were built in honor of the Virgin and other saints; kings and queens pledged allegiance to the Pope and asked his blessing in all important ventures, be they marital or martial. In the pre-Columbian Americas, the Aztec state was a religious state, or theocracy, that thrived in spite of more or less constant warfare carried out to procure captives for human sacrifices to assuage or please the gods. In Peru, the Inca emperor proclaimed absolute authority based on the proposition that he was descended from the sun god. In our own country, the Declaration of Independence, which is an expression of the social and political beliefs of the United States, stresses a belief in a Supreme Being. This document states that "all men are created [by God] equal," a tenet that gave rise to our own form of democracy because it implied that all people should participate in governing themselves. The fact that the President of the United States takes the oath of office by swearing on a Bible is another instance of the use of religion to legitimize political power.

In many nonliterate societies, religion is even more closely related to the political system. Among the Afikpo Ibo of Nigeria, for example, religion is a political force even though priests and diviners are not politically active and officials do not require supernatural approval to hold office.[20] The political power of religion is vested in the Afikpo guardian *erosi*, the impersonal spirits connected with nature. These awesome spirits are instrumental in such important affairs as prosperity, fertility, and general welfare. Politically, the *erosi* reinforce the men's village society, which is charged with maintaining order within the village. For example, if a person accused of a crime denies guilt, it is necessary to swear innocence on an *erosi* shrine. If one refuses, one is considered guilty; if one swears and is lying, the Afikpos believe the *erosi* will kill, or make seriously ill, such a liar within a short span of time.

---

[20]Phoebe Ottenberg, "The Afikpo Ibo of Eastern Nigeria," in James L. Gibbs, Jr., ed., *Peoples of Africa* (New York: Holt, Rinehart and Winston, 1965), pp. 3–39.

CHAPTER SUMMARY

Through political organization all societies maintain social order, manage public affairs, and reduce social disorder. No group can live together without persuading or coercing its members to conform to agreed-upon rules of conduct. To properly understand the political organization of a society, one needs to view it in the light of its ecological, social, and ideological context.

Four basic types of political systems may be identified. In order of complexity, these range from decentralized bands and tribes to centralized chiefdoms and states. The band, characteristic of hunting-gathering and some other nomadic societies, is a small autonomous group of associated families or kin occupying a common territory. Political organization in bands is democratic, and informal social control is exerted by public opinion in the form of gossip and ridicule. Band leaders are older men whose personal authority lasts only as long as members believe they are leading well and making the right decisions.

The tribe is composed of separate bands or other social units that are brought together by such unifying factors as descent, age grading, or common interest. With an economy usually based on farming or herding, the population of the tribe is larger than that of the band, although family units within the tribe are still relatively autonomous and egalitarian. As in the band, political organization is transitory, and leaders have no formal means of maintaining authority.

Many tribal societies vest political authority in the clan, an association of people who believe themselves to be descended from a common ancestor. A group of elders or headmen regulate the affairs of members and represent their group in relations with other clans. The segmentary lineage system, similar in operation to the clan, is a rare form of tribal organization based on kinship bond. Tribal age-grade systems cut across territorial and kin groupings. Leadership is vested in men in the group who were initiated into the age grade at the same time and passed as a set from one age grade to another until reaching the proper age to become elders.

Common-interest associations wield political authority in many tribes throughout the world. A boy joins one or another club when he reaches warrior status. These organizations administer the affairs of the tribe. Another variant of authority in tribes in Melanesia is the Big Man, who builds up his wealth and political power until he must be reckoned with as a leader.

As societies become more heterogenous socially, politically, and economically, the need for formal, stable, and permanent leadership increases. Chiefdoms are ranked societies in which every member has a position in the hierarchy. Status is determined by the position of an individual's descent group. Power is concentrated in a single chief whose true authority serves to unite his community in all matters. The chief may accumulate great personal wealth, which enhances his power base, and pass it on to his heirs.

The most formal of political organizations is the state. It has a central power which can legitimately use force to administer a rigid code of laws and to maintain order even beyond its borders. A large bureaucracy functions to uphold the authority of the central power. The state is found only in societies with numerous diverse groups. Typically, it is a stratified society, and economic functions and wealth are distributed unequally.

There are two kinds of social controls, internalized and externalized. Internalized controls are self-imposed by guilty individuals. These built-in controls rely on such deterrents as personal shame, fear of divine punishment, or magical retaliation. Although bands and tribes rely heavily upon them, internalized controls are generally insufficient by themselves. Every society develops externalized controls, called sanctions. Positive sanctions, in the form of awards or recognition by one's neighbors, is the position a society or a number of its members takes toward behavior that is approved; negative sanctions, such as threat of imprisonment or corporal punishment, reflect societal reactions to behavior that is disapproved.

Sanctions may also be classified as either formal—involving actual laws—or informal—involving norms but not legal statutes. Formal sanctions are organized and reward or punish behavior through a rigidly regulated social procedure. Informal sanctions are diffuse, involving the immediate approving or disapproving reactions of individual community members to a fellow member's behavior. Other important agents of social control are witchcraft beliefs and religious sanctions.

Sanctions serve to formalize conformity to group norms, including actual law, and to integrate the various social factions in a community. Some anthropologists have proposed that to define law is an impossible and perhaps undesirable undertaking. In considering law, it appears best to examine each society within its unique cultural context.

Law serves several basic functions. First, it defines relationships among the members of a society and thereby dictates proper behavior under different circumstances. Second, law allocates authority to employ coercion in the enforcement of sanctions. In centralized political systems this authority rests with the government and court system. Decentralized societies may give this authority directly to the injured party. Third, law redefines social relations and aids its own efficient operation by ensuring that there is room for change.

Western societies clearly distinguish offenses against the state, called crimes, from offenses against an individual, called torts. Decentralized societies may view all offenses as offenses against individuals. One way to understand the nature of law is to analyze individual dispute cases against their own cultural background. A dispute may be settled in two ways, negotiation and adjudication. All societies use negotiation to settle individual disputes. Negotiation involves the parties to the dispute themselves reaching an agreement, with or without the help of a third party. Adjudication, not found in some societies, involves an authorized third party issuing a binding decision. The disputing parties present their petitions, but play no part in the decision-making.

In addition to regulating internal affairs, political systems also attempt to regulate external affairs, or relations among politically autonomous units. In doing so they may resort to the threat or use of force.

War is not a universal phenomenon, since societies exist which do not practice warfare as we know it. Usually these societies are those that have some kind of naturalistic world view, an attitude that until recently had become nearly extinguished in modern industrial societies.

A major problem faced by any form of political organization is obtaining and maintaining people's loyalty and support. Reliance on force and coercion in the long run usually tends to lessen the effectiveness of a political system. A basic instrument of political implementation is legitimacy, or the right of political leaders to exercise authority. Power based on legitimacy stems from the belief of a society's members that obedience is "right," and therefore on the positive expectations of those who obey. It may be distinguished from compliance based on force, which stems from fear, and thus on negative expectations.

Religion is so intricately woven into the life of the people in both industrial and nonindustrial countries that its presence is inevitably felt in the political sphere. To a greater or lesser extent, governments the world over use religion to legitimize political power.

SUGGESTED READINGS

Bohannan, Paul, ed. *Law and Warfare, Studies in the Anthropology of Conflict.* Garden City, N.Y.: Natural History Press, 1967.

Examples of various ways in which conflict is evaluated and handled in different cultures are brought together in this book. It examines institutions and means of conflict resolution, including courts, middlemen, self-help, wager of battle, contest, and ordeal. It also has a selection discussing war—raids, organization for aggression, tactics, and feuds.

Cohen, Ronald, and John Middleton, eds. *Comparative Political Systems.* Garden City, N.Y.: Natural History Press, 1967.

The editors have selected some 20 studies in the politics of nonindustrial societies by such well-known scholars as Lévi-Strauss, S. F. Nadel, Marshall Sahlins, and S. N. Eisenstadt.

Fried, Morton. *The Evolution of Political Society: An Essay in Political Anthropology.* New York: Random House, 1967.

The author attempts to trace the evolution of political society through a study of simple, egalitarian societies. The character of the state and the means whereby this form of organization takes shape is considered in terms of pristine and secondary states, formed because preexisting states supplied the stimuli or models for organization.

Hoebel, E. Adamson. *The Law of Primitive Man: A Study in Comparative Legal Dynamics.* Cambridge: Harvard University Press, 1954; Atheneum, 1968.

This book combines the study of law and anthropology to develop a setting of ideas and methods for the study of law in "primitive" society. It then analyzes seven cultures (including Eskimo, Comanche, Trobriand Islanders, and Ashanti) with reference to the underlying legal forms which govern each. It ends with a discussion of the interrelationship between law and society.

Krader, Lawrence. *Formation of the State.* Englewood Cliffs, N.J.: Prentice-Hall, 1968.

This book describes the characteristics of the state-type of political organization in the process of trying to account for the way (or ways) in which states develop.

Nader, Laura, ed. *Law in Culture and Society.* Chicago: Aldine, 1969.

This is a well-balanced and thorough collection of articles on law in different cultures and societies.

12 | Religion and Magic

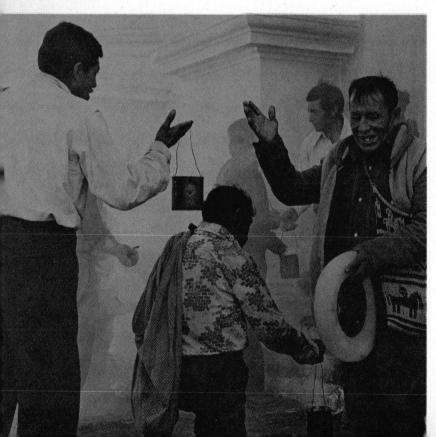

Ritual is religion in action, and prayer and the making of offerings are common forms of rituals. These Maya Indians are praying and making an offering on the steps of the church at Chichicastenango, Guatemala. Although the church is Roman Catholic, the ritual is distinctively Mayan, directed to deities who serve particular causes or protect against certain sicknesses.

PREVIEW

WHAT IS RELIGION?

Religion may be regarded as beliefs and patterns of behavior by which humans try to deal with what they view as important problems that cannot be solved through the application of known technology or techniques of organization. To overcome these limitations, people turn to the manipulation of supernatural beings and powers.

WHAT ARE RELIGION'S IDENTIFYING FEATURES?

Religion consists of various rituals—prayers, songs, dances, offerings, and sacrifices—through which people try to manipulate supernatural beings and powers to their advantage. These beings and powers may consist of gods and goddesses, ancestral and other spirits, or impersonal powers, either by themselves or in various combinations. In all societies there are certain individuals especially skilled at dealing with these beings and powers and who assist other members of society in their ritual activities. A body of myths rationalizes or "explains" the system in a manner consistent with people's experience in the world in which they live.

WHAT FUNCTIONS DOES RELIGION SERVE?

Whether or not a particular religion accomplishes what people believe it does, all religions serve a number of important psychological and social functions. They reduce anxiety by explaining the unknown and making it understandable, as well as provide comfort in the belief that supernatural aid is available in times of crisis. They sanction a wide range of human conduct by providing notions of right and wrong, setting precedents for acceptable behavior, and transferring the burden of decision making from individuals to supernatural powers. Through ritual, religion may be used to enhance the learning of oral traditions; and, finally, religion plays an important role in maintaining social solidarity.

According to their origin myth, the Tewa Indians of New Mexico emerged from a lake far to the north of where they now live. Once on dry land, they divided into two groups, the Summer People and the Winter People, and migrated south down both sides of the Rio Grande. During their travels, they made twelve stops before finally being reunited into a single community.

For the Tewa, all existence is divided into six categories, three human and three supernatural. Each of the human categories, which are arranged in a hierarchy, is matched by a spiritual category, so that when people die, they immediately pass into their proper spiritual role. Not only are the supernatural categories identified with human categories; they also correspond to divisions in the natural world.

From a Judeo-Christian vantage point, such a religion may seem, at best, irrational and arbitrary. It is neither—as has been shown by Alfonso Ortiz, a native-born Tewa anthropolgist. Ortiz argues that his native religion is not only logical and socially functional, it is the very model of Tewa society.[1] The Tewa have one of the few extant "dual organization" societies in the world; it is divided into two independent moieties, each having its own economy, rituals, and authority. The individual is introduced into one of these moieties, which are not based on kinship, and his or her membership is regularly reinforced through a series of life-cycle rituals that correspond to the stops on the mythical tribal journey down the Rio Grande. The rites of birth and death are shared by the whole community; other rites differ in the two moieties. The highest status of the human hierarchy belongs to the priests, who also help integrate this divided society; they not only mediate between the human and spiritual world, but also between the two moieties.

Tewa religion enters into virtually every aspect of Tewa life and society. It is the basis of the simultaneously dualistic/unified world view of the individual Tewa. It provides numerous points of mediation through which the two moieties can continue to exist as a single community. It sanctifies the community by providing a supernatural origin, and it offers divine sanction to those "rites of passage" that soften life's major transitions. In providing an afterworld that is the mirror image of human society, it answers the question of death in a manner that reinforces social structure. In short, Tewa religion, far from being arbitrary or illogical, gives a solid foundation to the stability and continuity of Tewa society.

All religions fulfill numerous social and psychological needs. Some of these—the need to confront and explain death, for example—appear to be universal; indeed, Malinowski went so far as to say that "there are no peoples, however primitive, without religion and magic."[2] Unbound by time, religion gives meaning to individual and group life, drawing power from "the time of the gods in the Beginning," and offering continuity of existence beyond death. It can provide the path by which people transcend their arduous earthly existence and attain, if only momentarily, spiritual selfhood. The social functions of religion are no less important than the psychological functions. A traditional religion reinforces group norms, provides moral sanctions for individual conduct, and furnishes the substratum of common purpose and values upon which the equilibrium of the community depends.

---

[1] Alfonso Ortiz, *The Tewa World* (Chicago: University of Chicago Press, 1969), p. 43.

[2] Bronislaw Malinowski, *Magic, Science and Religion* (Garden City, N.Y.: Doubleday, Anchor Books, 1954).

Because religion, as we shall see, fulfills important psychological and social functions, it has survived the various onslaughts of anticlericalism, rationalism, science, and technology.

Nineteenth-century evolutionists believed that science would ultimately destroy religion by showing people the irrationality of their myths and rituals. Indeed, the belief is still widespread that as scientific explanations replace those of religion, the latter should wither on the vine. But an opposite tendency has occurred; not only do traditional, "main line" religions continue to attract new adherents, but there has been a strong resurgence of fundamentalist religions with strong, anti-science biases.[3] Examples include the Muslim fundamentalism of the Ayatollah Khomeini in Iran and the Christian fundamentalism of Jerry Falwell and others in the United States. Moreover, interest in astrology and occultism continues to be strong in North America, and there are new religious options, such as the sects derived from Eastern religions.

Science, far from destroying religion, may have contributed to the creation of a veritable religious boom. It has done this by removing many traditional psychological props, while at the same time creating, in its technological applications, a host of new problems—threat of nuclear catastrophe, health threats from pollution, fear of loneliness in a society that isolates us from our kin and that places impediments in the way of establishing deep and lasting friendships, to list but a few which people must

now deal with. In the face of these new anxieties, religion offers social and psychological support.

The persistence of religion in the face of Western rationalism clearly reveals that it is a powerful and dynamic force in society. Although anthropologists are not qualified to pass judgment on the metaphysical truth of any particular religion, they can attempt to show how each religion embodies a number of "truths" about humans and society.

THE ANTHROPOLOGICAL APPROACH TO RELIGION

Anthony F. C. Wallace has defined religion as "a set of rituals, rationalized by myth, which mobilizes supernatural powers for the purpose of achieving or preventing transformations of state in man and nature."[4] What lies behind this definition is a recognition that people, when they cannot deal with serious problems that cause them anxiety through technological or organizational means, try to do so through the manipulation of supernatural beings and powers. This requires ritual, which Wallace sees as the primary phenomenon of religion, or "religion in action." Its major function is to reduce anxiety and keep confidence high, all of which serves to keep people in some sort of shape to cope with reality. It is this that gives religion survival value.

Religion, then, may be regarded as beliefs and patterns of behavior by which people try to control the area of the universe that is otherwise beyond their control. Since no known culture, our own included, has achieved complete certainty in controlling the universe, religion is a part of all known cultures. There is, however, consid-

---

[3] Richard J. Norelli and Robert R. Proulx, "Anti-Science as a Component in the Growing Popularity of Scientific Creationism," and Kenneth R. Stunkel, "Understanding Scientific Creationism," in Stephen Pastner and William A. Haviland, eds., *Confronting the Creationists* (Northeastern Anthropological Association Occasional Proceedings, No. 1, 1982, pp. 4–11, 51–60.

[4] Anthony F. C. Wallace, *Religion: An Anthropological View* (New York: Random House, 1966), p. 107.

Far from causing the death of religion, the growth of scientific knowledge, by producing new anxieties and raising new questions about human existence, may have contributed to the continuing presence of religion in modern life. North Americans continue to participate in traditional religions, such as Judaism (above), as well as imported sects, such as Hare Krishna (top right), and evangelicalism (bottom right).

erable variability here. At one end of the human spectrum are hunting and gathering peoples, whose scientific knowledge about the universe is limited, and who tend to see themselves more as part of, rather than masters of, nature. This is what we referred to in Chapter 11 as a naturalistic world view. Among hunters and gatherers religious behavior is apt to be an integral part of day-to-day behavior. At the other end of the human spectrum is Western civilization, with its wealth of scientific knowledge and its commitment to overcoming problems through technological and organizational skills. Here, religion is less a part of daily activities and tends to be restricted to specific occasions. Even so, there is variation. Religious activity may be less important to social elites, who see themselves as more in control of their own destinies, than it is to peasants or members of lower classes. Among them, religion may afford some compensation for a dependent status in society. It may also rationalize the system in such a way that these people may not seek to change their lot; after all, if there is hope for a better existence after death, then one may be more willing to put up with hard times in this life.

THE PRACTICE OF RELIGION

Much of the value of religion comes from the activities called for by its practice. Participation in religious ceremonies may bring a sense of personal transcendence, a wave of reassurance, security, and even ecstasy, or a feeling of closeness to fellow participants. Although the rituals and practices of religions vary considerably, even those rites that seem to us most bizarrely exotic can be shown to serve the same basic social and psychological functions.

Supernatural Beings and Powers

One of the hallmarks of religion is a belief in supernatural beings and forces. In attempting to control by religious means what cannot be controlled in other ways, humans turn to prayer, sacrifice, and ritual activity in general. This presupposes a world of supernatural beings which have an interest in human affairs, and to whom appeals for aid may be directed. For convenience, we may divide these beings into

> **Pantheons:** The several gods and goddesses of a people.

three categories: major deities (gods and goddesses), ancestral spirits, and non-human spirit beings. Although the variety of deities and spirits recognized by the world's cultures is tremendous, certain generalizations about them are possible.

GODS AND GODDESSES Gods and goddesses are the great and more remote beings. They are usually seen as controlling the universe, or, if several are recognized, each has charge of a particular part of the universe. Such was the case of the gods and goddesses of ancient Greece: Zeus was lord of the sky, Poseidon was ruler of the sea, and Hades was lord of the underworld and ruler of the dead. Besides these three brothers, there were a host of other deities, each similarly concerned with specific aspects of life and the universe. **Pantheons,** or collections of gods and goddesses such as those of the Greeks, are common in non-Western states as well. Since states have frequently grown through conquest, their pantheons often have developed as local deities of conquered peoples were incorporated into the national pantheon. Usually, creators of the present world are included, though this was not the case with the Greeks. Another frequent though not invariable feature of pantheons is the presence of a supreme deity, who may be all but totally ignored by humans. For example, the Aztecs of Mexico recognized a supreme pair, but they did not pay much attention to them. The reason for this is that, being so remote, they were not concerned with human affairs. Hence, attention was focused on those deities who were more directly concerned in human matters.

ANCESTRAL SPIRITS A belief in ancestral spirits is consistent with the widespread notion that human beings are made up of two parts, a body and some kind of vital spirit. For example, the Penobscot Indians, whom we met in Chapter 5, maintained that each person had a vital spirit which could even travel about apart from the body, while the latter remained inert. Given some such concept, the idea of the spirit being freed by death from the body and continuing to exist seems logical enough.

Where a belief in ancestral spirits exists, these beings are frequently seen as retaining an active interest, and even membership in, society. Like living persons, ancestral spirits may be benevolent or malevolent, but one is never quite sure what their behavior will be. The same feeling of uncertainty—how will they react to what I have done?—may be displayed toward ancestral spirits that tends to be displayed to those of a senior generation who hold authority over the individual. Beyond this, ancestral spirits closely resemble living humans in appetites, feelings, emotions, and behavior.

A belief in ancestral spirits of one sort or another is found in many parts of the world. In many African societies, however, the concept is particularly well developed. Here one frequently finds ancestral spirits behaving just like humans. They are able to feel hot, cold, and pain, and they may be capable of dying a second death by drowning or burning. They may even participate in family and lineage affairs, and seats will be provided for them, even though the spirits are invisible. If they are annoyed, they may send sickness or even death. Eventually, they are reborn as new members of their lineage, and in societies that hold such beliefs, there is a need to observe infants closely in order to determine just who it is that has been reborn.

Strong beliefs in ancestral spirits such as these are particularly appropriate in a society of descent-based groups with their associated ancestor orientation. More than this, though, they provide a strong sense of continuity in which past, present, and future are all linked.

ANIMISM One of the most widespread beliefs about supernatural beings is **animism,** which sees nature as animated by all sorts of spirits. In his search for the origin of all religious beliefs, Sir Edward Tylor invented the concept. Writing in 1873, he noted many examples of animism. For example, the Dayaks of Borneo believed rice had a soul, and they held feasts to contain the soul securely in order to prevent crop failure. The Koryaks of Asia, after killing a bear, would flay the animal, dress one of their people in the skin, and dance around chanting that they were not really responsible for killing the bear but that the Russians killed it.

The single term "animism" masks a wide range of variation. Animals and plants may all have their individual spirits, as may springs, mountains, or other natural features. So too may stones, weapons, ornaments, and so on. In addition, the woods may be full of a variety of unattached, or free-ranging, spirits. The various spirits involved are a highly diverse lot. Generally speaking, though, they are closer to people than gods and goddesses and are more involved in daily affairs. They may be benevolent, malevolent, or just plain neutral. They may also be awesome, terrifying, lovable, or even mischievous. Since they may be pleased or irritated by human actions, people are obliged to be concerned with them.

Animism is typical of those who see themselves as being a part of nature rather than superior to it. This takes in most hunters and gatherers and some food-producing peoples. Among them, gods and goddesses are relatively unimportant, but the woods are full of all sorts of spirits. Gods and goddesses, if they exist at all, may be seen as having created the world, and perhaps making it fit to live in. But it is spirits to whom one turns for curing, who help or hinder the shaman, and whom the ordinary hunter may meet in the woods.

ANIMATISM   While supernatural power is often thought of as being vested in supernatural beings, it doesn't have to be. The Melanesians, for example, think of *mana* as a force inherent in all objects. It is not in itself physical, but it can reveal itself physically. A warrior's success in fighting is not attributed to his own strength but to the *mana* contained in an amulet which hangs around his neck. Similarly, a farmer may know a great deal about horticulture, soil conditioning, and the correct time for sowing and harvesting, but nevertheless depends upon *mana* for a successful crop, often building a simple altar to this power at the end of the field. If the crop is good, it is a sign that the farmer has in some way appropriated the necessary *mana*. Far from being a personalized force, *mana* is abstract in the extreme, a power lying always just beyond reach of the senses. As R. H. Codrington described it:

Virtue, prestige, authority, good fortune, influence, sanctity, luck are all words which, under certain conditions, give something near the meaning. . . . *mana* sometimes means a more than natural virtue or power attaching to some person or thing. . . .[5]

---

[5]As quoted by Godfrey Leinhardt in "Religion," in Harry Shapiro, ed., *Man, Culture, and Society* (New York: Oxford University Press, 1960), p. 368.

> **Animism: A belief in spirit beings which are thought to animate nature.**
>
> **Animatism: A belief that the world is animated by impersonal spiritual powers.**

This concept of impersonal power was also widespread among North American Indians. The Iroquois called it *orenda;* to the Sioux it was *wakonda;* to the Algonquians, *manitu*. However, though found on every continent, the concept is not necessarily universal.

R. R. Marett called this concept of impersonal power **animatism.** The two concepts, animatism and animism, a belief in supernatural beings, are not mutually exclusive. They are often found in the same culture, such as in Melanesia, and also in the Indian societies mentioned above.

People trying to comprehend beliefs in supernatural beings and powers frequently ask how such beliefs are maintained. In part, the answer is through manifestations of power. By this is meant that, given a belief in animatism and/or the powers of supernatural beings, then one is predisposed to see what appear to be results of the application of such powers. For example, if a Melanesian warrior is convinced of his power because of his possession of the necessary *mana*, and he is successful, he may very well interpret this success as proof of the power of *mana*. "After all, I would have lost had I not possessed it, wouldn't I?" Beyond this, because of his confidence in his mana, he may be less timid in his fighting, and this could indeed mean the difference between success or failure.

Failures, of course, do occur, but they can be explained. Perhaps one's prayer was not answered because a deity or spirit is still angry about some past insult. Or perhaps our Melanesian warrior lost his battle—the obvious explanation is that he was not as successful in bringing *mana* to bear

In societies with occupational specialization, religious specialists are usually trained by formally organized religious bodies. This sequence of photos shows some events in the life of Theravada Buddhist monks.

Novices all eat together; their food is donated by local worshippers.

as he thought, or else his opponent had more of it. In any case, humans generally emphasize successes over failures, and long after many of the latter have been forgotten, tales will probably still be told of striking cases of the workings of supernatural powers.

Another feature that tends to perpetuate beliefs in supernatural beings is that they have attributes with which people are familiar. Allowing for the fact that supernatural beings are in a sense larger than life, they are generally conceived of as living the way people do, and are interested in the same sorts of things. For example, the Penobscot Indians believed in a quasi-human being called Gluskabe. Like ordinary mortals, Gluskabe traveled about in a canoe, used snowshoes, lived in a wigwam, and made stone arrowheads. The gods of the ancient Greeks had all the familiar human lusts and jealousies. Such features serve to make supernatural beings believable.

The role of mythology in maintaining beliefs should not be overlooked. Myths, which are discussed in some detail in Chapter 13, are explanatory tales which rationalize religious beliefs and practices. To us, the word "myth" immediately conjures up the idea of a story about imaginary events, but the people responsible for a particular myth usually don't see it that way. To them, myths are true stories, analogous to historical documents in our culture. Myths invariably are full of accounts of the doings of various supernatural beings. Hence, they serve to reinforce beliefs in them.

Religious Practitioners

PRIESTS AND PRIESTESSES In all human societies, there exist individuals whose job it is to guide and supplement the religious practices of others. Such individuals are highly skilled at contacting and influencing

The monastery is one of the sources of education for young boys.

The higher status of the abbot is indicated by the decoration of his fan.

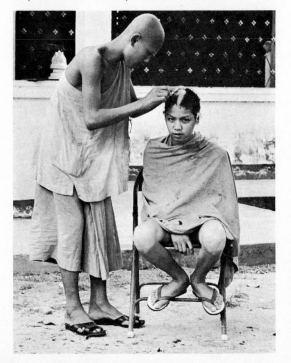

A novice has his head shaved; Thai monks are usually shaved on the day before the full moon.

A novice becomes a monk; his new name is written in Pali on the fan beside him.

supernatural beings and manipulating supernatural forces. Their qualification for this is that they have undergone special training. In addition, they may display certain unique personality traits that particularly suit them for their job. In societies with the resources to support occupational specialists, the role of guiding religious practices and influencing the supernaturals belongs to the **priest** or **priestess.** He or she is the socially initiated, ceremonially inducted member of a recognized religious organization with a rank and function that belongs to him or her as the tenant of an office held before by others. The source of power is the society and the institution in which the priest or priestess functions. The priest, if not the priestess, is a familiar figure in our own society; he is the priest, minister, pastor, rector, rabbi, or whatever the official title may be in some organized religion.

SHAMANS   Even in societies that lack occupational specialization, there have always been individuals who have acquired religious power individually, usually in solitude and isolation, when the Great Spirit, the Power, the Great Mystery, or whatever is revealed to them. Such persons become the recipients of certain special gifts, such as healing or divination; when they return to society they are frequently given another kind of religious role, that of the **shaman.**

In the United States, millions of people have learned something about shamans through their reading of the popular autobiography of Black Elk, a traditional Sioux Indian "medicine man," or Carlos Castaneda's apparently fictional accounts of his experiences with Don Juan, the Yaqui Indian shaman. Few of them may realize, however, that the faith healers and many other evangelists in their own society conform in every respect to our definition of

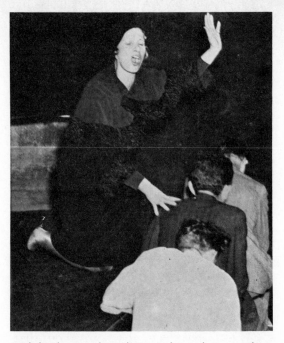

Faith healers, such as the one shown here, conform in every respect to our definition of the shaman. Thus, shamanism is by no means absent in modern, industrial societies.

the shaman. Thus, one should not get the idea that shamans are not to be found in modern, industrial societies, for they are. Furthermore, they may become more common, given the current revival of interest in the occult and supernatural which is taking place in the United States.

Typically, one becomes a shaman by passing through stages commonly related by many myths. These stages are often thought to involve torture and violent dismemberment of the body; scraping away of the flesh until the body is reduced to a skeleton; substitution of the viscera and renewal of the blood; a period spent in a nether region, or land of the dead, during which the shaman is taught by the souls of the dead shamans and other spirit beings;

and an ascent to a sky realm. Among the Crow Indians, for example, any man could become a shaman, since there was no ecclesiastical organization that handed down laws for the guidance of the religious consciousness. The search for shamanistic visions was pursued by most adult Crow males, who would engage in bodily deprivation, even self-torture, to induce such visions. The majority of the seekers would not be granted a vision, but failure carried no social stigma. While those who claimed supernatural vision would be expected to manifest some special power in battle or wealth, it was the sincerity of the seeker that carried the essential truth of the experience. Many of the elements of shamanism such as transvestitism, trance states, and speaking in undecipherable languages can just as easily be regarded as abnormalities, and it has been frequently pointed out that those regarded as specially gifted in some societies would be outcasts or worse in others. The position of shaman provides a socially approved role for otherwise unstable personalities.

> **Priest or priestess: A full-time religious specialist.**

> **Shaman: A person who has special religious power acquired through his or her own initiative and is thought to possess certain special abilities to deal with supernatural beings and powers.**

The shaman is essentially a religious entrepreneur, who acts for some human client. On behalf of the client, the shaman intervenes to influence or impose his or her will on supernatural powers. The shaman can be contrasted with the priest or priestess, whose "clients" are the deities. Priests and priestesses frequently tell people what to do; the shaman tells supernaturals what to do. In return for services rendered, the

Usually, the only religious specialist among hunters and gatherers is the shaman. Here, a shaman performs over a client whose leg was caught in a trap.

The shaman as a religious specialist may be found among peoples other than hunters and gatherers. In the Guatemalan community of Chichicastenango, a shaman pours an offering over an idol representing an ancient Maya deity.

shaman sometimes collects a fee—fresh meat, yams, a favorite possession. In some cases, the added prestige, authority, and social power attached to the status of shaman are reward enough.

One particular aspect of shamanism that some Westerners often find disturbing is the trickery which commonly goes with the job. The fact is that the shaman may put on quite a show for his or her client, involving not just going into a trance, but the performance of sleight-of-hand tricks and ventriloquism. In the arctic regions, for example, a shaman may summon spirits in the dark and produce all sorts of flapping noises and strange voices to impress the audiences. Somewhat less vigorous, but no less dramatic, is the following example of a shaman's performance among the Ona, a hunting and gathering people native to Tierra del Fuego, at the southern tip of South America.

ORIGINAL STUDY

An Ona Shaman Performs[6]

After allowing a quarter of an hour to elapse, Houshken said he was thirsty and went down to the nearby stream for a drink. It was a bright moonlight night and the snow on the ground helped to make the scene of the exhibition we were about to witness as light as day. On his return, Houshken sat down and broke into a monotonous chant, which went on until suddenly he put his hands to his mouth. When he brought them away, they were palms downward and some inches apart. We saw that a strip of guanaco hide, about treble the thickness of a leather bootlace, was now held loosely in his hands. It passed over his thumbs, under the palms of his half-closed hands, and was looped over his little fingers so that about three inches of end hung down from each hand. The strip appeared to be not more than eighteen inches long.

Without pulling the strip tight, Houshken now began to shake his hands violently, gradually bringing them farther apart, until the strip, with the two ends still showing, was about four feet long. He then called his brother, Chashkil, who took the end from his right hand and stepped back with it. From four feet, the strip now grew out of Houshken's left hand to double that length. Then, as Chashkil stepped forward, it disappeared back into Houshken's hand, until he was able to take the other end from his brother. With the continued agitation of his hands, the strip got shorter and shorter. Suddenly, when his hands were almost together, he clapped them to his mouth, uttered a prolonged shriek, then held out his hands to us, palms upward and empty.

[6] E. Lucas Bridges, *Uttermost Part of the Earth* (New York: Dutton, 1948), pp. 284–286.

Even an ostrich could not have swallowed those eight feet of hide at one gulp without visible effort. Where else the coil could have gone to I do not profess to know. It could not have gone up Houshken's sleeve, for he had dropped his robe when the performance began. There were between twenty and thirty men present, but only eight or nine were Houshken's people. The rest were far from being friends of the performer and all had been watching intently. Had they detected some simple trick, the great medicine-man would have lost his influence; they would no longer have believed in any of his magic.

The demonstration was not yet over. Houshken stood up and resumed his robe. Once again he broke into a chant and seemed to go into a trance, possessed by some spirit not his own. Drawing himself up to his full height, he took a step towards me and let his robe, his only garment, fall to the ground. He put his hands to his mouth with a most impressive gesture and brought them away again with fists clenched and thumbs close together. He held them up to the height of my eyes, and when they were less than two feet from my face slowly drew them apart. I saw that there was now a small, almost opaque object between them. It was about an inch in diameter in the middle and tapered away into his hands. It might have been a piece of semi-transparent dough or elastic, but whatever it was it seemed to be alive, revolving at great speed, while Houshken, apparently from muscular tension, was trembling violently.

The moonlight was bright enough to read by as I gazed at this strange object. Houshken brought his hands farther apart and the object grew more and more transparent, until, when some three inches separated his hands, I realized that it was not there any more. It did not break or burst like a bubble; it simply disappeared, having been visible to me for less than five seconds. Houshken made no sudden movement, but slowly opened his hands and turned them over for my inspection. They looked clean and dry. He was stark naked and there was no confederate beside him. I glanced down at the snow and, in spite of his stoicism, Houshken could not resist a chuckle, for nothing was to be seen there.

The others had crowded round us and, as the object disappeared, there was a frightened gasp from some of them. Houshken reassured them with the remark:

"Do not let it trouble you. I shall call it back to myself again."

The natives believed this to be an incredibly malignant spirit belonging to, or possibly part of, the *joön* from whom it emanated. It might take physical form, as we had just witnessed, or be totally invisible. It had the power to introduce insects, tiny mice, mud, sharp flints or even a jelly-fish or baby octopus into the anatomy of those who had incurred its master's displeasure. I have seen a strong man shudder involuntarily at the thought of this horror and its evil potentialities. It was a curious fact that, although every magician must have known himself to be a fraud and a trickster, he always believed in and greatly feared the supernatural abilities of other medicine-men.

PORTFOLIO 2

The Quiché Maya
of Chichicastenango

Early in 1524, when the Spaniard Pedro de Alvarado invaded the highlands of what is now Guatemala, he found the region heavily populated by Maya Indians. Organized into a number of small, warring states, these Maya were heirs to a rich civilization, by then over 1,000 years old. Today, more than 400 years after their conquest by the Spanish, Indians still outnumber non-Indians in Guatemala. What's more, they have shown great determination in continuing many of their old customs down to the present day. There are, for example, over a million speakers of Maya languages in the highlands today, and many rituals of pre-Columbian origin continue to be practiced by people who have been reckoned as Catholics ever since Spanish colonial times.

One of the most powerful of the preconquest states was that of the Quiché Maya. At one time they were able to impose their control over many of their neighbors, creating a small-scale empire of sorts. So stout was their resistance to Alvarado that he could not subdue them until he burned their capital, Utatlán, to the ground. Their modern-day descendants are pictured on the following pages, as well as elsewhere in this book.

Today the Quiché Maya live in and around the town of Chichicastenango. Mostly, they live outside the town, in well-built and sturdy homesteads of adobe and tile that are scattered all over the hills. Near these are their *milpas*, the plots of land where the traditional crops of corn, beans, and squash are grown. But although they are not town dwellers, they are very much of the town, for Chichicastenango is the center of their commercial, religious, political, and social life. As the people themselves see it, life outside the town is dull and monotonous, while everything that is joyful, exciting, and colorful takes place in town.

Like most Latin American towns, Chichicastenango is laid out in rectangular blocks, as much as the hilly terrain will permit, with a spacious plaza at the center. On most days of the week the

Mud brick houses and a hillside field near Chichicastenango.

Indians headed for market; in the background is the cemetery.

Yard goods, jackets for men, pottery, and boards for sale in the market.

The animal market is a few blocks from the main market.

A boy plays a marimba on the edge of a street.

Looming up over the market plaza is the imposing Catholic church.

A religious procession moves through Chichicastenango.

streets and plaza appear all but deserted. But on market days—Sundays and Thursdays—things are different. Before dawn Indians living around the countryside begin their long walk into town, converging throughout the morning on the plaza where the market is held. This becomes a beehive of activity, where people of all ages and sexes, non-Indians as well as Indians, are able to procure just about everything from pigs to coffins. As if the market were not colorful enough, added color is provided by the distinctive and sumptuous dress worn by the Indians, by which they proclaim their Quiché Maya identity.

Although the Quiché go to market to buy and sell, this is not the only, or even primary, reason they go. Market day is a great social occasion, with all sorts of things going on. And intertwined with all the commercial and social activity is important ceremonial activity. Dominating the plaza is the great Catholic church. This is approached by an impressive flight of stone steps, into which is built a stone altar on which smoldering ashes are always to be found. This is the altar to which the Quiché people come to offer copal incense to their non-Christian gods, just as their ancestors did before the coming of Alvarado. For centuries Catholic priests have objected to this, but Indian determination to continue the practice has prevailed. Besides offering incense, the Indians pray to their gods on the steps, and all day long they may be found there, as well as inside the church. On special holy days, they participate in religious processions through the marketplace.

That this mixture of commercial, ceremonial, and social activity predates Alvarado's conquest is highly probable, although obviously the details have changed considerably. Indeed, the general pattern of Quiché life as a whole seems to have changed little. But today, Indian resistance to change seems to have relaxed somewhat. Just where this will lead them remains to be seen.

Is, then, the shaman a fraud? The truth is that shamans know perfectly well that they are pulling the wool over people's eyes with their tricks. On the other hand, virtually everyone who has studied them agrees that shamans really believe in their power to deal with supernatural powers and spirits. It is this power that gives them the right as well as the ability to fool people in minor technical matters. In short, the shaman regards his or her ability to perform tricks as proof of superior powers.

The importance of shamanism in a society should not be underestimated. For the individual members of society, it promotes, through the drama of the performance, a feeling of ecstasy and release of tension. It provides psychological assurance, through the manipulation of supernatural powers otherwise beyond human control, of such things as invulnerability from attack, success at love, or the return of health. In fact, a frequent reason for a shamanistic performance is to cure illness. The treatment may not be medically effective, but the state of mind induced in the patient may be important to his or her recovery.

What shamanism does for society is to provide a focal point of attention. This is not without danger to the shaman. Someone with so much skill and power has the ability to work evil as well as good, and so is potentially dangerous. Too much nonsuccess on the part of a shaman may result in his or her being driven out of the group or killed. The shaman may also help maintain social control through the ability to detect and punish evil-doers.

The benefits of shamanism for the shaman are that it provides prestige, and perhaps even wealth. It may also be therapeutic, in that it provides an approved outlet for the outbreaks of an unstable personality. An individual who is psychologically unstable (and not all shamans are) may actually get better by becoming intensely involved with the problems of others. In this respect, shamanism is a bit like self-analysis. Finally, shamanism is a good outlet for the self-expression of those who may be described as being endowed with an "artistic temperament."

Rituals and Ceremonies

Religious ritual is the means through which persons relate to the sacred; it is religion in action. Not only is ritual the means by which the social bonds of a group are reinforced and tensions relieved, it is also one way that many important events are celebrated and crises, such as death, are made less socially disruptive and less difficult for the individuals to bear. Anthropologists have classified several different types of ritual, among them **rites of passage,** which pertain to stages in the life cycle of the individual, and **rites of intensification,** which take place during a crisis in the life of the group, serving to bind individuals together.

RITES OF PASSAGE In one of anthropology's classic works, Arnold Van Gennep analyzed the rites of passage which usher individuals through the crucial crises of their lives, such as birth, puberty, marriage, parenthood, advancement to a higher class, occupational specialization, and death.[7] He found it useful to divide ceremonies for all of these life crises into three stages: **separation; transition;** and **incorporation.** The individual would first be ritually removed from the society as a whole, then isolated for a period, and finally incorporated back into society in his or her new status.

_____

[7] Arnold Van Gennep, _The Rites of Passage_ (Chicago: University of Chicago Press, 1960).

Life Rites

✓ Van Gennep described the male initiation rites of Australian aborigines. When the time for the initiation is decided by the elders, the boys are taken from the village, while the women cry and make a ritual show of resistance. At a place distant from the camp, groups of men from many villages gather. The elders sing and dance, while the initiates act as though they are dead. The climax of this part of the ritual is a bodily operation, such as circumcision or the knocking out of a tooth. Anthropologist A. P. Elkin says,

This is partly a continuation of the drama of death. The tooth-knocking, circumcision or other symbolical act "killed" the novice; after this he does not return to the general camp and normally may not be seen by any woman. He is dead to the ordinary life of the tribe.[8]

The novice may be shown secret ceremonies and receive some instruction during this period, but the most significant element is his complete removal from society. In the course of these Australian puberty rites, the initiate must learn the tribal lore; he is given, in effect, a "cram course." The trauma of the occasion is a pedagogical technique which ensures that he will learn and remember everything; in a nonliterate society, effective teaching methods of this sort are necessary for both individual and group survival.

On his return to society, the novice is welcomed with ceremonies as though he had returned from the dead. This alerts the society at large that the individual has a new status—that they can expect him to act in certain ways and in return must act in the appropriate ways toward him. The individual's new rights and duties are thus

---

[8]A. P. Elkin, *The Australian Aborigines* (Garden City, N.Y.: Doubleday, Anchor Books, 1964).

Rites of passage: Religious rituals marking important stages in the lives of individuals, such as birth, marriage, and death.
Rites of intensification: Religious rituals that take place during a real or potential crisis for a group.
Separation: In rites of passage, the ritual removal of the individual from society.
Transition: In rites of passage, the isolation of the individual following separation and prior to incorporation.
Incorporation: In rites of passage, reincorporation of the individual into society in his or her new status.

clearly defined. He is spared, for example, the problems of "American teenage," a time when an individual is neither adult nor child but a person whose status is ill defined.

RITES OF INTENSIFICATION Rites of intensification are those rituals that mark occasions of crisis in the life of the group rather than individual. Whatever the precise nature of the crisis—a severe lack of rain which threatens crops in the fields, the sudden appearance of an enemy war party, or some other force from outside which disturbs everyone—mass ceremonies are performed to allay the danger to the group. What this does is to unite people in a common effort in such a way that fear and confusion yield to collective action and a degree of optimism. The balance in the relations of all concerned, which has been upset, is restored to normal.

An example of rites of intensification can be seen in this festival held in Chichicastenango, Guatemala. The carnival atmosphere is not unusual among peoples whose ceremonies are related to the agricultural cycle. For additional information on Chichicastenango, see Portfolio 2, pages 362–363.

While the death of an individual might be regarded as the ultimate crisis in the life of an individual, it is as well a crisis for the entire group, particularly if the group is small. A member of the group has been removed, and so its equilibrium has been upset. The survivors, therefore, must readjust and restore balance. They must, at the same time, reconcile themselves to the loss of someone to whom they were emotionally tied. Funerary ceremonies, then, can be regarded as rites of intensification that permit the living to express in nondisruptive ways their upset over the death, and that provide for social readjustment. A frequent feature of such ceremonies is an ambivalence to the dead person. For example, one

Life Rites

of the parts of the funerary rites of Melanesians was the eating of the flesh of the dead person. This ritual cannibalism, witnessed by anthropologist Bronislaw Malinowski, was performed with "extreme repugnance and dread and usually followed by a violent vomiting fit. At the same time it is felt to be a supreme act of reverence, love and devotion."[9] This custom, and the emotions accompanying it, clearly reveal the ambiguous attitude toward death: on the one hand, there is the desire to maintain the tie to the dead person, and on the other hand, one feels disgust and fear at the transformation wrought by death. According to Malinow-

---

[9]Malinowski, p. 50.

ski, funeral ceremonies provide an approved collective means of expressing these individual feelings, while at the same time maintaining social cohesiveness and preventing disruption of society.

The performance of rites of intensification does not have to be limited to times of overt crisis. In regions where the seasons differ enough so that human activities must change accordingly, they will take the form of annual ceremonies. These are particularly common among horticultural and agricultural people, with their planting, first fruit, and harvest ceremonies. These are critical times in the lives of people in such societies, and the ceremonies express a reverent attitude toward the forces of generation and fertility in nature on which peoples' very existence depends. If all goes well, as it often does at such times, participation in a happy situation reinforces group involvement. It also serves as a kind of dress rehearsal for serious crisis situations; it promotes a habit of reliance on supernatural forces through ritual activity which can be easily activated under stressful circumstances when it is important not to give way to anxiety and fear.

RELIGION, MAGIC, AND WITCHCRAFT

Among the most fascinating of ritual practices is application of the belief that supernatural powers can be compelled to act in certain ways for good or evil purposes by recourse to certain specified formulas. This is a classical anthropological notion of magic. Many societies have magical rituals to ensure good crops, the replenishment of game, the fertility of domestic animals, and the avoidance or cure of illness in humans. Although modern Western peoples, in seeking to objectify and de-mythologize their world, have often tried to suppress the existence of these fantastic notions in their

Viewing the body of the deceased is a common part of North American funeral rites. It is one expression of the desire to maintain a tie with the individual even after death. Other expressions of the same desire are common in the funeral rites of other cultures.

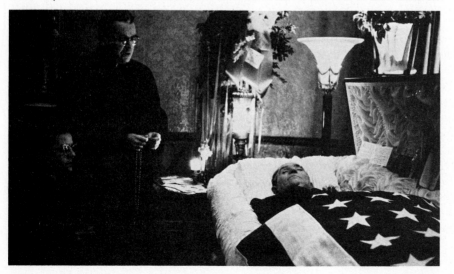

In North America an interest in and the practice of witchcraft have grown dramatically over the past 20 years.

own consciousness, they continue to be fascinated by them. Not only are books and films about demonic possession and witchcraft avidly devoured and discussed, but after some 40 years of poor sales, by 1967 sales of ouija boards in the United States passed the 2 million mark. Thirty years ago, about 100 newspapers carried horoscope columns, but by 1970, 1200 of a total of 1750 daily newspapers regularly carried such columns. Although it is certainly true that non-Western and peasant peoples tend to quite freely endow their world with magical properties, so do many Western peoples.

Sir James George Frazer made a strong distinction between religion and magic. Religion he saw as "a propitiation or conciliation of powers superior to man which are believed to direct and control the course of nature and human life."[10] Magic, on the other hand, he saw as an attempt to

[10]James G. Frazer, "Magic and Religion," in V. F. Calverton, ed., *The Making of Man: An Outline of Anthropology* (New York: Modern Library, 1931), p. 693.

manipulate certain perceived "laws" of nature. The magician never doubts that the same causes will always produce the same effects. Thus Frazer saw magic as a sort of pseudoscience, differing from modern science only in its misconception of the nature of the particular laws that govern the succession of events.

Frazer differentiated between two fundamental principles of magic. The first principle, that "like produces like," he called **sympathetic magic.** In Burma, for example, a rejected lover might engage a sorcerer to make an image of his scornful love. If this image was tossed in water, to the accompaniment of certain charms, the hapless girl would go mad. Thus the girl would suffer a fate similar to that of her image.

Frazer's second principle was that of **contagious magic**—the concept that things or persons which have once been in contact can afterward influence one another. The most common example of contagious magic is the permanent relationship between an individual and any part of his or her body, such as hair, fingernails, or teeth. Frazer cites the Basutos, a tribe in South Africa, who were careful to conceal their extracted teeth, because these might fall into the hands of certain mythical beings who could harm the owner of the tooth by working magic on it. Related to this is the custom, in our own society, of treasuring things that have been touched by special people.

Witchcraft

If blight seizes the groundnut crop it is witchcraft; if the bush is vainly scoured for game it is witchcraft; if termites do not rise when their swarming is due and a cold useless night is spent in waiting for their flight it is witchcraft; if a prince is cold and distant with his subjects it is witchcraft; if a magical rite fails to achieve its purpose it is witchcraft; if, in fact, any failure or misfortune falls upon anyone at any time and in relation to any of the manifold activities of his life it may be due to witchcraft.[11]

In this passage, E. E. Evans-Pritchard reveals the extent that witchcraft enters into the everyday life of the Azande, an African people. Although the Azande are not entirely typical in regard to witchcraft, since they believe that witches are simply ordinary persons who are born with a "substance" for witchcraft in their bodies, this list is an illustration of the widespread tendency on the part of some groups to explain many of the ordinary as well as extraordinary occurrences of life by reference to witchcraft.

The Azande and neighboring peoples distinguish between **witchcraft,** or an inborn and often unconscious capacity to work evil, and **sorcery,** or deliberate actions undertaken for the purpose of doing specific harm. Some anthropologists have attempted to generalize this distinction, but in many societies there is no division between the two types of evildoer. Perhaps a more practical classification is Lucy Mair's distinction between nightmare witches and everyday witches.[12] The nightmare witch is the very embodiment of a society's conception of evil, a being that flouts the rules of sexual behavior and disregards every other standard of decency. Nightmare witches, being almost literally the product of dreams and repressed fantasies, have much in common wherever they appear: both the modern Navajo and the ancient Roman, for

---

Sympathetic magic: Magic based on the principle that like produces like.

Contagious magic: Magic based on the principle that things once in contact can influence one another after separation.

Witchcraft: Among some peoples, an inborn and <u>unconscious</u> capacity to work evil, as distinguished from sorcery.

Sorcery: Deliberate actions undertaken by human beings for the purpose of doing specific harm.

---

example, conceived of witches that can turn themselves into animals and gather to feast on corpses. Everyday witches are real people, often the nonconformists, or social deviants of a group, those who are morose, who eat alone, who are arrogant and unfriendly. Such witches may be dangerous when offended and retaliate by causing sickness, death, crop failure, cattle disease, or any number of lesser ills; people thought to be witches are usually treated very courteously.

The Functions of Witchcraft

Why witchcraft? We might better ask, why not? As Mair aptly observed, in a world where there are few proven techniques for dealing with everyday crises, especially sickness, a belief in witches is not foolish, it is indispensable. No one wants to resign oneself to illness, and if the malady is caused by a witch's hex, then magical countermeasures should cure it. Not only does the idea of personalized evil answer the problem of unmerited suffering, it also provides an explanation for many of those happenings for which no cause can be dis-

---

[11] E. E. Evans-Pritchard, *Witchcraft, Oracles, and Magic among the Azande* (London: Oxford University Press, 1950), pp. 63–66.

[12] Lucy Mair, *Witchcraft* (New York: McGraw-Hill, 1969), p. 37.

covered. Witchcraft, then, cannot be refuted. Even if we could convince a person that his or her illness was due to natural causes, the victim would still ask, Why me? Why now? There is no room for pure chance in such a view; everything must be assigned a cause or meaning. Witchcraft provides the explanation, and in so doing, also provides both the basis and the means for taking counteraction. Moreover, the fact that certain kinds of antisocial behavior will result in an individual's being labeled a witch, and treated as such, tends to deter people from such behavior. A belief in witchcraft thus serves a function of social control.

PSYCHOLOGICAL FUNCTIONS OF WITCHCRAFT AMONG THE NAVAJO Widely known among American Indian tribes are the Navajo, who possess a detailed concept of witchcraft. Several types of witchcraft are distinguished. Witchery encompasses the practices of witches, who are said to meet at night to practice cannibalism and kill people at a distance. Sorcery is distinguished from witchery only by the methods used by the sorcerer, who casts spells on individuals, using the victim's fingernails, hair, or discarded clothing. Wizardry is not distinguished so much by its effects as by its manner of working; wizards kill by injecting a cursed substance, such as a tooth from a corpse, into the victim's body.

Whether or not a particular illness results from witchcraft is determined by **divination,** a magical procedure by which the identity of the witch is also learned. Once a person is charged with witchcraft, he or she is publicly interrogated and possibly tortured until there is a confession. It is believed that the witch's own curse will turn against the witch once this happens, so it is expected that the witch will die within a year. Some confessed witches have been allowed to live in exile.

According to Clyde Kluckhohn, Navajo witchcraft served to channel anxieties, tensions, and frustrations that were caused by the pressures from the white man.[13] The rigid rules of decorum among the Navajo

[13] Clyde Kluckhohn, "Navojo Witchcraft," *Papers of the Peabody Museum of American Archaeology and Ethnology,* 1944, 22(2).

In many societies witchcraft may be an important source of psychological assurance. Here we see a positive application of this fact. The man at the right is a Nigerian trained as a psychiatrist; helping him treat his patient is the local "witch doctor" who has considerable skill in dealing with severe emotional upsets. He has been incorporated into the staff of the clinic under the title "native therapist."

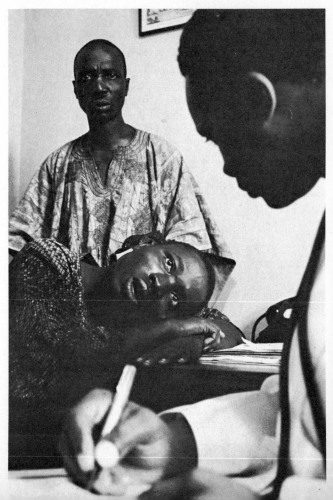

allow little means of expression of hostility, which is released in witchcraft accusations. Such accusations funnel pent-up negative emotions against individuals, without upsetting the wider society. Another function of accusations of witchcraft is that they permit the direct expression of hostile feelings against people to whom one would ordinarily be unable to express anger or enmity.

SOCIAL FUNCTIONS OF WITCHCRAFT AMONG THE NDEMBU   Victor Turner described the use of sorcery in a struggle for political power in a small village of the Ndembu of Africa.[14] Sandombu, a young man who had ambitions to the headmanship of Mukanza village, twice insulted the village headman, Kahali, in a challenge to his authority. This resulted in a fierce dispute, with each threatening the other with sorcery. Sandombu left for another village where a notorious sorcerer was supposed to live. A short time later, Kahali fell sick and died. There was no way to prove Sandombu's use of sorcery, but there was sufficient suspicion to prevent him from replacing Kahali as village headman. Instead, another man, not directly involved in the dispute, was chosen.

Turner shows that there is much more here than immediately meets the eye. Sandombu's insult to Kahali was a breach of the fundamental Ndembu principle that the older generation has authority over the younger. Further, Sandombu was of the same lineage as Kahali, and succession within the same lineage was looked upon with disfavor. Also, since Sandombu was sterile, and his sister barren, he had little basis for essential kin support. Though suspicion of sorcery was the ostensible cause of denying Sandombu headmanship, many other reasons lay beneath the surface.

---

[14]Victor W. Turner, *Schism and Continuity in an African Society* (Manchester: The University Press, 1957).

> **Divination: A magical procedure by which the cause of a particular event, such as illness, may be determined or the future foretold.**

The "social drama," as Turner calls it, shows how an accusation of sorcery was used to justify a political process and to effectively reaffirm such norms as the relationship between generations and the method of succession to authority. Belief in witchcraft, then, not only serves a number of psychological functions, it can also serve important social functions.

THE FUNCTIONS OF RELIGION

Just as a belief in witchcraft may serve a variety of psychological and social functions, so too do religious beliefs and practices in general. Here, we may summarize these functions in a somewhat more systematic way. One important psychological function is to provide an orderly model of the universe, the importance of which for orderly human behavior is discussed in Chapter 5. Beyond this, by explaining the unknown and making it understandable, the fears and anxieties of individuals are reduced. As we have seen, the explanations usually assume the existence of various sorts of supernatural beings and powers, which may potentially be appealed to or manipulated by people. This being so, a means is provided for dealing with crises: divine aid is, theoretically, available when all else fails.

A social function of religion is to sanction a wide range of conduct. In this context, religion plays a role in social control, which, as we saw in Chapter 11, does not rely on law alone. This is done through notions of right and wrong. If one does the right thing, one earns the approval of whatever supernatural powers are recognized by a particular culture. If, on the other hand, one does the wrong thing, one may suffer retribution through supernatural agencies. Religion does more than this, though; it sets precedents for acceptable behavior. We have already noted the connection between myths and religion. Usually, myths are full of tales of various supernatural beings, which in various ways illustrate the society's ethical code in action. So it is that Gluskabe, the Penobscot culture hero, is portrayed in the Penobscot myths as tricking and punishing those who mock others, lie, are greedy, or go in for extremes of behavior. Moreover, the specific situations serve as precedents for human behavior in similar circumstances. The Judeo-Christian Bible is rich in the same sort of material.

There is a psychological function tied up in all this. The moral code of a society, since it is held to be divinely fixed, lifts the burden of decision-making from the shoulders of the individual members of society, at least in important situations. It can be a tremendous relief to individuals to know that the responsibility for an important decision rests with the gods rather than with themselves.

Another social function of religion is its role in the maintenance of social solidarity. In our discussion of the shaman, we saw how such individuals provide focal points of interest, thus supplying one ingredient of assistance in maintaining the unity of the group. In addition, common participation in rituals, coupled with a basic uniformity of beliefs, helps to bind people together and reinforce their identification with the group. Particularly effective may be their participation together in rituals when the atmosphere is charged with emotion. The exalted feelings people may experience in such circumstances serve as a positive reinforcement, in that they "feel good" as a re-

sult. Here, once again, we find religion providing psychological assurance while providing for the needs of society.

One other area in which religion serves a social function is education. In our discussion of rites of passage, we noted that Australian puberty rites served as a kind of "cram course" in tribal lore. By providing a memorable occasion, initiation rites can serve to enhance learning and so help ensure the perpetuation of a nonliterate culture. Education may also be served as well by rites of intensification. Frequently, such rites involve dramas that portray matters of cultural importance. For example, among hunters and gatherers, dances may imitate the movement of game and techniques of hunting. Among farming people, a fixed round of ceremonies may emphasize the steps necessary for good crops. What this does is to help preserve knowledge that is of importance to a people's material well-being.

RELIGION AND CULTURE CHANGE

Although the subject of culture change is taken up in a later chapter, no anthropological consideration of religion is complete without some mention of revitalization movements. In 1931, at Buka in the Solomon Islands, a native religious cult suddenly emerged, its prophets predicting that a deluge would soon engulf all whites. This would be followed by the arrival of a ship laden with European goods. The believers were to construct a storehouse for the goods, and to prepare themselves to repulse the colonial police. Because the ship would arrive only after the natives had used up all their own supplies, they ceased working in the fields. Although the leaders of the cult were arrested, the movement continued for some years.

Young Melanesian men parade with mock rifles made of bamboo in a cargo cult ritual. Many of the believers are also Christians, converted by missionaries; the people see nothing contradictory in the two faiths.

This was not an isolated instance. Such "cargo cults"—and many other movements which have promised the resurrection of the dead, the destruction or enslavement of Europeans, and the coming of utopian riches—have sporadically appeared ever since the beginning of the century through-

> **Revitalization movements:** Social movements of a religious nature with the purpose of totally reforming a society.

out Melanesia. Since these cults are widely separated in space and time, their similarities seem to be due to similarities in social conditions. In these areas, the traditional cultures of the natives have been uprooted. Europeans, or European-influenced natives, hold all political and economic power. Natives are employed in unloading and distributing Western-made goods, but have no practical knowledge of how to attain these goods. When cold reality offers no hope from the daily frustrations of cultural deterioration and economic deprivation, religion offers the solution.

Revitalization Movements

From the 1890 Ghost Dance of the North American Indians to the Mau Mau of Africa to the "cargo cults" of Melanesia, extreme and sometimes violent religious reactions to European domination are so common that many anthropologists have sought to formulate their underlying causes and general characteristics. It has been suggested that all such religious innovations may be considered **revitalization movements.** Furthermore, revitalization movements are not restricted to the colonial world, and in the United States alone, hundreds of such movements have sprung up. Among the more widely known are Mormonism, which began in the nineteenth century, the more recent Unification Church of the Reverend Sun Myung Moon, and the cult of the Reverend Jim Jones. As these three examples suggest, these movements show a great deal of diversity, and some have been much more successful than others.

the normal state of society, in which stress is not too great and in which there are sufficient cultural means of satisfying needs. Under certain conditions, such as domination by a more powerful group, stress and frustration will be steadily amplified; this brings the second phase, or the period of increased individual stress. If there are no significant adaptive changes, the period of cultural distortion is ushered in, and stress

The People's Temple cult of the Reverend Jim Jones is an example of a revitalization movement that failed, as hundreds of followers with Jones himself committed mass suicide in an act that shocked the world.

A revitalization movement is a deliberate effort by members of a society to construct a more satisfying culture. The emphasis in this definition is on the reformation not just of one sphere of activity such as the religious, but of the entire cultural system. Such a drastic solution arises when a group's anxiety and frustration have reached such a degree that the only way to reduce the stress is to overturn the entire social system and replace it with a new one.

Anthropologist Anthony Wallace has outlined a sequence common to all expressions of the revitalization process.[15] First is

[15] Anthony F. C. Wallace, *Culture and Personality*, 2d ed. (New York: Random House, 1970), pp. 191–196.

becomes so chronic that the socially approved methods of releasing tension begin to break down. Steady deterioration of one culture may be checked at some point by a period of revitalization, during which a dynamic cult or religious movement grips a sizable proportion of the population. Often the movement will be so out of touch with reality that it is doomed to failure from the beginning; this was the case with the Ghost Dance, which was supposed to make the participants impervious to the bullets of the white men's guns. This was the case also with the cult of the Reverend Jim Jones, where the murder of a U.S. Congressman was followed by the mass suicide of Jones and many of his followers. More rarely, a movement may tap long-dormant adaptive forces underlying a culture, and a long-lasting religion may result. Such was the case with Mormonism. Wallace has observed that all religions stem from revitalization movements, including Judaism, Christianity, and Islam.

CHAPTER SUMMARY

Religion is a part of all cultures. It consists of beliefs and behavior patterns by which people try to control the area of the universe that is otherwise beyond their control. Among hunter-gatherer peoples religion is a basic ingredient of everyday life. As societies become more complex, religion is less a part of daily activities and tends to be restricted to special occasions.

Religion is characterized by a belief in supernatural beings and forces. Through prayer, sacrifice, and general ritual activity, people appeal to the supernatural world for aid. Supernatural beings may be grouped into three categories: major deities (gods and goddesses), nonhuman spirit beings, and ancestral spirits. Gods and goddesses are the great but remote beings. They are usually thought of as controlling the universe or a specific part of it. Animism is a belief in spiritual beings other than ancestors who are believed to animate all of nature. These spirit beings are closer to humans than gods and goddesses and are intimately concerned with human activities. Animism is typical of peoples who see themselves as a part of nature rather than as superior to it. A belief in ancestral spirits is based on the idea that human beings are made up of a body and soul. At death the spirit is freed from the body and continues to participate in human affairs. Belief in ancestral spirits is particularly characteristic of descent-based groups with their associated ancestor orientation. Animatism, as described by R. H. Codrington, may be found with animism in the same culture. Animatism is a force or power directed to a successful outcome which may make itself manifest in any object.

Beliefs in supernatural beings and powers are maintained, first, through what are interpreted as manifestations of power. Second, they are perpetuated because supernatural beings possess attributes with which people are familiar. Finally, myths serve to rationalize religious beliefs and practices.

All human societies have specialists—priests and priestesses and/or shamans—to guide religious practices and to intervene with the supernatural world. Shamanism, with its often dramatic ritual, promotes a release of tension among individuals in a society. The shaman provides a focal point of attention for society and can help to maintain social control. The benefits of shamanism for the shaman are prestige, sometimes wealth, and an outlet for artistic self-expression.

Ritual is religion in action. Through ritual social bonds are reinforced. Times of life crises are occasions for ritual. Arnold Van Gennep divided such rites of passage into rites of separation, transition, and incorporation. A ritual may consist of a sacrifice whose purpose is propitiation of the supernatural powers. A rite of reversal is a ritual in which there is a reversal of the normal values and customs. These may function as social safety valves.

Rites of intensification are rituals to mark occasions of crisis in the life of the group rather than the individual. They serve to unite people, allay fear of the crisis, and prompt collective action. Funerary ceremonies are rites of intensification that provide for social readjustment after the loss of the deceased. Rites of intensification may also involve annual ceremonies to seek favorable conditions surrounding such critical activities as planting and harvesting.

Ritual practices of peasant and non-Western peoples are often an expression of the belief that supernatural powers can be made to act in certain ways through the use of certain prescribed formulas. This is the classic anthropological notion of magic. Sir James Frazer saw magic as a pseudoscience and found two principles of magic, "like produces like," or sympathetic magic, and the law of contagion.

Witchcraft functions much like science in offering an explanation for unwanted events. Sorcery is the practice of witchcraft for evil purposes, and according to Clyde Kluckhohn, serves as an expression of hostile emotions against individuals without disturbing the norms of the larger group.

Religion serves several important social functions. First, it sanctions a wide range of conduct by providing notions of right and wrong. Second, it sets precedents for acceptable behavior. Third, religion serves to lift the burden of decision-making from individuals and places responsibility with the gods. Fourth, religion plays a large role in maintaining social solidarity. Finally, religion serves education. Ritual ceremonies enhance learning of tribal lore and so help to ensure the perpetuation of a nonliterate culture.

Domination by Western society has been the cause of certain religious manifestations in non-Western societies. In the islands of Melanesia, the cargo cult has appeared spontaneously at different times since the beginning of the century. Anthony Wallace has interpreted religious reformations as revitalization movements in which an attempt is made, sometimes successfully, to change the society. He believes that all religions stem from revitalization movements.

SUGGESTED READINGS

Lessa, William A., and Evon Z. Vogt, eds. *Reader in Comparative Religion: An Anthropological Approach*. New York: Harper & Row, 1972.

The articles collected in the book discuss the universality of religion as it corresponds to deep and inescapable human needs. It discusses religion as a system of ethics, a response to the processes of nature, and an answer to the uncertainties of experience. The collection shows the relationship of religion to philosophy, theater, science, and ethics.

Malinowski, Bronislaw. *Magic, Science and Religion, and Other Essays*. Garden City, N.Y.: Doubleday, 1954.

The articles collected here provide a discussion of a particular "primitive" people (the Trobriand Islanders) as illustration of conceptual and theoretical knowledge of humankind. The author covers such diversified topics as religion, life, death, character of primitive cults, magic, faith, and myth.

Norbeck, Edward. *Religion in Human Life: Anthropological Views*. New York: Holt, Rinehart and Winston, 1974.

The author presents a comprehensive view of religion based on twin themes: the description of religious events, rituals, and states of mind and the nature of anthropological aims, views, procedures, and interpretations.

Wallace, Anthony F. C. *Religion: An Anthropological View*. New York: Random House, 1966.

This is a standard textbook treatment of religion by an anthropologist who has specialized in the study of revitalization movements.

13 | The Arts

No human culture is known to be without some form of art, even though that art may be created for purely practical and utilitarian purposes. These textiles and religious objects for sale in the market at Chichicastenango, Guatemala, were not created to serve as objects of art, yet artistic they certainly are.

PREVIEW

WHAT IS ART?   p. 383 ∅

Art is the creative use of the human imagination to interpret, understand, and enjoy life. Although the idea of art serving nonuseful, nonpractical purposes seems firmly entrenched in the thinking of modern Western peoples, in other cultures art often serves what are regarded as important, practical purposes.

WHY DO ANTHROPOLOGISTS STUDY ART?

Anthropologists have found that art reflects the cultural values and concerns of a people. This is especially true of the verbal arts—myths, legends, and tales. From these, the anthropologist may learn how a people order their universe, and may discover much about a people's history as well. Too, music and the visual arts, such as sculpture, may provide insights into a people's world view and, through distributional studies, may suggest things about a people's history.

WHAT ARE THE FUNCTIONS OF THE ARTS?

Aside from adding enjoyment to everyday life, the various arts serve a number of functions. Myths, for example, set standards for orderly behavior, and the verbal arts generally transmit and preserve a culture's customs and values. Songs, too, may do this, within the restrictions imposed by musical form. And any form of art, to the degree that it is characteristic of a particular society, may contribute to the cohesiveness or solidarity of that society.

A rt is the product of a specialized kind of human behavior: the creative use of our imagination to help us interpret, understand, and enjoy life. Whether one is talking about a Chinese love song, a Pueblo pot, a Balinese dance, or a Persian bracelet, it is clear that everyone involved in the activity we call art—the creator, the performer, the participant, the spectator—is making use of a uniquely human ability to use and comprehend symbols and to shape and interpret the physical world for something more than just a practical or useful purpose. After all, if a Pueblo Indian wanted a useful container, a simply made, undecorated pot would do just as well as a carefully shaped, smoothed, and elaborately painted one, and could be more quickly and easily made. Yet Pueblo potters typically devote much time and technical skill to the production of pottery vessels that are esthetically pleasing not just to other Pueblo peoples but to many non-Pueblo peoples as well.

The idea of art serving nonuseful, nonpractical purposes seems firmly entrenched in the thinking of modern Western peoples. Today, for example, we may listen to the singing of a sea chanty purely for esthetic pleasure, as a form of entertainment. In fact, in the days of sail, sea chantys served very useful and practical purposes. They set the appropriate rhythm for the performance of specific ship-board tasks, and the same qualities that make them pleasurable to listen to today served to relieve the boredom of those tasks. Similarly, Bach did not compose his chorales, preludes, and fugues just to entertain; rather, they were composed to serve what were regarded as important religious ends. Such links between art and other aspects of culture are common in human societies around the world.

Whether a particular work of art is intended to be appreciated purely as such or

The idea of art serving nonuseful, nonpractical purposes is firmly entrenched in the thinking of modern Western peoples. Yet, many of the objects that they place in museums to be appreciated as objects of art were created to serve what were considered to be useful and practical ends.

to serve some practical purpose, it will in every case require the same special combination of the symbolic representation of form and the expression of feeling that constitutes the creative imagination. Insofar as the creative use of the human ability to symbolize is universal and either expresses or is shaped by cultural values and concerns, it is properly and eminently an area of investigation for anthropology.

There appears to be no culture in the world without at least some kind of storytelling, singing, or dancing, that gives esthetic pleasure. Reasoning backward from effect to cause, some writers in recent times have consequently proposed that humans may have an actual need or drive—either innate or acquired—to use their faculties of imagination. Just as we need food and shelter to survive, we may also need to nourish and exercise our active minds, which are not satisfied, except in times of crisis, with the mere business of solving the immediate problems of daily existence. Without the free play of the imagination there is boredom, and boredom may lead to a lack of productivity, perhaps even in extreme cases to death. It is art that provides the means and the materials for our imaginative play and thus helps to sustain life. According to this way of thinking, art is therefore not a luxury to be afforded or appreciated by a minority of esthetes or escapists, but a necessary kind of social behavior in which every normal and active human being participates.

As an activity or kind of behavior that contributes to well-being and helps give shape and significance to life, art must be at the same time related to, yet differentiated from, religion. The dividing line be-

Where art stops and religion begins in an elaborate tribal ceremony involving ornamental costumes, songs, and effigies is not always easy to say.

tween the two is not distinct: it is not easy to say, for example, precisely where art stops and religion begins in an elaborate tribal ceremony involving ornamentation, masks, costumes, songs, dances, effigies, and totems. Does religion inspire art, or is religion perhaps a kind of art in which the supernatural happens to be the central element?

This problem in semantics is not easy to solve, but it is often convenient to distinguish between secular and religious art, if not between art and religion. In what we call purely secular art, whether it is light or serious, it is clear that our imaginations are free to roam without any ulterior motives—creating and re-creating patterns, plots, rhythms, and feelings at leisure and without any thought of consequence or af-

termath. In religious art, on the other hand, the imagination is working still, but the whole activity is somehow aimed at assuring our well-being through propitiation, celebration, and acknowledgment of forces beyond ourselves. Whether categorized as secular or religious, at any rate, art of all varieties can be expected to reflect the values and concerns of the people who create and enjoy it; the nature of the things reflected and expressed in art is the concern of the anthropologist.

The following Original Study provides a good example of the way a people's art may inform us about the values and world view of those who have created it. Its author is Edmund Carpenter, a Canadian anthropologist who specializes in the study of art and the ways it communicates.

ORIGINAL STUDY

Eskimo Realities: The Act of Artistic Creation[1]

No word meaning "art" occurs in Eskimo, nor does "artist": there are only people. Nor is any distinction made between utilitarian and decorative objects. The Eskimo simply say, "A man should do all things properly." My use of both words here is strictly Western: by art I refer to objects which a Western critic would call art; by artist I mean any Eskimo.

Carving, like singing, isn't a thing. When you feel a song within you, you sing it; when you sense a form emerging from ivory, you release it.

As the carver holds the unworked ivory lightly in his hand, turning it this way and that, he whispers, "Who are you! Who hides there!" And then: "Ah, Seal!" He rarely sets out to carve, say, a seal, but picks up the ivory, examines it to find its hidden form and, if that's not immediately apparent, carves aimlessly until he sees it, humming or chanting as he works. Then he brings it out: Seal, hidden, emerges. It was always there: he did not create it, he released it; he helped it step forth.

---

[1] From *Eskimo Realities* by Edmund Carpenter © 1973 by Edmund Carpenter. New York: Holt, Rinehart and Winston, pp. 58–63.

I watched one white man, seeking souvenirs, commission a carving of seal but receive instead a carving of a walrus. Another, who wanted a chess set, though his explicit instructions were clearly understood, received a set in which each pawn was different. Ahmi—"it cannot be known in advance" what lies in the ivory.

Ohnainewk held a baby walrus tooth in his palm, turned it slightly, and there, unmistakably! Ptarmigan almost burst through the surface. As he cut lightly here, indented there, he spoke softly, diffidently; he was not passive, yet his act of will was limited, respectful: respectful to the form that was given.

The Eskimo language has no real equivalents to our words "create" or "make," which presuppose imposition of the self. The closest Eskimo term means "to work on," which also involves an act of will, but one which is restrained. The carver never attempts to force the ivory into uncharacteristic forms, but responds to the material as it tries to be itself, and thus the carving is continually modified as the ivory has its say.

Great Western artists sometimes thought in these terms and even expressed themselves so, but with one difference: they were exceptions in their own culture, independently reaching this attitude only after long experience and contemplation; whereas the Eskimo learn it as a mother-tongue and daily give it social voice and expression. It is their attitude not only toward ivory, but toward all things, especially people: parent toward child, husband toward wife.

We think of art as possession, and possession to us means control, to do with as we like. Art to them is a transitory act, a relationship. They are more interested in the creative activity than in the product of that activity.

THE ANTHROPOLOGICAL STUDY OF ART

In approaching art as a cultural phenomenon, the anthropologist has the pleasant task of cataloguing, photographing, recording, and describing all possible forms of imaginative activity in any particular culture. There is an enormous variety of forms and modes of artistic expression in the world. Because people everywhere continue to create and develop in new directions, there is no foreseeable point of diminishing returns in the interesting process of collecting and describing the world's ornaments, body decorations, variations in clothing, blanket and rug designs, pottery and basket styles, architectural embellishments, monuments, ceremonial masks, legends, work songs, social dances, and other art forms. But the process of collecting must eventually lead to some kind of analysis, and then perhaps to some illuminating generalizations about relationships between art and culture.

Probably the best way to begin a study of this problem of the relationships between art and culture is to examine critically some of the generalizations that have already been made about specific arts. Rather than trying to cover all forms of art we shall concentrate on just a few: verbal arts, music, and sculpture. We shall start with the verbal arts, for we have already touched upon them in our earlier discussions of religion (Chapter 12) and world view (Chapter 5).

VERBAL ARTS

1. give definitions
2. Then read some texts
3. ask students to judge

The term **folklore** was coined in the nineteenth century to denote the unwritten stories, beliefs, and customs of the European peasant as opposed to the traditions of the literate elite. The subsequent study of folklore, concentrating on folktales, has become a discipline allied to, but somewhat independent of, anthropology, working on cross-cultural comparisons of themes, motifs, and structures, generally more from a literary than an ethnological point of view. In general, both linguists and anthropologists prefer to speak of the oral traditions and verbal arts of a culture rather than its folklore and folktales, recognizing that creative verbal expression takes many forms and that the implied distinction between folk and "sophisticated" art is valid only in the context of civilization.

The verbal arts include narrative, drama, poetry, incantations, proverbs, riddles, word games, and even naming procedures, compliments, and insults, when these take elaborate and special forms. The narrative seems to be one of the easiest kinds of verbal arts to record or collect. Perhaps because it is also the most publishable, with popular appeal in our own cul-

ture, it has received the most study and attention. Generally, narratives have been divided into three basic and recurring categories: myth, legend, and tale.

Myth

The **myth** is basically religious, in that it provides a rationale for religious beliefs and practices. Its subject matter is the ultimates of human existence: where we and the things in our world came from, why we are here, and where we are going. Any aspect of these very large questions may be

The portable tape recorder has become the essential field tool of those who study the verbal arts. Here, tribal legends of the Ivory Coast, told to drum accompaniment, are being taped by a university faculty member, himself a native. No longer is the study of folklore limited to peoples of European background.

called a myth. As was noted in Chapter 12, the myth has an explanatory function; it depicts and describes an orderly universe, which sets the stage for orderly behavior.

Here is a typical origin myth traditional with the Fon of Dahomey in West Africa:

In the beginning the stars were visible both at night and in the daytime. The night stars were the children of the moon and day stars were the children of the sun. One day the moon told the sun that their children were trying to outshine them. To prevent this they agreed to tie up the stars in sacks and throw them in the ocean. The sun went first and cleared the daytime sky of stars. The sly moon, however, did not keep her part of the bargain, but kept all of her children in the night sky. The sun's children became all of the brightly colored fish in the ocean, and from that time the sun has been the mortal enemy of the moon, pursuing her to try to get revenge for the loss of the stars to the sea.

When there is an eclipse, the sun is trying to eat up the moon, and the people have to go out and beat on their drums to make the sun let her loose.

This myth may be encountered in a somewhat more elaborate form, with some more realistic and dramatic details, but the basic facts of the story will remain the same.

Such a myth, insofar as it is believed, accepted, and perpetuated in a culture, may be said to express a part of the **world view** of a people: the unexpressed but implicit conceptions of their place in nature and of the limits and workings of their world. This concept we discussed in Chapter 5. The concepts of world view and science are intimately related, and it may be said that myth is the science of cultures which do not employ scientific methods. Extrapolating from the details of the Fon myth, for example, we might arrive at the conclusion that the Fon personify and re-

Folklore: A nineteenth-century term first used to refer to the traditional oral stories and sayings of the European peasant, and later extended to those traditions preserved orally in all societies.

Myth: A traditional narrative of semi-historical events that explains ultimate questions of human existence.

World view: The conceptions, explicit and implicit, of a society or an individual of the limits and workings of one's world.

spect the forces of nature, and that they believe they have both the ability and the duty to influence the behavior of these forces. In their protectiveness toward the moon in the myth, the Fon would seem to be approving either deceitfulness or cleverness. But other interpretations might be that the Fon simply accept a mixture of goodness and badness in the workings of nature, or that they fear any change in the balance of things already established. At any rate it is characteristic of an explanatory myth, such as this one, that the unknown will be simplified and explained in terms of the known. This myth accounts in terms of human experience for the existence of fish and stars, for the movements of the sun and moon, and for the special phenomenon of the lunar eclipse. It is a product of creative imagination, and it is a work of art as well as a potentially religious statement.

The analysis and interpretation of myth have been carried to great lengths, becoming a field of study almost unto itself. It is certain that myth making is an extremely important kind of human creativity, and the study of the myth-making process and its results can give some valuable clues to the way people perceive and think about their world. But the dangers and problems of interpretation are great. Several questions arise. Are myths literally believed or perhaps accepted symbolically or emotionally as a different kind of truth? To what extent do myths actually determine or reflect human behavior? Can an outsider read into a myth the same meaning that it has in its culture? How do we account for contradictory myths in the same culture? New myths arise and old ones die: is it then the content or the structure of the myth that is important? All of these questions deserve, and are currently receiving, serious consideration.

Legend

Less problematical but perhaps more complex than myth is the legend. **Legends** are semihistorical narratives that account for the deeds of heroes, the movements of peoples, and the establishment of local customs, typically with a mixture of realism and the supernatural or extraordinary. As stories they are not necessarily believed or disbelieved, but they usually serve to entertain as well as to instruct and to inspire or bolster pride in family, tribe, or nation.

Here is an example of a short legend that instructs, traditional with the Western Abenakis of northwestern New England and southern Quebec:

This is a story of a lonesome little boy who used to wander down to the riverbank at Odanak or downhill toward the two swamps. He used to hear someone call his name but when he got to the swamp pond, there was no one to be seen or heard. But when he went back, he heard his name called again. As he was sitting by the marshy bank waiting, an old man came and asked him why he was waiting. When the boy told him, the old man said that the same thing

The telling of tribal legends and tales provides people with approved models of proper behavior. Here, a village elder on the Ivory Coast tells legends and tales to young boys as an important part of their education.

The telling of legends and tales is no less important in the education of children in the United States than it is on the Ivory Coast.

happened long ago. What he heard was the Swamp Creature and pointed out the big tussocks of grass where it hid; having called out it would sink down behind them. The old man said: "It just wants to drown you. If you go out there you will sink in the mud. You better go home!"[2]

The moral of this story is quite simple: swamps are dangerous places, stay away from them. When told well, the story is a lot more effective at keeping children away from swamps than just telling them: "Don't go near swamps."

The longer legends, sometimes in poetry or in rhythmic prose, are known as **epics.** In parts of West and Central Africa there are remarkably elaborate and formalized recitations of extremely long legends, lasting several hours, and even days. These long narratives have been described as veritable encyclopedias of the most diverse aspects of a culture, with direct and indirect statements about history, institutions, relationships, values, and ideas. Epics are typically found in nonliterate societies with a form of state political organization; they serve to transmit and preserve a culture's legal and political precedents and practices. The Mwindo epic of the Nyanga people, the Lianja epic of the Mongo, and the Kambili epic of the Mande, for example, have been the subject of extensive and rewarding study by French, British, and American anthropologists in the last few years.

Legends may incorporate mythological details, especially when they make appeal to the supernatural, and are therefore not always clearly distinct from myth. The leg-

[2] Gordon M. Day, quoted in the film *Prehistoric Life in the Champlain Valley*, by Thomas C. Vogelman and others (Burlington, Vt.: Department of Anthropology, University of Vermont, 1972).

> **Legends:** Semihistorical narratives coming down from the past that recount the deeds of heroes, the movements of peoples, and the establishment of local customs.

> **Epics:** Long oral narratives, sometimes in poetry or rhythmic prose, recounting the glorious events in the life of a real or legendary person.

---

end about Mwindo follows him through the earth, the atmosphere, the underworld, and the remote sky, and gives a complete picture of the Nyanga people's view of the organization and limits of the world. Legends may also incorporate proverbs and incidental tales, and thus be related to other forms of verbal art as well. A recitation of the legend of Kambili, for example, has been said to include as many as 150 proverbs.

For the anthropologist, the major significance of the secular and apparently realistic portions of legends, whether long or short, is probably in the clues they provide to what constitutes approved or model ethical behavior in a culture. The subject matter of legends is essentially problem-solving, and the content is likely to include combat, warfare, confrontations, and physical and psychological trials of many kinds. Certain questions may be answered explicitly or implicitly. Does the culture justify homicide? What kinds of behavior are considered to be brave or cowardly? What is the etiquette of combat or warfare? Is there a concept of altruism or self-sacrifice? But here again there are pitfalls in the process of interpreting art in relation to life. It is always possible that certain kinds of behavior are acceptable or even admirable with the distance or objectivity afforded by art, but are not at all so approved in daily life.

Jesse James was an outlaw who is to the United States what Robin Hood is to England. His exploits have become legendary through songs and stories, suggesting that chivalry and loyalty are higher values than mere adherence to the law.

In our own culture, murderers, charlatans, and rakes have sometimes become popular "heroes" and the subjects of legends; we would object, however, to the inference of an outsider that we necessarily approved or wanted to emulate the morality of Billy the Kid or Jesse James.

Tale

The term **tale** is a nonspecific label for a third category of creative narratives, those that are purely secular, nonhistorical, and recognized as fiction for entertainment, though they may as well draw a moral or teach a practical lesson. Here is a brief summary of a tale from Ghana,

known as "Father, Son, and Donkey":

A father and his son farmed their corn, sold it, and spent part of the profit on a donkey. When the hot season came, they harvested their yams and prepared to take them to storage, using their donkey. The father mounted the donkey and they all three proceeded on their way until they met some people. "What? You lazy man!" the people said to the father. "You let your young son walk barefoot on this hot ground while you ride on a donkey? For shame!" The father yielded his place to the son, and they proceeded until they came to an old woman. "What? You useless boy!" said the old woman. "You ride on the donkey and let your poor father walk barefoot on this hot ground? For shame!" The son dismounted, and both father and son walked on the road, leading the donkey behind them until they came to an old man. "What? You foolish people!" said the old man. "You have a donkey and you walk barefoot on the hot ground instead of riding?" And so it goes. Listen: when you are doing something and other people come along, just keep on doing what you like.

This is precisely the kind of tale that is of special interest in traditional folklore studies. It is an internationally popular "numskull" tale; versions of it have been recorded in India, the Middle East, the Balkans, Italy, Spain, England, and the United States, as well as in West Africa. It is classified or catalogued as exhibiting a basic **motif** or story situation—father and son trying to please everyone—one of the many thousands that have been found to recur in world folktales. In spite of variations in detail, every version of the tale will be found to have about the same basic structure in the sequence of events, sometimes called the syntax of the tale; a peasant father and son work together, a beast of burden is purchased, the three set out on a short excursion, the father rides and is criticized, the son rides and is criticized, both walk and are criticized, and a conclusion is drawn.

Tales of this sort with an international distribution sometimes raise more problems than they solve: Which one is the original? What is the path of its diffusion? Could it be sheer coincidence that different cultures have come up with the same motif and syntax, or could it be a case of independent invention with similar tales developing in similar situations in responses to like causes? A surprisingly large number of motifs in European and African tales are traceable to ancient sources in India. Is this good evidence of a spread of culture from a "cradle" of civilization, or is it an example of diffusion of tales in contiguous areas? There are, of course, purely local tales, as well as tales with such a wide distribution. Within any particular culture, it will probably be found possible to categorize local types of tales: animal, human experience, trickster, dilemma, ghost, moral, scatological, nonsense, and so on. In West Africa there is a remarkable prevalence of animal stories, for example, with such creatures as the spider, the rabbit, and the hyena as the protagonists. Many were carried to the slave-holding areas of the New World; the Uncle Remus stories about Brer Rabbit,

> **Tale:** **A creative narrative recognized as fiction for entertainment.**
>
> **Motif:** **A story situation in a folktale.**

Brer Fox, and other animals may be a survival of this tradition.

The significance of tales for the anthropologist rests partly in this matter of their distribution. They provide evidence for either cultural contacts or cultural isolation, and for limits of influence and cultural cohesion. It has been debated for decades now, for example, to what extent the culture of West Africa was transmitted to the southeast United States. So far as folktales are concerned, one school of folklorists has always found and insisted on European origins; another school, somewhat more recently, is pointing out African prototypes. But the anthropologist can be interested in more than these questions of distribution. Like legends, tales very often illustrate local solutions to universal human ethical problems, and in some sense they state a moral philosophy. The anthropologist sees that whether the tale of the father, the son, and the donkey originated in West Africa or arrived there from Europe or the Middle East, the very fact that it has been accepted in West Africa suggests that it states something valid for that culture. The tale's lesson of a necessary degree of self-confidence in the face of arbitrary social criticism is therefore something that can be read into the culture's values and beliefs.

Other Verbal Arts

Myths, legends, and tales, prominent as they are in anthropological studies, turn out to be no more important than the other verbal arts in many cultures. In the Yoruba

The famous confrontation between Brer Rabbit and the Tar Baby, from the Uncle Remus stories, as portrayed in the Walt Disney movie *Song of the South.*

culture of Nigeria, for example, indigenous explanatory myths are now rare (the beliefs of Christianity and Islam have largely replaced them), but riddles, proverbs, figures of speech, poetry, and drama are all lively and active verbal arts that deserve and are receiving attention. Yoruba poetry, rich in both lyrical and dramatic elements, has only recently been studied and made available to the rest of the world, chiefly through the efforts of the new Nigerian institutes and local studies programs. Subjects of the poetry include alliances and conflicts with neighboring peoples; military and political triumphs and reverses; treaties, annexations, resettlements; the encroachment of Europeans on the land of the Africans; and the undermining of the power of the chief by the missionary and the magistrate. Yoruba drama, previously not an especially popular verbal art, is being revived and cultivated and may be developing into a new and significant kind of creative activity.

In all cultures, the words for songs constitute a kind of poetry. Poetry and stories recited with gesture, movement, and props become drama. Drama combined with dance, music, and spectacle becomes a public celebration. The more we look at the individual arts, the clearer it becomes that they are often interrelated and interdependent. The verbal arts are in fact simply differing manifestations of the same creative imagination that produces music and the plastic arts.

THE ART OF MUSIC

The study of music in specific cultural settings, beginning in the nineteenth century with the collection of folksongs, has developed into a specialized field, called **ethnomusicology.** Like the study of folktales for its own sake, ethnomusicology is at the same time related to and somewhat independent of anthropology. Nevertheless, it is possible to sort out from the various concerns of the field several concepts that are of interest in general anthropology.

In order to talk intelligently about the verbal arts of a culture, it is, of course, desirable to know as much as possible about the language itself. In order to talk about the music of a culture, it is equally desirable to know the language of music—that is, its conventions. The way to approach a totally unfamiliar kind of musical expression is to learn first how it functions in respect to melody, rhythm, and form.

Elements of Music

In general, human music is said to differ from natural music—the songs of birds, wolves, and whales, for example—in being almost everywhere perceived in terms of a repertory of tones at fixed or regular intervals from each other: in other words, a scale. We have made closed systems out of a formless range of possible sounds by dividing the distance between a tone and its first overtone or sympathetic vibration (which always has exactly twice as many vibrations as the basic tone) into a series of measured steps. In the Western or European system, the distance between the basic tone and the first overtone is called the octave; it consists of seven steps—five "whole" tones and two "semitones"— which are named with the letters A through G. The whole tones are further divided into semitones, for a total working scale of twelve tones. Westerners learn at an early age to recognize and imitate this arbitrary system and its conventions, and it comes to sound natural. Yet the overtone series, on which it is partially based, is the only part of it that can be considered a wholly natural phenomenon.

One of the most common alternatives to the semitonal system is the pentatonic system, which divides the octave into five nearly equidistant tones. In Japan there is a series of different pentatonic scales in which some semitones are employed. In Java there are scales of both five and seven equal steps, which have no relation to the intervals we hear as "natural" in our system. In Arabic and Persian music there are smaller units of a third of a tone (some of which we may accidentally produce on an "out-of-tune" piano) with scales of 17 and 24 steps in the octave. There are even quarter-tone scales in India and subtleties of interval shading that are nearly indistinguishable to a Western ear. Small wonder, then, that even when we can hear what sounds like melody and rhythm in these systems, the total result may sound to us peculiar or out of tune. The anthropologist needs a very practiced ear to learn to appreciate—or perhaps even to tolerate—some of the music heard, and only some of the most skilled folksong collectors have attempted to notate and analyze the music of nonsemitonal systems.

Scale systems and their modifications comprise what is known as **tonality** in music. Tonality determines the possibilities and limits of both melody and harmony. Not much less complex than tonality is the matter of rhythm. Rhythm, whether regular or irregular, is an organizing factor in music, sometimes more important than the melodic line. Traditional European music is rather neatly measured into recurrent patterns of two, three, and four beats, with combinations of weak and strong beats to mark the division and form patterns. Non-European music is likely to move also in patterns of five, seven, or eleven, with complex arrangements of internal beats and sometimes polyrhythms: one instrument or singer going in a pattern of three beats, for

---

Ethnomusicology: The study of a society's music in terms of its cultural setting.

Tonality: In music, scale systems and their modifications.

---

example while another is in a pattern of five or seven. Polyrhythms are frequent in the drum music of West Africa, which shows remarkable precision in the overlapping of rhythmic lines. In addition to polyrhythms, non-European music may also contain shifting rhythms: a pattern of three, for example, followed by a pattern of two, or five, with little or no regular recurrence or repetition of any one pattern, though the patterns themselves are fixed and identifiable as units.

Although it is not necessarily the concern of anthropologists to untangle all these complicated technical matters, they will no doubt want to know enough to be aware of the degree of skill or artistry involved in a performance and to have some measure of the extent to which people in a culture have learned to practice and respond to this often important creative activity. Moreover, as with folklore, myths, and legends, the distribution of musical forms and instruments can reveal much about cultural contact or isolation.

Functions of Music

Even without concern for technical matters, the anthropologist can profitably investigate the function music has in a society. First, it is rare that a culture has been reported to be without any kind of music. Even the Tasadays of the Philippines, a group of forest dwellers only recently "discovered" by the outside world, have

adopted, if not invented, a bamboo jaw harp called a *kubing*. Kenneth MacLeish translates in these words the comments of the Tasaday *kubing* player: "If I play my kubing, it is because someone is listening. I really know how to play the *kubing*." Interestingly, these simple words seem to express the value music—in fact, all art—has in far more complex cultures: it is an individual creative skill which one can cultivate and be proud of, whether from a sense of accomplishment or the sheer pleasure of performing; and it is a form of social behavior through which there is a communication or sharing of feelings and life experience with other humans.

The social function of music is perhaps most obvious in song. Songs very often express as much as tales the values and con-

While songs and dances are often performed in Western society for enjoyment, in non-Western societies they are often more important as adjuncts to ritual. In the Mousgoum funeral ceremony shown below men are blowing horns and beating drums while the relatives of the dead man dance.

cerns of the group, but they do so with the increased formalism which results from the restrictions of closed systems of tonality, rhythm, and musical form. Early investigators of non-European song were struck by the apparent simplicity of pentatonic scales and a seemingly endless repetition of phrases. They often did not give sufficient credit to the formal function of repetition in such music, confusing repetition with repetitiveness or lack of invention. A great deal of non-European music was dismissed as "primitive" and formless, and typically treated as trivial.

Repetition is nevertheless a fact of music, including European music, and a basic formal principle. Consider this little song from Nigeria:

Repetition and rhythmic sounds are devices frequently employed by non-Western peoples in their music making. The same devices are the stock in trade of Western rock musicians such as the B'52s shown here.

> Ijangbon l'o ra,
> Ijangbon l'o ra,
> Eni r'asho Oshomalo,
> Ijangbon l'o ra.
> (He buys trouble,
> He buys trouble,
> He who buys Oshomalo cloth,
> He buys trouble)

Several decades ago, the Oshomalo were cloth sellers in Egba villages who sold on credit, then harassed, intimidated, and even beat their customers to make them pay before the appointed day. The message of the song is simple, and both words and music are the same for three lines out of four; the whole song may be repeated many times at will. What is it that produces this kind of artistic expression and makes it more than primitive trivia? A single Egba undoubtedly improvised the song first, reacting to a personal experience or observation, lingering on one of its elements by repeating it. The repetition gives the observation not emphasis but symbolic form, and therefore a kind of concreteness or permanence. In this concrete form, made memorable and attractive with melody and rhythm, the song was taken up by other Egba, perhaps with some musical refinements or embellishments from more creative members of the group, including clapping or drumming to mark the rhythm. Thus a bit of social commentary was crystallized and preserved even after the situation had passed into history.

Whether the content of songs is didactic, satirical, inspirational, religious, political, or purely emotional, the important thing is that the formless has been given form and feelings are communicated in a symbolic and memorable way that can be repeated and shared. The group is consequently united and probably has the sense that their experience, whatever it may be, has shape and meaning.

THE ART OF SCULPTURE

In the broadest sense, sculpture is art in the round. Any three-dimensional product of the creative imagination may be called a piece of sculpture: a ceremonial knife, a decorative pot, a hand-crafted lute, an ornamental gate, a funerary monument, or a public building displays the same essential artistic process as a statue, a mask, or a figurine. All of these human creations represent an imaginative organization of materials in space. The artist has given tangible shape to his or her feelings and perceptions, creating or recreating symbolically meaningful form out of formlessness. In a narrower sense, sculpture means only those artifacts that serve no immediate utilitarian purpose and are fashioned from hard or semipermanent materials. But it is difficult to state unequivocally what may or may not qualify as a piece of sculpture, even with this limitation. Are the beautiful and highly imaginative tiny brass figurines of Ashanti, for example, formerly used as weights for measuring out quantities of gold, not to be considered sculpture, even though the somewhat larger brass figurines of comparable design in Dahomey, which have never had a practical use, are obviously to be so considered? Or should we perhaps now call the Ashanti figurines sculpture, as we now do, because they are no longer put to use?

Art and Craft

Our use of the word "sculpture" in English seems to impose a distinction between types of creative activity where none may in fact exist. One solution is to substitute the more modern term "plastic art," but the phenomenon remains the same. Objects that are obviously skillfully made but still do not quite qualify as sculpture by virtue of being somewhat trivial, low in

symbolic content, or impermanent—by the standards of the culture—are generally known and considered as the products of craft (or, in modern times, industry). An automobile, for example, however beautifully it may be designed, however lovingly it may be displayed in front of the house as an object for admiration, and however cleverly we may interpret its parts and its functions as symbolic in our culture, is for us above all a mass-produced consumable, and to treat it as sculpture would be mis-

This page from a 1902 Sears, Roebuck catalog shows a kitchen stove fairly typical of the period. Though mass produced as a utilitarian item, such a stove today in good condition would fetch a price of several hundred dollars as an object of "art in the round." Although not created as a piece of sculpture, that is what it has, in effect, become.

Michelangelo's "David."

representing its *usual* value in our society. Furthermore, we must also consider the intention of the creator. What we call sculpture or plastic art is not ordinarily artistic by accident or through after-the-fact interpretation, but by design. Detroit does not intentionally produce sculpture.

As a type of symbolic expression, sculpture may be representational, imitating closely the forms of nature, or abstract, drawing from natural forms but representing only their basic patterns or arrangements. Representational sculpture is partly abstract to the extent that it generalizes from nature and abstracts patterns of ideal beauty, ugliness, or typical expressions of

emotion. Michelangelo's "David" is representational sculpture, clearly depicting a human being; it is also abstract insofar as it generalizes an ideal of masculine beauty, quiet strength, and emotional calm, therefore functioning symbolically. Henry Moore's gigantic women with holes through their midsections are abstractions, using nature but exaggerating and deliberately transforming some of its shapes for the purpose of expressing a particular feeling toward them.

West African Sculpture

West African sculpture, only comparatively recently studied and described in adequate detail, is an especially rich non-Western tradition that may help illustrate some of the anthropological aspects of representational and abstract sculpture, its subjects, materials, and meanings.

Ancestor worship and reverence of royalty have found expression in a realistic or portrait-style sculpture throughout the region of the Niger and Congo River basins. Probably the most dramatically realistic are the so-called Benin bronzes: hundreds of finely detailed heads of royal ancestors, produced first at the sacred Yoruba city of Ife (in present-day Nigeria) in the fifteenth century, and later in the Benin capital itself. Upon the death of a ruler of Benin, a memorial head was cast in bronze to be placed on the shrine of the departed ruler. Most of these heads were carried off to England at the end of the nineteenth century, and they have served as a forcible reminder to Westerners that the Mediterranean region is not the only source of fine realistic sculpture.

In addition to the Benin bronzes, the royal statues of the Bakuba kings in the Congo River region, the ancestor figures of the Guro on the Ivory Coast, the secular and satirical representations of Europeans by the Yoruba in Nigeria, and the small brasses depicting the royalty and animals of the Fon in Dahomey are also naturalistic in detail, and are obviously often intended to represent real persons or animals in characteristic moods or poses. Features and proportions may be somewhat stylized according to regional conventions of what is appropriate or possible in sculpture: heads may be disproportionately large, necks elongated, and sexual parts either exaggerated or minimized. It is interesting to note

Sculpture as an embellishment of architecture is illustrated by this Nigerian house. The relief carving was done in wet cement; note the bicycle and car used as decorative motifs.

that most of these sculptures come from cultures in which subsistence techniques were efficient enough to produce a surplus, which was used to support a variety of occupational specialists. The artist was one such specialist; much of the artists' work was commissioned by other specialists, such as priests and government officials.

The majority of West African sculpture is abstract or expressionistic—giving form to human feelings and attitudes toward gods, spirits, other humans, and animals. Generalizations about the nonrepresentational styles and purposes for the region are, however, almost impossible. Every West African culture that produces or has produced sculpture has its own identifiable styles, and this artistic cohesion undoubtedly reinforces the social unity of the group. A Fon recognizes a Yoruba mask, and is disassociated from whatever symbolic significance it has for the Yoruba. Materials as well as styles differ in neighboring cultures. The most common material is wood, but there is also regional use of brass, iron, terracotta, mud, and raffia. Sculpture may be rubbed with ash, smoked in banana leaves, oiled, waxed, painted, and adorned with cowrie shells, teeth, iron or brass nails, strips of metal, or cloth.

SYMBOLIC CONTENT The anthropologist is interested in exactly what is abstracted from nature, and why, in all these varieties of sculpture, whatever their style and material. The anthropologist is also interested in the extent to which traditions are perpetuated, and what meanings may be developing or changing. It appears that any single piece of sculpture in West Africa may be interpreted in terms of its symbolic significance for the group, and that generally such significance is well known by the people who make and look at the sculpture. Consequently the anthropologist has only to ask.

A small wooden figure of a person, with a head, rudimentary limbs, and a large trunk purposely riddled with holes may be found among the Balega of the northeast Congo region. The figure is known as a *katanda*, meaning the scattering of red ants when attacked; it is interpreted as symbolizing the bad effect of internal fighting on the unity of local descent groups. The *kanaga* mask of the Dogon in Upper Volta is an elongated head with triangular eyes, long pointed ears and nose, and a cap surmounted with an enormous crest, four or five times the size of the head, in the form of a double-armed cross. For young initiates the cross symbolizes a bird with outstretched wings, the beginning of active flight into life, and for older initiates of high rank its structure symbolizes a synthesis of contradictory or competing life forces. The *akua'ba* dolls of the Ashanti in Ghana, flat disc-headed figures on a long, narrow, legless body with a simple crosspiece for arms, are said to symbolize an Ashanti ideal of beauty in the high, wide forehead; the dolls are tucked into the waistcloths of young girls, who carry them like real babies, perhaps as talismans to assure their own physical development or that of their children.

RITUAL MASKS The widest variety of expression in African sculpture is certainly to be found in the ritual mask. Styles range from the relatively realistic and serene faces made by the Baule on the Ivory Coast to the frightening, violent, and extroverted faces with protruding eyes produced by the neighboring Ngere of Liberia. Theories about the symbolism of the masks have arisen beside the explanations of local informants, particularly in cases where certain masks are no longer produced or known. One of the more interesting is the notion that the unnatural features of some of the masks representing spirits of the dead are made systematically unnatural in order to suggest that the other world, or the spirit world, is somehow an opposite of this one: noses are long instead of short, ears are large rather than small, eye cavities are hollow rather than filled, and so on. The mask, as well as other sculpture, therefore becomes as much as the myth an expression of world view. The sculptor again gives shape and meaning to that which is unknown.

As in musical expression, sculpture also crystalizes feeling in a form that can be shared and perpetuated. Much, though not all, African sculpture is impermanent because of the impermanent nature of its materials (50 years has been suggested as an average lifetime for a wooden figure exposed to weather), but it is generally considered a great shame when a mask or piece of sculpture disintegrates. An important piece of sculpture may be replaced by imitation, copied and perpetuated so that the traditions and beliefs may be preserved. There is often a ritual in mask making, with great care taken to preserve and copy exactly the traditional specifications. Similarly, there is still in some places a special reverence in the process of sculpting in general, and the soul of the wood must be respected with attendant rituals and beliefs similar to what we have seen in relation to the drum. Traditional West African sculpture is currently in decline, but it is not by any means everywhere dead. An excursion beyond the major urban centers reveals continuing activity in this important kind of symbolic creativity.

CHAPTER SUMMARY

Art is the creative use of the human imagination to interpret, understand, and enjoy life. It stems from the uniquely human ability to use symbols to give shape and significance to the physical world for more than just a utilitarian purpose. Anthropologists are concerned with art as a reflection of the cultural values and concerns of people.

Oral traditions denote the unwritten stories, beliefs, and customs of a culture. Verbal arts include narrative, drama, poetry, incantations, proverbs, riddles, and word games. Narratives, which have received the most study, have been divided into three categories: myths, legends, and tales.

Myths are basically religious, with their subject matter the large questions of human existence. In describing an orderly universe, myths function to set standards for orderly behavior. Legends are semihistorical narratives that recount the exploits of heroes, the movements of people, and the establishment of local customs. Epics, which are long legends in poetry or prose, are typically found in nonliterate societies with a form of state political organization. They serve to transmit and preserve a culture's legal and political practices. Anthropologists are interested in legends because they provide clues as to what constitutes model ethical behavior in a culture. Tales are fictional, secular, nonhistorical narratives that sometimes teach moral or practical lessons. Anthropological interest in tales centers on the fact that their distribution provides evidence for cultural contacts or cultural isolation.

The study of music in specific cultural settings has developed into the specialized field of ethnomusicology. Almost everywhere human music is perceived in terms of a scale. Scale systems and their modifications comprise tonality in music. Tonality determines the possibilities and limits of melody and harmony. Rhythm is an organizing factor in music. Traditional European music is measured into recurrent patterns of two, three, and four beats.

The social function of music is most obvious in song. Like tales, songs may express the concerns of the group, but with greater formalism because of the restrictions imposed by closed systems of tonality, rhythm, and musical form.

Sculpture is any three-dimensional product of the creative imagination fashioned from hard or semipermanent materials. Sculpted objects, such as a statue, a ceremonial knife, or a public building, represent an imaginative organization of materials in space. A more modern term for sculpture is plastic art. Certain objects, although skillfully made, do not qualify as sculpture. This may be because by the standards of the culture they are trivial, low in symbolic content, or impermanent. Such objects are generally considered as the products of crafts—or in modern times, industry. Sculpture may be representational—imitating the forms of nature, or abstract—representing only basic patterns of natural forms. West African sculpture illustrates some of the anthropological aspects of representational and abstract sculpture in its subject matter, materials, and meanings.

SUGGESTED READINGS

Boas, Franz. *Primitive Art*. Gloucester, Mass.: Peter Smith, 1962.
   The book gives an analytical description of the basic traits of "primitive" art. Its treatment is based on two principles: the fundamental sameness of mental processes in all races and cultural forms of the present day, and the consideration of every cultural phenomenon in a historical context. It covers formal elements in art, symbolism, and style and has sections on "primitive" literature, music, and dance.

Fraser, Douglas. *Primitive Art*. Garden City, N.Y.: Doubleday, 1962.
   The book presents a systematic survey of non-Western art, aiming to place each style studied in relation to both its local setting and to other styles near and far away. The author covers the three main geographical areas of Africa, Asia-Oceania, and America. Good color illustrations.

Nettl, Bruno. *Music in Primitive Culture*. Cambridge, Mass.: Harvard University Press, 1956.
   The book is designed as an introduction to music in tribal societies and attempts to show the kinds of phenomena that characterize it. It provides examples of types of such music, shows how they have been studied, and provides general conclusions which have been drawn from them.

Otten, Charlotte M. *Anthropology and Art: Readings in Cross-Cultural Aesthetics*. Garden City, N.Y.: Natural History Press, 1971.
   This is a collection of articles by anthropologists and art historians with an emphasis on the functional relationships between art and culture.

Thompson, Stith. *The Folktale*. New York: Holt, Rinehart and Winston, 1960.
   The book serves as a guide to the study of the folktale, in both written and oral form. It includes an account of well-known Western folktales and their history, and a section on the classical folktale as reconstructed from literary remains. North American Indian tales serve as examples of tales in tribal and band societies. The final section provides some analysis of theory and methods in the field.

Wingert, Paul. *Primitive Art: Its Traditions and Styles*. London: Oxford University Press, 1962; World, 1965.
   The book serves as an introduction to "primitive" art, defining that term and examining various prevailing attitudes and approaches toward it. The method of approach places art in a cultural context, and analyzes objects from Africa, Oceania, and North America.

Workers using a computer in Niamey, Niger. In the past, the capacity to change has given cultures the capacity to adapt to new circumstances. In the twentieth century, culture change frequently involves the loss of whatever self-sufficiency a people may possess as they become more and more dependent on goods and commodities that they themselves do not produce. While the hope is that this will lead to a higher standard of living, such a system places people at the mercy of rises and dips in a world economy over which they have no control.

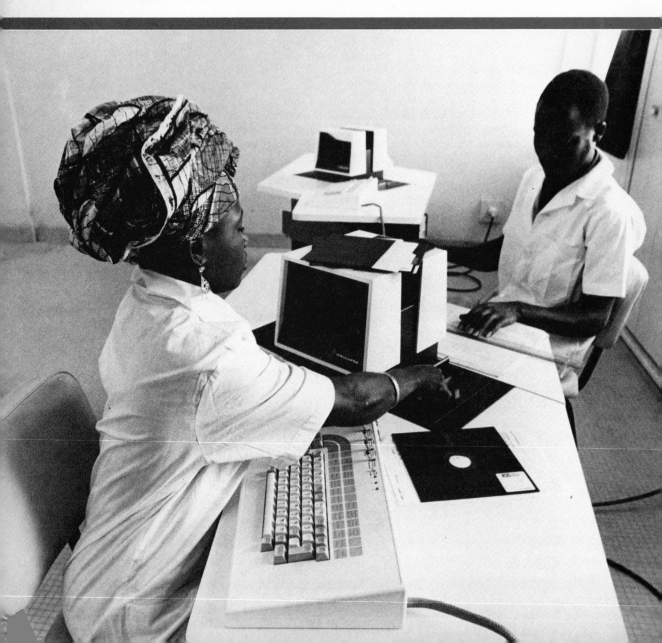

PART FIVE

CHANGE AND THE FUTURE

Solving the Problem of Adjusting to Changed Conditions

INTRODUCTION

Without the ability to conceive new ideas and change existing behavior patterns, no human society could survive. Human culture is remarkably stable, but it is also resilient and therefore able to adapt to altered circumstances. Throughout this book—as we studied the beginnings of human culture or the changes associated with the development of food production or the ways in which kinship organization evolves—we have seen that change is characteristic of all cultures. We need only look at the diversity of cultures that have appeared in the course of human history, all ultimately derived from the earliest hunter-gatherer base, to know that cultural change is continually and constantly taking place.

Understanding the processes of change, the subject of Chapter 14, is one of the most important and fundamental of anthropological goals. With colonialism and, later—beginning around the 1930s—with the spread of industrialization to undeveloped areas of the world, anthropologists began increasingly to see societies whose traditional organization, institutions, and customs were rapidly changing and even eroding away. After several generations of contact with industrialization and with European and North American commercialism, many traditional societies were experiencing serious and pressing conflicts both within and beyond their borders as their people grappled with the strain of changing from one mode of life to another. Early twentieth-century anthropologists were quick to recognize the need during the colonial era to apply programs and policies that would diminish the conflicts that seemed inevitably associated with contact between vastly different cultures. In addition, the anthropological approach has brought a needed objectivity and a fresh perspective to the problems of culture contact.

For many colonial areas of the world, the period after World War II was marked by a new national consciousness and a striving by these peoples to determine their own political destinies. But at the same time that these countries have thrown off the shackles of colonialism, they have more and more aspired to the standard of living enjoyed by Western industrialized societies. A major emphasis of post-World War II anthropology has been on the rapid and pervasive changes that were brought about by colonialism and continue today in the process of modernization. To know the dynamics of these changes is of the utmost importance for all of humanity, which has been affected by extraordinary changes in the very recent past and will certainly be affected by far-reaching changes in the immediate future.

The more anthropologists study change and learn about the various ways people go about solving their problems of existence, the more aware they become of a great paradox of culture. On the other hand, the basic business of culture is to solve problems, but in doing so inevitably new problems are created which themselves demand solution. Again throughout this book we have seen examples—the problem of forming groups in order to cooperate in solving the problems of staying alive, the problem of finding ways to overcome the stresses and strains on individuals as a consequence of their membership in groups, as well as the structural problems that are inherent in the division of society into a number of smaller groups, to mention but a few. It is apparent that every solution to a problem has its price, but so long as culture is able to keep at least a step ahead of the problems, all is reasonably well. This seems to have been the case generally over the past two million years.

When we see all of the problems that face the human species today (Chapter 15), most of them the result of cultural practices, we may wonder if we haven't passed some critical threshold where culture has begun to fall a step behind the problems. This is not to say that the future necessarily has to be bleak for the generations that come after us, but it would certainly be irresponsible to project some sort of rosy, science-fiction type of future as inevitable, at least on the basis of present evidence. To prevent the future from being bleak, humans will have to rise to the challenge of changing their behavior and ideas in order to conquer the large problems that threaten to annihilate them: overpopulation and its concomitant starvation, poverty, and squalor; urbanization and the snuffing out of the individual spirit; environmental pollution and poisoning; and the culture of discontent and bitterness that rises out of the widening economic gap separating industrialized and nonindustrialized countries. Anthropologists of the future may well play a role in helping people to adjust their own ideas and desires in order to ensure the survival of the human species. They may also play a part in helping people of the Western world to realign their thinking with regard to exploiting their environment and its natural resources. Anthropologists are well aware of examples throughout history that testify to the resilience of humans and to their facility for changing their behavior in the face of necessity. In its work for the future (Chapter 16), anthropology needs to continue its exploration of change in all human societies, in those that have vanished as well as those that are on the verge of slipping away, in African villages as well as in the great cities of North America.

14 | Culture Change

The capacity to change has always been an important feature of human cultures; without it, they would lack the capacity to adapt to changed conditions. Perhaps at no time has the pace of culture change equalled that to be seen in the world today, as symbolized by this picture of a woman of Upper Volta on her way to market on a motorbike. In the space of a single generation, many traditional peoples are attempting to undergo the kind of culture change that took the industrial societies of the West many generations to accomplish.

PREVIEW

WHY DO CULTURES CHANGE?

All cultures change at one time or another, for a variety of reasons. One cause is environmental change, which may require an adaptive change in culture. Another is that, purely by chance, or for some other reason, a people may change the way they perceive their environment and their place in it. Or, contact with other peoples may lead to the introduction of "foreign" ideas, bringing about changes in existing values and behavior. This may even involve the massive imposition of foreign ways through conquest of one group by another.

HOW DO CULTURES CHANGE?

The mechanisms of change are invention, diffusion, cultural loss, and acculturation. Invention occurs when someone within a society discovers something new that is then accepted by other members of the society. Diffusion is the borrowing of something from another group, and cultural loss is the abandonment of an existing practice or trait without replacement. Acculturation is the massive change that occurs with the sort of intensive, firsthand contact that has occurred under colonialism.

WHAT IS MODERNIZATION?

Modernization refers to a global process of change by which traditional, nonindustrial societies seek to acquire characteristics of industrially "advanced" societies. Although modernization has generally been assumed to be a good thing, and there have been some successes, it has frequently led to the development of a new "culture of discontent," a level of aspirations far exceeding the bounds of an individual's local opportunities. Sometimes it leads to the destruction of cherished customs and values people had no desire to abandon.

Culture is the medium through which the human species solves the problems of existence, as these are perceived by members of the species. Various cultural institutions, such as kinship and marriage, political and economic organization, and religion, mesh together to form an integrated cultural system. Because this system is adaptive, it is fairly stable and remains so unless either the conditions to which it is adapted, or human perceptions of those conditions, change. Archeological studies have revealed how elements of a culture may persist for long periods of time. For example, the calendar used a thousand years ago by the pre-Columbian Maya of Central America is still used in some modern Maya communities. Similarly, many of today's Maya live in houses resembling those built by their forbears during the height of Maya civilization (A.D. 250–870).

Although stability may be a striking feature of many cultures, cultural change does take place—we need only look at the incredible diversity of cultures today, all ultimately derived, in something like two million years, from a simple hunting-gathering base. Even more amazing is the fact that all nonhunting-gathering cultures have developed in the past 10,000 years. The causes of change are various. One common cause is change in the environment, which must be followed by an adaptive change in culture; another is individual variation in the way people within a culture perceive its characteristics, which may lead to a change in the way society in general interprets the norms and values of its culture. A third source of change is contact with other groups, which introduces new ideas and ways of doing things, eventually producing change in traditional values and behavior.

Change is characteristic of all cultures, but the rate and direction of change vary considerably from one to another and from time to time. Among the factors that influence the way change will occur within a given culture are the degree to which a culture encourages and approves flexibility; the particular needs of the culture at a specific time; and, perhaps most important of

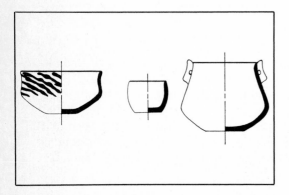

The invention of pottery containers in the Middle East. The picture, right, shows a clay-lined basin in the floor of a cooking area at ancient Jericho. The proximity of clay and fire must have led to accidental firing of clay on numerous occasions. The drawings above show early pottery vessels from Jarmo, Iraq.

all, the degree of "fit" between a new element and the existing cultural matrix.

Even when cultural changes appear to be beneficial and adaptive, they may well be difficult for individuals within the culture to accept. Thus cultural change is considered a social problem even though it is part of the necessary process of getting along in the world. New ways of doing things not only feel wrong, they also require relearning. An example of this can be seen in the reluctance of people in the United States to abandon completely the awkward and cumbersome old English system of weights and measures for the far more logical metric system, which has been adopted by just about everyone else on the face of the earth. Another can be seen in the continued British practice of driving on the left-hand side of the road, rather than on the right. Driving on the left is no more natural than driving on the right, but to someone from Britian it seems so, because of the body reflexes which have developed in the course of driving on the left. In this case the individual's very body has become adjusted to certain patterns of behavior that bypass any presumed "openness" to change.

MECHANISMS OF CHANGE

Cultural change may be slow, occurring over long periods of time, or it may be rapid, occurring over relatively brief periods of time. The processes or mechanisms involved in cultural change are invention, diffusion, cultural loss, and acculturation.

Invention

The term **invention** refers to the discovery, by a single individual, of a new practice, tool, or principle that eventually gains

> **Invention:** The discovery by a single individual of a new tool or principle that becomes socially shared.

the acceptance of others and thus becomes socially shared.

The term "invention" can be further broken down into "primary" and "secondary" inventions. Primary inventions are the chance discoveries of new principles; secondary inventions are improvements made by applying known principles.

An example of a primary invention is the discovery that the firing of clay makes the material permanently hard. Presumably, the firing of clay frequently took place by accident in ancient cooking fires. However, an accidental occurrence is not an invention unless some application of it is perceived. About 25,000 years ago, an application was perceived, for figurines were made of fired clay. Pottery vessels were not made, however, and the invention apparently did not reach the Middle East; if it did, it did not take root. It was not until some time between 7000 and 6500 B.C. that a significant application of fired clay was perceived in the Middle East with the making of cheap, durable, easy-to-produce containers and cooking vessels.

As nearly as we can reconstruct it, the development of the earliest known pottery vessels came about in the following way.[1] By 7000 B.C., cooking areas in the Middle East included clay-lined basins which were made as part of the floor, as well as clay ovens and hearths. In such a situation, the accidental firing of clay was inevitable. At

---

[1] Ruth Amiran, "The Beginnings of Pottery-Making in the Near East," in Frederick R. Matson, ed., *Ceramics and Man*, Viking Fund Publications in Anthropology, 1965, No. 41, pp. 240–247.

the time, clay was also used in house construction, in the modeling of figurines, and in lining storage pits. Hence, although people were familiar with the working of clay, it was not purposely fired, nor was it used for making containers other than the pit linings. For containers, stone vessels, baskets, and leather bags were in use.

Once the significance of fired clay—the primary invention—was perceived, then the application of known techniques to it—secondary invention—became possible. Clay could be modeled in the familiar way into the known shapes of baskets, leather bags, and stone bowls and then fired, either in an open fire or in the same ovens used for cooking food. In fact, the earliest known Middle Eastern pottery is imitative of leather and stone containers, and the decoration consists of motifs transferred from basketry, but which were ill suited to the new medium. Eventually, shapes and decorative techniques more suited to the new technology were developed.

The original pottery was handmade, and the earliest kilns were the same ovens that were used for cooking. As pottery making progressed, there were further technological refinements. As an aid in production, the clay could be modeled on a mat or other surface which the potter could move as work progressed. Hence, the potter could sit in one place and not have to move around the clay. A further refinement was to mount the movable surface on a vertical rotating shaft—an application of a known principle used for drills—which produced the potter's wheel and permitted mass production. Kilns, too, were improved for better circulation of heat by separating the firing chamber from the fire itself. By chance, it happened that these improved kilns produced enough heat to smelt some ores such as copper, tin, gold, silver, and lead. Presumably, this discovery was made by acci-

dent—another primary invention—and the stage was set for the eventual development of the forced draft furnace out of the earlier pottery kiln.

Primary inventions may set off rapid cultural change and stimulate other inventions, as the above example suggests. Indeed, cultural values and goals can themselves lead to inventions. This seems to be responsible for the many instances of particular inventions that had more than one discoverer: the theory of evolution through natural selection, for example, was discovered ("invented") by Wallace as well as Darwin; three men independently produced the telescope; and the steamboat had no less than four inventors—all of whom worked before Fulton's time. On the other hand, an invention's chance of acceptance is limited if it fails to fit into a society's pattern of established needs, values, and goals. Copernicus' discovery of the rotation of the planets around the sun and Mendel's discovery of the basic laws of heredity are instances of genuine creative insights out of step with the needs of their times. In fact, Mendel's work remained obscure until 16 years after his death when it was rediscovered by three scientists working independently in 1900. Mendel's discovery thus is an example of an idea whose time had come by 1900, in spite of its earlier failure.

While an invention must be reasonably consistent with a society's needs, values, and goals if it is to be accepted, this is not sufficient to assure its acceptance. Force of habit tends to be an obstacle to acceptance; people will generally tend to stick with what they are used to, rather than adopt something new which will require some adjustment on their part. Hence, an invention's chance of acceptance tends to be greater if it is obviously better than the thing or idea it replaces. Beyond this, much may depend on the prestige of the inventor

Diffusion from contemporary Western culture to the world's traditional cultures. Here, a Tahitian woman cuts her grass with a gasoline-powered lawnmower.

and imitating groups. If the inventor's prestige is high, this will help gain acceptance for the invention. If it is low, acceptance is less likely unless the inventor can attract a sponsor who has high prestige.

Diffusion

In cultural borrowing, or **diffusion**, the "inventor" is the introducer of a new cultural element from another society. Murdock[2] cites the European colonists who came to America, who borrowed not just the use of corn, squash, and beans from

[2] George P. Murdock, "How Culture Changes," in Harry L. Shapiro, ed., *Man, Culture and Society* (Chicago: University of Chicago Press, 1956).

> **Diffusion: The spread of customs or practices from one culture to another.**

American Indians, but the entire Indian way of producing them. Borrowing is so common that Malinowski,[3] for example, regarded it as being just as creative as other forms of cultural innovation, and Linton[4] suggested that borrowing accounts for as much as 90 percent of any culture's content. People never borrow all available innovations but exercise a high degree of selectivity, limiting their selections to those compatible with the existing culture. In modern-day Guatemala, for example, Maya Indians, who make up more than half of that country's population, will adopt West-

[3] Bronislaw Malinowski, *The Dynamics of Culture Change* (New Haven, Conn.: Yale University Press, 1945).

[4] Ralph Linton, *The Study of Man* (New York: Appleton, 1940).

Diffusion within the Western world: Popeye Bar in Escuintla, Guatemala.

ern ways if the value of these ways is self-evident and they do not conflict with traditional ways and values. The use of metal hoes, shovels, and machetes has long since become standard, for they are superior to stone tools, and yet they are compatible with the traditional cultivation of corn by men using hand tools. Yet certain other "modern" practices, which might appear advantageous to the Maya, tend to be resisted for reasons and in ways that are discussed in the following Original Study.

ORIGINAL STUDY

Persistence and Change in a Maya Community[5]

The basic Indian technological complex is still old, but it is by no means unmodified. It is Indian in so far as the women continue to form their pottery by the pre-Columbian coil method, as the tumpline has not been replaced, as the corn is cultivated by men and their hand tools without the use of the plow. On the other hand, the types of tools used (hoes, shovels, and machetes), the use of iron sheeting for roofing, and the use of an infinite number of similar items purchased in Guatemala City attest to the fact that European technology has been borrowed, perhaps as early as the arrival of the first Spaniards in Middle America. Indeed, the modern economy of Guatemala has been described as consisting of three technological layers: "[a] a thin veneer of modern industrial art; [b] the middle layer, a very substantial one, represents European technology of the centuries before the Industrial Revolution; [c] the bottom layer is what remains of the technology of the pre-Columbian Indians."[6]

To explain why the Indian economy has persisted in Chinautla constitutes a full research project in its own right. Here we can only comment on some aspects of the relationship between the Indian economy and the modernized setting of Guatemala. For instance, why is the bus so popular in the midst of the old Indian ways? This is so to the point where a lack of bus facilities creates confusion in the population, which depends more and more on this means of transportation. The answers given by informants vary, but in general the following theme recurred:

> On the bus I can get to the capital fast, sell my products, buy my staples, and before noon I can be home to take care of the household chores, go to the woods, or work on my pottery. On Saturday I can do all my errands in town and have some leisure time before returning to Chinautla. Or else I can complete my business in the city and return to Chinautla to participate in the rituals of the religious societies.

---

[5] Ruben E. Reina, *The Law of the Saints.* Copyright © 1966 by Bobbs-Merrill Company, Inc. Reprinted by permission of Ruben E. Reina, pp. 65–68.

[6] Sol Tax, *Penny Capitalism: A Guatemalan Indian Economy,* Smithsonian Institution, Institute of Social Anthropology, Pub. No. 16 (Washington, D.C.: Government Printing Office, 1953), p. 20.

The adoption of a modern custom, in this case transportation, proves efficient in terms of time, which has become economically and socially valuable. It also makes possible the conservation of other segments of the cultural tradition. The Chinautlecos have replaced an old, customary way of doing something by a new way that means profit in terms of money and energy, which they then can devote to other, culturally meaningful activities. Again, the new specialties in industry and in agriculture, like "huisquil" production, were adopted because they not only are financially profitable but do not conflict in time-space with the basic productions. They are interstitial activities and have little effect on the Indians' basic attitudes. Being day laborers in Guatemala City, for example, does not challenge their sense of identity as Indians or Chinautlecos; and while they work with the other day laborers, they have so far been quiet listeners and observers among them, avoiding labor unions so as not to get caught up in irrelevant regulations and activities.

On the other hand, the persistence of pottery-making without the use of the wheel also needs explanation. Women ask, "What else can we do with our time?" They claim there is little money to be made from pottery, but the time is available to them and at least a few cents extra can be earned in this way. Efficiency is again the theme, but in the sense that the woman's time has little economic value. She sees no use for the time she would save by using a potter's wheel; she cannot participate in charcoal-making or in agricultural activities because they, according to the traditional division of labor, are men's work. Tax's statement on the subject may be cited in summary:

> Actually, since her time has no economic value, the pots cost nothing to make, unless for some purchased materials. The family could clearly earn more money if she continued to make pots than if she stopped. The competition with the wheel-made pottery is, under such circumstances, only theoretical. So women continue to make pottery, and in the old-fashioned way.[7]

Although some Indian customs may be discarded and more modern ones adopted, nonetheless there are limits to this process. When innovation is carried to the point where it runs counter to basic elements of the social tradition, little comes of it. For example, there was only one person in Chinautla who engaged in intensive and specialized work in horticulture. A young Indian, who had learned the trade while working three years for a Chinese gardener in Guatemala City and whose family owns a property watered the year round by a natural spring, was, for a time, running a truck garden that was oriental in pattern. His full growing season was the summer, or dry season, from December to May or June. During these months he grew cash crops with market value only in Guatemala City, vegetables not eaten by the Indians or even by the rural Ladinos; in growing them, he used chemical fertilizers and DDT, having learned their use from the Chinese. The remainder of the year he grew a few vegetables, but most of his time was spent in the preparation of charcoal and

---

[7] Tax, p. 26.

some "milpa" work. However, unable to secure a "good" girl for a wife because of his unorthodox activities, he abandoned them for the traditional means of making a living, "milpa" and charcoal. He is now a "man," married, and no longer different and conspicuous.

A similar story can be cited about pottery, where the culture puts a value upon both skillful workmanship and consistency in producing the typical water jars. As it happened, there were several artistically inclined girls who were induced by the tourist trade to produce candleholders, figurines, and animals. In one case, a girl received three marriage proposals, but the negotiations were never successful because the boys' families always abandoned the arrangement after serious considerations of her reliability. Because of her failures, this girl decided at the age of twenty-two that she would not make any more figurines but would produce the same water jars as everyone else. The "tinajas" were of the first quality, and she aggressively took them into the market. Public opinion changed rapidly. Soon after the switch she had her fourth proposal, was married, and has not reverted to her figurines or toymaking. When she and her aunt were questioned about the change, there was much giggling and joking but never a straightforward discussion of the issue. The middle-aged aunt, with whom the girl lived before her marriage, continues with the figurines, mainly because she has nothing to lose.

While the tendency toward borrowing is so great as to lead Robert Lowie to comment, "Culture is a thing of shreds and patches," the borrowed traits usually undergo sufficient modifications to make this wry comment more colorful than critical. Moreover, the borrowed trait may modify existing cultural traits. An awareness of the extent of borrowing can be eye-opening. Beals, for example, reviews the numerous things we have borrowed from American Indians.[8] Domestic plants that were developed, or "invented," by the Indians— "Irish" potatoes, corn, beans, squash, and sweet potatoes—furnish nearly half the world's food supply. Among drugs and stimulants, tobacco is the best known, but others include coca in cocaine, ephedra in ephedrine, datura in pain relievers, and cascara in laxatives. All but a handful of drugs known today made from plants native to America were used by Indians, and over 200 plants and herbs which they used for medicinal purposes have at one time or another been included in the *Pharmacopeia of the United States* or in the *National Formulary*. Varieties of cotton native to the Americas cultivated by Indians supply much of the world's clothing needs, while the woolen poncho, the parka, and moccasins are universally familiar items. Not only has North American literature been permanently shaped by such works as Longfellow's *Hiawatha* and James Fenimore Cooper's *Leather-Stocking Tales*, but American Indian music has contributed to world music such ultramodern devices as unusual intervals, arbitrary scales, conflicting rhythms, and hypnotic monotony. These borrowings are so well integrated into our culture that few people are aware of their source.

[8] Alan R. Beals, with G. and L. Spindler, *Culture in Process*, 2d ed. (New York: Holt, Rinehart and Winston, 1973), p. 298.

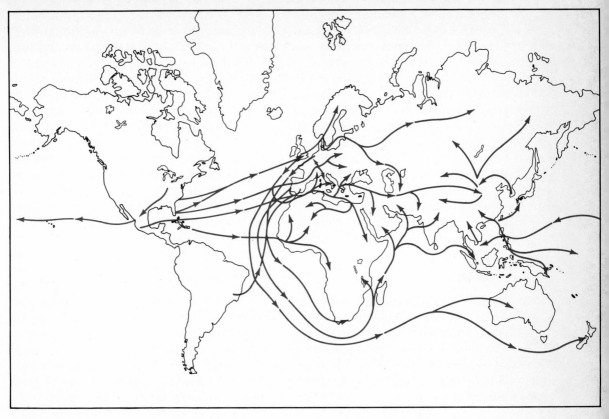

The diffusion of tobacco from its starting point in Virginia to England in 1586 and its rapid spread throughout the world.

In recent decades the Peace Corps has functioned as an agent of diffusion. Here a volunteer teaches songs to Afghan girls in Kabul.

In spite of the obvious importance of diffusion, there are probably more obstacles to accepting an innovation from another culture than there are to accepting one that is "homegrown." In addition to the same obstacles that stand in the way of "home-grown" inventions is the fact that a borrowed one is, somehow, "foreign." In the United States, for example, this is one reason why people have been so slow to accept the metric system of weights and measures, in spite of its clear superiority over the old English system. Hence, the ethnocentrism of the potential borrowing culture may act as a barrier to acceptance.

Cultural Loss

Most often, we tend to think of change as an accumulation of innovations; new things being added to those already there. We do so because this seems so much a part of the way we live. A little reflection, however, leads to the realization that frequently the acceptance of a new innovation leads to the loss of an older one. This sort of replacement is not just a feature of Western civilization. For example, at one time the art of making pottery came into widespread use among the Indians of northeastern North America. By the time Europeans arrived on the scene, this seemingly useful trait had been lost among some of them, and containers were made of basketry and birch bark instead. Actually, pottery is heavier and more breakable than baskets and birch bark containers, serious drawbacks for peoples who move about from one campsite to another and must carry their belongings themselves. Basketry and birch bark were better adapted to their way of life than pottery.

Often overlooked is another facet of the loss of apparently useful traits: loss without replacement. This phenomenon constitutes change just as surely as a new innovation.

An example of this kind of cultural loss is the absence of boats among the inhabitants of the Canary Islands, an archepelago isolated in the stormy seas off the coast of West Africa. The ancestors of these people must have had boats, for without them, they could never have transported themselves and their domestic livestock to the islands in the first place. Later, without boats, they had no way to communicate between islands. The cause of this loss of something useful was that the islands contain no stone suitable for making polished stone axes, which in turn limited the islanders' carpentry.[9]

Acculturation

The process of **acculturation** has received special attention from anthropologists. Acculturation results when groups of individuals having different cultures come into intensive firsthand contact, with subsequent massive changes in the original culture patterns of one or both groups. Its numerous variables include degree of cultural difference; circumstances, intensity, frequency, and amiability of contact; relative status of the agents of contact; who is dominant and who is submissive; and whether the nature of the flow is reciprocal or nonreciprocal. It should be emphasized that acculturation and diffusion are totally disparate terms; one culture can borrow from another without being in the least acculturated.

Anthropologists use the following terms to describe what may happen during acculturation:

1. **Substitution,** in which a pre-existing trait or complex may be replaced by one that fills its function, involving minimal structural change;

---

[9] Carleton S. Coon, *The Story of Man* (New York: Alfred A. Knopf, 1954), p. 174.

2. **Syncretism**, in which old traits blend to form a new system, possibly resulting in considerable cultural change;
3. **Addition**, in which new traits or complexes may be added, and structural change may or may not occur;
4. **Deculturation**, in which a substantial part of a culture may be lost;
5. **Origination** of new traits to meet the needs of the changing situation;
6. **Rejection**, in which changes may be so rapid that a large number of persons cannot accept them, resulting in either total rejection, rebellion, or revitalization movements.

As a result of one or a number of these processes, acculturation may then develop along several lines. Merger or assimilation occurs when two cultures lose their separate identities and form a single culture. Incorporation takes place when one culture loses autonomy but retains its identity as a subculture, such as a caste, class, or ethnic group; this is typical of conquest or slavery situations. Extinction is the phenomenon in which one culture loses its individual members until it can no longer function, and members either die out or join other cultures. In adaptation, a new structure may develop in dynamic equilibrium. In this last instance change may continue, but in the slow, "melting pot" form.

As an example of acculturation, we may look briefly at what happened to the Indians of northern New England following the invasion and colonization of the region by the British.[10] Outwardly, the Indians came to look and act much like the colonists among whom they now lived; they wore European-style clothing, used metal rather than stone tools, fought with guns rather than bows and arrows, emphasized the patrilineal transmission of important

---

[10]William A. Haviland and Marjory W. Power, *The Original Vermonters* (Hanover, N.H.: University Press of New England, 1981), p. 246.

> **Acculturation: Major culture changes that occur as a result of prolonged contact between societies.**
>
> **Substitution: In acculturation, replacement of a preexisting trait or complex by another that fills its function, with minimal structural change.**
>
> **Syncretism: In acculturation, the blending of old traits to form a new system.**
>
> **Addition: In acculturation, the addition of new traits or complexes.**
>
> **Deculturation: In acculturation, loss of a substantial part of a culture.**
>
> **Origination: In acculturation, the development of new traits to meet the needs of the changing situation.**
>
> **Rejection: In acculturation, changes may be so rapid that a large number of persons cannot accept them, resulting in either total rejection, rebellion, or revitalization movements.**

property, recognized distinctions of rank, were generally fluent in a European language (French), and even adopted Christianity (Catholicism). Such Indian practices as they did retain—hunting, fishing, the cultivation of corn, beans, and squash, use of canoes and snowshoes, and the smoking of tobacco—had long since been adopted by the colonists and were no longer distinctively Indian. Thus, the Indians became all but invisible to the non-Indians around them, even though they retained a core of values and traditions distinctively their own. The result is that when these Indians in the 1970s began to reassert their ethnic identity, most non-Indians didn't take them seriously; they just didn't *look* Indian.

Although the above illustration is taken from our own history, similar situations are taking place around the world today as the world's remaining tribal peoples are affected by the "development" of regions such as the Amazon basin. We shall have more to say about this later in this, as well as subsequent, chapters.

FORCIBLE CHANGE

Quite logically, instances of the acceptance of change are highest when the element of change results from a need within the society. This may represent a society's striving to adapt economically to the world-wide technological revolution, even though the ramifications of the change may be felt throughout the society. The changing roles of women in Africa, or, for that matter, in the United States, may be considered an example of such a change. However, changes are often imposed from outside a culture, usually by colonialism and conquest. We examined in Chapter 12 two examples of societies attempting to deal with such intrusions: the cargo cults of Melanesia and the Ghost Dance of the American Indian. Here we will look at some of the anthropological theories that attempt to explain the dynamics of changes that are forcibly imposed.

Colonialism and Conquest

One by-product of colonialism has been the growth of **applied anthropology** and the use of anthropological techniques and knowledge for certain "practical" ends. For example, British anthropology has often been considered the "handmaiden" of that country's colonial policy, for it typi-

cally provided the kind of information of particular use in maintaining effective colonial rule. In North America, nineteenth-century anthropologists were heavily committed to the usefulness of their discipline, and they were not infrequently to be found coming to the assistance of the American Indian peoples among whom they worked. Early in the present century the applied work of Franz Boas, who almost single-handedly trained a generation of anthropologists in the United States, was instrumental in reforming the country's immigration policies. In the 1930s, anthropologists carried out a number of studies in industrial and other institutional settings with avowedly applied goals. We shall say a bit more about some of these efforts in the last chapter of this book. With World War II came the first efforts at colonial administration beyond our own borders, especially in the Pacific, made by officers trained in anthropology. The rapid recovery of Japan was due in no small measure to the influence of anthropologists in structuring the U.S. occupation. Other North American experiments aimed at meshing the colonial culture with the native structure with the least possible disturbance also bore fruit. Although many of these studies were admittedly for purposes of military intelligence, they proved useful also in postwar programs.

On the other side of the coin, however, and reflected especially in the early literature of contact between Europeans with indigenous groups, is a complete lack of anthropological understanding, and often of humaneness. Such contacts frequently brought to many areas the decimation, misery, and community degeneration that is known colloquially as "culture crash." Severe disruption of traditional community life, with indications of social chaos or discord and personal or individual malaise,

Franz Boas, 1858–1942

Born in Germany, where he studied physics and geography, Boas came to the United States to live in 1888. His interest in anthropology began a few years earlier with a trip to Baffinland, where he met his first so-called primitive people. Thereafter, he and his students came to dominate anthropology in North America through the first three decades of the 1900s. Through meticulous and detailed fieldwork, which set new standards for excellence, Boas and his students were able to expose the shortcomings of the grandiose schemes of cultural evolution which had been proposed by earlier social theorists. His thesis that a culture must be judged according to its own standards and values, rather than those of the investigator, represented a tremendously liberating philosophy in his time.

Applied anthropology: The use of anthropological knowledge and techniques for the purpose of solving "practical" problems, often for a specific "client."

often came in the wake of colonial occupation. This by no means implies that traditional societies were frictionless before contact with "civilization," but rather that existing conflicts could be handled through established cultural institutions without prolonged disruptions of daily life. In these early cases, degeneration occurred because traditional institutions designed to deal with traditional stress or conflict could not,

Colonialism and colonization have frequently caused decimation and cultural disintegration, as was the case with most native American peoples. This picture shows Indians listening to a recorded speech made to them by President Woodrow Wilson. Throughout the Americas, Indians for the most part remain neglected minorities, almost 500 years after Columbus.

or were not allowed by a colonial power, to cope with new and rapid change that did not fit into the context of the traditional system. Too rapid change in a value system, for example, leaves other parts of the culture to catch up.

Sometimes, indigenous people show great strength and resiliency in the face of European domination, inventing creative and ingenious ways of expressing this. Such a people were the Trobriand Islanders under British rule. These people were introduced by missionaries to the rather staid, traditional British game of cricket, but were determined to "rubbish" (throw out) the British game, turning it into a real Trobriand contest. Neither "primitive" nor benignly accepted in its original form, Trobriand cricket was thoughtfully and creatively adapted into a sophisticated activity reflecting the importance of basic indigenous cultural premises. Exuberance and pride are displayed by everyone associated with the game, and the players are as much concerned with conveying the full meaning of who they are as with scoring well. From the individual application of face paint in preparation for the game to the team chanting of "rude" songs and to chorus-line dancing between the innings, there is little doubt that each player is playing for his own importance, for the fame of his team, and for the hundreds of attractive young women who usually watch the game.[11]

The most extreme cases of acculturation usually occur as a result of military conquest and displacement of traditional political authority by conquerors who know nothing about the culture they control. The indigenous people, unable to resist imposed changes and restricted in their traditional social, religious, and economic activities, may be forced into new activities that tend to isolate individuals and tear apart social integration. Slavery in the early years of the United States, possibly the best-known example to us, provides many explanations for problems in race relations once shrugged off as "racial inferiority." It should be pointed out that slavery in early America was not confined to the United States. As part of the prevailing economic system (known as "the plantation system") slavery was characteristic of the Caribbean Islands and coastal South America, as well as the southeastern United States. The racial problems the United States inherited from the slavery era are shared by these other areas in the Americas where slavery was practiced.

Rebellion and Revolution

When the scale of forced acculturation reaches a certain level, the possibilities for rebellion and revolution—such as the Cuban Revolution or the Red Revolution in China—are high.

The question of why revolutions come into being, as well as why they frequently fail to live up to the expectations of the people initiating them, is a problem. It is clear, however, that the colonial policies of countries such as England, France, Spain, Portugal, and the United States during the nineteenth and early twentieth centuries have created a world-wide situation in which revolution has become nearly inevitable. In numerous technologically undeveloped lands which have been exploited by more powerful countries for their natural resources and cheap labor, a deep resentment of the foreign rulers prevails. Lack of responsiveness to this feeling makes revolution or rebellion in some emerging nations

---

[11] Annette B. Weiner, review of "Trobriand Cricket: An Ingenious Response to Colonialism," *American Anthropologist*, 1977, 79:506.

the only alternative. On the basis of an examination of four revolutions of the past— English, American, French, and Bolshevik—the following conditions have been offered as precipitators of rebellion and revolution:

1. Loss of prestige of established authority, often as a result of the failure of foreign policy, financial difficulties, dismissals of popular ministers, or alteration of popular policies.
2. Threat to recent economic improvement. In France and Russia, those sections of the population (professional classes and urban workers) whose economic fortunes had previously taken an upward swing were "radicalized" by unexpected setbacks such as steeply rising food prices and unemployment.
3. Indecisiveness of government, as exemplified by lack of consistent policy; such governments appear to be controlled by, rather than in control of, events.
4. Loss of support of the intellectual class. Such a loss deprived the prerevolutionary governments of France and Russia of philosophical support, thus leading to their lack of popularity with the literate public.
5. A leader or group of leaders with charisma enough to mobilize a substantial part of the population against the establishment.

Apart from resistance to internal authority, such as in the English, French, and Russian revolutions, many revolutions in modern times have been struggles against an externally imposed authority. Such resistance usually takes the form of independence movements that wage campaigns of armed defiance against colonial powers. The Algerian struggle for independence from France and the American Revolution are typical examples.

Revolts are not without their own problems. Hoebel quotes Max Gluckman writing of rebellion to oust the incumbents of offices without attempting to alter the nature of these offices. According to Gluckman, rebellions:

"throw the rascals out" and substitute another set, but there is no attempt to alter either the cultural ideology or the form of the social structure. In political revolution, attempts are made to seize the offices of power in order to change social structure, belief systems, and their sym-

The Bolshevik uprising in Russia was not just a rebellion but a true revolution.

bolic representations. Political revolutions are usually turbulent, violent, and not long-lasting. A successful revolution soon moves to re-establish a stable, though changed, social structure; yet it has far-reaching political, social and sometimes economic and cultural consequences.[12]

It should be pointed out, however, that revolution is a relatively recent phenomenon, occurring only during the last 5000 years. The reason for this is that political rebellion requires a centralized political authority (or state) to rebel against, and the state has been in existence for only 5000 years. Obviously, then, in those societies, typified by tribes and bands and in other nonindustrial societies lacking central authority, there could not have been rebellion or political revolution.

REVITALIZATION MOVEMENTS One important aspect of rebellion and revolt as modes of forcible change is the revitalization process, already touched upon in Chapter 12. Revitalization may be defined as a deliberate attempt by some members of a society to construct a more satisfactory culture by the rapid acceptance of a pattern of multiple innovations.[13] Once primary ties of culture, social relationships, and activities are broken, and meaningless activity is imposed by force, individuals and groups characteristically react with fantasy, withdrawal, and escape.

Examples of revitalization movements have been common in the history of the United States whenever significant segments of the population have found their conditions in life to be at odds with the values of "the American Dream." For example, in the nineteenth century, periodic depression and the disillusionment of the decades after the Civil War produced a host of revitalization movements, of which the most successful was that of the Mormons. In the twentieth century, movements have repeatedly sprung up in the slums of major cities, as well as in depressed rural areas such as Appalachia. By the 1960s, a number of movements were becoming less inward-looking and more "activist"; a good example of this is the rise of the Black Muslim movement. The 1960s also saw the rise of revitalization movements among the young of middle-class and even upper-class families. In their case, the professed values of peace, equality, and individual freedom were seen to be at odds with the reality of persistent war, poverty, and constraints on individual action imposed by a variety of impersonal institutions. Their reaction to these things was expressed by their use of drugs, in their outlandish or "freaky" clothes, hair styles, music, speech, and in their behavior toward authority and authority figures.

By the 1980s, revitalization movements were becoming prominent even among older, more affluent segments of society, as in the rise of the Moral Majority. In these cases, the reaction is not so much against a perceived failure of "the American Dream" as it is against perceived threats to that dream, by dissenters and activists within their society, by foreign governments, by new ideas which challenge other ideas that they would like to believe, and by the sheer complexity of modern life.

Clearly, when value systems get out of step with existing realities, a condition of cultural crisis is likely to build up that may breed some form of reactive movement. Not all suppressed, conquered, or colonialized people eventually rebel against established authority, although why they do not is still a debated issue. When they do, how-

---

[12] E. Adamson Hoebel, *Anthropology: The Study of Man*, 4th ed. (New York: McGraw-Hill, 1972), p. 667.

[13] Anthony Wallace, *Culture and Personality*, 2d ed. (New York: Random House, 1970), pp. 188–199.

In Iran, the Ayatollah Khomeini led a revitalization movement which was in part revivalistic and in part revolutionary.

Revitalization movements that are revivalistic in nature are not restricted to Third World countries like Iran; in the United States Jerry Falwell is the leader of one such movement.

Transitional: A revitalization movement that attempts to speed up the acculturation process in order to share more fully in the supposed benefits of the dominant culture.

Millenarism: A revitalization movement that attempts to resurrect a suppressed pariah group which has long suffered in an inferior social position and which has its own special subcultural ideology.

Nativistic or revivalistic movement: A revitalization movement that tries to reconstitute a destroyed but not forgotten way of life.

Revolutionary: A revitalization movement from within directed primarily at the ideological system and the attendant social structure of a culture.

ever, resistance may take one of the following forms, all of which are varieties of revitalization movements. A culture may seek to speed up the acculturation process in order to share more fully in the supposed benefits of the dominant cultures—as in the example of the cargo cults—in which case it is called **transitional.** It may attempt to resurrect a suppressed pariah group that has long suffered in an inferior social standing and that has its own special subcultural ideology, and is then referred to as **millenarism;** the most familiar examples of this to us are prophetic Judaism and early Christianity. If a movement tries to reconstitute a destroyed but not forgotten way of life, as did the Ghost Dance of the Plains Indians, it is known as a **nativistic** or **revivalistic movement.** If the aim of the movement is directed primarily to the ideological system and the attendant social structure of a cultural system from within, it is then called **revolutionary.**

In the past few decades, Western countries have sent technological ''missionaries'' to teach people in other countries new ways of doing old tasks. Often, such ''missionaries'' are unaware of the side effects their new ways will have.

MODERNIZATION

One of the most frequently used terms to describe social and cultural change as these are occurring today is **modernization.** This is most clearly defined as an all-encompassing and global process of cultural and socioeconomic change whereby developing societies seek to acquire some of the characteristics common to most industrially advanced societies. If one looks very closely at this definition, one sees that ''becoming modern'' really means ''becoming like us,'' with the very clear implication that not being like us is to be antiquated and obsolete. Not only is this ethnocentric, it also fosters the notion that these other societies must be changed to be more like us, irrespective of other considerations. It is unfortunate that the term ''modernization'' continues to be so widely used. Since we seem to be stuck with it, the best we can do at the moment is to recognize its inappropriateness, even though we continue to use it.

The process of modernization may be best understood as consisting of four subprocesses, the first of which is technological development. In the course of modernization, simple traditional knowledge and techniques give way to the application of scientific knowledge and techniques borrowed mainly from the West. The second subprocess is agricultural development, represented by a shift from an emphasis on subsistence farming to commercial farming. Instead of raising crops and livestock for their own use, people turn more and more to the production of cash crops, with greater reliance on a cash economy and markets for the sale of farm products and purchase of goods. The third subprocess is industrialization, with a greater emphasis placed on inanimate forms of energy—es-

Structural differentiation. Where once most items in daily use were made at home, as in the quilting party shown above, today almost everything we use is the product of specialized production, as are the blouses shown below in a Japanese department store.

> **Modernization:** The process of cultural and socioeconomic change whereby developing societies acquire some of the characteristics of Western industrialized societies.

> **Structural differentiation:** The division of single traditional roles, which embrace two or more functions (for example, political, economic, and religious) into two or more roles, each with a single specialized function.

pecially fossil fuels—to power machines. Human and animal power become less important, as do handicrafts in general. The fourth subprocess is urbanization, marked particularly by population movements from rural settlements into cities.

As modernization takes place, other changes are likely to follow. In the political realm, political parties and some sort of electoral machinery frequently appear, along with the development of a bureaucracy. In education, there is an expansion of learning opportunities, literacy increases, and an indigenous educated elite develops. Religion becomes less important in many areas of thought and behavior as traditional beliefs and practices are undermined. The traditional rights and duties connected with kinship are altered, if not eliminated, especially where distant kin are concerned. Finally, where stratification is a factor, mobility increases as ascribed status becomes less important and achievement counts for more.

Two other features of modernization go hand in hand with those already noted. One, **structural differentiation,** is the division of single traditional roles, which embrace two or more functions, into two or more roles, each with a single specialized function. This represents a kind of fragmentation of society which must be counteracted by new **integrative mechanisms** if the society is not to disintegrate into a number of discrete units. These new mechanisms take such forms as new nationalistic ideologies, formal governmental structures, political parties, legal codes, labor and trade unions, and common-interest associations. All of these cross-cut other societal divisions and so serve to oppose differentiating forces. But these two forces are not the only ones in opposition in a situation of modernization; to them must be added a third, the force of **tradition.** This opposes the new forces both of differentiation and integration. On the other hand, the conflict does not have to be total. Traditional ways may on occasion facilitate modernization. For example, rural people may be assisted by traditional kinship ties as they move into cities if they have relatives already there to whom they may turn for aid. One's relatives, too, may provide the financing that is necessary for business success.

One aspect of modernization, the technological explosion, has made it possible to transport human beings and ideas from one place to another with astounding speed and in great numbers. Formerly independent cultural systems have been brought into contact with others. The cultural differences between New York and Pukapuka are declining, while the differences between fishing people and physicists are increasing. No one knows whether this implies a net gain or net loss in cultural diversity, but the world-wide spread of anything, whether it is DDT or a new idea, should be viewed with at least caution. That human beings and human cultural systems are different is the most exciting thing about them, yet the destruction of diversity is implicit in the world-wide spread of rock-and-roll, communism, capitalism, or any-

thing else. When a song is forgotten or a ceremony ceases to be performed, a part of the human heritage is destroyed forever.

An examination of some traditional cultures that have felt the impact of modernization or other cultural changes will help to pinpoint some of the problems these cultures have met. The cultures are the Pueblo Indians of the American Southwest, and the Skolt Lapps of Finland.

The Modern Pueblo Indians

The Pueblo Indians of the North American Southwest represent an interesting example of an entire culture that has been exposed to modernizing influences in the last century. The Pueblo, traditionally farming people with a population of about 200,000 have been studied by Edward Dozier, himself a Tewa Indian, and others.[14] Despite the influence for over 400 years of the Spanish and Anglo-American conquest, basic Pueblo culture and society have endured. Dozier attributes this to the retention of the large extended family and the community as primary units of socialization and the persistence of indigenous languages. The traditional network of kin and community relations has not been disturbed. Thus, these factors have formed the same personality types over the years and have continued to reproduce individuals faithful to Pueblo beliefs. Pueblo social structure has remained virtually intact because the Indians have been able to retain their basic ethical and moral concepts.

However, outside influences, primarily those of the materialistic and technological Anglo-American culture, have forced a number of cultural changes on the Pueblo.

---

[14] Edward P. Dozier, *The Pueblo Indians of North America* (New York: Holt, Rinehart and Winston, 1970), pp. 9–27.

Not surprisingly, many of these changes have arisen as a result of modifications in the Pueblo's traditional agrarian economy.

As a result of their exposure to and domination by Anglo-Americans, the Indians have abandoned subsistence farming as their primary economic occupation and have adopted the Western credit system and cash economy. Along with this, many facets of Pueblo life have changed. For example, the village, or *pueblo*, has lost many of its compact characteristics. Separate family adobe homes are replacing the traditional apartmentlike dwellings. Some of the more modernized villages include single-family dwellings similar to Anglo-American houses, complete with garage, lawn, trees, yard, and shrubbery. Many villages also have electricity, running water, and inside plumbing.

Family possessions also reveal the increased economic status of many of the Pueblos: the furnishings found in a modern Pueblo home are similar to those of many contemporary North American homes. In the Santa Clara pueblo of New Mexico, television antennas are as numerous as in any small U.S. town. Indeed, in some pueblos, the television set has replaced the traditional gathering of the bilateral kin group to listen to the old stories and legends. The formerly all-important corn-grinding equipment—*metates* and *manos*—is gone. Manufactured chairs and couches rest side by side with the trunk containing the ceremonial and dance paraphernalia. In many pueblos, the long pole suspended from the ceiling to hold the family's clothing and blankets has disappeared. While the Pueblos still wear their brightly colored dresses and shawls, they now purchase these items from stores rather than manufacture them themselves. Refrigerators and pantries have taken the place of the small back room where melons were stored and corn was

> **Integrative mechanisms:** Cultural mechanisms, such as nationalistic ideologies, formal governmental structures, political parties, legal codes, labor and trade unions, and common-interest associations, that oppose forces for differentiation in a society.

> **Tradition:** In a modernizing society, old cultural practices, which may oppose new forces of differentiation and integration.

stacked. The busy activities of the annual harvest time have been replaced by weekend shopping trips to the local supermarket.

In almost all pueblos, automobiles and pickup trucks furnish the transport once provided by horses and wagons. While farming on small land holdings continues, working for wages in nearby towns and cities has become an essential part of Pueblo life, and it does not seem probable that farming will ever return as the primary economic occupation. This is because Pueblo thinking remains customarily communal and small scale; those Pueblos who still practice farming are small operators compared to their profit-minded Anglo-American counterparts. The Indians tend to stick to their traditional planting of small plots of corn and garden crops rather than multiacre cash crops. Similarly, investment in land, livestock, and machinery are alien to Pueblo ways of thinking.

In spite of all the outward materialistic and economic changes, the Pueblo remain a communal people, maintaining much of their traditional social organization. Disagreements, which are common in every pueblo, are seen as family quarrels and have rarely broken up a village. In fact, many Pueblo communities occupy the

PORTFOLIO 3

"The Vanishing Cowboy"

In spite of its "melting pot" image of itself, the United States has long been a nation of subcultures, some of which have lasted longer than others. Of these, few have captured the public imagination like the cowboy subculture. Part of the reason for this was the early glorification of cowboy life by such notables as Theodore Roosevelt, the painter Frederick Remington, and the writer Owen Wister. These men, and those who came after them, tended to portray cowboys as heroic figures who epitomized such values of the larger culture as freedom, resourcefulness, and the ability to stand up for oneself and be one's own master. Even today, well into the space age, fascination with the cowboy continues, and Western novels still sell millions of copies. Indeed, some of today's space heroes of fiction, such as Buck Rogers, continue to act like cowboys, making their own decisions with casual disregard for authority and shooting it out with "bad guys," even though they ride spaceships rather than horses.

In view of the long-lasting interest in cowboys and all they supposedly stood for, it is of interest to note that the era of the true cowboy was short-lived, lasting at most for about a generation. To be sure, some elements of cowboy culture have survived to the present, but the cowboy himself has long since vanished, replaced by the domesticated ranch hand. The pictures that follow depict in brief the life of the cowhand today, on a ranch in Montana.

Cowboy culture came into being right after the Civil War, when by chance the right combination of elements existed: large numbers of tough ex-soldiers looking for something to do, a surplus of half-wild longhorn cattle in Texas, and refrigerated boxcars which could carry beef to the large Eastern markets without the meat spoiling on the way. Furthermore, the numbers of both Indians and buffalo had been drastically reduced on the plains, creating a kind of vacuum which allowed cattle to replace the buffalo as

Branding and calf pulling are still important activities on the ranch today.

Barbed wire—patented in 1874—changed the face of the West by denying the cowboy access to open rangeland. Yesterday's cowboy often attacked such fences with wire cutters; today's ranch hand spends much time patrolling and mending fences.

Today's ranch hand still ropes cattle from horseback, but fences help in the roundup.

Unlike the cowboy of old, today's ranch hand spends considerable time carrying feed to cattle.

the number one consumer of grass, and cowboys to replace Indians as harvesters of the number one grazing animal. Finally, the technology and techniques were there to be borrowed from the Mexican *vaqueros* south of the Rio Grande. The cowboy vocabulary reflects this, in words like *bandana, corral, rodeo,* and *sombrero,* or buckaroo (from *vaquero*), chaps (from *chaparejos*), lariat (from *la reata*), and ranch (from *rancho*). It is ironic that cowboys derived so much from the Mexicans, because as a rule, they held Mexicans in contempt.

Not only was true cowboy culture short-lived, but it differed significantly from the popular stereotype. True, it was a wild and free life, but it was also violent and brutal. On the range cowboys jockeyed for control of watering places and tried to monopolize choice rangeland through a variety of devious and unsavory tactics. The writer Alistair Cook put the situation aptly in the phrase: "out on the range, where seldom was heard a discouraging word, but the bellowing of poisoned cattle." In the cow towns, the death rate was ten to twenty times what it is in New York City today, where murders are not exactly unknown, and sensible citizens made it a point to stay out of those parts of town frequented by cowboys.

The era of the cowboy came to an end as the combination of factors that gave rise to it changed. The long cattle drives from Texas ended as more and more homesteaders and railroad lines interfered with them, and as new breeds of cattle derived from English and Scottish stock proved themselves superior to the longhorns, especially in the north. Then, too, the amount of open rangeland, most of which was government owned, diminished as railroads and homesteaders gobbled it up for themselves and as sheepmen competed for the remaining grazing land. Ultimately, the seemingly limitless rangelands proved quite limited. Barbed wire fences protected remaining grazing lands, while windmill-pumped tanks eliminated the need to range over vast areas for water.

A meeting of the Hopi tribal council. The Hopis and other pueblo peoples along with other Indians such as the Navajo constitute the fastest-growing segment of the population in the southwestern part of the United States today.

same sites they did for centuries before the Spanish came. One reason for the long life of the Pueblo community is found in the ways the Indians deal with deviants: discipline is harsh, and eviction from the community is not a rare punishment for a persistent wrongdoer. Another more important reason for the survival of the Pueblo is the integration found in Pueblo life-styles. Kroeber has described the integrative mechanisms of the Zuni; his description is as applicable to the other Pueblos:

Four or five different planes of systemization crosscut each other and thus preserve for the whole society an integrity that would speedily be lost if the planes merged and thereby inclined to encourage segregation and fission. The clans (among the Tanoans, extended families and moieties), the fraternities, the priesthoods, the kivas, in a measure the gaming parties, are all dividing agencies. If they coincided, the rifts in the social structure would be deep; by counter-

ing each other they cause segmentations which produce an almost marvelous complexity, but can never break apart the national entity.[15]

Just as the central core of Pueblo life remains, so do their religion and ceremonials, despite the fact that the farming life around which they were built no longer exists as the primary economic occupation. Pueblo religion still provides its members with recreational outlets and a strengthening of communal living and identity. Dozier theorizes that this may be sufficient to keep the religion alive and to maintain the positions required for the rich ceremonial and religious life. In the face of the Anglo-American economic influence, it is interesting that among many Pueblos there appears to be a

[15] Alfred L. Kroeber, quoted in Edward Dozier, *The Pueblo Indians of North America* (New York: Holt, Rinehart and Winston, 1970), p. 19.

religious upsurge, and many ceremonies which have long been in disuse have been resurrected and reenacted in a number of pueblos. This may be due to a revitalistic movement among the Indians, or it may have something to do with the Pueblo agricultural background. It has been observed that religion developed in an agricultural setting may survive in other settings. For example, the Yaquis, who like the Pueblos work for wages in the city, still believe and practice the ancient ceremonies of their religion. The same holds true for the Pueblo; while many of them work in neighboring cities, they continue to practice their age-old ceremonies.

Skolt Lapps and the Snowmobile Revolution

Unlike the tightly knit and communally organized Pueblo Indians who have successfully resisted many negative aspects of modernization, the Skolt Lapps of Finland have not.[16] The Skolt Lapps traditionally supported themselves by fishing and the herding of reindeer. Although they depended on the outside world for certain material goods, the resources crucial for their system were to be had locally and were for all practical purposes available to all. No one was denied access to critical resources, and there was little social and economic differentiation among people. Theirs was basically an egalitarian society.

Of particular importance to the Skolt Lapps was reindeer herding. Indeed, herd management is central to their definition of themselves as a distinct people. These animals were a source of meat, for home consumption or for sale in order to procure

outside goods. They were also a source of hides for shoes and clothing, sinews for sewing, and antler and bone for making certain things. Finally, reindeer were used to pull sleds in the winter and as pack animals when there was no snow on the ground. Understandably, the animals were the center of much attention. The herds were not large, but without a lot of attention, productivity suffered. Hence, most winter activities centered on reindeer. Men, operating on skis, were closely associated with their herds, intensively from November to January, periodically from January to April.

In the early 1960s, these reindeer herders speedily adopted snowmobiles, thinking that the new machines would make herding physically easier and economically more advantageous. The first machine arrived in Finland in 1962; by 1971, there were 70 operating machines owned by the Skolt Lapps and non-Lapps in the same area. Although men on skis still carry out some herding activity, their importance and prestige are now diminished. By 1967, only four people still used reindeer sleds for winter travel; most had gotten rid of draught animals. Those who had not converted to snowmobiles felt themselves unable to keep up with the rest.

The consequences of this mechanization were extraordinary and far reaching. The need for snowmobiles, parts and equipment to maintain them, and a steady supply of gasoline created a dependency on the outside world unlike anything that had previously existed. As traditional skills were replaced by snowmobile technology, the ability of the Lapps to determine their own survival without dependence on outsiders, should this be necessary, was lost. Snowmobiles are also expensive, costing on the order of $1000 (1973 dollars) in the Arctic. The needs of maintenance and for gasoline

---

[16] Pertti J. Pelto, *The Snowmobile Revolution: Technology and Social Change in the Arctic* (Menlo Park, Calif.: Cummings, 1973).

must be added to this initial cost. Accordingly, there has been a sharp rise in the need for cash. To get this, men must go outside the Lapp community for wage work more than just occasionally, as had once been the case, or else rely on such sources as government pensions or welfare.

The argument may be made that dependency and the need for cash are prices worth paying for an improved system of reindeer herding. But has it improved? In truth, the use of snowmobiles has contributed in a significant way to a disastrous decline in reindeer herding. By 1971, the average size of the family herd was down from 50 to 12. Not only is this too small a number to be economically viable, it is too small to maintain at all. The reason is that the animals in such small herds will take the first opportunity to run off to join another larger herd. What happened was that the old close, prolonged, and largely peaceful relationship between herdsman and beast changed to a noisy, traumatic relationship. Now, when men appear, it is to come speeding out of the woods on snarling, smelly machines that invariably chase animals, often for long distances. Instead of helping the animals in their winter food quest, helping females with their calves, and protecting them from predators, the appearance of men now means either slaughter or castration. Naturally enough, the reindeer have become suspicious. The result has been actual de-domestication, with reindeer scattering and running off to more inaccessible areas given the slightest chance. Moreover, there are indications that snowmobile harassment has adversely affected the number of viable calves added to the herds.

The cost of mechanized herding, and the decline of the herds, has led many Lapps to abandon it altogether. Now, the majority of males are no longer herders at all. This constitutes a serious economic problem, since few economic alternatives are available. The problem is compounded by the fact that participation in a cash-credit economy means that most people, employed or not, have payments to make. But this is more than just an economic problem, for in the traditional culture of this people, being a herder of reindeer is the very essence of manhood. Hence, the new non-herders are not only poor in a way that they could not be in previous times, but they are in a sense inadequate as "men" quite apart from this.

This economic differentiation with its evaluation of roles seems to be leading to the development of a stratified society out of the older egalitarian society. Differences are developing in terms of wealth, and with this, in life-styles. It is difficult to break into reindeer herding now, for one needs a substantial cash outlay. And herding now requires skills and knowledge that were not a part of traditional culture. Not everyone has these, and those without them are dependent on others if they are to participate. Hence, there is now a restricted access to critical resources, where once there had been none.

Modernization and the Third World

In the two examples that we have just examined, we have seen how modernization has affected tribal peoples in otherwise "modern" nations. Elsewhere in the so-called third world whole nations are in the throes of modernization. Throughout Africa, Asia, and Latin America, we are witnessing the widespread removal of economic activities from the family-community setting; the altered structure of the family in the face of the changing labor market; the increased reliance of young

Modernization among the Masai of East Africa. Young girls are being taught agriculture, a skill needed for adjustment to a settled way of life. The men of the tribe are being taught scientific methods of animal husbandry, such as vaccination against disease. As these changes take hold, the Masai will become more dependent on the outside world, and hence more vulnerable to fluctuations in a world economy over which they will have no control.

children on parents alone for affection instead of on the extended family; the decline of general paternal authority; schools replacing the family as the primary educational unit; the discovery of a generation gap; and many others. The difficulty is that it all happens so fast that traditional societies are unable to adapt themselves to it gradually. Changes that took generations to accomplish in Europe and North America are attempted within the span of a single generation in developing countries. In the process, they are frequently faced with the erosion of a number of dearly held values they had no intention of giving up.

Modernization: Must it Always Be Painful?

Although most anthropologists see the change that is affecting traditional, non-Western peoples caught up in the modern technological world as an ordeal, some scholars, like sociologist Alex Inkeles, see emerging from the process of modernization a new kind of person.[17] This person is a kind of prototype, who—whether from an African tribe, a South American village, or a North American city—will be open to accept and benefit from the changes in the modern world. The first element in Inkeles' definition of the modern person is a readiness for new experience and an openness to innovation and change. Here he is talking of a "state of mind, a psychological disposition, an inner readiness" rather than of specific techniques and skills an individual or group may possess because of an attained level of technology. In this sense, therefore, someone working with a wooden plow may be more modern in spirit than someone

[17] Alex Inkeles, "The Modernization of Man" in Myron Weiner, ed., *Modernization: The Dynamics of Growth* (New York: Basic Books, 1966), pp. 141–144.

in another part of the world who drives a tractor.

Second, an individual is more "modern" if he or she "has a disposition to form or hold opinions over a large number of the problems and issues that arise not only in [the] immediate environment but also outside of it. . ." Such people show awareness of the diversity of attitude and opinion around them rather than closing themselves off in the belief that everyone thinks alike and, indeed, is just like themselves. They are able to acknowledge differences of opinion without needing to deny differences out of fear that these will upset their own view of the world; they are also less likely to approach opinion in a strictly autocratic or hierarchical way.

Inkeles' view of modernization reflects the optimism that was characteristic of the Western world before the 1970s. The prevailing view was that not only could the non-Western world attain the high levels of development seen in Europe and North America, but even this was capable of improvement. Overlooked was the simple fact that the standard of living in the Western world is based on a rate of consumption of nonrenewable resources, where far less than 50 percent of the world's population uses a good deal more than 50 percent of these resources. North Americans, for example, who make up less than 10 percent of the world's population, consumed, in the early 1970s, about 66 percent of the world's annual output of copper, coal, and oil.[18] Such figures suggest that it is not realistic to expect most peoples of the world to achieve a standard of living comparable to that of the Western world in the near future, if at all. At the very least, the countries of the Western world would have to cut drastically their consumption of nonrenewable resources. So far, they have shown no disposition to do this, and if they did, their living standards would have to change. Yet more and more non-Western people, quite understandably, aspire to a standard of living such as Western countries now enjoy, even though the gap between the rich and poor people of the world is widening rather than narrowing. This has led to the development of what anthropologist Paul Magnarella has called a new "culture of discontent," a level of aspirations that far exceeds the bounds of an individual's local opportunities. No longer satisfied with traditional values, people all over the world are fleeing to the cities to find a "better life," all too often to live out their days in poor, congested, and diseased slums in an attempt to achieve what is usually beyond their reach. So far it appears that this, and not Inkeles' prototype, is the person of the future.

---

[18] Paul Magnarella, *Tradition and Change in a Turkish Town* (New York: Wiley, 1974), pp. 183–185.

CHAPTER SUMMARY

Although cultures may be remarkably stable, culture change is characteristic to a greater or lesser degree of all cultures. One cause of it may be a change in the environment, which requires an adaptive change in the culture. Another is individual variation in the way people within a culture perceive its characteristics; this may change the way the society interprets the norms and values of its culture. Finally, a culture may change as a result of contacts with other groups who introduce new ideas and ways, eventually bringing change in traditional values and behavior.

The rate and direction of culture change depends on several factors. These are the degree to which a culture encourages and approves flexibility; the particular needs of the culture at a specific time; and the degree of "fit" between the new trait and the existing cultural pattern. Individuals within a culture may find change difficult to accept, beneficial though it may appear to be.

The mechanisms involved in cultural change are invention, diffusion, cultural loss, and acculturation. Cultural change by means of invention is originated by an individual within the culture who discovers a new practice, tool, or principle. Other individuals adopt the invention, and it becomes socially shared. Primary inventions are chance discoveries of new principles, for example, the discovery that the firing of clay makes the material permanently hard. Secondary inventions are improvements made by applying known principles, for example, modeling the clay which is to be fired by known techniques into familiar objects. Primary inventions may prompt rapid culture change and stimulate other inventions. An invention's chance of being accepted depends on its superiority to the method or object it replaces. Its acceptance is also connected with the prestige of the inventor and imitating groups. Diffusion is the borrowing by one society of a cultural element from another. In general, some areas, such as technology, are much more susceptible to borrowing than are others, such as social organization. Cultural loss involves the abandonment of a cultural trait or practice without replacement. Anthropologists have given considerable attention to acculturation. It stems from intensive firsthand contact of groups with different cultures and produces major changes in the cultural patterns of one or both groups.

Colonial administration guided by an understanding of the native culture can avoid causing serious disruption of native culture. In most cases, however, colonialism has resulted in "culture crash": decimation, misery, and community degeneration. A struggle against externally imposed authority may be a rebellion, in which the aim is simply to oust the incumbents of offices, or it may be a revolution, in which attempts are made to change not only the incumbents but the nature of the offices, and to change belief systems and the social structure as well.

When value systems diverge too widely from the realities in a culture, a condition of cultural crisis may develop, and revitalization movements may appear. In a transitional revitalization movement, the culture tries to speed up the acculturation process in order to get more of the benefits it expects from the dominant culture. In millenarism it attempts to resurrect a pariah group with its subcultural ideology. Nativistic or revivalistic movements aim to reconstitute a destroyed but not forgotten way of life. Revolutionary movements try to reform the culture from within.

Modernization refers to a global process of cultural and socioeconomic change by which developing societies seek to acquire characteristics of industrially advanced societies. The process consists of four subprocesses; in order of appearance these are technological development, agricultural development, industrialization, and urbanization. Other changes follow in the areas of political organization, education, religion, and social organization. Two other accompaniments of modernization are structural differentiation and new forces of social integration. An example of modernization is found in the Pueblo Indians, who have retained their extended families and indigenous languages but adopted the U.S. economy and consumer goods. On the other hand, the Skolt Lapps of Finland have not been able to resist many aspects of modernization. With the coming of the snowmobile, this traditional reindeer herding economy was all but destroyed, with nothing to take its place.

SUGGESTED READING

Arensberg, Conrad M., and Arthur H. Niehoff. *Introducing Social Change: A Manual for Americans Overseas.* Chicago: Aldine, 1964.
    This is an excellent "eye opener," showing Westerners that what appear to be bad or inefficient ways of doing things have purpose and meaning in the matrix of the particular culture, and that failure to understand such customs can lead to disaster when programs of change, no matter how well meaning, are introduced.
Barnett, Homer G. *Innovation: The Basis of Cultural Change.* New York: McGraw-Hill, 1953.
    This is the standard work on the subject, widely quoted by virtually everyone who writes about change.
Kroeber, A. L. *Anthropology: Cultural Processes and Patterns.* New York: Harcourt, 1963.
    Several chapters of this work are given over to excellent discussions of innovation and diffusion. Particularly good are sections dealing with the histories of specific inventions.
Magnarella, Paul J. *Tradition and Change in a Turkish Town.* New York: Wiley, 1974.
    This book has been called one of the best anthropological community studies of the Middle East, but it is also an excellent introduction to the phenomenon known as modernization. There are none of the facile generalizations about modernization that one so often finds, and the author's view of the phenomenon, which is well documented, is quite different from that which was promoted in the optimistic days of the 1950s.
Tax, Sol, Sam Stanley, and others. "In Honor of Sol Tax," *Current Anthropology*, 1975, 16:507–540.
    Sometimes people who desire change set new goals for themselves and request help from anthropologists in reaching those goals. This is known as "action anthropology," a term invented by Sol Tax. Here, action anthropology is the subject of an up-to-date appraisal.

15 | The Future of Humanity

A Western Abenaki surveys an archeological site from which information about her own Native American heritage is being recovered. All around the world, ethnic groups are trying to either retain, or rediscover and reassert their own ethnic identities and traditions. A major question is: What is the future of human differences and how do they relate to the development of a global society?

PREVIEW

WHAT CAN ANTHROPOLOGISTS TELL US OF THE FUTURE?

Anthropologists cannot more accurately predict future forms of culture than biologists can predict future forms of life. They can, though, identify certain trends of which we might otherwise be unaware, and anticipate some of the consequences these patterns might have if they continue. They can also shed light on problems already identified by nonanthropologists by showing how these relate to each other as well as to cultural practices and attitudes of which "experts" in other fields are often unaware. This ability to place problems in their wider context is an anthropological specialty, and it is essential if these problems are ever to be solved.

WHAT PRESENT-DAY TRENDS ARE TAKING PLACE IN THE EVOLUTION OF CULTURE?

One major trend in present-day cultural evolution is toward the worldwide adoption of the products, technology, and practices of the industrialized world. However, this apparent gravitation toward a homogenized, one-world culture is opposed by another, very strong trend toward the development of culturally pluralistic societies. A third trend, of which we are just becoming aware, is that the problems created by cultural practices seem to be outstripping the capacity of culture to find solutions to problems.

WHAT PROBLEMS WILL HAVE TO BE SOLVED IF HUMANITY IS TO HAVE A FUTURE?

If humanity is to have a future, human cultures will have to find solutions to problems of population growth, crowding, food and other resource shortages, pollution, and a growing culture of discontent. One difficulty is that, up to now, there has been a tendency to see these as if they were discrete and unrelated. Thus, attempts to deal with one problem, such as short energy supplies, are often at cross purposes with attempts to deal with others, such as short food supplies, and vice versa. Another difficulty is that the importance of cultural values, such as food preferences, has not been given adequate attention in seeking solutions. Until these difficulties are understood and overcome, the problems are not likely to be resolved.

Anthropology is often described by those who know little about it as a backward-looking discipline. The most popular stereotype is that anthropologists devote all of their attention to the interpretation of the past and the description of present-day tribal remnants. Yet as we saw in Chapter 1, and will see again in Chapter 16, not even archeologists, the most backward-looking anthropologists, limit their interests to the past, nor are ethnologists uninterested in their own cultures. Moreover, anthropologists have a special concern with the future and the changes it may bring. Like all residents of Western industrialized societies, they wonder what the "postindustrial" society now being predicted will hold. They also wonder what changes the coming years will bring to non-Western cultures. As we saw in the preceding chapter, when non-Western peoples are thrown into contact with Western industrialized peoples their culture is rapidly changed, often for the worse, becoming both less supportive and less adaptive. How then can these threatened cultures adapt to the future?

THE CULTURAL FUTURE OF HUMANITY

Whatever the biological future of the human species, culture remains the mechanism by which people solve their problems of existence. Yet some anthropologists have noted with concern—and interpret as a trend—that the problems of human existence seem to be outstripping culture's ability to find solutions. The main problem seems to be that in solving existing problems culture inevitably poses new ones. The anthropologist Jules Henry once put it this way: "although culture is 'for' man, it is also 'against' him."[1] As we shall see, this is

Signs of a growing trend toward world-wide homogenization of culture include this supermarket in Mexico City that carries Bayer aspirin, Ritz crackers, and Nescafé, and these Zambian boys who earn their living by selling Coca-Cola.

[1] Jules Henry, *Culture against Man* (New York: Vintage Books, 1965), p. 12.

438

now posing serious new problems for human beings. What can anthropologists tell us about the culture of the future?

One-World Culture

A popular belief in recent years has been that the future world will see the development of a single homogeneous world culture. The idea that such a "one-world culture" is developing is based largely on the observation that developments in communication, transportation and trade so link the peoples of the world that they are increasingly wearing the same kinds of clothes, eating the same kinds of food, reading the same kinds of newspapers, watching the same kinds of television programs, and so on. The continuation of such trends, so this thinking goes, should lead North Americans traveling in the year 2100 to Tierra del Fuego, Peking, or New Guinea to find the inhabitants of these areas living in a manner identical or similar to them.

Certainly, it is striking the extent to which such things as Western-style clothing, transistor radios, Coca-Cola and McDonald's hamburgers have spread to virtually all parts of the world, and many countries—Japan, for example—have gone a long way toward becoming "Westernized." Moreover, if one looks back over the past 5000 years of human history, one will see that there has been a clearcut trend for political units to become larger and more all-encompassing, while becoming at the same time fewer in number. A logical outcome of the continuation of this trend into the future would be reduction of autonomous political units to a single one, encompassing the entire world. In fact, by extrapolation from this past trend into the future, some anthropologists have gone so far as to predict that the world will become politically integrated perhaps by the twenty-third century, but by the year 4850 at the latest.[2]

The simple extrapolation of past trends into the future is a technique commonly used by economists, sociologists, political scientists, politicians, planners, and "futurologists" of just about every sort. The fallacy of this technique, however, has been clearly indicated by the anthropologist George Cowgill as follows: "It is worth recalling the story of the person who leaped from a very tall building and on being asked how things were going as he passed the 20th floor replied 'Fine, so far.'"[3] In other words, we should not expect trends to continue indefinitely into the future.

To project into the future the increase in size and reduction in number of political units that we have seen in the past seems unwarranted at the moment, given the strong upsurge in separatist movements, many of them ethnically based, in all parts of the world today. Examples—by no means exhaustive—include French separatism in Canada, Puerto Rican nationalism in the United States, Basque and Catalonian nationalist movements in Europe, Scottish, Irish, and Welsh nationalist movements in Britain, Ukrainian nationalism in the Soviet Union, Kurdish nationalism in Turkey, Iran, and Iraq, Bangladesh separatism in Pakistan, Ibo separatists in Nigeria, and Namibian nationalists in southwestern Africa. These range in violence all the way from the successful fight for independence from Pakistan on the part of Bangladesh, to the nonviolence of Scottish and Welsh nationalism. In addition to these and other separatist movements, expansionist attempts on the part of some nations—the

[2] Carol R. Ember and Melvin Ember, *Cultural Anthropology*, 3rd ed. (Englewood Cliffs, N.J.: Prentice Hall, 1981), p. 245.

[3] George L. Cowgill, Letter, *Science*, 1980, 210:1305.

Soviets in Afghanistan, the Vietnamese in Cambodia, the Iraqis in Iran, the Guatemalans in Belize, for example—have not been notably successful. In short, far from growing in size and decreasing in number, political units at the moment are showing a strong tendency to come apart; to fragment into a greater number of smaller units.

Many people today sincerely believe that a single culture for all the world's people would be a good thing, for it might offer fewer chances for the kinds of misunderstandings to develop that, so often in the past few hundred years, have led to wars. Some anthropologists question this, though, in the face of evidence that traditional ways of thinking of oneself and the rest of the world may persist, even in the face of massive changes on other aspects of culture. Indeed, one might argue that the chances for misunderstandings actually increase; an example of this is the Penobscot Indian land claims case we mentioned in Chapter 5. Many non-Indian residents of the State of Maine simply cannot comprehend how a people who look and act so

much like themselves could not see things as they do.

Some have argued that perhaps a generalized world culture would be desirable in the future, because certain fully developed cultures of today may be too specialized to survive in a changed environment. Examples of this situation are sometimes said to abound in modern anthropology. When a traditional culture that is highly adapted to a specific environment, such as that of the Indians of Brazil, who are well adapted to a life in a tropical rain forest, meets European-derived culture and the social environment changes suddenly and drastically, the traditional culture often collapses. The reason for this, it is argued, is that its traditions and its political and social organizations are not at all adapted to the new ways. Usually, such societies adopt many of the cultural features of the Western societies to which they have been exposed.

A problem with this argument is that far from being unable to adapt, traditional societies in places like Brazil's Amazon for-

These Australian Aborigines are calling relatives to ceremonies over a short wave radio powered by solar batteries. Indigenous peoples can manage to adapt themselves to the modern world without losing their own distinctive identity, providing they are left alone to do so.

est are often given no chance to work out their own adaptations. In eastern Ecuador, for example, Jivaro Indians have so far managed to adapt themselves to the modern world without losing their own distinctive ethnic and cultural identity. But in Brazil, the pressures to "develop" the Amazon are so great that whole groups of people are swept aside as multinational corporations and agribusiness pursue their own particular interests. People do not have much chance to work out their own adaptations to the modern world if they are transported en masse from their homelands and deprived literally overnight of their means of survival so that more acreage can be devoted to sugar cane, from which alcohol is distilled to help fuel all the automobiles of Rio. This is precisely the sort of thing that not only has been, but still is taking place in Brazil right now.

There is an important issue at stake in such situations, for what has happened is that some of the world's people have defined others, indeed, whole societies, as obsolete. This is surely a dangerous precedent, which if allowed to stand means that any of the world's people may at some time in the future be declared obsolete by someone else.

The Rejection of Modernity

In spite of the worldwide adoption of such things as Coca-Cola and the "Big Mac," and in spite of pressure for traditional cultures to disappear, it is clear that cultural differences are still very much with us in the world today. In fact, there seems to be a strengthening tendency for peoples all around the world to resist, and in many cases retreat from, modernization. Manifestations of this to which we have already alluded are the separatist movements around the world, and the success so far of the Jivaro in retaining their own ethnic and cultural identity. A closer look at a people who are in no hurry to give up their traditional ways is afforded by the following original study.

ORIGINAL STUDY

Resistance to Modernization among the Kwaio[4]

When I first began fieldwork among the Kwaio of the Solomon Islands in the Southwest Pacific, in 1962, they were very striking in that they continued to practice their ancestral religion, their economy was still based on subsistence and the quest for prestige using strung shell valuables. Their preoccupation with traditional life was very striking then. I felt quite privileged to stumble on, not totally by accident, a Melanesian way of life which was very much like the kinds of societies that existed in the 1910s, the 1920s, the sort of thing Malinowsky encountered in the Trobriands. But here I was in the 1960s, filled with zeal that I could do ethnography better and in new ways and I was in a

---

[4] From an interview with Roger Keesing for KOCE-TV, Huntington Beach, Calif., held in Los Angeles, December, 1981.

strikingly conservative cultural enclave. Not that it had been isolated. These people had been in touch with things Western for almost a century by that time and the fathers and, in some cases, grandfathers of men who were my inform- ants had been in Queensland, in Fiji, and in the early labor trade. So, this was somehow a way of life that had endured despite their engagement with things Western. I've been back many times since then—seven times I think. I have lived there almost five years now totally and I'm in continuous touch with the community still. What's striking about them now is what was striking about them then but even more so. Whereas people in the third world are supposed to be hell-bent on modernization and are supposed to be increasingly caught up in the cash economy, the quest for transistors and Toyotas, these people still living in their mountain hamlets are quite consciously rejecting all that, or most of it, and continue to sacrifice pigs to their ancestors, use strung shell valuables for feasting and base their economy on subsistence self-sufficiency, and live in thatched houses built on mud floors. They have many options to change, to move out, to move to the coast, missionaries have been trying to convert them since about 1905, and before that many worked in the sugar fields of Queens- land. So this is a defiantly conservative stance. These people are really opting for the past rather than the present and the future as a deliberate conscious strategy of a better way to live.

When I first worked among the Kwaio I thought that this was a way of life, however fascinating, that was transient, and was going to disappear in the next decade. There was a Seventh Day Adventist hospital going in down the coast, the country was moving toward independence—slowly in those days—and the penetration of the modern world economy seemed to be increasing by leaps and bounds. So, my bets were that this way of life had a ten- or fifteen- year life span and that the people would move down to the coast in masses or in a slow trickle and become Christian and hence, committed in various ways to things Western. I'm surprised that that hasn't happened. It's happened a bit. The ranks get thinned year by year a little bit. But still, for example, when a religious ritual is conducted, there may be a 60- or 70-year old grandfather dancing along with his son, and his young grandson is being instructed in this. So, it's very much a living way of life still. Even people who work on planta- tions, say, come back and immediately pick up their pan pipes. I was quite struck in 1977 when I was back when a young man came in a seaplane he had chartered from Honiara, the national capital. He came wearing Western clothes, sunglasses, and looking very spiffy, and I didn't recognize him. He had a very prosperous, good-paying job by local standards and he said he would come home for Christmas. The next day I saw him at a feast I went to up in the mountains and he had discarded every stitch of his clothes and was stark naked in traditional fashion, sitting around playing pan pipes. Gone were the sunglasses and the wristwatch and the whole lot, you know. And what's strik- ing about this is that this kind of separation of an engagement with the Western world and then a return to the old one is a hundred and ten years old now. This has been going on since the 19th century, long before these people were "pacified." There is an incredible stability and resilience about this way of life.

North Americans often have difficulty adjusting to the fact that not everyone wants to be just like us. As children, we are taught to believe that "The American Way of Life" is one to which all other peoples aspire. But it isn't only people like the Kwaio who resist becoming "just like us." There are in the world today whole nations that, having striven to emulate Western ways, have suddenly backed off. The most striking recent case of such a retreat from modernity is Iran. With the overthrow of the Shah, a policy of deliberate modernization was abandoned in favor of a radical attempt to return to an Islamic republic out of a past "golden age." A somewhat similar though far less radical retreat from modernity seemed to be under way in the United States, which, in 1980, elected a government dedicated to a return to certain "traditional values" out of its past. It is interesting to note some other parallels between

> **Cultural pluralism: Social and political interaction within the same society of people with different ways of living and thinking.**

the two situations; in Iran, the government is headed by a fundamentalist religious leader and in the United States members of the administration and some members of congress have shown themselves to be particularly sympathetic to fundamentalist religious views;[5] in Iran, Western-style dress was outlawed for women, who were ordered to return to traditional-style clothing, while in the United States, women on the White House staff were told that pants were no longer acceptable dress, and were ordered to wear skirts.

Cultural Pluralism

If a single homogeneous world culture is not necessarily the wave of the future, what is? Some see **cultural pluralism,** in which more than one culture exists in a given society, as the future condition of humanity. Cultural pluralism is the social and political interaction within the same society of people with different ways of living and thinking. Ideally, it implies the rejection of bigotry, bias, and racism in favor of respect for the cultural traditions of other peoples. In reality, it has rarely worked out that way.

An example of one form of cultural pluralism may be found in New York City, where the Puerto Ricans, who have their own cultural traditions and values, exist side by side with other New Yorkers. The Puerto Ricans have their own language,

All large North American cities contain pockets of immigrant cultures; shown here is a Spanish market in New York City.

music, religion, food; some live in their own *barrio* or neighborhood. This particular pluralism, however, may be of a temporary nature, a stage in the process of integration into what is sometimes referred to as "standard American culture." Thus, the Puerto Ricans, in four or five generations, like the Italians, Irish, and Jews before them, may also become North Americanized to the point where their life-style will be indistinguishable from others around them.

The United States, then, does not have a truly culturally pluralistic society where distinct cultures flourish. Rather, it has attempted to be a "melting pot" society where many cultures are supposed to be absorbed into the mainstream of North American culture. This hasn't been altogether successful, however, and there are signs that a true pluralism may be emerging. Blacks, American Indians, Chicanos, and Puerto Ricans are proclaiming their intentions of retaining identifiable cultural identities. Moreover, other ethnic and religious minorities have not completely abandoned their individual identities. This could be the beginning of a trend away from the "melting pot" philosophy and toward real pluralism.

Some other examples of cultural pluralism may be found in Switzerland, where Italian, German, and French cultures exist side by side; in Belgium, where the French Walloons and the Flemish each have different cultural heritages; and in Canada, where French- and English-speaking Canadians live in a pluralistic society. An excellent example of a recently formed (1960) culturally pluralistic society is that of the Federal Republic of Nigeria, in West Africa.

NIGERIAN CULTURAL PLURALISM Nigeria, with a population in excess of 58 million, is heterogeneous, with a variety of cultures

and languages, nearly 100 of which have been recorded. The three chief languages are spoken by the country's three principal entities—the Ibo, Yoruba, and Hausa—each of which has its own customs, religion, and political organization.

For example, the Ibo, who live in southeast Nigeria, represent a combination of village groups related by a common language and culture. Their social organization is based on kinship groups, most of which practice ancestor worship and live on land containing spirit shrines. Ibo political organization is a form of democracy whose center is the village. Their religion is a combination of ancestor worship and belief in natural forces, but most Ibo have recently converted to Christianity.

Across Nigeria, the Yoruba live in southwestern Nigeria on the Guinea Coast, predominantly in large urban centers. These cities are basically communities of farmers and groups of people joined by kinship. Their political organization is stronger than that of the Ibo: they have powerful state governments, each with a king and bureaucracy. Traditional Yoruba religion had an elaborate pantheon; however, Christianity and Islam have made considerable inroads into the traditional beliefs.

In northern Nigeria live the Hausa and the pastoral Fulani peoples. The Hausa developed principles of kinship, chieftainship, and office in centralized emirates. A strong element of Islamic religion and social forms is found in Hausa society, and its members pride themselves on their tradition of literacy in Arabic.

In the last century, the pastoral Fulani settled in Hausaland and unseated the Hausas as the source of power in northern Nigeria. In Hausaland, many Fulani have given up their all-important cattle culture and have become assimilated into the

Hausa by marriage. Unlike the Hausa, the Fulani have an egalitarian form of political organization. The Fulani are Moslems; as pastoral nomads, they have played a major role in the spread of Islam in West Africa.

Thus, in Nigeria, a number of ancient, fully integrated, fully developed separate cultures are trying to exist side by side, united politically and economically into a modern republic. Although the policy of cultural pluralism is endorsed by many of the nation's diverse peoples, the Nigerian attempt at pluralism has had its problems. A few years ago, the Ibos sought to break away and establish their own independent state of Biafra in a bloody battle with other Nigerians. Unfortunately, this sort of trouble has been all too common in pluralistic countries; recent examples include the troubles in Northern Ireland, Lebanon, and Cambodia. Switzerland may be about the only country where pluralism has really worked out to the satisfaction of all parties to the arrangement, but that may be because they are all heirs to a common European cultural tradition, in spite of their linguistic differences. The more divergent cultural traditions are, the more difficult it appears to be to make pluralism work.

ETHNOCENTRISM   The major problem associated with cultural pluralism relates to the concept of ethnocentrism, the belief that one's own culture is better than all others. In its natural form, ethnocentrism identifies the positive way individuals feel about their own culture; it serves to strengthen the individual's ego and social ties to the group. In many societies, this concept is important because it provides the individual with a world outlook and eases that person's social integration and adjustment as well. Ethnocentrism is stronger than patriotism or loyalty, because is assumes that a culture is superior in every aspect—art, science, religion, poli-

The difficulty in making pluralistic societies work is illustrated by the recent fighting between Christians and Muslims in Lebanon. This 1982 photo shows a street in Beirut, that nation's capital.

tics, economics—to all other cultures.

In its virulent form, ethnocentrism is a form of cultural evangelism that is often characterized by militaristic or aggressive tendencies on the part of one culture as it tries to spread its beliefs to other cultures. Among big industrialized nations, ethnocentrism is often stretched to the point that the society may be blinded by its belief in its own "rightness." It is rationalized and made the basis for programs often detrimental to the well-being of other societies being influenced. This, of course, gives rise to social problems such as unrest, hostility, and outright war.

Melville Herskovits argued that any culture that institutionalizes ethnocentrism is, in the end, basing its policy on a psychocultural unreality.[6] No culture, he argued, is a commodity for export. No society can, by conquest or persuasion, influence another society to change its entire life-style. When such a practice is attempted, it must fail because the original culture is rarely entirely lost; some aspects of it always appear in some form.

Virulent ethnocentrism has been practiced by European countries, such as England, France, and Spain, in their colonial policies toward India, America, and Africa. The United States has also practiced a form of economic and political ethnocentrism. Interpreting through its own culture the

---

[6] Melville J. Herskovits, *Cultural Dynamics* (New York: Knopf, 1964).

Housing constructed of sheet metal for Blacks in Namibia, where temperatures climb above 100 degrees, provided by the government of South Africa. Under apartheid, blacks are supposed to live in separate reserves apart from whites, but because all menial work is performed by blacks, some must live in white areas. Those who do must live in barracks with others of the same sex; they are not permitted to have spouses or children with them, no matter how long their period of labor.

biblical injunction to help fellow humans, the United States, convinced that its way of life is best, has attempted to spread its way to various non-Western nations by extending to them economic and political aid. In many cases, such aid has led to the destruction of the country's traditional cultures, resulting in power struggles and bloodshed and the loss of economic and social welfare.

Perhaps the most memorable example of this form of ethnocentrism in recent history can be found in Nazi Germany. The Germans under Hitler thought themselves to be the master race destined to rule the world. They wished to impose their entire culture—art, policies, technology, language, religion—on the countries they conquered. Their ethnocentrism resulted in a devastating world war in which millions of people perished. Today, various degrees of institutionalized ethnocentrism can be seen in Russia, China, and other Communist societies, as well as in many non-communist countries in Africa, Latin America, the Far East, and the Middle East.

One thing that emerges clearly from the discussion so far is that we can no more accurately predict future forms of culture than biologists can predict future forms of life. The fact is that the cultural future of humanity will be shaped by decisions that we humans will be making in the future. That being so, it behooves us to have a realistic understanding of the way things are in the world today if those decisions are to be made intelligently. Accordingly, a number of anthropologists have decided to put their distinctive expertise—the ability to see things as a whole—to work on the world situation today. They are attempting to look at the world as it exists today as a kind of global society in which all the world's peoples are bound by interdependency. Combining this with another anthropological specialty—making cross-cultural comparisons—an interesting if unsettling picture emerges.

Global Apartheid

Apartheid, which is the official policy of the government of South Africa, consists of programs or measures that aim at the maintenance of racial segregation.[7] Structurally, it serves to maintain the dominance of a "white" minority over a non-white majority through the social, economic, political, military, and cultural constitution of society. Non-whites are denied effective participation in political affairs, are restricted as to where they can live and what they can do, and are denied the right to travel freely. Whites, by contrast, control the government including, of course, the military and police. Although there are 4.7 non-whites for every white, being white and belonging to the upper stratum of society tend to go together. The richest 20 percent of South Africa takes 58 percent of the country's income and enjoys a high standard of living, while the poorest 40 percent of the population receives but 6.2 percent of the national product.

What has South Africa to do with a global society? Structurally, the latter is very similar—almost a mirror image of South Africa's society, even though there is no official policy of global apartheid. In the world society about two-thirds of the population is non-white and one-third white. In the world as a whole, being white and belonging to the upper stratum tend to go together. Although this upper stratum is not a homogeneous group, including as it does communist and non-communist peoples, neither is the upper stratum of South Afri-

---

[7] Material on global apartheid is drawn from Gernot Kohler, "Global Apartheid," *World Order Models Project Working Paper Seven* (New York: Institute for World Order, 1978).

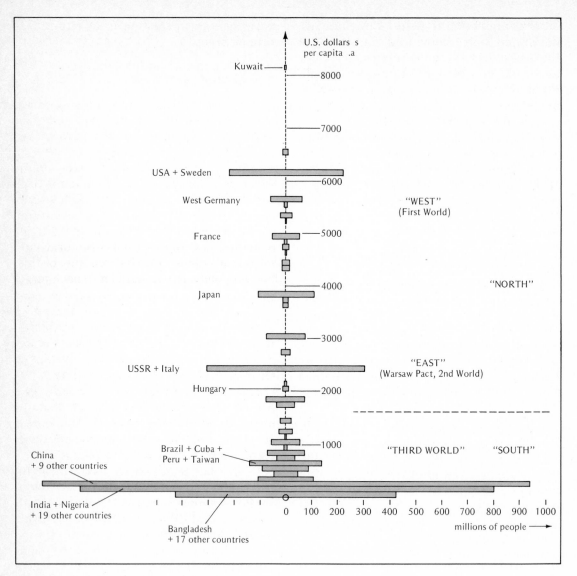

World income tree.

Vertical axis = GNP per capita (US$) intervals of 100
Horizontal axis = number of persons living at each income level.

can society, where there is friction between the English, who control business and industry, and the Afrikaners, who control the government and military. In the world, the poorest 40 percent of the population receives about 5.2 percent of the world product, while the richest 20 percent takes about 71.3 percent of world income. Life expectancy, as in South Africa, is poorest among non-whites. Most of the world's weapons of mass destruction are owned by whites: United States, U.S.S.R., France, and Britain. As in South Africa, death and suffering from war and violence is distributed unequally; in the world, 70 percent of the population suffers over 90 percent of violent death in all categories.

One could go on, but enough has been said to make the point: the parallels between the current world situation and that in South Africa are striking. We may sum up global apartheid as a de facto:

structure of world society which combines socioeconomic and racial antagonisms and in which (1) a minority of whites occupies the pole of affluence, while a majority composed of other races occupies the pole of poverty; (2) social integration of the two groups is made extremely difficult by barriers of complexion, economic position, political boundaries, and other factors, (3) economic development of the two groups is interdependent; (4) the affluent white minority possesses a disproportionately large share of the world society's political, economic, and military power. Global apartheid is thus a structure of extreme inequality in cultural, racial, social, political, economic, military and legal terms, as in South African apartheid.[8]

Since condemnation of South African apartheid has been close to universal, and since global apartheid is, if anything, even more severe, we ought to be much more concerned about it than we have been up to now.

PROBLEMS OF STRUCTURAL VIOLENCE

One of the consequences of a system of apartheid, be it official or unofficial, national or global, is a great deal of **structural violence;** that is, violence that is exerted by

---

[8]Kohler, p. 4.

> Structural violence: Violence exerted by situation, institutions, and social, political, and economic structures.

situations, institutions, social, political and economic structures. When a person dies of starvation, for example, it is because he or she has no access to food. As far as that person is concerned, the effect is violent, even though the system of food production and distribution was to blame, rather than the hostile act of a specific individual. The source of the violence was an anonymous structure, and this is what structural violence is all about. In what remains of this chapter, there is not sufficient space to go into all aspects of structural violence, but we can look at some aspects of it that have been of particular concern to anthropologists. They are of concern to other specialists, too, and anthropologists draw on the work of these specialists as well as their own, thereby fullfilling their traditional role as synthesizers (discussed in Chapter 1). Moreover, anthropologists are less apt than other specialists to see these aspects of structural violence as discrete and unrelated. Thus, they have a key contribution to make to our understanding of such modern-day problems as overpopulation, food shortages, pollution, and widespread discontent in the world.

Population Growth

One of the most critical problems facing humanity in the future is the so-called "population explosion." We are not sure yet whether urbanization and crowding themselves are serious problems, but there can be no doubt about the urgency of the crises that accompany rapid population increase, such as famine, poverty, social unrest, and psychological stress.

The fight against disease, carried on by such groups as the World Health Organization, has led to great increases in world population; the picture of a middle-class suburb in Nigeria typifies the problems of population growth and rising expectations.

Because of such factors as increased longevity, improved agricultural techniques, and advances in medicine, population has grown at a dramatically increasing rate throughout recent history.

This, in turn, has created serious new problems which so far have outstripped culture's ability to find solutions. Thus, we have a prime example of new problems being created as a direct result of culture's success at solving certain other problems.

Population growth is more than a simple addition of people. If this were so, the addition of 20 people a year to a population of 1000 would result in that population's being doubled in 50 years. But because the people added produce more people, the doubling time is actually much less than 50 years. Hence, it took the whole of human history and prehistory for the world's population to reach one billion people, which it had by 1850. By 1950, world population had reached almost 2.5 billion, representing an annual growth rate of about 0.8 percent. Between 1950 and 1960, the rate of growth had climbed to 1.8 percent (doubling time 39 years), and in the 1960s, fluctuated between 1.8 percent and 2 percent (doubling time 35 years at 2 percent).[9] There are now over four billion people in the world, with growth rates ranging from about 1 percent (Europe and North America) to 2.6 percent (Africa and South Asia) to close to 3 percent (Latin America).[10]

Food Shortage

The foremost question deriving from the burgeoning world population is simply, "How can so many people be fed?" On a worldwide scale, many people think humanity is faced with the prospect of possible exhaustion of its traditional food re-

[9] Paul R. Ehrlich and Anne H. Ehrlich, *Population, Resources, Environment* (San Francisco: Freeman, 1970), pp. 17–23.

[10] James R. Echols, "Population vs. the Environment: A Crisis of Too Many People," *American Scientist*, 1976, 64:166.

sources. Prior to World War II, sufficient food was produced in the world that all geographic regions except Western Europe were exporters of food. Until the 1960s, world food production more or less kept pace with population growth, although by the mid-sixties, food was becoming increasingly scarce. It was then that the "green revolution" was launched.

The green revolution represented a major effort to expand food production in the poor countries of the world. New high-yield strains of grains—especially wheat, rice, and corn—were developed, which could under the proper conditions double the yields of native grains. High energy inputs are required, especially in fertilizers and pesticides. Some dramatic results have come out of the green revolution.[11] India doubled its wheat crop in six years, and by early 1970 was on the verge of grain self-sufficiency. The Philippines ended half a century of dependence on imported rice and by the late sixties was an important exporter. These and other success stories led to a general air of optimism that the world could be provided with enough food to feed its population well into the future, although the originators of the green revolution were less optimistic; they warned that the program was only buying time and that controls on population growth were essential.

In spite of the accomplishments of the green revolution, the impressive output of North American agriculture, and improved fish catches (70 million tons in 1970 versus 22 million tons in 1950)[12], by 1973, population growth was again overtaking food production. In 1972, the world's surplus stocks

and excess production capacity stood at about 69 days; in 1973, the figure was down to 55 days and in 1974, to 33 days.[13] India, which was on the verge of grain self-sufficiency, now imports huge amounts of grain. By 1975, the Philippines had changed from a major exporter to a large-scale importer. Mexico, which exported 10 percent of its grain crop between 1965 and 1969, was forced by one of the world's fastest-growing populations to import 20 percent of its grain needs by the mid-1970s. Of 115 countries for which data are readily available, all but a few now import grain. Not one new exporter has emerged in the last 25 years, while many have gone the other way. Several developing and developed countries are importing more foods than they produce.

One response to this worsening food situation is to increase food production. There have been major advances in producing high-yield crops, but there is increasing doubt that the advances of the green revolution can be repeated. Nor is it likely that new sea-harvesting techniques will produce more seafood; already overfishing and the loss to "development" of estuaries, which are vital to the breeding of marine life, have resulted in declining catches. Intensification of agriculture—that is, conversion to mass production on huge holdings throughout the world—might increase yields, but this would go against cultural values in many areas. Such a plan would also entail production costs beyond the reach of the poorer countries. Finally, intensive agriculture relies on one-crop cultivation, making crops especially vulnerable to destruction by insects or diseases. Moreover, the widespread use of pesticides has led to the appearance of genetically resistant species of pests.

[11] Lester R. Brown, "The World Food Prospect," *Science*, 1975, 190:1058.

[12] Brown, p. 1059.

[13] Brown, p. 1053.

One possibility is to increase the amount of land in production. Since most of the world's unfarmed land is marginal, bringing it into production would be costly and would run a high risk of soil erosion, depletion, and conversion to desert. In the case of dry lands, costly irrigation is necessary, but most choice dam sites are already exploited, and some existing dams are becoming clogged with silt. Meanwhile, urban growth in North America and elsewhere continues to swallow up prime farmland, as coastal "development" has swallowed up the estuaries necessary for the breeding of marine life. All too often it is economically more profitable to subdivide land for development rather than to farm it or to leave it alone for the breeding of marine life. The problem is compounded by cultural values which equate "modernization" with abandonment of farming, which is seen as somehow less "advanced" than other economic pursuits.

In spite of these problems, land is available which can be brought into production, if care is taken not to overexploit it; here anthropologists can play a key role. For example, archeologists working at the ancient Mayan site of Tikal in northern Guatemala have recently discovered that large populations were supported in the past by a combination of kitchen gardening and raised field agriculture, with some slash-and-burn agriculture besides. At least one current research project is specifically designed to provide knowledge of these long-forgotten systems to aid present-day Guatemalans to increase agricultural production.[14] Similarly, studies of cultural adaptation in the Amazon basin have led anthropologist Betty Meggars to suggest that a program of intensive breeding of

Technological advances, such as the development of harvesting machines, allow increased food production. But these advances require fossil fuels, which are becoming more costly and are in shorter supply.

manatees—aquatic herbivorous animals —and water turtles for meat, coupled with fish culture and tree cropping, would be far more productive over the long run than the cattle raising and intensive farming now being promoted.[15] Cattle are ill suited to the region, and intensive farming more suited to temperate climates than the Tropics produces deterioration of the soil which probably is irreversible.

Although bringing more land into production, if not overdone, could produce some immediate benefits, it is not a long-term solution to the world's food problems. The large agricultural production of North America, as well as the success of the green revolution, depend upon huge inputs of fossil energy. Natural gas is essential for the manufacture of nitrogen fertilizers, as is coal for the manufacture of the steel used in

[14] Thomas P. Myers, ed., "Current Research," *American Antiquity* (July 1979), 44(2):610.

[15] Betty J. Meggars, *Amazonia* (Chicago, Aldine, 1971), p. 155.

farm machinery. Petroleum is essential for the manufacture of herbicides, fungicides, and pesticides, as well as for the running of machinery used to plant, cultivate, spray, irrigate, and harvest. Indeed, it takes as much energy to grow one acre of cauliflower as it does to build a six-passenger car, and the equivalent of 80 gallons of gasoline is used to produce an acre of corn.[16] It is estimated that growing raw agricultural commodities might require 60 to 180 percent more fuel energy in the next 25 years.[17] Yet as we all know fuel costs have been escalating and fossil fuels are in short supply (the present world "oil glut" to the contrary notwithstanding).

The consequences of short energy supplies are vividly indicated by the estimated one-million ton drop in India's wheat crop in the spring of 1975, which was brought about by a shortage of fuel for irrigation pumps.[18] A dependence on animal manure instead of manufactured fertilizer would help with the energy problem, but there is not enough of it, and it is being used increasingly as a fuel. Inevitably, sooner or later, fossil fuels will become scarcer, and as this scarcity becomes more acute, food production will decline. First, rising costs will deprive the poorer countries of fossil fuels (as has already happened to some degree), but ultimately all countries will feel the effects. Indeed, rising costs and diminishing returns are clearly linked to sharp price rises in food over the past decade.

---

[16] G. H. Heichel, "Agricultural Production and Energy Resources," *American Scientist*, 1976, 64:65; D. Pimentel, L. E. Hurd, A. C. Bellotti, M. J. Forster, I. N. Oka, O. D. Sholes, and R. J. Whitman, "Food Production and the Energy Crisis," *Science*, 1973, 182:448.

[17] Brown, p. 72.

[18] Brown, p. 1056.

In addition to becoming scarcer and more expensive, the petrochemicals necessary for chemical-intensive farming are known to have a long-term deleterious effect on farming, regardless of short-term benefits. For one thing, practices related to their use are resulting in loss of topsoil at an alarming rate, and for another, they lead to a loss of genetic variability in crops. In spite of this, the prevailing attitude that chemical-intensive farming is "more advanced" leads us to pursue it at almost literally all cost. A recent government study demonstrated conclusively that organic farming was viable on a commercial scale, and yet the U.S. Department of Agriculture has phased out its interest in organic farming. As the No. 2 man in the Department phrased it on a news program in the fall of 1982: "Common sense tells us it won't work."

The problem of food production is further compounded by cultural practices that call for the use of prime farmland for the production of nonedible crops. A prime example in North America is the devotion of some of the most fertile soils in Connecticut and the southeastern states to the production of tobacco. Not only is tobacco not edible, but it exacts a high cost since it is a direct cause of ill health in millions of people who smoke. In Brazil, millions of acres are being devoted to the production of sugar cane. Brazil is highly dependent on outside sources of fossil fuels for its energy needs and sees the production of alcohol from sugar cane as a major step toward less dependency on outside sources for energy. Other fuel-importing countries, including the United States, periodically consider stepped-up production of "gasohol," a mixture of gasoline and alcohol, which will require increased production not only of sugar cane but of sugar beets, potatoes, and grain for non-food purposes. It is ironic that we should add to the world's food-supply problems to produce a fuel that, for each unit of energy that one gets out of it, requires *more* than one unit to make.

The problem of food production is compounded by cultural practices which take prime farmland out of production. This picture shows the Columbia Dam, under construction on the Duck River in Tennessee. When completed, the impounded water will drown thousands of acres of excellent farmland. The Dam will not generate electricity, but is being built to provide flood control (which could be accomplished in other ways), recreation, and water for industry that may possibly, at some point in the future, come to the area.

Jack Corn/The New York Times

Another problem with feeding the world's billions has to do with cultural preferences for certain kinds of food. Changing the eating habits of people is difficult. For example, in North America, the dog population has become a problem. In the cities, their urine kills trees, and they constitute a serious litter and health problem. In rural areas, they are a serious menace to other livestock, especially sheep, and they are a menace to the health of children. Each year, and especially when the economy slows down, large numbers of dogs are abandoned to become strays, and as such they are responsible for attacks on people as well as livestock. Finally, a huge amount of food is unavailable for human consumption because it goes into pet food. In the United States, more than 3 billion dollars a year is spent on pet foods, which account for more than 5 percent of grocery sales. In spite of the fact that large numbers of abandoned dogs must be destroyed each year by humane societies, most Americans react with dismay and horror to the observation that dogs could be used as a significant source of high-quality protein food. To North Americans, dogs are pets, and the idea of eating dog meat is repulsive. Yet dogs are eaten in several other societies. In pre-Columbian Mexico, for example, dogs were sold in markets specifically for eating and were generally regarded as being quite tasty. In parts of Oceania, dog meat was preferred over pork, and early British visitors to Hawaii compared dog meat favorably with English lamb.[19]

On the other hand, many societies think that any food that comes from a can is unfit for human consumption. Totemic and religious taboos also affect the kinds of food

[19] Frederick Peterson, *Ancient Mexico* (New York: Capricorn Books, 1962), p. 170; M. Titcomb and M. K. Pukui, *Dog and Man in the Ancient Pacific*, cited by David B. Miller in *Science*, 1974, 186:394.

people will eat. Beef is disgusting to Hindus, and pork is sinful to Muslims and Jews. In certain non-Western societies, someone who unwittingly eats his totemic animal may vomit when he discovers what he has done.

Another example of the difficulty of changing eating habits can be seen in the experiences of some North American aid programs to countries with severe food shortages. The United States sent wheat to several countries—notably in South Asia —with severe food shortages. Wheat, especially North American wheat, is much higher in protein than the poor grade of rice these people had subsisted on. But the people, who were accustomed to eating rice for centuries, had no idea how to prepare wheat and did not like its taste. Many died of starvation because they were unable to switch to wheat as a substitute for rice.

This example also points to the importance of anthropology in helping solve some of the world's problems. If members of the U.S. foreign aid program had consulted qualified anthropologists, such an error would not have occurred; anthropologists would have been familiar with the eating habits of the people who were receiving the food and would have recommended another kind of food, or perhaps a program that taught South Asians how to cook and eat wheat. Although serious ethical problems are involved, future anthropologists may be faced with the task of trying to change people's cultural tastes and associated customs to enable their survival.

Pollution

Only recently has humanity come to realize the potentially disastrous consequences of overpopulation and unchecked industrialization on the environment for which we are completely dependent for life.

Pollution has become a direct threat to human health—in the air we breathe, in the water we drink, in the food we eat. Less direct, but just as dangerous, are those pollutants, such as chemical pesticides and inorganic nitrogen fertilizers, that may upset the earth's fragile ecosystems. For example, acid rain, an unintended by-product of industrial activity, is already damaging the productivity of those lands still used for timber and agricultural production, even when those lands lie far from the centers of industrial activity.

Modern humanity knows the causes of pollution, and realizes it is a danger to future survival. Why then can humanity not control this evil by which it fouls its own nest? The answer lies perhaps in philosophical and theological traditions. As we saw in Chapter 11, Western industrialized societies, using the Bible as a guide, believe that they have dominion over all the creatures of the earth and all that grows and lives on it. This exploitative world view, characteristic of all civilizations, extends to all natural resources. Only when it has been of any immediate advantage to them have Western peoples protected or replaced what greed and acquisitiveness have prompted them to take from their environment. In recent years, recognizing the seriousness of the environmental crisis people were creating for themselves, authorities have been forced to pass laws against such activities as hunting whales out of existence, dumping toxic wastes into streams and rivers, and poisoning the air with carbon monoxide fumes. That these laws have been at best only partially successful is indicated by the ban on aerosol sprays. The fluorocarbons in these sprays were contributing directly to the deterioration of the earth's ozone layer; yet since the ban was imposed, scientists have found that destruction of the ozone is proceeding twice as fast as predicted even without the ban.

One response to pollution is to seek escape. Here, research is aimed at finding cultural adaptations that will permit humans to extend their range and live in new environments, such as underwater. Experiments of this kind are costly and depend on resources that are becoming increasingly scarce. Moreover, living under such new conditions creates serious social and emotional problems which must be solved.

Pollution is a serious problem throughout the world. Some experts hold that pollution is a resource in the wrong place; there may be constructive uses for waste products, such as the use of garbage to generate gas or electricity.

This strip-mined landscape is symbolic of the Western world's cultural compulsion to "subdue the earth."

A large part of the problem in this and similar situations is a reluctance to perceive as disadvantageous practices that previously seemed to work well. What frequently happens is that practices carried out on one particular scale, or that were suited to one particular context, become unsuitable when carried out on another scale or in another context. Because they are trained to look at customs in their broader context, anthropologists would seem to have an important role to play in convincing people that changed conditions require changed behavior.

Members of many other societies have traditionally seen their environment in more symbiotic terms. They feel that the land and the forests are full of gods and spirits who hold great power over them. Such people believe there is a special relationship between themselves and their environment, including animals, plants, and natural forces. This kind of world view is particularly characteristic of hunter-gatherers. Hunters, for example, regard their game with respect, since their welfare depends on the animals. One avoids offending the animals, especially when their strength or cleverness makes them dangerous. Among the Tupians and other South American tribes, the concept of the "Lord of the Game Animals" is common. After the hunt, the Gaboon Pygmies implore the slain "Father Elephant" not to avenge himself on his killers, and many tribes in the northern woodlands address the bear politely and apologetically before attacking him. The Ainu of Japan capture bear cubs and raise them for a year or two; they then kill and eat the animals during a special ceremony. They hope that the bear soul will return loaded with gifts to his master, the "Old Man of the Mountains," and convey to him their wishes.

Among some agricultural peoples, plants are at the center of many animistic beliefs. For example, the Lamet, a tribe in Indochina, believe the soul of the rice is a kind of fluid that gradually collects at harvest time in a specific, consecrated part of the field; the crops harvested on that spot are used for sowing the following spring. The plant soul is also frequently visualized in animal or human form. Thus, the Indians in Peru believe in a Maize Mother and a Potato Mother. Similarly, in Indonesia, a Rice Mother is venerated, while the Grain Mother is likewise honored in parts of Europe.

Moreover, many non-Western societies stand in awe of natural forces, bestowing on them a special place in their religious system. For example, many people believe that rushing rapids, storms, the mountains, and the jungles possess awful powers. This is also true of fire, which warms and destroys. For farmers, the sun, rain, and thunder are important to their existence and are therefore often considered divine. Such world views may not prohibit the kind of environmental manipulation that causes severe pollution, but they certainly act as powerful restraining influences.

Birth Control

It should be evident from our discussions so far that many problems which beset the human species today can be solved only if population growth is arrested. This is particularly true so far as a permanent solution to the world's food crisis is concerned, but it is true for the solution of other problems as well. For example, practices which are essentially nonpolluting where populations are small become serious causes of pollution where populations are large. A significant reduction in birth rate actually took place in Western Europe and North America in the nineteenth century. By 1925, low birth rates in addition to low death rates resulted in relatively stable populations. The hope has been that the undeveloped world would experience a similar **demographic transition**—that Western technology, medicine, and hygienic practices would produce a decline in death rates, followed by a decline in birth rates, by mid-century. In essence, the green revolution was seen as a means of buying time for this to happen. As of 1976, there was almost no sign of a significant decline in birth rates. Since then, there have been some encouraging signs, as in China, where there has been a steep decline in fertility. But in South Asia, Africa, and some Latin American countries, the impact on fertility of programs to reduce birth rates is yet to be felt. In these countries, growing populations make it difficult even to maintain their present per capita share of food and other resources. Since food and other critical resources were not in short supply when the Western countries experienced the demographic transition, but they now are, it appears that the demographic transition is doomed to failure in the developing countries in the absence of effective birth control methods.[20] Such methods now exist, but whether or not these methods will be utilized on a vast enough scale depends on availability and cultural acceptance. Zero population growth goals

[20] Echols, pp. 165–173.

Chronic hunger stalks much of the world, as the result of cultural practices that have allowed population growth to outstrip our ability to provide sufficient food.

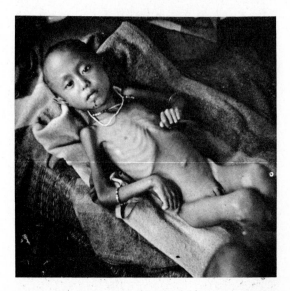

have been adopted in many countries, and programs for dissemination of birth control information have been developed in some 59 developing countries.

In many societies, the chief problem is to convince individuals to use birth control devices and techniques. Many of the world's peoples adhere to cultural customs and beliefs that are totally antithetic to the idea of birth control. For example, among the Kipsigis, a cattlebreeding people of East Africa, one of the primary duties of the young warrior is to enrich the tribe by begetting many children. In some societies, the number of children an individual has is a sign of prestige; if a man does not sire many children, he is looked down upon and thought a weakling. In other societies, particularly in the Middle East, motherhood and fatherhood are respected and desirable institutions. A male is not thought of as

> **Demographic transition:** A decline in the birth rate, following a decline in the death rate, in countries in which economic development has outstripped population growth.

a man nor a female a woman unless they produce a large number of children. Moreover, it is extremely difficult to convince a farmer to limit the size of his family when large families have been traditionally necessary to help with the great amount of manual labor nonmechanized agriculture requires. The problem is compounded by the fact that minorities often view birth control programs as subtle plots by the majority to diminish their numbers.

Perhaps the solution to the problem of birth control will be brought about indirectly with the application of some other technological advance. For example, in parts of India, the introduction of electricity into some rural areas has been a more effective means of birth control than any of the devices and information offered by government agencies. Apparently, lighting gave the inhabitants of these areas other leisure-time activities to engage in after dark. This connection is strengthened by the case of New York City in 1965, when a power failure that crippled the city overnight caused an upsurge in births nine months later.

The Culture of Discontent

Stabilization of the world's population appears to be a necessary step if the problems of the future are ever to be solved. Without this, whatever else is done, it seems inevitable that an inability to provide enough food will result in increased structural violence in the form of higher

death rates in the underdeveloped nations of the world. This will inevitably have an impact on the developed nations, with their relatively stable populations and high standards of living. It is hard to see how such nations could exist peacefully side by side with nations experiencing high death rates and low living standards.

Necessary though it may be in solving problems of the future, there is no reason to suppose that birth control will be sufficient by itself. The result would be only to stabilize things as they are. The problem is two-fold: over the past several years, the poor countries of the world have been persuaded that they should enjoy a standard of living comparable to that of the rich nations while at the same time the resources necessary to maintain such a standard of living are running out. As we saw in Chapter 14 this situation has led to the creation of a culture of discontent, whereby people's aspirations far exceed their opportunities. The problem involves not just a case of population growth outstripping food supplies; it is also one of urbanization exceeding the capacity to provide jobs, decent housing, sanitation, and adequate police and fire protection. And it is one of steady deterioration of the natural environment as a result of increasing industrialization.

What is required are some dramatic changes in cultural values and motivations, as well as in social institutions.[21] The emphasis on individual self-interest, materialism, and conspicuous production, acquisition, and consumption that is characteristic of the richer countries of the world needs to be abandoned in favor of a more human self-image and social ethic which can be created from values still to be found in many of the world's cultures. These include a world view that sees humanity as a part of nature rather than superior to it. Included, too, is a sense of social responsibility which recognizes that no individual or nation has the right to monopolize important resources. Finally, there is needed an awareness of the importance of the supportive ties among individuals such as are seen in kinship or other associations in the traditional societies of the world.

---

[21] Paul J. Magnarella, *Tradition and Change in a Turkish Town* (New York: Wiley, 1974), pp. 185–186.

CHAPTER SUMMARY

However humanity changes biologically, culture remains the chief means by which humans try to solve their problems of existence. Some anthropologists are concerned that there is a trend for the problems to outstrip culture's ability to find solutions. Rapid developments in communication, transportation, and world trade, some believe, will link people together to the point that a single world culture will result. Some feel that such a homogenized superculture would offer fewer chances for conflict between peoples than in the past. A number of anthropologists are skeptical of such argument, in view of the recent tendency for ethnic groups to reassert their own distinctive identities, and in view of the persistence of traditional ways of thinking about oneself and others, even in the face of massive changes in other aspects of culture. Anthropologists are also concerned about the tendency for many of the world's traditional societies to be treated as obsolete when they appear to stand in the way of "development."

Another possibility is that humanity may move in the direction of cultural pluralism, in which more than one culture exists in a society. In its ideal form, cultural pluralism rejects bigotry, bias, and racism. Some anthropologists maintain that pluralistic arrangements are the only feasible means for achieving global equilibrium and peace. A problem associated with cultural pluralism is ethnocentrism. All too often, it has led one group to force its ways on others, often leading to violent and bloody political upheavals.

Since future forms of culture will be shaped by decisions humans have yet to make, they cannot be predicted with any accuracy. Thus, instead of trying to foretell the future, a number of anthropologists are trying for a better understanding of the existing world situation. The picture which emerges is one of global apartheid, strikingly similar to South Africa's system of apartheid.

One consequence of any system of apartheid is a great deal of structural violence exerted by situations, institutions, and social, political, and economic structures. Such violence involves things like overpopulation and food shortages, which anthropologists are actively working to understand and help alleviate. One immediate challenge the world over is to provide food resources to keep pace with the burgeoning population. While such measures as bringing more land into production could bring temporary benefits, long-term solutions are needed. These largely depend on developing new energy sources as the world's supply of fossil fuels dwindles and utilizing animal manure rather than manufactured fertilizers. Another problem with feeding the world's exploding population has to do with cultural preferences for certain kinds of food. A people's eating habits often exclude food that is plentiful or nutritious and demand that which is scarce or of poor grade. Totemic and religious taboos also affect the kinds of food people will eat. Anthropologists of the future may be called on to help change people's cultural tastes and customs associated with food to enable their survival.

Pollution has become a direct threat to humanity. Western peoples have protected their environments only when it was immediately advantageous to do so; they have felt no long-term responsibilities toward the earth or its resources. Western societies could learn much from those non-Western peoples who see themselves as integral parts of the earth.

Meeting the problems of structural violence that beset the human species today probably only can be done if we are able to reduce the birth rate. Effective birth control methods are now available. Whether or not these methods are used on a vast enough scale depends on their availability and acceptance. Many of the world's peoples cling to cultural customs and beliefs which cause them to reject the idea of birth control.

Solving the problems of the global society depends also on lessening the gap between the living standards of poor and developed countries. This will call for dramatic changes in the values of Western societies with their materialistic, consumer orientation. All people need to see themselves as a part of nature rather than as superior to it. Also needed are a social responsibility which recognizes that no nation has a right to monopolize important resources and an awareness of the importance of supportive ties between individuals.

SUGGESTED READINGS

Alland, Alexander, Jr. *Human Diversity*. New York: Columbia University Press, 1971.
Chapter 5 of this book, "Of Mice and Men: Behavioral Genetics and Human Variation," traces the implications of certain kinds of cultural change for the biological future of humanity. Working from the supposition that humans are relatively free of behavioral programming, the author examines one way this freedom has enabled people to cope with diverse environments and how these environments in turn have shaped people both culturally and biologically.

Kahn, Herman, and Anthony J. Wiener. *The Year 2000*. New York: Macmillan, 1967.
To an anthropologist, the most interesting chapter of this book is Chapter 6, "Some Canonical Variations from the Standard World." It projects a number of possible cultural futures, including both a world of greater integration and one of greater disarray. Although there is much emphasis on technological factors throughout the book, this chapter focuses on cultural alternatives.

Magnarella, Paul J. *Tradition and Change in a Turkish Town*. New York: Wiley, 1974.
The last chapter of this book discusses the "culture of discontent" and suggests what steps must be taken if the developing predicament of humanity is to be surmounted in the future.

Meadows, Donella H., Dennis L. Meadows, Jorgen Randers, and William W. Behrens III, *The Limits to Growth*, 2d ed. New York: Universe Books, 1974.
In 1970, an international team of researchers gathered at MIT and constructed a preliminary model of the world in which all assumptions and parameters are explicit. From this, aided by computers, they examined their model to determine alternative patterns for the future of humanity. Their conclusions are important for all anthropologists interested in the future of the human species.

Wolf, Eric R. *Europe and the People Without History*. Berkeley: University of California Press, 1982.
One anthropologist who is looking at the world as a global society is Eric Wolf. In this book, Wolf pays particular attention to the ways that non-Western peoples participated in the making of the modern global society.

16 The Future of Anthropology

Anthropologist Stephen Pastner with Baluch tribesmen aboard their fishing vessel off the coast of Pakistan. Although anthropologists continue to study cultures in faraway places, more and more of them are studying aspects of their own culture.

PREVIEW

IS THE SUBJECT MATTER OF ANTHROPOLOGY DISAPPEARING?

It is sometimes supposed that with fewer "lost cities" and "missing links" left to find, and with the modernization of traditional, nonindustrial societies, anthropologists will be left with nothing to do. As it turns out, the supposition is false—anthropologists will have a great deal to keep them busy far into the future.

WHAT WILL ANTHROPOLOGISTS BE DOING IN THE FUTURE?

The traditional anthropological concern for non-Western, nonindustrial peoples will continue as anthropologists work to ensure that the world's surviving tribal and band societies are given the chance to work out their own destinies in the modern world. There is work to be done, too, gathering data on ways of life that may soon disappear, as well as furthering our understanding of the process of modernization. In addition, studies of North American culture are on the increase, and this trend will continue into the foreseeable future.

WILL THERE BE ANY PRACTICAL APPLICATION OF ANTHROPOLOGICAL KNOWLEDGE?

Anthropologists have always held that their discipline has practical utility, and some anthropologists have been applying their knowledge for a long time. Now, there is increased interest in applied anthropology as jobs are sought outside traditional academic settings. This trend brings with it the need for increased attention to questions of ethics.

Travelers have always been fascinated by the seeming strangeness of the behavior and beliefs of people in other places. Marco Polo, perhaps the most famous traveler of the thirteenth century, wrote to his Italian relatives of his amazement at the manners and morals of the Chinese court; the Spanish conquistadors were perplexed by the customs of the New World civilizations they eventually destroyed; modern travelers leave their jet with camera in hand, ready to record on film the landmarks of their destination and the dress of its inhabitants. Small wonder, then, that the work of the anthropologist that has captured the public imagination is that which takes place in faraway places—remote islands, deep forests, hostile deserts, or arctic wastes. When anthropology makes the pages of the *New York Times*, it is generally to report the "discovery" of a "last surviving stone age tribe," the uncovering of some ancient "lost city," or the recovery of the bones of some remote human ancestor. Thus a public image has been built up of the anthropologist as someone who is exclusively concerned with extinct "missing links," extinct civilizations, or present-day tribal peoples whose ways of life are on the verge of extinction as they are swept up in the worldwide process of modernization.

Not surprisingly, this stereotype of anthropologists and what they do has prompted some people to ask: Will anthropologists have anything to do in the future? After all, with the disappearance of tribal peoples, and with few "lost cities" or "missing links" left to discover, anthropologists will soon be left with nothing to study. As it turns out, nothing could be further from the truth. We have already seen, in the last chapters, some of the ways in which anthropologists are already involved in studying the problems of the future. And although it is true that anthropologists have emphasized studies of non-Western peoples, for reasons noted in Chapter 1, they have had a long-standing interest in their own culture. Many of them, as applied anthropologists, are putting their expertise to work in an attempt to find solutions to problems of various sorts. In short, anthropologists will have lots to do for some time to come. We began this book by looking at the nature of anthropology as a discipline, and in this last chapter we come full circle as we look at the future of the discipline.

THE DISAPPEARING PAST

In this part of the twentieth century, the time is long past when the anthropologist could go out and describe small tribal groups in out-of-the-way places which had not been "contaminated" by contact with Westerners. There are few such groups in the world today. Indeed, many classic ethnographies dealt with societies more affected by contact with Westerners than previously thought.

Anthropologists are increasingly concerned about the fast disappearance of the world's remaining tribal peoples for a number of reasons, and foremost among them is a basic issue of human rights. In the world today, there is a rush to develop those parts of the planet earth that have so far escaped industrialization, or the extraction of resources regarded as vital to the well-being of "developed" economies. These efforts at national and international development are planned, financed, and carried out by both governments and businesses, generally the huge multi-national corporations. Unfortunately, the rights of native peoples generally have not been incorporated into the programs and concerns of these organizations, even where laws exist that are supposed to protect the rights of such peoples. At the least, this leads to encroachments on the territories of native groups, who are thereby deprived of resources that they need to provide for their own well-being. At the same time, they are not given the education and health care that they require to carve a meaningful niche for themselves in the national society of which they are expected to become a part. Instead, they find that they must forfeit their indigenous identity and be pressed into a mold that allows them no latitude or motivation to rise above the lowest rung of the social ladder. From an autonomous people with pride and a strong sense of their own identity as a people, they are transformed into a deprived underclass with neither pride nor a sense of their own identity, often despised by more fortunate members of the national society.

This kind of "benign neglect," for example, has characterized much of the recent development of South America's Amazon Basin. Not infrequently, however, native people are faced with the further indignity of forced removal from their traditional homelands as entire communities are uprooted to make way for hydroelectric projects, grazing lands for cattle, mining operations, or the construction of highways. On occasion, in some parts of the world, this has led to actual **genocide**—the deliberate extermination of ethnic groups that are regarded as standing in the way of development. Although genocide rightly triggers public outrage when it is brought to public attention, it is far less common than the abuses of human rights just outlined. Nor are these abuses limited to the "developing nations" of the world; what has happened and what is still happening to the indigenous people of the Amazon Basin has much in common with what is happening to native peoples in Alaska and

> **Genocide:** Deliberate extermination of ethnic groups and societies that are seen as hindering economic progress.

Canada, as reserves of oil, gas, and other resources are developed, or in the southwestern United States as the mining of coal and its use for gasification and power generation are expanded.

Two organizations of anthropologists in the United States that are explicitly concerned with violations that threaten the human rights and survival of indigenous cultures the world over are Cultural Survival, Inc., and the Anthropological Resource Center, Inc. (ARC), both based in Cambridge, Mass. The former is exclusively concerned with cultural survival, whereas the latter is a public interest anthropology

ARC Inc. is a public interest anthropology group that carries out research on important public issues, and translates this into a program of public education aimed at promoting the participation of citizens in the political decision-making process. Among their activities have been studies of the social impact of nuclear power stations. Shown here is the plant at Three Mile Island, Pennsylvania.

group that deals with other issues as well. Neither organization is interested in preserving indigenous cultures in some sort of romantic, pristine condition, so that they will be there to study or to serve as "living museum exhibits," as it were. Their interest is to provide the information and support to help endangered groups to comprehend their situation, maintain or even strengthen their sense of self, and adapt to the changing circumstances. They do not regard "mainstreaming" these groups into national societies as necessarily desirable; rather, they should be allowed to work out their own ways of being different. Instead of designing projects and then imposing them on endangered societies, both Cultural Survival and ARC prefer to respond to the requests and desires of groups that see a problem and the need to address it. They can suggest ways to help, and they can activate extensive networks of anthropologists, other indigenous peoples who have already dealt with similar problems, and those government officials whose support can be critical to success. Generally, both organizations wish to facilitate the formation of effective national and international organizations of indigenous peoples. Although both groups are aware of the need to broaden the base of public support for the rights of indigenous peoples, Cultural Survival tends to work in a low-key, "behind the scenes" way, whereas ARC is more actively involved in educating the public and increasing its awareness of the problems.

Although the basic right of groups of people to be themselves and not be deprived of their own distinctive cultural identities is and should be our paramount consideration, there are other reasons to be concerned about the disappearance of the societies with which anthropologists have been so often concerned. For one thing, the need for information about them has become steadily more apparent. If we are ever

Anthropology as the rescuer of non-Western traditions is illustrated by this modern Hopi Indian pot. In the Tewa and Hopi pueblos, pottery making died out completely after the first century of Spanish rule. The renaissance of traditional pottery making, now the basic craft in the Tewa and Hopi pueblos of First Mesa, was made possible in part by nearby archeological excavations which provided the old designs for the new potters to copy. Shown below is Hopi potter Rachel Namingha painting a design on a jar.

to have a realistic understanding of that elusive thing called human nature, we need lots of good data on all humans. There is more to it than this, though; once a tribal society is gone, it is lost to humanity unless an adequate record of it exists. When this happens, humanity is the poorer for the loss. Hence, anthropologists are in a sense rescuing such societies from oblivion. Not only does this help preserve the human heritage, it may also be important to an ethnic group that, having become Westernized, wishes to rediscover and reassert its past cultural identity. As an example, native arts on the northwest coast of North America all but disappeared as a consequence of the Canadian government's decision that native practices such as potlatching (discussed in Chapter 7) had to stop. With the dropping of the ban on potlatching in 1951, there was a resurgence of ethnic pride and, in consequence, a revival of native arts. A key role in this was played by Bill Holm, an anthropologist at the University of Washington. Through an analysis of 400 of the finest old pieces of northwest coast art in museums, he was able to rediscover the esthetic rules that had governed the works of traditional wood sculptors. This has breathed new life into the work of native artists, who are again creating splendid works of art that are vital to traditional northwest coast social and ceremonial life.

In the case just cited, Bill Holm was not working as an applied anthropologist in the strict sense—that is, he was not putting his anthropological talents to work for a specific client, he was just "doing research." Yet, the practical outcome of his work was as if he had: The fact is, the distinction that is often made between "basic" and "applied" research is not nearly as clear as is often made out. Another example of how non-applied work may be useful in preserving another ethnic group's traditions is Weston LaBarre's study of the Na-

tive American Church, *The Peyote Cult*. When setting up new branches of this church, Indians have repeatedly consulted this meticulously complied ethnography for ritual details.

We should not, then, underrate the value of salvaging information about endangered traditions. The need for such work is urgent. So even though the survival of tribal societies is threatened today as never before, anthropologists will continue to be concerned with them, gathering whatever data can still be obtained.

The need for salvage applies to archeological as well as ethnological data. Here, we are not confronted with societies that are rapidly being Westernized or destroyed; rather, we are dealing with the remains of societies that are being drowned in reservoirs, covered by parking lots for shopping centers, or just plain bulldozed into oblivion. Archeological sites are being lost at an alarming rate, and this is a critical problem for three reasons. First, they are nonrenewable; second, they provide the essential data needed by anthropologists to understand the processes of change over extended periods of time; third they are part of the human heritage that belongs to all humanity and that no individual or group has the right to destroy. In the United States, concern over the loss of archeological resources led to the passage of legislation that requires the planning for any project that will utilize federal funds, or requires a federal license or permit, to assess the project's impact upon both prehistoric and historic sites. If it is determined that a project will adversely affect a site that is likely to produce significant information about past human activity, then steps must be taken to mitigate the project's impact. This may be done by redesigning the project, retrieving the archeological data before they are destroyed, or both.

These pictures of Jimbal Stela I before and after vandalism show the kind of destruction caused by the international antiquities trade. This Maya site was not discovered until 1965, and the stela was still in mint condition in 1967 when investigated by the author. By 1971, thieves had shaved off part of the face with a chain saw in an attempt to break the huge monument into pieces small and light enough to transport inconspicuously.

The archeological problem is not one of earth-moving alone. The last decade has seen the spectacular rise of an illicit international traffic in antiquities. So it is, for example, that ancient Maya monuments in the forests of Guatemala are broken up, smuggled out of the country, and reassembled to be purchased by art dealers and museums. Not only have prize pieces of Maya sculpture been destroyed, there has also been at least one murder connected with these operations. Although a number of museums and governments have acted to discourage such purchases, not nearly enough has been done to stem the illegal traffic in antiquities. For example, the United States for many years failed to implement a 1970 UNESCO convention designed to restrict severely this traffic in antiquities, and one of the largest markets for these objects consists of wealthy collectors in the United States. Although the House of Representatives quickly passed implementing legislation, it was always killed in the Senate, owing to opposition from art and antiquities dealers. Implementing legislation was finally passed by the Senate and ready for the President's signature in December 1982. Opposition from the art and antiquities lobby was overcome only by a compromise which specifies that the convention will not actually become effective in the U.S. until Britain, France, West Germany, Switzerland, Japan, and the Scandinavian countries also implement the convention. Meanwhile, the antiquities traffic goes on.

THE EMERGENCE OF MODERN SOCIETIES

Important though archeological and ethnological salvage work may be, anthropologists, as they must, are concerning themselves with the longer-range future and are opening up new fields of research. More and more anthropologists are turning their attention to studies of modernization, the process by which traditional, non-Western societies adopt some of the characteristics of industrially advanced countries, such as state governments, nationalism, and integration into industrial economies. This is a logical outcome of the special anthropological concern with the non-Western world, and it obviously involves anthropologists with problems of immediate concern. Some of these are: How should the so-called underdeveloped nations develop? What will be the effect of development on traditional ways? What traditional ways are worth preserving? How can this be done? How can a desired change be introduced into a traditional community with some chance of success?

In spite of increased interest on the part of anthropologists in studying modernization, such studies are not always easy to carry out. For one thing, more and more of the world's developing countries dislike the idea of Westerners coming in and studying them as if they were some strange form of life. In addition, many of the developing countries were once colonies of the West. In the past, anthropologists working in these countries had to obtain permission from colonial officials. Now, one way to express displeasure with the colonial past is to deny permission for anthropological studies to those whom colonial officials once allowed to work in their countries.

STUDIES OF NORTH AMERICAN CULTURE

In recent years, more and more U.S. anthropologists have become involved in studies of their own culture, in response to various developments. Among them are the disappearance of the kinds of indigenous cultures so often studied in the past, as well as the increased difficulty of conducting anthropological research abroad. In addition, the civil rights and related movements of the 1960s publicized the fact that there were important anthropological problems to be dealt with at home, as well as abroad. Many of these problems involved peoples anthropologists had previously studied in rural settings, especially American Indians and Latin Americans. As increasing numbers of these people moved into the cities of North America, anthropologists followed them.

Some have viewed this current interest of anthropologists in their own culture as something new; after all, so the conventional wisdom goes, this is the domain of sociology, rather than anthropology. But as we saw earlier in this book, anthropologists have always been interested in their own culture. Although they worked extensively in the United States during the years of the depression and World War II, this did not receive the publicity accorded work in faraway places. With the 1950s, the availability of large amounts of research money allowed anthropologists to work abroad as never before, resulting in the relative neglect of research at home. With the return of anthropologists to areas of research dominated by sociologists in the 1950s and 1960s, a new and fruitful area for cooperation between the two fields has opened up. The ethnographic techniques of the anthropologists offer a valuable supplement to the more traditional sociological techniques of census taking and administration of questionaires.

Much though it has to offer, the anthropological study of one's own culture is not without its own special problems. Sir Edmund Leach, a noted British anthropologist, puts it in the following way:

Surprising though it may seem, fieldwork in a cultural context of which you already have intimate first-hand experience seems to be much more difficult than fieldwork which is approached from the naive viewpoint of a total stranger. When anthropologists study facets of their own society their vision seems to become distorted by prejudices which derive from private rather than public experience.[1]

Probably the most successful anthropological studies of their own culture by North Americans have been done by those who first worked in some other culture. Lloyd Warner, for example, whose work we cited in Chapter 1, had studied the Murngin of Australia before he tackled Newburyport, Massachusetts. In addition to getting ourselves outside of our own culture before trying to study it ourselves, it would be a good idea to encourage anthropologists from Africa, Asia, and Latin America to do fieldwork in North America. Their outsider's perspective would serve as a valuable check on the reliability of our own studies of ourselves. But the special difficulties of studying one's own culture can be overcome, as long as one is acutely aware of them.

Jules Henry, an anthropologist who made a specialty of studying North American culture (after first studying Indians in Brazil), had the following to say about such endeavors:

I doubt that there is any country in the world more suitable for anthropological study as a whole than the United States, for not only do towns and institutions open their doors to research, but the United States Government Printing Office is an inexhaustible source of information on everything from how to repair a home freezer to analysis of the military budget, and Government officials are tireless in giving answers to all questions. Millions of pages of *The Congressional Record* provide a running ethnography on some of our most crucial concerns; and over and over again these millions of pages are condensed into brilliant reports by nameless anthropological geniuses employed by the Government. In addition to all this are our newspapers, particularly great journals like the *New York Times* . . . for not only do they carry a continuous report of our daily goings-on, but even their biases, their omissions, and their trivia provide deep insights into our culture. Whereas in primitive culture the anthropologist often has to work to ferret out information, in our great democracy the printing presses inundate him with it, and his greatest task is to sort it out and interpret it. So, although much of the material of which I speak comes from "research projects," much is derived from contemporary printing presses.[2]

In spite of all this, social scientists generally have been frustrated in their efforts to analyze ways of life in the United States in terms of a single, unitary system of ideas and activities. The problem is that the United States, in common with all of the so-called "modern" societies of the world, has within it a large number of more or less separate subcultures. Those who live by the standards of one particular subculture have their closest relationships with one another, receiving constant reassurance that their perceptions of the world are the only correct ones and coming to take it for granted that the whole culture is as they see it. Yet all these subcultures are connected and dependent not just on one another but on certain fundamental orientations and values common to most, if not all, North American subcultures as well.

---

[1] Edmund Leach, *Social Anthropology* (Glasgow: Fontana Paperbacks, 1982), p. 124.

[2] Jules Henry, *Culture against Man* (New York: Vintage Books, 1965), p. 4.

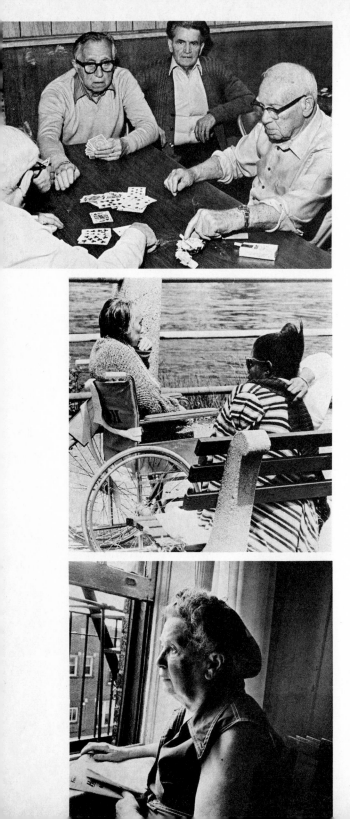

Urban anthropology: Anthropological studies of urban neighborhoods, slums, and ethnic enclaves, in order to learn about poverty, class and subcultural variation, problems of minorities, and how migrants to cities adapt to urban life.

Although anthropologists have studied such things as midwestern hamlets and Appalachian religious cults, many of their recent studies in the United States fall under the heading of **urban anthropology.** The term does not imply that anthropologists are necessarily trying to write holistic ethnographies of cities. Rather, they are studying urban neighborhoods, slums, and ethnic enclaves to try to understand poverty, class and subcultural variation, problems of minorities, and how migrants to cities adapt to urban life. Many of these migrants were earlier studied in rural settings by anthropologists, who have followed them into the city. Their prior knowledge of these people, in addition to their ability to collect information across cultural boundaries and their understanding of subcultural differences generally, uniquely suit anthropologists for this kind of research, and the information gained is of obvious importance in solving many of the problems of contemporary North American society. In particular, the work of anthropologists has been instrumental in demonstrating that a number of subcultural characteristics of urban immigrants once widely thought to be indicative of cul-

Anthropological studies of the elderly and their place in society are likely to become increasingly important, for a declining birth rate indicates that a significant percent of the U.S. population will be elderly by the year 2000.

tural breakdown are in fact adaptations to the new urban settings. By retaining many elements of the old rural culture, modifying them as necessary, and recombining them with new elements, the urban immigrants are able to cope with the new problems which beset them in the city.

In addition to finding anthropologists studying such diverse urban groups as Chicanos, blacks, hippies, longshoremen, street gangs, and so forth, one also finds them in institutional settings ranging all the way from small neighborhood bars to large city hospitals doing ethnographic work. Involved here are such specialties as educational anthropology and medical anthropology. The educational anthropologist may be concerned with studies of student

Some of the greatest health care problems in the United States have to do with health care delivery. For example, endless waiting in public clinics like this one is a standard feature of "health care" for the poor. Those who can pay generally receive better treatment.

subcultures, problems of bicultural education, and the structure of schools in their cultural or subcultural settings. The medical anthropologist may study the social structure of hospitals, ways of life in hospital wards, and community attitudes toward health and health care. As with studies in urban anthropology, the knowledge generated by studies such as these is potentially useful in the solution of social problems. For example, some of the greatest health problems in North America do not have to do with medical knowledge and capabilities but with health care delivery.

This can be seen most clearly, perhaps, in attempts to treat mental disorders. It has been well established that Western-style psychiatry has not been notably successful among culturally different peoples. What has proved successful, though, is community-based psychiatry, in which psychiatrists collaborate with traditional healers. In the United States, joint efforts of this sort have been undertaken among Navajo Indians, Puerto Ricans both on their home island and in New York City, and others. In these instances, and others outside of the United States, anthropologists have worked as cultural interpreters, explaining local beliefs and practices about disease and healing to the health care professionals, as well as explaining the subculture of these professionals to the locals. Not surprisingly, given the practical utility of work in educational and medical anthropology, many of those who specialize in these areas are applied anthropologists.

Anthropology and Jobs

For the most part, anthropologists have plied their trade as members of college and university faculties. Nonetheless, they have not seen their discipline as concerned exclusively with the accumulation and transmission of knowledge. For exam-

During World War II, anthropologists were hired by the government to study the adjustment of Japanese-Americans to the camps, such as this one in Manzanar, California, in which they were interned.

ple, the great English pioneer in anthropology Sir Edward B. Tylor viewed the discipline as a "reformer's science," and the North American pioneer Lewis Henry Morgan applied his anthropological knowledge by assisting the Seneca Indians in their fight against greedy landgrabbers. During the 1930s there was a strong trend toward the practical application of anthropological knowledge, and the field of applied anthropology grew accordingly. For example, a number of anthropologists were employed by government agencies to study such things as cultural aspects of dietary practices, resistance to innovation on the part of farmers, and effects of large-scale farming on the quality of life in local communities. Throughout World War II, they were hired to study Japanese-American internment camps in the United States, to analyze the national character of the Japanese, and to assist the war effort in other ways to be dis-

cussed later in this chapter. After the war, though, the rapid growth of higher education, and the availability of abundant money for basic research, brought about an almost exclusive concern with teaching and research. Now, reduced funding for basic research, as well as for higher education generally, and a growing demand for applied anthropologists in such areas as health planning, rural and urban development, cross-cultural administration, and cultural resource management are causing more and more anthropologists to take jobs outside of academic institutions.

Nonacademic jobs for people with an anthropological background exist in areas of business and government which are concerned with cross-cultural problems or which involve contact with peoples of different ethnic or other backgrounds. For example, corporations that do extensive business abroad or radio and TV stations with programming for specific ethnic groups may find anthropological expertise useful. In government, the Department of the Interior recognizes the importance of anthropological training in its administration of the Pacific Trust Territories and American Indian affairs. Conversely, some anthropologists have worked for the Indians themselves, rather than the government, especially in connection with Indian land claims. Indeed, the 1981 Praxis Award was won by James Wherry for his use of anthropological knowledge to win federal recognition for a band of Maliseet Indians living in Maine, making them eligible for millions of dollars of federal assistance. The Praxis Award is an international competition open to all projects, programs, or activities which illustrate the translation of anthropological knowledge into action.

Jobs for anthropologists are also to be found where there are problems of development, involving directed or desired change. The Agency for International Development is an example of a government agency that hires anthropologists to assist in development, and private management research firms also hire anthropologists for their skills in this area. Jobs are to be found, too, where there is a special concern for "grass roots" participation in areas or activities where there is a substantial difference between administrators and participants. This is all too often the case in the United States today, where those who deliver goods and services frequently wish to do so in ways that are more beneficial to themselves than they are to those who are to receive those goods and services.

The field of cultural resource management has undergone something of a boom as a result of recent state and federal legislation. As a result, more archeologists have been employed by the National Park Service to assist in the preservation, restoration, and salvage of archeological resources. Archeologists are also in some demand as consultants to engineering firms, since federal and many state regulations require that the impact of proposed construction projects on archeological resources be assessed in advance. But cultural resource management involves more than archeological sites; it also involves people—ethnic and other minorities, poor people, and others—who will be affected by planned projects of various sorts. Hence, many state and local agencies employ anthropologists to assist in planning.

On a larger scale, the World Bank in 1982 issued a policy directive requiring that the rights and autonomy of tribal peoples and minorities must be *guaranteed* in any development project in which the World Bank is involved.[3] This came about largely in response to the outcries of an-

thropologists about the extremely adverse and harsh affects of development projects on the indigenous peoples of the Amazon Basin, and it will require the services of anthropologists to prepare the necessary social impact studies.

In addition to the World Bank, agencies of the United Nations and agencies for development in other countries are increasingly calling on the services of anthropologists for social impact assessments. Across the board, there is a growing recognition of a need for truly humanistic social planning, as opposed to a "coldly" scientific approach. Anthropologists, with their humanistic tradition and sensitivity to cultural differences, would seem to be particularly well suited for such work. For precisely this reason, apparently, the popularity of anthropology in Europe is rising, while that of sociology is declining. Perhaps a similar trend will develop in the United States.

Questions of Ethics

The kinds of research and job opportunities outlined above raise a number of important questions concerning anthropological ethics. Who will make use of the findings of anthropologists, and for what purposes? In the case of a militant minority, for example, will others use anthropological data to suppress that minority? And what of traditional communities around the world—who is to decide what changes should, or should not, be introduced for community "betterment"? By whose definition is it "betterment," the community's or that of a remote national government? Then there is the problem of privacy. Anthropologists deal with people's private and sensitive matters, including things that people would not care to have generally known about them. How does one write about such matters and at the same time

[3] World Bank, *Tribal Peoples and Economic Development* (Washington, D.C.: World Bank, 1982).

protect the privacy of informants? Not surprisingly, because of these and other questions, there has been a hot debate among anthropologists over the past decade on the subject of ethics. In 1967, the American Anthropological Association adopted a statement on problems of anthropological research and ethics. Among other things, this expressed concern about conditions that might threaten the ability of anthropology to contribute to the general interests of human welfare. What concerned anthropologists was that their research findings might be used as a basis for policy formation, and that this policy might be to the detriment of the group from which those findings came.

This question has not always been a primary worry for anthropologists, although the anthropologists of the nineteenth and early twentieth centuries in the United States almost all felt a personal obligation to the people whom they studied. This sometimes involved them in fighting court battles on behalf of their informants, often at their personal expense.

In World War II, anthropologists were in great demand by the United States government, largely because of their familiarity with foreign cultures and the places

Destruction in Hiroshima after the first atomic bomb blast on August 6, 1945. A significant problem in applied anthropology is convincing a client to accept recommendations that are at odds with the client's preconceived notions. For example, toward the end of World War II, a group that included anthropologists predicted a Japanese surrender without the need to drop atomic bombs. Because it conflicted with the prevailing military view, it was not heeded, but evidence found after the war confirmed the correctness of their prediction.

where war operations were taking place. The anthropologists responded by preparing manuals for the troops, interpreting cultures for various agencies, and formulating policies for occupied areas. Perhaps the best-known by-product of these wartime activities was Ruth Benedict's *The Chrysanthemum and the Sword* (1946), an analysis of Japanese national character based on secondhand sources. Similar studies were made by Geoffrey Gorer and Weston LaBarre. Many of the conclusions of these studies have not stood up in the face of closer scrutiny based on firsthand observation.

Some of this wartime anthropological work was amazingly sound, but was not always listened to. A case in point is the work of the Foreign Morale Analysis Division of the Office of War Information. Headed up by an anthropologist-psychiatrist, it included several other anthropologists as well as psychiatrists and sociologists. This group correctly analyzed the deteriorating morale of Japanese soldiers and civilians as early as late 1944. Because it conflicted with the prevailing military view, it was largely ignored. In early 1945 the Division predicted a major blowup in Japan and, by spring, predicted a Japanese surrender between July and September 1945. Again they were ignored, but were later proved right when it was learned that the Japanese, in May 1945 (before any atomic bombs were dropped), made a decision to surrender before November.

The issue that made anthropologists in the United States reexamine the ethics of their ties to government was Project Camelot. This was a vast research project planned by the Department of Defense to find out the causes of social unrest leading to armed insurgency. From these data, ways of averting or suppressing armed rebellions could be found. Social scientists would thus be involved in the intervention of the U.S. government in the internal affairs of other nations. Project Camelot was canceled while still in the planning stages. Anthropologists had reacted vigorously, both because other nations might react by refusing to allow U.S. anthropologists to conduct any research within their borders, and because of the larger ethical issues involved. The traditional concern of the anthropologist for the welfare of the people under study, as that people see it, has been reawakened.

The present consensus among anthropologists about the ethics of their profession was summed up by Laura Nader in a recent interview:

Anthropologists have obligations to three different sets of people. First, to the people that we study; secondly, to the profession which expects us to report back our findings; and thirdly, to the organizations that fund the research. Some people would order them differently—one, two, three, three, two, one, or whatever—but those three are in the minds of most anthropologists. Now, sometimes the obligations conflict. If I do fieldwork among a group of people and I learn certain things that, if revealed, might come back to hurt them, then reporting my findings back to the profession is going to be secondary because first and foremost I have to protect my informants because they trusted me. In the case of the Zapotec, I was dealing with very sensitive materials about law and disputes and conflicts and so forth. And I was very sensitive about how much of that to report while people were still alive and while things might still be warm, so I waited on that. I'm just finishing my Zapotec monograph now. I've written certain things, but I waited for the most part, and I feel comfortable now releasing that information. With regard to a funder in that case, it was the Mexican government, and I feel that I have written enough to have paid off the $1200 which they gave me to support that work for a year. So, I've not felt particularly strained for my Zapotec work in those three areas. On energy research that I've done, it's been another story. Much of what people wanted me to do energy research for was . . . to tell people in decision-making positions about American consumers in such a way that they could be manipulated better, and I didn't want to do that. So what I said was I would be willing to study a vertical slice. That is, I would never study the consumer without studying the producer. And once you take a vertical slice like that, then it's fair because you're telling the consumer about the producer and the producer about the consumer. But just to do a study of consumers for producers, I think I would feel uncomfortable.[4]

[4] Laura Nader, Interview for KOCE–TV, held in Los Angeles, December 3, 1981.

ORIGINAL STUDY

Anthropologists at Work

Having looked at the promise and pitfalls of anthropological employment outside the college or university, we will conclude this chapter by looking at some examples of anthropological careers outside the traditional academic setting. Those that follow are three "Profiles of Anthropologists" that have been selected from the many which have appeared in the *Anthropology Newsletter* over the past few years.

Irving Wallach

Twenty-five years ago as a hungry Ph.D. candidate with a young and growing family to support, I departed Columbia University for the Washington job market. This led to a five year specialization in crosscultural communications and cultural diffusion via motion pictures. My first position was with the International Motion Picture Service at the State Department, which was involved in worldwide distribution of documentary films. As a member of the staff, I reviewed field reports and research proposals, and provided evaluation guidance to field officers in 78 foreign posts.

Upon leaving the State Department, I became a consultant for the Society for Applied Anthropology on a contract relating to multi-national documentaries. Recognizing the tremendous influence of Hollywood feature films in cross-cultural communication and diffusion, I accepted a position on the research staff of a major feature company. My assignment was to determine the types of films preferred by audiences in major foreign markets. I later undertook two years of research, including fieldwork in Japan, as a Foreign Area Training Fellow of the Ford Foundation. The purpose of my research was to delineate the process by which American films communicate with foreign audiences.

At American University, I worked on government contracts involving the planning of overseas studies. Gradually, I became involved in the growing EDP field. For the next six years with the Systems Development Corporation, I dealt with systems analysis and design, primarily in an experiment to determine which social science training best suited an individual to analyze and design systems. The results showed that while all social science training seemed appropriate, anthropologists learned and performed best initially, with sociologists and psychologists following in that order.

From 1965 to the present, my work has included both research and administrative activities with both nonprofit and government agencies relating to the criminal justice system. At Stanford Research Institute, I directed research which developed profiles of convicted adult felons and active juvenile offenders in Washington, DC. At another nonprofit agency, I directed and performed research on the role and function of the police in the Black community from both a police and community perspective. My training in social control and ethnic differences was directly applicable to this research which was expanded into a comparative study of the police function in tribal, pre-industrial and industrial societies.

Subsequently, I accepted administrative assignments for the State of New York and the District of Columbia involving Criminal Justice Grant Programs. I am presently Executive Director of the Office of Criminal Justice Plans and Analysis in Washington, DC.

My experience has convinced me that anthropologists can engage in a wide variety of interesting work which utilizes the insights provided by their training. All types of social science research are available to the adequately trained student. However, adequate training involves many skills which were not included in my graduate training; for example, methodologies other than participant observation and fieldwork techniques; quantitative skills, particularly statistics; and research and program administration.

While I recommend pursuit of a non-academic career, I must point out that the successful practitioner quickly prices himself out of the academic market. For those who cannot forego it, I suggest part-time teaching. This permits a transfer of applied research techniques and experience to the graduate student. From the perspective of my present position, I see a growing need for evaluators of social programs. Anthropological training is well suited to evaluation of community based programs, and graduate students may find this field worthy of their attention.[5]

Susan Peterson

My interest in natural decision-making and my curiosity about Honolulu's open-air market led me into a study of Hawaiian fishing and the fish market as part of my dissertation research at the University of Hawaii. At the AAA annual meeting in Toronto in 1972, a discussion about fish netting materials with John Cordell, who did fieldwork with fishermen in Brazil, resulted in my application to the Marine Policy and Ocean Management Program at Woods Hole Oceanographic Institution where John was a fellow from 1972–73.

[5] *Anthropology Newsletter* (October 1976) 17(8):18.

I arrived in Woods Hole in 1973 as a postdoctoral fellow, where I began to study fishermen and fishing methods throughout New England. With the collaboration of an economist, I received an 18-month grant from Sea Grant in the Department of Commerce to continue and expand the research. This involved research into fisher-related policy decisions being made at international, national and state levels. As a result of this research, I have served on the U.S. delegation to the International Commission for the Northwest Atlantic Fisheries, advised the New England Regional Commission, written model legislation for the Massachusetts lobster fishery, and presently am a member of the Mid-Atlantic and New England Fisheries Councils' Scientific and Statistical Committee.

In addition to research, my position at the Oceanographic involves some administrative work as one of three research associates on the staff of the Marine Policy program. Some of this is grant and contract proposal preparation for specific projects and program development as well as responses to RFP's put out by various government agencies. The Oceanographic is a private, non-profit organization, and while some programs such as educational and marine policy fellowships are funded through endowment, most science is funded by grants or contracts awarded for a specific proposal to the individual scientist.

Most of my administrative work is involved with the annual crop of post-doctoral fellows—social scientists who come to the Oceanographic for a year or two to learn how their disciplines can contribute to the development of ocean policy. Providing them with contacts in various government agencies, bibliographic information, background on ocean related scientific research, and some guidance on the scope of their research during their postdoctoral year gives me quasi-academic responsibilities.

It is important to ask what contributions anthropology can make in arenas outside of those in which it has traditionally operated. My experience has indicated that there are many possibilities. For example, part of my salary comes from a grant which supports a project of salt marsh research in which my contribution is a discussion of land tenure and use in marsh areas on Cape Cod. Anthropology also provides a valuable framework for marine policy research because it offers a means of combining social and cultural variables with such factors as number of boats, engine size, etc. Familiarity with statistical techniques and computers makes my work both manageable and credible. For example, one could not propose a management plan to put "some" or "many" lobstermen out of work; it is important to know the number of men, their ages, levels of capital investment, alternative work experience, and so forth.

Finally, an anthropological background is valuable because of its compatibility with interdisciplinary research. I have worked with economists, lawyers, biologists, chemists, mathematicians, geographers and planners on research as well as in the preparation of policy documents. Full-time research at this institution as well as in industry usually means that one works on a number of projects simultaneously. Although this takes some adjustment, I found being an anthropologist at the Oceanographic both personally and professionally rewarding.[6]

Margaret Knight

Margaret Knight is an anthropologist who has successfully applied a combination of anthropological and administrative skills in management settings. She holds an M.A. and M.B.A. from the University of Arizona and has worked for different agencies within the federal government. In this interview with *AN*, she discusses the uses to which she has put anthropology and her reasons for pursuing a business degree.

Margaret Knight never wanted a purely academic career and in graduate school knew that she preferred application to basic research, "I saw myself as eventually fitting between the university and the problem-solving world." Having nonacademic employment explicitly in mind as a career goal, Knight took an M.A. in anthropology and, rather than pursue a Ph.D., decided to look for a position where she could develop managerial experience.

She worked for a time as a supervisor of VISTA volunteers for the Pima County Adult Basic Education Project, directing programs aimed at expanding enrollment, developing student leadership, creating culturally relevant materials, and counseling Chicanos and Amerindians. She also worked as a coordinator for a social science education program for Medical and Nursing School faculty and students at the University of Arizona.

In 1974 Knight decided she wanted an M.B.A., and after 2 1/2 years as a full- and part-time student in the Business School at Arizona, she received one. We asked her why. "An M.B.A. supplied what I wanted to know—how the world of money operates. It's also a widely accepted professional degree. More importantly, it picks up where cognitive anthropology and linguistics leave off. The training teaches you to use decision and systems-theory in real settings. Some of the statistical and economic models have given me a whole set of new cognitive tools to apply to a wide area of behavior."

Since receiving the M.B.A., Knight has worked as a consultant for the United States Agency for International Development, participating in the design of an economic development project in Zaire. She outlined the native production and marketing system, laid out key points of impact for USAID technical assistance, developed learning objectives for USAID personnel, assisted in preparing the proposal and defended it during the State Department review process.

The project offered Knight the opportunity to combine anthropological and management skills. "I was able to take sophisticated business concepts such as 'return on investment,' 'risk coverage,' and 'marginal utility of labor' and quickly find their analogies in village farm and commercial practices."

---

[6] *Anthropology Newsletter* (May 1977) 18(5):11.

Most recently Knight, as an environmental specialist, has coordinated the Department of Interior's San Juan Basin Regional Uranium Study in New Mexico. The Project's goal is to provide a comprehensive analysis of the ecological, economic, political, and sociocultural aspects of uranium extraction and production, and presents another opportunity to combine cross-cultural and planning skills. "We are constructing a model that recreates the decisions of key actors in the development of uranium, i.e., the interacting subcultures of mining and oil companies, bureaucratic regulators, tribal leaders, community people, and environmental groups. I have also been focusing on what makes a 'good business deal' across two cultures; i.e., translating the costs, benefits and risks of cultural change into terms understandable to the business world."

Apart from these specific applications, Knight's anthropological training comes into play in a more general and pervasive manner as part of her basic approach to problem solving. "My education in anthropology has given me the broadest possible perspective one can have, several million years of human social and biological history around the globe. This perspective is ultimately optimistic, apolitical, and unselfish. With it, you can take in almost any information and store it for future use, and you can talk to almost anybody and learn something.

"Practically, my training in anthropology makes it second nature for me to think in terms of systems and networks. In my work, I try to develop a large model of a situation, gather data from real people, hypothesize about patterns, and test the hypotheses. I listen a lot, 'interview' every chance I get, and am less judgmental about differing viewpoints. In short, I think I'm able to see the 'big picture' better and faster."

We asked Knight about the Society of Professional Anthropologists, a Tucson-based group she cofounded with Barry Bainton. She considers SOPA valuable because it allows for the formalized sharing of ideas and coping skills among anthropologists engaged in applied activities. "SOPA has helped me in finding my last two jobs, renewing old friendships, and has most of all given me a solid peer group for personal motivation."

For the future, Knight's long-term goal is to achieve as broad a range of experience as possible. "Shifting contexts heightens your flexibility and separates the universal from situation-specific rules of how you get things done." Knight would like to remain in the food and mineral commodities area and go overseas again, perhaps in the private sector.[7]

---

[7] *Anthropology Newsletter* (February 1979) 20(2):13.

Whether or not one plans to make a career of it, the fact of the matter is that a background in anthropology is a tremendously useful thing. A few years ago, the anthropology department at Queen's College in New York City polled several hundred graduates who had been undergraduate majors in anthropology. Very few of these graduates had gone on in anthropology; most had become schoolteachers, or were employed by the city in various capacities, or had jobs on Madison Avenue, and were in fact doing all kinds of jobs. A significant majority of these graduates said that they had found undergraduate anthropology to have been tremendously helpful in enabling them to understand what they were doing.

Whatever they were doing, they were in some kind of organized social arrangement. Anthropology gave them a way of thinking about what they were living in, and how they were going to make a living in it. We taught them those specific skills. We taught them a point of view, to see how the world operates, and how you live in it.[8]

---

[8] Mervyn Meggitt, Interview for KOCE–TV, held in Los Angeles, December 3, 1981.

CHAPTER SUMMARY

In the public mind, anthropology is often seen as a search for the world's "last surviving Stone Age tribes," lost cities, or the bones of remote human ancestors. But with fewer such tribes, cities, and bones left to discover, so the conventional reasoning goes, anthropologists will soon be left with nothing to do. As it turns out, nothing could be further from the truth; anthropologists will be busy far into the future studying their own and other cultures.

Although the time is long past when anthropologists could go off to study traditional societies thought to be unaffected by Western influences, anthropologists continue to be concerned with traditional, non-Western peoples. For one thing, their efforts and expertise are needed to see that the world's remaining tribal and band societies are given the chance to work out their own destinies in the modern world. For another, they have a responsibility to gather whatever data can still be obtained on aspects of traditional ways of life that may soon disappear. They need to focus as well on the process of modernization as it takes place in traditional non-Western societies—whole nations within the so-called third world as well as smaller ethnic groups within nations.

Anthropolgal studies of North American culture are not new, but they are on the increase, and this will continue into the foreseeable future. Three reasons for this are the increased difficulties in working abroad, greater recognition of the importance of the problems that need to be dealt with in our culture, and the failure of the other social sciences to provide the kind of understanding that can be gained only through the use of anthropological techniques and knowledge. Although anthropologists have studied such things as midwestern hamlets and Appalachian religious cults, many of their recent studies come under the heading of urban anthropology. This does not necessarily imply that anthropologists are doing ethnographies of whole cities; mostly they are studying urban neighborhoods, slums, and ethnic enclaves in order to understand class and subcultural variation, problems of poverty and discrimination, and how migrants adapt to city life. Anthropologists may also be found in a number of institutional settings doing ethnographic work. Involved here are such new specialties as educational and medical anthropology. Much work in these specialties is of an applied nature.

Nonacademic jobs for people with an anthropological background exist in business and government where there is a concern with cross-cultural problems. They are also to be found where there are problems of development, involving desired or directed change. Anthropologists are particularly suited for work that necessitates truly humanistic social planning.

The changing role of the anthropologist brings with it the need for careful ethical evaluation of any proposed project. Of main concern are the welfare and privacy of the people who are subjects of anthropological studies.

SUGGESTED READINGS

ARC Newsletter. Cambridge, Mass: ARC Inc., P.O. Box 90, 02138.

The Anthropology Resource Center was founded in 1975 as the first public interest anthropology group in the United States. The *Newsletter* reports on the work of the center, which aims to carry out anthropological research on important public issues and to translate this work into a program of public education.

Bernard, H. Russell, and Willis E. Sibley, *Anthropology and Jobs.* Washington, D.C.: American Anthropological Association, 1975.

For those who want to know about future nonacademic job prospects in anthropology, this is the first place to look. Also available from the American Anthropological Association are *Getting a Job Outside the Academy, Federal Job Opportunities for Anthropologists, State Employment Opportunities for Anthropologists,* and *Training Programs for New Opportunities in Applied Anthropology.* Finally, career opportunities are indicated by the employment ads in every issue of the association's *Newsletter.*

Bodley, John H. *Anthropology and Contemporary Human Problems.* Menlo Park, Calif: Cummings, 1976.

This book, written for students at the introductory level, explains how the cross-cultural, evolutionary, and cross-disciplinary perspectives of anthropology are vital for a deeper understanding of the problems of modern industrial societies. The problems addressed in the book are overconsumption, adapting to the environment, resource depletion, hunger and starvation, overpopulation, and violence and war.

Cultural Survival Quarterly. Cambridge, Mass: Cultural Survival, Inc.

This periodical reports on threats to indigenous peoples around the world, as well as on actions taken by Cultural Survival and others to alleviate the situation. A "must" for anyone concerned about human rights violations in the world.

Shimkin, Dimitri B., Sol Tax, and John W. Morrison, eds. *Anthropology for the Future.* Urbana, Ill.: Department of Anthropology, University of Illinois, Research Report No. 4, 1978.

What are the key issues and desirable courses of action in anthropology today? In 1977, these questions were the focus of a conference attended by over 70 anthropologists, of which this volume is the final product. In it, one will find discussions of the new problems, techniques, and findings with which anthropologists will be concerned, at least in the immediate future.

Bibliography

Aberle, David F., 1961. "Culture and Socialization," in F. Hsu, ed., *Psychological Anthropology: Approaches to Culture and Personality*. Homewood, Ill.: Dorsey Press, pp. 381–399.

Aberle, David F., Urie Bronfenbrenner, Eckhard H. Hess, Daniel R. Miller, David H. Schneider, and James N. Spuhler, 1963. "The Incest Taboo and the Mating Patterns of Animals," *American Anthropologist*, 65:253–265.

Adams, Robert McC., 1966. *The Evolution of Urban Society*, Chicago: Aldine.

Al-Issa, Ihsan, and Wayne Dennis, eds., 1970. *Cross-cultural Studies of Behavior*. New York: Holt, Rinehart and Winston.

Alland, Alexander, Jr., 1970. *Adaptation in Cultural Evolution: An Approach to Medical Anthropology*. New York: Columbia University Press.

Alland, Alexander, Jr., 1971. *Human Diversity*. New York: Columbia University Press.

Amiran, Ruth, 1965. "The Beginnings of Pottery-Making in the Near East," in Frederick R. Matson, ed., *Ceramics and Man*. Viking Fund Publications in Anthropology, No. 41.

Anderson, Robert T., 1972. *Anthropology: A Perspective on Man*. Belmont, Calif.: Wadsworth.

Arensberg, Conrad M., 1961. "The Community as Object and Sample," *American Anthropologist*, 63:241–264.

Arensberg, Conrad M., and Authur H. Niehoff, 1964. *Introducing Social Change: A Manual for Americans Overseas*. Chicago: Aldine.

Bagby, P., 1953. "Culture and the Causes of Culture," *American Anthropologist*, 55:535–554.

Balandier, Georges, 1971. *Political Anthropology*. New York: Pantheon.

Banton, Michael, 1968. "Voluntary Association: Anthropological Aspects," *International Encyclopedia of the Social Sciences*, 16:357–362.

Barber, Bernard, 1957. *Social Stratification*. New York: Harcourt.

Barnett, H. G., 1953. *Innovation: The Basis of Cultural Change*. New York: McGraw-Hill.

Barnouw, Victor, 1963. *Culture and Personality*. Homewood, Ill.: Dorsey Press.

Barth, Frederick, 1960. "Nomadism in the Mountain and Plateau Areas of South West Asia," *The Problems of the Arid Zone*. UNESCO, pp. 341–355.

Barth, Frederick, 1961. *Nomads of South Persia: The Basseri Tribe of the Khamseh Confederacy*. Boston: Little, Brown (Series in Anthropology).

Barton, R. F., 1919. *Ifugao Law*. Berkeley: University of California Publications in American Archaeology and Ethnology, Vol. XV.

Bascom, Williams, 1965. "The Forms of Folklore-Prose Narratives," *Journal of American Folklore*, 78:3–20.

Bascom, William, 1969. *The Yoruba of Southwestern Nigeria*. New York: Holt, Rinehart and Winston.

Bateson, Gregory, 1958. *Naven*. Stanford, Calif.: Stanford University Press.

Beals, Alan R., 1972. *Gopalpur: A South Indian Village*. New York: Holt, Rinehart and Winston.

Beals, Alan R., with G. and L. Spindler, 1973. *Culture in Process*, 2d ed. New York: Holt, Rinehart and Winston.

Beattie, John, 1964. *Other Cultures: Aims, Methods and Achievements*. New York: Free Press.

Beidelman, T. O., ed., 1971. *The Transition of Culture: Essays to E. E. Evans-Pritchard*. London: Tavistock.

Belshaw, Cyril S., 1958. "The Significance of Modern Cults in Melanesian Development," in William Lessa and Evon Z. Vogt, eds., *Reader in Comparative Religion: An Anthropological Approach*. New York: Harper & Row.

Benedict, Ruth, 1959. *Patterns of Culture*. New York: New American Library.

Bennett, John W., 1964. "Myth, Theory and Value in Cultural Anthropology," in E. W. Caint and G. T. Bowles, eds., *Fact and Theory in Social Science*. Syracuse, N.Y.: Syracuse University Press.

Berdan, Frances F., 1982. *The Aztecs of Central Mexico*. New York: Holt, Rinehart and Winston.

Bernard, H. Russell, and Willis E. Sibley, 1975. *Anthropology and Jobs*. Washington, D.C.: American Anthropological Association.

Bernstein, Basin, 1961. "Social Structure, Language and Learning," *Educational Research*, 3:163–176.

Berreman, Gerald D., 1962. *Behind Many Masks: Ethnography and Impression Management in a Himalayan Village*. Ithaca, N.Y.: Society for Applied Anthropology (Monograph No. 4).

Berreman, Gerald D. 1968. "Caste: The Concept of Caste," *International Encyclopedia of the Social Sciences*, 2:333–338.

Bicchieri, M. G., ed., 1972. *Hunters and Gatherers Today: A Socioeconomic Study of Eleven Such Cultures in the Twentieth Century*. New York: Holt, Rinehart and Winston.

Bidney, David, 1953. *Theoretical Anthropology*. New York: Columbia University Press.

Birdwhistell, Ray L., 1970. *Kinesics and Context*. Philadelphia: University of Pennsylvania Press.

Black, Henry Campbell, 1968. *Black's Law Dictionary*. St. Paul, Minn.: West Publishing Company.

Bloch, Marc, 1961. *Feudal Society*. Chicago: University of Chicago Press.

Boas, Franz, 1962. *Primitive Art*. Gloucester, Mass.: Peter Smith.

Boas, Franz, 1966. *Race, Language and Culture*. New York: Free Press.

Bock, Philip K., 1970. *Culture Shock: A Reader in Modern Cultural Anthropology.* New York: Knopf.

Bodley, John H., 1976. *Anthropology and Contemporary Human Problems.* Menlo Park, Calif.: Cummings.

Bohannan, Paul, 1966. *Social Anthropology.* New York: Holt, Rinehart and Winston.

Bohannan, Paul, ed., 1967. *Law and Warfare: Studies in the Anthropology of Conflict.* Garden City, N.Y.: Natural History Press.

Bohannan, Paul, and George Dalton, eds., 1962. *Markets in Africa.* Evanston, Ill.: Northwestern University Press.

Bohannan, Paul, and John Middleton, eds., 1968. *Kinship and Social Organization.* Garden City, N.Y.: Natural History Press (American Museum Source Books in Anthropology).

Bohannan, Paul, and John Middleton, eds., 1968. *Marriage, Family, and Residence.* Garden City, N.Y.: Natural History Press (American Museum Source Books in Anthropology).

Bolinger, Dwight, 1968. *Aspects of Language.* New York: Harcourt.

Bornstein, Marc H., 1975. "The Influence of Visual Perception on Culture," *American Anthropologist,* 77(4):774–798.

Bradfield, Richard M., 1973. *A Natural History of Associations.* New York: International Universities Press.

Braidwood, Robert J., 1960. "The Agricultural Revolution," *Scientific American,* 203:130–141.

Braidwood, Robert J., and Gordon R. Willey, 1962. *Courses Toward Urban Life: Archeological Consideration of Some Cultural Alternatives.* Chicago: Aldine (Publications in Anthropology Series, No. 32).

Brew, John O., 1968. *One Hundred Years of Anthropology.* Cambridge, Mass.: Harvard University Press.

Bridges, E. Lucas, 1948. *Uttermost Part of the Earth.* New York: Dutton.

Brinton, Crane, 1953. *The Shaping of the Modern Mind.* New York: Mentor.

Brown, Lester R., 1975. "The World Food Prospect," *Science,* Vol. 190.

Bruner, Edward M., 1970. "Medan: The Role of Kinship in an Indonesian City," in William Mangin, ed., *Peasants in Cities: Readings in the Anthropology of Urbanization.* Boston: Houghton Mifflin.

Burling, Robbins, 1969. "Linguistics and Ethnographic Description," *American Anthropologist,* 71:817–827.

Burling, Robbins, 1970. *Man's Many Voices.* New York: Holt, Rinehart and Winston.

Butzer, K. W., 1971. *Environment and Anthropology: An Ecological Approach to Prehistory,* 2d ed. Chicago: Aldine.

Calverton, V. F., ed., 1931. *The Making of Man: An Outline of Anthropology.* Westport, Conn.: Greenwood.

Carneiro, Robert L., 1961. "Slash and Burn Cultivation among the Kuikuru and Its Implications for Cultural Development in the Amazon Basin," in J. Wilbert, ed., *The Evolution of Horticultural Systems in Native South America: Causes and Consequences.* Caracas: Sociedad de Ciencias Naturales La Salle, pp. 47–68.

Carneiro, Robert L., 1970. "A Theory of the Origin of the State," *Science,* 169:733–738.

Carpenter, Edmund, 1973. *Eskimo Realities.* New York: Holt, Rinehart and Winston.

Carroll, John B., ed., 1956. *Language, Thought and Reality: Selected Writings of Benjamin Lee Whorf.* New York: Wiley.

Chagnon, Napoleon A., 1968. *Yanomamö: The Fierce People.* New York: Holt, Rinehart and Winston (2d ed., 1977).

Chagnon, N. A., and William Irons, eds., 1979. *Evolutionary Biology and Human Social Behavior.* North Scituate, Mass.: Duxbury Press.

Chapple, Eliot D., 1970. *Cultural and Biological Man: Explorations in Behavioral Anthropology.* New York: Holt, Rinehart and Winston.

Chomsky, Noam, 1957. *Syntactic Structure.* The Hague: Mouton.

Chomsky, Noam, 1968. *Language and Mind.* New York: Harcourt.

Clark, W. E. LeGros, 1960. *The Antecedents of Man.* Chicago: Quadrangle Books.

Clifton, James A., ed., 1970. *Applied Anthropology: Readings in the Uses of the Science of Man.* Boston: Houghton Mifflin (Resources for the Study of Anthropology).

Clough, S. B., and C. W. Cole, 1952. *Economic History of Europe,* 3d ed. Lexington, Mass.: Heath.

Codere, Helen, 1950. *Fighting with Property.* Seattle: University of Washington Press (American Ethnological Society, Monograph 18).

Cohen, Mark N., in press. "Population Pressure and the Origins of Agriculture: An Archaeological Case Study from the Central Coast of Peru," in Charles Reed, ed., *The Origins of Agriculture.* The Hague: Mouton.

Cohen, Myron L., 1967. "Variations in Complexity among Chinese Family Groups: The Impact of Modernization," *Transactions of the New York Academy of Sciences,* 295:638–647.

Cohen, Myron L., 1968. "A Case Study of Chinese Family Economy and Development," *Journal of Asian and African Studies,* 3:161–180.

Cohen, Ronald, and John Middleton, eds., 1967. *Comparative Political Systems.* Garden City, N.Y.: Natural History Press.

Cohen, Yehudi, 1968. *Man in Adaptation: The Cultural Present.* Chicago: Aldine.

Coon, Carleton S., 1948. *A Reader in General Anthropology.* New York: Holt, Rinehart and Winston.

Coon, Carleton S., 1958. *Caravan: The Story of the Middle East,* 2d ed. New York: Holt, Rinehart and Winston.

Coon, Carleton S., 1971. *The Hunting Peoples.* Boston: Little, Brown.

Cottrell, Fred, 1965. *Energy and Society. The Relation between Energy, Social Changes and Economic Development.* New York: McGraw-Hill.

Courlander, Harold, 1971. *The Fourth World of the Hopis.* New York: Crown.

Cowgill, George L., 1980. Letter, *Science,* 210:1305.

Cox, Oliver Cromwell, 1959. *Caste, Class and Race: A Study in Dynamics.* New York: Monthly Review Press.

Dalton, George, ed., 1967. *Tribal and Peasant Economics: Readings in Economic Anthropology.* Garden City, N.Y.: Natural History Press.

Dalton, George, ed., 1967. *Economic Anthropology and Development: Essays on Tribal and Peasant Economics.* New York: Basic Books.

Darwin, Charles, 1967; orig. 1859. *On the Origin of Species.* New York: Atheneum.

Davenport, W., 1959. "Linear Descent and Descent Groups." *American Anthropologist,* 61:557–573.

Deevy, Edward S., Jr., 1960. "The Human Population," *Scientific American,* 203:194–204.

de Laguna, Frederica, 1977. *Voyage to Greenland: A Personal Initiation into Anthropology.* New York: Norton.

Despres, Leo A., 1968. "Cultural Pluralism and the Study of Complex Societies," *Current Anthropology,* 9:3–26.

Devereux, George, 1963. "Institutionalized Homosexuality of the Mohave Indians," in Hendrik M. Ruitenbeck, ed., *The Problem of Homosexuality in Modern Society.* New York: Dutton.

Dobyns, Henry F., Paul L. Doughty, and Harold D. Lasswell, eds., 1971. *Peasants, Power, and Applied Social Change.* London: Sage.

Douglas, Mary, 1958. "Raffia Cloth Distribution in the Lele Economy," *Africa,* 28:109–122.

Dozier, Edward P., 1970. *The Pueblo Indians of North America.* New York: Holt, Rinehart and Winston.

Driver, Harold, 1964. *Indians of North America.* Chicago: University of Chicago Press.

Dubos, Rene, 1968. *So Human an Animal.* New York: Scribner.

Durkheim, Émile, 1964. *The Division of Labor in Society.* New York: Free Press.

Durkheim, Émile, 1965. *The Elementary Forms of the Religious Life.* New York: Free Press.

Dubois, Cora, 1944. *The People of Alor.* Minneapolis: University of Minnesota Press.

Echols, James R., 1976. "Population vs. the Environment: A Crisis of Too Many People." *American Scientist,* Vol. 64.

Edmonson, Munro S., 1971. *Lore: An Introduction to the Science of Folklore.* New York: Holt, Rinehart and Winston.

Eggan, Fred, 1954. "Social Anthropology and the Method of Controlled Comparison," *American Anthropologist,* 56:743–763.

Ehrlich, Paul R., and Anne H. Ehrlich, 1970. *Population, Resources, Environment.* San Francisco: Freeman.

Eiseley, Loren, 1958. *Darwin's Century: Evolution and the Men Who Discovered It.* New York: Doubleday.

Eisenstadt, S. N., 1956. *From Generation to Generation: Age Groups and Social Structure.* New York: Free Press.

Elkin, A. P., 1964. *The Australian Aborigines.* Garden City, N.Y.: Doubleday, Anchor Books.

Ember Carol R., and Melvin Ember, 1981. *Cultural Anthropology,* 3d ed. Englewood Cliffs, N.J.: Prentice Hall.

Ember, Melvin, and Carol R. Ember, 1971. "The Conditions Favoring Matrilocal vs. Patrilocal Residence," *American Anthropologist,* 73:571–594.

Epstein, A. L., 1968. "Sanctions," *International Encyclopedia of the Social Sciences,* Vol. 14.

Erasmus, C. J., 1950. "Patolli, Pachisi, and the Limitation of Possibilities," *Southwestern Journal of Anthropology,* 6:369–381.

Erasmus, C. J., and W. Smith, 1967. "Cultural Anthropology in the United States since 1900," *Southwestern Journal of Anthropology,* 23:11–40.

Ervin-Tripp, Susan M., 1973. *Language Acquisition and Communicative Choice.* Stanford, Calif.: Stanford University Press.

Evans, William F., 1968. *Communication in the Animal World.* New York: Crowell.

Evans-Pritchard, E. E., 1937. *Witchcraft, Oracles, and Magic among the Azande.* London: Oxford University Press.

Evans-Pritchard, E. E., 1968. *The Nuer: A Description of the Modes of Livelihood and Political Institutions of a Nilotic People.* London: Oxford University Press.

Falk, Dean, 1975. "Comparative Anatomy of the Larynx in Man and the Chimpanzee: Implications for Language in Neanderthal," *American Journal of Physical Anthropology,* 43(1):123–132.

Farsoun, Samih K., 1970. "Family Structures and Society in Modern Lebanon," in Louise E. Sweet, ed., *Peoples and Cultures of the Middle East,* Vol. 2. Garden City, N.Y.: Natural History Press.

Firth, Raymond, 1952. *Elements of Social Organization.* London: Watts.

Firth, Raymond, 1957. *Man and Culture: An Evaluation of Bronislaw Malinowski.* London: Routledge.

Firth, Raymond, 1963. *We the Tikopia.* Boston: Beacon Press.

Firth, Raymond, ed., 1967. *Themes in Economic Anthropology.* London: Tavistock.

Forde, C. Daryll, 1955. "The Nupe," in Daryll Forde, ed., *Peoples of the Niger-Benue Confluence.* London: International African Institute (Ethnographic Survey of Africa. Western Africa, part 10), pp. 17–52.

Forde, C. Daryll, 1963. *Habitat, Economy and Society.* New York: Dutton.

Forde, C. Daryll, 1968. "Double Descent among the Yako," in Paul Bohannan and J. Middleton, eds., *Marriage, Family and Residence.* Garden City, N.Y.: Natural History Press, pp. 179–192.

Fortes, Meyer, 1950. "Kinship and Marriage among the Ashanti," in A. R. Radcliffe-Brown and C. Daryll Forde, eds., *African Systems of Kinship and Marriage.* London: Oxford University Press.

Fortes, Meyer, 1969. *Kinship and the Social Order: The Legacy of Lewis Henry Morgan.* Chicago: Aldine.

Fortes, Meyer, and E. E. Evans-Prichard, eds., 1962; orig. 1940. *African Political Systems.* London: Oxford University Press.

Foster, G. M., 1955. "Peasant Society and the Image of the Limited Good," *American Anthropologist,* 67:293–315.

Fox, Robin, 1968. *Kinship and Marriage in an Anthropological Perspective.* Baltimore, Md.: Penguin.

Fraser, Douglas, 1962. *Primitive Art.* New York: Doubleday.

Fraser, Douglas, ed., 1966. *The Many Faces of Primitive Art: A Critical Anthology.* Englewood Cliffs, N.J.: Prentice-Hall.

Frazer, Sir James George, 1931. "Magic and Religion," in V. F. Claverton, ed., *The Making of Man: An Outline of Anthropology*. Westport, Conn.: Greenwood, pp. 693–713.

Frazer, Sir James George, 1961 reissue. *The New Golden Bough*. New York: Doubleday, Anchor Books.

Freeman, J. D., 1960. "The Iban of Western Borneo," in G. P. Murdock, ed., *Social Structure in Southeast Asia*. Chicago: Quadrangle Books.

Freud, Sigmund, 1950; orig. 1913. *Totem and Taboo*. London: Routledge.

Freud, Sigmund, n.d. *Civilization and Its Discontents*. New York: Doubleday, Anchor Books.

Fried, Morton, 1960. "On the Evolution of Social Stratification and the State," in S. Diamond, ed., *Culture in History: Essays in Honor of Paul Radin*. New York: Columbia University Press, pp. 713–731.

Fried, Morton, 1967. *The Evolution of Political Society: An Essay in Political Anthropology*. New York: Random House.

Fried, Morton, 1972. *The Study of Anthropology*. New York: Crowell.

Fried, Morton, Marvin Harris, and Robert Murphy, 1968. *War: The Anthropology of Armed Conflict and Aggression*. Garden City, N.Y.: Natural History Press.

Friedl, Ernestine, 1962. *Vasilika, A Village in Modern Greece*. New York: Holt, Rinehart and Winston.

Friedl, Ernestine, 1975. *Women and Men: An Anthropologist's View*. New York: Holt, Rinehart and Winston.

Gamst, Frederick C., and Edward Norbeck, 1976. *Ideas of Culture: Sources and Uses*. New York: Holt, Rinehart and Winston.

Geertz, Clifford, 1963. *Agricultural Involution: The Process of Ecological Change in Indonesia*. Berkeley: University of California Press.

Geertz, Clifford, 1965. "The Impact of the Concept of Culture on the Concept of Man," in John R. Platt, ed., *New Views of Man*. Chicago: University of Chicago Press.

Geertz, Clifford, 1968. "Religion: Anthropological Study," *International Encyclopedia of the Social Sciences*, Vol. 13. New York: Macmillan.

Gelb, Ignace J., 1952. *A Study of Writing*. London: Routledge.

Gellner, Ernest, 1969. *Saints of the Atlas*. Chicago: University of Chicago Press (The Nature of Human Society Series).

Gibbs, James L., Jr., 1965. "The Kpelle of Liberia," in James L. Gibbs, ed., *Peoples of Africa*. New York: Holt, Rinehart and Winston.

Gleason, H. A., Jr., 1966. *An Introduction to Descriptive Linguistics*, rev. ed. New York: Holt, Rinehart and Winston.

Gluckman, Max, 1955. *The Judicial Process among the Barotse of Northern Rhodesia*. New York: Free Press.

Godlier, Maurice, 1971. "Salt Currency and the Circulation of Commodities among the Baruya of New Guinea," in George Dalton, ed., *Studies in Economic Anthropology*. Washington, D.C.: American Anthropological Association (Anthropological Studies No. 7).

Goode, William J., 1963. *World Revolution and Family Patterns*. New York: Free Press.

Goodenough, Ward, 1956. "Residence Rules," *Southwestern Journal of Anthropology*, 12:22–37.

Goodenough, Ward, 1961. "Comment on Cultural Evolution," *Daedalus*, 90:521–528.

Goodenough, Ward, ed., 1964. *Explorations in Cultural Anthropology: Essays in Honor of George Murdock*. New York: McGraw-Hill.

Goodenough, Ward, 1965. "Rethinking Status" and "Role: Toward a General Model of the Cultural Organization of Social Relationships," in Michael Benton, ed., *The Relevance of Models for Social Anthropology, ASA Monographs 1*. New York: Praeger.

Goodenough, Ward, 1970. *Description and Comparison in Cultural Anthropology*. Chicago: Aldine (Lewis H. Morgan Lecture Series).

Goodfellow, D. M., 1973. *Principles of Economic Sociology: The Economics of Primitive Life as Illustrated from the Bantu Peoples of South and East Africa*. Westport, Conn.: Negro Universities Press (reprint of 1939 edition).

Goodman, Mary Ellen, 1967. *The Individual and Culture*. Homewood, Ill.: Dorsey Press.

Goody, Jack, ed., 1972. *Developmental Cycle in Domestic Groups*. New York: Cambridge University Press (Papers in Social Anthropology, No. 1).

Goody, John, 1969. *Comparative Studies in Kinship*, Stanford, Calif.: Stanford University Press.

Graburn, Nelson H., 1971. *Readings in Kinship and Social Structure*. New York: Harper & Row.

Graham, Susan Brandt, 1979. "Biology and Human Social Behavior: A Response to van den Berghe and Barash," *American Anthropologist*, 81(2):357–350.

Greenberg, Joseph H., 1968. *Anthropological Linguistics: An Introduction*. New York: Random House.

Gulliver, P., 1968. "Age Differentiation," *International Encyclopedia of the Social Sciences*, 1:157–162.

Hallowell, A. Irving, 1955. *Culture and Experience*. Philadelphia: University of Pennsylvania Press.

Hammond, Dorothy, 1972. *Associations*. Reading, Mass.: Addison-Wesley (Modular Publications, 14).

Harlow, Harry F., 1962. "Social Deprivation in Monkeys," *Scientific American*, 206:1–10.

Harris, Marvin, 1965. "The Cultural Ecology of India's Sacred Cattle," *Current Anthropology*, 7:51–66.

Harris, Marvin, 1968. *The Rise of Anthropological Theory*. New York: Crowell.

Harris, Marvin, 1971. *Culture, Man, and Nature: An Introduction to General Anthropology*. New York: Crowell.

Hart, Charles W., and Arnold R. Pilling, 1960. *Tiwi of North Australia*. New York: Holt, Rinehart and Winston.

Haviland, W. A., 1970. "Tikal, Guatemala and Mesoamerican Urbanism," *World Archaeology*, 2:186–198.

Haviland, W. A., 1972. "A New Look at Classic Maya Social Organization at Tikal," *Ceramica de Cultura Maya*, No. 8, pp. 1–16.

Haviland, W. A., 1974. "Farming, Seafaring and Bilocal Residence on the Coast of Maine," *Man in the Northeast*, 6:31–44.

Haviland, W. A., 1975. "The Ancient Maya and the

Evolution of Urban Society," *University of Colorado Museum of Anthropology, Miscellaneous Series,* No. 37.

Haviland, W. A., 1983. *Human Evolution and Prehistory,* 2d ed. New York: Holt, Rinehart and Winston.

Haviland, W. A., and M. W. Power, 1981. *The Original Vermonters: Native Inhabitants, Past and Present.* Hanover, N. H.: University Press of New England.

Hawkins, Gerald S., 1965. *Stonehenge Decoded.* New York: Doubleday.

Hays, H. R., 1965. *From Ape to Angel: An Informal History of Social Anthropology.* New York: Knopf.

Heichel, G. H., 1976. "Agricultural Production and Energy Resources," *American Scientist,* Vol. 64.

Heilbroner, Robert L., 1972. *The Making of Economic Society,* 4th ed. Englewood Cliffs, N.J.: Prentice-Hall.

Helm, June, 1962. "The Ecological Approach in Anthropology," *American Journal of Sociology,* 67:630–649.

Henry, Jules, 1965. *Culture against Man.* New York: Vintage Books.

Herskovits, Melville J., 1952. *Economic Anthropology.* New York: Knopf.

Herskovits, Melville J., 1964. *Cultural Dynamics.* New York: Knopf.

Hewes, Gordon W., 1973. "Primate Communication and the Gestural Origin of Language," *Current Anthropology,* 14(1–2):5–24.

Hickerson, Nancy Parrot, 1980. *Linguistic Anthropology.* New York: Holt, Rinehart and Winston.

Hjelmslev, Louis, 1970. *Language: An Introduction,* Francis J. Whitfield, trans. Madison: University of Wisconsin Press.

Hodgen, Margaret, 1964. *Early Anthropology in the Sixteenth and Seventeenth Centuries.* Philadelphia: University of Pennsylvania Press.

Hoebel, E. A., 1954. *The Law of Primitive Man: A Study in Comparative Legal Dynamics.* Cambridge, Mass.: Harvard University Press, Atheneum, 1968.

Hoebel, E. A., 1960. *The Cheyennes: Indians of the Great Plains.* New York: Holt, Rinehart and Winston.

Hoebel, E. A., 1972. *Anthropology: The Study of Man,* 4th ed. New York: McGraw-Hill.

Hogbin, Ian, 1964. *A Guadalcanal Society.* New York: Holt, Rinehart and Winston.

Hostetler, John, and Gertrude Huntington, 1971. *Children in Amish Society.* New York: Holt, Rinehart and Winston.

Hsu, Francis, 1961. *Psychological Anthropology: Approaches to Culture and Personality.* Homewood, Ill.: Dorsey Press.

Hsu, Francis, 1977. "Role, Affect, and Anthropology," *American Anthropologist,* 79:805–808.

Hsu, Francis, 1979. "The Cultural Problems of the Cultural Anthropologist," *American Anthropologist,* 81:517–532.

Hubert, Henri, and Marcel Mauss, 1964. *Sacrifice.* Chicago: University of Chicago Press.

Hunt, Robert C., ed., 1967. *Personalities and Cultures: Readings in Psychological Anthropology.* Garden City, N.Y.: Natural History Press.

Hymes, Dell, 1964. *Language in Culture and Society: A Reader in Linguistics and Anthropology.* New York: Harper & Row.

Hymes, Dell, ed., 1972. *Reinventing Anthropology.* New York: Pantheon.

Inkeles, Alex, 1966. "The Modernization of Man," in Myron Weiner, ed., *Modernization: The Dynamics of Growth.* New York: Basic Books.

Inkeles, Alex, and D. J. Levinson, 1954. "National Character: The Study of Modal Personality and Socio-cultural Systems," in G. Lindzey, ed., *Handbook of Social Psychology.* Reading, Mass.: Addison-Wesley, pp. 977–1020.

Inkeles, Alex, Eugenia Hanfmann, and Helen Beier, 1961. "Modal Personality and Adjustment to the Soviet Socio-political System," in Bert Kaplan, ed., *Studying Personality Cross-culturally.* New York: Harper & Row.

Jennings, Francis, 1976. *The Invasion of America.* New York: W. W. Norton.

Johanson, Donald C., and Maitland Edey, 1981. *Lucy, the Beginning of Humankind.* New York: Simon & Schuster.

Jopling, Carol F., 1971. *Art and Aesthetics in Primitive Societies: A Critical Anthology.* New York: Dutton.

Jorgensen, Joseph, 1972. *The Sun Dance Religion.* Chicago: University of Chicago Press.

Kahn, Herman, and Anthony J. Wiener, 1967. *The Year 2000.* New York: Macmillan.

Kaplan, David, 1968. "The Superorganic: Science or Metaphysics," in Robert Manners and David Kaplan, eds., *Theory in Anthropology: A Sourcebook.* Chicago: Aldine.

Kaplan, David, 1972. *Culture Theory.* Englewood Cliffs, N.J.: Prentice-Hall (Foundations of Modern Anthropology).

Kardiner, Abram, 1939. *The Individual and His Society. The Psycho-dynamics of Primitive Social Organization.* New York: Columbia University Press.

Kardiner, Abram, and Edward Preble, 1961. *They Studied Men.* New York: Mentor.

Keesing, Roger M., 1975. *Kin Groups and Social Structure.* New York: Holt, Rinehart and Winston.

Keesing, Roger M., 1976. *Cultural Anthropology: A Contemporary Perspective.* New York: Holt, Rinehart and Winston.

Kerri, James N., 1976. "Studying Voluntary Associations as Adaptive Mechanisms: A Review of Anthropological Perspectives," *Current Anthropology,* 17(1).

Kessler, Evelyn, 1975. *Women.* New York: Holt, Rinehart and Winston.

Kleinman, Arthur, 1982. "The Failure of Western Medicine" in David Hunter and Phillip Whitten, *Anthropology: Contemporary Perspectives.* Boston: Little Brown.

Kluckhohn, Clyde, 1944. "Navajo Witchcraft." Cambridge, Mass.: Harvard University Press (Papers of the Peabody Museum of American Archaeology and Ethnology 22, 2).

Kluckhohn, Clyde, 1970. *Mirror for Man.* Greenwich, Conn.: Fawcett.

Kohler, Gernot, 1978. "Global Apartheid," in *World Order Models Project, Paper 7.* New York: Institute for World Order.

Kolata, Gina Bari, 1974. "!Kung Hunter-Gatherers:

Feminism, Diet, and Birth Control," *Science*, 185:932–934.

Krader, Lawrence, 1965. *Formation of the State*. Englewood Cliffs, N.J.: Prentice-Hall (Foundation of Modern Anthropology).

Kroeber, A. L., 1939. "Cultural and Natural Areas of Native North America," *American Archaeology and Ethnology*, Vol. 38. Berkeley, Calif.: University of California Press.

Kroeber, A. L., 1958. "Totem and Taboo: An Ethnologic Psycho-analysis," in William Lessa and Evon Z. Vogt, eds., *Reader in Comparative Religion: An Anthropological Approach*. New York: Harper & Row.

Kroeber, A. L., 1963. *Anthropology: Cultural Processes and Patterns*. New York: Harcourt.

Kroeber, A. L., and Clyde Kluckhohn, 1952. *Culture: A Critical Review of Concepts and Definitions*. Cambridge, Mass.: Harvard University Press (Papers of the Peabody Museum of American Archaeology and Ethnology, 47).

Kuhn, Thomas S., 1968. *The Structure of Scientific Revolutions*. Chicago: University of Chicago Press (International Encyclopedia of Unified Science, 2(27)).

Kurath, Gertrude Probosch, 1960. "Panorama of Dance Ethnology," *Current Anthropology*, Vol. 1.

Kuper, Hilda, 1965. "The Swazi of Swaziland," in James L. Gibbs, ed., *Peoples of Africa*. New York: Holt, Rinehart and Winston, pp. 497–511.

Kushner, Gilbert, 1969. *Anthropology of Complex Societies*. Stanford, Calif.: Stanford University Press.

La Barre, Weston, 1945. "Some Observations of Character Structure in the Orient: The Japanese," *Psychiatry*, Vol. 8.

Laguna, Grace A. de, 1966. *On Existence and the Human World*. New Haven, Conn.: Yale University Press.

Lanternari, Vittorio, 1963. *The Religions of the Oppressed*. New York: Mentor.

Leach, Edmund, 1961. *Rethinking Anthropology*. London: Athione Press.

Leach, Edmund, 1962. "On Certain Unconsidered Aspects of Double Descent Systems," *Man*, 214:13–34.

Leach, Edmund, 1962. "The Determinants of Differential Cross-cousin Marriage," *Man*, 62:238.

Leach, Edmund, 1963. "The Determinants of Differential Cross-cousin Marriage," *Man*, 63:87.

Leach, Edmund, 1965. *Political Systems of Highland Burma*. Boston: Beacon Press.

Leach, Edmund, 1982. *Social Anthropology*. Glasgow: Fontana Paperbacks.

LeClair, Edward, and Harold K. Schneider, eds., 1968. *Economic Anthropology: Readings in Theory and Analysis*. New York: Holt, Rinehart and Winston.

Lee, Richard B., 1969. "!Kung Bushman Subsistence: An Input-Output Analysis," in Andrew P. Vayda, ed., *Environment and Cultural Behavior*. Garden City, N.Y.: Natural History Press, pp. 47–49.

Lee, Richard B., 1984. *The !Kung: Foragers in a Changing World*. New York: Holt, Rinehart and Winston.

Lee, Richard B., and Irven DeVore, eds., 1968. *Man the Hunter*. Chicago: Aldine.

Leeds, Anthony, and Andrew P. Vayda, eds., 1965. *Man, Culture and Animals: The Role of Animals in Human Ecological Adjustments*. Washington, D.C.: American Association for the Advancement of Science.

Lees, Robert, 1953. "The Basis of Glottochronology," *Language*, 29:113–127.

Lehmann, Winifred P., 1973. *Historical Linguistics, An Introduction*, 2d ed. New York: Holt, Rinehart and Winston.

Leinhardt, Godfrey, 1964. *Social Anthropology*. London: Oxford University Press.

Leinhardt, Godfrey, 1971. "Religion," in Harry Shapiro, ed., *Man, Culture and Society*. London: Oxford University Press, pp. 382–401.

LeMay, Marjorie, 1975. "The Language Capability of Neanderthal Man," *American Journal of Physical Anthropology*, 43(1):9–14.

Lenski, Gerhard, 1966. *Power and Privilege: A Theory of Social Stratification*. New York: McGraw-Hill.

Lessa, William A., and Evon Z. Vogt, eds., 1972. *Reader in Comparative Religion: An Anthropological Approach*. New York: Harper & Row.

LeVine, Robert A., 1973. *Culture, Behavior and Personality*. Chicago: Aldine.

Lévi-Strauss, Claude, 1963. *Structural Anthropology*. New York: Basic Books.

Lévi-Strauss, Claude, 1963. *Totemism*. Boston: Beacon Press.

Lévi-Strauss, Claude, 1966. *The Savage Mind*. Chicago: University of Chicago Press.

Lévi-Strauss, Claude, 1969. *The Elementary Structures of Kinship*. Boston: Beacon Press.

Lévi-Strauss, Claude, 1971. "The Family," in Harry L. Shapiro, ed., *Man, Culture and Society*. London: Oxford University Press, pp. 333–357.

Lewis, I. M., 1965. "Problems in the Comparative Study of Unilineal Descent," in Michael Banton, ed., *The Relevance of Models for Social Organization* (A.S.A. Monograph No. 1). London: Tavistock.

Linton, Ralph, 1963. *The Study of Man*. New York: Appleton.

Little, Kenneth, 1964. "The Role of Voluntary Associations in West African Urbanization," in Pierre van den Berghe, ed., *Africa: Social Problems of Change and Conflict*. San Francisco: Chandler.

Livingstone, Frank B., 1973. "The Distribution of Abnormal Hemoglobin Genes and Their Significance for Human Evolution," in C. Loring Brace and James Metress, eds., *Man in Evolutionary Perspective*. New York: Wiley.

Lorenz, Konrad, 1974. *Civilized Man's Eight Mortal Sins*. Munich: Pieper Verlag.

Lounsbury, F., 1964. "The Structural Analysis of Kinship Semantics," in Horace G. Lunt, ed., *Proceedings of the Ninth International Congress of Linguists*. The Hague: Mouton, pp. 1073–1093.

Lowie, Robert H., 1948. *Social Organization*. New York: Holt, Rinehart and Winston.

Lowie, Robert H., 1956. *Crow Indians*. New York: Holt, Rinehart and Winston.

Lowie, Robert H., 1966. *Culture and Ethnology*. New York: Basic Books.

Lustig-Arecco, Vero, 1975. *Technology: Strategies for Survival*. New York: Holt, Rinehart and Winston.

Lyons, John, 1970. *Noam Chomsky*. New York: Viking.

Magnarella, Paul J., 1974. *Tradition and Change in a Turkish Town*. New York: Wiley.

Mair, Lucy, 1969. *Witchcraft*. New York: McGraw-Hill.

Mair, Lucy, 1971. *Marriage*. Baltimore, Md.: Penguin.

Malefijt, Annemarie de Waal, 1969. *Religion and Culture: An Introduction to Anthropology of Religion*. London: Macmillan.

Malefijt, Annemarie de Waal, 1974. *Images of Man*. New York: Knopf.

Malinowski, Bronislaw, 1922. *Argonauts of the Western Pacific*. New York: Dutton.

Malinowski, Bronislaw, 1945. *The Dynamics of Culture Change*. New Haven, Conn.: Yale University Press.

Malinowski, Bronislaw, 1951. *Crime and Custom in Savage Society*. London: Routledge.

Malinowski, Bronislaw, 1954. *Magic, Science and Religion*. Garden City, N.Y.: Doubleday, Anchor Books.

Marano, Lou, 1982. "Windigo Psychosis: The Anatomy of an Emic-Etic Confusion," *Current Anthropology*, 23:385–412.

Marshack, Alexander, 1976. "Implications of the Paleolithic Symbolic Evidence for the Origin of Language," *American Scientist*, Vol. 64.

Marshall, Lorna, 1961. "Sharing, Talking and Giving: Relief of Social Tensions among !Kung Bushmen," *Africa*, Vol. 31.

Mason, J. Alden, 1957. *The Ancient Civilizations of Peru*. Baltimore, Md.: Penguin.

Maybury-Lewis, David, 1960. "Parallel Descent and the Apinaye Anomaly," *Southwestern Journal of Anthropology*, 16:191–216.

McFee, Malcolm, 1972. *Modern Blackfeet: Montanans on a Reservation*. New York: Holt, Rinehart and Winston.

McHale, John, 1969. *The Future of the Future*. New York: Braziller.

Mead, Margaret, 1928. *Coming of Age in Samoa*. New York: Morrow.

Mead, Margaret, 1963. *Sex and Temperament in Three Primitive Societies*, 3d ed. New York: Morrow.

Mead, Margaret, 1970. *Culture and Commitment*. Garden City, N.Y.: Natural History Press.

Meadows, Donella H., Dennis L. Meadows, Jorgen Randers, and William W. Behrens III, 1974. *The Limits to Growth*. New York: Universe Books.

Meggars, Betty J., 1971. *Amazonia*. Chicago: Aldine.

Mesghinua, Haile Michael, 1966. "Salt Mining in Enderta," *Journal of Ethiopian Studies*, 4(2).

Middleton, John, ed., 1970. *From Child to Adult: Studies in the Anthropology of Education*. Garden City, N.Y.: Natural History Press (American Museum Source Books in Anthropology).

Mitchell, William E., 1973. "A New Weapon Stirs Up Old Ghosts," *Natural History Magazine*, December, pp. 77–84.

Mitchell, William E., 1978. *Mishpokhe: A Study of New York City Jewish Family Clubs*. The Hague: Mouton.

Montagu, Ashley, 1964. *The Concept of Race*. London: Macmillan.

Montagu, Ashley, 1964. *Man's Most Dangerous Myth: The Fallacy of Race*, 4th ed. New York: World Publishing.

Morgan, Lewis H., 1877. *Ancient Society*. New York: World Publishing.

Mowat, Farley, 1981. *People of the Deer*. Toronto: Bantam Books.

Murdock, George P., 1956. "How Culture Changes," in Harry L. Shapiro, ed., *Man, Culture and Society*. Chicago: University of Chicago Press.

Murdock, George P., 1960. "Cognatic Forms of Social Organization," in G. P. Murdock, ed., *Social Structure in Southeast Asia*. Chicago: Quadrangle Books.

Murdock, George P., 1965. *Social Structure*. New York: Free Press.

Murphy, Robert, 1971. *The Dialectics of Social Life: Alarms and Excursions in Anthropological Theory*. New York: Basic Books.

Murphy, Robert, and Leonard Kasdan, 1959. "The Structure of Parallel Cousin Marriage," *American Anthropologist*, 61:17–29.

Myers, Thomas P. ed., 1970. "Current Research," *American Antiquity*, 44(2):610.

Myrdal, Gunnar, 1974. "Challenge to Affluence: The Emergence of an 'Under-class,'" in Joseph O. Jorgensen and Marcello Truzzi, eds., *Anthropology and American Life*. Englewood Cliffs, N.J.: Prentice-Hall.

Nader, Laura, ed., 1965. "The Ethnography of Law," *American Anthropologist*, Part II, 67(6).

Nader, Laura, ed., 1969. *Law in Culture and Society*. Chicago: Aldine.

Naroll, Raoul, 1973. "Holocultural Theory Tests," in Raoul Naroll and Frada Naroll, eds., *Main Currents in Cultural Anthropology*. New York: Appleton.

Nash, Manning, 1966. *Primitive and Peasant Economic Systems*. San Francisco: Chandler.

Needham, Rodney, ed., 1971. *Rethinking Kinship and Marriage*. London: Tavistock.

Needham, Rodney, 1973. *Belief, Language and Experience*. Chicago: University of Chicago Press.

Nesbitt, L. M., 1935. *Hell-Hole of Creation*. New York: Knopf.

Nettl, Bruno, 1956. *Music in Primitive Culture*. Cambridge, Mass.: Harvard University Press.

Newman, Philip L., 1965. *Knowing the Gururumba*. New York: Holt, Rinehart and Winston.

Nimkoff, M. F., and Russell Middleton, 1960–1961. "Types of Family and Types of Economy," *American Journal of Sociology*, 66(3):215–226.

Norbeck, Edward, 1974. *Religion in Human Life: Anthropological Views*. New York: Holt, Rinehart and Winston.

Norbeck, Edward, Douglas Price-Williams, and William McCord, ed., 1968. *The Study of Personality: An Interdisciplinary Appraisal*. New York: Holt, Rinehart and Winston.

Nye, E. Ivan, and Felix M. Berardo, 1975. *The Family: Its Structure and Interaction*. New York: Macmillan.

Oliver, Douglas Z., 1964. *Invitation to Anthropology*. Garden City, N.Y.: Natural History Press.

O'Mahoney, Kevin, 1970. "The Salt Trade," *Journal of Ethiopian Studies*, 8(2).

Ortiz, Alfonso, 1969. *The Tewa World*. Chicago: University of Chicago Press.

Oswalt, Wendell H., 1970. *Understanding Our Culture*. New York: Holt, Rinehart and Winston.

Oswalt, Wendell H., 1972. *Habitat and Technology*. New York: Holt, Rinehart and Winston.

Oswalt, Wendell H., 1972. *Other Peoples Other Cus-*

toms: *World Ethnography and Its History.* New York: Holt, Rinehart and Winston.

Otten, Charlotte N., 1971. *Anthropology and Art: Readings in Cross-cultural Asthetics.* Garden City, N.Y.: Natural History Press (American Museum Sourcebooks in Anthropology).

Ottenberg, Phoebe, 1965. "The Afikpo Ibo of Eastern Nigeria," in James L. Gibbs, ed., *Peoples of Africa.* New York: Holt, Rinehart and Winston.

Otterbein, Keith F., 1971. *The Evolution of War.* New Haven, Conn.: HRAF Press.

Parker, Seymour, and Hilda Parker, 1979. "The Myth of Male Superiority: Rise and Demise," *American Anthropologist,* 81(2):289–309.

Pastner, Stephen, and William A. Haviland, eds., 1982. "Confronting the Creationists," *Northeastern Anthropological Association Occasional Proceedings* No. 1.

Pelto, Pertti J., 1966. *The Nature of Anthropology.* Columbus, O.: Merrill (Social Science Perspectives).

Pelto, Pertti J., 1973. *The Snowmobile Revolution: Technology and Social Change in the Arctic.* Menlo Park, Calif.: Cummings.

Penniman, T. K., 1965. *A Hundred Years of Anthropology.* London: Duckworth.

Peters, Charles R., 1979. "Toward an Ecological Model of African Plio-Pleistocene Hominid Adaptations," *American Anthropologist,* 81(2):261–278.

Peterson, Frederick L., 1962. *Ancient Mexico, An Introduction to the Pre-Hispanic Cultures.* New York: Capricorn Books.

Piddocke, Stuart, 1965. "The Potlatch System of the Southern Kwakiutl: A New Perspective," *Southwestern Journal of Anthropology,* 21:244–264.

Pimentel, David, L. E. Hurd, A. C. Bellotti, M. J. Forster, I. N. Oka, O. D. Sholes, and R. J. Whitman, 1973. "Food Production and the Energy Crisis," *Science,* Vol. 182.

Polanyi, Karl, 1968. "The Economy as Instituted Process," in E. E. LeClair, Jr., and H. K. Schneider, *Economic Anthropology: Readings in Theory and Analysis.* New York: Holt, Rinehart and Winston.

Pospisil, Leopold, 1963. *The Kapauku Papuans of West New Guinea.* New York: Holt, Rinehart and Winston.

Pospisil, Leopold, 1971. *Anthropology of Law: A Comparative Theory.* New York: Harper & Row.

Powdermaker, Hortense, 1966. *Stranger and Friend: The Way of an Anthropologist.* New York: Norton.

Premack, Ann James, and David Premack, 1972. "Teaching Language to an Ape," *Scientific American,* 277(4):92–99.

Price-Williams, D. R., ed., 1970. *Cross-cultural Studies: Selected Readings.* Baltimore, Md.: Penguin (Penguin Modern Psychology Readings).

Prins, A. H. J., 1953. *East African Class Systems.* Gronigen, The Netherlands: J. B. Walters.

Pumpelly, R., 1908. *Explorations in Turkestan: Expedition of 1904: Prehistoric Civilization of Anau.* Washington, D.C.: Publications of the Carnegie Institute, 1 (73).

Radcliffe-Brown, A. R., 1931. "Social Organization of Australian Tribes," *Oceania Monographs,* No. 1. Melbourne: Macmillan, 1931.

Radcliffe-Brown, A. R., 1952. *Structure and Function in Primitive Society.* New York: Free Press.

Radcliffe-Brown, A. R., and C. D. Forde, eds., 1950. *African Systems of Kinship and Marriage.* London: Oxford University Press.

Rappaport, Roy, 1968. *Pigs for the Ancestors.* New Haven, Conn.: Yale University Press.

Rathje, William L., 1974. "The Garbage Project: A New Way of Looking at the Problems of Archaeology," *Archaeology,* 27:236–241.

Redfield, Robert, Ralph Linton, and Melville J. Herskovits, 1936. "Memorandum of the Study of Acculturation," *American Anthropologist,* 38:149–152.

Reina, Ruben E., 1961. "The Abandonment of Primicias by Itza of San Jose, Guatemala, and Socotz, British Honduras," *Tikal Report.* Philadelphia: University of Pennsylvania Press (Museum Monographs, 10).

Reina, Ruben E., 1966. *The Law of the Saints.* Indianapolis: Bobbs-Merrill.

Rodman, Hyman, 1968. "Class Culture," *International Encyclopedia of the Social Sciences,* 15:332–337.

Russell, Bernard H., 1975. *Anthropology and Jobs.* Washington, D.C.: American Anthropological Association.

Sahlins, Marshall, 1961. "The Segmentary Lineage: An Organization of Predatory Expansion," *American Anthroplogist,* 63:322–343.

Sahlins, Marshall, 1968. *Tribesmen.* Englewood Cliffs, N.J.: Prentice-Hall (Foundations of Modern Anthropology).

Sahlins, Marshall, 1972. *Stone Age Economics.* Chicago: Aldine.

Salthe, Stanley N., 1972. *Evolutionary Biology.* New York: Holt, Rinehart and Winston.

Salzman, Philip C., 1967. "Political Organization among Nomadic Peoples," *Proceedings of the American Philosophical Society,* 3(2).

Sangree, Walter H., 1965. "The Bantu Tiriki of Western Kenya," in James L. Gibbs, ed., *Peoples of Africa.* New York: Holt, Rinehart and Winston.

Sapir, E., 1916. *Time Perspective in Aboriginal American Culture: A Study in Method.* Ottawa: Geological Society of Canada (Memoir 90, Anthropological Series, No. 13).

Sapir, E., 1917. "Do We Need a Superorganic?" *American Anthropologist,* 19:441–447.

Sapir, E., 1921. *Language.* New York: Harcourt.

Sapir, E., 1924. "Culture, Genuine or Spurious?" *American Journal of Sociology,* 29:401–429.

Schaller, George B., 1963. *The Mountain Gorilla.* Chicago: Chicago University Press.

Scheflen, Albert E., 1972. *Body Language and the Social Order,* Englewood Cliffs, N.J.: Prentice-Hall.

Schurtz, Heinrich, 1902. *Alterklassen und Männerbünde.* Berlin: Reimer.

Schusky, Ernest L., 1975. *Variation in Kinship.* New York: Holt, Rinehart and Winston.

Service, Elman R., 1958. *Profiles in Ethnology.* New York: Harper & Row.

Service, Elman R., 1966. *The Hunters.* Englewood Cliffs, N.J.: Prentice-Hall (Foundations of Modern Anthropology).

Service, Elman R., 1971. *Primitive Social Organization: An Evolutionary Perspective*, 2d ed. New York: Random House.

Shapiro, Harry, ed., 1960. *Man, Culture and Society*. New York: Oxford University Press.

Sharp, Lauriston, 1952. "Steel Axes for Stone Age Australians," in Edward H. Spicer, ed., *Human Problems in Technological Change*. New York: Russell Sage.

Shimkin, Dimitri B., Sol Tax, and John W. Morrison, eds., 1978. *Anthropology for the future*. Urbana, Ill.: Department of Anthropology, University of Illinois, Research Report No. 4, 1978.

Shinnie, Margaret, 1970. *Ancient African Kingdoms*. New York: New American Library.

Slobin, Dan I., 1971. *Psycholinguistics*. Glenview, Ill.: Scott, Foresman.

Smith, Raymond, 1970. "Social Stratification in the Caribbean," in Leonard Plotnicov and Arthur Tudin, ed., *Essays in Comparative Social Stratification*. Pittsburgh: University of Pittsburgh Press.

Speck, Frank G., 1920. "Penobscot Shamanism," *Memoirs of the American Anthropological Association*, 6:239–288.

Speck, Frank G., 1935. "Penobscot Tales and Religious Beliefs," Journal of American Folk-Lore, 48(187):1–107.

Speck, Frank G., 1940. *Penobscot Man*. Philadelphia: University of Pennsylvania Press.

Spencer, Herbert, 1896. *Principles of Sociology*. New York: Appleton.

Spiro, Melford E., 1954. "Is the Family Universal?" *American Anthropologist*, 56:839–846.

Spiro, Melford E., 1966. "Religion: Problems of Definition and Explanation" in Michael Banton, ed., *Anthropological Approaches to the Study of Religion* (A.S.A. Monograph#s). London: Tavistock.

Spitz, René A., 1949. "Hospitalism," *The Psychoanalytic Study of the Child*, Vol. 1. New York: International Universities Press.

Stanner, W. E. H., 1968. "Radcliffe-Brown, A. R.," *International Encyclopedia of the Social Sciences*, Vol. 13. New York: Macmillan.

Stephens, William N., 1963. *The Family in Cross-cultural Perspective*. New York: Holt, Rinehart and Winston.

Steward, Julian H., 1972. *Theory of Culture Change: The Methodology of Multilinear Evolution*. Urbana, Ill.: University of Illinois Press.

Stocking, George W., Jr., 1968. *Race, Culture and Evolution: Essays in the History of Anthropology*. New York: Free Press.

Swadesh, Morris, 1951. "Diffusional Cumulation and Archaic Residue as Historic Exploration," *Southwestern Journal of Anthropology* 7:1–21.

Swartz, Marc J., Victor W. Turner, and Arthur Tuden, 1966. *Political Anthropology*. Chicago: Aldine.

Tax, Sol, 1953. *Penny Capitalism: A Guatemalan Indian Economy*, Smithsonian Institution, Institute of Social Anthropology, Pub. No. 16. Washington, D.C.: Government Printing Office.

Tax, Sol, ed., 1962. *Anthropology Today: Selections*. Chicago: University of Chicago Press.

Tax, Sol, Sam Stanley, and others, 1975. "In Honor of Sol Tax," *Current Anthropology*. 16:507–540.

Thomas, W. L., ed., 1956. *Man's Role in Changing the Face of the Earth*. Chicago: University of Chicago Press.

Thompson, Stith, 1960. *The Folktale*. New York: Holt, Rinehart and Winston.

Trager, George L., 1964. "Paralanguage: A First Approximation," in Dell Hymes, ed., *Language in Culture and Society*. New York: Harper & Row.

Tuden, Arthur, 1970. "Slavery and Stratification among the Ila of Central Africa," in Arthur Tuden and Leonard Plotnicov, eds., *Social Stratification in Africa*. New York: Free Press.

Tuma, Elias H., 1971. *European Economic History: Theory and History of Economic Change*. New York: Harper & Row.

Tumin, Melvin M., 1967. *Social Stratification: The Forms and Functions of Inequality*. Englewood Cliffs, N.J.: Prentice-Hall (Foundations of Modern Sociology).

Turnbull, Colin M., 1961. *The Forest People*. New York: Simon & Schuster.

Turnbull, Colin M., 1972. *The Mountain People*. New York: Simon & Schuster.

Turner, V. W. 1957. *Schism and Continuity in an African Society*. Manchester: The University Press.

Turner, V. W., 1969. *The Ritual Process*. Chicago: Aldine.

Tylor, Edward Burnett, 1871. *Primitive Culture: Researches into the Development of Mythology, Philosophy, Religion, Language, Art and Customs*. London: Murray.

Tylor, Sir Edward B., 1931. "Animism," in V. F. Calverton, ed., *The Making of Man: An Outline of Anthropology*. New York: Modern Library.

Valentine, Charles A., 1968. *Culture and Poverty*. Chicago: University of Chicago Press.

Van Gennep, Arnold, 1960. *The Rites of Passage*. Chicago: University of Chicago Press.

Van Lawick-Goodall, Jane, 1972. *In the Shadow of Man*. New York: Dell.

Vansina, Jan, 1965. *Oral Tradition: A Study in Historical Methodology*, H. M. Wright, trans. Chicago: Aldine.

Vayda, Andrew P., 1961. "A Re-examination of Northwest Coast Economic Systems," *Transactions of the New York Academy of Sciences*, 2d. series, 23:618–624.

Vayda, Andrew P., 1961. "Expansion and Warfare among Swidden Agriculturalists," *American Anthropologist*, 63:346–358.

Vayda, Andrew P., ed., 1969. *Environment and Cultural Behavior: Ecological Studies in Cultural Anthropology*, Garden City, N.Y.: Natural History Press.

Vogelman, Thomas C., and others, 1972. Film: *Prehistoric Life in the Champlain Valley*. Burlington, Vt.: Department of Anthropology, University of Vermont.

Voget, F. W., 1960. "Man and Culture: An Essay in Changing Anthropological Interpretation," *American Anthropologist*, 62:943–965.

Voget, F. W., 1975. *A History of Ethnology*. New York: Holt, Rinehart and Winston.

Wagner, Philip L., 1960. *The Human Use of the Earth*. New York: Free Press.

Wallace, Anthony F. C., 1956. "Revitalization Movements," *American Anthropologist*, 58:264–281.

Wallace, Anthony F. C., 1965. "The Problem of the Psychological Validity of Componential Analysis," *American Anthropologist, Special Publication*, Part 2, 67(5):229–248.

Wallace, Anthony F. C., 1966. *Religion: An Anthropological View*. New York: Random House.

Wallace, Anthony F. C., 1970. *Culture and Personality*, 2d ed. New York: Random House.

Wallace, Ernest, and E. Adamson Hoebel, 1952. *The Comanches*. Norman: University of Oklahoma Press.

Wardhaugh, Ronald, 1972. *Introduction to Linguistics*. New York: McGraw-Hill.

Weiner, Myron, 1966. *Modernization: The Dynamics of Growth*. New York: Basic Books.

Westermarck, Edward A., 1926. *A Short History of Marriage*. New York: Macmillan.

White, Leslie, 1940. "The Symbol: The Origin and Basis of Human Behavior," *Philosophy of Science*, 7:451–463.

White, Leslie, 1949. *The Science of Culture: A Study of Man and Civilization*. New York: Farrar, Strauss.

White, Leslie, 1959. *The Evolution of Culture: The Development of Civilization to the Fall of Rome*. New York: McGraw-Hill.

Whiting, Beatrice B., ed., 1963. *Six Cultures: Studies of Child Rearing*. New York: Wiley.

Whiting, J., and J. Child, 1953. *Child Training and Personality: A Cross-cultural Study*. New York: McGraw-Hill.

Wilson, A. K., and V. M. Sarich, 1969. "A Molecular Time Scale for Human Evolution," *Proceedings of the National Academy of Science* 63:1089–1093.

Wingert, Paul, 1962. *Primitive Art: Its Tradition and Styles*. London: Oxford University Press; New York: World, 1965.

Wolf, Eric, 1966. *Peasants*. Englewood Cliffs, N.J.: Prentice-Hall (Foundations of Modern Anthropology).

Wolf, Eric, 1982. *Europe and the People without History*. Berkeley: University of California Press.

Wolpoff, Milford H., 1982. "*Ramapithecus* and Hominid Origins," *Current Anthropology*, 23:501–522.

Woolfson, Peter, 1972. "Language, Thought, and Culture," in Virginia P. Clark, Paul A. Escholz, and Alfred F. Rosa, eds., *Language*. New York: St. Martins.

World Bank, 1982. *Tribal Peoples and Economic Development*. Washington, D.C.: World Bank.

CREDITS (continued from p. iv)

Index

Terms in boldface type are defined in the running glossaries on the text pages indicated by boldface numbers. Text folios are in Roman type. Illustration folios are in italic type.

497

Brace, C. L., 84n, 166n
Brazilian Indians, and culture crash, 440–441
Breummer, F., 171
Bride price, 250, 251
Bride service, 251, 251
Brown, L. R., 451n, 453n
Burin (stone tool), 87
Burling, R., 113n
Bushmen (South Africa), 135

Calverton, V. F., 368n
Cannibalism, 157–158
Capital, 207, 207–208
Cargo cults, 372–373
Cargo systems, 211
Carpenter, E., 382–383
Carrying capacity, 180, 181
Castaneda, C., 358
Caste, 300–301, 301; Indian, theory on origin of, 306; and mobility, 304
Cave paintings (Upper Paleolithic), 87–88
Chagnon, N. A., *16, 19,* 41–44, 46n, 151n, 232n
Change, cultural, 46–48; acculturation, 414–416; causes of, 406; colonialism and conquest, 416–418; cultural loss, 414; by diffusion, 409–414; forcible, 416–421; introduction to, 402–403; by invention, 407–409; Mayan Indians, contemporary, 410–412; mechanisms of, 407–416; modernization, 422–432; rate and direction of, 406–407; rebellion and revolution, 418–421; and religion, 372–375
Cheyenne Indians (North America), 168; Elk Soldier Society, 335; warriors' clubs, 321
Chiefdom, 323, 323–324
Child, I. L., 142, 149
Child-rearing, 142–149, 230–232; of hunters and gatherers, 144–145; of migratory workers, 145–148; and nuclear families, 253–254; in Samoa, 140–141
Chimpanzees, behavioral adaptation in, 61–62
Chomsky, N., 124–125
Clan, 271, 271–272; as political organization, 319
Clark, V. P., 115n
Classic Neanderthal, 81
Code switching, 124, 125
Codrington, R. H., 355
Coercion, as social control, 341
Cognitive map, 139
Cohen, M. N., 186n

Cohen, R., 64n
Colonialism, change by, 416–418
Comanche Indians (North America), 167–168
Common-interest associations, 294–299; defined, **295;** men's and women's, 296–297; as political systems, 320–321; types of, 295–297; in urban world, 297–299
Complementary opposition, 320
Conjugal bond, 234, 235
Conquest, change by, 416–418
Consanguine family, 237, 237–238
Consanguineal kin, 234, 235
Conspicuous consumption, 215, 215–219
Contagious magic, 368, 369
Contrastive pairs, *236*
Convergent evolution, 168, 169
Coon, C. S., 175n, 190n, 212, 414n
Cooperative work, 203–204
Coppers, of Kwakiutl, 217–219
Cordell, J., 480
Core vocabulary, 112, 113
Cousins club (New York City Jews), 270, 276, 287
Cowboy culture, 426–427
Cowgill, G. L., 439
Crime, 336–338
Cro-Magnons, 84, 85; tools of, *86*
Cross-cultural comparisons, 19–20
Crow Indians (North America), balanced reciprocity among, 210; shamanism, 359
Crow system, of kinship terminology, **279,** 279–280
Cultural adaptation, 46
Cultural anthropology, 11, 12–20; subfields of, 13
Cultural deprivation theory, 19
Cultural diversity, and technology, 424
Cultural materialist, 37; L. B. White, 36
Cultural pluralism, 443, 443–447; Nigerian, 444–445; Puerto Ricans, in New York City, 443–444
Cultural relativism, 50, 51
Cultural Survival, Inc., 467–468
Cultural transmission (*see* Enculturation)
Culture, and biology, 4–5; and change (*see* Change, cultural); characteristics of, 31–38; concept of, 30–31; defined, **31;** of discontent, 459–460; evaluation of, 49–50; fieldwork, 39–44; functions of, 46; future

of, 438–449; and the individual, 48–49; integration of, 36–38; learned nature of, 34–35; loss and replacement, 414; North American, studies of, 471–484; and process, 44–50; and race, 34; shared nature of, 31–34; and society, 31–32; strain to consistency in, 38; symbolic basis of, 35–36
Culture areas, 168–174; defined, **169**
Culture-bound, 13; hypothesis, 21–22; theory, 12; theory of cultural deprivation, 19
Culture concept (*see* Culture, concept of)
✓ **Culture core, 174–175, 175**
Culture crash, 416–418
Culture of discontent, 432
✓ **Cultural ecology, 173;** procedures for, *173*
✓ **Culture type, 173,** 173–174

Dahomey, cooperative labor in, 203–204
Dancing societies, 297
Darwin, C., 24
Day, G. M., 387n
Dayaka (Borneo), anaimism of, 354
Death, rites of, 366–367
Deculturation, 415, 415
Deep structure, 124–125, 125
de Laguna, F., 16–18; photo, *17*
de Laguna, G., 4
Demographic transition, 458–459, 459
Density of social relations, 180–182; defined, **181**
Dentition, primate, 58; of Ramapithecines, 67–69, *70*
Dependence training, 142–143, 143, 252
Dependency ratio, 181–182
Descent group, 261, 261–270; evolution of, 275–276; forms and functions of, 270–276
Descriptive linguistics, 104, 109, 109
Descriptive system, of kinship terminology, 280, **281**
Devereux, G., 34n
Deviant behavior, 34, 156–158; in Pueblo Indians, 428
Dialects, 118–124; defined, **119**
Diffusion, 409, 409–414; from American Indian to mainstream U.S., 412
Dionysian personality, *150*
Displacement, in language, 65–66, 127, **127**
Divination, 370, 371

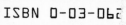
ISBN 0-03-06